Karl Barth

Karl Barth

A Life in Conflict

CHRISTIANE TIETZ
Translated by
VICTORIA J. BARNETT

Great Clarendon Street, Oxford, OX2 6DP,
United Kingdom

Oxford University Press is a department of the University of Oxford.
It furthers the University's objective of excellence in research, scholarship,
and education by publishing worldwide. Oxford is a registered trade mark of
Oxford University Press in the UK and in certain other countries

© Verlag C.H.Beck oHG, München 2019 For the English language edition (c) Christiane Tietz 2021

This translation is based upon the corrected second German edition.

The moral rights of the authors have been asserted

First Edition published in 2021

Impression: 1

All rights reserved. No part of this publication may be reproduced, stored in
a retrieval system, or transmitted, in any form or by any means, without the
prior permission in writing of Oxford University Press, or as expressly permitted
by law, by licence or under terms agreed with the appropriate reprographics
rights organization. Enquiries concerning reproduction outside the scope of the
above should be sent to the Rights Department, Oxford University Press, at the
address above

You must not circulate this work in any other form
and you must impose this same condition on any acquirer

Published in the United States of America by Oxford University Press
198 Madison Avenue, New York, NY 10016, United States of America

British Library Cataloguing in Publication Data
Data available

Library of Congress Control Number: 2020952990

ISBN 978-0-19-885246-9

Printed and bound in the UK by
TJ Books Limited

Links to third party websites are provided by Oxford in good faith and
for information only. Oxford disclaims any responsibility for the materials
contained in any third party website referenced in this work.

For Eberhard Jüngel

Preface

"Compared with Karl Barth we are all mere dwarfs."[1] This verdict, coming not from a friend but from an enemy, goes to the heart of the epochal significance of the theologian Karl Barth. For decades he dominated the debates far beyond his own discipline. He disagreed with the dominant theological convictions, opposed societal trends, and battled against political developments. Invariably he did this with courage and without mincing words.

Barth's lasting significance, which is also his lasting disruptive potential, rests in the fact that he emphatically clarified the absolute otherness of God over against the "world." In an era in which God and religion had become understood culturally, interpreted psychologically, and instrumentalized politically, the impact of this insight on theology was similar to that of Heidegger's stress on the fundamental difference between "Being" (*Sein*) and "Beings" (*Seiendes*) on philosophy, or the Expressionist protest in art against Naturalism.

Karl Barth was Swiss, but for many years was a professor in Germany. He was critical of National Socialism and the German church's conformity to it. Even after his dismissal from the university by the National Socialists and his return to Switzerland he remained tied to Germany as a critical contemporary. After the Second World War he summoned the Germans to confess their guilt and the Swiss to friendship with the Germans. He fought against German rearmament as against nuclear armament during the Cold War. His Swiss heritage gave him the freedom to take political positions while at the same time bringing him under attack as an outsider.

Barth always stood up for his convictions clearly. Even outside the theological world many admired his incorruptibility. Others were sharply critical of the stands he took. His writings were censored and he himself was under surveillance.

Similarly, his private situation was difficult. For almost forty years he lived with his wife and his mistress under one roof. All of them suffered under this arrangement but found no way out.

In the early decades following his death Barth's approach remained influential. In more recent years however many have put aside his theology as static and outdated, and described his personality as authoritarian.

Barth's personal and professional life, and the times in which he lived, were marked by conflict. It is now time, from a greater historical distance, to take a new

---

[1] Paul Althaus according to Loewenich, *Erlebte Theologie*, 60.

look at Barth's central concern to speak of God entirely differently from what was customary, and to reconstruct how his life, so filled with contradictions, and his thought, which sought to make contradictions and conflicts fruitful, influenced each other. Barth was unwavering, yet he also experienced self-doubt and loneliness. He was a harsh judge of others, but could also surprise, with his humor and twinkling eyes. And he was a friend to human beings.

Karl Barth: His Life from Letters and Autobiographical Texts, the biography by Eberhard Busch, Barth's personal assistant in the final years of his life, is foundational for any biographical treatment of Barth. This book owes much to Busch's work.

I dedicate this work to Eberhard Jüngel, a critical student of Barth and my professor, who taught me how inspiring Barth's theology is.

In Horgen, a town near the "Bergli," May 10, 2018.

Christiane Tietz

Acknowledgments

Work on this biography would not have been possible without the support of the Karl Barth-Archive in Basel and its director, Dr. Peter Zocher. I am deeply grateful to him for his prompt attention in providing me with materials and information.

Dr. Hans-Anton Drewes, the previous director of the Karl Barth-Archive, and Dr. Niklaus Peter, board member of the Karl Barth-Foundation Basel, took on the work of reading the manuscript and offering critical suggestions that improved it. In the past few years Niklaus Peter has been an important conversation partner about Barth's contemporary significance.

Pastor Dieter Zellweger, president of the commission that oversees Barth's literary estate, followed and supported my project with sympathetic interest, permitting the citations from Nelly Barth's letters.

Jakob and Thomas Lindt agreed to the publication of previously unpublished passages from a letter from Barth to their mother Gertrud Lindt.

I would like to express my deep thanks to the Berta Hess-Cohn Foundation of Basel for a publication stipend for the German edition.

I would not have been able to complete this book without my colleagues Johanna Breidenbach, Liliane Frei, Michael Pfenninger, and Dominik Weyl. They helped me collect the literature and in the final months of work spent their evenings, weekends, and holidays reading and correcting the manuscript. Through their encouraging feedback they—as well as numerous friends—helped me persevere throughout the arduous periods of writing this book.

I am deeply grateful to C. H. Beck publishers who published the original German edition of this book and to its editor Dr. Ulrich Nolte for his encouragement of this project and his valuable support. I am filled with joy that the English edition of this book is now being published by Oxford University Press.

Finally, my sincere thanks go to Victoria J. Barnett, who so wonderfully translated this book, with all her scholarly expertise and linguistic sensitivity.

Contents

List of Illustrations	xv
List of Abbreviations	xix

1. "I Belong to Basel": Ancestors and Childhood, 1886–1904 — 1
   - A Guildmaster, Pastors, and Scholars: Barth's Ancestors — 1
   - A Strict Love for Truth and Christian Discipline: His Parents — 8
   - "A Great Great Joy": Childhood and Youth — 12

2. "This Obscure Desire toward a Better Understanding":
   Studies, 1904–9 — 23
   - The Decision to Study Theology — 23
   - Student in Bern — 24
   - Wearing the Colors and Noncombative: In the Zofingia Association — 26
   - "Very Diligent and Quite Capable": Student in Berlin — 28
   - Once More in Bern and then Tübingen — 32
   - In Marburg at last — 35
   - His Work for *Die Christliche Welt* — 37

3. "Stumbling up the Steps to Calvin's Pulpit": Geneva, 1909–11 — 48
   - Vicar in Geneva — 48
   - Quite Demanding: The First Confirmation Instruction — 50
   - Theologian in the Congregation — 52
   - "In Such a Dreadfully Pious Environment" — 53
   - A Daughter from a Good Home: The Engagement to Nelly Hoffmann — 55
   - Farewell to Geneva — 56

4. "The Red Pastor": Safenwil, 1911–21 — 61
   - "This System of Employment Must Fall": Workers and Socialists — 62
   - A Theological Friendship: Eduard Thurneysen — 66
   - "The World…without Gods": The First World War — 68
   - "An Open House": Family Life — 73

5. "A Book for Those Who Were Also Concerned":
   The First *Epistle to the Romans*, 1919 — 84
   - Human Religion and the Divine Word — 84
   - "Like a Bomb on the Playground of the Theologians" — 90
   - "Without Windows to the Kingdom of Heaven": The Tambach Lecture — 91

6. "To Always Work Somewhat Faster": Göttingen, 1921–5 — 100
   - From Swiss Pastor to German Professor — 100

"Unavoidable Nonsense of the Academic Business"	103
"Almost Like a Buddy": Barth with His Students	109
"Lively Combat": Emanuel Hirsch and Other Colleagues	110
"Stranger from a Neutral Place": Karl Barth and the Germans	112

7. "Not a Stone Left Standing": The Second *Epistle to the Romans*, 1922 — 121
   - A Critical Turn — 121
   - The New Version of the *Epistle to the Romans* — 125
   - Critics and Admirers — 130
   - What is Dialectical Theology? — 133
   - Dialectical Traveling Companions: Brunner, Bultmann, Gogarten — 137
   - Fifteen Questions and Sixteen Answers: The Controversy with Harnack — 142

8. "The Need for Thinking Further": Münster, 1925–30 — 153
   - A Call and a Momentous Encounter — 153
   - Received with Joy, Departing in Discord — 156
   - In the Tunnel of the Semester — 158
   - Return to Bern? — 163
   - "The Church, the Church, the Church": Encounters with Catholicism — 165
   - Riding, House Music, and Travel — 167

9. A Troubled "Ménage à Trois": Charlotte von Kirschbaum — 177
   - A Long-Guarded Secret — 177
   - "I Never Knew That There Could Be Something Like This" — 178
   - "A Certain Double Life" — 183
   - Three under One Roof — 188

10. "A Swissman in the Middle of Germany": Bonn, 1930–5 — 199
    - Working on Theology — 199
    - The Humanity of God — 202
    - First Conflicts with German Nationalists: The Case of Günther Dehn — 206
    - Now's the Time for the Social Democrat Party: 1933 — 209
    - Warnings to the Church and a Letter to Hitler — 211
    - 1933 as a Year of Crisis in the Barth Household — 214
    - The Theological Dimension of Barth's Relationship to Charlotte von Kirschbaum — 220
    - Attacks on the Swissman — 223
    - Against the "German Greeting" — 225
    - The Break with his Dialectical Traveling Companions — 226
    - The Barmen Theological Declaration — 231
    - Suspension, Ban on Public Speaking, Dismissal — 239

11. "We Who Can Still Speak": Basel, 1935–45	268
Life Goes On: Professor in Basel	268
International Honors and Lack of Appreciation	270
Battle for the Confessing Church	272
Anti-Appeasement: The Call to the Czechs to Resist	277
The Political Responsibility of a Christian	280
Church Struggle and Refugee Aid	283
Ecumenical Silence at the Onset of the War	286
Family Intrigues and Grief	288
A Call for Military Resistance, and Swiss Censorship	290
A Friend of the Germans, Nonetheless	299
12. "In Political Respects a Dubious Will-o'-the-Wisp": Basel, 1945–62	314
War's End and the Declaration of Guilt	314
Back to Bonn and, Once Again, State and Church Issues	320
"God's Beloved Eastern Zone": Against Anti-Communism	324
A Pacifist after All? Protest against Rearmament and Nuclear Weapons	330
Yes to Ecumenism, but without the Catholics	336
The Master with the Crumpled Tie	341
The Discovery of Optimism in Prison	344
Courage, Tempo, Purity, Peace: Confession to Mozart	346
Children, Grandchildren, and the Rejection of His Desired Successor	347
13. "The White Whale": *Church Dogmatics*	362
"A Conceptual Helix": Barth's Monumental Work	362
The Threefold Form of the Word of God	364
God's Three Modes of Being	366
"God Is" Means "God Loves"	368
Whom God Elects	369
What God Commands	371
Why God Wants the Creation	372
Nothingness and the Shadow Sides of Creation	373
The Threefold Office of Christ and the Three Forms of Sin	375
The Light Shines Where It Wishes	376
The Baptism of Water and of the Spirit	377
14. "All Things Considered, a Little Tired": The Final Years, Basel, 1962–8	383
"Fantastic": A Calvinist in the United States	383
"Rules for Older People in Relation to Younger"	387
"As If Deeply Veiled": Charlotte von Kirschbaum Must Move Out	390
"Separated Brothers": In Conversation with Rome	394

A Late Friendship with Carl Zuckmayer 397
The Uncompleted Mammoth Work 399
At the End of His Life Journey 400

Epilogue 409
Chronology 413
Bibliography 417
Index 433

List of Illustrations

1.1. Fritz and Anna Barth, 1884, © Karl Barth-Archive in Basel. — 9
1.2. Anna Barth with Karl Barth, 1886, © Karl Barth-Archive in Basel. — 13
1.3. The Barth children in 1897: Peter, Karl, Gertrud, Heinrich and Katharina Barth, © Karl Barth-Archive in Basel. — 14
2.1. Karl Barth as a member of the Bern Zofingia Association in 1907, © Karl Barth-Archive in Basel. — 32
2.2. Karl Barth in Marburg, 1909, © Karl Barth-Archive in Basel. — 38
3.1. Calvin's pulpit in the Temple de l'Auditoire, Geneva, © Bibliothèque de Genève/Foto Atelier Boissonnas. — 49
3.2. Karl Barth's engagement to Nelly Hoffmann, 1911, © Karl Barth-Archive in Basel. — 57
4.1. The Reformed church in Safenwil, the old parsonage in the foreground, © Erhard Sommer, Kölliken, used with permission. — 62
4.2. Karl Barth with Eduard Thurneysen at the "Bergli," 1920, © Karl Barth-Archive in Basel. — 67
4.3. Nelly Barth in 1932, © Karl Barth-Archive in Basel. — 74
4.4. Karl and Nelly Barth with children Franziska, Markus, and Christoph in 1918, © Karl Barth-Archive in Basel. — 75
5.1. Karl Barth in front of the Safenwil parsonage in 1913, © Karl Barth-Archive in Basel. — 86
6.1. Karl Barth with son Hans Jakob in 1925, © Karl Barth-Archive in Basel. — 102
6.2. Karl Barth as a young professor in Göttingen, 1925, © Karl Barth-Archive in Basel. — 106
7.1. Friedrich Gogarten, Eduard Thurneysen, and Karl Barth at the "Bergli" at the founding of the journal *Zwischen den Zeiten*, 1922, © Karl Barth-Archive in Basel. — 142
8.1. The Barth family with a housekeeper, 1927, © Karl Barth-Archive in Basel. — 155
8.2. Karl Barth in 1925, © Karl Barth-Archive in Basel. — 159
9.1. Charlotte von Kirschbaum, © Karl Barth-Archive in Basel. — 178
9.2. The "Bergli" in Oberrieden, the garage with the "Törli" in the background, © Karl Barth-Archive in Basel. — 185
9.3. Karl Barth with Charlotte von Kirschbaum at the "Bergli" in 1929, © Karl Barth-Archive in Basel. — 187

xvi LIST OF ILLUSTRATIONS

9.4. Nelly Barth and Charlotte von Kirschbaum in Bonn,
© Karl Barth-Archive in Basel. 191
10.1. Karl Barth in Bonn, 1930, © Karl Barth-Archive in Basel. 200
10.2. Karl Barth in 1932, © Karl Barth-Archive in Basel. 208
10.3. Karl Barth with Charlotte von Kirschbaum in 1935 near
the "Bergli" in Oberrieden, © Karl Barth-Archive in Basel. 218
10.4. Karl Barth with his mother Anna Barth in 1928,
© Karl Barth-Archive in Basel. 219
10.5. Karl Barth with Emil Brunner, ca. 1935, © Karl Barth-Archive in Basel. 228
10.6. At the 1934 Barmen confessional synod: Karl Barth
(with pipe) on the left; the two other persons cannot be identified
with certainty, © Karl Barth-Archive in Basel. 232
10.7. Hans Asmussen, Karl Barth, and Heinrich Vogel in Doorn,
Netherlands, 1935, © Karl Barth-Archive in Basel. 238
11.1. Karl Barth in 1937, © Karl Barth-Archive in Basel. 273
11.2. Karl Barth in Moravia, 1935, © Karl Barth-Archive in Basel. 278
11.3. Hiking with his sons Christoph and Markus Barth in the summer
of 1941, a month after the death of son Matthias,
© Karl Barth-Archive in Basel. 290
11.4. Karl Barth as a soldier, 1940, © Karl Barth-Archive in Basel. 292
12.1. Karl Barth with Pierre Maury, 1945, © Karl Barth-Archive in Basel. 316
12.2. Barth's final home on Bruderholzallee. Photo: Christiane Tietz. 319
12.3. Karl Barth in Italy, 1954, © Karl Barth-Archive in Basel. 332
12.4. *Der Spiegel* cover of December 23, 1959, © DER SPIEGEL 52/1959. 335
12.5. Karl Barth with Willem A. Visser 't Hooft at a 1960 conference of
the World Student Christian Federation in Strasbourg,
© Karl Barth-Archive in Basel. 340
12.6. Karl Barth in Bossey, 1958, © Karl Barth-Archive in Basel. 343
12.7. Karl Barth and the painter Paul Basilius Barth in 1954,
© Karl Barth-Archive in Basel. 348
12.8. Karl Barth with grandson Dieter Zellweger in 1955,
© Karl Barth-Archive in Basel. 350
13.1. Karl Barth's study at the Bruderholzallee home in Basel, doorway to
Charlotte von Kirschbaum's office in the background. Photo:
Christiane Tietz. 363
13.2. Karl Barth with Charlotte von Kirschbaum at his desk in 1955,
© Karl Barth-Archive in Basel. 367
14.1. *Time Magazine* cover of April 20, 1962, https://time.com/ 384

14.2. Karl Barth at the Gettysburg battlefield, 1962,
    © Karl Barth-Archive in Basel.   387
14.3. Karl Barth and Charlotte von Kirschbaum, 1967,
    © Karl Barth-Archive in Basel.   392
14.4. Karl Barth with Nelly Barth, 1966, © Karl Barth-Archive in Basel.   393
14.5. Karl Barth with Hans Küng, 1966, © Karl Barth-Archive in Basel.   395

All photographs provided by the Karl Barth-Archive in Basel were used with kind permission.

List of Abbreviations

CD	*Church Dogmatics*
GA	Karl Barth Gesamtausgabe
KBA	Karl Barth-Archive
SP	Swiss Social Democrat Party
SPD	German Social Democrat Party

1
"I Belong to Basel"
Ancestors and Childhood, 1886–1904

"On the 10th of May, 1886, at midday as the clock struck twelve I came into the world. The constellation was propitious."[1] Echoing Goethe, these could have been the opening words of Karl Barth's autobiography, a project he ventured as he was approaching the age of eighty. Barth could have started with himself.

Yet he chose a different opening, setting the tone by quoting a hymn by the poet Paul Gerhardt: "What have we here or what are we/Of good what can earth give/That we do not alone from Thee/Our Father, aye receive?"[2] It resounds like a summary of Barth's theology: human beings are what they are solely through God.

For Karl Barth this also meant that a person's life does not start with himself but with his parents and their parents and grandparents. He began his autobiography with them. As he looked back at his life he wished to understand himself as "defined and limited" by them but also "free as himself."[3] He dug through archives and traced his family tree back as far as the Reformation to find out more about his ancestors. At the end he discovered that he was "somehow connected to them all" and could "somehow recognize" himself in them; they were part "of my present and my future as well."[4]

Unfortunately Barth's portrayal only went as far back as his grandparents' generation, but his examination of his own roots is revealing.[5]

A Guildmaster, Pastors, and Scholars: Barth's Ancestors

The Barth family came from Mülligen in the Swiss canton of Aargau.[6] Some five kilometers away above the Aare River is Habsburg Castle, the ancestral seat of the Habsburg royal house. Barth suspected somewhat sheepishly

> that one or another of my Barthian ancestors may have been in Morgarten in 1315 and in Sempach in 1386[7] . . . : not among the victorious original Swiss but on the wrong side, and there certainly not as noble knights in shining armor, but only among the lightly armed footmen or among the Habsburg hangers-on—one of those who in both battles would have been the first to run off in disgrace.[8]

Because the parish records in Mülligen were lost in a fire, Barth could find only one ancestor with the family name Barth as far back as the mid-eighteenth century, a "farmer named Hans Jakob who surely worked industriously in his field and stable."[9] His grandson, Karl Barth's great-grandfather Samuel Barth, moved from Mülligen to Little Basel (*Kleinbasel*), the sector of Basel on the right bank of the Rhine, and had a tobacco store there. He became a Basel citizen in 1816.

In turn his son, Franz Albert Barth, Karl Barth's paternal grandfather, studied theology and was initially a pastor in the canton of Basel-Country. In 1852 he began working as a teacher at the Upper School for Young Ladies (*Höhere Töchterschule*), a secondary girls' school founded in 1813 in the city of Basel at the initiative of the "Society for Enlivening and Encouraging the Good and the Public Benefit." In 1861 he became pastor of the Church of St. Theodore in Little Basel. He was "a quiet but active and faithful preacher, counselor and teacher... My father always spoke of him with the most affectionate respect."[10]

Political interest was natural in the household of Barth's grandparents. In contrast to other German-speaking Swiss, they opposed Napoleon III and supported the Germans in the 1870–1 Franco-Prussian War. Karl Barth recalled in particular one of his grandfather's "mementos of this preference": "a nutcracker with the unmistakable head and face of Bismarck (which had the effect that for a long time the words 'Bismarck' and 'nutcracker' meant one and the same thing to me)."[11]

Karl Barth's paternal grandmother came from an old Kleinbasel family, the Lotz's. Burkhard Lotz, the oldest ancestor he was able to trace, was a butcher who came to Basel from the Alsace and became citizen of Basel in 1543. Barth's great-grandfather Peter Friedrich Lotz was a silk dyer and a highly respected member of the appeals court, member of the City High Council, as well as guild master of the weavers' guild. He seems to have been quite a willful character, and Barth knew a number of stories about him. He had once "mailed all his colleagues on the High Council a washcloth."[12] When Lotz learned that he was to be publicly mocked during the Basel Carnival by one of the customary cliques (organized groups of pipers and drummers and others who march during Carnival), he quickly and impudently joined the head of the clique, armed with an umbrella, and marched with them for three days through the city, a "formidable act of civil courage."[13]

Karl Barth believed that his own vehement outbursts could be traced back to what the family called the "Lotz rage." It was a familiar feature of his father, even if he knew how to suppress it as he grew older. Nor was it foreign to his brothers. When a Lotz loses his temper, Barth wrote in the draft of his autobiography, "he gets piercing green eyes" and "then certainly doesn't always stay within the bounds of... what is right before God and is appropriate for making one popular among one's fellows... May I add to soften this that once the 'Lotz rage' has broken out, it dissipates rather quickly and adopts more humane emotions and manners."[14]

Barth however also traced a certain physical limberness to this side of the family. A distant cousin once told him that one had to be descended from the Lotz family to be able to "stand on one foot and bring the large toe of the other to the mouth... When my cousin had left I tried this secretly myself (at the time I was at least already a full professor in Basel) and in fact...!"[15]

The daughter of headstrong Peter Friedrich Lotz, Sara Lotz married Franz Barth. The couple had five sons and one daughter. Sara Lotz too was clear in her political positions. When the first liberal pastor arrived in Basel she closed "all the blinds of the parsonage on Rebgasse on the day of his installation... as though there had been a death in the family."[16]

Barth's maternal grandfather was a Sartorius, the son of Karl Friedrich Sartorius, about whom the family did not like to speak: "There was sufficient reason and justice to be ashamed of him, wish that he had never been born and to the greatest extent possible to keep quiet about him or only speak of him in whispered references."[17]

In his autobiographical draft Karl Barth did the opposite: he spent considerably more time on Sartorius than on the others.

> The decisive thing that drew me to him and captured my focus for a fairly long time was only this, that in no sense was he a shining light... rather he only appeared to me to be the most obviously lacking, poorest, unhappy figure among my ancestors that I knew of: as someone who unequivocally failed in the school of life and thus as a pariah demanded my attention.[18]

Barth did not wish to treat him condescendingly, since the process of dealing with him was "perhaps... in anticipation part of the portrait of my own life."[19]

Karl Friedrich Sartorius was born in 1793 near the Saxon city of Annaberg. He studied theology and philology in Leipzig and received his doctorate in 1815. In the same year he moved to Basel to become a teacher at a private school there. The school closed in 1818, but in the meantime Sartorius had become a teacher of German literature and history at the Basel humanistic *Pädagogium*, the second oldest secondary school in Switzerland.

Through his impressive speeches he soon drew the attention of the people of Basel. In 1819 he was appointed to the first chair for German literature at the University of Basel without needing to go through the customary procedure for appointments. In his public appearances he battled fervently for the new humanism, for truth, virtue, and beauty. Barth's impression however was that he dealt only eclectically with literature and philosophy. While some of those who heard him found his lectures academically deficient, others praised him as "a star of the highest order in the firmament of scholars from Raurach," a comparison that in

Barth's judgement was quite exaggerated, since in that era great scholars like the naturalist Peter Merian and the theologian Wilhelm Martin Leberecht de Wette were lecturing at the University of Basel.[20]

Privately however things at some point began to go wrong for Sartorius. "Here was where his ship, after a departure that promised happiness, blundered into a whirlwind that then led to his human, professional and civil ruin."[21] In 1823 he married Sophie Huber, the daughter of the architect Achilles Huber. Barth was convinced that they were deeply in love. In a short period of time the couple had four children.

The marriage appeared "at first to have been subjectively 'happy.'" "Even later I could find no sign that this relationship had been disrupted by another woman."[22] Barth determined that Sophie Huber must have been "a lovely, sensitive young woman to be sure, very impressionable to the nature and environment around her, but in terms of keeping these impressions up, let alone mastering them, she was simply in need of clear direction."[23] Therefore she fled to her parents through letters where she wrote about the household, her health, and the children, but never about "the intellectual intentions and activities of her Karl Friedrich. Was it because according to her own statements she wasn't really preoccupied by them? Or for her part was she simply not gifted enough intellectually?"[24]

Around 1830 the theologian and philologist Karl Ludwig Roth, a teacher in Basel who later became professor at the university, joined the household as the children's tutor. Barth thought it unlikely that there was a relationship between Roth and his great-grandmother. He believed however that because of Roth's dignified, academically respectable manner, for the parents of Sophie Huber he quickly took the place of Sartorius, who had no authority over his wife and could hardly impress her with his unproductive studies. Indeed, at home he had been "a lonely shadow figure."[25]

The situation became difficult as rumors began to spread through Basel that Sartorius drank too often and too much. Soon he no longer lived in the family country house but rented an apartment in town. After several public scandals related mostly to his misuse of alcohol he submitted his resignation to the university on November 12, 1832. When he attempted two days later to withdraw it, the university responded by noting his "academic incompetence" and the "poorness of his instruction."[26] Sartorius left Switzerland shortly thereafter and returned to the German Ore Mountains (*Erzgebirge*). On New Year's Day 1834 he preached a sermon once more in his Saxon homeland. Barth read it "again and again...always looking for something new that...might once more change the portrait of him...Unfortunately...in vain."[27] One year later, in 1835, Sartorius was dead.

Between the lines of Sartorius's final sermon was sadness about his own life, the loss of his family and the respect that he had once received, but also reproaches about his unfair treatment and self-blame. For Barth it was the "final...tortured...howl of a man...who...for this very reason was so helpless because he continued to believe that he could help himself."[28]

What Barth however did not find in the sermon—and perhaps as someone approaching the end of his own life he especially longed for it—was someone comforted by *"forgiven*...guilt," "the divine 'sympathy.'"[29] This was theologically unsatisfactory for Barth. On a human level however he was moved:

> what the sermon *actually* cries for is human sympathy: a taking part in the *misery* of this one existence and essence. One cannot and may not deny him this, particularly if one understands or thinks he understands genuine, divine "sympathy": this poor, helpless, and as far as one can tell stubborn to the very end— dear great-grandfather![30]

Karl Barth's maternal grandfather Karl Achilles Sartorius was the eldest son of this great-grandfather. He attended the *Pädagogium* where the extraordinary Germanist Wilhelm Wackernagel, a full professor at the University of Basel since 1835, became his teacher. In 1843 he began his theological studies in Basel and continued them in Berlin where he attended the lectures of the elderly Friedrich Wilhelm Joseph Schelling. After this he went to Heidelberg. From his time in Berlin he brought first editions of Schleiermacher's *Die christliche Sitte* as well as Schleiermacher's letters and sermons, which Karl Barth after the death of his grandmother "brought to Safenwil, to prevent others from getting these first. They have truly come in handy and to this day are an especially treasured ornament in my library."[31]

In 1849 Karl Achilles took a pastorate in Bretzwil in the canton of Basel-Country and married Margaretha Rickenbach, who bore one daughter but died only two years after the wedding. That same year he transferred to the St. Elisabeth Church in Basel. There he worked on behalf of a new church building, which was financed by the Basel patron and large landowner Christoph Merian. In 1864 the first worship service took place in the new St. Elisabeth Church, which is the most significant neo-Gothic church in Switzerland and seats 1,200. Karl Barth recalled that as a small child he had often been in the parsonage next to the church. There he received "an impression" of the "dignity and pastoral solemnity" of his grandfather, "which later I was unable to convey in the slightest to my own grandchildren."[32]

Already in 1854 Karl Achilles Sartorius remarried, to Johanna Burckhardt. The couple had nine children, of whom the seventh was Karl Barth's mother Anna. The eldest son of this second marriage was also named Karl and became a close student friend of Barth's father, who would name his son for him.

In Barth's view the theological profile of his grandfather was rather simple: despite the fact that he had experienced the "Schleiermacher atmosphere" during his studies, "in the following period [he] had gone over...to a rather primitive theological conservatism, which was softened only by the mild pietism of my good grandmother."[33] While in him Barth observed an "upright and warm Christocentrism" there was also the tendency toward a "stern and severe Reformed orthodoxy modified somewhat by a...Lutheran element."[34] In the battle of theological directions during that era[35] between liberal "Reformers," who sought to free themselves from outdated dogmas, reform the liturgy and eliminate the Apostolic Creed or make it optional, and the so-called "Positives," who for the sake of the church's substance wanted to preserve what in their eyes were the proven traditions, Karl Achilles Sartorius stood on the side of the latter. He combatted the spirit of materialism and atheism that was permeating the church with an "at times wrathful, at times somewhat fearful defensiveness."[36] He was "a typical representative of that ecclesial and pastoral glory which in a rather uptight and humorless manner contradicted the tendencies of that century, especially after 1848, and yet at the same time in its neo-Gothicism probably did not quite correspond to the Gospel," but which in its fidelity and devotion nonetheless possessed "its particular Christian luminosity."[37] Barth's mother Anna could recall her father's statement, in a tone both strict and despairing: "Anna, the teachings of the Bible and the Church are a building from which one cannot remove a single small stone, otherwise the entire thing collapses!"[38]

"Sociologically speaking...the highest, most distinguished aspect" of Barth's heritage, of which Barth was "not a little proud," was his maternal grandmother's family, the Burckhardts, for they were one of the original Basel families and made up at least a quarter of Barth's ancestry.

> Here we have been from the very beginning, neither in Aargau or even in Saxony, but in Basel, and not in Little Basel ("the lesser one") but in the Great Basel on the left bank of the Rhine, from where formerly at the entrance to the only bridge over the Rhine the *Lällenkönig* ("Tongue King"),[39] which can still be viewed in the Historical Museum, condescendingly stuck his tongue out toward Little Basel (originally part of Austria). "One certainly does not live there," my great uncle and godfather Hans Burckhardt-Burckhardt told my mother when she as an older woman temporarily settled in Little Basel.[40]

The Burckhardts had resided in Basel since the Reformation. Christoph Burckhardt arrived in Basel in 1521 and became a citizen in 1523. He made his money in the cloth and silk trade and married Gertrud Brand. Barth hung a portrait of the pair in his last study on Bruderholzallee.

The most significant theological ancestor from this line was Barth's great-great-grandfather Johannes Rudolf Burckhardt, who was the pastor at St. Peter's Church in Basel. A piece of furniture from his parsonage made its way to Karl Barth: his "modest, but for the needs of that time practically arranged (with openings for an inkpot, a sand pot, and the elongated, literally named 'feathers' of that era) writing desk."[41] Barth's great-grandfather Johannes Burckhardt took the desk with him to Bretzwil and Schaffhausen; ultimately, when Barth's grandmother Johanna Burckhardt wed Karl Achilles Sartorius, the desk returned to Basel, where for many years it stood in the St. Elizabeth's parsonage. Karl Barth received it as a gift from his grandmother in 1911 when he started his own ministry in Safenwil; he then took it with him at every stage. In his last residence it stood in the guestroom. Today it is in his old parsonage in Safenwil. "If such a faithful old writing desk could speak!"[42]

Johannes Rudolf Burckhardt was an influential pietist figure in Basel. This Protestant revival movement viewed the Christianity of that era as having become dormant and saw the governing church structures as hindrances. Instead, they sought to revive the personal piety of individual believers and create new forms for Christian communal fellowship. Burckhardt's friends included some of the leading figures in this revival movement like Nikolaus Graf von Zinzendorf, the founder of the Moravian Brotherhood.

Johannes Rudolf Burckhardt married three times. Barth's maternal great-grandfather, Johannes Burckhardt, was his twenty-first child, and one of his brothers was the father of the historian Jacob Burckhardt, who achieved world renown with his scholarship on the cultural history of Italian Renaissance art.

After a brief attempt to study medicine Johannes Burckhardt came into contact with the revivalist movement in Geneva and went to Tübingen to study theology. His friendship with Ludwig Hofacker, who became one of the most important preachers in the Württemberg revivalist movement, stems from this period. After his examinations in 1822 Burckhardt moved to Wuppertal, which was also under the revivalist influence. He hoped to become a missionary but instead was called as pastor of St. James Church in Basel. In 1826 he married Amalie Peyer, daughter of a patrician family from Schaffhausen. She was also the descendant of a long line of clergy; one of her ancestors was Heinrich Bullinger, the Reformer and successor of Huldrych Zwingli at the Zurich Großmünster Church. In 1827 they moved to Betzwil, southeast of Basel. Later he became director of the Schaffhausen branch of the Basel Mission, a mission society founded in 1815 and influenced by the Basel pietism. The couple had three daughters and one son.

Barth acknowledged in his memoirs that he had "received the strongest spiritual impression from this man."[43] According to Barth, Johannes Burckhardt was someone with "a living relationship to the living Lord Jesus Christ—and for that reason he was not gloomy, pessimistic...bigoted...stern, trying to repress his environment legalistically, but someone who was in the best sense an uplifting and pleasant pietist."[44]

As the second wife of Karl Sartorius junior, Johannes Burckhardt's youngest daughter Johanna became Karl Barth's grandmother. According to Barth she remained more faithful to the devout pietism of her father and grandfather, rather than conforming to her husband. She had a "certain sternness" which however "was to some extent outshone by a great goodness and solicitousness."[45] For that reason her grandchildren enjoyed visiting her even in her old age, and her tiny house on Nonnenweg 60 became "a center for the entire extended family."[46] Karl Barth's father, who had buried his own mother already in 1888, developed a close relationship to his mother-in-law.

Barth attributed his own interest in history to the impressions he had received in her home. Portraits of significant clergy from the history of Basel, a zograscope, as well as a depiction of the arrival of the Pilgrims in the New World, contributed to his sense that "everything there gave the air of an honorable past worthy of respect."[47]

A Strict Love for Truth and Christian Discipline: His Parents

Karl Barth's father Johann Friedrich (Fritz) Barth was born on October 25, 1856, as the youngest child of Franz Albert and Sara Barth.[48] Quite sickly as a child, for his parents he was a "worrisome child who needed much consideration and found it difficult to get used to the lively interactions with other children," therefore "at the beginning strongly introverted... and sensitive."[49]

After attending the parish school at St. Theodore's and the humanistic secondary school in Basel, he transferred in 1871 to the Basel *Pädagogium*, where he had the fortune to have renowned teachers. He met the art historian Jacob Burckhardt, the Hebrew scholar Emil Kautzsch, and in the 1873–4 academic year Friedrich Nietzsche, who at the time was professor of classical philology in Basel. With his "incisive critique of the modern condition, along with his distinguished reserved manner" Nietzsche made a "'lasting impact' on him."[50] In 1909 Fritz Barth recalled: "Personally I can only speak of Nietzsche with great regard, since as a student I had him as a teacher and did not experience the slightest dire influence from him."[51] He had not been a philosopher, but "a dithyrambic poet... who remained unchallenged by even the most extreme self-contradictions."[52] His idea "not to follow the paths of the crowd, but to keep in mind one's self and one's needs and abhor all superficiality, all mere knowledge that lacks the corresponding action"[53] seemed educationally fruitful. Fritz Barth's seatmate at the *Pädagogium* was Eduard Thurneysen, who became a theologian and remained a lifelong friend. Thurneysen's son Eduard became one of Karl Barth's closest friends.

Like his three brothers Fritz Barth studied theology. His teachers in Basel after 1874 were Franz Overbeck, the critic of Christendom and friend of Nietzsche, and the dogmatics scholar Julius Kaftan, who had been a student of Albrecht Ritschl. Barth also attended the historical lectures of Jacob Burckhardt and, in the 1876/7 winter semester, those of the still young Adolf Harnack in Leipzig. There however he was enthralled primarily by the musical offerings. During the 1878 summer

1.1. Fritz and Anna Barth, 1884, © Karl Barth-Archive in Basel.

semester he studied in Tübingen with Johann Tobias Beck, who understood how to connect pietistic biblical fealty with speculative thought in a Hegelian spirit. Fritz Barth later said of him: "he was not only a teacher, but became a spiritual father and led me out of the arid heath of self-sufficient criticism to the green pastures of God's word. To him I owe the fact that I may be certain and joyful in my faith even as a theologian."[54]

Following his studies Fritz Barth began in 1879 as a pastor in the small village of Reitnau in the Aargau Canton. In 1884 he married Anna Katharina Sartorius. In addition to his ministry Barth wrote a study on the church father Tertullian's understanding of Paul, which in 1881 earned him the academic degree of licentiate, which today would be analogous to a doctorate.[55]

In April 1886 he and his very pregnant wife moved to Basel, where he taught church history and New Testament at the Protestant Preachers' Seminary. The school had been established in 1876, amidst

> the lack, widely felt and often bewailed, of suitable proclaimers of the Gospel for the needs of our time... to be a place of education for those young men who at this time without any particular heed toward specific church forms, security and honor have decided to serve the Lord as witnesses, wherever and however He wants to use them, to rescue errant souls and to shepherd Christian congregations.[56]

Students with only secondary modern school certificates, who could not attend the university, were accepted. The study of the Bible was to stand at the center of the education. The committee tasked with calling faculty saw in Fritz Barth a "significant young theologian,"[57] and thus "Barth's arrival in the spring of 1886" was the beginning "of a first springtime of the preachers' seminary."[58]

Fritz Barth however remained in Basel only briefly. In 1889 he did his postdoctoral degree at the Theological Faculty in Bern and began to teach there as a lecturer.[59] The faculty hoped in him to engage a university teacher who would continue with the exegetical positions of lecturer Adolf Schlatter, who had moved in 1888 as a professor to Greifswald. In the end Fritz Barth was promoted in Bern in 1895 to full professor.[60]

In Bern Fritz Barth became involved among other things in the canton synod as well as the Protestant Church Welfare Society of Bern[61] and the Bern Committee for the Promotion of Church Charity, since for him Christian life included engagement against social abuses. He fought "especially warmly for the justified claims of the women's movement, of which he had become aware through numerous contacts with noble women."[62]

Academically Fritz Barth was open to historical-critical biblical scholarship, which examined the different layers of text, literary interdependence, and historical context. He thought that he owed it to his era to "respond to its doubts about the Gospel."[63] At the same time he was sympathetic for the conflict that this historical-critical perspective aroused among more devout Christians whose faith relied strongly on the Bible.

His first monograph, *Die Hauptprobleme des Lebens Jesu. Eine geschichtliche Untersuchung* ("The Main Problems of the Life of Jesus: A Historical Study"), appeared quite late, in 1899. It was among the almost overabundant number of publications at the time about the "historical Jesus."[64] His book sought "simply to portray, how it was and how it went, using the impartial questioning of the sources, as we learned from our unforgettable teacher... Burckhardt."[65] As did Jacob Burckhardt in his lectures and books, Fritz Barth in his text also addressed laypeople, "educated non-theologians."[66] His son may well have learned this openness from him. Some laypeople had won the impression through the new research that nothing could be said with certainty anymore about Jesus's life, whereas others already found it dangerous to talk of "problems" in the life of Jesus. Fritz Barth used Alpine images, as Karl Barth would later do, to encourage his readers to join him on his path to understanding:

> Whoever wants to climb a lofty Alpine peak cannot let himself be put off if at times he is enveloped in fog. Soon a fresh wind will rise and tear away the veil of fog; until then however one continues to climb, even when it seems dangerous; the main thing is that the path remains under one's feet and that one continues uphill.[67]

Things will certainly not reach the point of a conflict between faith and thought, between awe toward Jesus and the "strictest love of truth" "because all reality is part of God's world."[68] His son would define the relationship between rationality and faith differently.

In the summer of 1910 Fritz Barth became seriously ill with appendicitis and recovered only after several weeks. On February 25, 1912, he died of blood poisoning at the age of only fifty-five years.

Looking back at his own life, Karl Barth acknowledged he owed his father the "qualifications" for his "later relationship to theology." His father had "become and remained an enduring and often enough exhortative model in the quiet seriousness with which he devoted himself to Christian matters as a scholar and teacher."[69] At the same time Karl Barth was "incapable of making his (moderately) 'positive', as one said at the time... theological attitude and direction his own."[70] Karl Barth revered his father, but also suffered under his father's attempt to influence his son's life plans. Occasionally the repressed anger in statements in his letters to his father can be sensed. In 1909 there was a fierce argument when Karl Barth published a short essay with explicitly liberal views and his father criticized him for it.[71]

At Fritz Barth's funeral it was said of his theology what could be said of his son's thought as well: it had been important to him "that his theology was not grounded in the opinions of the time, which come and go, but rather upon the eternal foundation of God's revelation in Christ, to which the Holy Spirit bears witness."[72] In the final year of his life Karl Barth judged that his father had been among "those overlooked and a little scorned by the theological pillars of his era, great and small."[73] Even in his old age Karl Barth kept a portrait of his father above his desk.

Karl Barth's mother Anna Katharina Sartorius was born on April 15, 1863, in Basel.[74] She attended grammar school followed by five years at the Upper School for Young Ladies. She always emphasized to her children that "school had basically been only a happy time for her; she loved school not only as a place where one learned but as an opportunity to come into contact with people and life."[75]

She received confirmation instruction from her father, whose personality and office made a strong impression on her. "From early on her zest for life was maintained within a strict Christian discipline," her children later wrote, "and it was always the keynote of her existence that the life is meant to be lived in freedom, but bound by faith and that its beauty might also be enjoyed."[76]

At the age of almost twenty she began to oversee the household of her brother Karl Sartorius in Fleurier in the Neuchâtel Jura Mountains. In 1883 they moved together to Bennwil in the canton of Basel-Country. As the closest friend of her brother, Fritz Barth became acquainted with her when he visited them in Bennwil. In April 1884 the two became engaged; they married on August 28, 1884, and she took on the traditional duties of a pastor's wife, first in Reitnau and then in Basel and Bern. With her support her husband was able to invite students to their home one evening a week for conversation. Both Adolf Schlatter and Adolf Harnack were guests in the family home.[77] Like her husband, Anna Barth became involved in the Protestant Church Welfare Society of Bern and visited Protestant schools in the Catholic cantons of Valais and Fribourg. She was a committee member on the Friends of Young Ladies, which tried to protect young women from prostitution, as well as a board member of the Protestant Women's Aid of Bern, which offered support for women in difficult circumstances.

In 1918, six years after the death of her husband, Anna Barth moved back to her birth city of Basel to oversee the household of her youngest son Heinrich, and she followed him in 1929 back to Bern. In 1935 she became very ill and died on September 5, 1938, of the aftereffects of an "arterial sclerosis of the brain."[78]

Karl Barth's relationship to his mother was filled with tension. As a pastor he sent her his sermons for her critical comments. In 1920, when she disagreed with his theological changes, Barth had a dream about his own funeral: "but I only appeared to be dead and, already in my grave, protested vigorously. My mother suggested very amicably to close the grave, I would then go ahead and die (!!), but I managed to assert myself and then galloped over the cemetery back to life."[79] Her later letters in which she attempted to influence the marital situation of her son offer oppressive insight into her domineering character.[80] Some of her children[81] summarized at her funeral: "Her children and numerous grandchildren found in her a rare participation and empathy in all their affairs. Thus she became an understanding counselor for the young and the old."[82] As we shall see, at certain times in his life Karl Barth could not have said this.

"A Great Great Joy": Childhood and Youth

Karl Barth first saw the world's light in Basel on May 10, 1886, as the first child of Fritz and Anna Barth. The family resided in a small apartment house at Grellinger

"I BELONG TO BASEL" 13

1.2. Anna Barth with Karl Barth, 1886, © Karl Barth-Archive in Basel.

Street 42 in the east part of Basel. In 1888 they moved several houses down to a small row house at Number 36.

The baptism took place on June 20, 1886, in the Basel Münster Church. Barth was baptized by his grandfather Karl Achilles Sartorius. His three godparents were his paternal grandmother Sara Barth-Lotz, Anna Barth's brother Karl, who in the meantime had become a pastor in Pratteln in the canton of Basel-Country, as well as a brother of his maternal grandmother, the wealthy silk industrialist Hans Burckhardt-Burckhardt.

Karl Barth was joined by four siblings. There were two brothers, Peter and Heinrich, and two sisters, Katharina and Gertrud. Katharina, the elder sister, died at the age of six of diphtheria.

1.3. The Barth children in 1897: Peter, Karl, Gertrud, Heinrich and Katharina Barth, © Karl Barth-Archive in Basel.

Peter Barth studied theology in Bern and Marburg and in 1915 married Helene Rade, a daughter of Martin Rade, under whom he worked following his theology studies in Marburg. Peter Barth became a pastor in Switzerland but also continued to do academic work. In 1926 he began to edit the *Opera Selecta* (*Selected Works*) of John Calvin. He was assisted by a theology student, Dora Scheuner,[83] with whom he had an affair, which because of his continued marriage to Helene Rade led to great tensions with his mother Anna Barth. As president of the Bern Canton Theological Working Group, in March 1934 Peter Barth initiated a statement of solidarity by 600 Swiss pastors with the German Pastors Emergency League that was given to Martin Niemöller.[84] In 1940 Peter Barth became severely ill and died.

His younger brother Heinrich Barth contracted polio before he had reached one year and had difficulty walking throughout his life. He studied philosophy and ancient languages in Bern and Marburg, finishing in Berlin. From 1928 to 1960 he was professor of philosophy at the University of Basel. Shaped by the neo-Kantianism of Marburg, his philosophy influenced Karl Barth's second commentary on the Epistle to the Romans.

The youngest sister Gertrud Barth studied law but then became a pastor's wife. Her husband Karl Lindt was pastor from 1922 to 1926 in Beatenberg in Bern Canton and worked after that at the Church of the Holy Ghost in Bern.[85]

Karl Barth grew up in the city on the Aare River after his father's professional move to Bern in 1889. Initially the family lived on the edge of the city in an apartment building on Länggasse 75, near the Bremgarten woods, so that "among my earliest and deepest youthful memories are the many forests, fields and gardens."[86] Yet he also happily recalled the "arcades, fountains, and towers" of the Bern Old City.[87] In addition the Bernese Highlands, with their 4,000 meter high, motionless, icy giant peaks left a deep impression on the youth.

A note from the outline of another autobiography indicates how these natural impressions accompanied him his entire life. The first catchword he wanted to write about in the biography was "landscapes."[88] The influence of the natural world becomes even more evident in the images that Barth used to illustrate his theological thinking. He described his dialectical method for example as wandering on a mountain ridge where one could never stop but always had to keep moving forward, stepping neither too far to the left nor to the right.[89]

In 1895 the family moved to a semi-detached house on Höheweg 13 on the other side of Bern, in the Schosshalde district above the Aare River. In 1896 they moved to a parallel street, to Klaraweg 8, into a freestanding house built for the family.

Although Barth spent most of his childhood and youth in Bern, he never felt native to the city. "I belong to Basel."[90] Barth spent his youth among the natives of Bern, supposedly of a slow, steady mentality, "not without opposition against a temperament and intellectual tendency, under whose paralyzing resistance I not infrequently saw my father suffer."[91]

Barth's childhood was shaped by the Basel German children's songs of the theologian Abel Burckhardt, who composed this Christmas poem:

> The angel told the shepherds:/I tell you of a great great joy;/You dear people, let us be joyful,/This night the Savior has come to us/ . . . O little child Jesus in the ugly stall,/Have you come to me from the heavenly hall?/Have you come to me and then look for me/and are you my dear little brother?[92]

Even as an old man Barth related how he was "greatly indebted" to Burckhardt since his children's songs were

> the text-book in which, at the beginning of the last decade of the last century, I received my first theological instruction in a form appropriate to my then immaturity. And what made an indelible impression on me was the homely naturalness with which these very modest compositions spoke of the events of Christmas, Palm Sunday, Good Friday, Easter, the Ascension and Pentecost as things which might take place any day in Basel or its environs like any other important happenings. History? Doctrine? Dogma? Myth? No—but things actually taking place, so that we could see and hear and lay up in our hearts. For as these songs were sung in the everyday language we were then beginning to hear and speak, and as we joined in singing, we took our mother's hand, as it were, and went to the stall at Bethlehem, and to the streets of Jerusalem where, greeted by children of a similar age, the Saviour made His entry.[93]

The decisive influence of this early religious impression on Barth's later fundamental theological convictions is evident in the fact that the declaration above is in one of the final volumes of his main work, the *Church Dogmatics*. At that place in the text is the question of how one can speak of the presence of Jesus Christ when he lived 2,000 years ago.[94] Is it possible to bridge this historical distance? Barth explains that faith is not the pure remembering of a long-sunken past. Rather, in all the Christian celebrations like Christmas, Good Friday, and Easter, "the tacit presupposition of all these actions" is "that, preceding our remembrance, the One whom we remember is Himself in action now, today and here," that what took place back then "takes place today and will again take place tomorrow."[95] Barth acknowledged this view as seminal for his theological work:

> The yawning chasm of Lessing did not exist. The contemporaneity of Kierkegaard was not a problem. The Saviour Himself was obviously the same yesterday and today. All very naive, and not worth mentioning at all in academic circles? Yes, it was very naive, but perhaps in the very naiveté there lay the deepest wisdom and greatest power, so that once grasped it was calculated to carry one relatively unscathed—although not, of course, untempted or unassailed—through all the serried ranks of historicism and anti-historicism, mysticism and rationalism, orthodoxy, liberalism and existentialism, and to lead one back some day to the matter itself.[96]

Barth's parents sent the children for a time to Sunday school. Not much of it seems to have stayed with Barth. He reported that they had sung the song "*Wo findet die Seele die Heimat, die Ruh*" ("O where is the home of the soul to be found"): "Sweet rest, deep rest, heavenly rest!—I recall from the Sunday school of my childhood, how when I heard this sound I used to think of some African animal (probably a Kangaroo[97] or such)."[98] After one far too vivid description of Hell by the Sunday school teacher Barth's father preferred to teach the children at home.[99]

When Barth was older he attended elementary school and then the Free Gymnasium of Bern.[100] In 1859 this private boys' school had been founded during the Bern *Kulturkampf* between liberals and conservatives by Theodor von Lerber, a pietistically influenced classical philologist and secondary teacher who belonged to the "positive" (not the "liberal") camp of Swiss Christianity of that time. He came from an old Bern patrician family with some political influence in the city. Under the liberal government of his time Lerber feared the loss of humanistic and religious formation in the public schools and for that reason developed his Protestant school "as an alternative model to the secular ideal of education of the modern, liberal state."[101] Humanistic education was as natural in the Lerber School as the daily class in religion. The school was not simply to serve the personal edification of individuals, but to create strong personalities:

"Rock-solid men who remain standing in the storms of their times...not blowing with the wind...men who could sacrifice anything but their convictions."[102]

By the time Karl Barth entered the school it had left behind the strict biblicism of its founder and had been renamed "Free Gymnasium" several years before. The subjects of study emphasized were mathematics and the new natural sciences, rather than instruction in religion and Latin.[103] Yet Barth still enjoyed a quite fine humanistic education, even if he himself complained one day that he "was never so well instructed in the older languages" as was customary in German humanistic secondary schools.[104] His school day always began with a short morning devotion. There was prayer several times a day, sometimes very brief, as when Karl Barth recalled his mathematics teacher: "'Lord, bless us. Amen' was one of his shortest forms. But that really says everything."[105]

In 1900 Barth and his school friends founded a school club, "Studia," and in 1902 he became a member of the student organization "Patria"; both groups gave him numerous opportunities to give speeches.[106] Some friendships from his schooldays remained lifelong.

Even in elementary school he had no aptitude for arithmetic ("I have always been a poor calculator").[107] In secondary school too he had a "hostile antipathy" against mathematics and natural science that continued to pursue him during the 1920s "sometimes...even in my dreams."[108] His unattractive handwriting was complained about, but he quickly became "a bookworm."[109] He was especially interested in historical narratives and therefore history class. Again and again, beginning at the age of seven or eight, he avidly read the *Heldenbuch* ("The Book of Heroes") by Christian Niemeyer, "a bloodthirsty account" of the war of independence against Napoleon.[110] It left such an impact on him that even as an elementary student, when his teacher asked for a sentence with an accusative object, he replied without hesitation: "Napoleon established the Confederation of the Rhine."[111] By his own account, well into his adolescence warlike scenes and events dominated his "intellectual life."[112] He and his brothers spent many hours earnestly playing with tin soldiers. Barth's youthful memories include his four-year long membership in the Bern Cadet Corps, where he learned military discipline, how to shoot, and the basic elements of maneuvers, and where, despite only modest talent as a sharpshooter, he reached the level of sergeant.[113] In 1905 however he was exempted from military service due to his nearsightedness.[114]

Barth was naturally fascinated by Schiller's drama *William Tell* and the works of the poet Theodor Körner, who had died young in action, and began eagerly to write literature himself. During his summer holidays 1899 at the age of thirteen he prepared a collection of his writings and titled them "Karl Barth's Collected Works, dedicated to his grandmama."[115]

Because music was cultivated in the family home Barth learned to play the violin, efforts that in his own opinion "were less than fruitful."[116] Nor was he drawn to sports: "I left technical performances of any kind, as e.g. proper gymnastics... up to others without envy."[117]

Barth passed his final school certificate exams in 1904, "floundering in chemistry, physics and such," with a grade of 2.[118] For his graduation his family gave him a trip to Frankfurt and Cologne, which led him for the first time to Germany.

As a child Karl Barth was quite a rascal. At age twelve he wrote in his diary: "Today I beat up many and was beaten up by many. There is actually a wonderful poetry in this active and passive."[119] His school reports include remarks like "daydreams often" or "three hours of detention due to misbehavior." One of the fundamental theological concepts of the adult Karl Barth is his recurrent challenge that theology has to "stay focused on the essence of its topic" (i.e., "the living, personal and free God.") In one of his school report cards his attention to the class in religion was noted with a warning: "stay focused!"[120]

Notes

1. Paraphrase of the opening sentence from Johann Wolfgang von Goethe, *Aus meinem Leben. Dichtung und Wahrheit*, 10.
2. Barth, "Entwurf Autobiographie" (Autobiographical draft), KBA 11303, 1. Translation of Paul Gerhardt's *Ich singe Dir mit Herz und Mund* ("O Lord, I Sing with Lips and Heart"), in: https://hymnary.org/hymn/LH1941/569 (accessed August 26, 2020).
3. Barth, "Entwurf Autobiographie," 1.
4. Barth, "Entwurf Autobiographie," 48.
5. The accounts in this chapter come primarily from Barth's draft of his autobiography (KBA 11303). Over the course of his life Barth wrote several brief biographical outlines that are also referred to in this biography.
6. "At least according to the coat of arms known to us, the name 'Barth' can be traced back to '*Barte*,' i.e., the long lost term for the cutting edge of an ax or similar tool (e.g., a halberd)." Barth, "Entwurf Autobiographie," 2.
7. These refer to two violent battles between Swiss patriots and Habsburg loyalists; both battles play an important role in the legends about the founding of the Swiss Confederation.
8. Barth, "Entwurf Autobiographie," 3.
9. Barth, "Entwurf Autobiographie," 3.
10. Barth, "Entwurf Autobiographie," 4.
11. Barth, "Entwurf Autobiographie," 4.
12. Barth, "Entwurf Autobiographie," 6.
13. Barth, "Entwurf Autobiographie," inserted page after page 6.
14. Barth, "Entwurf Autobiographie," 6f.
15. Barth, "Entwurf Autobiographie," 7.
16. Barth, "Entwurf Autobiographie," 8.
17. Barth, "Entwurf Autobiographie," 10.
18. Barth, "Entwurf Autobiographie," 11.
19. Barth, "Entwurf Autobiographie," 11.

20. Barth, "Entwurf Autobiographie," 17. Raurach (Rauracien) is the countryside in northwest Switzerland surrounding Basel, bordered by the German Black Forest, French Vosges Mountains, and Swiss Jura Mountains. The area was originally inhabited by the Celtic tribe of Rauraei.
21. Barth, "Entwurf Autobiographie," 18.
22. Barth, "Entwurf Autobiographie," 19.
23. Barth, "Entwurf Autobiographie," 20.
24. Barth, "Entwurf Autobiographie," 20.
25. Barth, "Entwurf Autobiographie," 23f.
26. Barth, "Entwurf Autobiographie," 22.
27. Barth, "Entwurf Autobiographie," 27.
28. Barth, "Entwurf Autobiographie," 30.
29. Barth, "Entwurf Autobiographie," 29f.
30. Barth, "Entwurf Autobiographie," 30.
31. Barth, "Entwurf Autobiographie," 34.
32. Barth, "Entwurf Autobiographie," 37.
33. Barth, "Concluding Unscientific Postscript on Schleiermacher," *Theology of Schleiermacher*, 263.
34. Barth, "Entwurf Autobiographie," 35.
35. Cf. Pfister, *Kirchengeschichte der Schweiz*, 260-8.
36. Barth, "Entwurf Autobiographie," 35.
37. Barth, "Entwurf Autobiographie," 37f.
38. Barth, "Entwurf Autobiographie," 35.
39. A painted mechanical copper head.
40. Barth, "Entwurf Autobiographie," 39.
41. Barth, "Entwurf Autobiographie," 40.
42. Barth, "Entwurf Autobiographie," 41.
43. Barth, "Entwurf Autobiographie," 43.
44. Barth, "Entwurf Autobiographie," 43.
45. Barth, "Entwurf Autobiographie," 46.
46. Barth, "Entwurf Autobiographie," 47.
47. Barth, "Entwurf Autobiographie," 48.
48. Regarding this account of Barth's father, cf. Moritz Lauterburg, "Biographisches Vorwort," in Fritz Barth, *Christus unsere Hoffnung*, iii-xviii; "Ansprache von Herrn Pfr. Ben. Rikli," in Fritz Barth, *Professor D. Fritz Barth 1856-1912*, 5-12; Klauspeter Blaser, Article on Barth.
49. Lauterburg, preface, in Barth, *Christus unsere Hoffnung*, iv.
50. Lauterburg, preface, in Barth, *Christus unsere Hoffnung*, iv f.
51. Fritz Barth, "Jesus Christus, Gottes Antwort," in Barth, *Christus unsere Hoffnung*, 325.
52. Barth, "Jesus Christus, Gottes Antwort," in Barth, *Christus unsere Hoffnung*, 325.
53. Barth, "Jesus Christus, Gottes Antwort," in Barth, *Christus unsere Hoffnung*, 325. Fritz Barth however rejected Nietzsche's concept of the Superman (*Übermensch*) in which there was no more place for those who were weak and in need of help (326).
54. Fritz Barth, quoted in Lauterburg's preface to *Christus unsere Hoffnung*, vi.
55. Fritz Barth, "Tertullians Auffassung," 706-56.

56. "Evangelische Predigerschule in Basel. January 1876," cited in Ramstein, *Die Evangelische Predigerschule*, 137f., n. 111.
57. "Protokoll des Komitees," cited in Ramstein, *Die Evangelische Predigerschule*, 154.
58. Ramstein, *Die Evangelische Predigerschule*, 155.
59. According to information received by Michael Pfenninger from Professor Benedikt Bietenhard, Bern, in an email of January 22, 2018.
60. The governmental council decision of June 1895 promoted him to "Full Professor of Old and Medieval Church History"; in 1901 "general church history" was added. In fact however Fritz Barth continued to teach New Testament as well (according to information from Professor Benedikt Bietenhard, Bern, sent to Michael Pfenninger in emails of January 22 and 23, 2018).
61. This association offered support for Protestants in Swiss regions in which they were the minority, through the construction of and financial support for Protestant churches and schools.
62. Lauterburg, preface, in Barth, *Christus unsere Hoffnung*, xvi.
63. Fritz Barth, *Die Hauptprobleme des Lebens Jesu*, viii.
64. Albert Schweitzer's 1906 book *The Quest of the Historical Jesus* put an abrupt end to this direction in the scholarship for some time. Schweitzer was able to show that each of these attempts at reconstruction simply were reading into Jesus the author's own theological convictions (cf. Schweitzer, *Geschichte der Leben-Jesu-Forschung*, 47). In his explanations Schweitzer also mentioned Fritz Barth and his book "as representative of the modern-liberal popularization scholarship" (349) but did not discuss the book beyond that.
65. Barth, *Die Hauptprobleme*, v.
66. Barth, *Die Hauptprobleme*, v.
67. Barth, *Die Hauptprobleme*, iv.
68. Barth, *Die Hauptprobleme*, v.
69. "Autobiographical Sketches II. Bonn B. 1946," in *Karl Barth–Rudolf Bultmann: Letters 1922-1966* (GA 1), Appendix 38, 157. Translation revised.
70. Barth, "Concluding Unscientific Postscript," *Theology of Schleiermacher*, 261. Translation revised. This classification of his father's theology stands in a certain tension to how Albert Schweitzer categorized Fritz Barth "as representative of the modern-liberal popularization scholarship" (see n. 64 above).
71. See pp. 40–41.
72. "Ansprache," in Fritz Barth, *Professor D. Fritz Barth 1856–1912*, 7.
73. Barth, "Concluding Unscientific Postscript," *Theology of Schleiermacher*, 265. Translation revised.
74. Most details in this account of Anna Barth-Sartorius's life are from the brief biography written by her children for her funeral, *Zur Erinnerung an Frau Professor Anna Barth-Sartorius (15. April 1863–5. September 1938)*, undated. According to Peter Zocher this biography was presumably written by Gertrud Lindt, perhaps together with Heinrich Barth.
75. *Zur Erinnerung an Anna Barth-Sartorius*, 5.
76. *Zur Erinnerung an Anna Barth-Sartorius*, 5f.
77. Cf. Busch, *Karl Barth: His Life from Letters and Autobiographical Texts*, 10.

78. *Zur Erinnerung an Anna Barth-Sartorius*, 10.
79. Letter of July 16, 1920, to Eduard Thurneysen, *Karl Barth–Eduard Thurneysen Briefwechsel* I (GA 3), 411.
80. See pp. 217, 219–220.
81. See n. 74 above.
82. *Zur Erinnerung an Anna Barth-Sartorius*, 9.
83. Cf. *Karl Barth–Charlotte von Kirschbaum Briefwechsel* I (GA 45), 236, n. 4.
84. Cf. the letter of March 13, 1934, from Eduard Thurneysen to Peter Barth, *Barth–Thurneysen Briefwechsel* III (GA 34), 605 and n. 2; letter of March 25, 1934, to Thurneysen (616 and n. 18). The text of the statement of solidarity can be found in 933–4.
85. Cf. *Barth–von Kirschbaum Briefwechsel* I (GA 45), 41, n. 11.
86. "Autobiographical Sketches I. Münster, 1927," *Barth–Bultmann Letters* (GA 1), 151. Translation revised.
87. "Autobiographical Sketches I. Münster, 1927," *Barth–Bultmann Letters* (GA 1), 151. Translation revised.
88. Cf. "Notizzettel mit einem Aufriss für eine Biographie," KBA 11306.
89. See p. 135.
90. "Autobiographical Sketches I. Münster, 1927," *Barth–Bultmann Letters* (GA 1), 151. Translation revised.
91. "Autobiographical Sketches I. Münster, 1927," *Barth–Bultmann Letters* (GA 1), 151.
92. Burckhardt, *Kinder-Lieder von Abel Burckhardt*, 5.
93. Barth, *CD* IV/2, § 64, 112.
94. Cf. Barth, *CD* IV/2, § 64, 111f.
95. Barth, *CD* IV/2, § 64, 112.
96. Barth, *CD* IV/2, § 64, 113.
97. The German for the threefold "rest" is "*Ruh*," which is why he thought of a kangaroo.
98. Letter of August 13, 1947, to the family, KBA 9247.296.
99. Busch, *Karl Barth: His Life*, 13.
100. On the history of this school, see Bietenhard, "Freies Gymnasium Bern 1859–2009," 13–82.
101. Bietenhard, "Freies Gymnasium Bern," 1.
102. Lerber, cited in Bietenhard, "Freies Gymnasium Bern," 3.
103. For that reason in 1892 Lerber had forbidden the school from continuing to use his name; after that it was called the *Freies Gymnasium*.
104. "Autobiographical Sketches I. Münster, 1927," *Barth–Bultmann Letters* (GA 1), 152.
105. Letter of January 14, 1951, to E. Huber, KBA 9251.7.
106. Busch, *Karl Barth: His Life*, 29.
107. *Schweizerköpfe der Gegenwart*, 117.
108. "Autobiographical Sketches I. Münster, 1927," *Barth–Bultmann Letters* (GA 1), 152.
109. "Autobiographical Sketches I. Münster, 1927," *Barth–Bultmann Letters* (GA 1), 151.
110. "Autobiographical Sketches I. Münster, 1927," *Barth–Bultmann Letters* (GA 1), 151. Cf. Niemeyer, *Heldenbuch: Ein Denkmal der Grossthaten in den Befreiungskriegen von 1808-1815*.
111. "Autobiographical Sketches I. Münster, 1927," *Barth–Bultmann Letters* (GA 1), 151.

112. "Autobiographical Sketches I. Münster, 1927," *Barth–Bultmann Letters* (GA 1), 151. Translation revised.
113. Cf. "Autobiographical Sketches I. Münster, 1927," *Barth–Bultmann Letters* (GA 1), 151.
114. Cf. Barth, *Vorträge und kleinere Arbeiten 1909–1914* (GA 22), 488, n. 5.
115. Busch, *Karl Barth: His Life*, 27.
116. "Autobiographical Sketches I. Münster, 1927," *Barth–Bultmann Letters* (GA 1), 152.
117. "Autobiographical Sketches I. Münster, 1927," *Barth–Bultmann Letters* (GA 1), 152. Translation revised.
118. "Autobiographical Sketches I. Münster, 1927," *Barth–Bultmann Letters* (GA 1), 152. Translation revised.
119. Entry made in his Swiss school calendar for January 12, 1899.
120. Busch, *Karl Barth: His Life*, 25. Translation revised.

2
"This Obscure Desire toward a Better Understanding"
Studies, 1904–9

The Decision to Study Theology

By his own account, the immediate reason for Barth's decision to study theology was his confirmation instruction from 1901 to 1902 by Robert Aeschbacher, the pastor in Bern of the Nydegg Church and later of Bern's Munster Church. Aeschbacher was a pupil and friend of Barth's father and was said to be an outstanding preacher. According to Barth,

> in keeping with the style of the turn of the century, he was very apologetically inclined, but brought the whole problem of religion so closely home to me that at the end of the classes I realized clearly the need to know more about the matter. For this rudimentary reason, I resolved to study theology. I did not know then what I was undertaking, and now that I know this sphinx more closely I do not know if today I would have the courage to take this step.[1]

Barth made the decision to study theology on the very evening of his confirmation.[2] Aeschbacher had trained the young confirmation students properly in theology. From him Barth already learned Thomas Aquinas's proofs for the existence of God and the doctrine of the verbal inspiration of the Holy Scripture. At the same time Aeschbacher showed them the questionable aspects of both teachings.[3] He had acquainted Barth "so with the premises and problems of Christian knowledge" that his student felt "called to pursue these further. In this obscure desire—less toward proclamation than toward a better understanding!—I went to the university."[4]

In autobiographical notes on his life Karl Barth spoke quite extensively about his studies and the impressions that he received there. He repeatedly stressed clearly how well he had become acquainted with the historical-critical method of his era and that he, in contrast to his father, had subscribed entirely at the time to liberal theology. Here he probably overstated things.[5] He later described his subsequent development as a gradual move away from the influences on him during his studies.

Student in Bern

Karl Barth began his theology studies in Bern in the fall of 1904, while he continued to live with his parents. He attended his father's "Introduction to the Study of Theology" as well as several of his basic lecture courses on the New Testament and church history. In addition he attended an introduction to the New Testament taught by Rudolf Steck, who pushed the historical-critical method to its extremes. Steck went so far as to deny the authenticity of the main letters of Paul.[6] Barth took little interest in his "amiable but rather tediously exact analyses."[7]

He was introduced to the Old Testament by Karl Marti, a student of the historian of religion and orientalist Julius Wellhausen. Barth studied systematic theology under the liberal Hermann Lüdemann, who like Steck had been a student of Ferdinand Christian Baur, the Tübingen church and dogmatic historian and New Testament scholar. Like Schleiermacher, Lüdemann saw the key to religion in the religious consciousness of the Christian. The leading theses of his lecture always began with the words: "By virtue of his religious consciousness the Christian knows..."[8] He drew his ethical and epistemological insights from Immanuel Kant. Lüdemann too sparked nothing in Barth.

As this description of Barth's professors indicates, the Bern theological faculty at that time included a number of students of prominent scholars of liberal theology, who with their courageous theses overturned previous convictions. According to Baur the Gospel of John historically was much less reliable than the three other gospels. Wellhausen had completely reordered the five books of Moses historically. Now Barth learned from their students that as a scholar one had to trace the biblical texts historically. Barth "diligently" wrote down their lectures, but their "sound, but somewhat dry wisdom" did not really inspire him.[9] It was different with his father's lectures, which he "followed... with incomparably greater involvement" because his father spoke so vividly.[10] In general Barth was a neat student. He had his lecture notes and excerpts of biblical texts and theological works bound carefully and numbered them "Excerpts I," etc.

Barth was soon taking pleasure in independent theological work. During his holidays in the summer of 1905 he wrote his father that even now he was studying theological literature. He was busy with the so-called "synoptic question" of the interdependence of the gospels of Matthew, Mark, and Luke, and reported to his father: "I am so hot on the theological trail that today I had a vivid dream about the synoptic question, which took dramatic form for me, I don't know how."[11] Of the books he read, a philosophical work particularly captivated him: Immanuel Kant's *Critique of Practical Reason* was the "first book that truly moved me as a student."[12]

When one reads Karl Barth's first preserved theological work, *The Character of Religion in Ancient India*, written in 1905 presumably in the context of a class on religious history, the tone is surprising. The voice is not of a reserved student in the beginning semesters, but rather of a young man from a professorial household who apparently is accustomed to having confidence in himself and his viewpoints. Barth strikes an oddly didactic, almost precocious tone: "Let us not however get ahead of ourselves!"[13] He is quite quick to render theological verdicts. And unashamedly he rebukes the European church landscape. Barth expresses appreciation for the Basel Mission Society's critique of the Indian caste system; while it certainly did not meet with agreement in India, "even in Europe there would be in some places sour faces, or worse, when one wanted to touch on the privileged church seats of the nobility and the honorable!"[14]

Barth's text "Die Stigmata des Franz von Assisi" ("The Stigmata of Francis of Assisi"), which he probably worked on for his father's class in church history in summer 1905, gives instructive insight into his early view of historical-critical research. In his final years Francis of Assisi was said to have had stigmata similar to those of the crucified Jesus of Nazareth. It is astonishing that Barth devoted himself to what for a Reformed theologian was hardly an obvious theme. He began by making it clear that modern historical criticism had to dismiss the miracle tales handed down by the church as 90 percent ahistorical. At the same time he complained that historical research had long "succumbed to the opposite extreme and in part up to the present day [denied] all that was 'miraculous', i.e. everything that falls outside the world as it usually appears to us, the historical reality." Yet in the meantime one could no longer assume "*absolute* natural laws."[15] Barth concurs with Hamlet: "There are more things in heaven and earth.../ Than are dreamt of in your philosophy."[16] Historical consciousness, he believed, was different than it had been in the nineteenth century. To lend his position more weight Barth quoted Adolf von Harnack's 1899/1900 lecture *What is Christianity* (*Das Wesen des Christentums*): "The habit of condemning a narrative...only because it contains stories of miracles, is a piece of prejudice."[17]

Barth's reference to Harnack, who was to become his most important teacher in Berlin, is notable because it shows him in a position that was quite remote from the liberal critique of miracles. Barth however misunderstands Harnack. As if reacting to Barth's citation, Harnack noted in subsequent editions of the lecture that his position on the miracles had been "so misunderstood, as if I did indeed allow for miracles through a backdoor."[18] In the original lecture however he already had summarized: "we are firmly convinced that what happens in space and time is subject to the general laws of motion, and that in this sense, as an interruption of the order of nature, there can be no such things as miracles."[19] He merely meant that one cannot deny a source all historical value, even if it contains elements like accounts of miracles that don't hold up historically. Barth's false paraphrase of Harnack's view already anticipates his later conviction that there are things in Christian faith that don't correspond to natural laws and in that sense are "miracles," which nonetheless are real. The resurrection of Jesus will be for him such an event.[20]

In his text on the stigmata of Francis of Assisi Barth stresses further that reason and knowledge may not have the final word. Even historical observation is a matter of perspective for him: "Yet if we now apply the same [source criticism] we must nonetheless be quite clear that with this we enter completely *subjective* and *relative* terrain, which in itself can be just as unscholarly as remaining fixed e.g. on the oldest source."[21] In the awareness of its piecemeal nature one cannot forego critique. "Without critique, no historical scholarship."[22] In his analysis of the texts describing the stigmatization of Francis of Assisi Barth uses the historical method skillfully.

During his time as a student in Bern Karl Barth participated in the Christian Student Conferences in Aarau in the Aargau Canton. This annual meeting had been founded in 1897 for German-Swiss students in the context of the international student mission movement. It was an occasion where "all students who are concerned with the matter of God's kingdom could meet one another and come into contact with their teachers who were of the same mind."[23] Fritz Barth lectured here several times and became part of the committee of senior members. As a vicar and pastor Karl Barth continued to attend these meetings.

In the summer of 1906 Barth held his first theological lecture on "The Original Form of the 'Our Father,'" at the Bern Academic Protestant Theological Association. Once again he showed himself to be well-versed in historical source criticism as he sought out the original version of the prayer. But he referred to the boundaries of this approach, citing once more Harnack as his witness:

> Today we have taken a look at the workshop of historical criticism, which cannot stop by rights even before the highest and most holy, a prayer handed down as coming from the mouth of Jesus himself ... Yet as even *Harnack* acknowledges, the truly valuable thing in such a piece of handed down evangelical tradition can neither be given nor taken away by historical criticism. *"Thy Kingdom Come!"* ... this will be and will remain for all time the first prayer of a disciple of Jesus.[24]

In typically acerbic tone Barth sums up retrospectively that in Bern he had "learned to forget any horror I might have had" because there "I so thoroughly went through ... the earlier form of the 'historical-critical' school that the remarks of their later and contemporary successors could no longer get under my skin or even touch my heart—they could only get on my nerves, as all too familiar."[25]

Wearing the Colors and Noncombative: In the Zofingia Association

At the very beginning of his studies Karl Barth—like his father before him in Basel and his brothers in Bern—joined the student fraternity Zofingia, which had the

Couleur [a special band of colors, usually worn as a sash and on headwear] but did not engage in dueling. Here he "spent much time, money, and energy."[26] He was give the fraternity nickname "Sprenzel," which means "lightweight" or "puny."[27] The "Swiss Zofingia Association," known simply as Zofingia, had been founded in 1819 in Zofingen, Aargau Canton, by students from Bern and Zurich. In the years that followed students from other Swiss cities joined as well. As Charles Gilliard summarizes, they met with the goal "of uniting all the youth who were studying into one single association and thereby preparing the spiritual unity of Switzerland" and to combat the tendency among the various cantons to seek only their own self-interest. Only through this could Switzerland emerge "boldly over against foreign countries."[28] According to Barth, Zofingia wanted to create a space that transcended political or social partisanship, where "the most different viewpoints and stands found common ground in shared concern for the Fatherland."[29] There was disagreement among the students about how exactly this goal should be reached and what role German fraternity regulations should play. As their motto they took "*Patriae-amicitiae-litteris!*"—To Fatherland-Friendship-Scholarship.

Barth was not an uncritical participant in fraternity events in Bern. He complained to a fraternity brother elsewhere that the fraternity's ideals, which he thought were carried out better in the Basel branch of the fraternity, were practiced so little in Bern. He felt challenged: "If there is any place where the Zofingia ideals should be *practiced* and *fought for*, not just *talked about*, it's in Bern."[30] It disturbed him that in Bern the only concern was for the ideal of friendship.[31] And he was angry that changes were blocked: "'It has always been that way, therefore it is good!' That is the great wisdom of those in Bern!"[32]

In a January 1906 lecture Barth advocated a modernization of the fraternity and stronger consideration for the "social question," for the sake of greater emphasis on the ideal of "Patriae," the Fatherland. In those days whoever wasn't closing their eyes had to "emphasize the social problem as a specter of shocking reality."[33] The gains made by the Social Democrats in the 1903 German parliamentary elections were an "attendant symptom" of this.[34] The fact that there had not yet been such election results in Switzerland as in Germany, which was permeated by "a Byzantinean system of principalities" and "unbearable militarism," should not lead to "false optimism," as Barth provocatively warned "from the standpoint of a self-satisfied petit-bourgeois startled out of his peace and quiet."[35] Even though in Barth's observation the Swiss Social Democrats were first and foremost political agitators, he found their diagnosis of an ever-growing "gap between *capital* and *labor*,... between *rich* and *poor*" to be accurate.[36] It wasn't enough simply to take care of the poor with food. Ultimately the solution of the social question concerned the central task of humanity, it was a matter of the "twofold... *responsibility of the individual toward the divine, on the one hand, and toward humanity on the other hand.*"[37]

Concretely, Barth argued that Zofingia's contribution to the solution of the social question rested in "*awakening and strengthening the awareness of social responsibility*" among its members.[38] For as students they possessed a particular responsibility through "the high privilege that we are allowed to devote ourselves for years to the free study of the highest and most beautiful that is conceived in the human heart, and may experience such agreeable hours in a circle of friends and the realm of art," while their contemporaries already had to work for their living.[39] Here he dismissed any external social activities for the fraternity; there would be enough time for these in their subsequent careers. Instead Barth advocated that students of lesser financial means be admitted, not only the sons of "good society."[40] For this the financial burden for individuals had to be reduced by changing the fraternity culture. Finding a suitable wife from a good home through expensive festive events could not be as important as admitting other students. Barth's notes of the discussion that followed indicate that he found no receptive audience for his suggestions.[41] They were viewed as superfluous, typical of a newcomer, or in contradiction to the spirit of fraternity customs.

When Barth returned in the summer semester of 1907 to Bern from Berlin, he was elected after six ballots (and even then only barely) with three other theological students into the leadership of the Bern section of Zofingia; Barth was elected president. The publication of the Swiss Zofingia Association commented ironically that one need not fear that the Bern section would now become a "house of prayer" since the leadership, being Swiss, would consist of "proper confederates who always tend toward compromise."[42] Looking back at the semester the editors stated with relief:

> The semester began with great anxiety and great hopes. The elections brought a surprise: A heretic became the Pope. The other heretics rejoiced, the strict were filled with worry. But hopes and fears...were not fulfilled. The new church prince barely attempted to break with the old customs. Soon he was acting completely orthodox, completely according to the code of conduct. And in this he was right.[43]

"Very Diligent and Quite Capable": Student in Berlin

In the summer and fall of 1906 Karl Barth completed the church *Propaedeuticum*, an intermediary examination in a Bible survey course, church history, philosophy, and history of religions, with a grade of First. He wanted to continue his studies in liberal Marburg, but his father insisted on the faculties in Halle or Greifswald, which had been shaped by "positive theology." The compromise solution was finally Berlin, which was considered neutral and where Barth moved for the winter semester of 1906/7.[44] He resided at Hallesche Street 18 near the Anhalt train station. The building where he lived no longer exists.

To his later regret Barth overlooked the church historian Karl Holl, who launched the so-called Luther Renaissance at the beginning of the twentieth century. He "wisely" avoided Reinhold Seeberg, who taught history of dogma.[45] Barth did experience him however in 1924 when as a professor passing through Berlin he visited Seeberg's course on dogmatics. To his friends he described Seeberg as a "genuine…theological…centipede, who could wheedle anything out of the devil (about whom he had just expounded) and 'somehow' (popular word) knows what to do about everything. No, that *does* not do. It would be better to be a theological sheep than such a rascal."[46]

Barth studied dogmatics, the scholarly reflection about the contents of Christian faith, under Julius Kaftan, who emphasized Kant as the "philosopher of Protestantism."[47] The place of religion was not in theoretical knowledge; rather, religion was "a practical matter of the human spirit."[48] From him Barth heard that the issue was not to "make the understanding of religion and with that of Christendom dependent upon philosophical preconditions."[49] Philosophy could only develop a certain ideal of religion. If theology were oriented around that, then "Christendom" became "subordinate to a norm that was not of itself,"[50] thereby losing its "usefulness in the church" and with that its scholarly nature, which in fact consisted of "stating the truth already given in the faith of the congregation."[51]

Under Hermann Gunkel Barth became absorbed with the Old Testament and discovered through Gunkel's history of religions approach that "the Old Testament was concerned with something exciting."[52] Much later in his *Church Dogmatics* Barth would wrestle with Gunkel's theses.[53]

The most important figure in Berlin for Barth however would be Adolf von Harnack. Influential in academic policy, the church historian and liberal theologian was not uncontroversial, since he explored how theological and church developments were shaped by their historical settings. Barth attended his seminar on the Acts of the Apostles, learning there that when analyzing texts one always had to ask: "what is the author's opinion?"[54] Barth was fascinated by his seminar style: Harnack engaged in thorough text analysis, but also reported on current excavations and discoveries, never losing sight of "his topic."[55] That being said however the opening of the seminar struck Barth as peculiar:

> The beginning is staged in a particularly august fashion as two leopards suddenly spew out of the gates being opened at the same time, namely, Harnack and his amanuensis [his secretary], a very crafty and intelligent gentleman,[56] who at the same time is the seminar senior and carries the books behind his master like a poodle carries the stick. Then all rise and take their seats again just as formally and the Council is opened.[57]

For the seminar Barth wrote a paper on "Paul's mission work according to the Acts of the Apostles." To manage this paper he grew accustomed to a regular daily routine and worked unceasingly. He even shortened his Christmas holidays in Switzerland in order to be back in Berlin on time and get back to "acting the apostles."[58] Still, he allowed himself an occasional theater visit. At the end of the winter semester he was able to turn in a 158-page paper to Harnack.

Conceptually Barth relied on Harnack's thesis about the author of Acts. In his newly published book *Luke the Doctor* Harnack had argued against the predominant opinion in the research that the author of Acts and that of the Gospel of Luke were one and the same person, that is, Luke the physician and Paul's co-worker.[59] Methodologically Barth followed Harnack's belief that it is essential to explain the viewpoint and intention of the author in order to understand the text.[60] Barth showed that the author of the Acts of the Apostles "wanted to describe the triumph of the Gospel and its taking root in Asia and Europe, not however a 'history of the early period' of the Christian communities [which had been the majority opinion before Harnack]."[61]

Barth was particularly interested in how in Acts Paul's sermons and their "linkage" to the listener's religious pre-understanding were conceived. What is the relation of their current convictions to Christian faith? Paul would show the Jews that through diligent study of the Old Testament text it can "be *deduced*" that Jesus is the Messiah; among the Gentiles he connected through "general human...thought."[62] In light of the fact that Barth later rejected any kind of linkage to human pre-understanding, it is worth mentioning how he assessed this during his time as a student. The "view expressed of a pre-Christian religiosity among Jews and Gentiles" as "revelation" in Acts had in fact been the viewpoint of the historical Paul.[63] Over against that, what takes place in Jesus Christ was only a "higher...revelation."[64]

Harnack graded the work as quite in order. While in one place in the manuscript he made a wavy line over two pages, in other places he added a "correct" or "good." Harnack's comment at the end of the paper stated:

> The final section's treatment on "Paul in the economy of Acts of the Apostles" is too brief and doesn't satisfactorily address the problems. Conversely in the preceding sections some things are treated too extensively, including some unnecessary aspects that are brought in. On the whole, however, the essay is very diligent and quite capable, and its conclusions achieved prudently and deliberately and are solid.[65]

Barth's letters from that period document his enthusiasm for the theological atmosphere in Berlin. He reported to his school and student friend and fellow Zofinger Otto Lauterburg that after six weeks he already felt "like a different person" "who had come from the barren heath of theological skepticism...to green pastures."⁶⁶ The reason was that here no longer were the "Pauline letters bumped off according to the old-fashioned templates" as had been the case with Rudolf Steck in Bern, but that Harnack in his liberal approach was interested in content.⁶⁷ Barth wrote his father that he had now hung pictures of Harnack and Kaftan above his bed; "someday they will worthily adorn my parsonage—hopefully even more their spirit, which I would like to grasp better and more completely."⁶⁸ Harnack left the most lasting impression; in 1909 Barth described himself as a "disciple of Harnack."⁶⁹ After their theological paths had long since taken separate directions, in 1935 Barth wrote Harnack's daughter Agnes von Zahn-Harnack:

> Among the many Swiss students who were there together with me at the time, no one was more enthusiastic about your father's personality and manner of teaching than I was. Things went so far that due to the work I had to do for his seminar, which occupied me almost day and night for months, I almost completely neglected to take proper notice of the Kaiser-Friedrich-Museum [now called the Bode-Museum] and Berlin's other glories and by the end had seen and heard very little, although if I may say so, I had listened to your father very thoroughly.⁷⁰

Barth's knowledge of Kant enabled him to read *Ethics* by Lutheran theologian Wilhelm Herrmann, who had been professor of systematic theology in Marburg since 1879.⁷¹ In 1925 Barth still admitted: "I remember the days almost twenty years ago in Berlin when I read his ethics for the first time, as if it were today... From that point on I believe I have been self-driven in my attention to theology."⁷²

Herrmann's intent in his *Ethics*, which appeared in 1901, was "to come to an understanding even with those who don't wish to be Christians about what moral behavior would be."⁷³ He rejected a particular Christian ethic that substantively distinguished itself from a philosophical one. Every person was capable of recognizing what the moral good was.⁷⁴ At the same time however we recognize our powerlessness to accomplish the good. In that way we become open to the religious.⁷⁵ Herrmann considered this the point where the task of Christian ethics begins: it must make "Christian religion as a morally liberating force" comprehensible.⁷⁶ For only the Christian religion causes a person to be able to bring about the good. Faith was a "process in consciousness... from which one creates the strength and motives to a new willing," an "inner transformation."⁷⁷

Along with Herrmann's *Ethics* in Berlin Barth bought his "copy of Schleiermacher's *On Religion. Speeches to its Cultured Despisers*, in the edition by R. Otto, which I still use today [1968]. Eureka! Having apparently sought for 'The Immediate,' I had now found it... through Schleiermacher."⁷⁸ Barth later surmised that this was connected perhaps also to his love of Romantic literature, naming Joseph von Eichendorff and Novalis. After all, "I was (and am?!) a bit of a romantic myself!"⁷⁹

Once More in Bern and then Tübingen

After the semester in Berlin Barth was back in Bern for the 1907 summer semester. Most of his time was spent as president of Zofingia. By his own account he did not study seriously that semester, devoting his time instead to "student glories."[80] This was followed by four weeks as vicar in Meiringen, a congregation in the Bernese Highlands.

During this semester Barth experienced his first great love—to Rösy Münger, a young woman from Bern, whom he had met the year before.[81] His parents insisted that the relationship be ended, so that Karl Barth finally broke with her in May

2.1. Karl Barth as a member of the Bern Zofingia Association in 1907, © Karl Barth-Archive in Basel.

1910.[82] It is impossible to say how close Barth's relationship with Münger was, since they are said to have burned their letters to one another together when it ended.[83] In 1925 Münger died of leukemia.

Barth mentioned her twice later in letters to Charlotte von Kirschbaum.[84] In 1932 he recalled her when during a meeting of the Bern pastors' association he returned to a hall where in 1907 Rösy Münger had accompanied him to a Zofingia ball and "the affair with R.M. entered the decisive stage."[85] In 1933 he reported to Kirschbaum that he had a long conversation with a fraternity brother in which they spoke about Münger. At the time Barth had also met one of her cousins and heard "more about this past matter that is nonetheless still with me."[86] He wrote Kirschbaum that he was "very glad for the opportunity to reach a certain mutual understanding, at least retroactively, with all those who have grown older for their part,"[87] a comment that suggests that on the Müngers' side there had been a lack of understanding about Barth's breaking the relationship.

Barth later exchanged a few letters with Münger's sister, writing her in 1943: "I cannot imagine my life without her. Again and again she is there: questioning but friendly, and as gentle as she was . . . in life."[88] Barth admitted in his letter that in retrospect, "in that which was between your sister and me and didn't become more," he himself was "a puzzle."[89] In 1948 he told a friend that he had "never been able to forget" Rösy Münger.[90]

Barth's father had insisted in 1907 that his son put geographical distance between himself and Münger. Barth left Bern for that reason, "obeying the stricter authority of my father rather than my own inclinations,"[91] and went to Tübingen for the 1907/8 winter semester. There he lived at Neckargasse 10, right in Tübingen's old city with a view of the Neckar and quite close to the Hölderlin Tower.

He attended the lectures on the Gospel of Matthew by Adolf Schlatter, the Swiss New Testament and systematics scholar who had transferred from Greifswald to Tübingen, with a fierce inner aversion, since he had learned an entirely different approach to the Bible through historical criticism.[92] In addition Barth found Schlatter's "manner of argumentation" to be "unscholarly and imprecise and arbitrary."[93] In contrast, he studied under the Swiss professor of church law Fritz Fleiner "with pleasure."[94]

In November, December, and February, Barth traveled to nearby Bad Boll, on the northern side of the Swabian Jura, where he got to know Pastor Christoph Blumhardt. Blumhardt had succeeded in opening Württemberg pietism to modernity. In this the concept of the kingdom of God was central for him.

During Barth's semester in Tübingen he worked mostly on his final thesis, which was required by the examination regulations of the Bern Church. He chose the topic "The Concept of Christ's Descent into Hell in Church Literature up to Origen," that is, the idea that after his death Jesus Christ descended into the kingdom of the dead in order to preach to them. The preliminary work demanded weeks of extracting texts, since the library only allowed students to take four books home at a time. He took evening breaks at the Tübingen Royal Society Roigel, a student association directly below the old Tübingen castle. After spending the Christmas holidays in Bern and Bad Boll, on January 1, 1908 he complained to his school friend Willy Spoendlin: "Now I am sitting here again, smoking large amounts of tobacco and working on my final thesis. My youthful cheerfulness is now definitively buried for the 23rd time, day by day I become more of a dark ill-tempered dotard...Tübingen is a lousy dump and the theological faculty is a dive."[95] Barth often sat at his desk until midnight. In the process he was aware that his results would find little resonance among the professors in Bern, since he was drawing a great deal on Harnack.[96] Nor was he counting on the constant agreement of his father. "Already I'm hearing in my mind...Papa: You really slipped up a few times."[97]

Barth completed the thesis on January 27, 1908. At 194 pages it was again very extensive. He was attempting a purely church historical portrayal, without including any dogmatic positions, but working merely on the historical level left him with a hollow feeling.[98] "A chance reading," the introduction stated,

> led me to this topic. Admittedly without the strict necessity of the final thesis that comes once to every Bern theology student when his hour arrives...there would have been indeed little reason for me to address such a frequently examined question, which moreover at first glance has something so wondrous and bizarre. Yet I had the experience that precisely the study of this kind of religious phenomenon, as foreign as it may appear to us today, has its peculiar attraction, as long as one doesn't from the outset utilize it for a modern purpose whose very nature is foreign to it, whether that is to "rescue" at all costs a piece of Christian antiquity for dogmatics, or whether it is to illustrate how people once thought so imaginatively and inadequately and "what a glorious height we have achieved at last." (Goethe, *Faust* I) For that reason I have left the *dogmatic* question [that is, how contemporary people should view this earlier theological topic] untouched...I have therefore confined myself to the *exegetical-history of dogma* problem and posed the question: *which religious or theological motives led to establishing the concept of the Descensus ad inferos in Christian theology and the church*?[99]

Until the essay was finally graded Barth suffered under his own dissatisfaction with it: "There's a lot of hogwash in my final thesis, now it falls in Lüdemann's hands. Oh woe is me, woe is me."[100] Generally however his work did then receive a grade of Second. Barth drew the conclusion from all this: "Academic work in a narrow sense is not for me, however, I have come to see that with growing clarity... *sunt certi denique fines* [ultimately there are certain limits]."[101]

In Marburg at last

His father then did allow Karl Barth to go to Marburg for the 1908 summer semester. He lived at Hirschberg 4, very close to the old Marburg marketplace. For the rest of his life he would recall his enthusiasm that he could finally study under Wilhelm Herrmann: "There I found what I had been looking for: a theology built upon Kant's 'critique of practical reason.'"[102] "I absorbed Herrmann with every pore."[103]

Barth was fascinated by Herrmann's academic personality. In contrast to other German scholars who when appearing on the streets of university towns radiated a general "academic and scholarly solemnity" ("seldom without a whiff of Fichteian arrogance"), one sensed with Herrmann the conviction "that *theology*...as such could have its *own* academic seriousness," because there are facts "the knowledge of which simply requires academic *theology*."[104] Herrmann succeeded in making "the divine *address* to human beings" perceptible in his courses.[105] He was an "independent thinker," the "air of *freedom* wafted in his auditorium."[106] And

> even his *physical* countenance was lacking entirely any trait of sophisticated shrewdness, which particularly among "systematic" theologians can be recognized not infrequently even from far away. This was also absent in his *theology*. For that reason some found it naïve, complaining already as students in Marburg about the "upper-level confirmation instruction" that one received in his lectures.[107]

Herrmann's thought had been influenced by Kantian philosophy, from which however he distanced himself on essential points, and by the younger Schleiermacher. In his eyes Schleiermacher's speeches *On Religion* "were the most important and correct writings in Christian knowledge and confession to appear since the closing of the New Testament canon."[108]

For that reason Barth read Schleiermacher and again Kant intensively during his time in Marburg: "working through the 'Critique of Pure Reason' twice, from A to Z, with a ruler in hand."[109] As he worked he had the impression that he was "finally giving himself a sound theological foundation."[110] Barth recalled this period with the image of the "narrow ridge," on which he and many others at the time who were fascinated by Herrmann wandered, and on which they felt "free and superior" over against the liberal theology that had become outdated by Herrmann as well as against orthodoxy and positive theology.[111]

In retrospect Herrmann's "Christocentric impulse" was decisive for Barth.[112] According to Herrmann faith was ignited by the historical Jesus.[113] Access to him is possible through the tradition of the Christian community. The important thing in this for faith however is not primarily the knowledge of specific historical information about the life of Jesus, but rather the *living impression* of Jesus's *inner life* which is conveyed, that is, that which makes Jesus an ethical personality.[114] Human beings must experience that the ethical good that lives in Jesus also becomes alive *in them*.[115] Therefore for Christians the certainty of the truth of Jesus's inner life rests "not in what they make of the tradition, but rather in what the content of that tradition makes of them."[116] Generally speaking, then, the Christian religion is not about general thoughts about God and the world, but rather that through the historical figure of Jesus "God himself engages with us so that we are able to say that we recognize...God's effect on us and sense God's nearness."[117]

Later, in 1925, Barth criticized Herrmann for grounding the particular claim of theology in general philosophical considerations, thereby grounding it by human initiative. Whereas one had to "allow that which is grounded...to be subtly *un*grounded."[118] Instead of speaking of the self-groundedness of individual experiences in religion, one should refer to the sole "ground that is grounded in itself, which is truly not 'object' in any respect but is irreversible subject," namely, God.[119] Dogmatics may not begin with human thinking—here Herrmann was correct—as little however as it could begin with human experience. At the beginning of dogmatics stands "*God* in *God's* word."[120]

Barth goes straight to the point where he sees the distinction:

> That we are "grasping" the active *God* in the power of Jesus cannot be determined in hindsight based upon some corresponding experiences, as it should be... according to Herrmann's Christology. Rather, this fact is the beginning, the foundation and the precondition...There is no other path at all outside of the path from above to below. Orthodox Christology [which makes the beginning exactly so] is the glacial river that steeply flows down from a height of 3000 meters; there is something to be made of this. Herrmann's Christology...is the futile attempt to push a stagnant lagoon to the same heights using a hand pump. It simply doesn't work.[121]

Herrmann's one-sidedness however met with Barth's lasting approval: "A respectable theology is always one-sided."[122] One should not attempt to work here with small doses, lest one land with a "pharmaceutical theology."[123]

In addition to the work of Wilhelm Herrmann, the neo-Kantian philosophy represented by Hermann Cohen and Paul Natorp was important for Barth in Marburg.[124] In their work Barth discovered "an almost priestly serious philosophy."[125] Cohen was concerned with a "pure" philosophy: "*We* [as opposed to Kant and in particular the empiricists] *begin with thinking*. Thinking may have no other source outside of itself, if otherwise its purity is to be unlimited and unclouded."[126] It is essentially "origin" or "generation" and in its activity as well as in its content dynamic.[127] This conviction reaches its pinnacle in Natorp. For him experience is "an unending process, the object of knowledge never conclusively determined, but rather an...'unending task.'"[128] This approach by the Marburg philosophy was later to be fruitful for Barth's commentary on the Epistle to the Romans.[129]

In Marburg Barth also attended the lectures of New Testament scholar Wilhelm Heitmüller, for whom he also came to have high regard. In contrast he had more trouble with the New Testament scholar and church historian Adolf Jülicher, who had become renowned for his work on the parables of Jesus. Finally, the connection to the systematic theologian and Harnack student Martin Rade became important in a way that will be described shortly.

Several decades later Barth offered this description of his theological position at the end of his studies:

> At the conclusion, in opposition to the direction taken by my grandfathers and father I found that I had trained as a decided disciple in the "modern school" that dominated the era leading up to the First World War and was considered the only [school] fit for human beings, in which Christianity according to Schleiermacher and Ritschl was interpreted on the one hand as a phenomenon to be explored critically, on the other hand as an inner experience of a primarily moral nature.[130]

His Work for *Die Christliche Welt*

Following his written examinations in July 1908 Barth successfully completed a second four-week long period as independent vicar in Pruntrut in the Bernese Jura. After finishing his oral examinations on October 28, 1908—Barth passed the examinations with a general note of Second—he returned to Marburg from November 1908 to August 1909. Now he lived on Hainweg 1, below the Landgrafen Castle. During this period, at the home of Martin Rade, Barth got to know Rudolf Bultmann, who was to become a fellow traveler in the early years of dialectical theology.

Karl Barth returned to Marburg because Martin Rade[131] had offered him the position of editorial assistant at the journal *Die Christliche Welt*. In 1886, together with friends from his studies Rade had founded *Die Christliche Welt*, which became the most significant journal of liberal Protestantism at the time in Germany, and was now its editor in Marburg. He had initially asked Barth's friend Otto Lauterburg, who declined and suggested Barth. Rade then asked another fellow student, but Barth was in luck: "There—*deus ex machina* his mother declared out of orthodoxy her veto, and with a thunderbolt I moved into first place."[132] The offer came at the right time for Barth, for after his exams he had "the desire to breathe a little academic air without an exam before the

2.2. Karl Barth in Marburg, 1909, © Karl Barth-Archive in Basel.

transition to a practical office."[133] The new task gave him time to continue attending faculty classes.

Barth enjoyed his work for the magazine:

It consisted mainly of reading the many incoming manuscripts, forming my opinion about them in order to convey this to Martin Rade in the appropriate manner and finally to prepare the material that he selected for publication. Innumerable written paper, which I and then the master held to be less significant, disappeared into a kind of theological wolf's gulch for a more or less lengthy or eventually final waiting period... Rade in his own generous manner permitted me to do what I wanted within limits, and it was inevitable that from my...vantage point I seemed to myself, as something like an assistant helmsman, to be not a little important.[134]

With a wink, Barth recalled that during that period manuscripts from the greatest theologians, like Wilhelm Bousset, Hermann Gunkel, or Ernst Troeltsch, "had to pass through my censorship, first and last."[135]

During Rade's absence in the summer of 1909, Barth was even allowed to work independently and sign off on two issues. Since reviews were part of *Die Christliche Welt*, Rade soon permitted him to write a few of his own critiques. Showing the audacity of someone who had just passed his examinations, they are energetic and self-confident in their verdict: "I viewed them as masterpieces."[136]

During this year Barth achieved a solid overview of contemporary liberal theology, which he valued:

> Everything that I saw and heard in this environment had such a self-evident glory, this world, represented by so many capable and witty figures, circled so secure in itself, that surely I would have only laughed at anyone who had predicted to me back then that my own future might go in a different direction than in some extension of the Marburg theology and particularly that of the *Christliche Welt*.[137]

Barth recalled these semesters in Marburg, along with the summer semester of 1908, as his happiest time as a student.[138] After the year with Rade he moved "as one coming entirely from Marburg into life, the church, and my further theological reflection..."[139]

Barth's 1909 essay *Moderne Theologie und Reichsgottesarbeit* ("Modern Theology and the Work for the Kingdom of God") is a good expression of his position at that time and one of the first documents showing his theologically pugnacious nature. It appeared in the *Zeitschrift für Theologie und Kirche*, which had been published since 1907 by Martin Rade and Wilhelm Herrmann. In this brief text Barth shows why "it [is] incomparably more difficult...to enter the ministry of the pulpit, by the sickbed, or the club house" when one comes out of the faculties of "modern" theology in Marburg and Heidelberg "than out of those in Halle or Greifswald."[140]

Two things could be found in the "tool box" of the modern theologian that he viewed himself to be.[141] One was "*historical relativism*," which explored the texts and history of Christianity using historical methods and for that reason could not accept anything "absolute" in nature or the intellectual realm. For historical relativism the New Testament would be "a collection of religious texts like others," "Christianity a religious phenomenon like others...Jesus a...founder of a religion like others as well, and it treats their coming into being and history using the same methods that it uses for Avesta [the Zoroastrian scriptures] and Zoroaster."[142] The other item in the baggage of the modern theologian is "*religious individualism*," since morality as the precondition of religion is concerned solely with the individual who recognizes the moral good by himself.[143] There would be no generally valid revelation. Each person could take responsibility for himself or herself as to where truth is to be found. And there would be no general ethical norms: each must find that orientation in himself or herself. Modern theologians would no longer be able to calm their life of faith by appealing to church tradition, but rather they would have to take a stand as to whether this tradition is "the expression of their faith as well."[144] To others they could only "speak [of this] strictly individually experienced and experiential religion."[145] For that reason it is only natural and in no way problematic when someone influenced in this direction—in contrast to another's "zeal of evangelization"—cultivates a certain reserve in the first years of ministry.[146]

Barth's father was displeased by this publication by his son, who after all had just turned twenty-three. When Barth sent him the article, he replied that he would have advised against publication:

> for here too you place yourself vehemently on the side of the "moderns" in a way which has solely personal but in no way academically established character and of which perhaps you yourself in a few more years will no longer approve... Something that has been published ties you down... for the period following; at your age development should be taking place much more internally and not put on the open market, and in particular it is preferable to save such statements about principles for a time of greater maturity.[147]

Barth immediately sent a twenty-page reply in which he stressed that for him, the portrait of religion he had laid out in his essay "is not merely theology but rather genuine living experience."[148] He was repelled by his fellow students, who "already while at the university have the urge constantly to 'bear witness'": "Faith is not measured by the ability to talk about it. And that theology which most readily gives someone the tools for that is certainly not the best??"[149] Self-confidently he rebuffed his father's concern that he had tied himself down too early with this publication: "The main thing is that *I* don't feel tied down by a published paper, if I should later ever come to a different viewpoint, which a priori is not impossible, although it is unlikely."[150]

Barth's essay drew reactions in the same journal from two significant practical theologians: Ernst Christian Achelis from Marburg and Paul Drews from Halle.[151] Drawing on the theology of Albrecht Ritschl, both criticized Barth and faulted the missing references to Christ. Achelis noted that Barth's individualistic approach was too arbitrary. He also expressed surprise that Barth argued about the possibility of imparting faith before he had even started working as a pastor.[152] Drews argued against Barth that the limit of individualism lay in the fact that in Christianity one "[must] feel bound to Jesus and the values that have been given to us by him"; here is where "compelling authority" was to be found.[153]

Barth's father strongly advised him against countering. His son in the future would need "to engross himself, but not primarily in Kant and Schleiermacher, whom you have exploited far too one-sidedly, but instead in the Scripture, from which you have yet much, indeed everything, to draw."[154] His son retorted that the language of academic theology had to be different from that of a pastor. And: "accusations and objections of the kind you are making to me hurt [me] quite *physically*..., because they '*come at me*' in my full theological existence, instead of sympathetically complementing and helping, for which I remain open."[155]

Despite his father's advice Barth wrote a rebuttal that Rade also published in the *Zeitschrift für Theologie und Kirche*. His father reacted to this somewhat more conciliatorily:

> I am pleased by every attention that these articles may draw for you in Germany; I am not the one who prepares your path through life, rather God must do this, and God until now has led you benevolently despite all kinds of things that I don't yet understand. But I would like to say one thing to you again: *write if you must as much as you like; but don't let it all be published immediately* even if all the Rades... of the German cloud of scholars require it of you! You are not supposed to become a journalist; so store your cigars before you offer them; hopefully you have a long life ahead of you. *Ceterum censeo*.[156]

Rade had stirred up the controversy for journalistic reasons,[157] bringing the debate to a close with an "editorial concluding statement" in the final 1909 issue. Somewhat paternalistically he commented that he had accepted Barth's opening contribution because "we had in this little article a 'human document' that, with an honesty for which we can be thankful, allowed us to see into the soul of a brave theologian who at present is about to conclude his studies and devote himself to praxis."[158] Karl Barth was grateful for this "concluding blessing, which you have now spoken about my Cossack's ride."[159]

There would later be strong disagreements between the two men.[160] Nonetheless in 1939 Barth looked back with gratitude to Martin Rade and his wife Dora for what he had learned in Marburg: "from the never tiring industriousness and the openness for looking around in the church and the world, up to the fluttery black tie, which for many years reminded contemporaries of where and by whom I had spent my apprentice years."[161] When Barth in 1953 received Johannes Rathje's monograph on the life and work of Rade, he commented:

> One had to and still must appreciate Martin Rade even today: just as he was and apparently could not be otherwise, as well as the Marburg of that era—as I read it I thought I again saw the grey slate roofs of the city and the castle high up and the garden [of Martin Rade's residence] on Roter Graben!—and all the very able and sage people of that "world" as well...[162]

Notes

1. "Autobiographical Sketches I. Münster, 1927," *Barth–Bultmann Letters* (GA 1), 152. Translation revised.
2. Cf. Barth, "Systematische Theologie," *Lehre und Forschung*, 36. From his confirmation instruction Barth understood "that it might be a lovely and good thing not just to know and affirm the great propositions of the Christian creed but to understand them from within."
3. Barth, "Systematische Theologie," 35f.
4. "Selbstdarstellung" (1962 or 1963), KBA 11294, 1.
5. Cf. Chalamet, *Dialectical Theologians*, 65.
6. Cf. "Selbstdarstellung" (1962 or 1963), KBA 11294, 1.
7. Barth, "Concluding Unscientific Postscript," *Theology of Schleiermacher*, 261.
8. "Interview von Hans A. Fischer-Barnicol," *Gespräche 1964–1968* (GA 28), 137.
9. "Autobiographical Sketches I. Münster, 1927," *Barth–Bultmann Letters* (GA 1), 152.
10. "Autobiographical Sketches I. Münster, 1927," *Barth–Bultmann Letters* (GA 1), 152. Cf. Barth, *Theology of John Calvin*, 131.
11. Letter of August 23, 1905 to his father, cited in *Vorträge und kleinere Arbeiten 1905–1909* (GA 21), 46.
12. "Autobiographical Sketches I. Münster, 1927," *Barth–Bultmann Letters* (GA 1), 152. Regarding Kant's influence on Barth's theology, cf. the summary by Johann Lohmann, "Kant, Kierkegaard und der Neukantianismus," in Beintker, ed., *Barth Handbuch*, 42f.
13. "Der Charakter der Religion des alten Indiens," *Vorträge und kleinere Arbeiten 1905–1909* (GA 21), 2.
14. "Der Charakter," *Vorträge und kleinere Arbeiten 1905–1909* (GA 21), 6.
15. "Die Stigmata des Franz von Assisi," *Vorträge und kleinere Arbeiten 1905–1909* (GA 21), 9f.
16. William Shakespeare, *Hamlet*, Act 1:5 (New York: Simon and Schuster, 1992), 67.
17. Harnack, *Das Wesen des Christentums*, 24, cited in Barth, "Die Stigmata," *Vorträge und kleinere Arbeiten 1905–1909* (GA 21), 10. Barth shortened and slightly revised the citation, from *entspringt* in Harnack ("originates in prejudice") to *entspricht* ("is a piece of prejudice").
18. Harnack, *Das Wesen des Christentums*, 24, n. 1.
19. Harnack, *Das Wesen des Christentums*, 24.
20. Cf. *CD* III/2 §47, 446f.
21. "Die Stigmata," *Vorträge und kleinere Arbeiten 1905–1909* (GA 21), 24.
22. "Die Stigmata," *Vorträge und kleinere Arbeiten 1905–1909* (GA 21), 24.
23. "Zirkular zur ersten Konferenz" (Circular for the first conference), cited in Gruner, *Menschenwege und Gotteswege*, 156.
24. Barth, "Die ursprüngliche Gestalt des Unser Vaters," *Vorträge und kleinere Arbeiten 1905–1909* (GA 21), 146f.
25. Barth, "Concluding Unscientific Postscript," *Theology of Schleiermacher*, 261f.
26. "Autobiographical Sketches I. Münster, 1927," *Barth–Bultmann Letters* (GA 1), 152. Dueling had been banned in the Zofingia fraternity since 1863 but the ban wasn't successful. https://www.zofingia.ch/index.php/zofingia/geschichte/ (accessed May 2, 2018; additional information about the group's history is available there).

27. Cf. the editor's introduction to "Zofingia und Sociale Frage," *Vorträge und kleinere Arbeiten 1905–1909* (GA 21), 61.
28. Charles Gilliard, "Zofingia," *Historisch-Biographisches Lexikon der Schweiz*, vol. VII, 673.
29. Barth, "Zofingia," *Vorträge und kleinere Arbeiten 1905–1909* (GA 21), 84.
30. Letter of May 17/18, 1905, to Otto Lauterburg, cited in *Vorträge und kleinere Arbeiten 1905–1909* (GA 21), 63.
31. Cf. editor's introduction to "Zofingia und Sociale Frage," *Vorträge und kleinere Arbeiten 1905–1909* (GA 21), 64.
32. Letter of May 17/18, 1905, to Otto Lauterburg, *Vorträge und kleinere Arbeiten 1905–1909* (GA 21), 63.
33. Barth, "Zofingia," *Vorträge und kleinere Arbeiten 1905–1909* (GA 21), 63.
34. Barth, "Zofingia," *Vorträge und kleinere Arbeiten 1905–1909* (GA 21), 63.
35. Barth, "Zofingia," *Vorträge und kleinere Arbeiten 1905–1909* (GA 21), 73f. 75.
36. Barth, "Zofingia," *Vorträge und kleinere Arbeiten 1905–1909* (GA 21), 74.
37. Barth, "Zofingia," *Vorträge und kleinere Arbeiten 1905–1909* (GA 21), 76.
38. Barth, "Zofingia," *Vorträge und kleinere Arbeiten 1905–1909* (GA 21), 81.
39. Barth, "Zofingia," *Vorträge und kleinere Arbeiten 1905–1909* (GA 21), 82.
40. Barth, "Zofingia," *Vorträge und kleinere Arbeiten 1905–1909* (GA 21), 86.
41. Cf. Barth, "Zofingia," *Vorträge und kleinere Arbeiten 1905–1909* (GA 21), 100–3.
42. "Centralblatt des Schweizerischen Zofingervereins," vol. 47 (1906/7), 517f., cited in *Vorträge und kleinere Arbeiten 1905–1909* (GA 21), 67f.
43. "Centralblatt des Schweizerischen Zofingervereins," vol. 48 (1907/8), 279f., cited in *Vorträge und kleinere Arbeiten 1905–1909* (GA 21), 68.
44. Cf. "Autobiographical Sketches I. Münster, 1927," *Barth–Bultmann Letters* (GA 1), 304.
45. "Autobiographical Sketches I. Münster, 1927," *Barth–Bultmann Letters* (GA 1), 304.
46. Circular letter of November 26, 1924, to his friends, *Barth–Thurneysen Briefwechsel* II (GA 4), 287.
47. Cf. Kaftan, *Kant*; cf. Rohls, *Philosophie und Theologie*, 518f.
48. Kaftan, *Dogmatik*, 14.
49. Kaftan, *Dogmatik*, 11.
50. Kaftan, *Dogmatik*, 11.
51. Kaftan, *Dogmatik*, 11.
52. Barth, "Concluding Unscientific Postscript," *Theology of Schleiermacher*, 261.
53. Cf. Bergner, *Um der Sache willen*, index entry for "Gunkel."
54. Letter of December 13, 1906, to his father, cited in *Vorträge und kleinere Arbeiten 1905–1909* (GA 21), 151.
55. Cf. Barth's letter of November 1, 1906, to his father, cited in *Vorträge und kleinere Arbeiten 1905–1909* (GA 21), 150.
56. This was the mathematician, theologian, and philosopher Heinrich Scholz, later professor of philosophy of religion and systematic theology in Breslau from 1917–19, professor of philosophy in Kiel from 1919–28, and after 1928 in Münster, where after 1943 he became professor for mathematical logic and basic research. Barth later met often with him for critical exchanges; see pp. 157–158, 203, 213.

57. Letter of November 1, 1906, to his father, cited in *Vorträge und kleinere Arbeiten 1905–1909* (GA 21), 150. The reference to the leopards is an allusion to Friedrich Schiller's ballad *Der Handschuh* ("The Glove").
58. Letter of December 13, 1906, to his father, cited in *Vorträge und kleinere Arbeiten 1905–1909* (GA 21), 151.
59. Cf. Barth, "Die Missionsthätigkeit des Paulus nach der Darstellung der Apostelgeschichte," *Vorträge und kleinere Arbeiten 1905–1909* (GA 21), 159.
60. Cf. letter of December 13, 1906, to his father, cited in *Vorträge und kleinere Arbeiten 1905–1909* (GA 21), 151 and 160f.
61. Barth, "Die Missionsthätigkeit," *Vorträge und kleinere Arbeiten 1905–1909* (GA 21), 207.
62. Barth, "Die Missionsthätigkeit," *Vorträge und kleinere Arbeiten 1905–1909* (GA 21), 212.
63. Barth, "Die Missionsthätigkeit," *Vorträge und kleinere Arbeiten 1905–1909* (GA 21), 214.
64. Barth, "Die Missionsthätigkeit," *Vorträge und kleinere Arbeiten 1905–1909* (GA 21), 214.
65. Cited in Barth, "Die Missionsthätigkeit," *Vorträge und kleinere Arbeiten 1905–1909* (GA 21), 243, n. 144.
66. Letter of November 30, 1906, to Otto Lauterburg, cited in *Vorträge und kleinere Arbeiten 1905–1909* (GA 21), 148.
67. Letter of January 10, 1907, to his parents, cited in *Vorträge und kleinere Arbeiten 1905–1909* (GA 21), 152.
68. Letter of November 22, 1906, to his father, cited in *Vorträge und kleinere Arbeiten 1905–1909* (GA 21), 149, n. 2.
69. Postcard of November 5, 1909, to Paul Walter, cited in *Vorträge und kleinere Arbeiten 1905–1909* (GA 21), 149, n. 4.
70. Letter of December 23, 1935, to Agnes von Zahn-Harnack, cited in *Vorträge und kleinere Arbeiten 1905–1909* (GA 21), 148.
71. Regarding Herrmann's influence on Barth, see Chalamet, *Dialectical Theologians*.
72. Barth, "Die dogmatische Prinzipienlehre bei Wilhelm Herrmann," *Vorträge und kleinere Arbeiten 1922–1925* (GA 19), 551f.
73. Herrmann, "Vorrede zur ersten Auflage," in *Ethik*, v.
74. Cf. Herrmann, *Ethik*, 36f.
75. Cf. Hägglund, *Geschichte der Theologie*, 297.
76. Herrmann, *Ethik*, 2.
77. Herrmann, *Ethik*, 3 and 6.
78. Barth, "Concluding Unscientific Postscript," *Theology of Schleiermacher*, 262.
79. Barth, "Concluding Unscientific Postscript," *Theology of Schleiermacher*, 262. Translation revised.
80. "Music for a Guest—A Radio Broadcast," in Barth, *Final Testimonies*, 23. Translation revised.
81. Cf. Busch, *Karl Barth: His Life*, 42.
82. Cf. letter of December 13, 1948, to Karl Huber, KBA 9248.319; *Barth–von Kirschbaum Briefwechsel* I (GA 45), 191, ed. note 7. Regarding the date, cf. Busch, *Karl Barth: His Life*, 42.

83. Cf. Selinger, *Charlotte von Kirschbaum und Karl Barth*, 6.
84. See Chapter 9.
85. Letter of September 21, 1932, to Kirschbaum, *Barth–von Kirschbaum Briefwechsel* I (GA 45), 241.
86. Letter of September 26, 1933, to Kirschbaum, *Barth–von Kirschbaum Briefwechsel* I (GA 45), 338.
87. Letter of September 26, 1933, to Kirschbaum, *Barth–von Kirschbaum Briefwechsel* I (GA 45), 338.
88. Letter of May 19, 1943, to Gertrud Chr. Dallgard-Münger, KBA 9243.56.
89. Letter of May 19, 1943, to Gertrud Chr. Dallgard-Münger, KBA 9243.56.
90. Letter of December 13, 1948, to Karl Huber, KBA 9248.319.
91. "Autobiographical Sketches I. Münster, 1927," *Barth–Bultmann Letters* (GA 1), 153. Translation revised.
92. Cf. "Autobiographical Sketches I. Münster, 1927," *Barth–Bultmann Letters* (GA 1), 153.
93. "Interview von Hans A. Fischer-Barnicol," *Gespräche 1964–1968* (GA 28), 139.
94. "Autobiographical Sketches I. Münster, 1927," *Barth–Bultmann Letters* (GA 1), 153.
95. Letter of January 6, 1908, to Willy Spoendlin, cited in *Vorträge und kleinere Arbeiten 1905–1909* (GA 21), 246.
96. Cf. letter of January 21, 1908, to his parents, cited in *Vorträge und kleinere Arbeiten 1905–1909* (GA 21), 246.
97. Letter of January 28, 1908, to his parents, cited in *Vorträge und kleinere Arbeiten 1905–1909* (GA 21), 247.
98. Cf. Letter of January 28, 1908, to his parents, cited in *Vorträge und kleinere Arbeiten 1905–1909* (GA 21), 247.
99. Barth, "Die Vorstellung vom Descensus Christi ad inferos in der kirchlichen Literatur bis Origines," *Vorträge und kleinere Arbeiten 1905–1909* (GA 21), 249f.
100. Letter of June 9, 1908, to his parents, cited in *Vorträge und kleinere Arbeiten 1905–1909* (GA 21), 247.
101. Letter of December 14, 1908, to his parents, cited in *Vorträge und kleinere Arbeiten 1905–1909* (GA 21), 247.
102. "Interview von Hans A. Fischer-Barnicol," *Gespräche 1964–1968* (GA 28), 139.
103. "Autobiographical Sketches I. Münster, 1927," *Barth–Bultmann Letters* (GA 1), 153. In retrospect Barth generally classified Herrmann as "liberal." Christophe Chalamet believes that there are also conservative elements in Herrmann; cf. Chalamet, *Dialectical Theologians*, 59.
104. Barth, "Die dogmatische Prinzipienlehre bei Wilhelm Herrmann," *Vorträge und kleinere Arbeiten 1922–1925* (GA 19), 583.
105. Barth, "Die dogmatische Prinzipienlehre," *Vorträge und kleinere Arbeiten 1922–1925* (GA 19), 591.
106. Barth, "Die dogmatische Prinzipienlehre," *Vorträge und kleinere Arbeiten 1922–1925* (GA 19), 597.
107. Barth, "Die dogmatische Prinzipienlehre," *Vorträge und kleinere Arbeiten 1922–1925* (GA 19), 585.
108. Barth, "Concluding Unscientific Postscript," *Theology of Schleiermacher*, 262.

109. "Interview von Hans A. Fischer-Barnicol," *Gespräche 1964–1968* (GA 28), 137f.
110. "Autobiographical Sketches I. Münster, 1927," *Barth–Bultmann Letters* (GA 1), 153.
111. "Interview von Hans A. Fischer-Barnicol," *Gespräche 1964–1968* (GA 28), 140.
112. "Interview von Hans A. Fischer-Barnicol," *Gespräche 1964–1968* (GA 28), 142. Chalamet questions this description by Barth of what he had learned from Herrmann. It was much more the case that Barth had learned dialectical thinking from him. (Cf. Chalamet, *Dialectical Theologians*, 171ff.)
113. Cf. Herrmann, *Der Verkehr des Christen mit Gott*, 11.
114. Cf. Herrmann, *Der Verkehr*, 57.
115. Cf. Herrmann, *Der Verkehr*, 63: "We become most clearly aware of God's interaction with us through the event in which the person of Jesus is revealed to us through the power of its inner life."
116. Herrmann, *Der Verkehr*, 59.
117. Herrmann, *Der Verkehr*, 62.
118. Barth, "Die dogmatische Prinzipienlehre," *Vorträge und kleinere Arbeiten 1922–1925* (GA 19), 585.
119. Barth, "Die dogmatische Prinzipienlehre," *Vorträge und kleinere Arbeiten 1922–1925* (GA 19), 588.
120. Barth, "Die dogmatische Prinzipienlehre," *Vorträge und kleinere Arbeiten 1922–1925* (GA 19), 588.
121. Barth, "Die dogmatische Prinzipienlehre," *Vorträge und kleinere Arbeiten 1922–1925* (GA 19), 594f. Barth immediately relativizes this contrast when he asks whether this was truly Herrmann's opinion. "Didn't Herrmann always speak of this inner life, that its power was only because *God has revealed* himself in this life?" (595).
122. Barth, "Die dogmatische Prinzipienlehre," *Vorträge und kleinere Arbeiten 1922–1925* (GA 19), 599f.
123. Barth, "Die dogmatische Prinzipienlehre," *Vorträge und kleinere Arbeiten 1922–1925* (GA 19), 600.
124. Cf. Lohmann, "Kant, Kierkegaard und der Neukantianismus," in Beintker, ed., *Barth Handbuch*, 44f.; as well as Lohmann, *Karl Barth und der Neukantianismus*.
125. Barth, "Die dogmatische Prinzipienlehre," *Vorträge und kleinere Arbeiten 1922–1925* (GA 19), 583.
126. Cohen, *Logik der reinen Erkenntnis*, 13, cited in Lohmann, *Karl Barth und der Neukantianismus*, 69.
127. Cohen, *Logik der reinen Erkenntnis*, 13; cf. Lohmann, *Karl Barth und der Neukantianismus*, 70–2.
128. Lohmann, *Karl Barth und der Neukantianismus*, 133, with citations from Natorp, *Die logischen Grundlagen der exakten Wissenschaften*, 33f.
129. See Chapter 5.
130. *Schweizerköpfe der Gegenwart*, 118.
131. Regarding the relationship between Barth and Rade, cf. Christoph Schwöbel, introduction, in *Karl Barth–Martin Rade. Ein Briefwechsel*, 9–56.
132. Letter of August 9, 1908, to Otto Lauterburg, cited in *Vorträge und kleinere Arbeiten 1905–1909* (GA 21), 313.
133. Letter of April 27, 1947, to Johannes Rathje, *Offene Briefe 1945–1968* (GA 15), 119.

134. Letter of April 27, 1947, to Johannes Rathje, *Offene Briefe 1945–1968* (GA 15), 119.
135. Letter of April 27, 1947, to Johannes Rathje, *Offene Briefe 1945–1968* (GA 15), 120.
136. Letter of April 27, 1947, to Johannes Rathje, *Offene Briefe 1945–1968* (GA 15), 120.
137. Letter of April 27, 1947, to Johannes Rathje, *Offene Briefe 1945–1968* (GA 15), 120.
138. Cf. "Autobiographical Sketches I. Münster, 1927," *Barth–Bultmann Letters* (GA 1), 153.
139. Letter of April 27, 1947, to Johannes Rathje, *Offene Briefe 1945–1968* (GA 15), 121.
140. Barth, "Moderne Theologie und Reichsgottesarbeit," *Vorträge und kleinere Arbeiten 1905–1909* (GA 21), 341f. While Marburg and Heidelberg were the places for "modern," liberal theology at the time, Halle and Greifswald were dominated by "positive," more conservative theologians.
141. Cf. Barth, "Moderne Theologie," *Vorträge und kleinere Arbeiten 1905–1909* (GA 21), 344.
142. Barth, "Moderne Theologie," *Vorträge und kleinere Arbeiten 1905–1909* (GA 21), 343f.
143. Barth, "Moderne Theologie," *Vorträge und kleinere Arbeiten 1905–1909* (GA 21), 342.
144. Barth, "Moderne Theologie," *Vorträge und kleinere Arbeiten 1905–1909* (GA 21), 345.
145. Barth, "Moderne Theologie," *Vorträge und kleinere Arbeiten 1905–1909* (GA 21), 346.
146. Barth, "Moderne Theologie," *Vorträge und kleinere Arbeiten 1905–1909* (GA 21), 346.
147. Letter of June 17, 1909, from Fritz Barth, cited in *Vorträge und kleinere Arbeiten 1905–1909* (GA 21), 335.
148. Letter of June 18, 1909, to Fritz Barth, cited in *Vorträge und kleinere Arbeiten 1905–1909* (GA 21), 336.
149. Letter of June 18, 1909, to Fritz Barth, cited in *Vorträge und kleinere Arbeiten 1905–1909* (GA 21), 336.
150. Letter of June 18, 1909, to Fritz Barth, cited in *Vorträge und kleinere Arbeiten 1905–1909* (GA 21), 336.
151. Regarding this, cf. Schwöbel, introduction, *Karl Barth–Martin Rade*, 18.
152. Ernst Christian Achelis, "Noch einmal: Moderne Theologie und Reichsgottesarbeit," cited in *Vorträge und kleinere Arbeiten 1905–1909* (GA 21), 347–51.
153. Paul Drews, "Zum dritten Mal: Moderne Theologie und Reichsgottesarbeit," cited in *Vorträge und kleinere Arbeiten 1905–1909* (GA 21), 352.
154. Letter of September 29, 1909, from Fritz Barth, cited in *Vorträge und kleinere Arbeiten 1905–1909* (GA 21), 339.
155. Letter of September 30, 1909, to Fritz Barth, cited in *Vorträge und kleinere Arbeiten 1905–1909* (GA 21), 339.
156. Undated letter from Fritz Barth, cited in *Vorträge und kleinere Arbeiten 1905–1909* (GA 21), 340.
157. Cf. the letter of December 6, 1909, from Ernst Christian Achelis to Fritz Barth, cited in *Vorträge und kleinere Arbeiten 1905–1909* (GA 21), 340f.
158. Martin Rade, "Redaktionelle Schlußbemerkung," cited in *Vorträge und kleinere Arbeiten 1905–1909* (GA 21), 365.
159. Letter of November 24, 1909, to Martin Rade, in Schwöbel, ed., *Karl Barth–Martin Rade*, 70.
160. See pp. 69–71.
161. Letter of October 7, 1939, to Martin and Dora Rade, in Schwöbel, ed., *Karl Barth–Martin Rade*, 280.
162. Letter of March 19, 1953, to Johannes Rathje, *Offene Briefe 1945–1968* (GA 15), 338f.

3
"Stumbling up the Steps to Calvin's Pulpit"
Geneva, 1909–11

In September of 1909 Barth began his practical work as *pasteur suffragant*, assistant pastor, in the German Reformed congregation in Geneva.[1] At the end of October head pastor Adolf Keller transferred from Geneva to Zurich, so that Barth had to tend to the congregation alone until Keller's successor arrived in February 1910.[2]

Vicar in Geneva

The worship services took place in the small gothic chapel, Temple de l'Auditoire, adjacent to the great cathedral of St. Peter's. It was a space rich in history. Here the Geneva reformer John Calvin and his successor Theodore Beza had interpreted the Bible. The Scottish reformer John Knox had preached in the chapel. Later Barth expressed amazement to Keller about "how at the time I—100% a product of Marburg, who knew everything, but everything, better—entered the ministry and stumbled up the steps to Calvin's pulpit, with the inexperience, clumsiness, and unsurpassable confidence reminiscent of the comportment of a young Saint Bernard."[3]

His place of work contributed to the fact that during his time in Geneva, in addition to continuing his reading of Schleiermacher, Barth absorbed himself in Calvin's main work, *Institutes of the Christian Religion*, and his biblical commentaries.

Fully in the spirit of his first essay, *Moderne Theologie und Reichsgottesarbeit*, Barth introduced himself to his congregation in his opening sermon on September 26, 1909: "To be good friends, pathfinders, leaders in the sphere of the inner life ... we cannot do more ... We pastors and theologians have neither to administer nor to distribute religion; our task is always only to arouse, to encourage, and to shape religion."[4]

Barth prepared his sermons carefully, basing them on a written out manuscript. He was all the more disappointed that his sermons and other offerings found only little resonance. Thus in 1910 he wrote a peppery article in the parish newsletter on Reformation Day. It was sobering, he wrote, how few men appeared in the

3.1. Calvin's pulpit in the Temple de l'Auditoire, Geneva, © Bibliothèque de Genève/ Foto Atelier Boissonnas.

worship service on Sundays, given the number of church members. Even among the women, empty seats were often to be seen. Nor were other events well-attended. "In light of these circumstances there are friendly apologists who speak the following words of comfort: 1. Things are much worse in northern Germany. 2. Even here among us it used to be much worse. 3. In the French-speaking churches of Geneva it is just as bad."[5] In Barth's view however none of these relativizations mattered. He viewed the excuses caustically. His sense of being slighted is evident:

"Pastor, I am a modern human being. Darkness and clerical deception is not my thing; science has shown that...!" What do I hear there? I hung around the universities for five years to reach clarity about these matters, and now along comes Mr. Z., who knows everything, without having attended university, and *how* sure of himself! Please continue to speak, I would love to learn more. But isn't it true, here we are of the same mind: the culture war, that general bashing about church and dogmatics, that was forty years ago. Whoever is still fighting that battle shows that intellectually he is an outdated customer and belongs in the museum along with the dug-up mammoth bones. Educated people don't get worked up any more about the proofs of God and theories of creation, whether for or against. In the church as well we have more urgent things to do.[6]

He made it clear to his parishioners:

We therefore have an institute, a community, called "Church," which deals with the care of an area of life, the importance of which every human being should know, namely with the life of the soul, with the purpose and sense and content of existence, to put it into one word: with the *human being*, who surely (or?) doesn't merely work, eat, drink, and read the newspaper, but *lives*, or *should* live. 800 men have announced their interest in this community by letting their names be written in the membership roster [of this congregation]. Two other men have pursued all kinds of studies and continue to do so, in order to help the others with their thoughts as best as they can. A very small system has been put to work for this purpose, and everyone nods and says: It must be like this; there must be people who care for this business, just as there are men who light the lanterns; *it* must preach from time to time, just as *it* rains from time to time.[7]

Barth did not wish to accept these conditions: "...out of a congregation which exists on paper [there must become] a congregation that *lives* and that *works*."[8] Amazingly enough this article had a great effect. In the following weeks more men showed up in worship service.

Quite Demanding: The First Confirmation Instruction

In Geneva Barth had to give confirmation instruction.[9] As was customary there, it lasted only a half year. Barth prepared it carefully in writing and developed a different program for each year. The background knowledge of his confirmation students tended to be sparse. In a notice to the congregation about the 1909/10 course, pastor and vicar reported: "It was nothing unusual when bibles were opened and the Epistle to the Romans was looked for somewhere around the five books of Moses."[10]

In the first year Barth still relied somewhat on an existing catechism and confronted the confirmation pupils with quite demanding theological deliberations. After 1910 he followed a concept that he developed.[11] Each theme was introduced with several thesis statements (as was the case later in his work on dogmatics), which he dictated "like an old professor."[12] The sentences did not have to be learned by heart, but were to serve as "a coat hanger to hang things up to remember them."[13]

In the first hour he tried to make it clear to the confirmation pupils that the class was about them: "This has to do with you yourselves, and so you have to be present, not just your ears and your head. Instruction cannot be mere teaching and learning, we have to find each other personally, become good friends, if we are to speak about these things."[14] He wanted two-way questions and answers, they should pose questions themselves, and the goal was "learning from each other."[15] He expected of the confirmation pupils that they take the class seriously, not just sit it out: "No grumpiness, but rather a cheerful and serious concentration on the goal," and that they regularly attend either the children's Sunday school or the main worship service.[16]

In content the first course was like a religious pedagogical application of Wilhelm Herrmann's concept that human beings recognize the Good (in religious terms: God's command) through their reason, but are incapable of bringing it about through their own power; for this they need the experience of the inner life of Jesus. Barth demonstrated to the young people how for example this takes place in praying the Lord's Prayer. In this we recognize Jesus's inner life and are moved through this: "His prayer was the expression of his life, and so we see in his prayer how it is when a human being lives fully with God. Out of his prayer he himself speaks to us: be like this! and still more: a *power* comes from it, to be like this."[17] The decisive dynamic in the life of a person lies in such religious "experience" (*Erlebnis*); from a human perspective this is religion, but from the perspective of God it is revelation.[18]

In the final class of the first 1909/10 course Barth had the courage to ask his confirmation pupils whether they had understood the class.[19] Apparently he himself sensed that much of it had been quite demanding. Unfortunately their answers have not been preserved. Barth reassured himself and his confirmation pupils with the comment that "instruction...[can] not make someone a Christian, only God can do this."[20] He encouraged them that it was better to cancel confirmation than lie when asked about their faith. Faith means "to have the desire and intent to manage one's life according to the way of Jesus."[21] "Confirmation is then the truth when it becomes life."[22]

The second course was also influenced by Herrmann's theology. Confirmation instruction was not primarily about moral rules or specific intellectual insights. The purpose of the instruction was: "To become a living human being oneself, to see and comprehend Jesus oneself. Agreement or rejection of individual 'Christian' concepts doesn't matter. There must be diversity within Christendom."[23] Particularly in the early classes Barth more strongly took up the "life-world" of the young people and their questions, for example about happiness and the meaning of life. Barth's obvious concern now was to genuinely accompany them as they transitioned to adulthood.

Theologian in the Congregation

Barth wrote numerous small contributions for the parish newsletter, which for several months he also editorially oversaw. Some of these are true to life and realistic, some of them are theologically ambitious.

His reflection "From One Plate" is an especially colorful portrait. There Barth reports about a farm wedding that he had attended in 1909 in Hesse, where it was a custom for the bridal couple to eat the entire wedding meal using only one spoon, one fork, and one knife from only one plate. Barth used the image to illustrate Christian life. For Christians the satisfaction that "the dear God has filled one's own plate to the brim" wasn't sufficient.[24] True Christian joy exists when one shares with others. Admittedly this was not so easy. "For human beings are not just soft mollusks where all gives way wherever one pushes, rather they are indescribably bristly creatures with many edges and barbs."[25] Living with one another is something that must be learned. Through this "friction and competition in life, through [using] the same plate [God teaches us] human beings to become Christians."[26] When this happens, the person must say to herself: "this is not something you did on your own, you little bristly human being, it was God, who is completely other than you and who is at work to make something completely else out of the person you still are."[27]

Another contribution was titled "Did Jesus live? A Retrospective Easter Reflection." Here again the influence of Wilhelm Herrmann is unmistakable. Barth explained to the congregation that a number of scholars deny the question, while others attempt to show that while some aspects of Jesus's life are uncertain, "the fact of his life, his worldly work, his death under Caesar Tiberius... [is among] the greatest of certainties."[28] Barth welcomed this attempt, but distanced himself sharply from an organized protest that had taken place on February 20, 1910, in Berlin against the "denial of the historicity of Jesus":[29] "Protesting and demonstrating doesn't prove anything at all, at least not for us in Switzerland!"[30] Faith is not "accepting and holding external facts to be true."[31] The inner life of Jesus is the foundation of faith:

the image of his human character, which portrays itself to us as complete obedience to God, as complete love for his brothers and therefore as complete self-denial... When in light of this image of his character it becomes clear to us what *God is*, and we are *to become*, then we *believe*.[32]

After the 1910 confirmation Barth introduced so-called "evenings for the confirmed."[33] He wanted to keep those who had been confirmed in the congregation and help them further deepen their knowledge about Christianity. Adults were also permitted to attend these evenings. Initially Barth dealt with the history of missions, but then concentrated on theologians from the history of dogma. After a review of Socrates and Plato he went through Paul, John, and church fathers such as Origen and Augustine. These evenings alternated with discussion evenings about themes like "miracles" or "the resurrection of Jesus." Barth devoted the final weeks before he left Geneva to Paul's Epistle to the Romans. Barth benefited from paraphrasing what he had learned in his studies in a more generally understandable manner.[34] At the same time these preparations allowed him to discover that, despite his appearance of being very self-assured, he essentially had very little knowledge of the great theological tradition *before* the modern age. And that changed some things.

Barth had initially considered doing a doctorate in Marburg. Wilhelm Herrmann had recommended that he work on Schleiermacher's understanding of prayer.[35] At the beginning of 1911 however Barth grew more hesitant about whether this might truly be the right path for him because his interests had shifted. He explained to Wilhelm Loew, a fellow student friend from his years in Marburg, that "right now Schleiermacher... seems theologically unbelievably remote to me, and I don't feel that I am prepared enough to hammer out statements about Schl. and the 19th century until I have personally understood the analytics and dialectics of the religion of the Reformation on a very different level."[36] His reading of Calvin led him to discover major gaps in his knowledge. Now it was time first to go through Luther and Zwingli, scholastic theology and Augustine, perhaps the New Testament as well.[37] Apparently this insight had been provoked by the evenings for those who had been confirmed. Several months after introducing these gatherings he admitted to himself "that at the moment I am not at all theologically 'on my feet,' rather I sit facing the views of others who are wiser."[38]

"In Such a Dreadfully Pious Environment"

Through his new office Karl Barth was invited to the pastoral conferences of the German-speaking pastors in French Switzerland.[39] After the second meeting on May 30, 1910, he wrote to his parents in horror:

In such company I feel completely alien, I must often remind myself almost forcibly that I belong to this profession, whose comportment among most of its representatives comes across as so peculiar, and that I [am] not a "worldling," who for these standard-bearers of the Gospel, with their many prayers, eyes cast to the heavens, with their hands softly folded over their stomachs etc. has only the interested curiosity of someone who enjoys oddities... In such a dreadfully pious environment I feel ever more decidedly pagan tendencies.[40]

Barth was asked and agreed to give a lecture at the pastoral conference on October 5, 1910, in Neuchâtel. Later he viewed this as his attempt at a synthesis between Schleiermacher and Calvin, and wished that he had not submitted it for publication.[41] At the time however he wanted to arouse the pastors in attendance with his lecture "Christian Faith and History." Barth confidently believed that his reflections were far more substantive than those in *Faith and History*, the article by the Heidelberg systematician Ernst Troeltsch that had just appeared in the large new lexicon *Die Religion in Geschichte und Gegenwart*.[42] It is astonishing how certain young Barth was in his verdict of a successful scholar: Troeltsch "is an ambitious un-thorough fellow who does not see the simplest things and will lead theology into the swamp."[43]

Once again Barth pushed for immediate publication. His father reacted with resignation: "Getting this published would not seem to be so urgent; but that is up to you; you will then have to accept the responsibility for what you write."[44] Barth sent a special offprint to Troeltsch, who reacted with aplomb:

> in earlier years I thought I could assert this standpoint, but it proved to be untenable for me and at best effective only for the orthodox. I also understand the sense of superiority that can lead someone from this standpoint to condescend toward such a strongly tentative work like mine, and am happy to put up with that.[45]

In his contribution, in which he once again was recognizably a student of Wilhelm Herrmann, Barth wanted to clarify the relationship between faith and historical facts.[46] Faith is the "immediate consciousness of the present and the effectiveness of the superhuman, transcendent and therefore absolutely superior life force."[47] For what then does it need historical facts such as the life of Jesus? And how can faith's access to these be understood, when there is no immediacy possible toward them, but rather we can only access them as mediated through other human beings and their cultural achievements, such as the biblical text? Put differently: how do the immediacy and the mediated aspects of faith belong together?

Barth argued that to find their way to faith, human beings need human community, even when faith itself is the immediate experience of God. In contrast human beings within themselves find only the ethical law and the insight that they cannot empirically live up to that law.

Christian faith originates in "Christ outside of us,"[48] in Jesus's piety and his love for God and human beings, that is, simply in his inner life. Barth found Troeltsch's claim, that faith is about "the epistemological moment of piety"[49] and the relationship of faith to history is primarily a conceptual one, to be too cognitive; in this Troeltsch did not distinguish enough between the *doctrine* of faith and faith itself.

Barth reaches the conclusion: "Effective history is faith brought into effect."[50] Put differently: the historical fact of Jesus's life works upon us in that faith arises in us from it. Neither can be separated, nor do they need to be mediated retroactively. "Faith does not stand over against history, rather it is simply the extension or the *apprehensio* [the grasping] of history in the life of the individual."[51] Indeed, today's human being does not directly encounter the person Jesus and his inner life. But through another human being who has come alive through Jesus's inner life, his inner life will be mediated to us.

There was not much discussion of the lecture. The president of the conference, Pastor Adolph Hoffmann of the German Lutheran Church in Geneva, opened it unenthusiastically with the words: "Yes, I can see that Brother Barth is the smartest one among us."[52]

On March 29, 1911, Barth participated one more time in such a pastoral conference. Adolph Hoffmann now declared that a troublemaker like Barth wasn't wanted in their ranks.[53] Barth wrote Loew that he had been "thrown out as not 'biblical-devout-positive.'"[54]

A Daughter from a Good Home: The Engagement to Nelly Hoffmann

Barth's acquaintance and engagement to Nelly Hoffmann occurred during his time in Geneva. She had been in his first confirmation class.

Nelly Hoffmann was born on August 26, 1893, near the town of Rorschach on the Bodensee.[55] Since the beginning of the eighteenth century her family had resided in the Renaissance castle of Wiggen. Nelly's grandfather Joseph Marzell Hoffmann was a member of the Swiss national council and president of the executive of the canton St. Gallen; her father was Robert Hoffmann, the state clerk of St. Gallen. Robert Hoffmann had five daughters with his wife Anna Elisabeth, neé Hugentobler. Nelly was the youngest. One year after her birth her father died. Nelly was deeply affected by this: "With him something very essential was missing from my life."[56]

After her father's death the family left the castle, moving to nearby Goldach. The daughters attended school in St. Gallen. Their house included an extensive garden with large fir trees and Nelly had a lasting memory of their "eerie somberness" at dusk.[57] Among her "nicest childhood memories were the Rietli house with warm-hearted Aunt Fanny, her father's sister, which they reached by going through the meadows and vineyards."[58]

Several years later the family moved to Zurich. Nelly Hoffmann attended the Free Protestant School in the city center. In their apartment building there was a trapeze in the hall, "high enough that one could sing or recite over the heads of those in authority; Mama and Aunt were the loyal audience for my self-composed poetry."[59]

In 1905 the family moved once more for the sake of their daughters' education, to Geneva. Nelly Hoffmann again attended a private school, naturally now with classes in French, and then the Secondary and the Superior School. She received her first violin lessons at the age ten, initially from a private instructor and then later at the Geneva Conservatory. She enjoyed playing the violin: "My real joy was in music as soon as I was given a full-sized lovely-sounding Italian violin."[60]

As Pastor Adolf Keller had been, Vicar Karl Barth now became a frequent visitor of the family. "I was very interested in his sermons from the beginning," Nelly Hoffmann recalled,

> they would have still been very intellectual-theological, from his years of study in Berlin, Tübingen, Marburg. But I did not understand and recognize that. I think that his urgent questions and his search for a true interpretation of the text was what drew and interested me... So I was filled in two ways—with music and with questions of faith.[61]

On May 16, 1911, one year after her confirmation, Karl Barth asked if she wished to be his wife. The barely eighteen-year-old was unprepared for this. Up to that point he had been something like an older brother for her.

> I think I said: I thank you for this trust! Then I went outside—somewhere under the wide, open skies... Finally I knew: this question is greater, more important than everything I had aspired toward... Mama, just as surprised as I was, had confidence in this fiery young pastor... So it happened that we became engaged on a day in May in 1911.[62]

Farewell to Geneva

Barth delivered his final sermon in Geneva on June 25, 1911, on Matthew 10:26–7. The text, in which Jesus calls upon his disciples to proclaim his gospel, urges us: "You must proclaim that which is living in you to the people out there."[63] Barth emphatically linked this to his work as pastor and once again took up his Marburg

3.2. Karl Barth's engagement to Nelly Hoffmann, 1911, © Karl Barth-Archive in Basel.

article:[64] "To make apparent what is hidden within us, to let people know about the secret facts of a life that comes from and with God, as well as we can, to witness to that which lives in us, that is our obligation and our task."[65] The sermon certainly illustrates what Barth had learned in the meantime. He had discovered a dynamic of inner life that he had not yet known in Marburg: when the inner life has reached maturity, then it does not want to keep to itself but seeks to have an outside impact. This urge to express the religious inner life to others, is—and this too was new—strengthened by the love for other people, which one learns in the attitude of Jesus on the cross. It is in this very way that a genuine Christian congregation emerges.

Ultimately every Christian has this task. It is fulfilled however not through immediately trumpeting each inner experience to the world; the encounter with God leads one first of all into stillness and solitude. Barth explains, in phrases that in their tension almost anticipate his later renowned lecture, *The Word of God as the Task of Theology*,[66] but here the reason for the tension rests not in God but in human beings:

> Particularly when we have experienced something serious, great, and solemn, it is initially difficult for all of us to speak of it, and it must be difficult. But this initial reserve cannot be final, rather, it is only half of the matter. When God has spoken

to us, then we must initially be silent, but then we must also begin to speak, and only then is God's work in us completed.[67]

Barth's description of the resistance one can encounter when expressing one's inner life to others seems to be a reflection on his experiences in Geneva: "distrust towards life," "superficiality," "moral ambiguity," "spiritually going to seed," and "moralistic dullness."[68] This "resistance of the dull world" sometimes takes the "form of an open battle," at other times one encounters a "lazy..., sticky... mass of indifference."[69] Whoever encounters such things in proclaiming the Gospel feels "sad and deserted and useless."[70] But he should comfort himself that he has entered into the general course of life, and that which is hidden must become revealed.

Notes

1. Barth initially resided at Quai des Bergues 21, directly next to the Rhone outflow from Lake Geneva, and then after May 1910 at Avenue des Petits Délices 9 (cf. Busch, *Karl Barth: His Life*, 52).
2. Cf. Barth, "Konfirmandenunterricht 1909/10," *Konfirmandenunterricht 1909-1921* (GA 18), 1, n. 2.
3. Letter of May 20, 1956, to Adolf Keller, KBA 9256.148.
4. Inaugural sermon of September 26, 1909, cited in Busch, *Karl Barth: His Life*, 52.
5. Barth, "Etwas über die Kirche! Speziell über die deutsche reformierte in Genf und was davon zu halten sei," *Vorträge und kleinere Arbeiten 1909-1914* (GA 22), 215.
6. Barth, "Etwas über die Kirche!," *Vorträge und kleinere Arbeiten 1909-1914* (GA 22), 217.
7. Barth, "Etwas über die Kirche!," *Vorträge und kleinere Arbeiten 1909-1914* (GA 22), 215f.
8. Barth, "Etwas über die Kirche!," *Vorträge und kleinere Arbeiten 1909-1914* (GA 22), 218.
9. Cf. the editor's preface, *Konfirmandenunterricht* (GA 18), xxi–xxxiii.
10. "Konfirmanden-Abende," *Vorträge und kleinere Arbeiten 1909-1914* (GA 22), 56.
11. Cf. the editor's preface, *Konfirmandenunterricht* (GA 18), xxiii.
12. Letter of November 25, 1910, to Willy Spoendlin, cited in *Konfirmandenunterricht* (GA 18), xxiii.
13. Barth, "Konfirmandenunterricht 1910/11," *Konfirmandenunterricht* (GA 18), 57.
14. Barth, "Konfirmandenunterricht 1910/11," *Konfirmandenunterricht* (GA 18), 57.
15. Barth, "Konfirmandenunterricht 1909/10," *Konfirmandenunterricht* (GA 18), 1.
16. Barth,"Konfirmandenunterricht 1910/11," *Konfirmandenunterricht* (GA 18), 58.
17. Barth, "Konfirmandenunterricht 1909/10," *Konfirmandenunterricht* (GA 18), 21.
18. Cf. Barth, "Konfirmandenunterricht 1909/10," *Konfirmandenunterricht* (GA 18), 15: "what we from the human side call *religion* is from God's side *revelation*. The human being sees, and God allows himself to be seen. Both come together in the term *experience*."

19. Cf. Barth, "Konfirmandenunterricht 1909/10," *Konfirmandenunterricht* (GA 18), 54f.
20. Barth, "Konfirmandenunterricht 1909/10," *Konfirmandenunterricht* (GA 18), 54.
21. Barth, "Konfirmandenunterricht 1909/10," *Konfirmandenunterricht* (GA 18), 54. At that time the church constitution in Geneva did not require a particular confession of faith to be recited during the confirmation. Presumably Barth was expecting something more like a vow from his confirmation students (cf. Barth, "Konfirmandenunterricht 1909/10," *Konfirmandenunterricht* (GA 18), 55, n. 110).
22. Barth, "Konfirmandenunterricht 1909/10," *Konfirmandenunterricht* (GA 18), 55.
23. Barth, "Konfirmandenunterricht 1910/11," *Konfirmandenunterricht* (GA 18), 61f.
24. Barth, "Aus einem Teller," *Vorträge und kleinere Arbeiten 1909–1914* (GA 22), 21.
25. Barth, "Aus einem Teller," *Vorträge und kleinere Arbeiten 1909–1914* (GA 22), 22.
26. Barth, "Aus einem Teller," *Vorträge und kleinere Arbeiten 1909–1914* (GA 22), 23.
27. Barth, "Aus einem Teller," *Vorträge und kleinere Arbeiten 1909–1914* (GA 22), 23.
28. Barth, "Ob Jesus gelebt hat? Eine nachträgliche Osterbetrachtung," *Vorträge und kleinere Arbeiten 1909–1914* (GA 22), 41.
29. Editor's introduction to "Ob Jesus gelebt hat?," *Vorträge und kleinere Arbeiten 1909–1914* (GA 22), 37.
30. Barth, "Ob Jesus gelebt hat?," *Vorträge und kleinere Arbeiten 1909–1914* (GA 22), 41.
31. Barth, "Ob Jesus gelebt hat?," *Vorträge und kleinere Arbeiten 1909–1914* (GA 22), 42.
32. Barth, "Ob Jesus gelebt hat?," *Vorträge und kleinere Arbeiten 1909–1914* (GA 22), 43.
33. Cf. Barth, "Konfirmanden-Abende," *Vorträge und kleinere Arbeiten 1909–1914* (GA 22), 46–58.
34. Cf. the editor's introduction to "Konfirmanden-Abende," *Vorträge und kleinere Arbeiten 1909–1914* (GA 22), 49.
35. Cf. the letter of January 29, 1911, to Otto Lauterburg, cited in "Konfirmanden-Abende," *Vorträge und kleinere Arbeiten 1909–1914* (GA 22), 50, n. 4.
36. Letter of February 19, 1911, to Wilhelm Loew, cited in *Vorträge und kleinere Arbeiten 1909–1914* (GA 22), 50.
37. Cf. the editor's introduction to "Konfirmanden-Abende," *Vorträge und kleinere Arbeiten 1909–1914* (GA 22), 51.
38. Letter of February 19, 1911, to Wilhelm Loew, cited in *Vorträge und kleinere Arbeiten 1909–1914* (GA 22), 51.
39. Cf. the editor's introduction to Barth, "Der christliche Glaube und die Geschichte," *Vorträge und kleinere Arbeiten 1909–1914* (GA 22), 149.
40. Letter of May 30, 1910, to his parents, cited in *Vorträge und kleinere Arbeiten 1909–1914* (GA 22), 149.
41. "I did not undergo a sudden conversion, but thought I could easily unite idealistic-romantic and Reformation theology. Along these lines I allowed to be printed a large treatise on faith and history which would have been better left unprinted." "Autobiographical Sketches I. Münster, 1927," *Barth-Bultmann Letters* (GA 1), 154. Translation revised.
42. Cf. letter of October 4, 1910, to his parents, cited in *Vorträge und kleinere Arbeiten 1909–1914* (GA 22), 150. Cf. also Troeltsch, "Glaube und Geschichte," *Religion in Geschichte und Gegenwart* 1 (1901), vol. 2, 1447–56.
43. Letter of October 14, 1910, to Wilhelm Loew, cited in *Vorträge und kleinere Arbeiten 1909–1914* (GA 22), 151f. On March 15, 1911, at the student conference in Aarau Barth

heard Troeltsch speak in person on *Die Bedeutung der Geschichtlichkeit Jesu für den Glauben* ("The significance of Jesus's historicity for faith"); cf. editor's introduction to Barth, "Der christliche Glaube," *Vorträge und kleinere Arbeiten 1909-1914* (GA 22), 152.

44. Letter of October 10, 1910, from his father, cited in *Vorträge und kleinere Arbeiten 1909-1914* (GA 22), 151.
45. Letter of April 26, 1912, from Ernst Troeltsch, cited in *Vorträge und kleinere Arbeiten 1909-1914* (GA 22), 154. Cf. also Wittekind, *Geschichtliche Offenbarung und die Wahrheit des Glaubens*, 163-65.
46. Cf. Barth, "Der christliche Glaube," *Vorträge und kleinere Arbeiten 1909-1914* (GA 22), 155.
47. Barth, "Der christliche Glaube," *Vorträge und kleinere Arbeiten 1909-1914* (GA 22), 161.
48. Barth, "Der christliche Glaube," *Vorträge und kleinere Arbeiten 1909-1914* (GA 22), 188.
49. Troeltsch, "Glaube III," *Religion in Geschichte und Gegenwart* 1 (1901), vol. 2, 1438.
50. Barth, "Der christliche Glaube," *Vorträge und kleinere Arbeiten 1909-1914* (GA 22), 200.
51. Barth, "Der christliche Glaube," *Vorträge und kleinere Arbeiten 1909-1914* (GA 22), 201. Cf. on p. 200: "Christ's justice becomes my justice, Christ's piety becomes my piety."
52. Letter of October 14, 1910, to Wilhelm Loew, cited in *Vorträge und kleinere Arbeiten 1909-1914* (GA 22), 151.
53. Cf. the editor's introduction to Barth, "Der christliche Glaube," *Vorträge und kleinere Arbeiten 1909-1914* (GA 22), 149, 153.
54. Letter of April 9, 1911, to Wilhelm Loew, cited in *Vorträge und kleinere Arbeiten 1909-1914* (GA 22), 153.
55. Cf. Zellweger-Barth, "Lebenslauf," in *Nelly Barth-Hoffmann 26. August 1893-23. Oktober 1976*, 3-9.
56. Nelly Barth, cited in Zellweger-Barth, "Lebenslauf," in *Nelly Barth-Hoffmann*, 3.
57. Nelly Barth, cited in Zellweger-Barth, "Lebenslauf," in *Nelly Barth-Hoffmann*, 3.
58. Zellweger-Barth, "Lebenslauf," in *Nelly Barth-Hoffmann*, 3.
59. Nelly Barth, cited in Zellweger-Barth, "Lebenslauf," in *Nelly Barth-Hoffmann*, 4.
60. Nelly Barth, cited in Zellweger-Barth, "Lebenslauf," in *Nelly Barth-Hoffmann*, 4.
61. Nelly Barth, cited in Zellweger-Barth, "Lebenslauf," in *Nelly Barth-Hoffmann*, 4f.
62. Nelly Barth, cited in Zellweger-Barth, "Lebenslauf," in *Nelly Barth-Hoffmann*, 5.
63. Barth, Sermon of June 25, 1911, *Predigten 1911* (GA 51), 184.
64. See p. 39.
65. Barth, Sermon of June 25, 1911, *Predigten 1911* (GA 51), 184.
66. See pp. 133-136.
67. Barth, Sermon of June 25, 1911, *Predigten 1911* (GA 51), 187.
68. Barth, Sermon of June 25, 1911, *Predigten 1911* (GA 51), 190f.
69. Barth, Sermon of June 25, 1911, *Predigten 1911* (GA 51), 191.
70. Barth, Sermon of June 25, 1911, *Predigten 1911* (GA 51), 191.

4

"The Red Pastor"

Safenwil, 1911–21

In July 1911 a new ministry awaited Barth after the end of his time as assistant pastor. He had already given a trial sermon on April 2 in the parish of Safenwil in the canton of Aargau.[1] The *Kirchenpflege*, the parish governing council, recommended him afterward as the new pastor. Barth was elected unanimously at a meeting of the entire community on April 30,[2] and so on July 3 he was able to move into the parsonage in Safenwil. He was installed as pastor on July 9 by his father and in the presence of his fiancée.

It has been customary, even in Barth's own retrospective writings, to portray his encounter with the pressing social problems in Safenwil as responsible for a fundamental change in his thinking, away from the "inner life" of the Geneva period toward the themes of "God's kingdom," "socialism," and "God's word." Yet one already finds these subsequently key concepts in Barth's inaugural sermon on July 9, in which he delivered his theological calling card, so to speak. The goal of his work in the congregation was "that the kingdom of God come among us." This kingdom of God is utterly concrete and has a social dimension. "The kingdom of God is the seriousness, the truth, the love, the justice in human hearts, in homes and families, in public life."[3] He had chosen the ministry because he had grown certain that the word of God that speaks of this kingdom of God has an effect. Therefore Barth asked the congregation

> to give [me] the confidence that I will not speak to you of God because I happen to be pastor, but that I am a pastor because I *must* speak of God, if I wish to stay true to myself, that is my better self. I want to bring to you what has become the truth for myself.[4]

In contrast to when he had started in Geneva, now the thought that the fulfillment of his ministry depended on "the divine depths of [one's] own inner life" made him anxious.[5] But he was comforted "that I have something to offer, that is great and sufficient for you, even if I sometimes will be small and lacking... God has something to tell you through me, and indeed the greatest of all things: that God loves you and that you all may love one another."[6] Barth then spoke in a way that one might have expected only months later: what matters in the lives of Christians is that they live "for the sake of their brothers," in "a socialism"—here

4.1. The Reformed church in Safenwil, the old parsonage in the foreground, © Erhard Sommer, Kölliken, used with permission.

probably the word is seen for the first time in an explicitly positive, not just exemplary sense—"that is worthy of its name."[7]

Apparently there had already been a shift of some kind during Barth's period in Geneva. Having grown up without material want, during his time as assistant pastor he had become familiar with poverty for the first time.[8] Initially he had viewed social disparities as a necessity of nature. The study of Calvin had then opened his eyes for the social question. Calvin's concept of the city of God on earth showed him "that *Jesus* described the *kingdom of God* as a state of consummate love of God and brother."[9] Presumably rendering a passage from Calvin's *Institutes* (I, 17:4f) in the parish newsletter in Geneva had also given him cause for thought. In this text Calvin criticized the viewpoint that certain conditions had been imposed by God, "when God put the means to overcome them in our hands."[10] Poverty and social injustice did not have to be.[11] Barth's thinking had begun to change in Geneva, but the social circumstances in his new area of activity in Safenwil were to lead to a permanently new orientation.[12]

"This System of Employment Must Fall": Workers and Socialists

Safenwil was then a small parish of farmers and workers. Among the 700 people working in Safenwil were predominantly men and women workers who worked in the two local textile factories, twelve hours a day, earning barely enough to live on. Barth quickly took their side.[13] In 1927 he remembered:

> In the class difference that I saw concretely before me in my congregation, I was touched for the first time by the real problems of real life. The result was that for some years...my only theological work was reduced to the preparation of sermons and classes which I still did quite carefully. What I really studied were factory acts, insurance business and trade unionism and the like, and my attention was claimed by violent local and cantonal struggles, which were caused by my taking positions on behalf of the workers.[14]

Christianity for Barth was no longer a matter primarily of the inner life. Now it had to do with concrete external problems.

Several months after beginning his ministry, on December 17, 1911, Barth held a talk about "Jesus Christ and the social movement" in the workers union (*Arbeiterverein*), the local organizational body of the Swiss Social Democrat Party (SP). Here Barth for the first time praised socialism and social democracy at length. The "19th and 20th century social movement" was "the greatest and most forceful word of God to the contemporary world" and "a very direct advance of...the spiritual power that through Jesus entered into history and into life."[15] Barth found the continguity in that which the social movement and social democracy wanted: that "which they want...is what Jesus wanted as well."[16] For that reason one could "be a genuine follower and disciple of Jesus as an atheist and materialist and Darwinist."[17]

As a proletarian movement, socialism was a movement from below. Very similarly, Jesus was a worker and tended to the poor and oppressed. Whoever asserted that Jesus's gospel had been only directed at spirit and innerness was denying this message. For Jesus, there were not two worlds of spirit and material, of heaven and earth, "but rather only one reality of God's kingdom"; redemption for Jesus meant "that God's kingdom *comes to us* in the material and on earth."[18] Stated pointedly: "It is not that we should come to heaven, but that heaven should come to us."[19]

For this reason the church had to finally have the courage to proclaim that "social needs *are not meant to be*, in order to devote its *entire* energy for this '*they are not meant to be.*'"[20] Barth immediately applied this courage. He asked rhetorically: "Do these two things go together: Jesus and capitalism, the system of the unhemmed growth of private property?"[21] And he drew the consequence: "This system of employment must...*fall*, above all its fundamental pillar [must fall]:...the private ownership of the means of production."[22]

The workers of Safenwil were pleased with Barth's vote. In the months that followed leading socialists gathered at the new pastor's for evenings with socialist literature/reading.[23]

But not everyone in Safenwil was pleased about the new pastor taking political positions. Walter Hüssy, the thirty-two year-old son of one of the two local factory owners who had forty years earlier financially supported the construction of the Reformed church,[24] expressed his views about Barth's appearances in an open letter on February 1, 1912, in the *Zofinger Tagblatt*: Barth's "agitating speech" was an attempt "to sow discord between employers and employees."[25] Hüssy's criticism was directed primarily against Barth's demand to do away with the private ownership of the means of production. The independent property owners were after all those who "pull the cart" and therefore needed "a certain elbow room."[26] The Communist alternative had never worked.

Barth's response, appearing a few days later in the same newspaper, was impudent and blunt: "My honored sir, may I loan or give you a few good books from which you can teach yourself something about the essence of modern socialist theory?"[27] "You address me in my role as pastor, that I should 'have a mediating effect.' Oh yes, as *you* understand it, right? That would suit you! With your permission however as a pastor I set myself a different program, over which I owe no accounting to *you*."[28]

> Finally, just a word about your *phrase* that there is a difference between *theory and praxis*... What you mean by praxis is *private use*, and what I mean by theory is *justice*. You would be wise to keep justice and private use as far apart as possible and explain certain fateful biblical sayings as "old and therefore outdated." But we will wait and see whose light burns longer... You may be older than I, as you noted, but nonetheless are still young enough to develop better insights. I sincerely wish you that.[29]

At the same time Barth wrote Walter Hüssy's father that he hoped the incident would not cloud the good relationship between the manufacturer's family and the parsonage.[30]

Walter Hüssy reacted once more with an open letter in which he reproached Barth that he had lost "the ability... to reflect quietly and objectively about whether that which you strive for is also really achievable."[31] He withdrew from any further debate about the matter.

On the following Sunday, February 11, Barth's church was full. The slugfest of letters and the underlying problems were *the* village theme. Months later at the Hochuli Knitters, the other large local factory, the owners still anxiously asked on Monday mornings "whether and what 'he' had said in the sermon about capitalism."[32]

On February 12, 1912, the *Zofinger Tagblatt* published an article that had been submitted anonymously, "On the Red Danger in Safenwil."[33] Barth was pursuing "agitatorial subversive activities" and inciting the mood "quietly toward a class struggle." He relished his role "as red Messiah," but this in no way stated whether he "was also a good Christian."

The following day Gustav Hüssy, a cousin of Barth's adversary, resigned from his office as president of the Safenwil parish governing council "in protest."[34] The majority of the council however stood behind Barth. He reported to his father of a meeting that had taken place the same day without Hüssy:

> I am amazed by how the people spoke, although they were all farmers and not workers. All of them made statements against capitalism that would have surprised you; it is as if I had drawn a fifty year old spigot from the barrel, namely from the barrel of the people's soul of Safenwil.[35]

Only a half year after arriving in Safenwil it had become clear to Barth that "shrugging one's shoulders over taking a conscious position on practical matters" in such a place "absolutely doesn't work" for a pastor.[36] "I would think myself outrageous if I wanted to gaze from the window of my parsonage at these things and preach a neutral 'Gospel.'"[37]

Barth had previously succumbed to a similarly aggressive tone as in his reply to Hüssy. Feedback from the Basel theology professor Paul Wernle, to whom he sent his lecture and the correspondence, led him to think about the tone of his letter. Wernle accused him of answering "crudeness with crudeness and rudeness with rudeness," giving room in an unchristian fashion for the "principle of vengeance."[38] Barth admitted:

> When I read his attack, I truly, at least to my knowledge, didn't feel a *personal* sense of offence, rather a very focused *objective* desire to fight: so, *this* is how you are? Into battle with fury! Take up the sword of the Lord and Gideon! And then I hit back the way I did. I still know how when I was writing it, it was as if someone stood behind me and commanded: "Rapid fire! Rapid fire!" I truly didn't intend anything else but to run down an enemy of a good cause, as one should. But already fourteen days later, as the powder smoke has cleared, I must indeed acknowledge that I behaved in an Old Testament-like fashion. My gesture appeared less heroic to me, and I could sense all the egocentric aspects that had contributed to it.[39]

Barth resolved to do things differently the next time. There would however be few times when he succeeded in this.

In the years that followed Barth held numerous "socialist speeches" in Safenwil and elsewhere.[40] He compiled an extensive collection of material about workers' issues, for which he studied specialist literature as well as data about the living conditions of workers in Switzerland.[41] He met with Safenwil residents to educate them about labor policy themes and joined with other pastors interested in religious social issues.[42] There was no question that he now read journals such as the *Gewerkschaftliche Rundschau* ("Union Review") or *Textilarbeiter* ("Textile Worker").[43] Barth also wrote several political reports. In addition he spoke out about gambling and together with Nelly Hoffmann, who in the meantime had become his wife, became involved in a popular initiative aimed at an extensive ban on gambling casinos in Switzerland.[44]

Another area of engagement for Barth was the Blue Cross.[45] This movement had been founded in Geneva in 1877 to confront alcoholism through strict abstinence. Initially those who joined consisted only of people who, although they were not addicted, wanted to show solidarity with the necessary lifestyle for alcoholics. Contrary to the predominant medical opinion that prescribed only a permanent placement in a psychiatric setting, they believed that there was a possible cure for alcoholism: through faith in God. This concept motivated many pastors to become members. Because Barth had witnessed alcoholism's terrible effects,[46] he participated in gatherings after September 1911 and held office from January 1912 to May 1916 as president of the Safenwil Blue Cross. He contributed to meetings with bible studies and lectures.

In the summer of 1913 the council of the Safenwil workers union approached Barth with the request that he become a member (and thereby also a member of the SP) and also take over as local chair.[47] Barth refused. He explained the reason to his friend Wilhelm Loew:

> Not on principle, but for the moment, for practical considerations ... I do not see a theological barrier, on the contrary, but I don't feel that I am ready to undertake this 1. with regard to the political knowledge and finesse that are necessary for this, 2. with respect to combining this task with that of the ministry—I would want to be able to live both in a respectable fashion. So out of appropriateness for the time being I am not yet a complete Sozi (Socialist), but this can still happen.[48]

He experienced his refusal as a defeat, as "conformity to the miserable 'practical life.'"[49]

A year and a half later he had overcome his reservations. On January 26, 1915, he became a member of the SP.[50] He later believed that his congregation "over time found it quite interesting that people said: 'the red pastor of Safenwil.'"[51]

Despite all this social involvement, the core of Barth's professional activity remained preaching, in addition to confirmation instruction.[52] He often began preparing his sermons only on Saturday.[53] Since until early 1918 he always wrote out his sermons, he usually stood under enormous time pressure.[54] In tone his sermons were friendly, simply worded, with numerous examples from daily life, but always clear and challenging.

A Theological Friendship: Eduard Thurneysen

The Safenwil period also included the deepening friendship and beginning of joint theological work with Eduard Thurneysen. They had met in Marburg. Thurneysen took a pastorate in 1913 in the Aargau village of Leutwil, not far from Safenwil. Both enjoyed the possibility for a theological exchange. They visited each other often or took walks together. Since they had no telephones they regularly exchanged letters.[55] This frequent correspondence, which continued until 1935 when they became fellow lecturers in Basel, documents their common theological wrestling that was to lead to a new theological approach: "In those years, 1913–1921, Karl Barth and I were driven by the failures of theology, church and society, in the face of the need at that time, for that new departure that would lead to a turning point and new foundation for theology."[56]

In 1916 Eduard Thurneysen married Marguerite Meyer, the daughter of a secondary school teacher and a pianist. They had five children.

Through Thurneysen Barth became acquainted with the Zurich ironware dealer Rudolf Pestalozzi and his wife Gerty, neé Eidenbenz. Pestalozzi and Thurneysen worked in the Zurich Young Men's Christian Association, and Thurneysen had given Pestalozzi Barth's writings to read. As a result Pestalozzi contacted Barth for the first time in November 1912, requesting an article for the Association newsletter.[57] Pestalozzi liked the article Barth wrote: "If I may, I will knock at your door more often."[58] Thus developed another friendship that for Barth also meant some financial support. Barth would often spend his semester breaks at the "Bergli," the summer home in Oberrieden on Lake Zurich that the Pestalozzis owned after 1920.[59]

4.2. Karl Barth with Eduard Thurneysen at the "Bergli," 1920, © Karl Barth-Archive in Basel.

Through Eduard Thurneysen Barth also got to know Hermann Kutter.[60] At the time a pastor in the Zurich Neumünster Church, Kutter was the most important figure in Swiss religious socialism besides Leonhard Ragaz.[61] He was a sharp critic of the church of his era because it had withdrawn entirely to spiritual, inner themes, rather than taking seriously that the Christian message is also always a matter of the bodily, external existence of human beings.[62] Because many adherents of social democracy didn't believe in God, the church had a negative view of the movement, yet Kutter thought that in fact in its demands for justice and social reforms, social democracy was bringing into reality matters that the church had criminally neglected. "Others must now speak of what the church should be preaching, others put into practice the church's task...Others—today it's the Social Democrats."[63] While the church comforted itself that sin and evil were simply inevitable, "the Social Democrats declare that all evil must come to an end...in the world."[64] Kutter was therefore certain: "Yes, it is so: God's promises are fulfilled in the Social Democrats."[65] Barth was fascinated by these ideas and from Kutter learned "to speak the great word 'God' once again seriously, responsibly, and with weight."[66]

Barth also had personal contact with Leonhard Ragaz. As pastor at Basel's Münster Church, in 1903 Ragaz,[67] who came from a poor family, had drawn attention with a sermon preached on the occasion of a strike by the Basel masons. The strike was unsuccessful, but Ragaz corroborated the masons: "The *social movement* is simply far and away the most important thing that is occurring in our days"; it is giving rise to a "new...world...that develops out of the heart of the Gospel."[68] He too was certain that the kingdom of God comes in the transformation of social conditions. "Earthly conditions [are] not immutable orders. God is still at work and we should work with God so that the world is to be filled with God's glory."[69] Ragaz was convinced that for this to happen, the contemporary capitalist order had to be done away with.

Personally and in their correspondence Thurneysen and Barth repeatedly discussed the theology of Ragaz and Kutter, the relationship between their approaches, and which should be given preference and for what reason.[70] Additional stimulation in the clarification of their own theological position came from the Aarau student conferences where significant theological minds of that era such as Wilhelm Herrmann, Ernst Troeltsch, and Johannes Weiß delivered lectures.[71]

"The World...without Gods": The First World War

In retrospect Karl Barth saw the outbreak of the First World War and the support for that war among German theologians as decisive for his further theological development. He always particularly underscored one incident:

the dreadful Manifesto of the ninety-three German intellectuals[72] who identified with the war policy of Kaiser Wilhelm II and his chancellor [Theobald von] Bethmann-Hollweg. And among those who undersigned I had to discover with dismay the names of approximately all my German professors (with the honorable exception of Martin Rade!). This, along with the other things from German theologians that one got to read at the time, shook to the very foundation an entire world of theological exegesis, ethics, dogmatics, and preaching, that until then I had held to be credible in principle.[73]

Barth was convinced that Schleiermacher—in contrast to Fichte and perhaps Hegel as well—would not have signed the Manifesto,[74] but the position taken by his teachers also led him to doubt Schleiermacher's theology: "it was still the case that the entire theology which had unmasked itself in that manifesto, and everything which followed after it..., was grounded, determined, and influenced decisively by him!"[75]

In his memoirs Barth incorrectly dated the Manifesto to August rather than October 4, 1914.[76] In retrospect he confused this with an argument that he had beginning in August 1914 with Martin Rade.[77] In fact the ninety-three signatories did not include "the names of approximately all my German professors," but only those of Adolf von Harnack, Wilhelm Herrmann, and Adolf Schlatter—but thereby of course "the two most esteemed"—and not, in fact, Rade.[78]

What was the issue in Barth's conflict with Rade?[79] During this period Barth had continued to read *Die Christliche Welt*, the journal edited by Rade. Here Rade wrote along these lines: "The calm, order and security with which our mobilization has been undertaken is wonderful. The angels in heaven must take a delight in this as well."[80] Such statements led Barth on August 31, 1914, to write Rade and deplore "how throughout Germany right now love of fatherland, lust for war and Christian faith have fallen into a hopeless confusion."[81] He acknowledged

> that Germany must wage this war that, justly or unjustly, it now has, with defense and offense, with 42cm mounted guns and breaches of neutrality, with mass executions and the destruction of cities... But why in this wholly worldly, sinful necessity do you not leave God out of the game? Through utter silence, if you like... To cease with all religious references to what the Germans now have to do would also be a protest. But not to pull God in this way into the matter, as though the Germans along with their big cannons may now feel mandated by God, as though in this moment they are permitted to shoot and burn with clear consciences. Not *that*! And you preach particularly this, a clear conscience now, now, where the bad conscience might be the only Christian possibility in face of the worldly, sinful necessity that now exists.[82]

No longer was the Gospel the point of orientation for theological statements about war, rather there "is now a German battle religion set into force, veiled in Christian references through much talk of 'sacrifice,' etc."[83] It illustrated that even beforehand, the Gospel had merely been a "varnish" for the theological positions for which *Die Christliche Welt* stood.[84]

As Karl Barth then heard from his brother Peter, who had met with Rade in Marburg, of the numerous wounded soldiers in the streets of the town and read reports by German soldiers whose eyes had been put out,[85] he softened his criticism of *Die Christliche Welt* somewhat in conversation with Thurneysen: "How such details when immediately experienced must affect one's emotional reactions! Can one be surprised by the catastrophe of Christliche Welt-Christendom? How would we persist in such a situation? Admittedly it remains a catastrophe despite everything, this behavior of our friends over there."[86]

Rade was deeply hurt by Barth's letter.[87] If nothing else he himself had deplored Germany's shared guilt for the war and spoken out against incitement against foreigners. Because of this *Die Christliche Welt* had been accused of betraying the fatherland.[88] He replied to Barth that the outbreak of the war had shaken him equally. The difference between him and Barth consisted in the fact that Barth was "neutral." Barth had not had

> the *experience*. Just as I don't have the experience of this war as a soldier who goes to the front has, or similarly of some others who are closer to important events than I was. In one thing however I am ahead of you: the experience of how this war has come over the *soul of my people*.[89]

Rade described how this occurred:

> The calm, clear mobilization that was unclouded by any morally discordant note. The order, the lack of alcohol, the certainty of how it was set into motion and the leadership. (Do not the angels in heaven then rejoice over everything that is *good* in this world?) And behind this phenomenon of a glorious solidarity on the whole, thousands and thousands of ways of devotion and the willingness of each individual to sacrifice... For such an overwhelming thing there is only One possible ground and instigator: *God*.[90]

Naturally Jesus and God as revealed in him and in the Gospel were indispensable. But one also finds God there "where Jesus Christ does not yet encounter us."[91] Here God is revealed differently than in Jesus; here God comes as the *deus absconditus*, the hidden God,[92] "over us... as the pure power of which we initially sense nothing but our absolute dependence."[93] Not only did God allow this war, that would be a "weak... God"; no, God was the active reason for these events.[94] Indeed, the "will to war" was a sin. But God took "responsibility for fate of war," and therefore it was "*also* pious to get out of the war whatever good that one can."[95] Both letters, Barth's accusation and Rade's justification, were published together in 1914.

On October 1 Barth wrote back to Rade. In the meantime he had received additional theological position statements on the war from Germany, which showed him that in a certain sense Rade still represented a moderate position. He acknowledged this. And yet: "Within me some of the high regard for the German nature has now collapsed forever, I know... because I see that, except for a few pieces of debris, the philosophy and Christianity of you Germans are now perishing in this war psychosis."[96]

In mid-October 1914 Barth received an entire collection of "printed material about the war" from Wilhelm Herrmann.[97] It is likely that the Manifesto was among these documents.[98] He wrote to Herrmann on November 4, formulating his critique in questions so that his respect for the professor, as well as his irritation, were visible throughout.

First: up to that point Barth had admired German scholarship for its "thoroughness and objectivity" and its "critical sensibility."[99] But had these characteristics been proven in the treatment of the current war, if one so quickly took positions on its antecedents and course without meticulous study of the records of both sides? Secondly: Herrmann's use of the category of "experience" (*Erlebnis*) had been important for Barth until then. What however would become of this category when Christians in Germany now believed that they had to "experience" the war as holy? Where was the Christian experience of God as a criterion? And finally: how could the fellowship with Christians abroad be preserved, when German Christians were denying all German guilt for the war, placing the guilt solely on other nations?

The question that had the most lasting impact on Barth was whether this appeal to an immediately compelling "experience" could justify everything, including the war, as the will of God.[100] Since the late nineteenth century through Wilhelm Dilthey and others, the concept of "experience" over against the dominance of the natural sciences had been used to describe the humanities' claim to truth. Since the turn of the century the term had really become a "buzzword."[101] In the context of the First World War, for example in Ernst Jünger's book *Der Kampf als inneres Erlebnis* ("Struggle as Inner Experience," 1922), by its inherent immediacy from which one could not escape, it had taken on a political and religious meaning. In contrast Barth was convinced "that the dear God is surely neutral."[102]

The war's shattering effects on Barth are illustrated in a November 15, 1915, lecture in Basel on "Wartime and God's Kingdom." Barth begins with the provocative claim: "Everywhere, ethics have moved to the trenches."[103] Ethics, the state, socialism, pacifism, and Christianity all belonged to "the world" and as such were not in the condition to overcome the world as it is. "World is world" and remains world.[104] The new comes only from God, from God "as God is known in the life and word of Jesus."[105] All other gods are not true gods; through the war, in which all of them have become "battle grey," "the world [had become] ... without Gods."[106] God however was "something entirely different ... from everything other than what appears to me to be true and right."[107] God could not be "put to one's own purpose." For Barth the issue was no longer whether in the encounter with God the inner life of Jesus is clear to us as the reply to the ethical demand, but rather "whether God's will that is revealed to us here claims us, makes such a compelling impression on us, that we must recognize and acknowledge: this God *is* God."[108] The Christian hope in this God is the source of life.[109]

The disappointing reaction of the international socialist movement to the war made it clear to Barth that socialism, too, was fully of this world and could not bring the kingdom of God by itself, but rather in the best case was one "of the most important reflections"[110] of God's kingdom. The socialists too were "filled with *enthusiasm for the war*," and therefore "no better" than the others.[111] When Barth visited him in the fall of 1914 Hermann Kutter took the side of Germany in an "incomprehensible" manner.[112] Leonhard Ragaz wrote a text in 1915 that irritated Barth, arguing that in light of the world war it could no longer be a matter of reconciling the kingdoms of God and of the world, but only "to represent the kingdom of God in its contrast to the kingdom of the world."[113] Barth asked himself:

> Is it then self-evident that "*we*" "*represent*" the kingdom of God ...? ... Have we then grasped, experienced, the kingdom of God at all, in its radical seriousness? ... Not a word about the "knowledge of God," of "conversion," of "waiting" for the kingdom of God ... all of which is in fact the apriori of all "representing!"[114]

Later Barth always reported that both ways of thinking that had fascinated him to that point, liberal theology and religious socialism had become fundamentally problematic for him through their position on the war.[115]

Disappointment in Ragaz and Kutter did not change Barth's political position: he continued to be an avowed socialist and Social Democrat, and, as previously noted, in January 1915 already had become a member of the SP. In 1917 Barth sent Kutter a volume of sermons by Thurneysen and himself, *Seek God and You Shall Live!*, with the comment: "We would like to give you this little book together as a small sign of our respect and gratitude. Here from beginning to end you will rediscover without difficulty the traces of your own life's work, whose fruits have become so important to both of us."[116] Nonetheless Barth now defined the relationship between the kingdom of God and socialism in a new way, drawing a clear distinction between the two.[117]

The theology of both Blumhardts was also responsible for this shift.[118] Kutter and Ragaz had attempted in their religious socialism to pursue their thinking politically, but Barth now believed this had to happen differently. In mid-April 1915 Barth and Thurneysen visited Bad Boll together and heard Christoph

Blumhardt preach. After this Barth began to study his theology more intensively and that of his father Johann Christoph Blumhardt, and from that point they played an important role in the conversations between Barth and Thurneysen.[119] In a review titled "Waiting for the Kingdom of God," Barth praised Christoph Blumhardt's 1916 devotional book *Haus-Andachten nach Losungen und Lehrtexten der Brüdergemeine*, conceived as "a greeting to all who with us wish to wait for the kingdom of God," as "the most immediate and insistent word of God and in the world's crisis that wartime has yet brought forth."[120] Blumhardt's point of departure was God.[121] For Blumhardt, too, God reigned, but this had not led him to a "war theology."[122] God's lordship did not happen everywhere, but rather only in Jesus, the savior of the world; the Good had begun in him "and extends into our time as well."[123] The human task above all was to wait for God and God's lordship over the world in a "still, watchful manner directed toward God."[124] This led Barth to a new way of thinking about God and the world.

This dynamic of waiting was also reflected in his sermons. He now asked himself how when he spoke he could do justice to God and God's mission. A sermon in Safenwil from January 16, 1916, makes this particularly clear. A few days previously there had been a local wedding party with much drunkenness where his confirmation students had also been drunk.[125] In his sermon Barth asked whether Safenwil didn't need a different pastor, a pastor

> from whose sermons and whose life the love of God emanates with such power that you have to feel it, that you are being moved, whether you wish to or not... You should have a man who can speak to you of God in such a way that the mountain lying on top of you is moved, that such things that have just taken place simply become impossible naturally... I very apparently am not able to speak to you in such a way... because apparently in myself there is something very deeply not in order with God.[126]

Three weeks later he raised this: "You have the wish for me to be *a false prophet*... The false prophet is *the pastor who pleases the people*."[127] But to have a pastor in the village means "to have eternal unrest in the village, [to have] a person who in the most uncomfortable way will continually question everything and will give unexpected replies to all questions."[128] It was disquieting for him, too, that God's word stood in opposition to everything. In the years that followed this sense of unrest would never let go of Barth. And it would bear theological fruits.

"An Open House": Family Life

After her engagement to Karl Barth, Nelly Hoffmann[129] had moved with her mother back to Zurich and preoccupied herself there with preparing her dowry. She had actually planned to study music, but for the sake of this new private perspective she abandoned these plans. From June to October 1912 she traveled to England as a governess. During this period the engaged pair had a lively correspondence.

Karl Barth and Nelly Hoffmann married on March 27, 1913, in the Bern Nydegg church where the bridegroom had already been confirmed. Adolf Keller, who had briefly been Barth's teaching pastor in Geneva, married the pair. Barth's father was not there; he had died the year before. The wedding party celebrated at Barth's mother's home in Bern "in a modest setting and a rather small circle."[130] Not even twenty years old, Nelly Barth was now a pastor's wife and had a large house and garden to take care of.

There were soon four children. On April 13, 1914, their daughter Franziska Nelly came into the world. This was followed by the birth of Karl Markus (called Markus) on October 6, 1915. Christoph Friedrich was born on September 29, 1917, and Robert Matthias (called Matthias) on April 17, 1921. Nelly Barth deeply loved the children, and Karl Barth delighted in them as well. "Fränzeli...yesterday encountered a large snail during her wanderings and shook herself with horror at this little animal that the dear God of course in his delight in creation had created along with the slime. Something isn't right here, either with Fränzeli or with the snail."[131]

4.3. Nelly Barth in 1932, © Karl Barth-Archive in Basel.

4.4. Karl and Nelly Barth with children Franziska, Markus, and Christoph in 1918, © Karl Barth-Archive in Basel.

It was not very easy for Nelly Barth "to have an open house despite the required frugality."[132] She suffered at times to have to run such a large household.[133] When in 1919 the couple contemplated changing to a parish in Bern, she hoped that they could now move only into an apartment, so that the household duties and staff could be reduced, making everything "smaller, easier to oversee."[134]

The correspondence from this period between Thurneysen and Barth makes it apparent that Nelly quickly became accustomed to Barth's strong character without becoming subdued in the process. During visits that the two received she did not hesitate to take her own position.[135]

Nelly also gave her opinion on Barth's professional duties. Still recovering from the birth of son Markus she gave Karl Barth differentiated advice in a letter about choosing a sermon from a series of sermons he had already delivered. The one she found "to be very decisive," another "clearly explanatory... and yet simple," the third had "the advantage that it especially 'sends a positive message.'"[136] In any case he needed to "shorten rather than lengthen in reworking" the sermon "because in the Münster church you have to speak very slowly indeed, otherwise there's an echo. And in a deep voice."[137]

In addition to her many duties Nelly continued to play the violin. Preserving her own sphere apparently mattered a great deal to her. There is an instructive letter exchange connected to Eduard Thurneysen's engagement to Marguerite. Thurneysen complained to Karl Barth of his irritation at a letter from Marguerite, who had written him that she was unable to see him because she had an organ lesson. He "feared this organ along with the piano and Bach and Beethoven, as if they wanted to take my bride from me into another world into which I am only very little able to follow."[138] He asked for Barth's advice, since Barth had indicated to him that there had been similar frictions at the beginning of his own relationship. Through Barth, Nelly Barth let Thurneysen know that he should

> not think at all that it was self-evident that the wife gave up or postponed all her own deepest interests in art in order to be filled post-haste with Kutter etc. That was not how it went. If the woman was worth something, then she must fight for her cause, assert it in the relationship until the time had come from *within* that she was no longer exchanging one thing for *another*, but rather simply continued to live on, in an uninterrupted line *with* her previous domain as something new (but also bringing him something new).[139]

Barth added his recollection that at the beginning of their relationship he had

> allowed stupid complexes to arise against the violin-the violin teacher-the violin case-violin virtuosos, sometimes taking the form that I myself on Saturday evenings, rather than writing my sermon, would scratch out a Bach concerto until 11 p.m. in my anxiety, my compulsion, my paranoia.[140]

But his friend could rest assured: "Everything, everything will end well, and indeed pretty soon."[141]

Because Karl Barth stipulated in his final will that the letters between him and his wife not be included in his literary estate, to date it has hardly been possible to reconstruct the details of their further relationship from written sources. According to Barth's own description the marriage in its early years was "amidst all difficulties a happy story."[142] Nelly cared for her husband tenderly and was grateful for his attention. In 1915 she wrote to him:

> Your letter moved me, it is *so* kind. And the picture! I cannot say how happy it makes me... The longer I look at it, the more I find it is fully you. The dear high forehead and the expression that is so much calmer and more concentrated than earlier. The face I love! It is truly a comfort to me until I have you here yourself.[143]

Notes

1. Cf. editor's foreword, *Predigten 1911* (GA 51), xiii.
2. Cf. the telegram of April 30, 1911, from the Safenwil parish governing council, KBA 14110.

3. Inaugural sermon of July 9, 1911, in Safenwil, *Predigten 1911* (GA 51), 198.
4. *Predigten 1911* (GA 51), 199.
5. *Predigten 1911* (GA 51), 200.
6. *Predigten 1911* (GA 51), 200f.
7. *Predigten 1911* (GA 51), 204.
8. Cf. Barth's 1914 lecture "Evangelium und Sozialismus" in which he explains how he came to combine the Gospel and socialism, *Vorträge und kleinere Arbeiten 1909–1914* (GA 22), 730.
9. Barth, "Evangelium und Sozialismus," *Vorträge und kleinere Arbeiten 1909–1914* (GA 22), 730f.
10. Barth, "Gott lenkt und der Mensch soll denken! Aus Calvins Institutio (1559)," *Vorträge und kleinere Arbeiten 1909–1914* (GA 22), 263.
11. Cf. Barth, "Evangelium und Sozialismus," *Vorträge und kleinere Arbeiten 1909–1914* (GA 22), 731, which has an implicit but clear reference to the Calvin text.
12. Cf. "Autobiographical Sketches I. Münster, 1927," *Barth–Bultmann Letters* (GA 1), 154.
13. Cf. editor's foreword, *Predigten 1911* (GA 51), x–xi, as well as the editor's introduction to Barth, "Menschenrecht und Bürgerpflicht," *Vorträge und kleinere Arbeiten 1909–1914* (GA 22), 361.
14. "Autobiographical Sketches I. Münster, 1927," *Barth–Bultmann Letters* (GA 1), 154. Translation revised. See also Barth, "Concluding Unscientific Postscript," *Theology of Schleiermacher*, 263.
15. Barth, "Jesus Christus und die soziale Bewegung," *Vorträge und kleinere Arbeiten 1909–1914* (GA 22), 387.
16. Barth, "Jesus Christus," *Vorträge und kleinere Arbeiten 1909–1914* (GA 22), 407.
17. Barth, "Jesus Christus," *Vorträge und kleinere Arbeiten 1909–1914* (GA 22), 391.
18. Barth, "Jesus Christus," *Vorträge und kleinere Arbeiten 1909–1914* (GA 22), 396. Here Barth is adopting well recognizable basic concepts from Hermann Kutter, *Sie müssen!* (see p. 68).
19. Barth, "Jesus Christus," *Vorträge und kleinere Arbeiten 1909–1914* (GA 22), 396.
20. Barth, "Jesus Christus," *Vorträge und kleinere Arbeiten 1909–1914* (GA 22), 395.
21. Barth, "Jesus Christus," *Vorträge und kleinere Arbeiten 1909–1914* (GA 22), 402.
22. Barth, "Jesus Christus," *Vorträge und kleinere Arbeiten 1909–1914* (GA 22), 399.
23. Cf. the editor's introduction to Barth, "Jesus Christus," *Vorträge und kleinere Arbeiten 1909–1914* (GA 22), 380f.
24. Cf. the editor's introduction regarding the open letter to Walter Hüssy, *Offene Briefe 1909–1935* (GA 35), 4.
25. Open letter from Walter Hüssy to Barth, February 1, 1912, *Vorträge und kleinere Arbeiten 1909–1914* (GA 22), 409f.
26. Open letter from Walter Hüssy to Barth, February 1, 1912, *Vorträge und kleinere Arbeiten 1909–1914* (GA 22), 409f.
27. Reply to the open letter from Walter Hüssy, February 6, 1912, *Vorträge und kleinere Arbeiten 1909–1914* (GA 22), 412.
28. Reply to the open letter from Walter Hüssy, February 6, 1912, *Vorträge und kleinere Arbeiten 1909–1914* (GA 22), 412.

29. Reply to the open letter from Walter Hüssy, February 6, 1912, *Vorträge und kleinere Arbeiten 1909–1914* (GA 22), 416f.
30. Cf. the editor's introduction to Barth, "Jesus Christus," *Vorträge und kleinere Arbeiten 1909–1914* (GA 22), 382.
31. Open letter from Walter Hüssy to Barth, February 9, 1912, *Vorträge und kleinere Arbeiten 1909–1914* (GA 22), 417.
32. Letter of April 16, 1912, to Wilhelm Loew, *Vorträge und kleinere Arbeiten 1909–1914* (GA 22), 439.
33. KBA 12225.
34. Cf. the introduction to Barth's letter to Walter Hüssy, *Offene Briefe 1909–1935* (GA 35), 5.
35. Letter of February 13, 1912, to his father, cited in *Vorträge und kleinere Arbeiten 1909–1914* (GA 22), 383.
36. Letter of April 26, 1912, to Paul Wernle, cited in *Vorträge und kleinere Arbeiten 1909–1914* (GA 22), 385.
37. Letter of April 26, 1912, to Paul Wernle, cited in *Vorträge und kleinere Arbeiten 1909–1914* (GA 22), 385.
38. Letter of May 6, 1912, from Paul Wernle, cited in *Vorträge und kleinere Arbeiten 1909–1914* (GA 22), 385.
39. Letter of May 31, 1912, to Paul Wernle, cited in *Vorträge und kleinere Arbeiten 1909–1914* (GA 22), 386.
40. According to Barth's own handwritten notes on an envelope, in which he preserved thirty-two keywords for concepts for lectures. Cf. the editor's foreword, *Vorträge und kleinere Arbeiten 1909–1914* (GA 22), xi.
41. Cf. Barth, "Die Arbeiterfrage 1913/14," *Vorträge und kleinere Arbeiten 1909–1914* (GA 22), 573–682.
42. Cf. the editor's introduction to "Die Arbeiterfrage 1913/14," *Vorträge und kleinere Arbeiten 1909–1914* (GA 22), 575 and 577; the editor's introduction to Barth, "Politik, Idealismus und Christentum bei Friedrich Naumann," *Vorträge und kleinere Arbeiten 1914–1921* (GA 48), 48.
43. Cf. the letter of December 15, 1913, to Wilhelm Loew, cited in *Vorträge und kleinere Arbeiten 1909–1914* (GA 22), 576. Barth there explained to his friend: "This year socialism has strongly taken the upper hand, at least in me."
44. Cf. the editor's introduction to Barth, "Aufruf an die Aargauischen Blaukreuzvereine 1914," *Vorträge und kleinere Arbeiten 1914–1921* (GA 48), 21f.; the "Spielbankinitiative 1914" (42–5).
45. Cf. the editor's introduction to the "Einladung zum aargauischen Abstinententag 1913," *Vorträge und kleinere Arbeiten 1909–1914* (GA 22), 559–61.
46. Cf. Barth's speech at the "Blaukreuzfest" in Rupperswil 1913, with its reference to concrete cases, *Vorträge und kleinere Arbeiten 1909–1914* (GA 22), 710f.
47. Cf. the editor's introduction to Barth, "Die Arbeiterfrage 1913/14," *Vorträge und kleinere Arbeiten 1909–1914* (GA 22), 574.
48. Letter of 16 July 1913 to Wilhelm Loew, cited in *Vorträge und kleinere Arbeiten 1909–1914* (GA 22), 574.

49. Letter of 9 July 1913 to his mother, cited in *Vorträge und kleinere Arbeiten 1909-1914* (GA 22), 574.
50. Cf. the editor's introduction to Barth, "Krieg, Sozialismus und Christentum (II)," *Vorträge und kleinere Arbeiten 1914-1921* (GA 48), 105.
51. Barth, "Gespräch mit Wuppertaler Theologiestudenten 1968," *Gespräche 1964-1968* (GA 28), 508.
52. Barth's confirmation class (cf. the editor's foreword, *Konfirmandenunterricht 1909-1921* (GA18), xxviii, with notes 25f.) took place at 6:30 in the mornings, because Barth very deliberately, although not without arguments with the factory, scheduled the class during the factory hours for the youth. He didn't want to burden them beyond their regular work hours.
53. Cf. the letter of June 5, 1915, to Eduard Thurneysen, *Briefwechsel Barth-Thurneysen* I (GA 3) 51.
54. Cf. the editors' foreword to Barth, *Predigten 1914* (GA 5), vii.
55. Three comprehensive volumes of this correspondence have been published in the Barth *Gesamtausgabe* for the years 1913-1921 (GA 3), 1921-1930 (GA 4), and 1930-1935 (GA 34). At the beginning Barth still wrote letters by hand, about which Thurneysen occasionally complained. This changed at Christmas 1926 when Nelly Barth gave him a Remington typewriter. Cf. letter of December 26, 1926, to Thurneysen, *Briefwechsel Barth-Thurneysen* II (GA 4), 450.
56. Thurneysen, foreword, *Briefwechsel Barth-Thurneysen* I (GA 3), vi. Regarding this "new departure" cf. the next chapter.
57. Cf. the editor's introduction to "Frömmler," *Vorträge und kleinere Arbeiten 1909-1914* (GA 22), 480.
58. Letter of December 11, 1912, from Rudolf Pestalozzi, cited in *Vorträge und kleinere Arbeiten 1909-1914* (GA 22), 480.
59. Cf. the letter of January 21, 1948, from Rudolf Pestalozzi, KBA 9348.90.
60. Cf. *Schweizerköpfe der Gegenwart*, 119. Regarding Kutter's influence on Barth, cf. Hans-Anton Drewes, *Das Unmittelbare bei Hermann Kutter*.
61. Regarding this, cf. Christian Link, "Barth und der religiöse Sozialismus," in Beintker, ed., *Barth Handbuch*, 71-5.
62. Cf. Kutter, *Sie müssen!*, 178.
63. Kutter, *Sie müssen!*, 258.
64. Kutter, *Sie müssen!*, 261.
65. Kutter, *Sie müssen!*, 261.
66. Barth, "Concluding Unscientific Postscript," *Theology of Schleiermacher*, 263.
67. Concerning his beginnings cf. Buess and Mattmüller, *Prophetischer Sozialismus*, 65-77.
68. Leonhard Ragaz, "Ein Wort über Christentum und soziale Bewegung (Matth. 22, 34-40)," in Ragaz, *Religiöser Sozialist*, 31f.
69. Ragaz, *Das Evangelium und der soziale Kampf der Gegenwart*, 23.
70. Cf. *Briefwechsel Barth-Thurneysen* I (GA 3), index entries "Kutter" and "Ragaz."
71. Cf. Busch, *Karl Barth: His Life*, 78.
72. This is a reference to the manifesto *An die Kulturwelt* ("To the world of culture"), which was published in the *Frankfurter Zeitung* Nr. 275 on October 4, 1914 (cited in

Härle, "Der Aufruf der 93 Intellektuellen," 209f.; regarding the history of its origin and dating, see Härle, 210–13):

"As representatives of German academia and art we raise before the entire world of culture a *protest against the lies* and defamations with which our enemies strive to taint the pure cause of Germany in the hard battle for existence that has been forced upon it..."

"*It is not true* that Germany is to blame for this war. Neither the people, nor the government, nor the Kaiser wanted it. On the part of Germany the ultimate has been done to prevent it... *It is not true* that our conduct of the war has disregarded the laws of international law. It [Germany's conduct] knows no undisciplined atrocity. In the east however the earth is soaked with blood of women and children slaughtered by Russian hordes, in the west *Dum Dum* bullets tear apart the breasts of our soldiers. Those who ally themselves with the Russians and Serbs and offer the world the disgraceful theater of setting the *Mongols* and *Negros* [NB: a more offensive term was used here] on the white race have the least right to gesture at being the defenders of European civilization."

"*It is not true* that the battle against our so-called militarism is not a battle against our culture, as our enemies hypocritically pretend. Without German militarism, the German culture would have been uprooted long ago... Believe us, believe that we will fight this battle to the end as a people of culture, to whom the legacy of a Goethe, a Beethoven, a Kant is just as holy as its hearth and its soil..."

73. Barth, "Concluding Unscientific Postscript," *Theology of Schleiermacher*, 263f. On Barth's agitation about his theological teachers' positions on the war, see also his letter of January 4, 1915, to Willy Spoendlin: "What a collapse of the intellectual ideals, not only in practice but in the ethos as well, in the quiet theory!... And German scholarship, with its objectivity, its critical sense, its enthusiastic idealism—everything has gone to the devil, everything has been sacrificed to Moloch's 'Necessity knows no law.'" Cited in *Offene Briefe 1909–1935* (GA 35), 22–4.
74. Cf. Barth, "Concluding Unscientific Postscript," *Theology of Schleiermacher*, 264.
75. Barth, "Concluding Unscientific Postscript," *Theology of Schleiermacher*, 264. Barth also took note of the similarly problematic proclamation of September 4, 1914, "To the Protestant Christians Abroad" (*An die evangelischen Christen im Auslande*). Cf. Hans-Anton Drewes, "Die Auseinandersetzung mit Adolf von Harnack," in Beintker et al., eds., *Karl Barth in Deutschland*, 192. To the point that Barth's theological turning away from his teachers did not first occur in 1914, but already before then, cf. Georg Pfleiderer, "1. Liberale Phase," in Beintker, ed., *Barth Handbuch*, 185.
76. Cf. Härle, "Der Aufruf der 93 Intellektuellen," 212f.
77. Cf. Härle, "Der Aufruf der 93 Intellektuellen," 215–19.
78. Cf. Härle, "Der Aufruf der 93 Intellektuellen," 218. Many of the signatories became aware of the statement's wording only after it appeared. Härle summarizes: "The naïve gullibility of the authors of the Manifesto toward the Kaiser's information politics was the consequence of an unpolitical, i.e. a de facto Kaiser-loyal and conservative self-understanding, among wide circles of intellectuals" (214).
79. Regarding the correspondence about the war question, cf. Schwöbel's introduction to *Karl Barth–Martin Rade*, 27–35. After Barth's departure from Marburg Barth remained in good contact with Rade (cf. 20).

80. Martin Rade, "Glossen *Zum Kriege*," *Die Christliche Welt* 1914 (33:781), cited in *Offene Briefe 1909–1935* (GA 35), 29, n. 48.
81. Letter of August 31, 1914, to Rade, *Offene Briefe 1909–1935* (GA 35), 27.
82. Letter of August 31, 1914, to Rade, *Offene Briefe 1909–1935* (GA 35), 27f.
83. Letter of September 4, 1914, to Thurneysen, *Briefwechsel Barth–Thurneysen* I (GA 3), 10.
84. Cf. letter of September 4, 1914, to Thurneysen, *Briefwechsel Barth–Thurneysen* I (GA 3), 10.
85. During the war, wartime propaganda that reported of atrocities perpetrated by the opposing side played an important role in every country involved. Cf. Horne and Kramer, *German Atrocities 1914*. Regarding the distrust of German soldiers, who had been told of "Belgian atrocities" (23) toward the civilian population in Belgium, as well as the violent actions of the German troops already in the very first days of the invasion, cf. 13–38.
86. Letter of September 25, 1914, to Thurneysen, *Briefwechsel Barth–Thurneysen* I (GA 3), 12.
87. Letter of September 25, 1914, to Thurneysen, *Briefwechsel Barth–Thurneysen* I (GA 3), 11.
88. Cf. Schwöbel's introduction, *Karl Barth–Martin Rade*, 30.
89. Letter of October 5, 1914, from Martin Rade, *Offene Briefe 1909–1935* (GA 35), 36.
90. Letter of October 5, 1914, from Martin Rade, *Offene Briefe 1909–1935* (GA 35), 37.
91. Letter of October 5, 1914, from Martin Rade, *Offene Briefe 1909–1935* (GA 35), 39.
92. Here Rade is referring to Martin Luther's concept of *deus absconditus* (the hidden God), which Luther developed as the antonym to *deus revelatus* (the revealed God). For Luther this *deus revelatus* was revealed in Jesus Christ as a loving, merciful God toward human beings. But in the history of the world it was not only this merciful God who was at work. Because God is omnipotent, God is also at work where things happen that stand in opposition to God's grace; here God is working as *deus absconditus*. According to Luther however one cannot derive an insight into God's nature from this action of God. One can only recognize God's nature in Jesus Christ. Cf. the English translation of Martin Luther, *De servo arbitrio (On the Bondage of the Will)* (1525) in *Luther's Works*, vol. 33 (1972): 3–295.
93. Letter of October 5, 1914, from Martin Rade, *Offene Briefe 1909–1935* (GA 35), 39.
94. Cf. letter of October 5, 1914, from Martin Rade, *Offene Briefe 1909–1935* (GA 35), 38.
95. Letter of October 5, 1914, from Martin Rade, *Offene Briefe 1909–1935* (GA 35), 41.
96. Letter of October 1, 1914, to Martin Rade, *Offene Briefe 1909–1935* (GA 35), 20.
97. Cf. the letter of November 4, 1914, to Wilhelm Herrmann, cited in Schwöbel, ed., *Karl Barth–Martin Rade*, 113.
98. This differs from Härle, "Der Aufruf der 93 Intellektuellen," 217. But Barth refers explicitly in his letter of reply to Herrmann's signature under the text and addresses the contents of the text in points (1) and (3) of his reply. Cf. letter of November 4, 1914, to Wilhelm Herrmann, Schwöbel, ed., *Karl Barth–Martin Rade*, 114f.
99. Cf. letter of November 4, 1914, to Wilhelm Herrmann, Schwöbel, ed., *Karl Barth–Martin Rade*, 114.

100. Cf. letter of November 23, 1914, to Martin Rade, Schwöbel, ed., *Karl Barth-Martin Rade*, 121. Cf. also the letter of October 30, 1914, from Thurneysen, *Briefwechsel Barth-Thurneysen* I (GA 3), 18.
101. Konrad Cramer, "Erleben, Erlebnis" in Ritter et al., *Historisches Wörterbuch*, vol. 2, 708.
102. Letter of January 4, 1915, to Willy Spoendlin, cited in *Offene Briefe 1909-1935* (GA 35), 22.
103. Barth, "Kriegszeit und Gottesreich," *Vorträge und kleinere Arbeiten 1914-1921* (GA 48), 186.
104. Barth, "Kriegszeit und Gottesreich," *Vorträge und kleinere Arbeiten 1914-1921* (GA 48), 193.
105. Barth, "Kriegszeit und Gottesreich," *Vorträge und kleinere Arbeiten 1914-1921* (GA 48), 193.
106. Barth, "Kriegszeit und Gottesreich," *Vorträge und kleinere Arbeiten 1914-1921* (GA 48), 195.
107. Barth, "Kriegszeit und Gottesreich," *Vorträge und kleinere Arbeiten 1914-1921* (GA 48), 201.
108. Barth, "Kriegszeit und Gottesreich," *Vorträge und kleinere Arbeiten 1914-1921* (GA 48), 202.
109. Barth, "Kriegszeit und Gottesreich," *Vorträge und kleinere Arbeiten 1914-1921* (GA 48), 197.
110. Barth, "Religion und Sozialismus," *Vorträge und kleinere Arbeiten 1914-1921* (GA 48), 214.
111. Cf. Barth, "Krieg, Sozialismus und Christentum (I)," *Vorträge und kleinere Arbeiten 1914-1921* (GA 48), 89f.
112. Cf. the letter of September 25, 1914, to Thurneysen, *Briefwechsel Barth-Thurneysen* I (GA 3), 12.
113. Ragaz and Brunner, "Von Gottesreich und Weltreich," 276.
114. Letter of August 6, 1915, to Thurneysen, *Briefwechsel Barth-Thurneysen* I (GA 3), 69f. Throughout Rade's text however there is only brief mention of the knowledge and waiting for God.
115. In 1927 Barth summarized: the outbreak of the First World War signified "for me two aberrations: first, in the teaching of all my theological mentors in Germany, who seemed to me to be hopelessly compromised by their failure in the face of the ideology of war; and then in socialism, which I had credulously enough expected, more than I had the Christian church, to avoid the ideology of war, but to my horror I saw it doing the very opposite in every land." "Autobiographical Sketches I. Münster, 1927," *Barth-Bultmann Letters* (GA 1), 154. Translation revised. Similarly in Barth, "Rückblick," in *Festschrift für D. Albert Schädelin*, 4.
116. Cited in Drewes, *Das Unmittelbare bei Hermann Kutter*, 189.
117. Cf. Christian Link, "Barth und der religiöse Sozialismus," in Beintker, ed., *Barth Handbuch*, 73f. Among others, Marquardt has a different reading in *Theologie und Sozialismus* (70), attempting to show that "Barth...above all in this [is] fully a religious socialist of Kutter's provenance, since at the very least he framed his talk of God...from the political, specifically the social reality, but even in the latest expressions of his theology also implicitly developed from it."

118. Regarding this, cf. Gerhard Sauter, "Barth und Blumhardt," in Beintker, ed., *Barth Handbuch*, 76–80.
119. Regarding this cf. the editor's foreword to Barth, "Auf das Reich Gottes warten," *Vorträge und kleinere Arbeiten 1914–1921* (GA 48), 275.
120. Barth, "Auf das Reich Gottes warten," *Vorträge und kleinere Arbeiten 1914–1921* (GA 48), 288. For a description of the book's primary concern, see Blumhardt, *Haus-Andachten nach Losungen und Lehrtexten der Brüdergemeine*, v.
121. Cf. Barth, "Auf das Reich Gottes warten," *Vorträge und kleinere Arbeiten 1914–1921* (GA 48), 291.
122. Barth, "Auf das Reich Gottes warten," *Vorträge und kleinere Arbeiten 1914–1921* (GA 48), 289.
123. Barth, "Auf das Reich Gottes warten," *Vorträge und kleinere Arbeiten 1914–1921* (GA 48), 295.
124. Barth, "Auf das Reich Gottes warten," *Vorträge und kleinere Arbeiten 1914–1921* (GA 48), 299.
125. Cf. the sermon of January 16, 1916, on Psalm 14:7, *Predigten 1916* (GA 29), 20, n. 2.
126. Sermon of January 16, 1916, on Psalm 14:7, *Predigten 1916* (GA 29), 24f.
127. Sermon of February 6, 1916, on Ezekiel 13:1–16, *Predigten 1916* (GA 29), 46.
128. Sermon of February 6, 1916, on Ezekiel 13:1–16, *Predigten 1916* (GA 29), 50.
129. With respect to the following account, cf. Zellweger-Barth, "Lebenslauf," in *Nelly Barth-Hoffmann*, 5f.
130. Letter of February 23, 1913, to Thurneysen, *Briefwechsel Barth–Thurneysen* I (GA 3), 3.
131. Letter of June 17, 1915, to Thurneysen, *Briefwechsel Barth–Thurneysen* I (GA 3), 57. Barth writes in a similarly loving tone in his letter of July 5, 1915, to Thurneysen, *Briefwechsel Barth–Thurneysen* I (GA 3), 60f.: "Fränzeli now runs in all directions from us, here to pick flowers and there to gently pet a large dog and there to eat dirt."
132. Zellweger-Barth, "Lebenslauf," in *Nelly Barth-Hoffmann*, 6.
133. Information given to the author by Dieter Zellweger.
134. Letter of August 16, 1919, from Nelly Barth, from her private papers, quoted with the kind permission of Dieter Zellweger, president of the Nachlasskommission Karl Barth.
135. Cf. e.g. letters to Thurneysen of May 14, June 17, July 8, 1915, in *Briefwechsel Barth–Thurneysen* I (GA 3), 42, 56, and 62.
136. Letter of October 12, 1915, from Nelly Barth, from her private papers, quoted with the kind permission of Dieter Zellweger, president of the Nachlasskommission Karl Barth.
137. Letter of October 12, 1915, from Nelly Barth, from her private papers, quoted with the kind permission of Dieter Zellweger, president of the Nachlasskommission Karl Barth.
138. Letter of July 9, 1915, from Thurneysen, *Briefwechsel Barth–Thurneysen* I (GA 3), 63.
139. Letter of July 14, 1915, to Thurneysen, *Briefwechsel Barth–Thurneysen* I (GA 3), 64.
140. Letter of July 14, 1915, to Thurneysen, *Briefwechsel Barth–Thurneysen* I (GA 3), 64.
141. Letter of July 14, 1915, to Thurneysen, *Briefwechsel Barth–Thurneysen* I (GA 3), 64.
142. Letter of February 28, 1926, to Kirschbaum, *Barth–von Kirschbaum Briefwechsel* I (GA 45), 24.
143. Letter of October 16, 1915, from Nelly Barth from her private papers, quoted with the kind permission of Dieter Zellweger, president of the Nachlasskommission Karl Barth.

5
"A Book for Those Who Were Also Concerned"

The First *Epistle to the Romans*, 1919

What Barth later called "the decisive material turning point" in his theological path occurred during his time as pastor in Safenwil.[1] The shock about the theological positions taken by his most important teachers in light of the world war, initially an ethical problem, made Barth aware "that their exegetical and dogmatic premises were not right either."[2] Barth asked himself whether the customary way of dealing with biblical texts at that time was suitable, whether it sufficed to look at them historically-critically. And how must the relationship between God and the world be defined, how must faith be conceived, if one was to avoid arriving at such positions?

When Barth and Thurneysen spoke about these matters it was also about the pastor's task in the congregation. They asked themselves how pastors could speak of God, if God's own word indeed was distinct from everything worldly. Later Barth recalled that in one of their meetings Thurneysen "whispered...half aloud" that "what we needed for preaching, instruction, and pastoral care was a 'wholly other' theological foundation."[3]

Human Religion and the Divine Word

When he later looked back at his life Barth described that "wholly other" that now began often and with different nuances. It was always however the turn to the Bible, to the Word of God that is encountered there, which in his eyes brought about the decisive clarification.[4] In the earliest such account, which he prepared in 1927 for the faculty in Münster, he wrote:

> The following morning[5] I found myself, surrounded by a stack of commentaries, before the apostle Paul's Epistle to the Romans, with what seemed to me to be the newly posed question about what really stood there. From the notes that I then made, there arose what later became the well-known, controversial book...In the first instance, I wrote the book really only for myself and for the private edification of Eduard Thurneysen and those who were also concerned.[6]

Even at the end of his life Karl Barth looked back at these days:

> The morning after Thurneysen had whispered that general observation to me, I [sat down] under an apple tree [and] began, at least with all the tools then at my disposal, to turn to the Epistle to the Romans... I began to read it as if I had never read it before: not without deliberately writing down step by step the things that I was discovering... I read and read and wrote and wrote.[7]

Barth attempted an exegesis of Paul's Epistle to the Romans that continued his insights into the difference between God and the world that he had developed during the past years. At the center of this was a new way of listening to the biblical text. His commentary on the Epistle to the Romans emerged, which three years later Barth completely rewrote for the second version. In his exegesis of Paul's Epistle he drew fruitfully from the impetus of numerous other authors. In addition to the exegetes,[8] Kutter and both Blumhardts, as well as Dostoevsky, Carl Spitteler, Kierkegaard, Overbeck, Plato and Kant, played a role.[9] Barth clarified later:

> So at that time (and indeed later), I read the biblical text with many different kinds of spectacles, as I unabashedly made known. But by using all those different kinds of spectacles, what I honestly wanted to express (and was convinced I was expressing) was the word of the Apostle Paul.[10]

The process by which the *Epistle to the Romans* was written is well documented in Barth's letters to Thurneysen from the Safenwil period. Barth mentions the project for the first time on July 19, 1916: "Meanwhile we [Nelly and Karl Barth] have been living on very quietly; strangely enough I am mainly pursuing exegetical research on the Epistle to the Romans, going so deep that I could even be seen brandishing Cremer's *Biblico-Theological Lexicon of New Testament Greek*."[11] Barth worked with enthusiasm and spent lengthy periods trying to understand individual passages. Thurneysen and both men's wives, as well as Hermann Kutter, frequently had to listen to passages from Barth's text.[12]

Even as he was still writing Barth was already trying to find a publisher for the book. Three Swiss publishers turned the book down.[13] Only after his friend Rudolf Pestalozzi guaranteed to cover any deficit did the G. A. Bäschlin publishing house in Bern accept it in September 1917.[14]

At the same time Barth remained skeptical:

> My Epistle to the Romans often appears to me to be a real *tower of Babel*. Perhaps it would be better to burn it ceremonially at the conclusion rather than allow it to be published. Does the dear Lord really want this scribbling? It is indeed just one more new theology.[15]

5.1. Karl Barth in front of the Safenwil parsonage in 1913, © Karl Barth-Archive in Basel.

Thurneysen advised him not to burn it: "Under no circumstances may you burn the Epistle to the Romans, perhaps you can give a strong little adage in the preface that prevents people from understanding it only 'theologically.' But [the manuscript] itself will take care of that."[16] After a four-week study break in Zurich during which he was able to devote himself completely to the manuscript, Barth finished it on June 3, 1918.[17] The fair copy for the publisher, in which Barth reworked and expanded the draft once more, was completed on August 16, 1918.[18]

Shortly after that Barth complained to Thurneysen:

> Now the Epistle to the Romans is finished, but no real joy about it is arising. The whole thing stands there like a sheep, but without the victory banner and such

things. And now the necessity of a... preface has great importance for me. Nelly is rejecting all my new drafts as dull, over-humble, and ragazisch [a reference to Leonhard Ragaz]. At the moment I can simply think of *nothing* more that could be said... So now as punishment for all the scribbling I am in a small special hell.[19]

Finally he summed up in a brief preface that the work was intended to be

no more than a preliminary undertaking, which begs for cooperation. If only many who are more competent would appear on the scene to bore for water in the same place. Should I however be mistaken in this joyful hope for shared new questions and investigations of the biblical message, then this book has time to— wait. The Epistle to the Romans waits as well.[20]

Barth corrected the publishers' proofs in the fall of 1918. At Christmas 1918, one and a half months after the war ended, he held the first printed copy of his work with the simple title *The Epistle to the Romans* in his hands.[21] The publication date was following year, and for that reason it is always described as the "1919 Epistle to the Romans."[22]

Barth's language in *Epistle to the Romans* was influenced by the characteristic style of the expressionism shaken by the war, as one encounters in the paintings of Max Beckmann or Otto Dix and the literature of Gottfried Benn or Georg Heym.[23] Barth uses powerful, bold formulations and pits them against each other, restlessly and underscoring the contrasts. He wanted to provoke and shake things up. He had hardly any hope in human beings. He wanted to lift God up into view.

The correct understanding of Barth's text requires, first of all, paying attention to his particular view of the biblical texts that continue even today to speak to people.[24] At the time all historical-critical exegetes would have subscribed to the book's first sentence: "Paul spoke to his contemporaries as a son of his times."[25] They would have viewed the exegetical task in positioning Paul in his era. And they would have emphasized the historical distance, which is the reason why we cannot apply Paul's statements directly to ourselves.

Barth however continues:

Yet *far more* important than this truth is the other, that as Prophet and Apostle of the Kingdom of God, he speaks to all human beings of all ages. The differences between then and now, there and here, should be taken into consideration. But the purpose of this consideration can only be the realization that these differences have *no* importance in the nature of the objects. The historical-critical method of biblical investigation has its right: it points to a preparation of understanding that is nowhere superfluous... Nevertheless, all my attention has been oriented toward seeing *through* the historical into the spirit of the Bible, which is the eternal spirit. What was once serious is still so today, and what is serious today and not merely quirk and coincidence—stands in direct connection with what was once serious. If we rightly understand ourselves, our questions are the questions of Paul; and if the light of his answers shines for us, those answers must be ours.[26]

Barth believes that in his interpretation he can—and must—leap over the historical ditch between back then and today. For in his epistle Paul is not representing a theological program or reflecting his own personal religiosity. Paul has "to deliver a message from *God*."[27] This message is

> a living word, perpetually regenerating itself anew out of its origins, not a sophisticated finished system... [It is] the message of a creative, fruitful examination of the essence of all things, which does not wish only to be heard but—to be *listened* to, that does not just count on [people] taking notice but on [their] participating, not only on reason but on understanding, not only on sympathy but on collaboration.[28]

The message from God with which Paul is concerned appears with a truth claim with which human beings must wrestle, or even more: from which human beings may not withdraw. On the surface, a historically distanced look at the biblical text may appear to be particularly objective, but according to Barth it bypasses the issue addressed by the text. This is the message from God. God's power is wholly creative and redemptive. It is "not one of the worldly powers that create nothing new but always and ultimately lead us around in circles."[29] Yet human beings confuse God with the world, worship themselves and their cultural achievements instead of God.[30] It is necessary however to worship God, for:

> *God* wants to be the Redeemer. *God* wants to be right through *God's* power. For only that which *God* does and fulfills is something genuinely and decisively new and helpful. However powerfully it may be expressed, in the [human being's] own desire to be vital and great... lies the old principle of the realm of death. God must act *alone* if redemption is to come.[31]

Barth now consistently distinguishes between God's actions and those of human beings, indeed he contrasts them. The kingdom of God, Barth is now convinced in contrast to his religious-social writings, comes about solely through God and not through human beings.[32] With that Barth is adopting a central insight of the Reformers: the position of human beings toward God is dependent solely upon God; in the language of the Reformers: the human being is justified before God through God's grace alone.

The flip side of this is that Barth locates all human activities *entirely* on the side of human beings, in the world that has not yet been redeemed through God. The statements that follow are clearly distinct from his convictions during his studies. But Barth with this also distances himself from religious socialism as well as from any theology of war.

Religion for Barth does not belong on the side of God, but rather on the side of the "world." Religion comes from human beings; it needs God only as the confirmation of what human beings themselves are capable of. In religion people orient themselves toward what *they* find holy and what *they* consider to be moral. They do not inquire seriously however whether this is God's orientation. In religion "everything is always already complete without God. God is supposed to be good enough to carry out and crown what human beings began on their own."[33]

Similarly, state and politics are something purely human. The state is based upon "an incorrect premise...its orientation toward force (*Gewalt*), i.e. toward the human beings who are separated from God."[34] Force is necessary only because human beings do not follow God's will. The nature of concrete political praxis, too, clearly does not correspond to the values of the kingdom of God. Barth's verdict is sharp: "As a battle for power *all* politics is...*fundamentally* dirty."[35] For Barth there is no doubt that "flamethrowers, mine detectors, gas masks, bombers and submarines are simply not the equipment of the kingdom of heaven."[36]

For this reason Christians can take their position toward the state with a certain equanimity; they are able to

> not take all the strange things the state also demands of *us* so seriously that we get involved in a battle with the state *over these things*. We combat the state fundamentally, radically and—*pay* taxes, *give* to Caesar what belongs to Caesar, *join* the Party, *fulfill* the functions to which we are obligated, within the not yet exploded realm of the political—and unfortunately also the *church*-political [realm.][37]

But false deference and the deification of political events cannot be allowed: "Performing one's duty without great fanfare and without illusions, but *no* compromising of God!... *no* Christian patriotism, *no* democratic mood of a crusade. Strike and general strike and battles in the streets, if it must be, but *no* religious justification and glorification of it!"[38]

Thus Barth reaches a comprehensive cultural critique: "Church and mission, personally strong convictions and morality, pacifism and social democracy do not represent the Kingdom of God, but rather in new forms the old kingdom of humanity."[39]

Barth's cultural critique reflects the spiritual situation of the wartime and postwar period, as it was expressed paradigmatically in Oswald Spengler's *The Decline of the West* (vol. 1, 1918) or Albert Schweitzer's *The Decay and the*

Restoration of Civilization (1923). Barth however placed no hope in a cultural reconstruction through which a "new world" could arise. Culture belonged entirely on the side of the old; human beings were not themselves in the position to create something truly new.

But there is a kingdom of God that had already begun, there where for Barth lies the turning point in human history, the change from the old era to the new, where in the "course of so-called history...the new element of the true history [that is, the history of God] that flows against it [becomes] visible": Jesus Christ.[40] He is the "divine Yes" to humankind.[41] He brings the old world of humanity to an end, and in him begins the new world of God.[42] He is the event of God's grace, a new beginning between God and humanity that is grounded solely in God.[43]

This "sole significance of God" corresponds on the human side the "sole significance of faith."[44] Through faith human beings come under the dominion of God.[45] It is "the step beyond the own, visible, subjectively possible and probable: toward where nothing else besides God's word holds us."[46] The believing person *takes* this step: "he dares this with a certainty that is not of this world, he absorbs the divine promise in his will."[47]

In the first version of his commentary on the Epistle to the Romans Barth consistently thinks "with God as the starting point."[48] He judges negatively everything human that isn't grounded in God's reality; all of it is the old human. "There can and may be no autonomy *next* to God, no lordless powers *outside of* God's power."[49]

"Like a Bomb on the Playground of the Theologians"

A few years after the book appeared the verdict of Catholic dogmatic theologian Karl Adam was: "As soon as it appeared for the first time Barth's *Epistle to the Romans* hit...like a bomb on the playground of the theologians."[50] Among younger theologians something like a "Barth congregation" soon formed.[51] In his review of the book Emil Brunner, at the time a pastor in the canton of Glarus and already in conversation with Barth for some time, praised Barth for making it clear that he was familiar with modern biblical scholarship, but also for noting correctly "that the biblical scholarship of our days bypasses the essential" in that its adherents, "rather than regarding the picture in the picture book, are analyzing the paper and color, because the actual task—observing and understanding the picture—seems 'unscholarly' to them."[52] In contrast Barth was attempting to genuinely understand Paul.

Fifty years later the philosopher Hans-Georg Gadamer praised the book in *Wahrheit und Methode* (3rd ed., 1972) as a milestone in modern hermeneutics, because in its search for the *subject matter* in Paul it had reopened the question of how to understand a text. Barth had undertaken a "critique" of liberal theology that was not directed so much at the critical history per se as at the theological self-satisfaction that considered its results an understanding of Holy Scripture. In this respect Karl Barth's Epistle to the Romans, despite its rejection of methodological reflection, is a kind of hermeneutical manifesto.[53]

Some of Barth's contemporaries accused him of "intellectualism," including Alfred Dedo Müller, a Saxon pastor who later became professor of practical theology in Leipzig. Müller feared that Barth's approach would mean the neglect of socially responsible actions: "Intellectualism is [namely] everywhere present where an existing vital impulse gets stuck in thought, where its path into life is not channeled,... where the urge toward the living embodiment of concepts is devoured by intellectual activity which is enjoyed with the highest satisfaction."[54] Then again, others found in Barth a contempt of reason and scholarship.[55]

Inevitably there were critical voices from the exegetical disciplines. The Marburg New Testament scholar Adolf Jülicher, under whom Barth had studied, judged that Barth had decided individual exegetical questions very quickly and to some extent also arbitrarily.[56] Barth had proceeded like the heretic Marcion, "with the same sovereign arbitrariness...with the same particularly dualistic one-sidedness, in animosity towards world, culture and convention, which tirelessly keeps on rolling out a few favorite ideas for us."[57] Barth represented a "modern gnosticism," a "radical dualism of all or nothing" and cultivated a "wrath at those who sought the middle ground."[58] With this however Barth denies history, in contrast to Paul. Barth's book did not attempt to truly understand the historical Paul. It was not a contribution to exegetical research; rather, it was merely an interesting product for church historians since Barth contrary to his claims had indeed developed a dogma.[59]

"Without Windows to the Kingdom of Heaven": The Tambach Lecture

Several months after the *Epistle to the Romans* appeared, Barth was invited to Tambach, Thuringia, September 22–5, 1919, to support a conference of the newly founded German Religious-Social Association, since they wished to have one of the "Swiss fathers of religious socialism" in attendance.[60] Barth gladly accepted: "At present I feel drawn toward Germany as nowhere else, because in this hour nowhere but there would I expect this community in the recognition of *genuine* need and *genuine* hope."[61] Barth quickly added however that he was neither father nor child of religious socialism. In contrast to Ragaz, for him the "main focus of the matter" was "no longer in the relationship between the two self-contained concepts of 'religion' and 'socialism,' but rather in posing the Socratic question, the question of God itself."[62]

Barth was finally asked to give a lecture about the topic "The Christian in Society." In it he further developed his thoughts from the commentary on the Epistle to the Romans. The lecture was heard by "people who had been deeply moved by the turbulence of the last years and now as Christians were searching for new paths in political and church life. The main theme was the position of Christians and therefore naturally that of the church toward socialism and the working class."[63]

Barth however boldly deviated from the assigned lecture title. He spoke not primarily about Christians in society, but about Christ.[64] Society is not left to its own devices only because the Christian being spoken of here is "*the Christ.*"[65]

Christ and society are in no respect organically connected, they "fall apart."[66] For

> the divine is something complete in itself, self-contained, new in kind, different from the world... It does not allow itself to be divided and distributed precisely because it is more than religion. It does not allow itself to be used. It wants to tear down and build up. It is complete in itself or it is nothing at all.[67]

All attempts to do so, as if "the world of God [had] open windows to our social life," were attempts to "secularize" Christ.[68] Instead the issue was to "engage God *with seriousness.*"[69]

Conversely too there was no window: society is "without windows to the kingdom of heaven."[70] Whoever attempts to "clericalize" worldly society and provide it with a church superstructure is deceiving it precisely about the God for whom one can only wait.[71]

The theologian's task can be only the "priestly *pondering* of that hope [for Christ] and need [of the separation between Christ and World], for it is through this [pondering] that the solution's way to us, which lies in God, is made more clear."[72] Barth describes the "standpoint"—which can hardly still be named as such—that the theologian therefore must take, using striking imagery: "our position in relation to the situation is a moment in a *movement*, comparable to a freeze-frame portrait of a bird in flight," and indeed *the* "movement that cuts vertically from above through all of these movements [such as the religious-social] as their hidden, transcendent meaning and engine."[73] As in his *Epistle to the Romans* Barth specifically warns: "We are concerned here with *God*. Not with religion, but with the movement that proceeds *from God*, with our being moved by *him*."[74] Religious experience, piety, was secondary, merely form.

Christ too comes entirely from God. Barth now no longer lets Christ encounter us "in the course of... history."[75] "Christ is the unconditionally *New* from *above*, the way, the truth, and the life of *God* in the midst of humankind."[76] Christ's resurrection from the dead is "the perpendicular line which cuts through all of our pieties and experiences, essentially passing them by. It is the breakthrough...and the appearing of the world of God..."[77] It is "wholly other," entirely different.[78] Here the "miracle of the *revelation* of God" takes place.[79]

This miracle corresponds on the side of human beings "the miracle of *faith*," that brings us "into critical opposition" to our entire life in this world.[80] One could say that Barth here was taking exception to the view that all life is always something like a resonance of divine life. The horror of the catastrophe of the world war, in which life had destroyed life, sat too deeply in him. No, in his eyes genuine life was measured alone in the living God. Therefore "all the 'validities' of life" had to be subjected "to a fundamental negation." They had to be compared to God as God is life itself.[81]

Barth did not however stay with this negation, for from God it is possible to esteem the world:

> God's judgement on the world is the establishment of his own righteousness. To allow oneself to be "thrown back" to the beginning is not an empty negation if we are really "thrown back" to the beginning, upon God. For only with God can we truly be positive. The *negation* that proceeds from God and points to God is positive, whereas all *positions* that are not built on God are negative.[82]

The world has no meaning in and of itself. But it receives meaning and hope from God, because God is its origin and its redeemer.

For the first time the concepts now appeared explicitly that were to lead to the description of Barth's new approach as "dialectical theology." With these ideas Barth is reaching back to an idea conceived by Hegel, a description of world history as a process of thesis, antithesis, and a synthesis that "suspends" the two into a higher unity. Barth turns this idea around. The synthesis is his starting point, concretely: the "*kingdom of God*," caused by God, "creation, redemption, the completion of the world by God and in God," the "advancing rule of God."[83] Only from the kingdom of God can a Yes be spoken to the world, can the world be regarded as something good. And only from this Yes is a No to the world necessary, clearly naming that and in what sense the present world is different from what would be in accordance to God.

> The synthesis is the original thing. The antithesis—above all, apparently the thesis itself—arises out of it. The insight into the genuine transcendence of the divine origin of all things permits, no, commands us to conceive of that which is and exists *as such* in God, in its connection with God. The direct, simple, methodical way leads us necessarily first to *affirm* the world as it is, not negate it. To find ourselves in God means to reconcile ourselves to the task of affirming him in the world as it is, and not in some false transcendental dream world. The

genuine and radical negation that we obviously intend in our protest movements can grow only out of this affirmation. The true antithesis can only grow out of the thesis, the true antithesis that originally grows out of the synthesis.[84]

The reverse however is also true: if one totally negates the world and sees it critically, based upon God, one can again draw something positive from the relative possibilities of the world:

> Only from the standpoint of the antithesis that has its roots in the synthesis can one accept the validity of the thesis so calmly. In this way [like Dostoevsky and like Jesus in his parables] the only one who can speak [is one] who stands in *absolute* criticism of life and who therefore... can also always refrain from a *relative* criticism of life. Such a person can just as well recognize the *analogy* of the *divine* in the *worldly things*, from a place of ultimate quietness, and rejoice in it...[85]

Affirmation and negation of life remain in a permanent tension, "rest comes in God alone."[86] God however means unrest for the world: "the 'other side' now unsettles us; with its absence in the present realm and with its knocking on the closed doors of this present realm it is the reason for our unrest."[87]

But precisely in this dialectical unrest is action in this world possible:

> Precisely *because* we have been offered a view onto the day of Jesus Christ, when God will be all in all, we have the freedom of being either naively with God or critically with God. If we want to understand ourselves properly, we must follow from above to below, and never the other way around. For the final thing, the eschaton, the synthesis, is *never* the continuation, the outcome, the consequence or the next stage of the penultimate. It is exactly the opposite. It is the radical interruption of every penultimate thing, yet precisely because of that [it is] its original meaning and moving power as well.[88]

Barth and his commentary on the Epistle to the Romans became known in Germany through the Tambach lecture.[89] Through the conference initiator, Otto Herpel, *The Epistle to the Romans* came to the attention of the jurist Alexander Münch, through whom the Munich pastor Georg Merz discovered it. Merz later recalled: "Presumably at the time there was hardly any reader who pounced on the book as fervently as Alo [Alexander Münch] and I did."[90] Merz was convinced "that in the *Epistle to the Romans* a new Reformation is imminent,"[91] and therefore urged Albert Lempp, owner of Chr. Kaiser Publishers in Munich (for which Merz was the theological advisor), to purchase the rights for the book and to distribute the remaining 700 copies of the first version in Germany.[92]

Several years later Barth looked back at this lecture: "Here I suddenly found a circle of people, with the prospect of larger circles, to whose disquiet my efforts offered answers—answers that quietly became new questions in the communication that now began with these German contemporaries."[93] Barth's work on the second version of his *Epistle to the Romans* commentary would soon begin, emerging out of these new questions.[94]

Barth left Safenwil two years later, in October 1921. His impression was that the congregation's pain at this parting was subdued. In his last letter from Safenwil he noted, "with insignificant exceptions the citizens of Safenwil are showing only *one* desire, which is to regain their peace soon."[95] Yet this doesn't seem to be entirely true. When Barth's successor was installed, one faction in the congregation indeed wished him to finally "preach... the *familiar* God" again, but another faction hoped that the new pastor would also speak about "the *unfamiliar* God... that was proclaimed by Pastor Barth."[96]

Notes

1. *Schweizerköpfe der Gegenwart*, 118. To the development of Barth's concept of theology, cf. Christoph Schwöbel, "The Task of Theology," in Jones and Nimmo, ed., *Oxford Handbook of Karl Barth*, 195–212.
2. Barth, "Rückblick," in *Festschrift für D. Albert Schädelin*, 4.
3. Barth, "Concluding Unscientific Postscript," *Theology of Schleiermacher*, 264.
4. Cf. e.g. Barth, "Rückblick," 4f.: "As the First World War ended, many of us had arrived at the conclusion that the new that was apparently announcing itself had to consist very simply in our 'beginning at the beginning' once again, i.e., we had to allow the Bible itself to speak decisively in our thinking and in our proclamation, more receptively and objectively than before." Cf. also *Schweizerköpfe der Gegenwart*, 119.
5. Regarding the day that preceded this morning, Barth does not mention here Thurneysen's whispering, but rather the agreement between the two "that for the further clarification of the situation, one would have to devote oneself again to academic theology." "Autobiographical Sketches I. Münster, 1927," *Barth–Bultmann Letters* (GA 1), 154f.
6. "Autobiographical Sketches I. Münster, 1927," *Barth–Bultmann Letters* (GA 1), 155.
7. Barth, "Concluding Unscientific Postscript," *Theology of Schleiermacher*, 264f. Translation revised.
8. Barth regarded as "*especially* valuable for me": John Calvin, Johann Albrecht Bengel, Carl Heinrich Rieger, Frédéric Godet, Johann Tobias Beck, Adolf Schlatter, Hans Lietzmann, Theodor Zahn, Hermann Kutter, Friedrich Zündel, and Albert Schweitzer. Cf. the afterword to the first version (1919) of *Der Römerbrief* (GA 16). Cited from the editor's preface, xviii.
9. Cf. Barth, "Concluding Unscientific Postscript," *Theology of Schleiermacher*, 265, with regard to the two versions of the Epistle to the Romans; "Selbstdarstellung," KBA 11294, 2. Regarding the contemporary status of the research on these various influences on the two versions, cf. the corresponding articles in Beintker, ed., *Barth Handbuch* as

well as Hake, *Die Bedeutung der Theologie Johann Tobias Becks*; Hong, *Leben vor den letzten Dingen*; Barrett, "Karl Barth"; and Eberhard Harbsmeier, "Karl Barth und Søren Kierkegaard. Kierkegaard im Streit der dialektischen Theologie," in Leiner and Trowitzsch, eds., *Karl Barths Theologie*, 317-30. The influence of Barth's philosopher brother Heinrich Barth on Barth's concept of the *"Ursprung"* is explicated in Lohmann, *Karl Barth und der Neukantianismus*, 206-316.

10. Barth, "Concluding Unscientific Postscript," *Theology of Schleiermacher*, 265. Translation revised.
11. Letter of July 19, 1916, to Thurneysen, *Briefwechsel Barth-Thurneysen* I (GA 3), 146.
12. Cf. editor's foreword, *Der Römerbrief* (first version) (GA 16), xi.
13. Cf. Barth's foreword in the 1963 reprint of *Der Römerbrief* (first version) (GA 16), 6.
14. Cf. editor's foreword, *Der Römerbrief* (first version) (GA 16), xi.
15. Letter of February 11, 1918, to Thurneysen, *Briefwechsel Barth-Thurneysen* I (GA 3), 265.
16. Letter of February 12, 1918, from Thurneysen, *Briefwechsel Barth-Thurneysen* I (GA 3), 266.
17. Cf. the letter of June 4, 1918, to Thurneysen, *Briefwechsel Barth-Thurneysen* I (GA 3), 279; editor's foreword, *Der Römerbrief* (first version) (GA 16), xiii.
18. Cf. editor's foreword, *Der Römerbrief* (first version) (GA 16), xiii f.
19. Letter of August 19, 1918, to Thurneysen, *Briefwechsel Barth-Thurneysen* I (GA 3), 288. The image of the "sheep without the victory banner" is a reference to the Agnus Dei, the Christian symbol for the resurrection of Jesus Christ: a sheep *with* the victory banner.
20. Barth, *Der Römerbrief* (first version) (GA 16), 4. In the foreword Barth explicitly "reverently and gratefully" mentions his father who had died in 1912, "whose entire life's work was a confirmation of this insight" that the "wisdom of yesterday" and the "wisdom of tomorrow... are one and the same" (3).
21. Cf. the editor's foreword, *Der Römerbrief* (first version) (GA 16), xvii. One thousand copies of the volume were published by Bäschlin, although in Switzerland only 300 were sold. (Cf. Barth's foreword in the 1963 reprint of the book (6).)
22. Regarding this, cf. Cornelis van der Kooi, "Erster Römerbrief," in Beintker, ed., *Barth Handbuch*, 189-94, and Frank Jehle, "Intellectual and Personal Biography I: The Young Barth (1886-1921)," in Jones and Nimmo, ed., *The Oxford Handbook of Karl Barth*, 29-32. See also Anzinger, *Glaube und kommunikative Praxis*, 128-236; Kooi, *Anfängliche Theologie*, 63-119; and McCormack, *Critically Realistic Dialectical Theology*, 135-82.
23. Cf. Brazier, "Barth and Expressionism."
24. Regarding Barth's new view toward the biblical texts see also his 1917 lecture, "Die neue Welt in der Bibel," *Vorträge und kleinere Arbeiten 1914-1921* (GA 48), 317-343. The Bible is concerned not with religion, not with "the correct human thinking about God, but rather the correct divine thinking about human beings. What stands in the Bible is not about how we should speak with God, but rather what God is saying to us" (335).
25. *Der Römerbrief* (first version) (GA 16), 3. Preface. The English translation by Edwin C. Hoskyns is a translation of the second version and of Barth's prefaces for both versions. It has been consulted for the preface but revised by Victoria Barnett, and in

the subsequent notes below translations are by Victoria Barnett. Page numbers cited are from the German critical edition.
26. Barth, *Der Römerbrief* (first version) (GA 16), 3. Preface.
27. Barth, *Der Römerbrief* (first version) (GA 16), 12.
28. Barth, *Der Römerbrief* (first version) (GA 16), 12.
29. Barth, *Der Römerbrief* (first version) (GA 16), 21.
30. Cf. Barth, *Der Römerbrief* (first version) (GA 16), 33f.
31. Barth, *Der Römerbrief* (first version) (GA 16), 398.
32. Cf. Kooi, "Erster Römerbrief," in Beintker, ed., *Barth Handbuch*, 191.
33. Barth, *Der Römerbrief* (first version) (GA 16), 401.
34. Barth, *Der Römerbrief* (first version) (GA 16), 519.
35. Barth, *Der Römerbrief* (first version) (GA 16), 502.
36. Barth, *Der Römerbrief* (first version) (GA 16), 519.
37. Barth, *Der Römerbrief* (first version) (GA 16), 519.
38. Barth, *Der Römerbrief* (first version) (GA 16), 520f.
39. Barth, *Der Römerbrief* (first version) (GA 16), 42.
40. Barth, *Der Römerbrief* (first version) (GA 16), 85.
41. Barth, *Der Römerbrief* (first version) (GA 16), 21.
42. Cf. Barth, *Der Römerbrief* (first version) (GA 16), 13.
43. Barth now explicitly bids farewell to the category of "experience," which he had learned from Herrmann and had become so offensive to him in the German war rhetoric (cf. Kooi, "Erster Römerbrief," in Beintker, ed., *Barth Handbuch*, 193f.). Whoever thought that one had to experience grace and that only through experience was its truth shown, places experience over God. Grace however is "true in itself. Grace is no 'event,' no 'experience.' ... Unquestionably grace does not remain without events and experiences, but it is primarily the divine precondition, ... the altered context of the world, into which our life is integrated." *Der Römerbrief* (first version) (GA 16), 206f.
44. Barth, *Der Römerbrief* (first version) (GA 16), 117.
45. Cf. Anzinger, *Glaube und kommunikative Praxis*, 183.
46. Barth, *Der Römerbrief* (first version) (GA 16), 138.
47. Barth, *Der Römerbrief* (first version) (GA 16), 138.
48. Kooi, "Erster Römerbrief," in Beintker, ed., *Barth Handbuch*, 191.
49. Barth, *Der Römerbrief* (first version) (GA 16), 219.
50. Adam, *Die Theologie der Krisis*, 325. On the reactions to the first *Epistle to the Romans*, see the editor's preface to *Der Römerbrief* (second version) (1922) (GA 47), xii ff.
51. Ernst Friedrich Karl Müller, "Karl Barth's Römerbrief," cited in the editor's preface, *Der Römerbrief* (second version), xiii.
52. Brunner, "'Der Römerbrief' von Karl Barth. Eine zeitgemäß-unmoderne Paraphrase" (1919), in Moltmann, ed., *Anfänge der dialektischen Theologie*, vol. 1, 80.
53. Gadamer, *Wahrheit und Methode*, 481.
54. Alfred Dedo Müller, cited in the editor's preface to *Der Römerbrief* (second version) (GA 47), xx f.
55. Such as Walter Köhler; cf. the editor's preface to *Der Römerbrief* (second version) (GA 47), xxi.

56. Cf. Adolf Jülicher, "Ein moderner Paulus-Ausleger" (1920), in Moltmann, ed., *Anfänge*, vol. 1, 91–3.
57. Jülicher, "Ein moderner Paulus-Ausleger," Moltmann, ed., *Anfänge*, vol. 1, 95.
58. Jülicher, "Ein moderner Paulus-Ausleger," Moltmann, ed., *Anfänge*, vol. 1, 95.
59. Cf. Jülicher, "Ein moderner Paulus-Ausleger," Moltmann, ed., *Anfänge*, vol. 1, 97.
60. Letter of June 22, 1919, from Otto Herpel, *Vorträge und kleinere Arbeiten 1914–1921* (GA 48), 547.
61. Letter of June 22, 1919, from Otto Herpel, *Vorträge und kleinere Arbeiten 1914–1921* (GA 48), 547.
62. Letter of June 22, 1919, from Otto Herpel, *Vorträge und kleinere Arbeiten 1914–1921* (GA 48), 548.
63. From the recollections of the German pacifist and pastor Günther Dehn who attended, in Dehn, *Die alte Zeit*, 217.
64. Cf. Dehn, *Die alte Zeit*, 220.
65. Barth, "The Christian in Society," in *The Word of God and Theology*, 36.
66. Barth, "The Christian in Society," in *The Word of God and Theology*, 37.
67. Barth, "The Christian in Society," in *The Word of God and Theology*, 38.
68. Barth, "The Christian in Society," in *The Word of God and Theology*, 38.
69. Barth, "The Christian in Society," in *The Word of God and Theology*, 38.
70. Barth, "The Christian in Society," in *The Word of God and Theology*, 39.
71. Cf. Barth, "The Christian in Society," in *The Word of God and Theology*, 40.
72. Barth, "The Christian in Society," in *The Word of God and Theology*, 41.
73. Barth, "The Christian in Society," in *The Word of God and Theology*, 42.
74. Barth, "The Christian in Society," in *The Word of God and Theology*, 43. Translation revised.
75. Barth, *Der Römerbrief* (first version) (GA 16), 85.
76. Barth, "The Christian in Society," in *The Word of God and Theology*, 44. Translation revised.
77. Barth, "The Christian in Society," in *The Word of God and Theology*, 44.
78. Barth, "The Christian in Society," in *The Word of God and Theology*, 66.
79. Barth, "The Christian in Society," in *The Word of God and Theology*, 45.
80. Barth, "The Christian in Society," in *The Word of God and Theology*, 46.
81. Barth, "The Christian in Society," in *The Word of God and Theology*, 47.
82. Barth, "The Christian in Society," in *The Word of God and Theology*, 49.
83. Barth, "The Christian in Society," in *The Word of God and Theology*, 51.
84. Barth, "The Christian in Society," in *The Word of God and Theology*, 52.
85. Barth, "The Christian in Society," in *The Word of God and Theology*, 55–6.
86. Barth, "The Christian in Society," in *The Word of God and Theology*, 59.
87. Barth, "The Christian in Society," in *The Word of God and Theology*, 63.
88. Barth, "The Christian in Society," in *The Word of God and Theology*, 67. Translation revised.
89. Cf. Georg Merz, "Die Begegnung Karl Barths mit der deutschen Theologie," 157, cited in *Vorträge und kleinere Arbeiten 1914–1921* (GA 48), 553f.
90. Georg Merz, *Wege und Wandlungen*, 211, cited in *Vorträge und kleinere Arbeiten 1914–1921* (GA 48), 555.

91. Letter from Georg Merz to Eduard Thurneysen, cited in Thurneysen's letter of April 6, 1927, *Briefwechsel Barth–Thurneysen* II (GA 4), 487.
92. Cf. the editor's preface to "Der Christ in der Gesellschaft," *Vorträge und kleinere Arbeiten 1914–1921* (GA 48), 555, and Barth's preface to the 1963 reprint of the first version of the *Epistle to the Romans*, *Der Römerbrief* (first version) (GA 16), 6. In his preface to the 1963 reprint Barth wrote that the reason for reprinting was the interest in his theological development: "Again and again it seems that there are brave young doctoral students, as well however as those who have graduated and are working in the various vineyards of scholarship about God, who find it correct and important in their scholarship to pore over certain dimensions or even certain stages in my thought, knowledge and confession, in their sequence and their connections, in order then to announce to their contemporaries, based upon their findings, what they should think of me." *Der Römerbrief* (first version) (GA 16), 5f.
93. "Autobiographical Sketches I. Münster, 1927," *Barth–Bultmann Letters* (GA 1), 155.
94. See Chapter 7, including its discussion of further significant lectures during the period between the first and second versions of the *Epistle to the Romans*.
95. Letter of October 9, 1921, to Eduard Thurneysen, *Briefwechsel Barth–Thurneysen* I (GA 3), 526.
96. Letter of November 27, 1921, to Eduard Thurneysen, in *Briefwechsel Barth–Thurneysen* II (GA 4), 14f.

6
"To Always Work Somewhat Faster"
Göttingen, 1921–5

From Swiss Pastor to German Professor

Barth never thought that his path would lead him out of the ministry. Nor had he prepared for this direction. "I wanted to become a pastor and was so for twelve years, without regarding myself as either called or suitable for the office of academic scholarship and teaching."[1] He was therefore surprised by the letter that he received on January 31, 1921. It was from the Reformed Göttingen pastor Johann Adam Heilmann, who had been trying for years to establish a Reformed professorship in Göttingen.[2] Heilmann asked Barth if he could imagine taking the new honorary professorship for Reformed Systematic Theology: "would you like to serve theology students and the Reformed Church here as professor?"[3] Heilmann had already been turned down several times, primarily because the position was not particularly well funded and because, so as not to water down publicly the Lutheran profile of the faculty, the person taking it should not become a member of the faculty but would only have associate status.[4]

Barth had been suggested for the Göttingen professorship by the Reformed professor in Erlangen, Ernst Friedrich Karl Müller. Müller had been asked himself if he didn't want to move to Göttingen, but had turned it down and in a letter to Heilmann mentioned Barth in passing as a substitute: "Among the Swiss one could consider someone like Barth, the son of the Bern professor who died early. I don't know him personally, but know him only as the author of the original, socially inspired commentary on the Epistle to the Romans."[5] Thus Barth had his first commentary on the Epistle to the Romans to thank for the invitation to become professor. Only after Heilmann had already sent his letter to Barth did a critical vote reach him, from the Basel linguistic scholar Jacob Wackernagel, who had taught in Göttingen from 1902 to 1915. Wackernagel warned against appointing Barth: "He is somewhat of a wild chap in the manner of his theological work...as well as in the manner of his behavior."[6]

Barth refused to give a trial lecture as was customary in such appointment procedures. He had no time for a lecture "at random"; he was "still pastor," and therefore one could not require that he "already prove [himself] as an academic."[7] But he was prepared to give a trial sermon. They invited him for February 27, 1921. His sermon was regarded as "carefully worked out" and "full of ideas," and

Barth's preaching style as "adequate, heart-winning," albeit too demanding of most listeners. In general he was found to be "suitable...for the appointment."[8]

Karl and Nelly Barth were unsure whether they should move to Göttingen: "We have to give up *too much* in Switzerland and there is no real *necessity*."[9] Moreover Barth was irritated that Basel church history professor Ernst Staehelin and Bern Lecturer for Old Testament Max Haller had also been put on the list of candidates, which indicated that there was no clear rationale for the position.[10] At the same time he was concerned about losing the freedom he had possessed up to now. He was also daunted by the prospect of *teaching* theology. Before him opened "like a gaping maw the necessity of conveying information, some kind of information (what kind of—and what about?) to an undefined bunch or even just a small bunch of German theology students."[11] He complained to Thurneysen:

> If for all the world I only *knew* a bit more; but with every look at a theological book I see a thousand things that are "fabulously new" to me, but about which I obviously should give exhaustive information soon. I realize only now what a sieve my head is; I simply have forgotten almost everything that I knew at the university and must somehow start from the very beginning and above all with the greatest care must practice the necessary diligence if I am not to betray my extensive ignorance. But it will come to daylight anyway...To put it briefly, I sometimes feel like weeping.[12]

Barth saw a particular difficulty in that until then he had hardly studied the specific profile of Reformed theology, with the exception of Calvin. Later, six years after his appointment as professor, he dared to admit "that at that time I did not even possess the Reformed Confessions, and had certainly never read them."[13] Now the time had come to assess the situation realistically. Müller, whom Barth consulted, suggested to him "in an official acceptance statement to emphasize explicitly that you will *gradually* familiarize yourself."[14]

Despite his reservations Barth accepted

> because of the immediate sense that as things were my place was among the theology students of Germany and not elsewhere, and in the blind confidence that things out there somehow must and would work out both with scholarship—and also with the care for my cheerfully growing flock of children.[15]

Shortly before Barth's departure Thurneysen, who in the meantime had transferred to a pastorate in St. Gallen, sent one last letter to Safenwil that shows how intensively both had experienced the challenge:

> How good indeed were those years before there was any *"Seek God...,"* no *Epistle to the Romans...*, before we were offered professorships and the

Christliche Welt and before publishing houses began to get interested in "us." How good as well were and still are *the* years where the full significance of all "our" insights and non-insights manifested themselves solely in our rapid walks back and forth along the Friesenweg,[16] and neither Jülicher nor especially Harnack, but rather at most the residents of Holziken and Schöftland, glancing at the street, could shake their heads at the two strange wanderers between two worlds... Why is everything so painfully strange, abnormal, in fits and starts, feverish, apocalyptic? What kinds of earthquake region did we unknowingly slip into, in the moment where we believed we should read the New Testament a little bit differently, more accurately than our teachers who were of course also honorable men? Where we could not ignore Blumhardt and could *no* longer really believe Schleiermacher (do you still recall the spot on our nightly path in Leutwil where we said that out loud for the first time?). Where we also became restless at the still proper comfortable seat at the Kutter table and moved on. In any case: this very strange path is irreversible.[17]

Barth reacted with a reserved tone of moving on: "I must now go there and go out on a limb in a manner that seems very impossible to me, and for the time being you must, just as impossibly, scamper on 'in place.'"[18]

Their new life in Göttingen began on October 20, 1921.[19] The family had initially purchased a site near the forest, but then decided instead to buy the

6.1. Karl Barth with son Hans Jakob in 1925, © Karl Barth-Archive in Basel.

house of Arthur Titius at Nikolausberger Weg 66, a neighborhood of villas in the town's northeast.[20] Titius had taught systematic theology in Göttingen, but had just left the city for Berlin.

An encouraging letter from Thurneysen greeted Karl Barth shortly after his move: he and Nelly were surely

> busy with setting up the new command post, soon the gun supports will be mounted, the pivoted tower set up and above all the flag will be raised. On Monday you will already be sitting again at the little green desk, a few last cigar stubs and tobacco in the usual drawer, and the battle can begin... Only that instead of the people of Safenwil, the Germans stand there, and instead of the splashes in Switzerland, the great long waves wash up on board, announcing that the ship is now upon the high sea.[21]

For the family the change was not difficult. Fortunately Nelly Barth, through her numerous moves as a child, was used to building a new life in a different place.[22] The children soon became accustomed as well.[23] At the end of their time in Göttingen, on April 6, 1925, the family's fifth and last child, Johann Jakob (called Hans Jakob) was born.

"Unavoidable Nonsense of the Academic Business"

Barth began his first Göttingen semester with a one-hour lecture on the Letter to the Ephesians, which was attended by fifty to sixty listeners—among only 180 theology students in Göttingen, including ten Reformed—as well as a two-hour lecture on the Heidelberg Catechism, with at least fifteen students.[24] Barth had been appointed in Göttingen with the task of teaching "introduction to the Reformed confession, Reformed doctrine, and Reformed congregational life."[25] Given this profile, a lecture about the Letter to the Ephesians did not immediately suggest itself. Barth's decision to do so indicates the importance for him of New Testament exegesis[26] and that through his work in the ministry and on the Epistle to the Romans he felt at home in this métier. Over against his exegesis of the Epistle to the Romans he intensified his work on contemporary research.[27] He managed however to do a thorough interpretation only for the first chapter of the Letter to the Ephesians, offering short sketches of the other five chapters in the last lecture session of the semester.

Barth struggled with the Heidelberg Catechism at the beginning; to him it was a "decidedly questionable work."[28] Above all the first question "what is your only comfort in life and in death" disturbed him, since it was conceived from the human perspective. And he was glad to be able to show that this perspective "fortunately through the answer is immediately blown up":[29] "That I am not my own, but belong—body and soul, in life and in death—to my faithful Savior, Jesus Christ."

Like many professors in their first semester Barth found it burdensome to have to prepare so much text every week for him to get through each forty-five-minute period of the three lecture classes. He complained to Thurneysen that on lecture days he "got up at 6 am and then—gulping down a bowl of soup at 8—I work like crazy until the stroke of 12, when at full gallop I run the four blocks to my lecture rostrum."[30] He wrote to Friedrich Gogarten, at the time a pastor in Thüringen, that he was "making zealous efforts to partly darn and partly cover up the holes in my academic cloak. The students come and listen to me as if I were a real professor, without knowing how nervous I often am whether my quota will suffice each time for an hour."[31] Barth had no doctorate or postdoctoral degree to show, and so such statements are certainly not intended as false modesty. After the first months in Göttingen he asked himself how he would be able to master some academic material truly thoroughly:

> Will one ever be able to say that of me, or among all the reputable scholars surrounding me will I always be merely this rambling... *Zigeuner*, who has only a few pots with holes in them to call his own and because of that occasionally burns down a house?[32]

After surviving his first Göttingen semester, Barth wrote his Swiss friends a letter that reveals the inner agony that he had to endure beyond the heavy schedule. Now on vacation, he was growing more conscious of "my thorn in the flesh, my horrible theological ignorance, aggravated by my very miserable memory that tenaciously only retains *very* decisive things... in the quiet that now surrounds me... as when I, constantly speaking, can be under the sweet illusion that I still knew something."[33] At the end of the second semester he continued to complain:

> I already feel thoroughly in need of a vacation, sometimes I think that I have never been as tired as now. This stems first of all from the unique business of such an academic position. It is the same thing that tires out a worker behind his machine: I must always work somewhat faster than would be my natural tempo, in order for all the world to have *something* prepared before it is 7 a.m. again. That is a serious strain on one's nerves (almost always a night shift!) and is even more unsatisfying because necessarily so much is not as well thought-out and its expression is not as well worked-out as I would like... Oh, the lovely, lovely gestation period in Safenwil! I am convinced that much of the wretchedness in theology must not be attributed to the stupidity and ill-will of theologians but simply to the unavoidable nonsense of the academic business. Even an archangel would become banal with this endless pulling of slimy threads.[34]

Dejected at the end of his first year in Göttingen he summed up: "... one would do better to pack in this theological business in *every* way and go somewhere to cultivate sycamore-fig trees or somehow sit on a hill, armed with an hourglass, and wait for what comes next."[35]

At the same time however he also experienced his new task as a relief: he no longer stood, as he had when preaching in Safenwil, under the "duress to speak even rhetorically impressively about the dear God." Rather, he enjoyed in the lecture class the given "certain ... good ... distance from the Holy of Holies ... one tells about this and that, one develops, one quotes, one celebrates a little Reformed triumph against the Lutherans, one has a little attack against Schleiermacher."[36] In a December 1921 letter to Switzerland Barth brooded over this distinction in particular, because he had preached again on the third Sunday in Advent and agonized over the sermon until two in the morning:

> It is simply not the same thing as a lecture, because a sermon really has to be something whole, has to lead somewhere, should conclude with some special: This! Whereas as a professor one imparts very nicely and indiscriminately for the duration of an hour, in order then to break off sedately with "*sed quia sonat hora iam non possum ulterius progredi*" ["and since the hour is striking I can no longer continue"].[37]

Barth was enthusiastic about the Göttingen library where he "may move about with the privilege of the lecturer," but stiffened before the collection there of "the abysses of books that have already been poured out about dear God."[38] For the still inexperienced university teacher, the library vault and its amenities generated a "mystical awe of scholarship ... and with trepidation I asked myself in the sinister thousand-voiced isolation, what it actually meant that I should have been brought into *this* corner of hell."[39]

In the following semesters in Göttingen Barth's lectures focused on Reformed theology, to expand his knowledge. He offered four-hour lecture courses on "The Theology of Calvin" in the 1922 summer semester, "The Theology of Zwingli" in the 1922/3 winter semester, "The Theology of the Reformed Confessions" in the 1923 summer semester, and "The Theology of Schleiermacher" in the 1923/4 winter semester. At the conclusion he felt that he was in the position to present his own dogmatic approach, a three semester lecture course, "Instruction in the Christian Religion," which began in the summer semester of 1924. In addition he continued to offer exegetical lectures.[40]

Barth's lecture in the 1922 summer semester on "The Theology of Calvin" is an example to be explored more closely since it gives a clear picture of the development of his Reformed profile.[41] Here he was able to build on the basic knowledge he had acquired in Geneva. He was now completely engaged by the Geneva Reformer:

6.2. Karl Barth as a young professor in Göttingen, 1925, © Karl Barth-Archive in Basel.

Calvin is a waterfall, a jungle, something demonic, something coming directly down from the Himalayas, absolutely Chinese, wonderful, mythological. I am utterly lacking in the organs, the suction cups, to only imbibe this phenomenon, let along correctly portray it. I take in only a thin stream of water and I can only convey in turn a thin extract of this thin stream of water. I would well and gladly sit and spend the rest of my life only with Calvin.[42]

He now lectured four times a week in the mornings from 7 to 8 a.m., to thirty to forty listeners.[43] At the beginning he dealt extensively with the relationship between the Reformation and the Middle Ages, comparing the three great Reformers, Luther, Zwingli, and Calvin, before portraying Calvin's theology in the context of his life. He could only offer a thorough treatment up to the summer of 1538; in the final three lecture classes he offered a cursory overview of the years 1538–41, and didn't deal at all with the years leading up to Calvin's death in 1564.

Barth believed that studying Calvin was not just important for the sake of historical education. Far more, "[w]e open books from the past in order to come to ourselves. The *living, speaking, working* past *is* the present."[44] He therefore ascribed the lecture under Cicero's motto that Calvin had quoted: "*historia vitae magistra*"—"history is life's teacher."[45] It was a matter of conducting a conversation with Calvin in which Calvin was the teacher so that we "make...our own sense of it" and at the conclusion "possibly...say something very different from what Calvin said."[46] Such a judgement however was not possible prematurely, for one must always read significant authors "with a certain *humility*" and "with a certain free and understanding *humor*..., presuming that the author is probably *always* right in some sense even when wrong."[47]

The preoccupation with Calvin helped Barth in his clarification of the place of ethics in theology as distinct from Luther's thought. Barth had discovered something in Luther that became central in his interpretation of the Epistle to the Romans: the emphasis on the "vertical line of the knowledge of God in Christ,"[48] which radically interrupts human thought and action. But one must then question further:

> What does the attack of the *vertical mean* for what takes place *horizontally*? What becomes of all that we will and work on this side of the line of death that is suddenly made visible, that we *have to* will and work because as people in time we are always on this side of that line of death...?[49]

Even if for Luther the ethical questions were by no means insignificant, he had not thought further theologically on this issue.

> Rather maliciously we might compare Luther's ethical writings to the Echternach spring procession in which there is one step backward for every two steps forward, so tirelessly upon any possible resolve to do good works does the weight lie: "Yet do not think that through this you can get to heaven."[50]

Since with this the question about the good ethical life remained open, Zwingli and Calvin became necessary. For Barth they represented the "second turn in the Reformation."[51] He interpreted Calvin's life path as precisely this clarification, since after 1536 in Geneva he took "the step from waiting for God to acting to his glory most impressively."[52] Calvin had

> in the Spirit *dared*...to take a *step*, a dangerous step, an earthly step, yet a step that he could not avoid taking...This is the secret of life in general...to look to what is everlasting, and then however to live and *act* in the world of the transitory precisely in light of this perspective.[53]

The planning of the 1924 summer semester led Barth to a difficult conflict with the faculty. Two years before, the faculty had decided to list Barth's honorary professorship in the personnel listings under the subtitle "Outside the faculty," indicated there following the lecturers.[54] In Barth's recollection his lectures were listed on the faculty bulletin board "along with the teacher who instructed students in how to play the harmonium and organ; *that's where* Reformed theology was put."[55] The background was apparently Barth's success among the Lutheran students. Carl Stange, a colleague in systematic theology, was said to have told Barth that it was "damaging to the [regular] faculty classes" when Lutheran students listened to his homiletical exercises.[56]

At the end of 1923 the dean of the faculty Alfred Rahlfs approached Barth with the resolute request that he change the listing of his summer semester 1924 "Prolegomena to Dogmatics" to "Prolegomena to *Reformed* Dogmatics."[57] Barth had accepted previous slights without resistance. Now however he rebelled, because this insertion aroused the impression that he himself would "endorse the character of Reformed theology as a kind of sectarian special doctrine compared to Lutheran theology, which in Göttingen behaves like *the* dogmatics, ethics, and so on."[58] In reality he too was acting with the "claim to general validity."[59] Following a fruitless back and forth over the title and announcement, the faculty sent the systematic theology colleague Georg Wobbermin to Barth. Over the course of a five-hour conversation things became too much for Barth, who slammed his fist ("effectively real...!"[60]) on the table and put as his final suggestion the German version of the title of Calvin's main work, *Instruction in the Christian Religion*,[61] with the subtitle "Prolegomena" ("introductory remarks"); otherwise he would turn to the appropriate minister in Berlin. The faculty gave in. Barth informed his students at the beginning of the first class about the background of the title—adding that on *his* manuscript the title was: "Prolegomena to Dogmatics."[62]

Barth's "Instruction in the Christian Religion" became his first attempt to delineate his own dogmatics. He now had to leave behind the "free... prophecy, as we loved it before."[63] His students experienced this as well. Walther von Loewenich, later a Luther scholar, recalled his disappointment about this lecture: "I had come to Göttingen filled with the impression of the 'prophetic' Karl Barth and instead found the professor of theology."[64] But the students sensed how Barth, in discussing the Reformed orthodox theology, was struggling for a new kind of dogmatic thought. Hermann Zeltner, later a professor of philosophy, expressed how many experienced these lectures in Göttingen: "In these lectures on dogmatics by Karl Barth... theological history was made, and we can say that we were there."[65] It was plain that this led to a certain "elite esoteric consciousness" among Barth's students: "As 'Barthians' we thought ourselves better than other theologians who had not yet been seized by the great turning point."[66]

Once more Barth pulled himself from one lecture session to the next. Since this lecture class also met at 7 in the mornings and the preceding night was the decisive phase of his preparation, it once happened that at the beginning of the lecture he had to admit: "Sirs, last night at two I got such a headache that I could no longer work; I beg your pardon if I stop after a half hour, we can of course have a discussion for the rest of the time."[67]

It was not easy for Barth to think about subject, concept, and method of theology. He complained to his friends:

> Yes, my goodness, now the dog has to get into the water... If only we had kept our mouths shut back then... However we never, and this was the calamity, *remained silent*, and now we have the reward: the accursed "Barth movement"... i.e. very banally, dozens, no, hundreds, who truly want to know how it will go further, and desire to hear from us after the A the B and C as well... but I sometimes feel... as if I'd most like to announce the liquidation of this.[68]

"Isn't it as if we sat in a car that is driving us dead straight somewhere where only heaven knows? It seems that all we can do is use the horn so that we don't drive over too many chickens."[69]

Barth organized his lecture around thesis statements, as he had done with his confirmation class. First however he warned his students that dogmatics was a "mortally dangerous undertaking,"[70] because here we speak ourselves and therefore must pose the question to ourselves: *What* do *you* want to say about *God*?[71] This question "put a pistol to the breast of the theologian."[72] "Every dogmatician is a rider on Lake Constance."[73]

Barth made his own position clear in distinction to the traditions of the nineteenth century when he defined dogmatics as "*academic reflection on the word of God*," not on religion or religious consciousness.[74] It was important to him that in this he was not asserting as a dogmatician that he could speak directly about God (which could not stand up to modern critique of metaphysics).[75] The point of departure for his dogmatics was the situation of the Christian preacher[76] who namely "*dare[s] to speak about God*."[77] And he dares this because he accepts the "*witness...that God himself has spoken*."[78] Only because God has spoken ("*deus dixit*") does the preacher—and with him the dogmatician who refers to his sermon—feel justified to speak of God.[79]

"Almost Like a Buddy": Barth with His Students

At the very beginning of his time in Göttingen Barth was disappointed about the professional level, particularly among the few Reformed students whom he found to be "unfortunately mostly... somewhat 'stupidly' uninterested and like schoolboys."[80] After the third week of the semester however he reported to Eduard Thurneysen that in the practical exercises that were part of the lecture courses the "liveliest questions and answers" arose.[81] The students pushed Barth to express and ground his position more precisely. Barth made every effort to do so.

In addition to the courses he regularly invited students (including those not studying theology) to open evenings at his home. In every semester these had a main theme, for example, modern literature or political autobiographies, but were also devoted to theological questions.[82] They had the "form of a kind of cozy 'exercise'... The participants (always around thirty) devise small works or outlines about the current status of their opinions on the church, authority, revelation and similar basic concepts and then discuss these under my wise guidance."[83]

Barth quickly developed a good relationship to the Göttingen students, which was probably also due to his appearance. Walther von Loewenich recalled:

> In his appearance Barth seemed completely unconventional. He wore a simple gray suit and a black hat that was somewhat crumpled. He received students during his office hours in a house jacket or, in the Swiss manner, in shirtsleeves. He placed no value on professional distance, instead dealing with his students almost like a buddy. The (already then) renowned man did not act that way in the slightest; if anything he intimated that he still had to hold his own against a strong group of opponents.[84]

"Lively Combat": Emanuel Hirsch and Other Colleagues

The relationship to his Göttingen colleagues proved to be difficult; this was also tied to the particular way in which the Reformed professorship had been designed. Barth continued to hope for an improvement in his position. At a conversation in Emden in September 1923 with representatives of the Reformed Federation however he was given little hope that his position could be transformed into that of full professor.[85]

Before his move to Göttingen Barth had already corresponded about theological topics with Emanuel Hirsch, who had been professor for church history there since 1921.[86] Barth found their first personal encounter in Göttingen oppressive, because he experienced Hirsch in an argument about politics. Hirsch appeared to him as "rabidly (more rabid, one could simply say fanatical, than came to light in the letters) German-national."[87] Barth was however soon impressed by how "truly horribly much" Hirsch knew.[88] Among the students there was a saying of Hirsch's that emphasized his industriousness: "Whoever has never worked with the scissors beneath his chin won't amount to anything as a scholar."[89]

An intense exchange soon developed between the two, also because they lived on the same street: "Lively combat alternates with identifying many things in common, but the contact remains close and thought-provoking."[90] Barth solicitously then asked his friends:

> Could one of you invite him for a few weeks to Switzerland in the summer, his health is declining pitiably because of his work style and he should really remain for the church for several more years. It would be a positive relief for me if I could drag him along in August and set him down somewhere on a meadow with milk and cheese.[91]

After the occupation of the Ruhr by French and Belgian soldiers in January 1923 however it came to energetic arguments between Hirsch and Barth, "in which 'Swiss! Foreigner! Rabble-rouser! Disturber of the peace!' were just thrown at me," and Barth gave back as good as he got.[92] Although they reconciled immediately afterward, the relationship soon became "somewhat bad...and half-hearted."[93] There was a further conflict in March 1923, when Barth sharply criticized Hirsch's thirty theses on nation, state, and Christendom, accusing him of having completely "betrayed [Christendom] to the Prussians."[94] Particularly "in Christ" they were not of one mind.[95] After this Hirsch broke off contact for two months.[96] Barth had destroyed the *"centrum concordiae"* ["the centerpoint of harmony"],[97] the "conviction...that the Gospel is the only Holy thing for the other person as well."[98] The relationship remained tense for the rest of his life. Hirsch would play an infamous role in Barth's 1934/5 dismissal.[99]

Professionally Barth took little interest in Carl Stange, the systematic theologian.[100] Barth's fellow countryman from Basel, Alfred Bertholet, who was professor of Old Testament, soon signaled to Barth that while Stange was superficially friendly, behind Barth's back he intrigued against him. Barth thus had the feeling that he stood "right in the middle with a Janus-face...or even with a single sheep face" and didn't know "which of the voices I should now believe."[101] Theologically Barth felt distant to Hirsch as well as to Stange, because both "are betraying...Christendom to history," that is, they wanted to make its significance and truth plausible out of its historical appearance.[102] Nonetheless during Barth's first two semesters in Göttingen Hirsch, Stange, and Barth, often accompanied by their wives, met regularly for theological conversation. One would give a talk about an agreed-upon subject that they would then discuss.[103]

Barth had a more positive impression of Erik Peterson, who had taught church history and Christian archaeology in Göttingen as a lecturer since 1920.[104] In July 1921 Peterson had sent Barth a postcard in which he portrayed to him how necessary he would be in Germany. He had just heard a lecture "in which the innermost heart of the matter and all its tensions was never made the point of the lecture, rather only the abstractions and formulations of a bad theology gone stale!... Please come therefore by winter and help me in my isolation."[105] Upon arriving in Göttingen Barth found Peterson to be "a delightful figure;" Peterson was "thoroughly convinced" of the "fallacy of earthly things" and took "supportive sympathy in my attempt as well."[106] Barth sat in on Peterson's lectures on Thomas Aquinas in the 1923/4 winter semester.[107] Peterson's later critique of dialectical theology would thoroughly preoccupy Barth.[108]

After his first year in Göttingen Barth consolidated his impressions of German professors in a critical conclusion:

> The German professors simply *are* just as bad as their reputation, it's only that when one faces them one loses all desire to proceed against them *in such a way* as the Swiss religious-socialists tended to do and occasionally we along with them. Eschatology on the one hand and a zoological garden on the other are the only possible viewpoints from which one can regard these "little creatures" of our dear God, in their full derangement, which is then again completely and impeccably combined with so much sanity, amiability, disposition and—piety. I can only realize with astonishment that *this* is now my "neighbour" and that I myself from a *different* point of view *certainly* offer the *same* enigmatic picture, full of deathly poison and praising God the Lord.[109]

In the spring of 1923 he considered himself happy because he only saw his colleagues occasionally for a few minutes.[110]

In his letters to friends Barth described his colleagues in pronounced portraits and rendered severe judgements. He called Lietzmann "a youthful mercurial little man with a shark-like face," or he spoke of Hirsch's "dotty, Berlin-like, academic, Wingolf [a German fraternity]-fraternity-like" manner that made him "gulp."[111] But he was also ready to revise his judgements, for instance after a personal encounter, and then warned himself: "It is indeed very appropriate to speak very cautiously about how the places in heaven and in hell will be distributed."[112]

When Barth left Göttingen in 1925 he was relieved that there was no farewell meal with the Göttingen faculty, but happy to note, after a number of farewell visits with Nelly, that they had also found friends in the town.[113]

"Stranger from a Neutral Place": Karl Barth and the Germans

Barth and his wife occasionally took excursions in the countryside around Göttingen, often on bicycle. To Switzerland he reported: "The surrounding area is quite pleasant, although the Germans talk quite inappropriately of 'mountains,' 'summits,' and similar things... that among us would hardly be called a real dung heap. But it is all very friendly, and I always took special pleasure in the large, wide hollows and heights."[114]

During the summers Barth enjoyed the annual Handel Festival, which had been held in Göttingen since 1920. Nelly Barth, who met often with other professors' spouses to play music, even played in the festival orchestra in the summer of 1923.[115]

Many in Germany quickly became interested in the new Göttingen professor, so that Barth soon had to discover unwillingly that he could "have a lecture on each finger somewhere in these endless plains...where everywhere there are corners and nests, where it is just buzzing in reason and unreason, in Yes and No, dialectic, resurrection, God is God and all kinds of drivel."[116] Barth jokingly considered simply changing his style and only "grinning...while holding a monologue, entirely indifferent to whether anyone wants to hear it and what comes of it."[117] Especially his lectures, which he often held several times, contributed to a more precise development of his approach. It was not seldom that they lasted two full hours. Many of those attending sought a theological conversation with him and visited him in Göttingen, and he visited many. At the conclusion of his time in Göttingen in 1925 Barth had a good network in Germany. Despite this great resonance, however, Barth sometimes wished to escape his routine entirely. He fantasized about taking a long world trip with his friends. "*That* would be something. The West is going to decline despite all the lectures by and about us,"[118] he wrote in 1923, referring to the book by Oswald Spengler, *The Decline of the West*, which had recently appeared.

Barth followed the political developments in Germany primarily through a local Göttingen newspaper, so that after French and Belgian troops marched into the Ruhr valley he asked his Swiss friends to send him a few newspaper articles from Switzerland about this incident so that he could better assess how it should be judged. He was irritated by the dedication of a monument in Göttingen for members of the university community who had fallen in the First World War (a third of the student body), where he encountered the "German-ethno-nationalism." He was irritated by formulations in speeches like "the individual must die for the State to live," "Goods and Blood," "German oak forests," and "when the next war begins."[119] Barth wrote to his friends that he had, "more bitterly and more angry than for a long time become aware...of [his]...fully and incurable foreignness in this world."[120] Occasionally he attended events held by the Wingolf fraternity, where he was also outraged by the nationalism.

At the beginning of his first winter in Göttingen Barth noted with distress the tense economic situation in Germany.[121] He attempted to at least assist Göttingen by publishing a request for help in the *Appenzeller Sonntagsblatt* (a Swiss newspaper) that appeared on September 30, 1922. The reality in Germany was "more serious...than the reports about it reaching foreign newspapers."[122] Pensioners and widows, as well as students and orphans, had it particularly hard and scarcely knew how they were to survive. Students presumably could barely heat their rooms in the winter, they could no longer purchase important books.

> I know that the Swiss are overrun with questions of this nature. But I see the conditions here and cannot stop thinking how it could be helped here with a *few*, let alone *many* Swiss francs, and dare to ask: help me to offer at least *a little* relief for the many who are threatened and cornered![123]

Around 3,000 Swiss Francs and 85,000 Marks were collected, which in the period of hyper-inflation came to around four million Marks,[124] which were quickly distributed, as the price for one pound of margarine was 1,000 Marks. Nelly Barth also became involved in the summer of 1922 to help the suffering Germans. During her August vacation in Klosters she hung a leaflet to collect money for the Germans.[125]

As conditions worsened that winter Barth was moved by how the hunger, cold, and sickness affected people and how the Germans nonetheless celebrated Christmas: "What an irrepressible mood and disposition this people has! What boors we are in comparison!"[126] Personally he was glad about the Swiss "hinterland,"[127] that is about the financial support from his homeland, and that he was earning some money with the commentary on the Epistle to the Romans—money however that through inflation immediately lost its value. At the same time he felt a certain "embarrassment of the rich man, which until now I have never known and in light of which, *if* I had recognized it, several sermons perhaps would have remained unpreached."[128]

Looking back Barth called the Göttingen years "sour years... for I not only had to learn and teach continuously but also, as an advocate of a new trend in theology, I had to vindicate and protect myself in all directions in the form of lectures and public discussions."[129] But although in Germany he had been "a stranger from a neutral place"[130] and deeply enjoyed vacations at Lake Zurich, in House "Bergli," and in the Swiss mountains: he returned "always with pleasure back to Germany and the German people."[131]

Notes

1. "Autobiographical Sketches II. Bonn, B. 1946," *Barth–Bultmann Letters* (GA 1), 157. Translation revised.
2. Regarding the lengthy 170-year long history of the establishment of this professorship, cf. Freudenberg, "Die Errichtung der Professur für Reformierte Theologie"; the call to Barth is described on 254–7. Only an honorary professorship was established because its stipend, in contrast to that of a full professor, could be negotiated (253).
3. Letter of January 29, 1921, from Johann Adam Heilmann, cited in Freudenberg, "Errichtung," 257.

4. Cf. Freudenberg, "Errichtung," 251. Barth's salary was similar to that of a pastor, at that time 25,000 Reich Marks annually. His salary consisted of contributions from the state, the confederation of Reformed Churches in Lower Saxony, and the Protestant Reformed Church of the province of Hanover. More than half came in the form of a guaranteed contribution for six years from the North Western Synod of the Reformed Church of the United States (cf. 254).
5. Letter of October 23, 1920, from Ernst Friedrich Karl Müller to Johann Adam Heilmann, cited in Freudenberg, "Errichtung," 256.
6. Letter of January 29, 1921, from Jacob Wackernagel to Johann Adam Heilmann, cited in Freudenberg, *Karl Barth und die reformierte Theologie*, 19.
7. Letter of February 16, 1921, to Eduard Thurneysen, *Briefwechsel Barth–Thurneysen* I (GA 3), 468.
8. Report of March 2, 1921, by G. J. Smidt to the Consistory of the Protestant-Reformed Church of the province of Hanover, cited in Freudenberg, *Karl Barth und die reformierte Theologie*, 27f.
9. Letter of February 16, 1921, to Thurneysen, *Briefwechsel Barth–Thurneysen* I (GA 3), 469.
10. Cf. Letter of February 16, 1921, to Thurneysen, *Briefwechsel Barth–Thurneysen* I (GA 3), 468.
11. Letter of February 2, 1921, to Thurneysen, *Briefwechsel Barth–Thurneysen* I (GA 3), 464.
12. Letter of May 18, 1921, to Thurneysen, *Briefwechsel Barth–Thurneysen* I (GA 3), 488f.
13. "Autobiographical Sketches I. Münster, 1927," *Barth–Bultmann Letters* (GA 1), 156.
14. Letter of May 27, 1921, from Ernst Friedrich Karl Müller, cited in Freudenberg, *Karl Barth und die reformierte Theologie*, 1. Barth had also asked Martin Rade for advice in light of this "stone in my peaceful pond." (Letter of January 31, 1921, to Martin Rade, in Schwöbel, ed., *Karl Barth–Martin Rade*, 153). Rade advised him to accept (155f.).
15. "Autobiographical Sketches I. Münster, 1927," *Barth–Bultmann Letters* (GA 1), 156.
16. The Friesenweg is a path that owes its name to the legend that the people from the (northern German) region of Frisia left the North Sea because of a famine and moved to Switzerland, on some nights however leaving their graves to wander back to the sea along the same path they had come along. Cf. Lienert, *Schweizer Sagen und Heldengeschichten*, 22–5.
17. Letter of October 6, 1921, from Thurneysen, *Briefwechsel Barth–Thurneysen* I (GA 3), 524f.
18. Letter of October 9, 1921, to Thurneysen, *Briefwechsel Barth–Thurneysen* I (GA 3), 525.
19. From Barth's pocket 1921 calendar (his calendars are in the KBA). Just before the move Barth had spent several days at the "Bergli"; cf. his letter of October 9, 1921, to Thurneysen, *Briefwechsel Barth–Thurneysen* I (GA 3), 526.
20. Cf. the letters to Thurneysen of July 17, September 17–18, 1921, and Thurneysen's reply of September 22, 1921, *Briefwechsel Barth–Thurneysen* I (GA 3), 503 and 518f.
21. Letter of October 22, 1921, from Thurneysen, *Briefwechsel Barth–Thurneysen* II (GA 4), 3. (Thurneysen was suggesting that the small conflicts in Safenwil would be nothing compared to the conflicts Barth would encounter in Germany.) There are no existing pocket calendars from Barth during his time in Germany, differently from after

his return to Switzerland in 1935. Barth's regular letters to Thurneysen and their mutual friends are almost like a journal, however.

22. Cf. Barth-Zellweger, "Lebenslauf," in *Nelly Barth-Hoffmann*, 6: "Our mother's flexibility helped that this big step in 1921 could be dared. Who back then would have thought, after Nelly already in youth must change residences six times, that six additional moves would be endured before the final move to the house on Bruderholzallee 26?"

23. Cf. letter of January 22, 1922, to Thurneysen, *Briefwechsel Barth–Thurneysen* II (GA 4), 28.

24. Cf. letter of November 18, 1921, to Thurneysen, *Briefwechsel Barth–Thurneysen* II (GA 4), 9.

25. Letter of August 16, 1921, from the Prussian Minister for Scholarship, Art, and General Education Carl Heinrich Becker, cited in *Briefwechsel Barth–Bultmann* (GA 1), 215.

26. Cf. the editor's foreword to Barth, *Erklärungen des Epheser- und des Jakobusbriefes 1919-1929* (GA 46), vii.

27. Cf. the editor's foreword to Barth, *Erklärungen des Epheser- und des Jakobusbriefes 1919-1929* (GA 46), ix.

28. Letter of November 18, 1921, to Thurneysen, *Briefwechsel Barth–Thurneysen* II (GA 4), 9. Regarding Barth's lecture, see Reichel, *Theologie als Bekenntnis*, 34-74.

29. Letter of November 18, 1921, to Thurneysen, *Briefwechsel Barth–Thurneysen* II (GA 4), 9.

30. Letter of February 11, 1922, to Thurneysen, Rudolf Pestalozzi, and Peter Barth, *Briefwechsel Barth–Thurneysen* II (GA 4), 39f.

31. Letter of November 16, 1921, to Friedrich Gogarten, in Göckeritz, ed., *Friedrich Gogartens Briefwechsel*, 174.

32. Letter of December 11, 1921, to Thurneysen, Rudolf Pestalozzi, and Peter Barth, *Briefwechsel Barth–Thurneysen* II (GA 4), 21. Barth is referring to the Roma/Sinti people, using the German equivalent slur of "gypsy," which reflects the prejudices of that era (as does his description).

33. Circular letter of March 26, 1922, to his friends, *Briefwechsel Barth–Thurneysen* II (GA 4), 59.

34. Circular letter of July 7, 1922, to his friends, *Briefwechsel Barth–Thurneysen* II (GA 4), 91.

35. Circular letter of July 7, 1922, to his friends, *Briefwechsel Barth–Thurneysen* II (GA 4), 93. The images of the sycamores and the hill are references to the Old Testament prophets Amos and Jonah, who wanted to distance themselves from God's commission.

36. Letter of November 18, 1921, to Thurneysen, *Briefwechsel Barth–Thurneysen* II (GA 4), 8.

37. Circular letter of December 11, 1921, to his friends, *Briefwechsel Barth–Thurneysen* II (GA 4), 18f.

38. Letter of November 6, 1921, to Thurneysen, *Briefwechsel Barth–Thurneysen* II (GA 4), 6.

39. Letter of November 6, 1921, to Thurneysen, *Briefwechsel Barth–Thurneysen* II (GA 4), 6.

40. Barth held lectures on the Epistle of James (winter semester 1922/3), 1 Corinthians 15 (summer semester 1923), 1 John (winter semester 1923/4), Philippians (summer semester 1924), Colossians (winter semester 1924/5), and the Sermon on the Mount (summer semester 1924). Cf. the list of courses in the Karl Barth-Archive.
41. Regarding this, cf. Freudenberg, *Karl Barth und die reformierte Theologie*, 87–160; editor's foreword, *Theologie Calvins* (GA 23), vii–xvi.
42. Letter of June 8, 1922, to Thurneysen, *Briefwechsel Barth–Thurneysen* II (GA 4), 80.
43. Cf. the circular letter of May 9, 1922, to his friends, *Briefwechsel Barth–Thurneysen* II (GA 4), 71.
44. Barth, *Theology of John Calvin*, 8.
45. Cf. Barth, *Theology of John Calvin*, 1.
46. Barth, *Theology of John Calvin*, 4.
47. Barth, *Theology of John Calvin*, 6.
48. Barth, *Theology of John Calvin*, 49.
49. Barth, *Theology of John Calvin*, 49.
50. Barth, *Theology of John Calvin*, 76.
51. Barth, *Theology of John Calvin*, 49.
52. Barth, *Theology of John Calvin*, 235. Translation revised.
53. Barth, *Theology of John Calvin*, 293. Translation revised.
54. Contrary to the original plan of the faculty, however, Barth's certificate of appointment read "Honorary Professor *in* the Theological Faculty" (cf. Freudenberg, *Karl Barth und die reformierte Theologie*, 30). Author's italics.
55. "Interview von Hans A. Fischer-Barnicol," *Gespräche 1964–1968* (GA 28), 152.
56. Circular letter of May 17, 1922, to his friends, *Briefwechsel Barth–Thurneysen* II (GA 4), 77.
57. Letter of December 22, 1923, from Alfred Rahlfs, *Barth–Bultmann Letters* (GA 1), appendix 2, 113.
58. Letter of December 31, 1923, to Alfred Rahlfs, *Barth–Bultmann Briefwechsel* (GA 1), 213.
59. Letter of December 31, 1923, to Alfred Rahlfs, *Barth–Bultmann Briefwechsel* (GA 1), 213.
60. Circular letter of February 5, 1924, to his friends, *Briefwechsel Barth–Thurneysen* II (GA 4), 221.
61. To his friends he acknowledged that he was "not without quiet pleasure" at this suggestion, since this was also the title of the dogmatics by the renowned liberal Göttingen scholar Albrecht Ritschl. Cf. *Briefwechsel Barth–Thurneysen* II (GA 4), 221.
62. Editor's foreword to Barth, *"Unterricht in der christlichen Religion"* (GA 17), viii. Regarding this cf. Hinrich Stoevesandt, "Die Göttinger Dogmatikvorlesung. Grundriß der Theologie Barths," in Beintker et al., eds., *Karl Barth in Deutschland*, 77–98.
63. Letter of January 30, 1924, to Thurneysen, *Briefwechsel Barth–Thurneysen* II (GA 4), 217.
64. Loewenich, *Erlebte Theologie*, 50.
65. Cited in Loewenich, *Erlebte Theologie*, 51.
66. Loewenich, *Erlebte Theologie*, 51.
67. Loewenich, *Erlebte Theologie*, 52.

68. Circular letter of February 5, 1924, to his friends, *Briefwechsel Barth–Thurneysen* II (GA 4), 222f.
69. Circular letter of February 5, 1924, to his friends, *Briefwechsel Barth–Thurneysen* II (GA 4), 224.
70. Barth, *The Göttingen Dogmatics* (GA 17), § 1 The Word of God as the Problem of Dogmatics, 3.
71. Cf. Barth, *Göttingen Dogmatics* (GA 17), § 1 The Word of God as the Problem of Dogmatics, 6.
72. Barth, *Göttingen Dogmatics* (GA 17), § 1 The Word of God as the Problem of Dogmatics, 6. Translation revised.
73. Barth, *Göttingen Dogmatics* (GA 17), § 1 The Word of God as the Problem of Dogmatics, 6.
74. Barth, *Göttingen Dogmatics* (GA 17), § 1 The Word of God as the Problem of Dogmatics, 7. Translation revised.
75. Cf. Barth, *Göttingen Dogmatics* (GA 17), § 1 The Word of God as the Problem of Dogmatics, 10.
76. Cf. circular letter of May 18, 1924, to his friends, *Briefwechsel Barth–Thurneysen* II (GA 4), 252.
77. Barth, *Göttingen Dogmatics* (GA 17), § 3 Deus Dixit, 45; cf. § 8 The Scripture Principle, 201; § 11 Pure Doctrine, 265.
78. Barth, *Göttingen Dogmatics* (GA 17), § 3 Deus Dixit, 45.
79. Cf. Barth, *Göttingen Dogmatics* (GA 17), § 3 Deus Dixit, 56.
80. Letter of November 18, 1921, to Thurneysen, *Briefwechsel Barth–Thurneysen* II (GA 4), 9.
81. Letter of November 27, 1921, to Thurneysen, *Briefwechsel Barth–Thurneysen* II (GA 4), 14.
82. Cf. the circular letters to his friends of May 18, 1924, and June 7, 1925, *Briefwechsel Barth–Thurneysen* II (GA 4), 252 and 329.
83. Circular letter of December 20, 1923, to his friends, *Briefwechsel Barth–Thurneysen* II (GA 4), 209.
84. Loewenich, *Erlebte Theologie*, 50.
85. Cf. circular letter of September 24, 1923, to his friends, *Briefwechsel Barth–Thurneysen* II (GA 4), 187.
86. Regarding the relationship between the two, cf. Buff, "Karl Barth und Emanuel Hirsch." Hirsch sent Barth his book *Die Reich-Gottes-Begriffe des neueren europäischen Denkens*, in which he addressed Barth. Through Barth's *Epistle to the Romans*, which "emphasizes...the religious-ideal side," the religious socialism movement was "in danger of becoming seriously religious, i.e. to go over to an Enthusiastic sect that looks toward the coming of the Lord with fanatical fervor, which has hardly anything to do with the socialistic teaching of society." (Hirsch, *Reich-Gottes-Begriffe*, 32, n. 16) In the letter that accompanied this Hirsch however asked Barth "not to misunderstand his comments as an un-collegial lack of friendliness." (Buff, "Karl Barth und Emanuel Hirsch," 16.)
87. Letter of November 6, 1921, to Thurneysen, *Briefwechsel Barth–Thurneysen* II (GA 4), 5.

88. Circular letter of December 12, 1921, to his friends, *Briefwechsel Barth–Thurneysen* II (GA 4), 23.
89. Loewenich, *Erlebte Theologie*, 54. Hirsch was said to put a sharp pair of scissors under the chin to prevent himself from falling asleep when reading at night (cf. Wolfgang Trillhaas, "Emanuel Hirsch in Göttingen," in *Zeitschrift für Theologie und Kirche* 81 (1984), 227).
90. Circular letter of May 9, 1922, to his friends, *Briefwechsel Barth–Thurneysen* II (GA 4), 73.
91. Circular letter of May 9, 1922, to his friends, *Briefwechsel Barth–Thurneysen* II (GA 4), 73.
92. Circular letter of January 23, 1923, to his friends, *Briefwechsel Barth–Thurneysen* II (GA 4), 131.
93. Circular letter of February 28, 1923, to his friends, *Briefwechsel Barth–Thurneysen* II (GA 4), 152.
94. Circular letter of May 18, 1923, to his friends, *Briefwechsel Barth–Thurneysen* II (GA 4), 163. Cf. Freudenberg, *Karl Barth und die reformierte Theologie*, 67.
95. Cf. circular letter of May 18, 1923, to his friends, *Briefwechsel Barth–Thurneysen* II (GA 4), 163. Cf. also the letter of March 31, 1923, to Thurneysen (158).
96. Cf. letter of May 29, 1923, to Thurneysen, *Briefwechsel Barth–Thurneysen* II (GA 4), 171.
97. Letter of March 31, 1923, to Thurneysen, *Briefwechsel Barth–Thurneysen* II (GA 4), 158.
98. Buff, "Karl Barth und Emanuel Hirsch," 26.
99. See p. 239.
100. Cf. Freudenberg, *Karl Barth und die reformierte Theologie*, 64.
101. Circular letter of December 11, 1921, to his friends, *Briefwechsel Barth–Thurneysen* II (GA 4), 19.
102. Circular letter of December 12, 1921, to his friends, *Briefwechsel Barth–Thurneysen* II (GA 4), 23.
103. Regarding the content of the conversations cf. Freudenberg, *Karl Barth und die reformierte Theologie*, 59, n. 219.
104. Regarding the relationship of the two, cf. Peterson, *Theologie und Theologen* and Barbara Nichtweiß, "Lebendige Dialektik. Zur Bedeutung Erik Petersons für die theologische Entwicklung Karl Barths," in Beintker et al., eds., *Karl Barth in Deutschland*, 313–30.
105. Cited in Nichtweiß, "Lebendige Dialektik," in Beintker et al., eds., *Karl Barth in Deutschland*, 313.
106. Letter of November 6, 1921, to Thurneysen, *Briefwechsel Barth–Thurneysen* II (GA 4), 6f.
107. Regarding the core ideas, see Nichtweiß, "Lebendige Dialektik," in Beintker et al., eds., *Karl Barth in Deutschland*, 318–22; concerning the impression that these considerations about "natural theology" made on Barth, see the circular letter of December 20, 1925, to his friends, *Briefwechsel Barth–Thurneysen* II (GA 4), 211.
108. See pp. 202–203.

109. Circular letter of June 28, 1922, to his friends, *Briefwechsel Barth–Thurneysen* II (GA 4), 88.
110. Cf. circular letter of May 18, 1923, to his friends, *Briefwechsel Barth–Thurneysen* II (GA 4), 164.
111. Circular letters of November 26, 1924, and May 9, 1922, to his friends, *Briefwechsel Barth–Thurneysen* II (GA 4), 287f. and 73.
112. Circular letter of November 26, 1924, to his friends, *Briefwechsel Barth–Thurneysen* II (GA 4), 288.
113. Cf. circular letter of October 25, 1925, to his friends, *Briefwechsel Barth–Thurneysen* II (GA 4), 378.
114. Circular letter of March 26, 1922, to his friends, *Briefwechsel Barth–Thurneysen* II (GA 4), 62.
115. Information to the author from Dieter Zellweger.
116. Circular letter of July 7, 1922, to his friends, *Briefwechsel Barth–Thurneysen* II (GA 4), 92.
117. Circular letter of July 7, 1922, to his friends, *Briefwechsel Barth–Thurneysen* II (GA 4), 93.
118. Circular letter of May 18, 1923, to his friends, *Briefwechsel Barth–Thurneysen* II (GA 4), 169.
119. According to Barth's summary in his circular letter of November 26, 1924, to his friends, *Briefwechsel Barth–Thurneysen* II (GA 4), 286f.
120. Circular letter of November 26, 1924, to his friends, *Briefwechsel Barth–Thurneysen* II (GA 4), 287.
121. Cf. letter of November 18, 1921, to Thurneysen, *Briefwechsel Barth–Thurneysen* II (GA 4), 11.
122. Open letter to the *Appenzeller Sonntagsblatt* (first letter), *Offene Briefe 1909–1935* (GA 35), 51.
123. Open letter to the *Appenzeller Sonntagsblatt* (first letter), *Offene Briefe 1909–1935* (GA 35), 52.
124. Cf. the open letter to the *Appenzeller Sonntagsblatt* (second letter), *Offene Briefe 1909–1935* (GA 35), 54.
125. Information to the author from Dieter Zellweger.
126. Circular letter of December 18, 1922, to his friends, *Briefwechsel Barth–Thurneysen* II (GA 4), 122.
127. Circular letter of December 18, 1922, to his friends, *Briefwechsel Barth–Thurneysen* II (GA 4), 121.
128. Circular letter of December 18, 1922, to his friends, *Briefwechsel Barth–Thurneysen* II (GA 4), 121.
129. "Autobiographical Sketches I. Münster, 1927," *Barth–Bultmann Letters* (GA 1), 156.
130. "Autobiographical Sketches I. Münster, 1927," *Barth–Bultmann Letters* (GA 1), 156.
131. "Autobiographical Sketches I. Münster, 1927," *Barth–Bultmann Letters* (GA 1), 156.

7

"Not a Stone Left Standing"

The Second *Epistle to the Romans*, 1922

A Critical Turn

Before Karl Barth moved to Göttingen there had been a new "turn"[1] in his theological thinking that shaped the content of his work in Göttingen. The external cause was that after Barth's Tambach lecture the *Epistle to the Romans* sold well and Albert Lempp, director of the Chr. Kaiser Publishers, planned a new edition.[2] Yet Barth was suspicious of this success.[3] Was what had been portrayed there still too comfortable? Had it truly been made clear how very distinct God is from the world? Must not there be more emphasis on the distance between God and world?

Barth's involvement with the work of Franz Overbeck had led him further. Overbeck, the Basel New Testament scholar, church historian, and friend of Friedrich Nietzsche, had presented a profound critique of Christendom in which he drew a distinction between a "primal history" and the history of Christendom. The primal history is the era of the New Testament, with its expectation of the imminent return of Jesus Christ, followed by a radical repudiation of the world. For Overbeck, Christendom's conformation to the world, as had occurred most recently in the cultural Protestantism of the nineteenth century, signified an apostasy from these beginnings.[4]

In spring 1920 Barth read a posthumously published book with writings by Overbeck and reviewed it under the title "*Unerledigte Anfragen an die heutige Theologie*" ("Unresolved inquiries for contemporary theology"). Overbeck in his book had written critically: "Modern Christendom itself is only performing the work of gravediggers... It endeavors to smooth over Christian dogmatics by conforming it to modern thought. With that however it is only expunging the last traces that Christendom has in life."[5] Barth believed that every theology student had to read this critique of Christendom as the introduction for their studies since it made clear "that one essentially cannot be something like a theologian."[6] Overbeck's book led the reader "into the desert..., at a place... where he can neither lie nor sit, nor stand, rather absolutely can only move, where he can neither acquire nor possess, nor feast, nor distribute, rather only hunger and thirst [cf. Matt. 5:6], ask, seek, and knock [cf. Matt. 7:7f]."[7]

Barth was aware that Overbeck had not wanted to present a new theological agenda. But Barth nonetheless believed that in Overbeck he could discover "statements slipping out almost involuntarily about a more insightful and farsighted theology, the only kind perhaps still possible." This included the sentence: "Theology cannot again be justified except with audacity."[8] Later Barth would describe this as the basic principle of his own theology.[9] Now he saw in Overbeck above all the admonition that whoever today wishes to be a theologian must first "remain standing...in shock and awe and without screaming for positive suggestions" before the "narrow gate...of Overbeck's negation."[10] In Overbeck it became clear for Barth that in his *Epistle to the Romans* he had still taken it too much for granted that he knew something of God. With a wink he noted to a fellow pastor that in *Epistle to the Romans* he had spoken so grandiosely of "God" that his "printer once no longer had enough 'Gs' in his lettercase."[11]

One of the first documents in Barth's renewed attempt is a lecture of April 17, 1920, given at the Christian Student Conference in Aarau on the topic "Biblical questions, insights, and perspectives." He was to treat the question of what the Bible had to offer "in certain knowledge about the meaning of world events."[12] Already in the first minutes of his talk Barth made it clear that he wasn't thinking of asking this, that the Bible deals first of all and finally with the knowledge of God as our origin, and only from there with the knowledge of "ourselves" and "our present moment in history."[13] Theologically one always had to begin with the knowledge of God: "The knowledge of God is...the presupposition that we... always *start with* in our attempts to search for meaning."[14]

In Barth's conviction the knowledge of God stands at the center of the Bible. Our problem however is that we do not allow ourselves to be determined by this knowledge and do not live according to it. For that reason, the biblical texts arouse unrest in us, and rightly so.

Religion in Barth's eyes is the human attempt to evade this disquiet. It placates human beings that everything is still in order with them. Yet religion's "existence is only justified when it continually overcomes itself."[15] Its task would be "to point to the X that stands above the world *and* church."[16] Instead, it adorns itself with feelings and symbols, with morality, dogma, and cult, in order to cover up its own relativity. "Trust in God is recommended to the astonished world as a thoroughly attainable and very useful requisite for life...Without blushing one speaks of 'Christian' manners, families, clubs and institutions...[In religion] the human being has taken possession of the divine and put it under his management."[17] In religion human beings attempt to build God into their lives and satisfy their needs with God.

God however—as Barth formulated it, similarly to the religious scholar Rudolf Otto—is "the *wholly* other."[18] As this wholly other, God wants to be "Lord of our life, the eternal Lord of the world."[19] God is not part of this world. The kingdom of God of which the Bible speaks does not pick up on something that exists in the world, rather it is something radically new and therefore a great No to this world.

That nonetheless out of God's No something positive can emerge, out of death life again, is by no means self-evident, but comes solely through God. Barth gives two examples for this: the resurrection and the forgiveness of sins. The resurrection is not the natural course of life, as when spring comes after winter, but rather in it something new happens that the world was not able to bring about on its own. Resurrection is "the absolute, pure miracle."[20] The forgiveness of sins as well is not something that can be derived from the world. Forgiveness of sins does not mean to take into consideration that a person has had a difficult life or didn't mean to do something evil. Forgiveness of sins comes, when it comes, non-derivably. Both resurrection as well as forgiveness are grace that only God can give.

What can a person do for this? Nothing at all. We can only practice "patience" and "waiting," in a "sudden stopping, focused gazing, and tense listening."[21] Barth rediscovered this stance in Matthias Grünewald's depiction of John the Baptist in the crucifixion in the Isenheim Altar, "in the way his pointing hand is twisted in an almost impossible manner," pointing away from himself to the crucified.[22]

The students attending Barth's lecture remained unimpressed.[23] Barth's Berlin teacher Adolf von Harnack however was outraged. He had addressed the conference beforehand and stayed to listen to Barth. Barth reported later of Harnack's reaction: "since Kierkegaard...the subject had never been made *so* bad as just now!"[24] One day later the two met again in the home of the Basel church historian Eberhard Vischer. Barth told Thurneysen afterward:

> Both gentlemen [thought]...I should better keep my view of God...to myself, and not make it an "export article" (!). Finally I was scolded as a Calvinist and intellectualist and released with the prediction that according to all experiences of church history I would found a sect and would receive inspirations.[25]

Barth did not let himself be intimidated, instead challenging Thurneysen and himself:

> Both of us must now get down to business to prepare for new deeds. It is obvious that the idol is tottering. Harnack gives the impression of a basically broken man, he really knew astonishingly little outside of his lofty little jokes.[26]

For his part Harnack wrote to Vischer that in Barth human religiosity was being destroyed:

> The consideration that this kind of religion cannot be converted at all into real life, but rather can only appear above it like a meteor and indeed an exploding one, does not much soften the impression, because one must always again ask oneself: how can a *pastor*, who should still be a *spiritual counselor*, judge in such a manner? My impression was softened only through the personal discussion on

Sunday, giving me a little hope that Barth could still change, if he liberates himself from his arbitrarily worked out biblicism.[27]

In intensive conversations with Friedrich Gogarten in Safenwil in October 1920, it became clear to Barth what had to happen with the *Epistle to the Romans*. On a bicycle trip they took together to visit Barth's brother Peter in Madiswil he decided "to upend the whole thing and rebuild it."[28] After Gogarten's departure he wrote Thurneysen that the *Epistle to the Romans* had started "to shed its skin, i.e., I received the inspiration that as it is, it is impossible to simply publish it, rather it must be reformed in head and its members."[29] The first edition seemed to Barth "all at once … sloppy, cluttered, fuzzy etc.," it gave "constant occasion for misunderstandings and errors"[30] and was "far too much disposed toward Hurra!"[31] Barth immediately informed his publisher in Munich that the first edition could not be republished, and began with a new draft.[32]

Eduard Thurneysen reacted to Barth's news with relief, for in the first version he had "always sensed the struggling, the blurred manner of style and, that means, of knowledge in certain places."[33] Thurneysen was enthused about the first sample pages from the new draft that Barth sent:

> Now everything is more concise, reserved, filled out, dense … the modern-blurred manner is gone, one immediately gets the most central messages and is surrounded by the whole outrageous, staring strangeness and steepness of the new knowledge. It appears to me that you are writing this time not so much with "the joy of discovery" as with a certain wrath and not without your own horror.[34]

From the end of October 1920 to the beginning of September 1921 Barth worked on the entirely new version of what later would be called the "Second Epistle to the Romans."[35] Thurneysen was intensively involved in the reworking, reading, and commenting, chapter by chapter. Barth adopted many of his suggestions word-for-word,[36] which was also possible since Thurneysen in the meantime had learned to be faithful to Barth's way of speaking.[37] Barth mentioned this situation in the preface to the new version: "No specialist will find out where in our winning team the thoughts of the one begin and those of the other end."[38]

Shortly before his move to Göttingen Karl Barth thanked his friend once again emphatically:

> If nothing else, I want to give you *very* heartfelt thanks after all for all the effort and time that you now and for eleven months devoted to combing through this thing, putting aside the fact that without you I probably would still today be stuck grumpily with Schleiermacher or socialism, and never would have written either the first or the second Epistle to the Romans, and certainly would never have been in the strange situation now to turn this in to the professor as well.[39]

Thurneysen replied to Barth with similar gratitude: "What a musty corner I would be sitting in today without you and the sharp tempo that you set, and the grace that I could keep up with you. I lived and live by your urge and drive to move ahead."[40]

In his work on the text Barth repeatedly had to "pause in shock at seeing the change that is in process."[41] He consciously said farewell to the influences of Kutter and Ragaz that could still be found in the first version.[42] He believed that although he certainly had not yet reached the "true face of all these dark runes," that is, Paul's central concepts, he was however "a *little* closer to the subject matter ... than then."[43] He was glad that now the "pantheistic shimmer was gone," but felt "during the chopping down of all the rampant shoots ... like ... Abraham when he had to sacrifice Isaac."[44] He bolstered himself: "But now it is time to go forward, the jungle has been entered."[45] After Barth had decided to move to Göttingen he tried with all his might to complete the manuscript for the second version beforehand. "For me this hot summer will remain ... unforgettable. I wander back and forth as if I were drunk between desk, dining table, bed, at every kilometer the next is already in sight."[46] The second version appeared shortly before Christmas 1921; 1922 was the publishing date.

The New Version of the *Epistle to the Romans*

In his preface to the new version Barth records that in terms of the first version "not a stone has been left standing."[47] For all that, even this version was only a "temporary result."[48] At the same time the "fronts had been moved."[49] Now he had "moved the position that had been achieved [in the first version] ... to points farther along, establishing and fortifying these anew."[50] For the attack on human beings and their world is now even more radically executed. Barth takes up the diagnosis of a principal and not merely historical crisis, as can be found in the early 1920s in the work of Ernst Bloch, Georg Lukács, Paul Tillich, and others.[51] Barth insisted that this crisis came about through God himself, and could not be overcome in any way by human beings.

In his preface Barth names four factors that had influenced the new version: "*First* and foremost: the continued preoccupation with Paul."[52] Further was the aforementioned all too positive reception of the volume as well as his study of Franz Overbeck.[53] In addition came Kierkegaard and Dostoyevsky, toward whom Thurneysen in particular had pointed him, as well as Kant and Plato, as they had been conveyed to him by the texts of his brother Heinrich.[54]

Heinrich Barth had held a lecture on "The Knowledge of God" at an Aarau student conference on March 24–6, 1919, that had led Barth "to envisage the wholly other of the kingdom of God much more powerfully."[55] In a platonic continuation of Marburg neo-Kantianism, Heinrich Barth had stressed that the origin from which all knowledge comes is not an unending extension of the earthly, but rather is radically beyond the world.[56] No passage exists between what is given in this world and God as the origin: "If we are to speak of God and the divine, it must be through something completely new, absolutely superior, through something which in principle surpasses that [thing-oriented] way of thinking."[57] The origin possesses the "only legitimate..., genuine...and true... transcendence."[58] Because of this, the philosophical movement of thought (*Denkbewegung*) must turn around and begin with the origin. Its transcendence cannot be derived from what has already become, rather, "orientation toward the origin means an everlasting breaching of what has become."[59] Heinrich Barth related this conception of radical transcendence mainly to the platonic idea as something divine; his brother then applied it to the Christian God.

Karl Barth found this thought process was confirmed in Søren Kierkegaard, who assumed an "infinite qualitative difference"[60] between God and human:

> What drew us to him in particular, what delighted and instructed, was the unrelenting critique, in its cutting and separating, in which we saw him tackle all the speculation that blurs the infinite qualitative difference between God and human. Thus in that second phase of the revolution in which we found ourselves he became and was for us one of the roosters whose voice appeared to announce, from near and far, the breaking of a truly new day.[61]

In his preface to the new version Barth responded to various criticisms of the first version of *Epistle to the Romans*. Some had alleged that his text was too complicated, whereby "*simplicity* is the sign of the divine."[62] Barth countered "that it does not even occur to me to believe that I speak or write 'the divine.' To my knowledge 'the divine' is not at all to be found in books."[63]

Others in turn insinuated a biblicism in Barth in which he all too naively reached for the biblical text. Barth responded that he was simply attempting to understand the biblical statements, and indeed also those that were objectionable to modern consciousness.[64] "Strictly speaking, the entire 'biblicism' that can be detected in me consists of the fact that it is my prejudice that the Bible is a good book and that it is worthwhile for someone to take its thoughts at the very least as seriously as their own."[65]

In the context of the charge of biblicism he was suspected of being an "enemy of *historical criticism*."[66] Barth therefore again emphasized that he "explicitly acknowledged" the "right and necessity" of historical-critical research.[67] But he was disturbed by "its stopping with an explanation of the text that I cannot call an explanation but merely the first primitive attempt at one."[68] As Barth similarly had made clear in his introductory sentences to the first version of *Epistle*, from Calvin one could learn the real meaning of critical understanding. Calvin too had initially worked out "what is said," but then he thought about it for a long time, until the wall between the first and the sixteenth century became *transparent*, until Paul *spoke* there and the sixteenth century human being *heard* here, until the conversation between the original document and the reader became focused completely on the *subject matter* (which here and there *can* not be a different one!).[69]

Barth then formulated the famous statement: "For me, those who do historical-criticism must be *more critical!*"[70] To read a New Testament text truly "critically," that is, "with discrimination," means to measure all its statements in terms of the decisive subject matter about which its speaks and relate them to it.[71] In reading critically "the connection of the words to the Word in the words must be uncovered."[72]

Finally, in his preface Barth gets back to the charge that in the first version he had not interpreted the biblical texts at all, but rather had far more applied his own theological system to the texts. Barth acknowledges that his starting point was a theological basic idea:

If I have a "system," it consists of the fact that as much as possible I keep my eye on that which Kierkegaard called the "infinite qualitative difference" of time and eternity, in its negative and positive significance. "God is in heaven, you upon earth" [cf. Eccles. 5:2].[73]

In his new interpretation of the Epistle to the Romans Barth carries out this thought more consistently than in the first version. There is no passage from human beings to God. Even when God is revealed, God does not enter this world. To portray this Barth uses striking images: The human world and the world of God intersect like "two planes, a known and an unknown."[74] The line of intersection of these two planes however is not apparent, it "wants to be recognized."[75] Where can it be seen? Only in the one single "point of the line of intersection," in Jesus of Nazareth.[76] In our world however this point of connection between God and human beings has "no extension at all."[77] That which is historically noticeable about Jesus is only something inner worldly.

The effect, or much more the astonishing meteoric craters and caverns by which this [point of connection] makes itself noticeable within what is historically visible, are not the other world that in Jesus touches our world, even if they are called "the life of Jesus." And to the extent that this our world is touched in Jesus by the other world, it ceases to be historically, temporally, materially, directly visible.[78]

Stated differently: God cannot be discovered historically. God is known in Jesus Christ as the unknown God.[79] Knowledge of God is a radical eschatological event that stands at right angles to temporality and historicity.[80]

Jesus Christ's special significance for the knowledge of God comes through his resurrection.[81] Through this he has been established as the son of God. Even this establishment however cannot be grasped historically.[82] Barth describes the resurrection using an image from Kierkegaard: "In the resurrection the new world of the Holy Spirit touches the old world of the flesh. But it touches it like a tangent does a circle, without touching it, and precisely by *not* touching it, it touches it as its boundary, as *new* world."[83] Jesus Christ bridges the distance between God and humanity, but in such a way that he precisely underscores it.[84]

Again and again, Barth pounds the point home: the distinction between God and human beings is not only one of degree, as if all the goodness of human beings occurs in God in a multiplied fashion. The distinction between God and human beings is categorical, fundamental. No human conception of God is adequate for describing God.

> God, the pure boundary and pure beginning of everything that we are, have, and do, who stands in infinite qualitative distinction over against human beings and all that is human, is never ever identical to what we call God, experience as God, expect and adore, the absolute Stop! against all human disquiet and the absolute Onward! toward all human quiet, the Yes in our No and the No in our Yes, the First and the Last... and as such the Unknown, never ever however one thing among others in the center that is known to us, God the Lord, Creator and Redeemer—that is *the living God!*[85]

Thus all differences between people become relative:

> Measured by the standards of God, human merits lose their height, their seriousness, their scope, they become relative. Even the highest, most intellectual, most justifiable contradictions among human beings appear here as they are: in their natural, inner-worldly, profane "materialistic" significance. The valleys are lifted up, the mountains made low [Isa. 40:4]. The "battle of the good against the bad" is over. Human beings appear on *one* line.[86]

God encounters the entire world, then, as its judge. Thus the history of the world comes to its end: "the judgement of God is the *end* of history, not the beginning of a new second history. History is over, it will not be continued."[87]

But the matter does not rest there. God does not just bring things to their end, but through God all is made new:

> The One who judges is also the One who puts everything in order... The most radical execution of history, the No under which all flesh comes, the absolute crisis that God means for the world of human beings, of time and things, is also the recurrent thread running through its Being and its Being-So.[88]

God indeed judges human beings and their world. But at the same time God desires the life of those who are judged.[89] Out of the negation through God something positive springs forth: "The transitory *is*, recognized as such, the allegory to the everlasting. The final submission to God's wrath is the belief in God's justice. For as the *unknown* God, God becomes *known*."[90]

In his first version of the *Epistle to the Romans* Barth had described the "already now" and the "not yet" of the kingdom of God, and of the new, faithful I in each case, as a process brought about by God *within* history.[91] Now he emphasizes in both cases the "not yet." The kingdom of God is not a germinating seed within history.[92] There is no continuity at all between human action and divine action; only God acts in a good way. Human action never belongs on the side of God. For that reason the *fundamental* ethical deed of human beings is the surrender of their actions to God's judgement.[93]

Human faith, too, is entirely the miracle and act of God. It is not a "human attitude" or "disposition," but rather "void."[94] Faith is miracle, beginning, creation, election through God, it is the "impossible possibility."[95] If a person comes to faith, this is always divine grace.[96] "For that reason faith is never finished, never given, never ensured, viewed from the psychological perspective it is always and always again the leap into the unknown, into the darkness, into thin air."[97] The believing subject cannot be determined as such:

> through faith we are what *we* are *not*. What...looms into everyday human life as something that cannot be described or can only be evoked as vacuum, what from the side of all human comprehension always and everywhere only is negated, and precisely with that always and everywhere is thoroughly witnessed to, what from our perspective can only appear as the center between two infinitely continuing branches of a hyperbola, and precisely as such is in an impossible manner End and Beginning—that is the New Person, the subject of the predicate "faith." *I am not* this subject, so long as it as subject, as that which it is, is absolutely beyond, the radical Other, to everything that I am. And—*I am* this subject, so long as that which it does, its predicate—faith—consists simply in the constitution of identity between it and me... *Solely* through faith am I what I am (not!).[98]

According to Barth this dynamic, entirely determined by God and beyond this world, is the essence of Christian eschatology and characterizes the attitude of Christian faith toward the world: "Christendom that is not completely and totally eschatology has completely and totally nothing to do with *Christ*."[99]

Barth distinguishes sharply between faith characterized in this way and religion: the problem of religion is that it thinks "it is the condition...for God's positive relationship to humankind."[100] While indeed people who believe also have feelings, convictions, attitudes, piety, these however are not what is essential.[101] Barth arrives at this conclusion:

Therefore no religious message, no news and instruction about the divinity or the deification of human beings, but rather the message from a God who is completely other, and of whom the human being as human will never know nor have, and from whom for that very reason salvation comes.[102]

Even the Christian church belongs on the side of religion.[103] It is the

> attempt to make the divine human, to make it time-bound, to make it material, to make it worldly, to make it into a practical Something and all of this for the wellbeing of human beings... all in all: the attempt to make the incomprehensible and yet so unavoidable path... comprehensible.[104]

That its existence is nonetheless justified does not depend upon it, but again only on God.[105]

With the complete separation of God and the world that is implemented in the second *Epistle to the Romans*, Barth took the Reformation's doctrine of justification, that the justification of human beings before God depends not on the human but alone upon God, to its extreme. He smashed all human self-assurance and all religious precepts that had been taken as obvious. His concern was that first of all one "endures in this situation."[106] Precisely this was faith.[107]

Critics and Admirers

Barth was already professor in Göttingen when his revision appeared. The attention drawn by the book was correspondingly large. Paul Althaus, at that time professor in Rostock, criticized the book for its description of the relationship between God and history. In his view, Barth's approach of a "complete transcendence of divine life over against history"[108] led to the dissolution of the concept of revelation as well as to the renunciation of a Christian ethic characterized by concrete content. Barth's concept of God, with its emphasis on eternity, otherness, and the unknowness of God, had not been won from biblical texts or Christian belief, but was simply being presupposed by Barth.[109] A relationship between God and the human being could no longer be spoken of here. While it was indeed asserted that God was the origin, the Creator, this was not developed at all.[110] God was only great "through the failure of human beings."[111] With that Barth was going too far beyond Reformation theology: "Either the human or God, [for Barth] that applies not only, as with the Reformers, within the question of justification, but fully in general and in every respect."[112] From that follows in Barth: "Every direct religious assessment of history is invalidated. 'God in history'—that doesn't exist."[113] But when Barth negates the historicity of the revelation, the concept of God loses all content.[114]

Barth was bypassing the fact that God is revealed in moral law as well. In the concrete earthly duties that we must fulfill, God passes on responsibility to us.[115]

> History points to God, not only as its *boundary* but as the *Lord* who gives the vocation and the hour and demands the deed. In that through the transitory, lesser, highly this-sided relationships of our world we nonetheless discover responsibilities that have the tone of an unconditional commitment, we learn to believe in eternity.[116]

Later, during the Third Reich, Barth would turn precisely against such an *unconditional* commitment to something internal to history, also as an opponent of Althaus.[117]

The Tübingen theologian Adolf Schlatter was critical that Barth detached the Epistle to the Romans from the context of its own era and was interpreting it as a timeless word for us today.[118] By underscoring God as the wholly Other he was emptying the concept of God, rendering theology as thinking about God "as foolishness."[119] Schlatter warned against Barth's idea that faith was "a leap into the void," for faith needed content

> that is accessible for our perception and can be appropriated by us with a reasoned judgement. It receives this content through Christ. That is the statement that comes from Paul...with that, a deep gap opens up between [Barth's] interpretation and the Epistle to the Romans. Paul did not leap into the void, rather he followed Jesus.[120]

Barth welcomed this critique of Schlatter, for it was proof for him that he had gone his own way over against the positive theology represented by Schlatter.[121]

In contrast Rudolf Bultmann, professor in Marburg since 1921, praised Barth's book as standing together with Schleiermacher's *On Religion: Speeches to Its Cultural Despisers* and Rudolf Otto's *The Idea of the Holy*, in that it seeks "to prove *the independence and absoluteness of religion.*"[122] Bultmann agreed with Barth's distinction of faith from religious experiences and feelings and historically describable processes. Despite this esteem he found Barth's definition of faith to be too speculative. Faith does after all take place in human consciousness; it is "the paradoxical fact of the appropriation of justification through the human being (*this* human being) in human consciousness."[123] Bultmann also praised Barth's concern to work out "the subject matter" of the Epistle to the Romans. But he could not recognize that Barth really interrogated the individual statements of the Epistle and measured whether in them the subject matter was being expressed. And that

> everywhere in the Epistle to the Romans the subject matter must have won adequate expression is truly an impossible precondition, if one doesn't want to

construct a modern dogma of inspiration, and such a thing does certainly seem to stand behind Barth's exegesis... no person—including Paul—[speaks] only from the subject matter itself... Other spirits are speaking through him as well besides the *pneuma Christou* [the spirit of Christ].[124]

Barth reacted to Bultmann's critique in the preface to the third edition of his *Epistle to the Romans* (which essentially was an unrevised reprint of the second version) with the message that he was completely unable to make this distinction between biblical passages in which the spirit of Christ was speaking and others in which this was not the case. The spirit of Christ could not be found directly in any passage in the text of Paul's Epistle to the Romans. "*Everything* is litera [letter], the voice of 'other' spirits."[125] "The spirit of Christ is not a position from which one can lecture Paul or whomever."[126]

The critique of the young Dietrich Bonhoeffer followed a direction similar to that of Bultmann. Bonhoeffer fundamentally shared Barth's approach based upon revelation, but was critical that Barth didn't manage to conceive of "the new I... in unity with the empirical total-I"; the new I remained the "heavenly double" of the empirical I.[127] This bypasses the historicity of human beings. When one must then believe that one's own empirical I coincides with the new I, "this pushes the act of faith in an erroneous direction. Faith [correctly understood] knows only an outward-going direction towards cross and resurrection."[128]

Barth's second *Epistle to the Romans* had even greater influence than the first. Even today it draws attention. A few years ago the novelist Martin Walser made it the basis for his book *Über Rechtfertigung, eine Versuchung* ("On Justification, a Temptation"). Walser's theme is the basic human need to justify ourselves, that is, the wish to feel and know that we are justified. As a rule, human beings attempt justification through their deeds, yet do not manage this, succumbing instead to a continual compulsion that they must be right: "To be right is the accepted substitute for justification."[129] Today the passive nature, the aspect of grace in justification, is rejected: "When we are doing well, we attribute our well-being to ourselves. That is, to our works. There may be fewer of those who still experience their success as grace. We would rather call it luck. Or chance. Or, so we appear greater to ourselves, justice."[130] The need for true justification however is not satisfied by having to be right and with doing well. In contrast Karl Barth had managed to "opt out of this contest of having to be right, because he could not numb the immemorial need to seek justification."[131] Here Barth's cultural critique had its starting point: "Karl Barth's book is the practiced destruction of the scenery of culture that makes us forget that at one time justification was our need."[132] Barth insisted that only God could justify human beings.[133] His book keeps us awake "to the lack of something through God's absence."[134] Walser felt this lack himself: "When I hear from an atheist, and even from one who 'confesses,' that there is no God, then I think: But God is missing. To me."[135]

What is Dialectical Theology?

Barth's book did not only find resonance in the review journals of the theological guild. Many younger pastors were stirred up by his approach, and as a consequence Barth had to clarify in several lectures how he now understood the task of theology.

Karl Barth was invited to Schulpforta on the Saale river for a pastoral conference on July 25, 1922, to give an introduction into his theology under the title "The Need and Promise of Christian Proclamation." He began with the comment that he did not really wish to speak about "his theology"; there was no "cathedral or fortress" here into which he could introduce them.[136] What he was attempting was basically "a kind of *marginal note*."[137] He then portrayed to the pastors how the situation of preaching had led him to think about where the correct path lay between the two points of reference of the sermon: "the problematic of human living on the one side and the content of the Bible on the other."[138] He however had not found a way to mediate between these two poles. His theology was "the expression of this desperate situation and the question of the pastor when he dares to take on this task... a description as true as possible to the pressure under which the human sinks."[139] The question that had preoccupied him as he wrestled with Paul's Epistle to the Romans was: "What does preaching mean? Not: how does one *do* it? But rather how *can* one do it?"[140]

The situation on Sunday mornings was something very special, since here people—"even if it is only an old grandma"[141]—come to church with the expectation that there something special is going to happen. They come with the question whether the Gospel of God is dependable, whether "*the* Word, which promises grace in *judgement*, life in *death*, the beyond in the *here and now*, *God's* word" is really true.[142] The preacher must take this question, which is aimed at the ultimate, seriously. He may not shrug off his listeners with penultimate answers that evade this question.

For the promise that the preacher is speaking God's Word is in effect. He must understand his task in the sense of this promise. But it can only be believed that the preacher speaks God's Word. Therefore Barth summarizes: "Utter the words, *Veni creator spiritus*! (Come Creator, Holy Spirit!), which is for now...more hopeful than triumphant, as if one had already had it. Once you have heard this sigh, you have been introduced to 'my theology.'"[143]

Barth worked out a further clarification of his approach in his epochal lecture "The Word of God as the Task of Theology," which he held on October 3, 1922, at the invitation of Martin Rade, at a gathering of the Association of Friends of the *Christliche Welt* in Elgersburg, Thuringia. Barth traveled to the lecture from Göttingen without having completed his text. The last third of it was "written in a mood of desperation on my knees on the train a few hours before I held it!!"[144]

Barth began his lecture before 300 to 400 listeners with the statement: "We theologians endure hardship because of our vocation; a hardship in which we can perhaps try to soothe ourselves, but never find comfort."[145] This hardship consisted not of variations in mood, not in the insecure social standing of pastors in the contemporary world, not even in the backward nature of the church leadership. The hardship rested far more "in the subject matter, in the task that confronts us."[146]

The task of theologians was: "*We ought to speak of God.*"[147] Barth derived this from the expectation that people placed upon theologians. They did not need theologians for life's usual problems, but on the basis of their "existential need."[148] They were seeking God as "the answer to the ultimate question."[149] People needed theologians not for life, "but to *die*," on "the path on the razor-sharp ridge between *time* and *eternity*," "on the *boundaries* of humanity."[150] The God question affects all people, whether they are religious or not. "The human in his humanity cries out for God . . . not for solutions, but for *salvation*. Not for something human again, but for God, yet for God as the Savior of his *humanity*."[151]

Friedrich Schleiermacher in particular had failed to see this:

> With all due respect to the brilliance of his life's work, I hold Schleiermacher to *not* be a good theological teacher for now, because as far as I can see, his work leaves fatally unclear the fact that the human as human finds himself in *need*, that is, in inescapable need. His work also leaves unclear that the entire stock of so-called religion, including Christianity, *participates* in this need. Thus he is vague on the point that speaking of God means something *other* than speaking about the human in a somewhat higher pitch.[152]

The answer to the existential questions of human beings can only come from outside, from God: The

> answer to the question, the end of the existential need, is the absolutely new event: the impossible *itself* becomes possible, *death* becomes life, *eternity* becomes time, and *God* himself becomes human. There is *no* way that leads to this *new* event; *no* human faculty that can apprehend it.[153]

Theologians should speak of God, but since they are human beings, according to Barth they cannot "speak God's word, that Word which can only come from God: The Word, *that God becomes human.*"[154] Theology has tried in two ways to address this conflict: the path of dogmatism and the path of criticism. Barth rejected both.

On the *path of dogmatism* one presents the "Christological, soteriological, and eschatological perspectives."[155] Here one makes concrete statements about

God and human beings. In terms of content the human need through the strong doctrine of sin is indeed correctly described and the attempt is made to explain the concept of God. But here the word "God" is turned "into an object, a thing... in our pragmatic way, we approach it like we would a myth: Here it is! Now believe it!"[156]

Barth rejects the *critical path* as well. It is the path of negation, where "anyone who wants to participate in God is bid to die as human being... to become purely receptive."[157] God, according to this path, is not an opposite, a something, rather "pure, all-filling Being. God is without any qualities."[158] This is the "way of mysticism."[159] In the negation of the human, the location is given where one can at best speak of God; but this does not actually speak of God.[160]

The only appropriate way for Barth is the *dialectical path*. He presumes the truth of both ways, but also the knowledge of their insufficiency. In the living center between the dogmatic statement about God and the mystical self-questioning of the human is the realization that "God (but truly God!) becomes human (but truly human!)."[161] "The true dialectician knows that this center is incomprehensible and invisible. He allows himself to be carried away into direct communication about it as seldom as possible..."[162]

The dialectical path for Barth is a path along a ridge:

> Along this narrow cliff ridge we can only walk—and keep walking, for if we stand still we will fall. It might be to the right or to the left, but it will definitely be down. Thus the only thing left is an appalling spectacle for all those overcome by dizziness, where we keep looking from one side to the other, from the position to its negation and the negation to its position. The only thing to do is to clarify the "Yes" in the "No" and the "No" in the "Yes," pausing no longer than a moment in the gaze of the "Yes" or the "No."[163]

Barth illustrated this dialectical dynamic in a series of examples: One had to

> speak of the glory of God in creation... only to swiftly and strongly emphasize the complete hiddenness in which God is for our eyes in nature... the image of God in humans is by no means to be spoken of apart from the warning once and for all that the human as we know him is a fallen creature, whose misery we know more about than his glory. That being said, however, sin should not be spoken of except to point out that we would not recognize it if it were not already forgiven us.[164]

There is no possibility to settle down conceptually in the No or the Yes. Dialectical theology is constantly in movement on the narrow ridge. The church history professor Erich Foerster from Greifswald (which is in a flat region of Germany) described the difficulty of Barth's theological approach this way: "For the son of the Swiss mountains this aspect may not seem so terrible as for the millions who live in the lowlands."[165]

When along this dialectical path it happens that God's word is truly spoken, then according to Barth this was not because of the theologians but because of God, in that "in the dialectician's unambiguous and ambiguous assertions, the living truth in the center, the reality of God, asserts *itself*."[166] Methodologically this could not be forced: "the possibility that God speaks when the human speaks of God is not contained in the dialectical way as such. It arises where even this way *leads up to the abyss*."[167]

The "hardship" of theologians, that they must speak of God but are not able to, was further developed by Barth in a third claim: "We ought to *know both*, that we ought to speak of God and cannot, *and precisely in this way, give God the glory*."[168] In this attitude rests "our promise."[169] For in human speaking, the speaking of God can occur; because of that the theologian can "speak loudly and strongly from the hope, from the hidden glory of our vocation, instead of speaking from the need."[170]

Which form of "dialectics" is encountered here now, in contrast to the period of the first *Epistle to the Romans*?[171] While Barth picked up anew on Hegel's thinking about thesis and antithesis, he no longer held possible a "suspension" (*Aufhebung*) of the contradiction in a synthesis on a higher level. Rather, the "contradiction... that is *precisely not* to be mediated on a higher level... [must] be held open, in the interest of truth."[172] If the thesis therefore states: As theologians we must speak of God, and the antithesis is: As human beings, we are unable to do so, then the statement that connects these—the theologian should know both these things, and with that honor God—holds both, thesis and antitheses, in a state of tension, and at the same time points to the reason for theological speech, namely, that God spoke of himself. The dogmatic path is one-sidedly fixated on the thesis; the critical path on the antithesis. Responsible theological, simply dialectical speech knows that both must be conceived at the same time.[173]

But for Barth the "*inner dialectic of the subject matter*"[174] is even more important than this method, for God's action toward human beings is itself dialectic, it occurs in the dialectic of judgement and grace.[175] Precisely in the No to the human being God is seeking "the relationship to the human."[176] The Yes that is spoken in this relationship does not however relativize the No.[177]

Finally, the existence of human beings also takes place dialectically.[178] Human beings are created by God, and they go toward God's future.[179] But the salvation of the judged and pardoned human being cannot be seen in the present; it lies entirely in the future of God.[180] The unity between the human being as she is here on earth and the new human being as she is in the eyes of God, exists in faith. This brings Barth to the "dialectical" formula: "By faith we are what *we are not*."[181]

Dialectical Traveling Companions: Brunner, Bultmann, Gogarten

It was essential for the impact of dialectical theology that it was not only represented by Barth and Thurneysen, but that an entire group of theologians quickly came together, at least for a few years,[182] who thought along similar lines. They included Emil Brunner, Rudolf Bultmann, and Friedrich Gogarten.

The pastor Emil Brunner began corresponding with Karl Barth on April 1, 1916, because he had read Barth's Safenwil sermon on "The Pastor Who Pleases the People" and wanted to let Barth know that something in him said "a simple loud Yes to it," even if he wasn't sure that he was "'fully' in agreement with it."[183] Brunner praised Barth that in his sermon

> the last corner of the pastor's gown and all church ointment [had] disappeared, and a hearty German is spoken with the people, plainspoken, no frills, as I believe I have never heard. The people will have to notice finally that the things of God are just as real and pressing as some kind of livestock deal or a foreclosure... If only people notice *this* and God begins to become understandable as someone who interrupts them at home and in the alleys, then finally the fog that the church allows around God is ripped apart.[184]

The son of a primary school teacher, Brunner was born in Winterthur and had been confirmed by Hermann Kutter. After studying theology in Zurich and Berlin he successfully completed his assistant pastorate under Kutter.[185] In 1916 he became pastor in Obstalden in the canton of Glarus. That year he began fifty years of correspondence with Karl Barth that ended only with Brunner's death. In the same year, on May 23, 1916, they encountered one another for the first time at a religious-social conference in Brugg.[186] Three-quarters of a year later, on February 5–6, 1917, they got to know each other personally at Thurneysen's rectory in Leutwil.[187]

Brunner, like Barth and many other theologians, had the impression during those years of the world war that a new theological awakening was necessary.[188] At the same time he had the feeling—as Brunner wrote Barth in his third letter—that in his own search he was going in circles.[189] Barth replied that it was exactly the same for him; this only showed that God "is not to be found in the psychological labyrinth of our religious experiences."[190] One should not take the state of one's mood seriously either positively or negatively, rather we must "with eyes closed, so to speak, hold...to God," and direct ourselves toward "God...in God's *objectivity*," for only God was constant and reliable, not our religious inner lives.[191]

In Brunner Barth quickly discovered a "traveling companion" and in July 1916 suggested they address each other in the familiar "Du."[192] Barth sent him the book of sermons that he had co-published with Thurneysen, *Seek God and You Shall Live!* By Brunner's own account he read it with great delight, because it avoided every kind of church jargon. In the book was "something living...that bristles with all its might against letting itself be encapsulated in the old dead words."[193] In their sermons Barth and Thurneysen dared, "in a very unmodern way, to start with God but not with some doctrine rather with God's deeds, with the God who builds God's kingdom on earth."[194]

Brunner wrote an emphatic appreciation of Barth's first *Epistle to the Romans*.[195] In his eyes the book was "a *hit*," "a revolution of 'theological' thought."[196] Here one heard "finally at last *Paul*, called to be an apostle of Jesus Christ."[197] Barth had carried through Kutter's revolution,[198] for he was thinking "so to speak from the standpoint of God."[199] Barth was saying "what must now be said" and posed "the subject matter, not put off by the public."[200]

Brunner's 1924 book *Die Mystik und das Wort* ("Mysticism and the Word") is a sign of the closeness he sought to Barth. Here Brunner portrayed mysticism and Christian faith brusquely against each other: mysticism was "the finest, most sublime form of nature-worship, paganism, the objectification of the spirit."[201] Christian faith draws a sharp distinction between God and humans; in contrast mysticism allows the I to flow together with the universe.[202] Only the word brings clarity and light; mysticism however hedges around the word, it develops "only in 'mystical semi-darkness.'"[203] "Mysticism seeks the twilight and silence. Faith finds the day in the word... *Either mysticism or the word*."[204] Starting from this insight, Brunner turns sharply against Schleiermacher, who had transformed Christian faith into mysticism through his appeal to feeling.[205] Brunner for that reason in his book wants to uncover "the contrasting nature of that 'which Schleiermacher wanted' and of the apostles' and Reformers' world of faith."[206]

Barth wrote Brunner that he viewed him

> with the highest admiration as you slaughter the man, surely an act of the highest merit that will not only make an impression, but an epoch. You know, I *could* not give it to an individual historical figure and his work because I can't lose the feeling that in such an extirpation however right it is, "somehow" it would be an injustice. But perhaps that is only my clumsiness and short-sightedness and ignorance, which leaves me "waiting" (despite all the disgust with which Schleiermacher fills me), whether there were not indeed something to it.[207]

Despite the closeness to Barth that Brunner felt, he believed that on certain points he could not agree with him.[208] Already in 1921 they fought about the question of the relationship between the philosophical idea of God and the Christian revelation of God. Brunner was disturbed by how decidedly Barth took his position: "Must then the conceptual clock of the other always indicate exactly the same hour as yours, so that it shows a 'proficient way of thinking'?...For the sake of the matter...I would like to ask you to write your fellow truth-seekers somewhat less pope-like."[209] Brunner asked Thurneysen whether he might use his influence over Barth "so that he may be preserved from holding himself to be the dear Lord."[210] This reached Barth and he implored Brunner: "My dear friend, please take everything in the ambiguity and harmlessness with which it is intended, and above all: please don't take me—and you yourself so bloody earnestly, you dreadful seeker of truth with all your systematic suction cups and tentacles!"[211] The relationship remained full of tension even in the years to follow.

Barth knew Rudolf Bultmann from his time studying in Marburg; they had often encountered each other at Martin Rade's home. In 1916 Bultmann became "extraordinary professor" for New Testament in Breslau, then in 1920 full professor in Gießen before transferring in 1921 to Marburg. Bultmann had written critically about Barth's first *Epistle to the Romans*. While he welcomed its "religious cultural criticism," in its positive expositions Bultmann could hardly "see anything other than an arbitrary trimming of the Pauline myth of Christ."[212] He praised Barth's second version however positively[213] and at that point wrote him in the "hope of future cooperation."[214] The two met in October 1922 in Elgersburg in conjunction with Barth's lecture, "The Word of God as the Task of Theology," for a conversation that Bultmann wished to continue.[215] Barth in 1923 felt something like a "wireless telegraphy between you and me. I feel as if the certain agreement, with furrowed brow and shaking head, that you bring to my goings-on, is the most normal behavior that I can expect from others toward me."[216]

Bultmann explicitly agreed with dialectical theology and its critique of liberal theology in his February 1924 lecture in Marburg, "Die liberale Theologie und die jüngste theologische Bewegung" ("Liberal Theology and the Most Recent Theological Movement").

> The object of study in theology is God, and the charge against liberal theology is that it has not dealt with God, but with human beings. God means the radical negation and suspension of human beings; therefore theology, whose object is God, can only...have as its content [the word of the Cross]...[this] however is...[a scandal] for human beings. And so the charge against liberal theology is that it attempted to avoid this...[scandal] or...to soften [it].[217]

Liberal theology represented a pantheistic view of history, in which God's work was not associated with individual historical events or persons, as in the Old Testament, but rather with the development of the true, good, and beautiful in the history of humanity. With that however "the human being is deified."[218] Bultmann repeatedly warns that God is "absolutely beyond this world," calling *all* human action "into question."[219] No human action can be identified directly with the will of God. The justification of the human being before God is always God's judgement, never a fact on the human side.[220] "The new human is always the One beyond this world whose identity with the human on this side can only be believed in faith."[221]

Barth heard Bultmann's lecture in Marburg in person. He reported contentedly to his friends in Switzerland: "Marburg has now truly become one of the points on the map of middle Europe on which the eye can rest with satisfaction."[222] For several years Bultmann and Barth worked together—always however using the formal "Sie."

Friedrich Gogarten[223] had been a student of Adolf von Harnack and Ernst Troeltsch. In 1914 he published his book *Fichte als religiöser Denker* ("Fichte as a Religious Thinker"), which he had originally submitted to Ernst Troeltsch as his dissertation in Heidelberg, but then let it be published without a doctoral examination process. Since 1917 Gogarten had been a pastor in Stelzendorf, Thuringia. He broke radically with the cultural Protestantism of his teachers after the First World War.

In 1920 Gogarten drew attention with his essay *"Zwischen den Zeiten"* ("Between the Times").[224] In it he picked up on the diagnosis of that era that was then customary, which spoke of a "turning of the times," leading to a "new humanity" and a "new time."[225] Over against this Gogarten's diagnosis was that the world stood "between the times."[226] He concurred that the old times had passed. But the contemporary situation was characterized thoroughly by peoples' distrust of their own concepts as well. Through that the human being had become free: "The room became free for the God question. Finally."[227] The new time had not yet begun:

> The times fell away from each other and now time stands still... Let us protect ourselves in this hour from nothing so much as the consideration of what we should now do. We stand in this hour not before our wisdom, rather we stand before God. This hour is not our hour. *We* have now no time. *We* stand between the times.[228]

Barth warmly thanked Gogarten for this *"Stop"* and asked him: "Please raise your voice *loudly*! You have the thing to say that in Germany now must be said, and which one will perhaps more willingly buy from you than from us Swiss."[229]

On September 30 of the same year Gogarten held a widely regarded lecture on the Wartburg on *"Die Krisis der Kultur"* ("The Crisis of Culture").[230] Gogarten deliberately did not name a concrete example of the crisis and protested against deriving from the crisis any premature call for change.[231] He disagreed with Oswald Spengler's thesis in *The Decline of the West* that while religion as a cultural force was also subject to this crisis, it could at the same time transform it.[232] The present moment was not the beginning of something new but it must be held out as such in order that an encounter with God be reached. In light of the reality of God *everything* human, evil as well as good, was

> an apparition without substance. For right now it is being shown how everything, how all reality, has become a mirror for human beings in which they look at their own essence, sensationalizing their smallness and pitiful nature. It cannot last this way before God's light.[233]

Only after the world has gone through this judgement, this crisis, would it be able to receive once more a possible value. The crisis was not an internal world criticism of this or that, but rather a radical critique. Analogously to this critique, however, a Yes to the world was not possible based upon this or that good, but rather only based upon the world become new from the "eternal Word of God."[234] A religion that understood itself as part of culture could not be further helpful here, rather only a religion that passes "judgement...on the culture"[235] as a human undertaking, and indeed on the culture as a whole—and therefore on religion as well. Ultimately however God alone implements this judgement.

After the Wartburg lecture Gogarten traveled to Switzerland. He first visited Eduard Thurneysen, who wrote Barth that he was "astonished by how much there is in common between him and us. He comes from a very different side than we do, has wandered through all the wrong tracks and detours of mysticism and romanticism, but he now stands very close to us."[236] Shortly thereafter Gogarten spent several days with Karl Barth in Safenwil, whereupon Barth wrote the aforementioned letter to Thurneysen, that he had to start the *Epistle to the Romans* once more from the beginning. One month after the visit to Barth Gogarten thanked him for the time together:

> It seems to me as if I had known you forever and as if what we talked about during those brief days were things...that I together with you had always known. It is, I believe, good that I can only see you seldom. For through being together with you my thoughts are inspired in so many ways that it will take awhile before I can work through it all...It gladdens me to know of you and to sense the fellowship with you and your work.[237]

Following up, they sent each other publications and exchanged about the theological developments in Germany. Gogarten and Barth were often mentioned by others in one breath.[238] After 1921 they used the familiar "Du" with each other.

In August 1922 Barth, Thurneysen, and Gogarten, along with Georg Merz, decided at the "Bergli" to found a new journal, taking the name of Gogarten's diagnosis of their era: *Zwischen den Zeiten*.[239] Merz took over the editorial direction. From 1923 on, the magazine, with a printing of 2,000, shaped the

7.1. Friedrich Gogarten, Eduard Thurneysen, and Karl Barth at the "Bergli" at the founding of the journal *Zwischen den Zeiten*, 1922, © Karl Barth-Archive in Basel.

theological debates. It opened with Barth's lecture on "The Need and Promise of Christian Proclamation."[240]

Fifteen Questions and Sixteen Answers: The Controversy with Harnack

Beginning in the 1920s, the dialectical theology represented by Barth and his companions was deeply debated. This is illustrated by Barth's fight with Adolf von Harnack. Harnack turned not only against the *Epistle to the Romans* but against the entire approach of dialectical theology on January 11, 1923, with *"Fünfzehn Fragen an die Verächter der wissenschaftlichen Theologie unter den Theologen"* ("Fifteen Questions to the Despisers of Academic Theology among the Theologians"). Martin Rade published it in *Die Christliche Welt*. Barth responded immediately with "Sechzehn Antworten an Herrn Professor von Harnack" ("Sixteen Answers to Professor von Harnack"), which appeared on February 8 in *Die Christliche Welt* as well. Harnack reacted with an open letter of March 8 to which Barth replied on April 26. With an "Afterword" on May 24 Harnack had the last word. The debate was noted that same year as far as the United States.[241]

In Barth and those like him Harnack diagnosed a theology that had departed from scholarship. He in contrast advocated that theology was scholarship and must remain so. Historical criticism had proven the many-voiced nature of the biblical texts. Simply speaking naively of "the 'Bible'" meant giving up the scholarly engagement with the biblical texts.[242] To understand these texts, one needed historical knowledge and critical reflection and could not, as Barth apparently wanted, simply "wait...until they beam into the heart."[243] Only historical work made it possible to gain a clear portrait of the person of Jesus Christ and to prevent people from following an *"imaginary* Christ."[244]

According to Harnack the cultural and moral critique of dialectical theology led ultimately to an atheistic culture and morality, for the joy of dialectical theology at the paradox prevents people from forming themselves toward an ethical personality shaped by awe and love. This was possible only through the preaching that God is completely and undialectically majesty and love.

In his answer Barth rejected the charge that he was a despiser of "the" academic theology, showing instead that the theology he had criticized had distanced itself from its basic *theme*, the *"one revelation of God,"* in which God had made himself known to human beings.[245] He rejected narrowing the academic nature of theology to historical-critical thinking: the "academic nature" of theology consisted of its "being tied to the memory that its object was *previously subject* and must repeatedly be so."[246] God is subject because God reveals himself to human beings; only when understood in this way can God be the object of theology. The value and convincing power of theology measured itself by God and God's revelation, not by the random, updated daily opinion of other university disciplines about what scholarship is. The task of theology, to convey the word of Christ, is one with the task of the sermon. In his ethical approach Harnack was bypassing the reality of sin, which is *"apostasy* of the human being from *God"* and cannot simply be overcome by exhortations to awe and love.[247]

Harnack reacted with the accusation that Barth's approach transformed "the theological lectern into a preacher's pulpit."[248] By refuting every possibility for being educated toward God through his reflections, he was cutting "every band between faith and the human, as did Marcion."[249] Harnack concluded his response with a pessimistic outlook for the Gospel: "If your approach achieves dominance, then it will no longer even be taught, rather given exclusively over to the hands of the revival preachers who create their own understanding of the Bible freely and set up their own dominion."[250]

Barth's reply to this open letter was astonishingly feisty. If nothing else Harnack had been his honored teacher and was twice his age. He encountered Harnack in this letter "as the finished and knowing one..., who [had] no time and no ear for answers other than those he would give himself, as well as for other questions than his own based upon the experience and reflection of a rich human life."[251] Then

Barth repeated his critique of theological scholarship that was narrowed to historical criticism.

In his brief "afterword" Harnack recorded once more that "revelation" was "not a scholarly term," and closed in a conciliatory tone. He had been moved in this debate by "no other intention... than to reach clarity with a theologian who was a friend."[252] For his part Barth later thanked Harnack in a private letter for the "thoroughly noble and conciliatory manner" of the debate. At the same time, he confessed that Harnack's objections had deepened his "insights... into the historical and objective relativity" of his own theological attempt, which beset him "day and night."[253]

Notes

1. Cf. "Autobiographical Sketches I. Münster, 1927," *Barth–Bultmann Letters* (GA 1), 155.
2. Cf. Letter of October 30, 1920, to Thurneysen, *Briefwechsel Barth-Thurneysen* I (GA 3), 437.
3. Cf. editor's foreword, *Der Römerbrief* (second version) (GA 47), 7f.
4. Cf. Friedrich Wilhelm Graf, "Overbeck, Franz Camille," *Religion in Geschichte und Gegenwart* (4), vol. 6, 758.
5. Overbeck, *Christentum und Kultur*, 100.
6. Barth, "Unerledigte Anfragen an die heutige Theologie," *Vorträge und kleinere Arbeiten 1914-1921* (GA 48), 637.
7. Barth, "Unerledigte Anfragen," *Vorträge und kleinere Arbeiten 1914-1921* (GA 48), 637.
8. Barth, "Unerledigte Anfragen," *Vorträge und kleinere Arbeiten 1914-1921* (GA 48), 658. Barth quotes (imprecisely) from Overbeck, *Christentum und Kultur*, 48: "A theology [is] not to be refounded other than with audacity." Regarding Barth's misinterpretation of the quotation—Overbeck was not at all considering founding theology anew—cf. Eberhard Jüngel, "Die theologischen Anfänge. Beobachtungen," in Jüngel, *Barth-Studien*, 62ff.
9. Cf. Barth, "Möglichkeiten liberaler Theologie heute," *Schweizerische theologische Umschau* 30 (1960), 101: "Theology [is] no longer to be justified... other than with audacity."
10. Barth, "Unerledigte Anfragen," *Vorträge und kleinere Arbeiten 1914-1921* (GA 48), 660. There were different reactions to this text by Barth, which appeared together with a sermon by Thurneysen in 1920. Eberhard Vischer was among the critical voices. He criticized the "theological skill" (which Barth "truly masterfully" understood) to evade Overbeck's fundamental critique of Christendom and theology through the parasitical attempt "to claim [Overbeck] for one's own theology and play it off against the theology of the other." (Vischer, "Overbeck und die Theologen," 126.)
11. Letter of July 23, 1920, to Gottfried Ludwig, cited in *Vorträge und kleinere Arbeiten 1914-1921* (GA 48), 628.

12. Letter of September 15, 1919, from Mattheus Vischer, cited in *Vorträge und kleinere Arbeiten 1914–1921* (GA 48), 663.
13. Barth, "Biblical Questions, Insights, and Vistas, 1920," *The Word of God and Theology*, 74.
14. Barth, "Biblical Questions," *Word of God and Theology*, 75.
15. Barth, "Biblical Questions," *Word of God and Theology*, 83.
16. Barth, "Biblical Questions," *Word of God and Theology*, 83. Translation revised.
17. Barth, "Biblical Questions," *Word of God and Theology*, 83. Translation revised.
18. Barth, "Biblical Questions," *Word of God and Theology*, 87. Translation revised. Cf. Otto, *The Idea of the Holy*, 27–31.
19. Barth, "Biblical Questions," *Word of God and Theology*, 87. Translation revised.
20. Barth, "Biblical Questions," *Word of God and Theology*, 97.
21. Barth, "Biblical Questions," *Word of God and Theology*, 84 and 80.
22. Barth, "Biblical Questions," *Word of God and Theology*, 82.
23. Cf. letter of April 20, 1920, from Thurneysen, *Briefwechsel Barth–Thurneysen* I (GA 3), 381.
24. Letter of December 23, 1935, to Agnes von Zahn-Harnack, cited in *Briefwechsel Barth–Thurneysen* I (GA 3), 410f., n. 2.
25. Letter of April 20, 1920, to Thurneysen, *Briefwechsel Barth–Thurneysen* I (GA 3), 379f.
26. Letter of April 20, 1920, to Thurneysen, *Briefwechsel Barth–Thurneysen* I (GA 3), 380.
27. Letter of April 26, 1920, from Adolf von Harnack to Eberhard Vischer, cited in *Der Römerbrief* (second version) (GA 47), xx.
28. Letter of November 16, 1921, to Gogarten, in Göckeritz, ed., *Friedrich Gogartens Briefwechsel*, 173.
29. Letter of October 27, 1920, to Thurneysen, *Briefwechsel Barth–Thurneysen* I (GA 3), 435. "Reformiert an Haupt und Gliedern" ("reformed in head and its members") is a quotation from the 1415 Reform Council of Konstanz.
30. Letter of October 27, 1920, to Thurneysen, *Briefwechsel Barth–Thurneysen* I (GA 3), 436.
31. Letter of October 27, 1920, to Thurneysen, *Briefwechsel Barth–Thurneysen* I (GA 3), 436.
32. Cf. the letter of October 30, 1920, to Thurneysen, *Briefwechsel Barth–Thurneysen* I (GA 3), 437.
33. Letter of October 28, 1920, from Thurneysen, *Briefwechsel Barth–Thurneysen* I (GA 3), 436.
34. Letter of October 28 1920, from Thurneysen, *Briefwechsel Barth–Thurneysen* I (GA 3), 436.
35. On the question of the dating of the work's completion, cf. the editor's foreword in Tolstaja, ed., *"Das Römerbriefmanuskript habe ich gelesen,"* 11f. and 16f.
36. Cf. *Der Römerbrief* (second version) (GA 47), xxxiv, and the letter of February 22, 1921, to Thurneysen, *Briefwechsel Barth–Thurneysen* I (GA 3), 472.
37. Cf. the editor's foreword in Tolstaja, ed., *"Das Römerbriefmanuskript habe ich gelesen,"* 13f., in reference to the letter of March 21, 1921, from Thurneysen (103): "…I know… that your style has an effect on me and [I] want to be vigilant."
38. *Der Römerbrief* (second version) (GA 47), 24.

39. Letter of September 27, 1921, to Thurneysen, *Briefwechsel Barth-Thurneysen* I (GA 3), 520.
40. Letter of September 30, 1921, from Thurneysen, *Briefwechsel Barth-Thurneysen* I (GA 3), 523.
41. Letter of November 4, 1920, to Thurneysen, *Briefwechsel Barth-Thurneysen* I (GA 3), 438.
42. Cf. the letters of November 4 and 12, 1920, to Thurneysen, *Briefwechsel Barth-Thurneysen* I (GA 3), 438 and 441.
43. Letter of November 4, 1920, to Thurneysen, *Briefwechsel Barth-Thurneysen* I (GA 3), 438.
44. Letter of November 4, 1920, to Thurneysen, *Briefwechsel Barth-Thurneysen* I (GA 3), 438.
45. Letter of November 4, 1920, to Thurneysen, *Briefwechsel Barth-Thurneysen* I (GA 3), 438.
46. Letter of August 3, 1921, to Thurneysen, *Briefwechsel Barth-Thurneysen* I (GA 3), 508.
47. *Der Römerbrief* (second version) (GA 47), 5. The English translation by Edwin C. Hoskyns is not cited here and in the subsequent notes below; translations are by Victoria Barnett. Page numbers cited are from the German critical edition.
48. *Der Römerbrief* (second version) (GA 47), 5.
49. *Der Römerbrief* (second version) (GA 47), 6.
50. *Der Römerbrief* (second version) (GA 47), 5.
51. Cf. Korsch, *Dialektische Theologie nach Karl Barth*, 23-6.
52. *Der Römerbrief* (second version) (GA 47), 6 and note 4. In 1919 in Safenwil Barth had given a series of sermons on the Letter to the Ephesians and in 1920 on 2 Corinthians.
53. Cf. *Der Römerbrief* (second version) (GA 47), 6f.
54. Cf. *Der Römerbrief* (second version) (GA 47), 7.
55. Letter of April 13, 1919, to Thurneysen, *Briefwechsel Barth-Thurneysen* I (GA 3), 325.
56. Cf. Beintker, *Die Dialektik in der "Dialektischen Theologie,"* 226f.
57. Heinrich Barth, "Gotteserkenntnis," in Moltmann, ed., *Anfänge der dialektischen Theologie*, vol. 1, 236.
58. Heinrich Barth, "Gotteserkenntnis," in Moltmann, ed., *Anfänge*, vol. 1, 238.
59. Heinrich Barth, "Gotteserkenntnis," in Moltmann, ed., *Anfänge*, vol. 1, 239.
60. Søren Kierkegaard, *Einübung im Christentum*, 26: God is "separate from being human through an infinite difference in quality."
61. Barth, "Dank und Reverenz," in *Evangelische Theologie* 23 (1963), 339f.
62. *Der Römerbrief* (second version) (GA 47), 9.
63. *Der Römerbrief* (second version) (GA 47), 9.
64. *Der Römerbrief* (second version) (GA 47), 19.
65. *Der Römerbrief* (second version) (GA 47), 20.
66. *Der Römerbrief* (second version) (GA 47), 11.
67. *Der Römerbrief* (second version) (GA 47), 11.
68. *Der Römerbrief* (second version) (GA 47), 11.
69. *Der Römerbrief* (second version) (GA 47), 13.
70. *Der Römerbrief* (second version) (GA 47), 14.
71. Cf. *Der Römerbrief* (second version) (GA 47), 14.

72. *Der Römerbrief* (second version) (GA 47), 14.
73. *Der Römerbrief* (second version) (GA 47), 16f.
74. *Der Römerbrief* (second version) (GA 47), 48f.
75. *Der Römerbrief* (second version) (GA 47), 49.
76. *Der Römerbrief* (second version) (GA 47), 49.
77. *Der Römerbrief* (second version) (GA 47), 49.
78. *Der Römerbrief* (second version) (GA 47), 49f.
79. *Der Römerbrief* (second version) (GA 47), 58f.
80. Kooi, "Zweiter Römerbrief," in Beintker, ed., *Barth Handbuch*, 197.
81. *Der Römerbrief* (second version) (GA 47), 50.
82. *Der Römerbrief* (second version) (GA 47), 51.
83. *Der Römerbrief* (second version) (GA 47), 51f.
84. *Der Römerbrief* (second version) (GA 47), 53.
85. *Der Römerbrief* (second version) (GA 47), 451f.
86. *Der Römerbrief* (second version) (GA 47), 111.
87. *Der Römerbrief* (second version) (GA 47), 111.
88. *Der Römerbrief* (second version) (GA 47), 111f.
89. Cf. Kooi, "Zweiter Römerbrief," in Beintker, ed., *Barth Handbuch*, 197.
90. *Der Römerbrief* (second version) (GA 47), 112.
91. Cf. Beintker, "Dialektische Theologie," in Beintker, ed., *Barth Handbuch*, 203.
92. *Der Römerbrief* (second version) (GA 47), 332 and 406f.
93. Kooi, "Zweiter Römerbrief," in Beintker, ed., *Barth Handbuch*, 199.
94. *Der Römerbrief* (second version) (GA 47), 169.
95. *Der Römerbrief* (second version) (GA 47), 160ff., 89, and 189.
96. *Der Römerbrief* (second version) (GA 47), 190.
97. *Der Römerbrief* (second version) (GA 47), 138.
98. *Der Römerbrief* (second version) (GA 47), 204f.
99. *Der Römerbrief* (second version) (GA 47), 430.
100. *Der Römerbrief* (second version) (GA 47), 175.
101. Cf. *Der Römerbrief* (second version) (GA 47), 63f.
102. *Der Römerbrief* (second version) (GA 47), 47.
103. Cf. *Der Römerbrief* (second version) (GA 47), 454.
104. *Der Römerbrief* (second version) (GA 47), 455.
105. Cf. *Der Römerbrief* (second version) (GA 47), 530f.
106. Letter of July 23, 1920, to Gottfried Ludwig, cited in *Vorträge und kleinere Arbeiten 1914–1921* (GA 48), 628.
107. Cf. Letter of July 23, 1920, to Gottfried Ludwig, cited in *Vorträge und kleinere Arbeiten 1914–1921* (GA 48), 628.
108. Althaus, "Theologie und Geschichte," *Zeitschrift für Systematische Theologie* 1 (1923), 741.
109. Cf. Althaus, "Theologie und Geschichte," 742f.
110. Cf. Althaus, "Theologie und Geschichte," 743.
111. Althaus, "Theologie und Geschichte," 743.
112. Althaus, "Theologie und Geschichte," 743.
113. Althaus, "Theologie und Geschichte," 744.

114. Cf. Althaus, "Theologie und Geschichte," 746.
115. Cf. Althaus, "Theologie und Geschichte," 748f.
116. Althaus, "Theologie und Geschichte," 748.
117. See p. 236.
118. Cf. Schlatter, "Karl Barths 'Römerbrief'," in Moltmann, ed., *Anfänge*, vol. 1, 142f.
119. Schlatter, "Karl Barths 'Römerbrief'," in Moltmann, ed., *Anfänge*, vol. 1, 146.
120. Schlatter, "Karl Barths 'Römerbrief'," in Moltmann, ed., *Anfänge*, vol. 1, 146.
121. Cf. the foreword to the third edition, *Der Römerbrief* (second version) (GA 47), 26.
122. Bultmann, "Karl Barths 'Römerbrief' in zweiter Auflage," in Moltmann, ed., *Anfänge*, vol. 1, 119. Regarding Barth's relationship to him, see Konrad Hammann, "Barth und Bultmann," in Beintker, ed., *Barth Handbuch*, 96–101.
123. Bultmann, "Karl Barths 'Römerbrief'," in Moltmann, ed., *Anfänge*, vol. 1, 132.
124. Bultmann, "Karl Barths 'Römerbrief'," in Moltmann, ed., *Anfänge*, vol. 1, 141f.
125. *Der Römerbrief* (second version) (GA 47), 27.
126. *Der Römerbrief* (second version) (GA 47), 29. Bultmann reacted to this again in a letter of December 31, 1922, *Briefwechsel Barth–Bultmann* (GA 1), 8–12.
127. Bonhoeffer, *Act and Being*, 99.
128. Bonhoeffer, *Act and Being*, 100. Translation revised.
129. Walser, *Über Rechtfertigung*, 29.
130. Walser, *Über Rechtfertigung*, 40.
131. Walser, *Über Rechtfertigung*, 27.
132. Walser, *Über Rechtfertigung*, 29.
133. Cf. Walser, *Über Rechtfertigung*, 51.
134. Walser, *Über Rechtfertigung*, 86.
135. Walser, *Über Rechtfertigung*, 81.
136. Barth, "The Need and Promise of Christian Proclamation, 1922," *Word of God and Theology*, 102.
137. Barth, "Need and Promise," *Word of God and Theology*, 103.
138. Barth, "Need and Promise," *Word of God and Theology*, 106.
139. Barth, "Need and Promise," *Word of God and Theology*, 106.
140. Barth, "Need and Promise," *Word of God and Theology*, 108.
141. Barth, "Need and Promise," *Word of God and Theology*, 109.
142. Barth, "Need and Promise," *Word of God and Theology*, 111.
143. Barth, "Need and Promise," *Word of God and Theology*, 128.
144. Letter of October 9, 1922, to Thurneysen, *Briefwechsel Barth–Thurneysen* II (GA 4), 107.
145. Barth, "The Word of God as the Task of Theology, 1922," *Word of God and Theology*, 174.
146. Barth, "The Word of God," *Word of God and Theology*, 176.
147. Barth, "The Word of God," *Word of God and Theology*, 177.
148. Barth, "The Word of God," *Word of God and Theology*, 177.
149. Barth, "The Word of God," *Word of God and Theology*, 177.
150. Barth, "The Word of God," *Word of God and Theology*, 177–8.
151. Barth, "The Word of God," *Word of God and Theology*, 179.
152. Barth, "The Word of God," *Word of God and Theology*, 183.

153. Barth, "The Word of God," *Word of God and Theology*, 184.
154. Barth, "The Word of God," *Word of God and Theology*, 185. Translation revised.
155. Barth, "The Word of God," *Word of God and Theology*, 186.
156. Barth, "The Word of God," *Word of God and Theology*, 187.
157. Barth, "The Word of God," *Word of God and Theology*, 187–8.
158. Barth, "The Word of God," *Word of God and Theology*, 188.
159. Barth, "The Word of God," *Word of God and Theology*, 188.
160. Barth, "The Word of God," *Word of God and Theology*, 190.
161. Barth, "The Word of God," *Word of God and Theology*, 190. Translation revised.
162. Barth, "The Word of God," *Word of God and Theology*, 190.
163. Barth, "The Word of God," *Word of God and Theology*, 191.
164. Barth, "The Word of God," *Word of God and Theology*, 191.
165. Foerster, "Marcionitisches Christentum," in *Die Christliche Welt* 35 (1921), 819. Foerster sharply criticized Barth because of his damning approach to the culture that nonetheless "[holds] the hand that writes down this curse" (820). "The Professor ... sits at his desk and *writes* these words or stands at his lectern and *calls* them into the crowd, and then in the next moment he grabs his cigar and turns on the electric lamp" (820).
166. Barth, "The Word of God," *Word of God and Theology*, 194.
167. Barth, "The Word of God," *Word of God and Theology*, 194. Translation revised.
168. Barth, "The Word of God," *Word of God and Theology*, 195.
169. Barth, "The Word of God," *Word of God and Theology*, 196.
170. Barth, "The Word of God," *Word of God and Theology*, 197.
171. See pp. 93–94.
172. Beintker, "Dialektische Theologie," in Beintker, ed., *Barth Handbuch*, 200.
173. Cf. Beintker, "Dialektische Theologie," in Beintker, ed., *Barth Handbuch*, 201.
174. Barth, *Der Römerbrief* (second version) (GA 47), 16.
175. Cf. Beintker, "Dialektische Theologie," in Beintker, ed., *Barth Handbuch*, 202f.
176. Beintker, "Dialektische Theologie," in Beintker, ed., *Barth Handbuch*, 202.
177. Cf. Beintker, "Dialektische Theologie," in Beintker, ed., *Barth Handbuch*, 202.
178. Cf. Beintker, "Dialektische Theologie," in Beintker, ed., *Barth Handbuch*, 203.
179. Cf. Beintker, "Dialektische Theologie," in Beintker, ed., *Barth Handbuch*, 204.
180. Cf. Beintker, "Dialektische Theologie," in Beintker, ed., *Barth Handbuch*, 203.
181. Barth, *Der Römerbrief* (second version) (GA 47), 204.
182. Regarding the later conflicts, see pp. 226–230.
183. Letter of April 1, 1916, from Emil Brunner, *Barth–Brunner Briefwechsel* (GA 33), 3.
184. Letter of April 1, 1916, from Emil Brunner, *Barth–Brunner Briefwechsel* (GA 33), 3. Regarding the following, cf. Frank Jehle, "Barth und Brunner," in Beintker, ed., *Barth Handbuch*, 90–5.
185. Cf. *Barth–Brunner Briefwechsel* (GA 33), 8, n. 5.
186. Cf. letter of June 9, 1916, from Brunner, *Barth–Brunner Briefwechsel* (GA 33), 5.
187. *Barth–Brunner Briefwechsel* (GA 33), 15, n. 2.
188. Cf. letter of July 3, 1916, from Brunner, *Barth–Brunner Briefwechsel* (GA 33), 7–10.
189. Cf. letter of July 3, 1916, from Brunner, *Barth–Brunner Briefwechsel* (GA 33), 9.
190. Letter of July 9, 1916, to Brunner, *Barth–Brunner Briefwechsel* (GA 33), 11.

191. Letter of July 9, 1916, to Brunner, *Barth–Brunner Briefwechsel* (GA 33), 11 and 13.
192. Letter of July 9, 1916, to Brunner, *Barth–Brunner Briefwechsel* (GA 33), 14.
193. Letter of January 30, 1918, from Brunner, *Barth–Brunner Briefwechsel* (GA 33), 17.
194. Letter of January 30, 1918, from Brunner, *Barth–Brunner Briefwechsel* (GA 33), 18.
195. See p. 90.
196. Letter of November 28, 1918, from Brunner, *Barth–Brunner Briefwechsel* (GA 33), 24.
197. Letter of November 30, 1918, from Brunner, *Barth–Brunner Briefwechsel* (GA 33), 32.
198. Cf. the letter of November 28, 1918, from Brunner, *Barth–Brunner Briefwechsel* (GA 33), 24.
199. Letter of November 30, 1918, from Brunner, *Barth–Brunner Briefwechsel* (GA 33), 33.
200. Letter of November 28, 1918, from Brunner, *Barth–Brunner Briefwechsel* (GA 33), 24.
201. Brunner, "Einleitung zu Die Mystik und das Wort," in Moltmann, ed., *Anfänge*, vol. 1, 280.
202. Cf. Brunner, "Einleitung zu Die Mystik," in Moltmann, ed., *Anfänge*, vol. 1, 281f.
203. Brunner, "Einleitung zu Die Mystik," in Moltmann, ed., *Anfänge*, vol. 1, 283.
204. Brunner, "Einleitung zu Die Mystik," in Moltmann, ed., *Anfänge*, vol. 1, 283.
205. Brunner, "Einleitung zu Die Mystik," in Moltmann, ed., *Anfänge*, vol. 1, 284.
206. Brunner, "Einleitung zu Die Mystik," in Moltmann, ed., *Anfänge*, vol. 1, 287.
207. Letter of October 27, 1923, to Brunner, *Barth–Brunner Briefwechsel* (GA 33), 84.
208. In his review of the first *Römerbrief* Brunner had deliberately withheld this criticism because he was of the opinion that Barth's "one-sidedness is necessary now." (Letter of December 5, 1918, from Brunner, *Barth–Brunner Briefwechsel* (GA 33), 35) Regarding Brunner's criticism more specifically, see pp. 226–227.
209. Letter of May 15, 1921, from Brunner, *Barth–Brunner Briefwechsel* (GA 33), 61.
210. Letter from Brunner to Thurneysen, presumably of May 15, 1921, cited in *Barth–Brunner Briefwechsel* (GA 33), 61, n. 1.
211. Letter of May 26, 1921, to Brunner, *Barth–Brunner Briefwechsel* (GA 33), 62.
212. Bultmann, "Ethische und mystische Religion," 740.
213. See p. 131.
214. Letter of May 25, 1922, from Bultmann, *Barth–Bultmann Letters* (GA 1), 2, n. 2.
215. Cf. Letter of October 25, 1922, from Bultmann, *Barth–Bultmann Letters* (GA 1), 3 and n. 5.
216. Letter of October 9, 1923, to Bultmann, *Barth–Bultmann Letters* (GA 1), 8.
217. Bultmann, "Die liberale Theologie und die jüngste theologische Bewegung," in *Glauben und Verstehen*, vol. 1, 2.
218. Bultmann, "Die liberale Theologie," in *Glauben und Verstehen*, 8.
219. Bultmann, "Die liberale Theologie," in *Glauben und Verstehen*, 14.
220. Cf. Bultmann, "Die liberale Theologie," in *Glauben und Verstehen*, 24.
221. Bultmann, "Die liberale Theologie," in *Glauben und Verstehen*, 24.
222. Circular letter of March 4, 1924, to his friends, *Briefwechsel Barth–Thurneysen* II (GA 4), 231.
223. Regarding his career, see Göckeritz, ed., *Friedrich Gogartens Briefwechsel*, xviii–xxi.
224. Gogarten, "Zwischen den Zeiten," in Moltmann, ed., *Anfänge*, vol. 2, 95–101.
225. Cf. Graf, "Either–Or. The Narrative of 'Crisis' in Weimar Germany and in Historiography," 604.

226. Gogarten, "Zwischen den Zeiten," in Moltmann, ed., *Anfänge*, vol. 2, 95.
227. Gogarten, "Zwischen den Zeiten," in Moltmann, ed., *Anfänge*, vol. 2, 100.
228. Gogarten, "Zwischen den Zeiten," in Moltmann, ed., *Anfänge*, vol. 2, 100f.
229. Letter of June 16, 1920, to Gogarten, Göckeritz, ed., *Friedrich Gogartens Briefwechsel*, 153.
230. The lecture was published under the title "Die Krisis unserer Kultur" ("The Crisis of our Culture"). Gogarten's concern however was more fundamental and directed not only against Western culture (cf. Göckeritz, ed., *Friedrich Gogartens Briefwechsel*, 157, n. 9; there too regarding the date).
231. Cf. Gogarten, "Die Krisis unserer Kultur," in Moltmann, ed., *Anfänge*, vol. 2, 101f., and Gogarten's letter of May 24, 1920, to Martin Rade, in Göckeritz, ed., *Friedrich Gogartens Briefwechsel*, 157, n. 9.
232. Cf. Schneider, "Oswald Spenglers 'Der Untergang des Abendlandes,'" 200f.
233. Gogarten, "Die Krisis unserer Kultur," in Moltmann, ed., *Anfänge*, 108.
234. Gogarten, "Die Krisis unserer Kultur," in Moltmann, ed., *Anfänge*, 108.
235. Gogarten, "Die Krisis unserer Kultur," in Moltmann, ed., *Anfänge*, 120.
236. Letter of October 11, 1920, from Thurneysen, *Briefwechsel Barth-Thurneysen* I (GA 3), 432.
237. Letter of November 22, 1920, from Gogarten, Göckeritz, ed., *Friedrich Gogartens Briefwechsel*, 162.
238. Cf. letter of November 16, 1921, to Gogarten, Göckeritz, ed., *Friedrich Gogartens Briefwechsel*, 174.
239. Cf. Beintker, "Barths Abschied von 'Zwischen den Zeiten,'" 202.
240. Cf. Barth, "Need and Promise," *Word of God and Theology*, 101–29.
241. Cf. the circular letter of December 20, 1923, to his friends, *Briefwechsel Barth-Thurneysen* II (GA 4), 210. For the chronology, cf. the editor's introduction to "An Prof. Dr. Adolf von Harnack, Berlin, 1923," *Offene Briefe 1909–1935* (GA 35), 55–8.
242. Harnack, "Fünfzehn Fragen an die Verächter der wissenschaftlichen Theologie unter den Theologen," *Offene Briefe 1909–1935* (GA 35), 59.
243. Harnack, "Fünfzehn Fragen," *Offene Briefe 1909–1935* (GA 35), 60.
244. Harnack, "Fünfzehn Fragen," *Offene Briefe 1909–1935* (GA 35), 62.
245. Barth, "Sechzehn Antworten an Herrn Professor von Harnack," *Offene Briefe 1909–1935* (GA 35), 62.
246. Barth, "Sechzehn Antworten," *Offene Briefe 1909–1935* (GA 35), 62.
247. Barth, "Sechzehn Antworten," *Offene Briefe 1909–1935* (GA 35), 65.
248. Harnack, "Offener Brief an Herrn Professor K. Barth," *Offene Briefe 1909–1935* (GA 35), 68.
249. Harnack, "Offener Brief," *Offene Briefe 1909–1935* (GA 35), 69. Adolf von Harnack had presented a major study about Marcion, a heretic in the early church who attributed the creation of the world to a demiurge, distinct from the true, good God; from this world one had to be redeemed through Christ (cf. Harnack, *Marcion. Das Evangelium vom fremden Gott*). The accusation was often made during these years that Barth was a "Marcionite."
250. Harnack, "Offener Brief," *Offene Briefe 1909–1935* (GA 35), 72.

251. Barth, "Antwort auf Herrn Professor von Harnacks offenen Brief," *Offene Briefe 1909–1935* (GA 35), 73.
252. Barth, "Antwort," *Offene Briefe 1909–1935* (GA 35), 87f. The two met one last time in November 1925 in Münster when Harnack was there for a lecture series. On that occasion there was a longer personal conversation.
253. Letter of April 16, 1924, to Harnack, cited in *Offene Briefe 1909–1935* (GA 35), 58, n. 16.

8
"The Need for Thinking Further"
Münster, 1925–30

A Call and a Momentous Encounter

In June 1925 a new career perspective seemed to open up for Karl Barth. Through the mediation of Eduard Thurneysen Barth was invited to succeed Hermann Kutter, who was to retire in 1926, at the Neumünster Church in Zurich. Kutter himself had suggested Barth for this pastorate.[1] Barth however could hardly imagine accepting:

> I am plagued by the memory of how very much, how even much *more* [than in academia] I ultimately truly *failed* as pastor of Safenwil...The perspective of having to hold children's instruction, and of having to intervene in all possible practical questions...is truly dreadful for me; simply because I feel: I cannot *accomplish* it.[2]

It would indeed be lovely to return to Switzerland. But had he not in the meantime become an important voice in Germany, and were not some things that he had started there still a long way from being completed?

Barth stopped considering the Zurich position after the news reached him in July 1925 that he was in line for the extraordinary professorship in "Dogmatics and New Testament Exegesis" at the faculty in Münster.[3] In the process he was to be called immediately as a full professor, which was unusual.[4] Barth did not react as euphorically as one might have expected, given his difficulties with his colleagues in Göttingen. He wrote Eduard Thurneysen:

> News from Berlin: I am to go to *Münster* already in the fall as a personal full professor to take a "regular extraordinary professorship" and must decide by 1 August. A bad story. Our lovely home here! And the vast, vast distance to Switzerland! And the very unfamiliar world of Münster! But there is not much to do about it. The financial improvement that I need for my five uneducated children is considerable. The surviving dependents' benefits are also worth something and the full professorship all the more. I am still negotiating the teaching assignment [i.e., the exact description of the professorship], which has

not yet been determined, but I will certainly accept it, not without the ulterior motive that this will not be our final station.[5]

Barth already had close ties to the Münster faculty. On February 19, 1922, it had bestowed on him an honorary doctorate in theology "because of his numerous contributions to the revision of the religious and theological question," as the certificate stated. Barth was visibly pleased when he received the letter about his honorary doctorate.[6] Not having attained a doctoral degree, to him it signified a further academic recognition. He wrote Thurneysen with delight: "In heaven (at least in that corner where the opposition has gathered) perhaps some alienation about this honor, on earth this afternoon a simple black coffee."[7] In thanks he dedicated his publication *Die Auferstehung der Toten. Eine akademische Vorlesung über I. Kor. 15* ("The Resurrection of the Dead: An Academic Lecture on 1 Corinthians 15") to the faculty in 1924.[8] In an infamous process however Münster withdrew the honorary doctorate in 1939 and gave it back to Barth only in 1946.[9]

After Barth had decided to follow the call to Münster he tried to suggest Thurneysen, who was still a pastor in St. Gallen, as his successor in Göttingen, but Thurneysen refused. For one thing, he did not feel that he was academically in the position to accept, for another he had experienced too closely how difficult the academic path for Barth had been. Finally, the nexus made no sense to him: Because Barth was going from Göttingen to Münster, he should now go to Göttingen?[10] "I must remain with what *I* do best. Please spare me any further inquiries!"[11]

Before his move to Münster Barth spent the 1925 summer holidays with his family and friends on the North Sea island of Baltrum[12] and afterwards stayed several more days without the family at the "Bergli" in Oberrieden. He enjoyed the riding and conversations with Thurneysen and Merz. And there he became acquainted with Charlotte von Kirschbaum. They fell in love with each other. She began to work for him and, although Barth remained married, she became his life companion. In 1929 she moved into Nelly and Karl Barth's household (see Chapter 9).

The move to Münster was overshadowed by the difficulties of finding a buyer for their home in Göttingen and a new home in Münster.[13] While the family soon was able to buy a house and planned to move in mid-November, the takeover became difficult because of the renter who still lived there. Finally Barth went so far as to pursue a court case against the renter, winning the case at the end of February 1926.[14] For that reason Nelly Barth remained with the children in Göttingen for the first semester; only at the beginning of March 1926 could the family move into their own home in Münster. At the lovely address of Himmelreichallee ("Kingdom of Heaven Alley") 43 they now lived in a brick

8.1. The Barth family with a housekeeper, 1927, © Karl Barth-Archive in Basel.

house directly between the Münster central cemetery and the old Zoological Garden in the western end of the town, with wide expansive fields nearby.

Until his family moved in, Karl Barth lived "terribly lonely" in a rented room on Warendorfer Strasse 73, close to the main train station.[15] Barth missed the family with the "five little crawling creatures... who are otherwise rolling around me."[16] He enjoyed all the more the Christmas days in Göttingen: "It is unbelievable how lively and teeming it is!"[17] Somewhat disconcertedly he realized for the first time that the children, although four of them had been born in Switzerland, meanwhile spoke high German to each other and only spoke the Swiss German dialect with their parents.[18] He also felt a little superfluous during his visit: "everything went very well even without me. The children are rolling happily through life and Nelly was in good control... of them."[19] Barth admired that Nelly knew "unbelievably well how to deal with" the children, "whereas the 'Papa'... was more an object of entertainment and amusement."[20] Charlotte von Kirschbaum spent the New Year's days in Göttingen. On February 24, 1926, as the family was still in Göttingen, she visited Karl Barth in Münster—a dramatic reunion.

Received with Joy, Departing in Discord

In general Barth got along better with his colleagues in Münster.[21] With surprise he noted that he was "almost warmly welcomed... from all sides in the professors' lounge."[22] He attributed this to the "smaller amount of self-importance... that [makes] everyone more peaceful than the Göttingen pincers."[23] The faculty meetings reminded Barth of a "council of schools meeting" in Switzerland, "only with somewhat more cultured language"; through the very lengthy conversations people "got to know one another quite well."[24]

At the beginning Barth was outraged by the low requirements that his colleagues set for the students' final works for graduation. He decided that he would not conform to these.[25] In examinations he expected solid basic knowledge of Reformed orthodoxy. One result of this, as he could proudly report to Thurneysen at the beginning of his fourth semester, was that the price of the relevant standard textbook since his move to Münster had gone up from three to twelve Marks.[26] At his final examinations in Münster Barth summarized with satisfaction: "I could clearly ascertain that since I have been part of things the level in dogmatics, ethics and philosophy has gone up markedly, simply because word gets around that demands are made and if necessary people are failed."[27]

He had an ambivalent relationship to Wilhelm Stählin, who taught practical theology and had come to Münster in 1926. Stählin was an important theological figure in the youth movement (*Jugendbewegung*) and in 1923 had been part of the founding of the Berneuchen Circle, which strove for church renewal through a deepened liturgical consciousness. Barth was not very happy about his appointment, since he did not care for Stählin's manner of preaching.[28] He reported to his friend from student days, Wilhelm Loew, of the ambivalent beginning of their work together: "In our private conversations we strongly contradict each other after five minutes at the latest. But I like him as a person and colleague and... in faculty matters and in taste I am usually in agreement with him."[29]

In his autobiography Stählin's recollections of Barth were reserved:

> Barth's humor often had something of the satirical sharpness that is attributed to natives of Basel, and his lack of readiness to allow for thinking other than his own made the work together not always easy, also in the faculty... Back then in any case I—and not just I—sometimes suffered under him and in terms of what I myself had to offer, I felt inhibited and paralyzed by the halo of his infallibility.[30]

In particular Barth's criticisms of his sermons stuck with Stählin:

> Once, when I was invited to the Barths' with my wife, he said: "I am always in church but your sermons are execrable; every time I want to spring up on to the

bench and hold a counter-sermon." What then was so execrable about my sermons, I wanted to know. "You always take the congregation into consideration and want to address them; whoever is there should be no concern of yours. You should objectively proclaim God's word!" I countered that Karl Barth as the pastor of farmers in Safenwil surely preached differently than in an academic service in Göttingen. He disputed that in the most energetic fashion and claimed that no, he had never made any distinction. Whereupon his wife stepped in: "Karli, you don't believe that yourself!"[31]

Despite the ill feelings between them, Barth and Stählin in January 1929 jointly authored a protest statement against a film about Luther after the two had attended the screening together. The film falsified the historical truth and turned questions related to the content of the Reformation "into psychological thrills and excitements."[32]

Barth's relationship to the New Testament scholar Otto Schmitz was also tense. Explicitly distinguishing it from the journal *Zwischen den Zeiten*, in 1928 Schmitz had revived the magazine *Die Furche*, a publication that had already appeared between 1910 and 1924.[33] Despite the "penetrating power" of *Zwischen den Zeiten* Schmitz was critical of the journal's "one-sidedness." "It stands, as its name says, 'between the times.' Over against this, the '*Furche*', appropriately for its name ['the furrow'], wants to stand in time, in our time, but to take up the seed of eternity in itself and lead it into time."[34] Schmitz had a leading position in the German Christian Student Association (DCSV), which had emerged out of the Awakening movement (*Erweckungsbewegung*), and in 1929 he coined its motto: "Germany's studying youth for Jesus."[35] Barth's stance toward the DCSV was reserved.[36] He was suspicious of the positive view of their own Christian identity and attitude toward God. At a lecture on "Justification and Sanctification" that he held before the group in June 1927 he emphasized that while a Christian knows what *God* is doing with him, he knows nothing *of himself* "except that I am lost, sick from head to toe."[37]

Only shortly before Barth's departure from Münster did the logician, philosopher, and Protestant theologian Heinrich Scholz enter Barth's view; Scholz moved to Münster in 1928.[38] They knew each other from the Harnack seminar in Berlin; now Scholz became a "new very unlikely friend."[39] Charlotte von Kirschbaum enthusiastically attended a lecture he gave about Kant in the 1929/30 winter semester. In his last months in Münster Scholz visited the Barth home regularly.[40] Since he played the piano well he often played music together with Nelly Barth.[41] And although he worked with mathematical formulas, influenced by Bertrand Russell and Alfred North Whitehead, Barth found a certain closeness to him and they understood each other well. Scholz was one "of the very few who came from very different pastures ... with whom one soon feels as if one is, so to speak, wall to wall and with whom in any case it's easy to reach understanding by a rhythmic knocking on the wall!"[42] The two began an intense argument about the academic nature of theology,

> partly over the telephone, partly through written theses, partly in nighttime conversations...above all however through Lollo [Charlotte von Kirschbaum], who attends his Kant lecture daily and afterward must stand up to him with coffee and cake for at least an hour so that I can learn the necessary things at 11 o'clock.[43]

Barth found these conversations so fruitful that he almost regretted in 1930 that he had to move to the University of Bonn.[44] The two were able to continue the debate in Bonn, however, for Barth invited Scholz in 1930 to speak to his seminar on the question of the academic nature of theology.[45] Scholz had high regard for Barth as well and asked him to perform the church wedding with his second wife in March 1930.[46]

In his last semester in Münster Barth held the office of dean and attempted to get Friedrich Gogarten appointed as his successor, although he thought that "despite all the objective closeness neither his theological nor his personal manner are that appealing."[47] For Barth was of the opinion, as was by the way Rudolf Bultmann,[48] that Gogarten should finally receive a professorship. The faculty however did not want Gogarten on any terms, so that Barth spent his final weeks in Münster fighting with his colleagues. The other members of the faculty wanted to appoint Emil Brunner, Adolf Köberle, or Otto Piper. Barth interceded in a special vote for Gogarten,[49] but finally Otto Piper received the position.

In the Tunnel of the Semester

The letters that Karl Barth wrote to his friends from Münster show that in the beginning he again suffered under the burden of teaching, which now consisted of seven hours. He still had the feeling that he "talked...away, as if I knew something," and he was "still always the rider over *Lake Constance*."[50] Even when he heard that some in Münster were already referring to his "erudition," he must "often slog away for many weeks with depression of the nastiest kind, plans to escape to a Swiss pastorate in the countryside and such things."[51] "The constant pressure of the burdens of thinking further" seemed to him to be particularly onerous duties of a professor.[52] He could not let stand the unclarities and aporia that appeared on his theological conceptual path, rather he had to try to reach further clarification. He felt it demanding that he and other leading thinkers of dialectical theology were "surrounded by countless people who listen to us, who are only waiting to let themselves be led by us."[53] Again he was working late into the nights; even at midnight his pipe was often "a *long* way from going out... because the matter must go on implacably the next day."[54]

Bit by bit however he began to deal better with his teaching obligations. After the first two semesters in Münster the complaints in his letters to friends subsided. Barth now observed in himself "a certain leathery calm toward everything I face."[55] But as late as the beginning of the twelfth semester in February 1927 he wrote of going down "into the tunnel of the semester."[56] And at Christmas 1928 he hoped for himself from "Santa Claus" that he would "bring the possibility of a life that I might spend certainly not as a theologian, rather perhaps as the director of a small stationery shop or a cigar store."[57]

A group of students had followed him to Münster and at the beginning dominated his seminars. Barth was somewhat "concerned about how it will be when this stratum is gone and I am alone with the Westphalians, who are in any case *tough* company, a little reminiscent of the manner of the students in *Bern*."[58] In order to get to know the Münster students better, he continued his tradition of holding open evenings. There they read for example the sermons of the Dutch

8.2. Karl Barth in 1925, © Karl Barth-Archive in Basel.

pastor Hermann Kohlbrügge,[59] who had long worked in the Dutch Reformed congregation in Elberfeld and whose sermons were influential far beyond that. Kohlbrügge's contemporary followers felt close to Barth's theology since they also rejected any discoverable sanctification.[60] They also discussed the 1926 book *Das Jahrhundert der Kirche. Geschichte, Betrachtung, Umschau und Ziele* ("The Century of the Church: History, Reflection, Review, and Goals") by the national-conservative theologian and general superintendent Otto Dibelius. Barth found the book insignificant, but in Germany it was drawing strong attention.[61]

Barth's lectures and seminars met with lively interest, although only in Bonn would it come to overfilled events.[62] Barth began his teaching in Münster in the 1925/6 winter semester with the conclusion of his lecture on "Instruction in the Christian Religion," now covering the doctrine of redemption. It was Barth's only comprehensive treatment of eschatology.[63] In addition he held a four-hour lecture on the Gospel of John.

In the summer of 1926 Barth undertook the history of Protestant theology since Schleiermacher; he repeated this lecture in the 1929/30 winter semester. He was conscious of the danger that in his critical positioning against the theological developments in so-called modern theology he might become "too big for his britches"[64] and hoped

> to speak of *all* [theologians] with the greatest possible meekness and shared distress. If the lecture was to *succeed*, it must have the form of a "doctor's round" by the head doctor in an infirmary, where as we know a convoy of assistants, medical students, nurses etc. is there when at every bed the records of fevers etc. are assessed.[65]

At the same time he commented self-critically: "from which of all the diseases that one sees the people working on does one not effectively suffer *oneself*?"[66]

In the 1926/7 winter semester Barth gave a further three-semester cycle on "dogmatics," in which he again started anew. While he used his Göttingen lecture on "Instruction in the Christian Religion" as the "framework," in his own perspective "here too almost no stone has been left standing" as he revised it for Münster.[67]

Given the expectation of many that Barth would not just say what was theologically no longer possible but rather finally unfold in a positive sense a new theology, Barth felt under pressure to publish this lecture. He was uncertain as to whether he should "present this as food now so longed for by the people and as tasteless muck to the enemies of truth."[68] In November 1926 he asked Thurneysen for his honest opinion. Thurneysen realized that friends and foes of their theology would take an especially critical look at Barth's first own book on dogmatics. The risky task was: "To climb these aged hoary Dolomites, peak by peak, while the guests of the theological Hotel Splendid enjoy themselves watching from the terrace, and some of them would even take delight when you fall right before their eyes."[69] After Thurneysen began reading the manuscript in January 1927 he was however "for immediate publication, in order to open the eyes of the many, many, who still see you from the viewpoint of the Epistle to the Romans, to that which today must be tackled."[70] Georg Merz, editorial director of *Zwischen den Zeiten*, initially opposed publication.[71] Barth himself wrestled with it for over six months before he decided in mid-June 1927 to issue the first volume of his own dogmatics. His decision did not make him happy: "No one has ever approached the publication of dogmatics with such a ducked head."[72] The volume appeared in December 1927, cautiously titled *Die christliche Dogmatik im Entwurf. Erster Band: Die Lehre vom Worte Gottes. Prolegomena zur christlichen Dogmatik* ("Christian Dogmatics in Outline. First Volume: The Doctrine of the Word of God. Prolegomena to Christian Dogmatics").[73]

Karl Barth begins the book with the confession that it was "the attempt of a beginner in this area."[74] This was surely not meant as a gesture to win the goodwill of the reader. He was only presenting an "outline" because he first wanted to portray "the *problems* of a genuine dogmatics," since at present there was not any genuine dogmatics.[75] At the same time, with his book Barth wanted to intercede with "a protest against the (unfortunately the entirety of—with a number of exceptions[76]) modern Protestantism."[77]

Barth was aware that the publication of his own dogmatics would incur the accusation that he was departing from his original policy of only attempting "a kind of *marginal note*" with his theology.[78] After all, he had hoped with his *Epistle to the Romans* specifically not to present a theology.[79] Now that he was doing precisely that, he summarized with a powerful image:

> If I look back at my path, I seem to myself to be someone who, tentatively ascending the stairs of a dark church tower, unintentionally grabbed a rope from the bell instead of the railing, and now must hear with shock how the large bell from above him has rung, and not just noticeably to him. He did not intend this and he can and will not want to repeat it. Shaken by the experience, he will continue to climb as cautiously as possible. If my previous work here and there has worked and should continue to work as a peripheral commentary and corrective, this could not and cannot be my intent. I was and am a normal theologian who has available not God's word but at best a "doctrine of the word of God." I feel neither justified nor obligated to pause in the pose of a prophet, in the position of a breakthrough, in which apparently I have been seen by some for a moment, and in which they now again and again like to see me for their joy and comfort. I had to and have to therefore take on the bad appearance, unavoidably like every theologian, as if I "make a theology" out of the word of God or the truth and reality of God's kingdom... I have followed and continue to my path *on the earth* before and after the Epistle to the Romans. Concretely this means for me

(very simply, since I was given the corresponding professorships) that without being able to ask what will come of it, I must and have gotten involved in Christian dogmatics.[80]

Barth organizes his text again in paragraphs that begin with pointed thesis statements. As in his Göttingen period Barth explains that dogmatics is the doctrine of the word of God, to the degree that it comes from the sermon in which "through the means of the human word God's own word is proclaimed to people."[81] For the first time in a publication he now speaks of the "three forms of God's word":[82] the sermon, the Bible, and God's revelation in the *primal history* to which the prophets and apostles testify."[83] The Holy Scripture and the sermon that interprets it are only testimonies of this original *deus dixit* (God has spoken) of primal history.[84] The path of theological knowledge runs backwards, it comes from the sermon and only through that and the Bible can it recognize God's original speaking. But the path of justification runs in reverse: "from above to below, from the ... revelation to the Holy Scripture, to the church sermon."[85] Holy Scripture and the sermon that interprets it have authority only because God's revelation exists.

Because God for Barth was the wholly Other, and the relationship between God and human beings can only be produced from the side of God, for Barth God's revelation is "God's word without justification in another. It is God's speaking justified in itself."[86] God's word is not at human disposal and God remains Lord of God's revelation when people preach, hear, or recognize God's word.[87]

In the following Barth explains God's revelation as the revelation of Father, Son, and Holy Spirit. Barth thus does not begin, as had been customary in dogmatics up to then, with general observations about theology as scholarship, about human beings, or God. Barth was to retain and pursue this basic decision in his main work, *Church Dogmatics*.[88]

For his exegetical courses in Münster Barth also reached back to something he had already taught in Göttingen. In the 1926/7 winter semester he lectured again about the Letter to the Philippians, in summer 1927 once more about the Letter to the Colossians, and in the 1928/9 winter semester about James for the second time. Here however he once again only reached the end of the second chapter.

As something new, Barth in summer 1928 and winter 1928/9 offered lectures on ethics. Here too Barth oriented himself around his concept of "God's word": ethics seeks "in God's word the answer to the question about the goodness of human action."[89] Christian ethics to him was the exegesis of God's commandment, which he explained in a Trinitarian fashion as the commandment of God the creator, reconciler, and redeemer. Barth still speaks in this ethic of "orders of creation," such as work and family, which follow from the "commandment of life,"[90] a concept that he later would vehemently combat.[91]

Barth also offered seminars in Münster for the first time. The thematic spectrum ranged from Anselm of Canterbury and Thomas Aquinas, through Calvin and Luther, up to Schleiermacher and Albrecht Ritschl.[92] As is customary today as well, students gave presentations. Barth was not especially squeamish in his critiques of the presentations. It sometimes happened that a student broke out in tears or a father complained in a letter about Barth's behavior.[93]

Barth was especially preoccupied with his seminar on the medieval theologian Thomas Aquinas' *Summa Theologiae* in the winter semester of 1928/9. He experienced dealing with Aquinas as

> incredibly instructive but simply eerie because the man went to work with a meticulousness that up to now e.g. has not allowed us to formulate one single objection. He also knew everything, absolutely everything, if one subtracts the one thing he did not know: that the human being is a scoundrel [a robber and murderer, briefly: a sinner].[94]

Barth admitted to Thurneysen that he felt simply "bowled over" and would have to "become a Catholic"—if he had not been already convinced by the Protestant conception of the human being that emphasized sinfulness.[95]

Return to Bern?

In the summer of 1927 the dogmatics professor Hermann Lüdemann submitted his resignation in Bern for reasons of age so that the professorship of dogmatics there became free.[96] Albert Schädelin joined others to urge that Barth be appointed. He was an old school friend who had been pastor since 1911 at the Bern Münster Church and had been convinced by Barth's dialectical approach. Eduard Thurneysen also hoped very much for Barth's return to Bern, to have Barth once again in Switzerland. There Barth could work "in a smaller but manageable circle where he could have an influence" and could shape the future German-speaking generation of Swiss pastors.[97] In contrast it would be almost impossible for a Swiss in Germany to have such influence on the church, so that in the Prussian church it would fall to Barth only "to be active through commentary."[98] Thurneysen also feared that "a possible turn to the right in Prussian politics" could harm Barth's "situation with the ministry so that chances that exist today might disappear tomorrow."[99]

After Barth in August 1927 had received numerous letters of recruitment from Bern, he thought it was his duty to accept a possible offer from the church of his homeland.[100] Barth's children hoped deeply for Switzerland, "of which they have high hopes for something like an eternal vacation stay with only snowy mountains and the ringing of cowbells and among people who 'don't talk and cackle so loud,' as Stöffeli [Christoph Barth] defined the difference between Germans and Swiss on this occasion."[101] At the same time there were a number of things that held Barth back from returning to Switzerland. The prospect of "Swiss and Bern narrowness" oppressed him.[102] He was aware of how much he "simply [felt] at home in Germany, [belonged] to the Germans,"[103] and his "heart trembled... thinking about all the unchanged, unpleasant constellations" that would await him in Switzerland.[104] In particular the argument with Leonhard Ragaz that would then be necessary seemed fruitless to him,[105] because according to Thurneysen's reports the religious socialist in his thinking was becoming more and more dogmatic and had become close to a Baptist theology.[106]

In Bern too, however, there were objections to Barth. In a letter to the editor of the Bern newspaper *Der Bund* a liberal pastor recalled in September 1927 that up to then in Bern the "three direction system" had worked well, in which there was a balance at the theological faculty of liberal reformers, "mediators," and "positives."[107] With Rudolf Steck's death in 1924 and Lüdemann's resignation, the faculty had just lost two liberal professors, so that it was basically clear that as a critic of liberal theology Barth could not be appointed. In addition Barth's theology had been "repudiated and characterized as sect-like...by the most renowned scholars."[108] Barth's "undercutting of everything that exists," especially the state itself, which he had identified as the "beast from the bottomless pit,"[109] was confusing and dangerous.[110] After this view was published, numerous readers' letters reached the newspaper scolding the author. Ernst Schürch, the head editor of the *Bund*, saw the need for an editorial. There he indeed praised Barth's effectiveness: "We cannot overlook the fact that movement, life, a new pulse appears to come from Barth and that even people who are not in agreement with him on every matter declare that they have much to thank him for."[111] But he too questioned Barth's position toward the state:

> Barth says very categorically that the state to him, "call [it]...what you will... [is] the beast from the bottomless pit." How then can he stand in the service of the state? Is it then merely a matter for the faculty or perhaps also for the state, which is about to accept an intellectual leader, an educator of our country's clergy for the service of the state?[112]

Precisely because all Swiss knew that their state was "the work of human beings," Barth's comparison was more than superfluous.[113] People wanted to celebrate "1928, the Bern Reformation year[114] in the spirit of a Christian community that supports and interfuses with the state."[115]

Despite these public objections the Bern governmental council voted in October 1927 to appoint Karl Barth, at the same time however the council determined that the next professor's chairs to become free were to be occupied by liberals—a perspective that further reduced Barth's inclination to go to Bern.[116]

The offer of 12,000 Swiss francs as annual salary was not negotiable and so low that it would hardly have sufficed for the family.[117] At the same time in Germany they were trying to retain Barth, with the offer of a substantial improvement in his salary, and presented to him how greatly he was needed in Germany.[118] On November 3, 1927, Barth asked his friend Thurneysen to travel to Bern to sound out whether he would "decisively be ruining something there" if he did turn it down.[119] After Thurneysen described to him the inflexible state church situation in the canton of Bern and the mediocrity of the theology there,[120] Barth opted on November 13 for a letter to Bern that would mean "with 99% probability the end of it":[121] He would accept the appointment only if the salary were raised to 15,000 francs and the decision to fill the next positions that became free with liberal theologians were reversed.[122] The government did not agree to this. Instead of Barth, the liberal New Testament scholar Martin Werner became professor.[123]

"The Church, the Church, the Church": Encounters with Catholicism

In retrospect Barth saw the significance of his time in Münster primarily in the "encounter and acquaintanceship with a very formidable form of Roman Catholicism."[124] The foundation for this was "a circle of friends, most of them theologically interested laypeople,"[125] who met every month or so to discuss central theological questions. The conversations particularly concerned two Catholic nineteenth-century scholars who at the time, there as elsewhere, had come once again into view: the important pioneer for ecumenism Johann Adam Möhler and the dogmatics scholar Matthias Joseph Scheeben, who had proposed his own dogmatic project based upon divine mystery.[126]

In Münster Barth also met for the first time with the Catholic philosopher of religion Erich Przywara, S. J.[127] In a 1923 article the Jesuit Przywara had praised dialectical theology (he readily named its advocates in one breath "Barth-Gogarten-Thurneysen")[128] as the consequent carrying out of Luther's concept of the "sole real and sole effective God."[129] There was an "original and genuine rebirth of Protestantism" happening in dialectical theology—and not in the so-called Luther Renaissance around Karl Holl.[130]

> Luther would belong [here] if to any group in today's Protestantism and is its father. For when God is on principle the "God over us," then there cannot be any "religious experience" that has an effect on God, there can be no work of God that would be recognizable as such. Everything that is somehow divine is on principle diametrically opposite to everything human and visible.[131]

Przywara observed however that in Luther there was a sudden change from this "God over us" to a "God in us." Luther's sole effective God was "ultimately the transformation of his vehement longing into something divine," that is, he brought God into his own self-understanding.[132] In Luther "human beings... ultimately make themselves nothing with respect to God, in order to absorb God in themselves and thus to be 'like God.'"[133]

Over against this, Catholic theology emphasized "the tension of 'God in us *and* above us.'"[134] Przywara found this viewpoint expressed in the principle of the Fourth Lateran Council of 1215: "between creator and creature there can be noted no similarity so great that a greater dissimilarity cannot be seen between them."[135] Przywara developed further the Catholic doctrine of the *analogia entis*, the analogy in being, not for the sake of closeness between God and creature, as is often claimed, but precisely in order to avoid such an identification of the human being with God.[136] Later Barth criticized the *analogia entis*, among other things because in it he saw a form of natural knowledge of God.[137]

In their first personal meeting in February 1929 in Münster however Barth was fascinated by Przywara, who held a talk on the Catholic principle of the church, participated in Barth's seminar on Thomas Aquinas, and spent two evenings in conversation with Barth.[138] Pleased, Barth reported afterward to Thurneysen that Przywara was in that respect in agreement with them: "We human beings are all rascals!"[139] Barth was also concerned with "how according to his doctrine the dear God, at least within the Catholic Church, just overflows human beings with grace," and that in his thought God is simultaneously in and beyond human beings, but both only through God.[140] And he was impressed by Przywara's intellectual brilliance, noting that one regarded him

> like a squirrel that swings from treetop to treetop, always the Council of Trent and the Council of the Vatican behind him, Augustine by heart and inside him, Thomas, Duns Scotus, Molina etc., always the Church, the Church, the Church, but truly the Church as highly vibrant and moving in manifold ways, around the firm pole of the dogma that is becoming ever more manifest.[141]

Thurneysen had experienced Przywara in a similar fashion in personal conversation:

> He ran back and forth like a dancing mouse between all the figures on the contemporary world stage, whether Heidegger or Gogarten or Buber or Grisebach or Husserl, gnawed at them all and then suddenly looked quickly out of his own hole victoriously, in order to disappear into it elusively... I think that the Devil himself would lose with him.[142]

Riding, House Music, and Travel

Barth had a sense of well-being in Münster and its surroundings. He took riding lessons and rode weekly with three of his colleagues, a jurist, a doctor, and a philosopher, sometimes in an indoor riding arena and sometimes in the open country.[143] With a certain chutzpah he occasionally gave this activity precedence over his academic obligations. In the summer of 1928 he wrote his dean, Otto Schmitz:

> Dear Dean and colleague! Yesterday's riding was so refreshing for me that I could not bring myself to cancel the next lesson, as I basically wanted to, for the sake of the faculty meeting. I certainly don't dare skip it entirely, but please permit me to come much too late... Each time I simply have to take a shower and put something else on before I am again ready to conduct business after this activity, but I will indeed be there, suddenly.[144]

Comments about his children that can occasionally be found in Barth's letters to friends are always quite tender. On the occasion of his 41st birthday in 1927 he reported to Thurneysen about the "little children's tribute by the bed of the just-awakened Papa."[145] Because his eldest made good progress in piano lessons and playing music together became possible, Barth once again took violin lessons, so that he began again to practice like "a little boy."[146]

Barth was often traveling to give lectures, which were very popular. He was invited by university bodies or church and cultural institutions.[147] He shortened the train trips by reading authors like Edgar Wallace.[148] He found it more difficult to hold individual lectures than to teach a lecture course over the semester. Whereas in the lecture courses one "can yield easily to the illusion that this or that delicate point was previously explained in § so and so, or will definitely be explained later at the appropriate occasion," the necessary condensation and understandability of the individual lectures meant that one "is very differently aware of the gaps and questionability of all kinds in what one says."[149] Not least through his busy lecture activity, however, during his time in Münster Barth acquired "the following that immediately made him the theological spokesman for the Confessing Church in the [German] church struggle."[150]

During these years Barth observed that he became somewhat dulled toward his supporters as well as his opponents.[151] With a mixture of indifference and sarcasm he wrote one critic that he regarded himself as "so definitively and devastatingly debunked" by him and his fellows that he wished to ask them "in the future to concern yourselves with more useful matters than with the ever new murder of a corpse."[152] In pietistic circles, which agreed with him in many ways, Barth did not really feel at home: "It will always be the case that one finally and at the last, particularly among the pious people, feels strangely alone, even among those who attest to their gratitude with great words."[153]

From May 28 to June 3, 1926 Karl Barth traveled together with his wife and a group of students for one week in the Netherlands. In Groningen he held two lectures on Philippians 3, preached and had an extensive disputation with professors, students, and pastors.[154] In Amsterdam he spoke to a congress for Inner Mission about "Church and Culture."[155] For some time in the Netherlands there had been followers of his theology who called themselves "Barthians," had studied his *Epistle to the Romans* and attentively followed *Zwischen den Zeiten*.[156] A monograph written about Barth's theology had already appeared, written by the Groningen dogmatic scholar Theodorus L. Haitjema.[157] Barth "was *startled* positively about this echo and the expectations that people there place on us. To that extent I felt the entire time as if I were choked by the trust and openness with which people received me."[158] Besides the agreeable mentality of the Dutch, which he experienced as a "very happy mix of German and western manner," Barth enjoyed the tobacco, tea, and ocean air.[159] At the Rijksmuseum in Amsterdam they twice viewed with astonishment Rembrandt's monumental works, especially "The Night Watch."[160] Following his childhood fondness Barth did not want to miss also studying the paintings of the sea battles of Admiral de Ruyter in detail.[161] When Barth came to the Netherlands again in 1927, now to Utrecht and Leiden, he was once more taken by the open and interested manner of the Dutch students, professors, and other listeners.[162]

Barth spent the summer of 1926 at the "Bergli" in Oberrieden. Because of a riding accident in which he had bruised his shoulder and had a thigh contusion he had to spend part of the holiday almost completely immobile, lying on the veranda. Although for a while he could not write, stand, or walk, and had to start the new semester on crutches, Barth had the impression that things "could have been much worse."[163] He had barely avoided crashing into the power pole that was only a few steps away.

In the summer of 1927 Barth traveled with his family and his lover Charlotte von Kirschbaum on vacation near Wernigerode in the Harz mountains. Barth used the time to dictate the final version of *Die christliche Dogmatik im Entwurf. Erster Band: Die Lehre vom Worte Gottes. Prolegomena zur christlichen Dogmatik* to Charlotte von Kirschbaum, who typed the manuscript.[164] After this intensive work together it was clear that he no longer wished work and life without Charlotte. Only two years now separated them from an agonizing *ménage à trois*.

The most important, closest person who accompanied Barth on his path during these years remained Eduard Thurneysen. Until then he had still been in St. Gallen. Now several things changed for him. In 1927 the responsible election commission suggested him as the first minister at the Basel Münster Church, but at the election meeting of parishioners he was rejected by 85 votes against 45.[165] According to his report to Barth the reason was: "Thurneysen is a Barthian, and 'we don't want one of them on the venerable pulpit of the Münster Church!' His proclamation is too gloomy, he takes away every possibility for human beings to cooperate [in God's work]. Barthian theology in general is a postwar phenomenon, antihuman, etc."[166] As surprised as Thurneysen was by this outcome, he was glad that this rejection had been due to a genuine objective difference: "the matter concerned and concerns nothing other than the question: Gospel or humanism."[167] Barth could also gain something from this rejection, since it illustrated that Thurneysen and he "*still* are tempestuous enough to cause offense, *still* have the elbow room that one loses to a great extent when in government" and had "not yet been released from the position of opposition in the visible church."[168] Thurneysen courageously put himself up for a second election meeting and now, since this time a number of people emphatically supported him with their vote, was put forward for election with 127 against 73 votes.[169] One week later he was elected as so-called *Antistes* (the head pastor of a Reformed church in Switzerland), by the Basel Münster congregation, with 896 votes against 213. He began his work in this prominent preaching post at the end of June 1927.[170] On November 10, 1927, Thurneysen was awarded an honorary doctorate in theology at the University of Gießen.[171] In the 1929 summer semester he began teaching practical theology at the University of Basel.

After 1929 Barth's geographical horizons widened. Until then he had only known Switzerland, Germany, and the Netherlands. Now he traveled to Italy, England, Scotland, Denmark, France, Austria, Czechoslovakia, Hungary, and Transylvania.[172] Barth experienced these journeys as his personal "ecumenical movement."[173] While they did not lead him "to cancel or extenuate anything at all of that which I had come to know formerly in my hermitage as the one all-essential,"[174] the strange regions and their history, as well as their current situation and their people, altered the point of reference for his thinking. Out of the one church that was important to him now became "many churches."[175] His own sense was it was these experiences abroad that preserved him from the nationalism and provincialism that captivated so many others during the 1930s.[176]

In November 1929 Barth encountered a figure who would later be central to National Socialism. As dean he had to attend a university memorial ceremony on the anniversary of the battle of Langemarck on November 10, 1914. The speaker was Captain (ret.) Hermann Göring. Göring demanded a military reckoning with Germany's enemies and stressed: "In heaven only God, on earth only Germany."[177] Barth found this new ideology so ludicrous that initially he attributed no particular significance to it—a mistake, as he confessed in retrospect: "I fundamentally erred back then in not seeing the danger of the already rising National Socialism, which from the very beginning, in its ideas and methods, in its leading figures, seemed so absurd to me."[178]

Shortly before, a new professional change for Barth had appeared on the horizon. In September 1929 he received a letter from the Prussian Ministry of

Culture with an appointment to the University of Bonn, the chair in systematic theology.[179] The salary offered was generous and Bonn was less remote than Münster,[180] so that Barth accepted the appointment shortly afterward.

Privately, a significant change happened in the final months in Münster: on October 15, 1929, Charlotte von Kirschbaum moved in with the family. They had planned the move even before the Bonn appointment and then carried it through as planned. In the final Münster semester Charlotte von Kirschbaum had been so helpful to Barth in his work that Barth only one month after her move wrote Thurneysen: "I am almost amazed that I could ever do it without her."[181]

Notes

1. Cf. the letters of June 11 and 15, 1925, from Thurneysen, *Briefwechsel Barth–Thurneysen* II (GA 4), 337 and 342.
2. Letter of June 13, 1925, to Thurneysen, *Briefwechsel Barth–Thurneysen* II (GA 4), 341.
3. Cf. letter of July 22, 1925, to Thurneysen, *Briefwechsel Barth–Thurneysen* II (GA 4), 359, and Neuser, *Karl Barth in Münster*, 9.
4. Cf. Neuser, *Karl Barth in Münster*, 9.
5. Letter of July 22, 1925, to Thurneysen, *Briefwechsel Barth–Thurneysen* II (GA 4), 359.
6. This document is cited in Neuser, *Karl Barth in Münster*, 7.
7. Letter of January 31, 1922, to Thurneysen, *Briefwechsel Barth–Thurneysen* II (GA 4), 35.
8. Published in Munich in 1924.
9. See p. 280.
10. Cf. letter of July 29, 1925, from Thurneysen, *Briefwechsel Barth–Thurneysen* II (GA 4), 362f.
11. Letter of July 30, 1925, from Thurneysen, *Briefwechsel Barth–Thurneysen* II (GA 4), 364.
12. Cf. letter of August 11, 1925, to Thurneysen, *Briefwechsel Barth–Thurneysen* II (GA 4), 364.
13. Cf. letter of November 17, 1925, to Thurneysen, *Briefwechsel Barth–Thurneysen* II (GA 4), 385.
14. Cf. letter of February 24, 1926, to Thurneysen, *Briefwechsel Barth–Thurneysen* II (GA 4), 404.
15. Letter of October 27, 1925, to Kirschbaum, *Briefwechsel Barth–von Kirschbaum* I (GA 45), 6.
16. Letter of November 3, 1925, to Kirschbaum, *Briefwechsel Barth–von Kirschbaum* I (GA 45), 8.
17. Letter of January 2, 1926, to Thurneysen, *Briefwechsel Barth–Thurneysen* II (GA 4), 392.
18. Cf. circular letter of January 17, 1926, to his friends, *Briefwechsel Barth–Thurneysen* II (GA 4), 395f.
19. Circular letter of January 17, 1926, to his friends, *Briefwechsel Barth–Thurneysen* II (GA 4), 400. Ellipsis is in the original.
20. Letter of February 5, 1926, to Kirschbaum, *Briefwechsel Barth–von Kirschbaum* I (GA 45), 15.

21. In May 1927, that is, before an invitation from Bern reached him, Barth was promoted at the suggestion of the faculty to a "regular full professorship." Cf. his letter of May 15, 1927, to Thurneysen, *Briefwechsel Barth–Thurneysen* II (GA 4), 499.
22. Letter of November 3, 1925, to Kirschbaum, *Briefwechsel Barth–von Kirschbaum* I (GA 45), 8.
23. Circular letter of January 17, 1926, to his friends, *Briefwechsel Barth–Thurneysen* II (GA 4), 398.
24. Circular letter of January 17, 1926, to his friends, *Briefwechsel Barth–Thurneysen* II (GA 4), 398.
25. Cf. circular letter of January 17, 1926, to his friends, *Briefwechsel Barth–Thurneysen* II (GA 4), 398f.
26. Letter of April 7, 1927, to Thurneysen, *Briefwechsel Barth–Thurneysen* II (GA 4), 491. The reference is to Heinrich Heppe, *Die Dogmatik der evangelisch-reformierten Kirche, dargestellt und aus den Quellen belegt* (1861). In this work statements on the dogmatic themes were compiled from the most important Reformed theologians from the second half of the sixteenth to the eighteenth century. Barth wrote a preface for the new 1935 edition that had been reviewed by Ernst Bizer.
27. Letter of October 6, 1929, to Thurneysen, *Briefwechsel Barth–Thurneysen* II (GA 4), 678.
28. Cf. the circular letter of January 17, 1926, to his friends, *Briefwechsel Barth–Thurneysen* II (GA 4), 399.
29. Letter of October 13, 1926, to Wilhelm Loew, cited in Neuser, *Karl Barth in Münster*, 12.
30. Stählin, *Via Vitae*, 220f.
31. Stählin, *Via Vitae*, 221.
32. "Protestschreiben der Professoren Karl Barth, Karl Bauer und Wilhelm Stählin vom Januar 1929," cited in Neuser, *Karl Barth in Münster*, 75.
33. Cf. Neuser, *Karl Barth in Münster*, 13.
34. *Die neue 'Furche,' Mitteilungen zur Förderung einer deutschen christlichen Studentenbewegung* 329, July 15, 1929, 91, cited in Neuser, *Karl Barth in Münster*, 13.
35. Otto Schmitz, "Die Aufgabe der D.C.S.V. in der gegenwärtigen Lage," cited in Neuser, *Karl Barth in Münster*, 14.
36. Cf. Neuser, *Karl Barth in Münster*, 14.
37. Barth, "Rechtfertigung und Heiligung," *Vorträge und kleinere Arbeiten 1925–1930* (GA 24), 71.
38. Cf. Neuser, *Karl Barth in Münster*, 19.
39. Letter of December 29, 1929, to Thurneysen, *Briefwechsel Barth–Thurneysen* II (GA 4), 693.
40. Letter of December 29, 1929, to Thurneysen, *Briefwechsel Barth–Thurneysen* II (GA 4), 693.
41. Cf. Zellweger-Barth, "Lebenslauf," in *Nelly Barth-Hoffmann*, 7.
42. Letter of December 29, 1929, to Thurneysen, *Briefwechsel Barth–Thurneysen* II (GA 4), 694.
43. Letter of January 26, 1930, to Thurneysen, *Briefwechsel Barth–Thurneysen* II (GA 4), 702.
44. Cf. Letter of January 26, 1930, to Thurneysen, *Briefwechsel Barth–Thurneysen* II (GA 4), 704.

45. See p. 203.
46. Cf. letter of January 26, 1930, to Thurneysen, *Briefwechsel Barth–Thurneysen* II (GA 4), 704.
47. Letter of November 16, 1929, to Thurneysen, *Briefwechsel Barth–Thurneysen* II (GA 4), 686.
48. Cf. letter of November 14, 1929, from Bultmann, *Barth–Bultmann Letters* (GA 1), 47, n. 54.
49. Cf. Neuser, *Karl Barth in Münster*, 62, and the letter of November 16, 1929, to Thurneysen, *Briefwechsel Barth–Thurneysen* II (GA 4), 688.
50. Letter of November 3, 1925, to Kirschbaum, *Briefwechsel Barth–von Kirschbaum* I (GA 45), 7.
51. Circular letter of January 17, 1926, to his friends, *Briefwechsel Barth–Thurneysen* II (GA 4), 397.
52. Letter of August 5, 1928, to Thurneysen, *Briefwechsel Barth–Thurneysen* II (GA 4), 597.
53. Circular letter of January 17, 1926, to his friends, *Briefwechsel Barth–Thurneysen* II (GA 4), 397.
54. Circular letter of January 17, 1926, to his friends, *Briefwechsel Barth–Thurneysen* II (GA 4), 397.
55. Letter of February 4, 1927, to Thurneysen, *Briefwechsel Barth–Thurneysen* II (GA 4), 459.
56. Letter of May 15, 1927, to Thurneysen, *Briefwechsel Barth–Thurneysen* II (GA 4), 501.
57. Letter of December 21, 1928, to Thurneysen, *Briefwechsel Barth–Thurneysen* II (GA 4), 640.
58. Circular letter of January 17, 1926, to his friends, *Briefwechsel Barth–Thurneysen* II (GA 4), 398.
59. Cf. letter of November 8, 1926, to Thurneysen, *Briefwechsel Barth–Thurneysen* II (GA 4), 442.
60. Cf. Neuser, *Karl Barth in Münster*, 57.
61. Cf. the letter of December 21, 1928, to Thurneysen, *Briefwechsel Barth–Thurneysen* II (GA 4), 639.
62. Cf. Neuser, *Karl Barth in Münster*, 10f. Cf. the list of classes in the KBA.
63. Cf. the editor's foreword, Barth, *"Unterricht in der christlichen Religion,"* vol. 3: *Die Lehre von der Versöhnung/Die Lehre von der Erlösung 1925/1926* (GA 38), viii f.
64. Letter of April 22, 1926, to Thurneysen, *Briefwechsel Barth–Thurneysen* II (GA 4), 409.
65. Letter of April 22, 1926, to Thurneysen, *Briefwechsel Barth–Thurneysen* II (GA 4), 409.
66. Letter of April 22, 1926, to Thurneysen, *Briefwechsel Barth–Thurneysen* II (GA 4), 409.
67. Letter of November 8, 1926, to Thurneysen, *Briefwechsel Barth–Thurneysen* II (GA 4), 441.
68. Letter of November 8, 1926, to Thurneysen, *Briefwechsel Barth–Thurneysen* II (GA 4), 441.
69. Letter of November 27, 1926, from Thurneysen, *Briefwechsel Barth–Thurneysen* II (GA 4), 447.
70. Letter of January 27, 1927, from Thurneysen, *Briefwechsel Barth–Thurneysen* II (GA 4), 456.

71. Cf. letter of December 26, 1926, to Thurneysen, *Briefwechsel Barth–Thurneysen* II (GA 4), 450.
72. Letter of June 17, 1927, to Thurneysen, *Briefwechsel Barth–Thurneysen* II (GA 4), 507.
73. Cf. letter of December 16, 1927, from Thurneysen, *Briefwechsel Barth–Thurneysen* II (GA 4), 552.
74. Barth, *Die christliche Dogmatik im Entwurf*, vol. 1: *Die Lehre vom Worte Gottes* (GA 14), 3.
75. Barth, *Die christliche Dogmatik im Entwurf* (GA 14), 6. Author's italics.
76. Exceptions for him were both Blumhardts, Isaak August Dorner, Søren Kierkegaard, Hermann Friedrich Kohlbrügge, Hermann Kutter, Julius Müller, Franz Overbeck, and August Vilmar (cf. Barth, *Die christliche Dogmatik im Entwurf* (GA 14), 4f.).
77. Barth, *Die christliche Dogmatik im Entwurf* (GA 14), 6.
78. See p. 133.
79. See pp. 85–86.
80. Barth, *Die christliche Dogmatik im Entwurf* (GA 14), 7f.
81. Barth, *Die christliche Dogmatik im Entwurf* (GA 14), 33.
82. Barth, *Die christliche Dogmatik im Entwurf* (GA 14), 58. This thought can already be found in the *Göttingen Dogmatics*.
83. Barth, *Die christliche Dogmatik im Entwurf* (GA 14), 64.
84. Cf. Barth, *Die christliche Dogmatik im Entwurf* (GA 14), 67.
85. Barth, *Die christliche Dogmatik im Entwurf* (GA 14), 165.
86. Barth, *Die christliche Dogmatik im Entwurf* (GA 14), 172.
87. Cf. Barth, *Die christliche Dogmatik im Entwurf* (GA 14), 173.
88. See Chapter 13.
89. Barth, *Ethik I* (GA 2), § 1 Leitsatz, 1.
90. Barth, *Ethik I* (GA 2), § 7, 193; cf. § 9, 367.
91. See p. 234.
92. Cf. the list of Barth's courses in the KBA.
93. Cf. the letter of May 26, 1928, to Thurneysen, *Briefwechsel Barth–Thurneysen* II (GA 4), 579.
94. Letter of December 21, 1928, to Thurneysen, *Briefwechsel Barth–Thurneysen* II (GA 4), 638.
95. Letter of December 21, 1928, to Thurneysen, *Briefwechsel Barth–Thurneysen* II (GA 4), 638.
96. Cf. *Briefwechsel Barth–Thurneysen* II (GA 4), 514, n. 3.
97. Letter of August 15, 1927, from Thurneysen, *Briefwechsel Barth–Thurneysen* II (GA 4), 513.
98. Letter of August 15, 1927, from Thurneysen, *Briefwechsel Barth–Thurneysen* II (GA 4), 513.
99. Letter of August 15, 1927, from Thurneysen, *Briefwechsel Barth–Thurneysen* II (GA 4), 514.
100. Cf. the letter of August 21, 1927, to Thurneysen, *Briefwechsel Barth–Thurneysen* II (GA 4), 516.
101. Cf. the letter of August 21, 1927, to Thurneysen, *Briefwechsel Barth–Thurneysen* II (GA 4), 517.

102. Letter of October 24, 1927, to Thurneysen, *Briefwechsel Barth–Thurneysen* II (GA 4), 534.
103. Letter of October 24, 1927, to Thurneysen, *Briefwechsel Barth–Thurneysen* II (GA 4), 536.
104. Letter of September 17, 1927, to Thurneysen, *Briefwechsel Barth–Thurneysen* II (GA 4), 522.
105. Cf. letter of September 17, 1927, to Thurneysen, *Briefwechsel Barth–Thurneysen* II (GA 4), 520-22.
106. Cf. letter of September 15, 1927, from Thurneysen, *Briefwechsel Barth–Thurneysen* II (GA 4), 518.
107. Cf. "Um die Wahl eines Professors für die systematische Theologie," *Der Bund*, Nr. 407, September 22, 1927, 3. Regarding the directions, see p. 6 in this volume.
108. Cf. "Um die Wahl," *Der Bund*, 3.
109. Barth, "The Christian in Society," *The Word of God and Theology*, 58. In his Tambach lecture Barth had urged an "objectivity" within existing world relations as well, because the correct Christian position could not be reduced to protest against everything that exists. In this context he spoke of the "freedom to move on the ground of this aeon as well... even in the house of the state, which is the beast from the bottomless pit [an image from Revelation 13], whatever it wants to be called" (58). Despite his choice of words Barth here was specifically not urging a radical rejection of the state.
110. Cf. "Um die Wahl," *Der Bund*, 3.
111. Ernst Schürch ("E. Sch."), "Um eine Professur," *Der Bund*, Nr. 413, September 26, 1927, 1.
112. Ernst Schürch ("E. Sch."), "Um eine Professur," *Der Bund*, 1.
113. Ernst Schürch ("E. Sch."), "Um eine Professur," *Der Bund*, 1.
114. The 400th anniversary of the Bern Disputation, leading in 1528 to the Reformation in Bern.
115. Ernst Schürch ("E. Sch."), "Um eine Professur," *Der Bund*, 1.
116. Cf. the letter of October 27, 1927, to Thurneysen, *Briefwechsel Barth–Thurneysen* II (GA 4), 542.
117. Letter of November 10, 1927, from Thurneysen, *Briefwechsel Barth–Thurneysen* II (GA 4), 548. 12,000 Swiss francs at that time corresponds to an annual salary today of approximately 76,000 Swiss francs.
118. Cf. the letters of October 24 and 27, 1927, to Thurneysen, *Briefwechsel Barth–Thurneysen* II (GA 4), 534 and 541.
119. Letter of November 3, 1927, to Thurneysen, *Briefwechsel Barth–Thurneysen* II (GA 4), 544.
120. Letter of November 10, 1927, from Thurneysen, *Briefwechsel Barth–Thurneysen* II (GA 4), 547.
121. Letter of November 13, 1927, to Thurneysen, *Briefwechsel Barth–Thurneysen* II (GA 4), 550.
122. Cf. *Briefwechsel Barth–Thurneysen* II (GA 4), 551, n. 2.
123. Cf. the letter of December 29, 1927, from Thurneysen, *Briefwechsel Barth–Thurneysen* II (GA 4), 553.
124. *Schweizerköpfe der Gegenwart*, 119. To Barth's stance toward Roman Catholicism cf. Keith L. Johnson, "Barth and Roman Catholicism," in Jones and Nimmo, ed., *Oxford Handbook of Karl Barth*, 147-61.

125. Neuser, *Karl Barth in Münster*, 38.
126. Cf. Neuser, *Karl Barth in Münster*, 39.
127. Cf. Neuser, *Karl Barth in Münster*, 40–6.
128. Cf. e.g. Przywara, "Mystik und Distanz," in *Ringen der Gegenwart*, vol. 1, 497.
129. Przywara, "Gott in uns und Gott über uns," in *Ringen der Gegenwart*, vol. 2, 548.
130. Przywara, "Gott in uns," in *Ringen der Gegenwart*, vol. 2, 553.
131. Przywara, "Gott in uns," in *Ringen der Gegenwart*, vol. 2, 553.
132. Przywara, "Mystik und Distanz," in *Ringen der Gegenwart*, vol. 1, 497.
133. Przywara, "Mystik und Distanz," in *Ringen der Gegenwart*, vol. 1, 498.
134. Przywara, "Mystik und Distanz," in *Ringen der Gegenwart*, vol. 1, 498.
135. This is the official Vatican translation: https://www.papalencyclicals.net/councils/ecum12-2.htm (accessed April 14, 2020).
136. Cf. Przywara, "Mystik und Distanz," in *Ringen der Gegenwart*, vol. 1, 498, and Przywara, *Religionsphilosophie katholischer Theologie*, 22–7.
137. Cf. Barth, *Church Dogmatics* I/1, preface, xiii.
138. Cf. Neuser, *Karl Barth in Münster*, 44–46.
139. Letter of February 9, 1929, to Thurneysen, *Briefwechsel Barth–Thurneysen* II (GA 4), 652f.
140. Letter of February 9, 1929, to Thurneysen, *Briefwechsel Barth–Thurneysen* II (GA 4), 652.
141. Letter of February 9, 1929, to Thurneysen, *Briefwechsel Barth–Thurneysen* II (GA 4), 652.
142. Letter of January 26, 1930, from Thurneysen, *Briefwechsel Barth–Thurneysen* II (GA 4), 708.
143. Letter of May 26, 1928, to Thurneysen, *Briefwechsel Barth–Thurneysen* II (GA 4), 578.
144. Letter of July 12, 1928, to Dean Otto Schmitz, cited in Neuser, *Karl Barth in Münster*, 66.
145. Letter of May 15, 1927, to Thurneysen, *Briefwechsel Barth–Thurneysen* II (GA 4), 498.
146. Letter of May 26, 1928, to Thurneysen, *Briefwechsel Barth–Thurneysen* II (GA 4), 578.
147. Cf. the summary in the editor's foreword to Barth, *Vorträge und kleinere Arbeiten 1925–1930* (GA 24), ix f.
148. Cf. letter of January 26, 1930, to Thurneysen, *Briefwechsel Barth–Thurneysen* II (GA 4), 699.
149. Letter of February 26, 1927, to Thurneysen, *Briefwechsel Barth–Thurneysen* II (GA 4), 466.
150. Neuser, *Karl Barth in Münster*, 62.
151. Cf. letter of February 26, 1927, to Thurneysen, *Briefwechsel Barth–Thurneysen* II (GA 4), 468.
152. Description of his reply to that critic in letter of February 26, 1927, to Thurneysen, *Briefwechsel Barth–Thurneysen* II (GA 4), 468.
153. Letter of August 21, 1927, to Thurneysen, *Briefwechsel Barth–Thurneysen* II (GA 4), 515.
154. Cf. the circular letter of June 4, 1926, to his friends, *Briefwechsel Barth–Thurneysen* II (GA 4), 414–16.
155. Cf. Barth, "Die Kirche und die Kultur," *Vorträge und kleinere Arbeiten 1925–1930* (GA 24), 6–40.

156. Cf. the circular letter of June 4, 1926, to his friends, *Briefwechsel Barth–Thurneysen* II (GA 4), 415.
157. The German translation of this work is Haitjema, *Karl Barths "kritische" Theologie*.
158. Circular letter of June 4, 1926, to his friends, *Briefwechsel Barth–Thurneysen* II (GA 4), 415.
159. Circular letter of June 4, 1926, to his friends, *Briefwechsel Barth–Thurneysen* II (GA 4), 414.
160. Cf. circular letter of June 4, 1926, to his friends, *Briefwechsel Barth–Thurneysen* II (GA 4), 415.
161. Cf. circular letter of June 4, 1926, to his friends, *Briefwechsel Barth–Thurneysen* II (GA 4), 417f.
162. Cf. letter of April 7, 1927, to Thurneysen, *Briefwechsel Barth–Thurneysen* II (GA 4), 490f.
163. Cf. letter of September 2, 1926, to Thurneysen, *Briefwechsel Barth–Thurneysen* II (GA 4), 429.
164. Cf. letter of August 15, 1927, from Thurneysen, *Briefwechsel Barth–Thurneysen* II (GA 4), 514, n. 2.
165. Cf. letter of March 23, 1927, from Thurneysen, *Briefwechsel Barth–Thurneysen* II (GA 4), 475.
166. Letter of March 23, 1927, from Thurneysen, *Briefwechsel Barth–Thurneysen* II (GA 4), 475f.
167. Letter of March 23, 1927, from Thurneysen, *Briefwechsel Barth–Thurneysen* II (GA 4), 476.
168. Letter of March 25, 1927, to Thurneysen, *Briefwechsel Barth–Thurneysen* II (GA 4), 479f.
169. Cf. letter of March 30, 1927, from Thurneysen, *Briefwechsel Barth–Thurneysen* II (GA 4), 483.
170. Cf. letter of April 6, 1927, from Thurneysen, *Briefwechsel Barth–Thurneysen* II (GA 4), 485f.
171. Cf. letter of November 10, 1927, from Thurneysen, *Briefwechsel Barth–Thurneysen* II (GA 4), 549.
172. Cf. Barth, *How I Changed my Mind*, 39f.
173. Barth, *How I Changed my Mind*, 40.
174. Barth, *How I Changed my Mind*, 40.
175. Barth, *How I Changed my Mind*, 40.
176. Cf. Barth, *How I Changed my Mind*, 40.
177. Cited in Neuser, *Karl Barth in Münster*, 63.
178. Barth, "Zwischenzeit," in *Magnum. Die Zeitschrift für das moderne Leben*, 38.
179. Cf. *Briefwechsel Barth–Thurneysen* II (GA 4), 676, n. 1.
180. Cf. letter of September 26, 1929, from Thurneysen, *Briefwechsel Barth–Thurneysen* II (GA 4), 675.
181. Letter of November 16, 1929, to Thurneysen, *Briefwechsel Barth–Thurneysen* II (GA 4), 686.

9
A Troubled "Ménage à Trois"
Charlotte von Kirschbaum

A Long-Guarded Secret

The closeness of the relationship between Karl Barth and Charlotte von Kirschbaum remained publicly unknown for a long time, even though already during their lifetimes there were countless rumors about their relationship.[1] After Barth's death his personal assistant, Eberhard Busch, intimated in his biography of Barth that Barth's personal situation had been difficult,[2] but for a long time there were no written documents published from which closer details emerged.[3]

Only in 1991[4] did Barth's descendants decide to change this.[5] The third volume of the correspondence between Barth and Eduard Thurneysen, which appeared in 2000 and covered the years 1930–5, therefore also included letters in which the problems of the relationships between Karl Barth, Charlotte von Kirschbaum, and Nelly Barth became evident.[6] Also published were letters from Charlotte von Kirschbaum to Eduard Thurneysen and three letters from Barth to his wife Nelly, which Barth at the time had given Thurneysen to read. Barth's will stipulated that the letters between him and his wife were not part of his literary estate.[7] But the commission handling the literary estate consulted legal counsel and became convinced "that in the sense of the Testator the three letters in the context of his correspondence with Thurneysen are not to be viewed as running counter to this decision."[8] Thus after 2000 the love relationship between Karl Barth and Charlotte von Kirschbaum, and the conflicts that this generated in Barth's marriage to Nelly Barth, became publicly known.[9]

When the letters between Charlotte von Kirschbaum and Karl Barth from the years 1925–35 appeared in 2008, it became possible to trace the conflicts in the marriage in detail, and a portrayal emerged of the deep love between these two human beings. Barth's children, who were von Kirschbaum's designated heirs, had already decided in 1985 that these letters should be published.[10] In 1993 Franziska and Markus Barth confirmed this decision again:

> As the only still living children of Karl Barth we decided after lengthy consideration and at the urging of people close to and far from [us] for the publication of this in part very intimate correspondence. In light of the gossip that has circulated since the mid-1920s we believe that the time has come to reveal the light

and dark sides of the very special and unique love that connected our father with our "Aunt Lollo."

Our dear mother, Nelly Barth, unfortunately does not speak in this collection of letters. *Karl Barth: His Life from Letters and Autobiographical Texts* by Eberhard Busch properly brings out how difficult the three-way life in the same house was: "unbearable," we children say in retrospect. And yet our mother held up through this, thereby contributing her significant part of the work of our father. She knew indeed how indispensable Lollo von Kirschbaum's theological assistance and unceasing participation was for carrying out this great work. That it never came in human terms to a break in our family life was magnanimous of our mother and we are thankful to her from the bottom of our hearts.[11]

The letters published in 2008 illustrate how all three suffered from the situation, but also how each, at least in their respective view, tried to behave responsibly toward the other two.[12]

"I Never Knew That There Could Be Something Like This"

Charlotte von Kirschbaum[13] was born on June 25, 1899, in Ingolstadt. She was the daughter of Major General Maximilian von Kirschbaum and his wife Henriette, born the Baroness of Brück. She grew up with one older and one younger brother.[14] Her father died on the French front in the First World War.

9.1. Charlotte von Kirschbaum, © Karl Barth-Archive in Basel.

After graduating from the Upper Girls School Charlotte von Kirschbaum moved in 1915 to the Munich Women's School, where she was in the "department for childhood education." In 1917 she passed the certification for governess. From 1917 until 1919 she worked in the Munich ambulance division of the Bavarian army. During the first half of 1920 she was employed as a stenographer for an attorney and then for the Bavarian Vereinsbank until the end of 1921.

The following year she began a nursing apprenticeship at the Bavarian Red Cross. She concluded this training in general nursing on May 7, 1927. From September 1925 to August 1926 she worked in the City Hospital of Krefeld. In April 1927 she began training at the Social Women's School in Munich. In March 1929 she graduated with an "outstanding" grade in the examination for "Charity Caregiver."

Charlotte von Kirschbaum had been in regular contact since 1921 with Georg Merz, who one year later would found the journal *Zwischen den Zeiten* with Karl Barth. They met almost daily to discuss theology, most likely including Barth's theology. Von Kirschbaum probably had already seen Barth in 1922 and 1923 during his visits to Merz' parish. In July 1924 Merz took her along for the first time to the "Bergli." When the two were there again in the summer of 1925, she met Karl Barth for the first time in August.[15]

After this first meeting they began a correspondence. Many of the letters from Karl Barth's hand from the years up to 1932 have been preserved, but only a single letter from Charlotte von Kirschbaum. It is her first love letter to Karl Barth, from February 27, 1926. Thus one hears her voice from these years only indirectly, through Barth's reactions to her. Presumably this gap arose because Barth demanded that they destroy their letters, which he did—understandable, for a married man—but which von Kirschbaum neglected to do.[16]

Barth's first letters to von Kirschbaum illustrate how quickly they felt close to one another. From the very beginning Barth addressed her with the familiar "Du" and her nickname "Lollo." He sent her theological texts, was delighted by her interest in his work, and he soon spoke openly with her about his uncertainty about how he should structure his lecture on dogmatics[17] and about his difficulties with professorial duties.[18] He described to her his loneliness in Münster[19] and mentioned to her knowing of a sense of sadness that all people have "in the very depths of their being," as surely she did as well.[20] Charlotte von Kirschbaum responded to his moods and acknowledged already at the beginning of their exchange, that it was good he was there.[21]

Karl Barth and his wife invited Charlotte von Kirschbaum to celebrate New Year's Eve 1925 with them in Göttingen. These were "very good" days for Barth.[22] Now he was particularly delighted when he received mail from her:

> Dear Lollo! ... I always make myself especially comfortable when I discover your handwriting in my mail, and then I read and consider it two to three times and

see you before me in your strict deaconess dress or perhaps the white outfit with the red belt that my powers of imagination have added, and say: Hello, and how fine that you are here![23]

After his move to Münster Barth urged von Kirschbaum to visit him before his family arrived.[24] She came for one day on February 24, 1926. After this visit Barth wrote to her:

> I want to write you many, many things, but I will leave them unwritten. I spent the night afterwards almost sleepless, and I have to look repeatedly at the corner of my desk where you were sitting, and wrestle with the great puzzle that you represent for me... Enough, I don't want to talk foolishness. Write me one kind word... you are such a better person than I am, and it feels to me as if I have disappointed you terribly.[25]

Charlotte von Kirschbaum replied immediately:

> Dear Karl, I should write you one *kind* word? I cannot. I can only say one thing to you, which perhaps I *may* not even say: I simply know since last Wednesday that I love you, more than I can comprehend. I do not know whether I didn't want to know it before or if I have been going through this world with closed eyes. But now it is so and it is hard. Do you now believe that I am no different from all of us?[26]

Barth promptly responded, now with a long letter. He was relieved that her open letter had brought "further clarity and simplicity to the situation."[27]

> Despite all the gravity and bitterness that now comes, I am even happy about it. Not only for the reason that lies nearest: because... now yes, on with it, there's nothing to do about it, it is simply so: because I love you as well, "more than I can comprehend." But rather also because I now know that I am not alone in my need and can speak very openly to you about the way in which we must now *help* each other or perhaps moreso, must *allow* ourselves to be *helped*.[28]

Barth continued:

> Until last Wednesday I thought (although I have long seen more than you, with shock, how I rejoiced in every trusting word that you said or wrote me), everything could be allowed to develop in the context of a lovely friendship. As it then became *so* evident in our conversation how unbelievably well and naturally we fit together, all of a sudden the situation appeared so insincere that I *had* to imply what I saw. And now you see it as well.[29]

In this first love letter Karl Barth attempted to be honest with Charlotte and draw a realistic picture of the situation that now existed:

> But now we must think of the present and the future. If we were both single, the discovery that has now been irrevocably made would be one of those moments of spring, joy and life with which God sometimes blesses us foolish, wrongheaded creatures in the midst of our darkness. As things stand, this same discovery is a moment of pain and renunciation at whose necessity we—once again with faith in God's justice—may wonder at as little as we can take the other for granted.[30]

Barth immediately saw how difficult this new love would be for his wife:

> you along with me will be clear about how this discovered reality will be hard and difficult first of all for my dear, true, valiant Nelly. You have seen our family life. The story of our marriage until now was for all the difficulties a happy story. We knew that there was no "smooth" marriage. But we were not prepared for such an incident. I believe I understand, at least a little, how this became possible (I mean, from the perspective of our marriage). You will understand that I do not speak to you about this.[31]

In the realization of his love for Charlotte, Barth was aware of his guilt toward his wife and children:

> in any case this means that what now *is*—however one deals with this... for me, but also for you, is in the first line a culpability toward *her*. I cannot even think about my dear five children without accusing myself that I am not with my *entire* heart with their mother and *only* with their mother. I ask you above all to bear *this* heaviness with me.[32]

How should things go further? In his long letter Barth ruled out the possibility of a purely spiritual love between them: "That is nothing for us. We want to remain healthy and admit to ourselves that this thoroughly concerns an earthly human love between us, which under other circumstances would have led us to become man and wife."[33] But he also rejected "bidding ourselves farewell with a gloomy face" and not seeing each other again: "that too would be forced and not at all worthy of ourselves. If it becomes evident that we are not strong enough to do this differently, then we can still grasp this drastic remedy."[34]

What then did Barth imagine instead of this? First of all it was important to him that Nelly know. And so he wrote her immediately.[35] At the same time he made clear to Charlotte that there could be no further steps in the direction of the mutual attraction they had now acknowledged. To him this would mean failure and unfaithfulness, not only toward his wife, but also toward his duties in the church and theology. He was all too aware of "the incongruity between what I am saying and what I am." But he could "not in any case endorse that incongruity of the personal and the factual or even *desire* to let it rest alone ... rather [would have to] *fight* against it."[36]

Barth concluded:

> We would not love each other if we would not recognize that the affection between us (we can and will not deny its reality, nor diminish it) is something that we only see and treat as a possibility that is indeed true, indeed given, not something to get rid of, but also with no possibility for *any* further development.[37]

Barth suggested that they see each other less often and be especially careful at meetings at the "Bergli," which nonetheless they should not intentionally avoid.[38] Also, the entire matter should remain between Nelly, her, and him, for if they were to speak about this with others it would only become all the more difficult.[39] Perhaps they should also exchange fewer letters (and not speak of "it" in the letters).[40] At the same time Barth encouraged her and himself now to turn with full energy to the work.[41] And she should not feel so bound by her declaration of love that she could not give her heart to another man.[42] Barth closed with the words:

> How is everything so wondrous and sad and great in our lives, my little Lollo, if one ponders: how we now stand with one another and what has now been inflicted upon us and how we should now help ourselves in our helplessness. With this letter to you (a strange document of "Barthian theology," utterly unique in its manner) I have written a little from my heart of my own needs. How much I want that this would also be a little help for you. If you want to reply to me (as the final written word of *this* matter), please do so quickly as long as I am still alone here ... I would be happy to have some affirming echo, that we have understood and will understand each other. The calamity began (or much more: was revealed) with this mutual "understanding." Now this should be revealed for our own well-being that we *truly* understand each other.[43]

Barth appears in this letter to have an exact idea of how things should proceed further between them, but already the next day he wrote her another letter, an "afterword."[44] He declared that his certainty and decisiveness about what was now to be done had not been easy for him, but rather was gained in a struggle with himself.

> I believe that it is so that we will feel the wound for our entire lives, and with the now achieved honesty, praise God, we want to stick to it in the future as well,

[and] where we encounter each other to look each other in the eye openly and—to know what we know.[45]

But in light of the uneasiness they both felt, he had the impression that he had to take leadership and show a solution.[46]

For three weeks Kirschbaum did not respond to his letters, which weighed terribly on Barth.[47] Finally, on April 1, Nelly Barth visited Kirschbaum in Krefeld for what was obviously a good conversation, as Kirschbaum now wrote back to Barth, apparently in agreement with him.[48]

"A Certain Double Life"

After Nelly had visited Charlotte Karl Barth invited Kirschbaum once more to Münster.[49] In May 1926 she visited Barth and his family for several days. After her departure there were lengthy, now troubled discussions between Barth and his wife.[50]

It is difficult to find out how Nelly Barth herself felt about the situation, since very few of her letters have been published. One knows her view of things almost exclusively from the letters of others. Nelly was visibly depressed by the fact that Barth did not attempt to find his way back to a fulfilled marriage with her.[51] He told his wife that he had not been *seeking* a substitute for what was lacking in his marriage, but rather simply had *found* Kirschbaum, and only then did he notice what had been missing in his marriage.[52] While Barth in May 1926 weighed the option of taking an absolute distance to Kirschbaum, he had the impression that this would be almost impossible for him. After conversations with his wife he wrote Kirschbaum:

> It was *very* close to the point where I sat down and with clenched teeth wrote you: yes, we'll choose "Breslau" [the nickname for the radical distance] as the least of the impending evils. But I am now *not* writing that to you and also ask you to wait for the time being with *this* decision. Not only because at the moment I simply cannot bring myself to it, but also because it still is not yet certain to me that this is necessary for God's will, hence our obedience.[53]

Barth admitted to her: You belong

> to my life (perhaps even more than I to yours)... so that it truly would be like tearing my eyes out... if I wanted to ask you to disappear from my life. One is permitted to consider *carefully* in advance whether such tearing out of one's eyes is necessary and required.[54]

At the time he asked himself whether "peace" could not be reached when

> I love Nelly as my wife and, since *this* position can only be filled once, love you now as my dear indispensable comrade Lollo, each in a very different relationship and under an entirely different order, without things having to become contentious.[55]

Barth at the time was decided "not [to] do in*justice*." At the same time he noted that for him it was "something im*possible* to care" for Charlotte von Kirschbaum "only a little less."[56] Barth's view of the situation changed noticeably: "we continue our marriage with all seriousness under the just as serious acknowledgment of the reality that Lollo is *also* there and that I now love her and *will* love her."[57] He was aware that from that point he could not avoid a "certain *double* life," but expected on his part that he would spare each of them as much pain as possible as well as love them as much as possible.[58] Barth's further letters to Kirschbaum from this early period of their relationship are filled with emotional ups and downs: between the sense of oppression through the problems of the situation, and the confidence that there would somehow be a good solution,[59] between the attempt to be the rational and sovereign one, and the power of his feelings that he could not deny.[60] He felt that she understood him,[61] asked her to write him often,[62] again and again expressing his worry about her health and fearing that she might work too much.[63] He also had to admit to himself that it would be difficult for him to genuinely give her the freedom for another man.[64]

On July 11, 1926, Barth and Kirschbaum met in Düsseldorf to visit an exhibition about health care, social welfare, and physical training.[65] As the meeting approached Barth behaved like a young man in love for the first time; he suggested to her that he could get up very early to reach a train that would arrive in Düsseldorf already at 6:44 a.m. so that they could spend as much time together as possible.[66] Following the meeting he sent her a poem that expressed the joy and pain of a time spent together but too briefly.[67] Soon afterward Barth found it unnatural that she was not with him every day.[68]

In the late summer of 1926 Charlotte von Kirschbaum again visited the "Bergli," where Barth spent his vacations; his family was there from August 6 to September 8.[69] In the meantime all their friends who were there knew of their love.[70] Before Kirschbaum's arrival Barth had lengthy conversations about the relationship with Georg Merz as well as Rudi and Gerty Pestalozzi,[71] and had the feeling that only Gerty completely understood them.[72]

Only two brief letters from Barth have been preserved from the period between these new days together in 1926 on Lake Zurich and the spring of 1929, as well as a poem he wrote after Christmas 1926. The poem tells of how the two of them— who were not searching for a partner (or new partner)—found each other. He had come to terms with the fact that "one is ultimately, ultimately—alone." Love had "broken" over them, "expressed full of guilt, full of joy, full of pain."[73] To have shared in this gave them both peace but also robbed them of it. Barth in his poem asked for her forgiveness for the pain that this gave her, but thanked her as well: *"Does it hurt you?* I am so sorry—*forgive* me! But my dearest, hear also *this*: *I thank you!"*[74]

Soon Kirschbaum was supporting Barth in his theological work. As previously noted, in August 1927 she typed up the manuscript for the first volume of *Die christliche Dogmatik im Entwurf* during the Barth family vacation in the Harz mountains. For that he dictated to her what he had previously written by hand and fine-tuned his wording as he dictated.[75]

During this vacation Charlotte and Nelly both had the feeling of an either/or.[76] Karl Barth however took the hands of both women.[77] To Eduard Thurneysen, who was visiting with his family in the Harz and with whom Barth spoke openly, this scene became a symbol for the problem of the ménage à trois. Even if Karl Barth believed that he wanted to love both of them in the same way, Nelly Barth simply had to think differently about his behavior than the two others. Thurneysen saw clearly "that ... each had made for themselves a very different idea about this form of being together, of closely being together."[78]

After this vacation Barth missed Kirschbaum in his daily life. He therefore suggested to her on January 1, 1929, that she move into his home.[79] She was to

9.2. The "Bergli" in Oberrieden, the garage with the "Törli" in the background, © Karl Barth-Archive in Basel.

continue to work with him, and for the outside one should speak of her as his "secretary."[80]

In the 1929 summer semester Barth was freed from teaching through a research semester. From April to September 1929 he spent it with Kirschbaum on the "Bergli."[81] In order to continue the work on *Die christliche Dogmatik im Entwurf* (a project that he then did not carry out), he asked her to prepare the following: She should work through the reviews of his writings looking for the "most important or most questionable points," get a general idea of the central key words of his theology, which he had collected in an "index card file ('Zeddelkasten'),"[82] and look for suitable quotations from Luther's sermons. During this period he also wished her to work through his Münster lecture manuscripts of dogmatics, parts two and three from 1927/8, and note the problematic points.[83]

Barth was happy that their work together now went beyond her typing his manuscripts:

> I would so like it if you could join in with joy and we could work together with that special fanaticism, without which no respectable work in any area comes into being. You know, I also imagine that it would be so lovely if then our love could finally reach firm ground or background, receiving objectivity and substance... so much that perhaps one can forget a little the irrational nature of this entire situation.[84]

Barth confessed to her in wonder:

> Tell me, what *is* it, that we now can *almost* no longer exist without one another? That even from far away there is *such* an attraction? And is nowhere more comfortable than with the other, and in fact so close as possible with the other? I never knew that there could be something like this.[85]

During the research semester they worked together in the so-called "Törli," two rooms over a garage built by the Pestalozzis a little above their own vacation home for their car.[86] Instead of working on his Dogmatics, Barth preferred to use the free time for detailed readings. "In the morning I do time with Augustine, afternoons with Luther, in between we teach each other in Latin and English and Lollo excerpts Luther sermons."[87] However much they enjoyed work and leisure together, the time could not be carefree.

While Barth was at the "Bergli" with Kirschbaum, his family spent their summer vacation at Beatenberg in the Bern Canton. In early August 1929 Barth drove to Nelly and the children and had serious talks with his wife. Nelly Barth had the impression that her husband was cold and only played a role toward her.[88] She tried to make it clear to him how difficult the situation was for her, and

9.3. Karl Barth with Charlotte von Kirschbaum at the "Bergli" in 1929, © Karl Barth-Archive in Basel.

mentioned the possibility of divorce.[89] Out of empathy for Barth, however, Nelly also tried to declare her willingness that Kirschbaum move in.[90]

Barth complained to Kirschbaum that his wife saw "only herself and her distress,"[91] but did have to admit that Nelly Barth could not seriously agree to such a "triangle." For Barth, the "triangle" meant a relationship arrangement, which had to include "thinking and acting in strict commonality."[92] Because of that the majority could not decide here, Barth and Charlotte von Kirschbaum could not, so to speak, overrule Nelly Barth. "*Three* people belong to this, and indeed three people...prepared for the *whole*."[93] Barth therefore wrote Kirschbaum on August 9, 1929, from Beatenberg that it would be necessary to drop the plan for her moving in.[94] He did not wish to force his wife to do something that she ultimately opposed.[95] Barth understood: "Here we could only make ourselves more miserable as three (and in the realization of the impossibility of this 'as three') than we already are."[96] Kirschbaum and he would now have to "be satisfied with the bitter small amount that still remains for us."[97] Meanwhile Barth considered himself

> free... with respect to the possibilities that still remain for us. I *will* soon return to you on the Bergli... We *will* continue to write each other. In the farther future we

will also see each other for the few times when this is possible. I must then simply step up and accept the responsibility to resolve these smaller questions in our sense and in contradiction to Nelly's own opinion.[98]

This decision of Barth's did not last long. In his next letter, of September 27, 1929, he spoke once more about Kirschbaum coming with the family to Bonn.[99] His letters from this period show that in his view there was ultimately no other option. They tell about his difficulties with Nelly,[100] his horror about how little he felt attracted to her, and his wrestling with truly devoting himself to her.[101] Barth felt terribly alone without his friend who understood him so well; he longed for his "little sister."[102] And he was deeply disturbed when Kirschbaum did not write him for a time: was she ill, depressed, no longer "*my* Lollo"?[103] Kirschbaum was during these weeks indeed uncertain about what the right path was. She was sad and depressed and accused him of turning away from her lovelessly.[104]

Three under One Roof

On October 15, 1929, Charlotte von Kirschbaum did then move into the family home in Münster. Thus began an almost forty-year long "*Notgemeinschaft,*"[105] as they called this arrangement to their children and close friends.[106] Kirschbaum conformed entirely to Barth's life path. Financially she became dependent on him. Already by early 1929 she had stopped earning her own money. For her work as his collaborator she earned from that point 100 Marks monthly from Barth, which corresponded approximately to the monthly pay of an untrained laborer.[107]

Even after she moved in, the two spent long vacations together at the "Bergli" so that "family vacations [became]...a rarity."[108] At the same time Kirschbaum got along well with the children and often looked after them. It saddened her that she and Barth would never have children together: "You must not think that I don't love your children. I love them greatly, each one, and everything that sometimes rises up in me in rejection comes from the fact that they—are not yours and mine."[109] She often accompanied him from that point on his professional travels and in March 1930 moved with the family to Bonn. Their two offices adjoined and shared a door, and were jokingly called "Vatican City."[110]

The family situation was difficult. Letters from this period reveal a sensitive, uncertain Barth, who repeatedly expresses his wish that everything should be different.[111] After a good half year of living together Kirschbaum complained to Eduard Thurneysen about the situation.[112] She could feel how Nelly Barth internally protested against the arrangement and how she for her part rebelled against this protest:

> The situation is completely so that Nelly *and* I only get through the days with great effort and that each moment can endanger *everything.* I realize so well that

I should be so much calmer and confident internally in order to get along well with Nelly even on a basic level and not encounter her protest against our situation only with rebellion. Now we are simply banished, incredibly, to a place that pulls the lid off everything and no longer allows us any illusions about where we are. And sometimes one may however because of that even know more than before that it is *grace* to be in this situation.[113]

It was harder for Barth to deal with Kirschbaum's negative feelings[114] than with those of his wife. In June 1930 he therefore expected of Charlotte "a very great progress in the school of Angels," that is, "the patience of angels."[115] It disturbed him unspeakably when she talked about something that had made her "apoplectic" or "crazy."[116] He tried to make her stop this; otherwise the project of living together would soon be over and he himself would go crazy, "for with this attack of yours from behind I *can* not bear the already almost impossible situation toward Nelly...if there is something that slowly but surely drives me to desperation it is when *you* now allow yourself *as well* to torment me with hysterical behavior."[117] Other letters reveal a reversed dynamic: he struggled with his negative, hopeless emotions and she reacted quietly and calmly.[118]

In early August 1930, a few months after their move together to Bonn, Nelly wrote several letters to Barth's mother—also saying this to Barth—that she could no longer live like this.[119] It appeared correct to her "that I should silently step aside until a new path opens for me."[120]

One letter from Nelly to Barth's mother is especially moving. In it she reports how Barth visited her in mid-August during the summer holidays in the Swiss mountain village of Adelboden. He came alone, without Charlotte. She was so happy that she and the children finally had him completely to themselves.[121] She had the feeling that she could again find energy if she would only be allowed to put together their new home in Bonn by herself, without Charlotte—in a way in which Karl Barth would feel comfortable there. Charlotte could move out and live nearby, come over to work together after his lectures and stay until the evening.[122] "I would then give her *less* trouble. I could encounter her somewhat more freely, see her come into my home in which I could breathe and more easily build it up according to the possibilities given me."[123] She could also then feel gratitude toward Karl and Charlotte for such a solution, more so than now, where Charlotte wanted to be a "martyr" for her.[124]

Only several days after Barth's arrival in Adelboden Nelly gave him an ultimatum: Charlotte must look for an apartment outside their home; in her presence she had "no air to breathe and no room to live."[125] Barth told her however that she would not receive his and Kirschbaum's agreement with this plan with good will.[126] They both had the impression that the situation was "not...ripe for an extreme decision toward one or the other side."[127] In light of Nelly's demand

Charlotte wished to tell her that she had not been sufficiently open for Nelly's distress during their first year of living together.[128]

At the end of August Karl and Nelly Barth agreed to try three more months together as a trio and afterward to consider how things should go on.[129] The situation remained difficult. Kirschbaum, following a visit to her mother in Munich, wrote Eduard Thurneysen of her worry

> whether this way must not lead *necessarily* to a catastrophe, and whether it makes any sense at all to take it up again. Only the fact that every other solution appeared *even more* futile and unfeasible let me return. And here? Oh yes, here I am again and again so badly off that the option of making a quick end is *very* close to me. I also see that the greatest difficulty is that Nelly and I have so little appreciation for each other. But we must perhaps be glad and thankful for each moment in which at least there is an *effort* not to make the path for one another even in detail more difficult.[130]

Although Barth also attempted to encounter his wife more amicably and openly, in the agreed upon three months the situation did not improve. Even after that however there was no external change. In June 1931 Nelly wrote to Eduard's wife Marguerite that she had to "lie much, much in tears."[131] In April 1932 she told Eduard Thurneysen that she could simply not go on.[132]

Charlotte was just as depressed, calling the situation in Bonn in 1932 a "battle scene"[133] and expressing her "right" to Barth very emotionally.[134] Then again she ensured him: "It is all just as it is, and it is fine."[135]

Barth tired of the arguments and hoped for peace and quiet. The conflicts at home burdened him in addition to his sense of total isolation in the emerging difficult church-political situation in Germany and his feeling that he was unable to fulfil his theological responsibility.[136] Eduard Thurneysen, to whom all three poured out their hearts, was so distraught in July 1931 that he had to vent to an outside friend:

> You can imagine that the fate of the Barth household lies also on us like a heavy crisis throughout the years. How much, how very much reflection and talking together and bearing it has already taken place, how many conversations with everyone involved, how much sighing together and contemplation between Karl and myself! One has tried to help, to solve. I thought for a long time that the right thing was not to take it all so tragically, above all not to turn this into an unresolvable tragedy through our thinking and talking. Therefore I tried as it were to hold on frantically [to the notion], that here against all appearances were some possible and sustainable conditions. But it became clearer that this is truly the gravest, most urgent matter. And when all the attempts to solve and help, for which one strove, failed, then one fell silent and thought, one simply has to live,

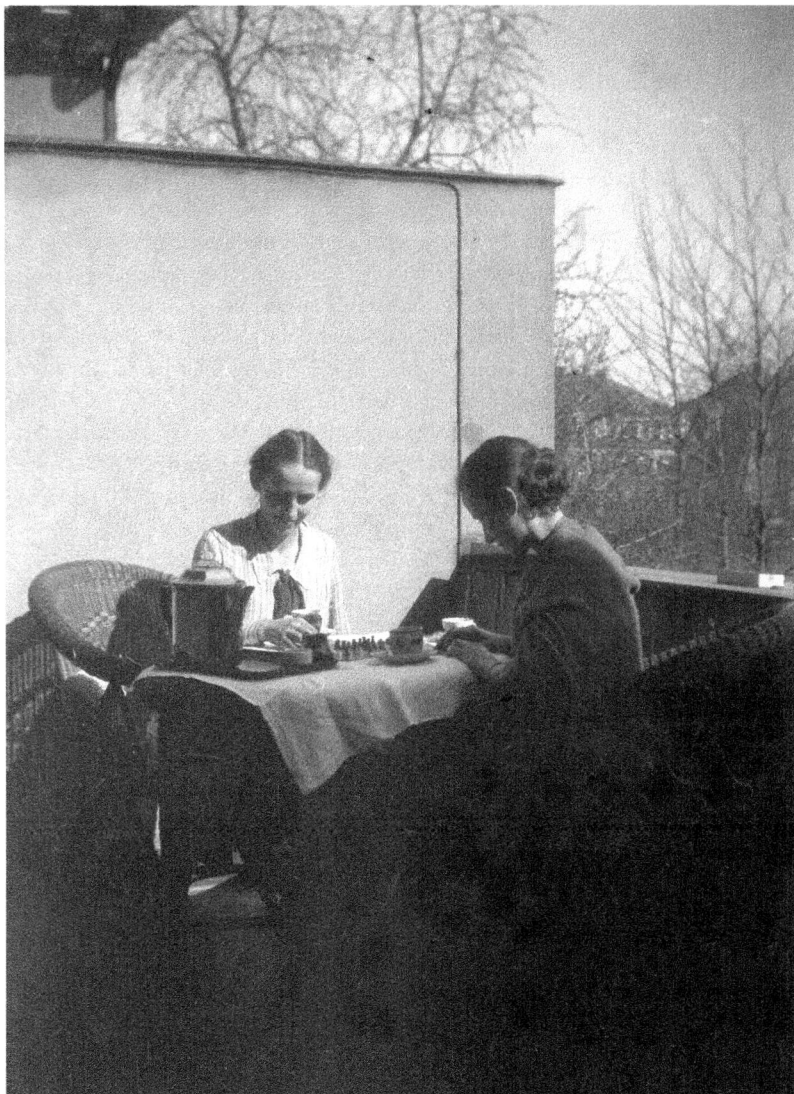

9.4. Nelly Barth and Charlotte von Kirschbaum in Bonn, © Karl Barth-Archive in Basel.

at least make an attempt to live, even if it seemed almost impossible, and now just see to it that all those involved stay really alive, internally and externally, and do whatever is possible so that the path that has now been followed doesn't become entirely unbearable and hopeless. But how should it be any different than that even for me everything, everything was and is always reminding me ... so that one can only say: this cannot go on, it should not go on![137]

Notes

1. Cf. my paper "Karl Barth and Charlotte von Kirschbaum," in *Theology Today* 74:2 (2017): 86–111, much of it reprinted in this chapter but in a new translation. The rest of this paper, again in a new translation, can be found in chapter 10.
2. Cf. Busch, *Karl Barth: His Life*, 185ff.
3. In the second volume of the Barth–Thurneysen correspondence, which covers the years 1921–30 (i.e., the period during which Barth got to know Kirschbaum) and which first appeared in 1974, Thurneysen as editor decided to replace personal references to Kirschbaum as well as to the related marital problems with ellipses [...]. This was done out of "consideration especially toward Nelly Barth, who was still alive." (Hinrich Stoevesandt, writing in the third volume: "Zur Editionsgeschichte des Briefwechsels zwischen Karl Barth und Eduard Thurneysen," *Briefwechsel Barth–Thurneysen* III (GA 34), xxi). In no way did Thurneysen conceal Kirschbaum's scholarly significance, but he did not wish that Barth's private life at that point become public.
4. Between Nelly Barth's death in 1976 and 1991, no volumes of the *Gesamtausgabe* appeared in which these private questions could have been touched on.
5. Cf. Stoevesandt, "Editionsgeschichte," *Briefwechsel Barth–Thurneysen* III (GA 34), xx f.
6. Cf. Stoevesandt, "Editionsgeschichte," *Briefwechsel Barth–Thurneysen* III (GA 34), xxi.
7. Cf. Stoevesandt, "Editionsgeschichte," *Briefwechsel Barth–Thurneysen* III (GA 34), xxii.
8. Stoevesandt, "Editionsgeschichte," *Briefwechsel Barth–Thurneysen* III (GA 34), xxii.
9. Two books about Charlotte von Kirschbaum appeared before this volume of correspondence: Köbler, *Schattenarbeit*, and Selinger, *Charlotte von Kirschbaum and Karl Barth*. For the 2004 German edition of Selinger's book the third volume of the Thurneysen–Barth correspondence was also consulted.
10. Cf. editor's foreword, *Briefwechsel Barth–von Kirschbaum* I (GA 45), xix. The decision was made by Franziska, Markus and Christoph Barth; Matthias and Hans Jakob Barth were already deceased.
11. Franziska and Markus Barth, "Entwurf zu einem Vorwort für die Ausgabe der Briefe zwischen Karl Barth und Charlotte von Kirschbaum," cited in *Briefwechsel Barth–von Kirschbaum* I (GA 45), xix.
12. Cf. Stoevesandt, "Editionsgeschichte," *Briefwechsel Barth–Thurneysen* III (GA 34), xxi. Two further volumes of the correspondence between Barth and Kirschbaum are being planned.
13. Cf. Familie Barth Basel, "Charlotte von Kirschbaum. Einige Angaben aus ihrem Leben," in *Briefwechsel Barth–von Kirschbaum* I (GA 45), xxxii–xxxiv; Rolf-Joachim Erler, "Biographische Daten zu Charlotte von Kirschbaum von 1899–1935" (xxxv–xli), and Stoevesandt, "Charlotte von Kirschbaum," in Beintker, ed., *Barth Handbuch*, 54–8.
14. Her brother Maximilian Eduard Karl was born two years before her and became a customs official and then later a lieutenant-colonel in the army. Her younger brother Hans Friedrich Karl was born in 1902 and went missing in action in the Second World War in 1944. In 1912 the family moved to Amberg in Oberpfalz. Cf. *Briefwechsel Barth–von Kirschbaum* I (GA 45), xxxv.
15. It cannot be the case that Barth already arrived at the "Bergli" on August 12, 1925 (per Erler, "Biographische Daten," *Briefwechsel Barth–von Kirschbaum* I, xxxviii), since on

August 17 Barth wrote Thurneysen from a boat trip on the North Sea (cf. letter of August 17, 1925, to Thurneysen, *Briefwechsel Barth–Thurneysen* II, 365f.).

16. Cf. Stoevesandt, "Charlotte von Kirschbaum," in Beintker, ed., *Barth Handbuch*, 55.
17. Cf. letter of October 4, 1925, to Kirschbaum, *Briefwechsel Barth–von Kirschbaum* I (GA 45), 3.
18. Cf. letter of November 3, 1925, to Kirschbaum, *Briefwechsel Barth–von Kirschbaum* I (GA 45), 7.
19. Cf. letters of October 27 and November 3, 1925, to Kirschbaum, *Briefwechsel Barth–von Kirschbaum* I (GA 45), 6 and 8.
20. Letter of November 3, 1925, to Kirschbaum, *Briefwechsel Barth–von Kirschbaum* I (GA 45), 9.
21. Cf. Letter of November 3, 1925, to Kirschbaum, *Briefwechsel Barth–von Kirschbaum* I (GA 45), 7.
22. Letter of January 17, 1926, to Kirschbaum, *Briefwechsel Barth–von Kirschbaum* I (GA 45), 13.
23. Letter of February 5, 1926, to Kirschbaum, *Briefwechsel Barth–von Kirschbaum* I (GA 45), 14f.
24. Cf. the letters of 18, 19, 20, 21, and February 23, 1926, to Kirschbaum, *Briefwechsel Barth–von Kirschbaum* I (GA 45), 17–21.
25. Letter of February 26, 1926, to Kirschbaum, *Briefwechsel Barth–von Kirschbaum* I (GA 45), 21. The first ellipsis is in the original letter.
26. Letter of February 27, 1926, from Kirschbaum, *Briefwechsel Barth–von Kirschbaum* I (GA 45), 22.
27. Letter of February 28, 1926, to Kirschbaum, *Briefwechsel Barth–von Kirschbaum* I (GA 45), 23.
28. Letter of February 28, 1926, to Kirschbaum, *Briefwechsel Barth–von Kirschbaum* I (GA 45), 23; ellipsis in the original letter.
29. Letter of February 28, 1926, to Kirschbaum, *Briefwechsel Barth–von Kirschbaum* I (GA 45), 23f.
30. Letter of February 28, 1926, to Kirschbaum, *Briefwechsel Barth–von Kirschbaum* I (GA 45), 24.
31. Letter of February 28, 1926, to Kirschbaum, *Briefwechsel Barth–von Kirschbaum* I (GA 45), 24.
32. Letter of February 28, 1926, to Kirschbaum, *Briefwechsel Barth–von Kirschbaum* I (GA 45), 24f.
33. Letter of February 28, 1926, to Kirschbaum, *Briefwechsel Barth–von Kirschbaum* I (GA 45), 28.
34. Letter of February 28, 1926, to Kirschbaum, *Briefwechsel Barth–von Kirschbaum* I (GA 45), 28.
35. Cf. the letter of March 1, 1926, to Kirschbaum, *Briefwechsel Barth–von Kirschbaum* I (GA 45), 31.
36. Letter of February 28, 1926, to Kirschbaum, *Briefwechsel Barth–von Kirschbaum* I (GA 45), 25.
37. Letter of February 28, 1926, to Kirschbaum, *Briefwechsel Barth–von Kirschbaum* I (GA 45), 27.

38. Cf. letter of February 28, 1926, to Kirschbaum, *Briefwechsel Barth–von Kirschbaum* I (GA 45), 28f.
39. Cf. letter of February 28, 1926, to Kirschbaum, *Briefwechsel Barth–von Kirschbaum* I (GA 45), 28.
40. Cf. letter of February 28, 1926, to Kirschbaum, *Briefwechsel Barth–von Kirschbaum* I (GA 45), 28 and 30.
41. Cf. letter of February 28, 1926, to Kirschbaum, *Briefwechsel Barth–von Kirschbaum* I (GA 45), 29.
42. Cf. letter of February 28, 1926, to Kirschbaum, *Briefwechsel Barth–von Kirschbaum* I (GA 45), 29.
43. Letter of February 28, 1926, to Kirschbaum, *Briefwechsel Barth–von Kirschbaum* I, 30.
44. Letter of March 1, 1926, to Kirschbaum, *Briefwechsel Barth–von Kirschbaum* I (GA 45), 30.
45. Letter of March 1, 1926, to Kirschbaum, *Briefwechsel Barth–von Kirschbaum* I (GA 45), 31.
46. Cf. letter of March 1, 1926, to Kirschbaum, *Briefwechsel Barth–von Kirschbaum* I (GA 45), 31.
47. Cf. letter of March 20, 1926, to Kirschbaum, *Briefwechsel Barth–von Kirschbaum* I (GA 45), 33f.
48. Cf. letter of April 2, 1926, to Kirschbaum, *Briefwechsel Barth–von Kirschbaum* I (GA 45), 34f.
49. Cf. letter of April 29, 1926, to Kirschbaum, *Briefwechsel Barth–von Kirschbaum* I (GA 45), 42.
50. Cf. letter of May 25, 1926, to Kirschbaum, *Briefwechsel Barth–von Kirschbaum* I (GA 45), 45.
51. Cf. letter of May 25, 1926, to Kirschbaum, *Briefwechsel Barth–von Kirschbaum* I (GA 45), 46.
52. Cf. letter of May 25, 1926, to Kirschbaum, *Briefwechsel Barth–von Kirschbaum* I (GA 45), 46.
53. Letter of May 25, 1926, to Kirschbaum, *Briefwechsel Barth–von Kirschbaum* I (GA 45), 45.
54. Letter of May 25, 1926, to Kirschbaum, *Briefwechsel Barth–von Kirschbaum* I (GA 45), 46.
55. Letter of May 25, 1926, to Kirschbaum, *Briefwechsel Barth–von Kirschbaum* I (GA 45), 45.
56. Letter of June 7, 1926, to Kirschbaum, *Briefwechsel Barth–von Kirschbaum* I (GA 45), 49.
57. Letter of August 8, 1926, to Kirschbaum, *Briefwechsel Barth–von Kirschbaum* I (GA 45), 72.
58. Cf. letter of August 8, 1926, to Kirschbaum, *Briefwechsel Barth–von Kirschbaum* I (GA 45), 73.
59. Cf. for example the letters of April 2 and June 7, 1926, to Kirschbaum, *Briefwechsel Barth–von Kirschbaum* I (GA 45), 34 and 50. Barth was disturbed by the tension "that what is as clear as daylight and of deep necessity between us now has to be a matter *toward the outside*, always and everywhere, that creates embarrassment and offense." (Letter of July 13, 1926, to Kirschbaum (58).)

60. Cf. for example the letter of June 15, 1926, to Kirschbaum, *Briefwechsel Barth-von Kirschbaum* I (GA 45), 51.
61. Cf. letter of July 30, 1926, to Kirschbaum, *Briefwechsel Barth-von Kirschbaum* I (GA 45), 66.
62. Cf. for example the letter of June 25, 1926, to Kirschbaum, *Briefwechsel Barth-von Kirschbaum* I (GA 45), 52.
63. Cf. for example the letters of July 23 and August 5, 1926, to Kirschbaum, *Briefwechsel Barth-von Kirschbaum* I (GA 45), 61 and 71.
64. Cf. letter of July 2, 1926, to Kirschbaum, *Briefwechsel Barth-von Kirschbaum* I (GA 45), 56.
65. Cf. letter of June 25, 1926, to Kirschbaum, *Briefwechsel Barth-von Kirschbaum* I (GA 45), 52, n. 1.
66. Cf. letter of July 3, 1926, to Kirschbaum, *Briefwechsel Barth-von Kirschbaum* I (GA 45), 57.
67. Letter of July 13, 1926, to Kirschbaum, *Briefwechsel Barth-von Kirschbaum* I (GA 45), 59f.
68. Cf. letter of July 30, 1926, to Kirschbaum, *Briefwechsel Barth-von Kirschbaum* I (GA 45), 65.
69. Cf. the letters of August 5 and 11, 1926, to Kirschbaum, *Briefwechsel Barth-von Kirschbaum* I (GA 45), 71 and 74; letter of September 7, 1926, to Thurneysen, *Briefwechsel Barth-Thurneysen* II (GA 4), 432.
70. Cf. letter of July 30, 1926, to Kirschbaum, *Briefwechsel Barth-von Kirschbaum* I (GA 45), 66.
71. Cf. letter of August 4, 1926, to Kirschbaum, *Briefwechsel Barth-von Kirschbaum* I (GA 45), 68.
72. Cf. letter of August 5, 1926, to Kirschbaum, *Briefwechsel Barth-von Kirschbaum* I (GA 45), 70f. Barth was concerned that "a cloud of gossip is arising around us," but believed that the most important thing was "that Nelly and you come to some kind of clear relationship... to one another." (Letter of August 4, 1926, to Kirschbaum, 69).
73. Poem of December 28, 1926, *Briefwechsel Barth-von Kirschbaum* I (GA 45), 75.
74. Poem of December 28, 1926, *Briefwechsel Barth-von Kirschbaum* I (GA 45), 75.
75. Cf. Stoevesandt, "Charlotte von Kirschbaum," in Beintker, ed., *Barth Handbuch*, 56.
76. Cf. the letter of April 18, 1933, from Nelly Barth to Eduard Thurneysen, *Briefwechsel Barth-Thurneysen* III (GA 34), 396.
77. Cf. the letter of April 18, 1933, from Nelly Barth to Eduard Thurneysen, and Thurneysen's letter of May 14, 1933, to Nelly Barth, *Briefwechsel Barth-Thurneysen* III (GA 34), 396 and 408f.
78. Letter of May 14, 1933, from Thurneysen to Nelly Barth, *Briefwechsel Barth-Thurneysen* III (GA 34), 408.
79. Cf. letter of August 7, 1929, to Kirschbaum, *Briefwechsel Barth-von Kirschbaum* I (GA 45), 98 and 100.
80. Cf. letter of March 21, 1929, to Kirschbaum, *Briefwechsel Barth-von Kirschbaum* I (GA 45), 81.
81. Cf. letter of September 27, 1929, to Kirschbaum, *Briefwechsel Barth-von Kirschbaum* I (GA 45), 104 and n. 1.
82. Cf. letter of March 21, 1929, to Kirschbaum, *Briefwechsel Barth-von Kirschbaum* I (GA 45), 78, n. 2. In 1928 Barth had started collecting citations on certain topics in

file boxes for his dogmatic work, a task that Kirschbaum now continued. The file boxes are arranged according to central key words, for example, "predestination," and subdivided by subtopics. There are citations from the Bible, the church fathers and medieval authors, Reformers and Old Protestant dogmatists, more recent authors as well as passages from the dogmatic texts of Barth's era. They constitute the foundation for Barth's lengthy excursuses in *Church Dogmatics*.

83. Cf. letter of March 21, 1929, to Kirschbaum, *Briefwechsel Barth–von Kirschbaum* I (GA 45), 79. Later too he still asked her to read literature "to my way of thinking" (letter of April 2, 1931, to Kirschbaum (176)), wording that indicates his strong impression that she was capable of thinking theologically entirely like him.

84. Letter of March 21, 1929, to Kirschbaum, *Briefwechsel Barth–von Kirschbaum* I (GA 45), 78.

85. Letter of March 21, 1929, to Kirschbaum, *Briefwechsel Barth–von Kirschbaum* I (GA 45), 81.

86. Cf. the letter of March 21, 1929, to Kirschbaum, *Briefwechsel Barth–von Kirschbaum* I (GA 45), 80, n. 12.

87. Letter of April 29, 1929, to Thurneysen, *Briefwechsel Barth–Thurneysen* II (GA 4), 660.

88. Cf. the letter of August 7, 1929, to Kirschbaum, *Briefwechsel Barth–von Kirschbaum* I (GA 45), 98.

89. Cf. the letter of August 7, 1929, to Kirschbaum, *Briefwechsel Barth–von Kirschbaum* I (GA 45), 98f.

90. Cf. letter of August 9, 1929, to Kirschbaum, *Briefwechsel Barth–von Kirschbaum* I (GA 45), 101.

91. Letter of August 7, 1929, to Kirschbaum, *Briefwechsel Barth–von Kirschbaum* I (GA 45), 98.

92. Cf. letter of August 9, 1929, to Kirschbaum, *Briefwechsel Barth–von Kirschbaum* I (GA 45), 100.

93. Letter of August 9, 1929, to Kirschbaum, *Briefwechsel Barth–von Kirschbaum* I (GA 45), 101.

94. Cf. letter of August 9, 1929, to Kirschbaum, *Briefwechsel Barth–von Kirschbaum* I (GA 45), 101.

95. Cf. letter of August 9, 1929, to Kirschbaum, *Briefwechsel Barth–von Kirschbaum* I (GA 45), 101.

96. Letter of August 9, 1929, to Kirschbaum, *Briefwechsel Barth–von Kirschbaum* I (GA 45), 103.

97. Letter of August 9, 1929, to Kirschbaum, *Briefwechsel Barth–von Kirschbaum* I (GA 45), 102.

98. Letter of August 9, 1929, to Kirschbaum, *Briefwechsel Barth–von Kirschbaum* I (GA 45), 102.

99. Cf. letter of September 27, 1929, to Kirschbaum, *Briefwechsel Barth–von Kirschbaum* I (GA 45), 105f.

100. Cf. letter of September 27, 1929, to Kirschbaum, *Briefwechsel Barth–von Kirschbaum* I (GA 45), 106: "The *shadows* of this week consist for me in the fact that I truly have *much* trouble in coming to terms with Nelly's manner. There was a trip through the town to find a wedding gift that was made really difficult, also technically, by her and my so utterly different attitude toward life... Yes, one *longs* for a quiet, easy (clouded

at most by an occasional little half-hour of Saturn) life together in Törli." The reference to Saturn concerns Kirschbaum's melancholy moods; she had ordered a horoscope to herself that argued that Saturn's influence was "like a leaden weight" (cited in a letter of October 4, 1929, to Kirschbaum (114, n. 2)).

101. Cf. letter of October 12, 1929, to Kirschbaum, *Briefwechsel Barth–von Kirschbaum* I (GA 45), 123f.
102. Cf. letter of September 27, 1929, to Kirschbaum, *Briefwechsel Barth–von Kirschbaum* I (GA 45), 108.
103. Letters of October 1 and 3, 1929, to Kirschbaum, *Briefwechsel Barth–von Kirschbaum* I (GA 45), 111f. and 113.
104. Cf. letter of October 4, 1929, to Kirschbaum, *Briefwechsel Barth–von Kirschbaum* I (GA 45), 114f. Shortly before her move in with the family Barth tried to explain to Kirschbaum that he had viewed her depressive periods in summer 1929 at the "Bergli" like a "warning": "What awaits us [with the move] is perhaps the most difficult test in both of our lives, and it is not *allowed* that we fail. It is not allowed that it then comes to light that our belonging together could only thrive and prove itself at best in the sun of the Bergli... I indeed like *the* Lollo who says: I don't want to, Karl! genuinely gladly, and she may and should truly also come, but just truly *come*, while it is entirely forbidden to opt out and be elsewhere than to be with her full attention." (Letter of October 6, 1929, to Kirschbaum (118).)
105. Translated literally, *Notgemeinschaft* means "an emergency or necessary community," but also "a community in distress."
106. Cf. *Briefwechsel Barth–von Kirschbaum* I (GA 45), 287, n. 3.
107. Cf. letter of October 1, 1929, to Kirschbaum, *Briefwechsel Barth–von Kirschbaum* I (GA 45), 111.
108. Zellweger-Barth, "Lebenslauf," in *Nelly Barth-Hoffmann*, 6.
109. Letter of March 18, 1932, to Kirschbaum, *Briefwechsel Barth–von Kirschbaum* I (GA 45), 218; cf. also the letter of October 4, 1934, 392: "Oh, it will truly be painful till the end of days that *our* little child will never be.—But I want to forget this again."
110. Cf. letter of September 12, 1930, to Kirschbaum, *Briefwechsel Barth–von Kirschbaum* I (GA 45), 155.
111. Cf. for example the letters of April 4 and September 9, 1930, to Kirschbaum, *Briefwechsel Barth–von Kirschbaum* I (GA 45), 130 and 151.
112. Thurneysen was the one friend who apparently was best able to empathize with the situation; in the years that followed he became something like a counselor to all three (cf. for example his letter of July 8, 1930, *Briefwechsel Barth–Thurneysen* III (GA 34), 16f.).
113. Letter of June 14, 1930, from Kirschbaum to Thurneysen, *Briefwechsel Barth–Thurneysen* III (GA 34), 15.
114. Cf. the letter Barth had already written on April 7, 1929, to Kirschbaum, *Briefwechsel Barth–von Kirschbaum* I (GA 45), 93, in which he asks her not to cry again and be angry when they see each other again at the "Bergli."
115. Cf. letter of June 16, 1930, to Kirschbaum, *Briefwechsel Barth–von Kirschbaum* I (GA 45), 135 with n. 9.
116. Cf. letter of August 21, 1930, to Kirschbaum, *Briefwechsel Barth–von Kirschbaum* I (GA 45), 140.
117. Letter of August 21, 1930, to Kirschbaum, *Briefwechsel Barth–von Kirschbaum* I (GA 45), 140.

118. Cf. letter of September 24, 1931, to Kirschbaum, *Briefwechsel Barth–von Kirschbaum* I (GA 45), 205.
119. Cf. the letters of August 4 and 5, 1930, from Nelly Barth to Anna Barth, *Briefwechsel Barth–Thurneysen* III (GA 34), 31.
120. Letter of August 5, 1930, from Nelly Barth to Anna Barth, *Briefwechsel Barth–Thurneysen* III (GA 34), 31.
121. Cf. letter of August 18, 1930, from Nelly Barth to Anna Barth, *Briefwechsel Barth–Thurneysen* III (GA 34), 35f. At the same time she was anxious about the necessary conversation with her husband: "I have a self-consciousness before it, before my own talking, which wants then to bring forward my own *wish*. I want to be open from the heart to Karl and not say anything forced, anything harmful. *Must* it then be that we once again hope, wish past each other, ... hurt each other to the bone?" (36).
122. Cf. letter of August 18, 1930, from Nelly Barth to Anna Barth, *Briefwechsel Barth–Thurneysen* III (GA 34), 36.
123. Cf. letter of August 18, 1930, from Nelly Barth to Anna Barth, *Briefwechsel Barth–Thurneysen* III (GA 34), 36.
124. Cf. letter of August 18, 1930, from Nelly Barth to Anna Barth, *Briefwechsel Barth–Thurneysen* III (GA 34), 36.
125. Letter of August 21, 1930, [I] to Kirschbaum, *Briefwechsel Barth–von Kirschbaum* I (GA 45), 138.
126. Cf. letter of August 21, 1930, [I] to Kirschbaum, *Briefwechsel Barth–von Kirschbaum* I (GA 45), 139.
127. Cf. the letter of August 12, 1930, from Karl Barth and Kirschbaum to Thurneysen, *Briefwechsel Barth–Thurneysen* III (GA 34), 34. The letter was a reaction to Nelly Barth's declaration already at the beginning of August of an either/or.
128. Cf. Kirschbaum's postscript to the letter of August 12, 1930, from her and Barth to Thurneysen, *Briefwechsel Barth–Thurneysen* III (GA 34), 35.
129. Cf. the letter of August 25, 1930, to Kirschbaum, *Briefwechsel Barth–von Kirschbaum* I (GA 45), 144.
130. Letter of October 19, 1930, from Kirschbaum to Thurneysen, *Briefwechsel Barth–Thurneysen* III (GA 34), 47.
131. Cf. the letter of June 4, 1931, from Nelly Barth to Marguerite Thurneysen, *Briefwechsel Barth–Thurneysen* III (GA 34), 147.
132. Cf. the letter of April 22, 1932, from Eduard Thurneysen, *Briefwechsel Barth–Thurneysen* III (GA 34), 332f.
133. Letter of March 18, 1932, from Kirschbaum, *Briefwechsel Barth–von Kirschbaum* I (GA 45), 217. Cf.: "Life there is so hard, and I often have no more strength at all to resist any longer against all this sad misery" (217).
134. Letter of September 24, 1932, to Kirschbaum, *Briefwechsel Barth–von Kirschbaum* I (GA 45), 246.
135. Letter of March 17, 1932, to Kirschbaum, *Briefwechsel Barth–von Kirschbaum* I (GA 45), 216.
136. Cf. letter of September 24, 1932, to Kirschbaum, *Briefwechsel Barth–von Kirschbaum* I (GA 45), 246.
137. Letter of July 7, 1931, from Eduard Thurneysen to an unnamed correspondent, *Briefwechsel Barth–Thurneysen* III (GA 34), 921.

10

"A Swissman in the Middle of Germany"

Bonn, 1930–5

In the summer semester of 1930 Karl Barth moved to Bonn. As of March 19 he lived with his family and Charlotte von Kirschbaum at Siebengebirgsstrasse 18. With respect to church politics the years that now followed would be the most intense and dramatic in Barth's life.

He had a successful debut in Bonn; Barth got along well with most of his new colleagues. From the beginning he felt especially close to the New Testament scholar Karl Ludwig Schmidt,[1] "who in any case thanks to the health and frankness of his nature is an agreeable colleague [of the kind] that I did not have in Münster."[2] The two went riding regularly.[3] Starting with the 1930/1 winter semester Fritz Lieb joined his Bonn circle of friends. As a theology student in 1921 Lieb had already assisted Barth with parish work in Safenwil. He too moved to Bonn in 1930 and in 1931 was appointed extraordinary professor for "Eastern Christianity in the past and present."[4] In 1931 Ernst Wolf joined the faculty as professor of church history and Christian archaeology. In his own work Wolf linked Barth's theology with that of Luther. In different ways Schmidt, Lieb, and Wolf became Barth's companions and allies. Wolf however became the most important, and Barth was always able to rely on his support.[5]

Working on Theology

For Barth the years in Bonn became the "liveliest and richest years" of his teaching career.[6] Students thronged to his classes.[7] In July 1931 the young Dietrich Bonhoeffer, at the time a lecturer in Berlin, came to Bonn for three weeks. He participated in several of Barth's classes and visited him at home. Afterwards he reported to his Swiss friend Erwin Sutz enthusiastically:

> I have, I believe, seldom regretted not having done something in my theological past as much as I now regret that I did not go to hear Barth sooner...it is... surprising in the nicest way to see how Barth still stands beyond his books. There is an openness, a willingness to listen to a critical comment...and with this such concentration and with a vehement insistence on the topic at hand...I am impressed by his discussion even more than by his writing and lectures. There

10.1. Karl Barth in Bonn, 1930, © Karl Barth-Archive in Basel.

he is really fully present. I have never seen anything like it nor thought it possible... This is really someone from whom one could learn something, and there one sits in poor, desolate Berlin and is discouraged because there is no one there from whom one can learn theology...[8]

Barth began his teaching in Bonn by repeating his two lecture courses on ethics given in Münster. This was followed by his Prolegomena to Dogmatics, but "in a new version."[9] Helmut Gollwitzer, then a student of Barth's and soon to become his doctoral student, reported that students were also involved in the reworking of the new version. Barth met with them during the summer of 1931 for a weekly society [a course for advanced students] in which the previous text of *Die christliche Dogmatik im Entwurf. Prolegomena* was discussed. The discussions took place with a certain "lack of respect"[10] for the teacher:

We spared him nothing. When several paragraphs had been ploughed through, sentence by sentence, Barth ended the meeting with the comment that for the next time we would need to compile a list of necessary corrections for the new edition. In response Karl Gerhard Steck[11] said: "What do you mean by 'corrections?' You cannot leave a single line of this stuff!"[12]

Barth actually wanted to spend only one semester reworking the book, but it dawned on him during his preparations for the society that presumably it would become "an entirely new book, as in 1920 the *Epistle to the Romans*, with many new loopholes and underground passageways."[13] Shortly after the beginning of the 1931 summer semester the scope of the text had expanded so much that he complained to Thurneysen: "The dogmatics in its new reworking is taking on dimensions that are making me very nervous for the summer holidays, in which it must be finished."[14] Barth agonized about making progress on it. "I have very often spent a whole string of fruitless hours and must repeatedly upend the work of entire days and start anew. Will the time never come when one can get genuine wisdom out of oneself with some fluency and elegance, and get it down on paper?"[15]

Once again Barth sent the individual paragraphs for a critical reading to Eduard Thurneysen, who comforted his friend:

> everything is thoroughly clear and the explanation is immersed in a rare fluency, very simply but at the same time each subsequent point stands forcefully next to the previous one. Something here has truly been brought to completion... The book will be no less of a cornerstone than was the Epistle to the Romans.[16]

Thurneysen was to prove correct in his estimation of the first volume of the work that would later be called *Church Dogmatics* and was to be Barth's life's work.

Barth's classes on Schleiermacher drew particular attention. According to Gollwitzer the students in Bonn came armed for "a great bloodbath and were looking forward to... the funeral feast. But we were treated to nothing of the sort."[17] Instead, Barth made it clear to them that Schleiermacher had central significance for modern theological history and that every serious theologian had to deal with him. Gollwitzer never forgot how one day he discovered portraits of the theological antipodes Schleiermacher and Harnack in the stairwell of the Barth home, and asked Barth with irritation, "Herr Professor, I thought you were opposed to them!?" Barth replied: "Despite everything they belong; and we too must be glad if we are allowed to belong," then adding that "the theological court [has] indeed to be distinguished from the Final Judgement."[18]

Despite the concentrated theological work there was no shortage of humor in Barth's classes. Gollwitzer related: "One morning—'The Blue Angel' was the current film sensation—Barth reported that 'last night I dreamt of Marlene

Dietrich.' We looked at him with envy: 'Oh, something nice?' 'She was very properly dressed and said to me: 'Karl Barth, give me a Bible!'"[19]

The Humanity of God

Barth's meetings with students in the summer of 1931, listening to their critique for a new version of *Die christliche Dogmatik im Entwurf,* were related to the fact that since the end of the 1920s he had once again undergone a theological transformation. It had become clear to him that he had to think beyond the 1927 work.

The occasion for this further change was first of all an argument with Erik Peterson that had begun in 1925; Peterson's critique had already been reflected in Barth's *Die christliche Dogmatik im Entwurf,* but only now led to broader consequences. Added to that was Barth's work on the medieval theologian Anselm of Canterbury.

In the spring of 1925 Peterson had given a lecture in Bonn against the methodological approach of dialectical theology, titled "What is Theology?" There he argued critically with Barth's claim that whoever avoided positive theological statements and persisted in the dialectical way of speaking was honoring God and doing theology with greatest seriousness.[20] Peterson took the opposing position that the seriousness of the dialectical thinker, at least, had nothing to do with the seriousness of God. Even more: dialectic was ultimately disobedience against God. For since Jesus Christ, God is "concretely visible and ... utterly undialectically there."[21] Only the one who conceives of God as concrete authority, whom one must concretely believe and obey, can honor God. Theology had certain presuppositions that must lead to genuine insights and clarifications in which—differently from what dialectical theology does—"in principle nothing is being left open."[22]

The premise of all theological thinking must be that God has become human in Jesus Christ and therefore that the knowledge of God is possible. Only in this way can there be any meaningful talk of revelation: "a revelation that cannot be recognized within certain parameters is simply not revelation."[23] Only in Jesus Christ, but then really in him, does God speak; in Jesus Christ's words and deeds God speaks and illustrates who God is. This is the foundation of Christian theology. For Peterson, this theology finds its proper form in dogma, that is, in the clear truth-claiming formulation of Christian doctrine.

Peterson wrote Barth that his lecture had "aroused a scandal and sensation" in the Bonn theological audience; he felt it was "the best that I have done up to now."[24] Barth read other things by Peterson and was torn both ways, admitting to Bultmann: "I have not read anything for some time that has so stimulated and angered me as these brilliant and in every respect insolent pamphlets."[25]

In October 1925 Barth answered Peterson's critique in his presence, in a lecture in Göttingen on "Church and Theology."[26] In Barth's view the discussion that followed was not very productive, "because P. simply did not confront it, instead declaring that he hadn't understood me."[27] In contrast Peterson had the impression that Barth had "not by any means [viewed] the problem in the sharpness with which it must be seen." Nonetheless Barth had found "it necessary to take my side...in the discussion."[28]

Barth's original concern in his lecture was to defend his dialectical theology. In fact however two significant shifts from his earlier texts can be observed:[29]

Firstly, Barth now emphasized that revelation itself was not dialectical and no paradox. It was much more the case that only the thinking and speaking of the theologian must proceed dialectically, since the theologian is simply human. With that, Barth was defending a different dialectic over against Peterson than what he had advocated previously.[30] Barth still believed that one must speak in pairs of concepts, naming in part the old pairs such as "grace and judgement," and "should *and* not-being able."[31] But he spoke now not of "belief *and* unbelief," but instead of "belief *and* obedience," and with respect to the world of "creation *and* providence."[32] In other words, he named not only paradoxical or contrasting pairs, but also conceptual pairs that fundamentally belonged together and described a positive interrelationship between God and humanity.[33]

Secondly, within certain limits Barth agreed with Peterson's accent on dogma as well as his thesis that the church was absent in contemporary Protestant theology. The "misery" of contemporary Protestant theology had a great deal to do with the fact that it found no church "that has the courage to tell us unambiguously: to the extent that we have something to say, this and that is dogma *in concretissimo*."[34] Theology needs this. While it does not live, as Peterson postulates, "from dogma," nonetheless it lives "*also* from dogma."[35]

In his 1927 *Die christliche Dogmatik im Entwurf* Barth took up Peterson's critique for the first time.[36] Peterson wrote retrospectively about this discussion with Barth, that "I inaugurated the turn toward dogma, whereas Barth on this point (as he told me) allowed himself to be influenced by me."[37]

The essence of theology was clarified further for Barth in his deepened study of Anselm of Canterbury. In summer 1930 he held a seminar about Anselm's text *Cur deus homo*, inviting philosopher Heinrich Scholz at the end of the semester to give a lecture about Anselm's famous "ontological proof of God."[38] Here Anselm extrapolated the necessity of God's existence from the determination that God was that "than which no greater can be conceived."

Barth could not let go of the topic. At the end of the summer holidays he wrote Thurneysen:

> Yes, Anselm! When I undertook at the beginning of the vacation to pursue the theme of my last seminar a little further for myself...I had no idea how far the

matter would take me...I fear that it will become almost a short book and am deeply concerned that it will be of much less interest for all of you than for me.[39]

The little book appeared in 1931 under the title: *Fides quaerens intellectum: Anselms Beweis der Existenz Gottes im Zusammenhang seines theologischen Programms* (published in English as: *Anselm: Fides Quaerens Intellectum*).

In his work on Anselm Barth discovered that theological knowledge "emerges out of the question of truth, which is always already positively decided in God" and that it can "depend on the reference to truth in the creed of the Christian church."[40] Stated briefly: theology always begins with the church's faith in Jesus Christ; it does not establish this faith. For that reason the task of theology is "to *reflect* on that which has been said" already in the confession of faith.[41] In this, theology is fulfilling a fundamental need of faith. Barth chose for the title of his book Anselm's formula, *"fides quaerens intellectum"*—faith seeking understanding. If theology begins with what for the faithful is the already certain existence of God, then for it—and this is the significant epistemological change over against the dialectical conception—God is also knowable.[42] From this point on, this understanding of theology defines Barth.

At the same time Barth persists in the conviction that in theology God can only be known through *human* reason and that only in *human* language can God be spoken of.[43] To picture this tension between God and human theology, Barth uses the figure of *analogy*, the equivalent. This already appears in his earlier texts, but now becomes a determinative conceptual structure. The dialectical way of speaking moves more into the background.[44] Human speech about God can be an "analogy"[45] that corresponds to God: *Because* God in Jesus Christ has spoken about himself, one human being can speak to another of God appropriately.

This initially very formal consideration led Barth to fundamental shifts in content. Now he pondered more intensively *how* God spoke of himself in Jesus Christ. From now on Barth's dogmatic thought would be devoted to the question: What about God and human beings is knowable in Jesus Christ?[46] In Barth's writings the love of God for humanity, which is shown in Jesus Christ, and the covenant that God through Jesus has entered into with humanity, now move into the foreground.

That which in this "christological concentration" seems to be a narrowing of his thought was experienced by Barth himself as a much greater freedom, clarity, and unambiguity.[47] While he was accused in this focus on Jesus Christ of "withdrawing entirely behind a 'great wall of China,'" and of only denying the world, Barth observed the opposite effect on himself: an openness to the world around him, for general intellectual history, the wisdom of classic antiquity and literature. "I do not think that I have ever lived more gaily in the real world, than precisely in this period, which brought with it for my theology what appeared to many to be a monkish concentration." Through this christological concentration he was "*simultaneously* very much more churchly *and* very much more worldly."[48]

In his 1956 lecture on "The Humanity of God" Barth once again offered an accounting of this change. In his theological turn away from the liberal and religious-social toward the dialectical theology of the two versions of the *Epistle to the Romans* he had been preoccupied with the "*godliness* of God," "the overwhelming height and distance, the strange, indeed, wholly other, with which a human being must deal when they take the name of God upon their lips." Focused completely on this, he had not been able to also speak appropriately about the "humanity of God" and in his talk of the infinitely qualitative difference had spoken "indeed somewhat terribly inhumanely."[49]

With that however he had overlooked the significance of Jesus Christ: in Christ God's "friendliness toward human beings" appeared.[50] For in Christ

> it has been once and for all established that God does not exist without human beings. Not as if God needs an other, and in particular human beings, in order to...truly be God...But...God in God's freedom really does not want to be without human beings, but rather *with* them...[51]

In *Church Dogmatics* Barth formulated this pointedly: "there is a Godlessness of human beings, but there is no 'humanlessness' of God."[52]

This has fundamental ethical consequences: "We have to regard and deal with *every human being*, even one who is most strange, villainous, or miserable, under the premise that, based upon the eternal decision of God's will, Jesus Christ is also *their* brother and God is also *their* father."[53] Barth's view of culture changed as well. Indeed, culture constantly attests to the fact that the human being "is *not* good, but rather to a great extent is a perfect monster."[54] But because the person acting here "is a being in whom God is interested," in culture God allows "*likenesses* of God's own eternally good will and action to occur ever and again."[55] Therefore the world does not stand generally in contradiction to the reality of God. Through God's working, things that correspond to and are analogies of God's relation to the world come into being. For Barth one of the most beautiful analogies was the music of Mozart.[56]

This theologically required friendly gaze turned toward our neighbor was reflected in a contribution by Barth to a 1934 newspaper. Along with the novelists Hermann Hesse and Thomas Mann Barth had been asked which book from the previous year he found essential. Where Hermann Hesse briefly referred among other things to Mann's *Joseph and His Brothers*, Mann praised various biographies and non-fiction books, such as those by Ernst Bloch and Karl Mannheim, that were characterized by their critical relevance to the times and their literary skills. In contrast, Barth named three novels, Alexander Lernet-Holenia's *Die Standarte*, Frank Thiess's *Der Weg zu Isabelle*, and *"Das Herz ist wach". Briefe einer Liebe*, ed.

by M. B. Kennicott, adding that his expectation of a modern novel was that it portrayed human beings as they were. He expected the novel

> to present to me in the human beings of today, my contemporaries, human beings as they always are—as well as the reverse: to present to me, in human beings as they always are, my contemporaries. That [the novel] delivers the proof on each page that the author loves these people... Further: that the book conveys in entirety only what its author has seen in these people... Finally: that it has a form corresponding to the picture of the human being that has been presented, internally necessary, rigorous, and also memorable, such that I cannot soon forget the person who has been shown to me in his time-bound and timeless shape, but rather must live with him, perhaps must live with him ever and again.[57]

Barth's formulation in 1934 is all the more astonishing when one considers that he experienced the developments in Germany during those years as "an enormous revelation of human lies and brutality on the one hand, and of human stupidity and fear on the other."[58]

First Conflicts with German Nationalists: The Case of Günther Dehn

One of Barth's first extended encounters with the dark side of human beings was the public controversy about the theologian and religious socialist Günther Dehn. They had first met in 1907, as young theology students in Barth's parents' home in Bern. Dehn later related how they had sat next to each other at dinner and he would have liked "a conversation" with Barth

> about church and theological conditions, especially in Switzerland, but there was no opportunity. While he spoke a sufficient amount, it was always only about his fraternity, the Zofingia... That this student would later one day become the famous theologian Karl Barth was completely obscured to me that evening. In any case the aura of future greatness did not rest on him then.[59]

In 1919 Dehn then heard Barth's Tambach lecture, which affected him "like a huge liberation."[60] Since then they had been on friendly terms.[61]

In 1928 Dehn held a lecture in Magdeburg on "Church and Reconciliation among the Nations," which took up the basic ideas of Barth's theology and was directed against interpreting the death of soldiers as a Christian sacrifice.[62] Dehn argued: When the death of a soldier was understood as Christian sacrifice, "this portrayal ignores the fact that the one who was killed also wanted to kill. Thus the parallel with the Christian supreme sacrifice becomes impossible."[63]

When Dehn in December 1930 received an offer of a professorship in practical theology at the University of Heidelberg, Gottfried Traub published a critical article on Dehn's lecture in the German nationalist paper *Eiserne Blätter* ("Iron Papers"), which led the Heidelberg faculty to withdraw the invitation to Dehn.[64]

In 1931 Dehn then received an offer of a professorship in Halle. This time German nationalist and National Socialist students attempted to prevent his taking office.[65] They decided to leave the University of Halle because of his appointment. At the request of Dehn and Gertrud Staewen,[66] a social pedagogical worker and friend of the Barth family, Karl Ludwig Schmidt and Karl Barth in October 1931 co-authored a short declaration sent to the rector of the University of Halle "that they are personally and objectively in solidarity with Dr. h.c. Dehn."[67] For them, the *objective* solidarity—in contrast to another protest letter from colleagues that merely criticized the students' disturbance of academic teaching[68]—was especially important so that students understood: "You will encounter a Dehn again at so many other universities...Dehn is not alone."[69]

At Dehn's first lecture class on November 3, 1931, the students distributed leaflets: "Pastor Dehn wants to educate German children in the crassest and most cowardly pacifism. Should we look on as such a person receives a chair at our university?"[70] In December 1931 Dehn published the documents about his case with the clear-sighted afterword, which however was again viewed as provocative: "It is simply not true that this fanatical love of the Fatherland, religiously-colored, if you like, but in truth detached from God, truly helps the Fatherland. On the contrary, it will lead the Fatherland to ruin."[71]

In response, Barth's former Göttingen colleagues Emanuel Hirsch and Hermann Dörries, a church historian who had been teaching in Göttingen since 1929, formulated an opposition statement, arguing that every person had to acknowledge "that the nation and its freedom, for all the questionable aspects of creaturely life, are goods that God hallows for Christians as well, demanding the full devotion of heart and life." From that follows "the confession to our people's passionate will to freedom, which is being oppressed and defiled by enemies who are grasping for power and possession."[72]

Barth was asked by several colleagues to say something more about the matter. Although since 1925 in addition to his Swiss citizenship he had possessed Prussian and therefore German citizenship,[73] he initially refused, giving as a reason that he did not want to get involved as a Swiss citizen: "My decisive reluctance to go along with your wish consists simply in the fact that as a *Swiss* I am not obviously the man called to act in this matter as *the praeceptor Germaniae*."[74] Hardly had he sent off this reply, however, when he wrote an article that was published on February 15, 1932, in the *Frankfurter Zeitung*.[75] There he emphasized that Dehn's viewpoint was a consequence of the dialectical theological approach, in which it was a matter of "understanding church and Gospel...on the basis of their foundation and content documented in the Holy Scripture rather than on the

10.2. Karl Barth in 1932, © Karl Barth-Archive in Basel.

basis of the Christian or other form of piety of the respective current age."[76] Whoever took a position against Dehn had to be against all of dialectical theology. *"The enemy is not just named Günther Dehn!"*[77]

This led to a public clash between Barth and Hirsch. Hirsch wrote an open letter, published on February 27, 1932, in the journal *Deutsches Volkstum*, that Barth's answer illustrated once again that he was not in the position to

> correctly understand and convey someone else's line of thought when [he] disagrees with it. For years now those working in theology who arouse your displeasure bear it as their cross that your polemic does not go without misrepresentations, and we have all come to understand that at your end this is not due to ill will, but rather that this shows an insurmountable limit to your intellectual ability.

Moreover, Hirsch argued, Barth faced German destiny in the role of an observer. Hirsch did not expect someone living in Germany as a guest to feel like a German, but truly indeed that "the lack of an ultimate sense of absolutely belonging to our people and state limits your understanding of German affairs, which you must learn inwardly to respect." The "consideration of the foundation and right of all human existence" is the required "objectivity when doing theological work." This human existence essentially includes "becoming part of the nation [Volk] and state and the historical hour and historical task of the nation and state"; underlining this specific context is an expression of obedience to God, who has located human existence in that specific context.[78] In light of such formulations and their later consequences one understands why Barth in his own thinking even years later still explicitly opposed orienting theological thought toward the circumstances and contexts in which it occurs, and underscored the orientation toward God's action in Jesus Christ as the essential objectivity of theology.

In his reply of April 17, 1932, Barth noted that Hirsch made no distinction between theology and politics. He did not recognize anything "above and beyond political excitement" as it exists in "God," "Gospel," and "Church."[79]

Hirsch reacted once more with an open letter that insisted that Barth as a Swiss could not understand what Germans were currently going through. Hirsch himself viewed his task as a professor of theology to help his church "in the right manner and with the right guidance, to position itself in the current German reality that God has laid before them."[80]

The thematic substance of the fronts along which the conflicts of the following years would play out had been marked by the conflict around Dehn. Hirsch and Barth exchanged private letters in April and May, but these could not overcome the rift between them.[81]

In light of the ongoing demoralizing conflicts Dehn himself applied in the fall of 1932 for a one-year leave of absence. He was given this on April 22, and on November 21, 1933, he was dismissed from his position under paragraph 4 of the Law for the Restoration of the Civil Service passed on April 7, 1933.[82]

Barth's colleague in Bonn, Karl Ludwig Schmidt, had to leave the faculty in 1933 as well due to this paragraph, since he was a member of the Social Democrat party (SPD).[83] Schmidt emigrated to Switzerland but left his children with family friends in Germany; his son Andreas Schmidt was taken in for a while by the Barth family.[84] Barth had happy memories of this time, writing Schmidt in 1956: "Do you still remember how during your childhood in Bonn you once offhandedly commented 'Aunt Lollo is the only reasonable person in this (namely ours) household!' Somewhat painful for the rest of us, but in fact proof of your sharp eye, apparently already then in existence and at work!"[85]

Now's the Time for the Social Democrat Party: 1933

On January 30, 1933, the day of Hitler's appointment as Reich Chancellor, Barth wrote Thurneysen that he should be "calm and unworried. The Nazis won't do anything to me."[86] At the time Barth somewhat innocently believed that he had "a 'stormtrooper' who is a very active member of the society and seminar...who acknowledges me as someone having a special providential mission, parallel to that of Adolf, and will certainly keep the brown henchmen away from me."[87]

In light of the ideological changes, which in Barth's view had long since settled firmly in theology and indeed were being promoted by it, in a March 1933 lecture

Barth insured himself of the theological foundations from which he even now did not think he could depart. He delivered this lecture, "The First Commandment as Theological Axiom," in Denmark.[88] The first commandment states: "I am the Lord your God, who brought you out of Egypt, out of the house of slavery. You shall have no other gods before me." (Ex. 20:2–3, NRSV) Barth believed that to obey this commandment we must orient ourselves exclusively toward God's self-revelation in Jesus Christ and reject all other sources of knowledge. Otherwise one was doing "natural theology." Barth drew the conclusion:

> In view of the first commandment as theological axiom, the unavoidable fight against natural theology is a fight for correct obedience in theology...theology today [should]...bid farewell to each and every form of natural theology and dares...in that narrowness, that isolation, to depend utterly on the God who is revealed in Jesus Christ.[89]

Barth would draw the consequences of this theological insight in the Barmen Declaration of Faith, as well as in his reactions to the "German [Hitler] greeting" and the civil service loyalty oath. The more that National Socialism revealed itself as the repudiation of the first commandment, the more intensely and extensively Barth waged his battle.

In light of his public engagement Barth decided it was necessary in the spring of 1933 to clarify the new government's view of him. Like Schmidt, he was a member of the SPD: out of protest against the political developments he had already joined the party on May 1, 1931.[90] He paid his membership dues until June 1933; the party was dissolved in July.[91] On April 4, 1933, Barth sent the following unsolicited inquiry to his superior, Prussian minister of culture Bernhard Rust: did the National Socialist government have the intention of ending his professorship in Bonn, given his membership in the SPD?[92] Barth stressed that his SPD membership was purely for "practical political...reasons" and had "nothing to do" with his teaching activity, "which is determined and bound solely through the confession of the Protestant church." He continued:

> My academic activity cannot have anything to do with the fight against the old or support for the new political system, but instead is determined solely by the command of theological objectivity. I couldn't however accept a demand to leave the SPD as a condition for the continuation of my teaching duties, since I cannot expect anything good from denying my political convictions or neglecting to make them known, as this step would mean, neither for my listeners nor the church nor the German people.[93]

Barth's letter concluded with the request for clarification so that he could know how he should plan his future.

Rust replied to Barth that he had no intention of restricting his teaching activities.[94] When an official letter reached Barth in early August 1933 that all civil servants had to leave the SPD, he drew the conclusion, based on his correspondence with Rust, that this requirement had already been clarified and that he did not have to take such a step. In the controversies to come however Barth's SPD membership proved to be far more problematic than Rust's reply had suggested.

Warnings to the Church and a Letter to Hitler

For the church in Germany, the early months of 1933 were shaped by the growing influence of the "German Christian" movement and the new government's policy of *Gleichschaltung* to conform the church and other institutions to Nazi state goals. The "German Christian" movement had been founded in 1932 with the goal of creating space for National Socialist ideology within the (Protestant) church. Its guidelines from June 6, 1932, had clearly announced this intent:

> We confess an affirmative faith in Christ, one suited to a truly German spirit of Luther and heroic piety... We want to bring to our church the reawakened German sense of life and to revitalize our church... We want our church to be front and center in the battle that will decide the life or death of our people... We recognize in race, ethnicity, and nation orders of life given and entrusted to us by God, who has commanded us to preserve them. For this reason race-mixing must be opposed... We are conscious of Christian duty toward and love for the helpless, but we also demand that the people be protected from those who are inept and inferior.[95]

In addition the German Christians were advocating a change to the German Protestant Church Federation, which had existed since 1922 to unite the various regional churches. Instead, they demanded a unified Protestant Reich Church, with the suspension of the previous democratic structures and led by a Reich bishop.[96] The National Socialist government also sought in this way to conform the church to the new regime.

The crisis that emerged out of these processes[97] was unleashed by the circumstances surrounding the election as Reich Bishop of Friedrich von Bodelschwingh, director at the time of the Bethel institutions and the candidate of the Young Reformation Movement, which opposed the "German Christians." He had been elected on May 27, 1933, under circumstances that had not yet been fully clarified in terms of new church law. In response the "German Christians" proposed the Königsberg pastor and long-time Nazi party member Ludwig Müller as the opposing candidate. Prussian minister of culture Rust announced a state of emergency in the church and on June 24 August Jäger was appointed church commissar for Prussia. That same day Bodelschwingh declared his resignation.

Barth was pressed by different sides to comment on the situation. He wrote his opinion between June 14 and 25, titled *Theological Existence Today!*, as the situation intensified.[98] His publisher Lempp insisted on going to press quickly, so that the text was already available on July 1, 1933. It met with an enormous echo. By July 1934, when the text was confiscated, 37,000 copies had been printed.[99]

Barth began his essay by reporting that he had been urged to state his position on the current "church concerns and problems."[100] But: "the decisive thing that I am trying to say today about these concerns and problems" consisted

> very non-currently and impalpably simply in this... that I am attempting to proceed here in Bonn with my students in lectures and exercises to do theology and only theology, just as before and as if nothing had happened—perhaps in a slightly raised tone but without making a direct connection. Somewhat like the Benedictine chanting of the hours in the nearby [abbey of] Maria Laach is doubtlessly proceeding, even in the Third Reich, according to the rules without interruption and diversion. I am of the opinion that this too is a statement, in any case a church-political statement and indirectly even a political statement![101]

Barth continued that rather than speaking "to the situation" it would be better as a theologian to address "the issue."[102] For the church it was essential that it meet the claim of the word of God "to be proclaimed and heard."[103] The danger of the current era was that

> amidst the power of other claims we no longer understand the intensity and exclusivity of the claim of the divine word as such, and therefore suddenly we no longer understand this word at all... That under the stormy impression of certain "forces, principalities, and powers"[104] we seek God elsewhere than in God's word, and God's word elsewhere than in Jesus Christ, and Jesus Christ elsewhere than in the Holy Scripture of the Old and New Testaments, and are therefore those who do not seek God at all.[105]

Each church reform, including external forms, must emerge from the "life... of the church itself... from obedience to God's word, or it is not *church* reform."[106] With the appointment of a state church commissar however this had been taken out of the church's hands. And with the establishment of a superior bishop's office in the Protestant church, the state's "Führer principle, embodied in the figure of Adolf Hitler and his subordinates," would be introduced into the church.[107]

Barth accused the "German Christians" of subordinating the church's purpose to the German people. The church indeed believed that God installed the state to be the bearer of law and order, but it did not believe in a certain state or specific form of state. The church proclaimed the gospel "also *in* the Third Reich, but not *under* it and not in *its* spirit."[108] Correspondingly:

> The community of those who belong to the church is not determined by blood or through race, but rather through the Holy Spirit and baptism. If the German Protestant Church were to exclude Christians of Jewish descent or treat them as second-class Christians, then it would have ceased to be a Christian church.[109]

With that Barth took a clear position against the adoption of the "Aryan paragraph"[110] from the Law for the Restoration of the Civil Service (April 7, 1933) for church law.

Barth concludes his text with a warning to German theology and the church:

> For that reason the church and theology cannot hibernate, even in a totalitarian state, and cannot accept a moratorium or be conformed to the state. The church is the natural boundary for everything, including the totalitarian state. For the people live even in a totalitarian state from the word of God, the content of which is: "forgiveness of sins, resurrection of the flesh and eternal life." Church and theology have to serve this word for the people. Therefore they are the boundary of the state. They are this for the salvation of the people, for *the* salvation that neither the state nor the church can create, but which the church is called to proclaim. The church must be *allowed* to remain true and must *want* to remain true to its characteristic objectivity. In the *particular* concern that has been assigned to the theologian he must remain *awake*, a lonely bird on the roof,[111] that is on earth but also under the open, wide and absolutely open heaven. If only the German Protestant theologian would stay awake, or, if he happens to have fallen asleep, today, today would awaken once more!"[112]

After the article's publication Barth received almost one hundred letters agreeing with him,[113] including one from Heinrich Scholz: "in the hour of the greatest danger you have been the theologian who rescued us from suffocation and led us back to the word that already seemed to be intended for crucifixion."[114] Non-theologians also took note of Barth's text. Thomas Mann, who had emigrated to Switzerland, wrote in his diary on August 29, 1933: "This evening read with extraordinary sympathy the text by Karl Barth, 'Theological Existence Today.' What a fearless, brave and pious man! And how symbolic, how not-only-theological, everything that he says is! His ironic politeness toward the German leaders is downright amusing."[115]

On July 1, 1933, Barth even sent his text to Adolf Hitler himself, writing in the cover letter outspokenly: "Protestant theology must go its own way, even in the new Germany, unrelenting and untroubled. I request your understanding for this necessity."[116] Whether Hitler responded to Barth is not known.

On July 11, 1933, the new constitution of the German Protestant Church was signed[117] and church elections were scheduled for July 23. Together with several colleagues and friends Barth founded a candidates list "Für die Freiheit des Evangeliums" ("For the Freedom of the Gospel").[118] In Bonn it competed with the "German Christians" and the Young Reformation Movement, which also rejected the political church aims of the "German Christians" but was more nationalist. The "German Christians" in Bonn achieved an absolute majority, but six candidates from the "For the Freedom of the Gospel" list were elected as Protestant congregational representatives:[119] Barth himself, Charlotte von Kirschbaum, Barth's colleagues Hans Emil Weber, Ernst Wolf, and Gustav Hölscher, as well as Otto Bleibtreu, a court assessor who later became Barth's lawyer.[120]

1933 as a Year of Crisis in the Barth Household

In the spring of 1933, as the political situation in Germany became increasingly difficult, Barth's domestic situation escalated. In March Nelly Barth began to consider the possibility of a divorce.[121] She summoned Karl Barth—as she explained to Eduard Thurneysen—"to a totally truthful decision, because it has turned out that the [three-way] *Notgemeinschaft* is not supported by the love for each other by each of us that alone would have allowed it to 'live.'"[122]

During these days Barth wrote Charlotte von Kirschbaum that on the one hand he tended toward a divorce, but on the other hand asked himself whether they had truly exhausted all other possibilities.[123] Charlotte however hoped that in light of the growing political difficulties she could be with Barth *legally*.[124] She recognized that Nelly could not live in the three-way constellation, but also that a return to the original marriage, as Nelly wished, was impossible:

> I think of Nelly with much sad sympathy. She really cannot live like this, it is destroying her, but the other thing, that which *she* wishes, will be even less possible. The longer this goes on the more I have the impression that she is dying of undernourishment next to you.[125]

In reality both of them—as Kirschbaum explicitly wrote—had long since divorced from Nelly and would only "avoid the risk as seen from the outside."[126] At the same time she assured Barth that she would stay with him, whichever path he now decided to take.[127]

Karl responded on March 31, 1933, to Nelly's wish for a decision with a long letter in which he once more explained his idea of a three-way *Notgemeinschaft*. This *Notgemeinschaft* meant that each one—bound and not bound in a particular fashion with the other two—has a special place, a special security, but also a special burden and pressure, without having to end our marriage legally and outwardly, and without having to deny and suppress that which connects me to Lollo.[128]

Barth tried to make clear to her that in this he had never considered a *Notgemeinschaft* in which he had the same relationship to each woman.[129] At the same time he now acknowledged that it was impossible for Nelly to live this way.[130]

For Karl Barth the option of returning to his marriage to Nelly without Charlotte was now as before ruled out; he felt himself "helpless" to do so.[131] It was clear to him that Nelly understandably would never stop hoping for this, but this very hope made their three-way relationship impossible because Nelly did not recognize that the *Notgemeinschaft* for Barth was not his free, even arbitrary choice, but rather simply a "necessity."[132] The necessity for him was "that on the one hand we—you and I—as it has become even more clearly evident in these seven years than before, are strangers to each other and in my conviction will remain so, while in the same way Lollo's inner belonging to me is a reality," and that on the other hand he did "not wish to annul the legal and external existence of our marriage."[133] He acknowledged his guilt to her: "that at a stage in which apparently I was not mature enough for such a decision, I asked you if you would be my wife, that I then couldn't be to you what a husband should be to his wife, and that finally I could not remain faithful to you as promised."[134]

Barth continued that he now felt a divorce was correct,[135] but a divorce in which Nelly and he would continue to be responsible and solicitous of one another.[136] For that reason only a divorce agreed upon by both was possible.[137] A divorce could also be an expression of love between them:

> I think: we can admit to each other that the attempt at a *Notgemeinschaft* in its form up to now has failed to such an extent that we must hold it as futile for the future, and so we see no other possibility than to forsake the legal-public form of our marriage. In doing this, we give each other the freedom and the room to live our lives as we *can* live them... [we] want... to show our respect for one another and express the love, from *within* that indestructible relationship between us to seriously look and enter on the path to a "*divorce*" of our legal-external marriage. As things are, I now don't know any other way either.[138]

Nelly replied however that she did not want a divorce, but instead preferred to continue living in the three-way relationship.[139] Karl countered that a divorce that would give them both distance and room to live was the only way in which they could still "prove faithfulness" to each other.[140] This wording sounds sarcastic, but is understandable when one considers how deeply all three were suffering from the situation and that Barth felt seriously obligated for the welfare of his wife. To him a divorce meant not the end of their relationship but was its necessary alteration.[141] For all three the divorce could be "something like a small door out of a prison that has truly become unbearable for all of us."[142] He now wanted to marry Charlotte von Kirschbaum.[143]

Barth even made a suggestion to his wife regarding what could happen with the children in the case of a divorce; depending upon their agreement he himself wanted to take both older sons, Markus and Christoph.[144] Barth concluded his letter with the words: "Now it is a matter of proving the unity that we have owed each other until now. I would like to call you to this rescue of the meaning of our marriage."[145]

The developments of April and May 1933 illustrate how convoluted the situation was. Nelly wrote Eduard Thurneysen that she knew "indeed for some time... that our community, however it may be, *is* recognized by God"; for her, acquiescing to a divorce would mean "blotting out the hope of our marriage."[146] She too felt "the responsibility toward the church congregation" and asked: "Am I not his wife, should I not prevent that he *must* divorce me?"[147]

On April 11 Dorothee Stoevesandt, a family friend, had a lengthy conversation with Nelly in which Nelly read both of her husband's letters to her.[148] Afterward Stoevesandt wrote to Karl Barth herself. She believed she had the "right" to do so, in light of the understanding of the Bible she had learned from him. In her letter she reminded Barth of his wife's loneliness in the three-way *Notgemeinschaft* up to now, which in fact had been "two and one." Nelly for him was like poor Lazarus or like the person "fallen 'among murderers'" (whom the Good Samaritan had helped) "as commanded by God." Barth should not attempt to cast off "the cross" that had been laid upon him.[149] That same day her husband, Karl Stoevesandt, wrote Barth as well and reminded him of his prominent position and his responsibility for the church.[150]

Charlotte was disheartened by Dorothee Stoevesandt's letter, which Barth showed to her:

> I am very sad. The "opinionated" letter from D. St. yesterday has confronted me with the full misery with N. I would like to be able to cry to the world: "This is all not *true*. It is all very different." But I know that one cannot do that. And that indeed we are *not* able to justify our path and that all *those* who shout out these obvious matters, like in this letter, are the ones who are right.[151]

Barth had the similar impression that the Stoevesandts were not really trying to put themselves in the place of the three, instead speaking too much "from an 'unassailable' place."[152] He replied to them that it was *he*, not them, "who was there in the twenty years... of marriage with Nelly, certainly with 'covered' eyes, as well as without the inner remorse over what I was doing—but nonetheless

I myself was there."[153] When they now accused him of having not done enough, they were failing to recognize that "we all cannot do what we should be able to, in the combination of guilt and guidance and nature given to us."[154] Barth protested that he did not have the intent, even in a divorce, of evading the particular responsibility of a marriage. "Even a divorced marriage remains a marriage."[155] He definitely wished to bear the cross of this marriage. "One cannot cast off one's cross, but perhaps one can put it on the one shoulder when one has chafed the other."[156]

Barth's mother opposed a divorce as well.[157] Kirschbaum tried to explain the situation to her: they had arrived at thoughts of a divorce "only from the point of utter hopelessness." "And now we stand before the question: must we endure a path that has become hopeless, hopeless with respect to the internal situation of three people, until one of us perishes, or may we now attempt a new path?"[158]

On April 19, 1933, even before his reply to the Stoevesandts, Barth wrote his wife that he accepted her decision *against* a divorce, although he was as before of the view that she would eventually arrive at this point.[159]

> But if we do not yet have your agreement to this of your own free will, then that is how it is, and there should and will hopefully be no lack of good will from Lollo and me as well to contribute to making this entire situation under these circumstances bearable, although from our perspective this cannot be something other than a more or less lasting temporary measure.[160]

On May 3, 1933, Nelly Barth then agreed to a divorce. Surprised by this change, Karl and Charlotte now did not see themselves in the position to agree to it. They had the impression that Nelly did not genuinely want this divorce:

> Yesterday Nelly agreed to a divorce, just as suddenly as two days before she had rejected it. It has become *completely* clear to us for the first time that now we may *not* do this, since *every* precondition for even the smallest agreement, in which alone K. wanted this step, is absent. Now we continue *as before*, N. at the moment astonishingly relieved.[161]

Yet the situation at home remained difficult. Charlotte shared her resignation and her inability to bear the situation with Thurneysen. She repeatedly rebelled against it.[162] And she could not feel any gratitude toward Nelly for her decision to continue on this three-way path, which Nelly however apparently expected and which only showed how much she misunderstood the situation.[163] At the same time Charlotte was distressed that she was not able to be a better companion to Nelly and that she also didn't even "feel a little love" for her.[164]

For her part Nelly complained to Marguerite Thurneysen that she no longer received Barth's correspondence to read and felt even more excluded than before this crisis.¹⁶⁵ "Whoever would look at our days could testify that I have retreated to my lonely place, without accusing, without *any* attempt to demand something kind."¹⁶⁶

In the summer of 1934 Nelly seems to have suffered so greatly under depression that she could no longer manage the household. Charlotte tried to help, but this only made the situation more tense, since Nelly now viewed this realm as having been stolen from her as well.¹⁶⁷

Occasionally however the letters following the great crisis of spring 1933 reveal a more carefree mood, at least between Karl Barth and Charlotte von Kirschbaum.¹⁶⁸ This may have been not least because the church demands of that period had become so great that private problems moved into the background. Both declared repeatedly to one another how much they loved and needed each other.¹⁶⁹ Charlotte understood his sense of isolation in the church situation but also grasped how necessary his voice was for the church: "Do not let yourself become weary. You are *very* alone, but it is very, very necessary. I told Lempp that I would rather go alone with you into the desert than [go] with others in filled churches."¹⁷⁰ At times it was easier for them to accept the situation as it was:

> Perhaps it will not be otherwise possible than that we must pay the price, well and truly, for our strange life, with all the worries and dejection that are spared others. But what do we want?—that is simply our life, against which we cannot grumble, just as we cannot let it be taken from us.¹⁷¹

10.3. Karl Barth with Charlotte von Kirschbaum in 1935 near the "Bergli" in Oberrieden, © Karl Barth-Archive in Basel.

One problem of the *Notgemeinschaft* was certainly that from the very beginning so many people felt justified in commenting on it. Letters were very often shown to third parties.[172] Gerty Pestalozzi and Eduard Thurneysen tried to empathize with the different difficulties of all three and avoided advising a certain course. Others however were very certain as to what was right and what was wrong. There were repeated conversations with Karl and Nelly Barth's siblings as well as with his mother.[173] Things went so far that in 1935 Charlotte rebelled against further judgements by Barth's sister Gertrud Lindt: was there something specifically to blame in this three-way relationship "that *we* must ask ourselves but *you* cannot ask us, or you need to have a different kind of insight into the concrete difficulties of our life together and [could] ask us this as a genuine attempt to help us with these difficulties."[174] Barth suffered similarly from the interventions of others. In 1933 as they considered the option of a divorce Barth wrote his mother how weary he was to have to discuss all this with her.

10.4. Karl Barth with his mother Anna Barth in 1928, © Karl Barth-Archive in Basel.

I would be so happy if you could now say to yourself that a forty-seven year-old man must ultimately know what he is doing when after a twenty year marriage he arrives at such a decision, and if you could place this confidence in your son, who after all is not unknown to you, which he does not want unprincipledly.[175]

His mother replied the next day that God's commandments applied to everyone, adding ruthlessly: "What good is the most discerning theology when it suffers a shipwreck in your own home."[176]

Barth tried to free himself from such opinions. He comforted himself and Charlotte with the insight: "Yes, how differently people are reflected in the eyes of others, and how good it is indeed that in the best case there is 'somehow' a not inappropriate snapshot, whereas no one ever is able to view and judge the entire film."[177]

The Theological Dimension of Barth's Relationship to Charlotte von Kirschbaum

On several occasions Barth expressed his belief that without Charlotte von Kirschbaum he would never have been able to do his theological work as he had. In 1947 he wrote a pastor in Neuenburg: "Without her my work could not have had the scope that it has achieved." He added: "it is not just a matter of her versatile technical collaboration but primarily in how she has accompanied me."[178] In the foreword to volume III/3 of *Church Dogmatics*, written in 1950, he declared to his readers

> what they and I owe to the twenty years of work quietly accomplished at my side by *Charlotte von Kirschbaum*. She has devoted no less of her life and powers to the growth of this work than I have myself... I know what it really means to have a helper.[179]

Kirschbaum had her own interest in theology. She passed examinations in 1933 that would have permitted her to study theology even without a high school exam.[180] She participated on her own in the Confessing Church theological working conference in January 1935 in Bad Oeynhausen, having conversations there with leading figures.[181] She also wrote some short theological texts and the small 1949 monograph *Die wirkliche Frau*.[182] Nonetheless she does not appear to have missed being in the public sphere herself. When Georg Merz suggested in early 1932 that she edit a book of devotions, she refused because she did not want to give up her anonymity.[183]

Kirschbaum's work was indispensable for the material richness of Barth's theology, as is evident in his *Church Dogmatics*. It is undisputed that she collected citations for his index card file and observed the critique of his theology among contemporaries. This led some to suspect that she, and not Karl Barth, was the author of the exegetical and historical excursuses in *Church Dogmatics*.[184] The few preserved handwritten excursuses in the Karl Barth-Archive in Basel however show Barth's handwriting, not that of Kirschbaum, and it can hardly be assumed that Barth copied out her texts by hand before she then typed them. He would have been able to make his own additions or revisions when he dictated the text.[185]

Karl Barth, Charlotte von Kirschbaum, and Nelly Barth were all aware of Barth's responsibility for the theology and church of his times. In his first love letter to Charlotte in 1926 Karl made clear to her that he had to deal with the situation in a manner appropriate to his responsibility for his work.[186] He was immediately aware of the discrepancy between what he said and what he did, and decided to fight against it. "Not for the sake of morality, but rather for the sake of the issue with which I had been tasked and have taken up, which I may not *wish* to damage, inwardly or outwardly, and which I may not *wish* to compromise."[187] He added: "It makes no difference whether the world knows of this or not. I have never preached morality, but indeed discipline as the reverse of faith and hope."[188] Once he realized that he could not live without Kirschbaum he decided for this three-way *Notgemeinschaft*.

Yet, this assessment shifted under the painful domestic pressures of 1933. Barth continued to fear provoking offense, but came to the conclusion

> that in any case bourgeois habit may not be the highest viewpoint and measure here. And then since many aspects of my authority in Christian-church circles are all too unreal anyway... the real aspect of this authority will be untouched by the examination that will surely arise through this event.[189]

Just as Barth's concern (that his authority as a theologian might be affected by a divorce) shaped his private life, so too his private experience ultimately influenced his theology as well. This was already evident in his very first love letter to Charlotte von Kirschbaum. Barth wrote her that a harsh tone dominated his theology:

> By pointing to the question, to the claim that is directed at human beings and toward the judgement to which they are subject and *must* subject themselves, I have taken much from many (and indeed [much that is] beautiful and lovely and high!). Arguably I think that I have often spoken too sharply, with too much certainty, and at the same time have had to sacrifice too little concretely myself.[190]

He continued: "a strange result of our 'experience' will be that my course this summer on the newer history of theology [his lecture course on the history of

Protestant theology since Schleiermacher] will turn out much milder, more compassionate, most reserved, than would otherwise have been the case!"[191]

Theologically Barth interpreted his situation as a tension between "order"[192] and that "which unwillingly has come over us out of the mysterious guilty depths of human nature," between the "sacredness of the commandment" and the fact "that you and I (I don't know on what level) are together,"[193] between the "right" that his wife had on her side and the "elemental experience."[194]

Barth however perceived yet another tension, namely between his culpability toward his wife and the right of his love for Charlotte:

> the shadow of guilt and suffering and denial under which you and I stand is there and will be there, but it is not the only thing there. Rather there is a certain *right*, admittedly difficult to describe, that we have for each other, and we may and will be *happy* in this right.[195]

Barth was convinced that this "could not simply be the work of the devil, it *must* somehow have some sense and a right to live, that we—no, I will speak only for myself—that I love you so much and see no possibility of stopping it."[196] He even had the sense that somehow in this situation God was acting,[197] hoped that God would show them the right way,[198] and spoke of the "*two* who have been given to me."[199]

Barth did not evade these tensions and tried to hold firm to the two realities of his life. In 1947 he declared in a letter:

> The way I am, I could and still can neither deny the reality of my marriage nor of my love. It is true that I am married, and I am a father and grandfather. It is also true that I love. And it is also true that these two facts are not in concordance with each other. Because of that we decided after a certain hesitation at the beginning not to resolve the problem through a separation of the one or the other... I find myself in a situation in which there are only imperfect solutions. I do not doubt for a moment that the seventh commandment in its Christian interpretation implies monogamy and the insolubility of the marital bond. In order to preserve my responsibility toward this commandment I had and have only the choice of choosing the least imperfect solution: in place of a separation of the one or the other, the permanent crisis that... is very difficult for all three involved to bear. I must also endure that this is even difficult for my friends to recognize and understand that with this decision I endeavor to live in order, not in disorder.[200]

At the same time, in Barth's eyes even a divorce would not have been disorder, since it is made possible in civil law.

Disorder in the face of God's order is not permitted, but why should a re-ordering, as occurs through the possibility of civil divorce despite all difficulties and sadness that it brings and must necessarily bring along with it, in the most extreme cases not only be allowed especially in light of the divine order, but even commanded?[201]

It would be wrong simply to identify civil marriage, as a human order, with the divine order. "It too... *is* only a human order that is *related* to the divine order within specific limitations, limitations that in those most extreme cases may and under certain circumstances must be transgressed."[202] No one should be too certain as to *how* God's order in his life and in the lives of others should be concretely realized: We can "not determine for ourselves and others the *how* of this order, or what *form* the crosses that [we] respectively have to bear will take, with the same unambiguity and finality... as for the *That* [of that order], from which there is certainly no escape."[203]

Charlotte von Kirschbaum expressed a very similar view in a February 1935 letter. The *Notgemeinschaft* was a form of responsibility, an "order in disorder."[204] She was convinced that order, God's commandment and responsibility could be found in both relationships; not only was there a "marriage" between Barth and his wife, but in the relationship between him and Charlotte as well.[205]

In 1947 Barth summarized how he viewed himself in his relationship to the two women and what this meant for his theology:

> The very fact is that the greatest earthly blessing bestowed upon me in my life is simultaneously the harshest judgement against my earthly life. So I stand before God's eyes, without being able to escape God in the one way or another... It is entirely possible that because of this there is an element of experience in my theology, or better put: an element of lived life. In a very concrete manner I have been forbidden from becoming the legalist that under other circumstances I could have become.[206]

Attacks on the Swissman

During the second half of 1933 Barth was attacked on many occasions for his public statements. The speaker for the "German Christians," Bishop of Hamburg Franz Tügel, declared in August in a brochure, *Unmögliche Existenz! Ein Wort wider Karl Barth*:

> Back then, the edition of Barth's "Epistle to the Romans" was for me—and surely not just for me—a great comfort and support out there on the front in the service

of the men's church (*Männerkirche*). This Protestant word about the sacred greatness of God helped us, those who truly "sat in the darkness and shadow of death," giving us a final ray of light for the path. On the desolate retreat of a victorious army which had been betrayed of victory, through the villages and cities of France, Belgium and Luxembourg, where from behind slightly opened curtains we were greeted by sneering faces, in the return to a Fatherland torn apart... such a theology as Barth was teaching at the time was a hardening bath for us who could barely still come to terms with this world.

Barth's essay *Theological Existence Today!* however was a theology "in a vacuum." Tügel thus closed that the "German Christians" today had "only him as enemy and no other!"[207]

Above all Barth was accused of doing not theology, as he claimed, but politics. Here the issue was raised again and again that he was Swiss, a democrat, and member of the SPD: he was opposed to state and nation, his behavior and thought posed a danger to the state. Barth did not let himself be distracted by this and even publicly emphasized the freedom that he possessed as a Swiss citizen:

I know indeed in what way I am, and amidst the German theology and church also totally and stalwartly wish to remain, a Swiss—namely in what one can read in the very secular Gottfried Keller: Hail to us, among the free it is still the custom/[to speak] a passionately free word! And I admittedly believe that—if there is to be any talk at all of my homeland identity card—I cannot better prove my love for and my affiliation to Germany than by being in that sense—a Swissman in the midst of Germany but in contrast to many Germans. Show me by what right people for that reason want to dispose of me![208]

Regarding the relationship between theology and politics he declared:

Where is it then written that one cannot be a good Christian and theologian if he belonged to the SPD, and if, with regard to the Reichstag fire, his reason tells him something other than what reason tells some others... Politics for me has always been a matter of second order. I allowed and allow myself to have my own opinions in this matter. But I have never confused these opinions of mine with that which I have to preach and teach, because (in contrast to the "German Christians"!) I am certain that in church and theology the Holy Scripture should lead the word, not political opinions.[209]

In the fall of 1933, in confidential conversations with opposition pastors held in the home of Berlin Pastor Gerhard Jacobi, Barth made it clear that his theological orientation would nonetheless have unambiguous consequences in the church-political sphere. Charlotte von Kirschbaum took notes, and Erica Küppers, a friend of Kirschbaum and Barth, reported on one of the conversations in a November 11, 1933, circular letter to friends.[210]

In these conversations Barth expressed his conviction that one could neither cooperate with the "German Christians" nor with the current church government, and had to oppose all the regulations that were in contradiction to the nature of the church.[211] Barth compared the situation with the persecution of Christians during the third century, when sacrifices before the portrait of Caesar represented a denial of Christ.[212]

Küppers also reported in her circular letter about Barth's meeting with the U.S. ecumenical official Pastor Charles S. Macfarland that same day. Macfarland was about to meet with Hitler. Barth is reported to have told him that he should relay a message to Hitler: "the fact that he named Ludwig the child [Ludwig Müller] Reich bishop was exactly as catastrophic as if he had named Lieutenant v. Köpenick [a famous impostor who posed as a Prussian officer in the early twentieth century] Reich military minister!"[213] Küppers' letter did not remain in confidential circles, but reached the Gestapo and the Prussian Ministry of Culture.[214] This was to play an important role in Barth's subsequent dismissal.

Against the "German Greeting"

On July 22, 1933, the order went out that all civil servants in the scope of their duties had to greet people with "Heil Hitler!"[215] Barth did not comply with the request of the Bonn University rector, sent to the professors on October 27, to begin and end their lecture classes with this greeting. He usually began his lectures with a brief meditation, in the context of which a greeting would not have been suitable.[216]

The departmental student organization then demanded that Barth's students still receive him with this greeting. Most did not do this, whereupon several received a reprimand.[217] Barth now advised his listeners to fall in line, even if he still did not use the greeting in that setting, and added Luther's motto "Sin boldly!," leaving no doubt about his view of the matter.[218] Summoned by the rector, Barth declared that he felt free or not to comply with a request; he would need to receive a command.[219] On December 14, 1933, the rector commanded him to use the greeting in lecture classes. Barth then submitted a complaint two days later to minister of culture Bernhard Rust. The Hitler greeting was "the symbolic act of recognizing the totalitarian claim of national unity in the sense of the National Socialist state," but

> theology, even when it is taught at university and in a state-owned building, is unequivocally and exclusively about the matter of the church, which is the proclamation of the Gospel. The totalitarian claim of national unity cannot be

applied here, because in it [in the matter of church] it finds its corresponding limit, namely as it here encounters a different, superior claim to totality... To make entirely clear what I mean here, I add: I would deem it right if the carrying out of the "German greeting" were completely banned in the entire Protestant and Catholic theological lectures. In this place it must be characterized by the church as well as by the state as improper.[220]

Barth's letter went through the official channels via the university rector's office, so that the rector immediately added:

Herr Professor Barth is opposed to the current state. In my opinion he is looking for reasons that must lead to his dismissal, but also could awaken the impression that he is being persecuted for his engagement for religion and church. I think that he is counting on his departure in the foreseeable future, at the same time hoping however that this departure will make him a "prominent case," a martyr in the eyes of the world.[221]

The Break with his Dialectical Traveling Companions

Since the mid-1920s Barth's relation to his companions in the dialectical breakthrough had changed. As did he, his earlier comrades-in-arms now presented their own concepts in which their previously shared critique moved into the background and they dared positive theological statements that went in very different directions.[222]

Between Emil Brunner and Barth the conflict arose about ethics and the problematic of "natural theology" as well as the question about an eristic that could make Christian faith understandable for people who are not Christians.[223]

Already in 1918 Brunner had warned that one could not simply disregard "human responsibility and activity"[224] as Barth did. In Barth's first *Epistle to the Romans* the human being was "annihilated... and [turned into] a marionette."[225] In Barth's thought there was an exaggerated dualism of ethics and God, so that a positive relationship between the acts of human beings and the Kingdom of God no longer existed.[226]

Brunner formulated his alternative in 1932 in his book *Das Gebot und die Ordnungen*, which he understood as an ethic of dialectical theology.[227] Thurneysen and Barth already had the impression since 1920 that Brunner relativized the radical No to the impossibility of a human path to God.[228] In the years that followed they watched his development attentively, Barth more rigorously than Thurneysen. In 1930 Thurneysen therefore warned Barth ironically: "Be gentle with the young man—Emil! He certainly deserves a good thrashing like all the others, but he should not be surrendered... protect him, it will not be in vain!"[229]

Brunner insisted that the *questions* of human beings, and indeed their questions today, had to be taken seriously. The answers from the Bible had to be "answers 'oriented' by these questions."[230] He read Barth's *Christian Dogmatics in Outline* from 1927 with this purpose. He appreciated Barth's starting with the church sermon, yet missed the eristic perspective: "The sermon proclaims the word—yes indeed; but it says it to the *human being*... Barth himself understands how to really speak to real human beings. But there is a great danger that his principles and position seduce others... no longer to *speak* but to *declaim*."[231] Brunner therefore sought a "point of contact" in human beings through which they could be approachable for the word of God. Despite the danger of thereby asserting bridges between humans and God, he asked "about the relation between the 'natural human beings' and the word of God," wanting to pose "therefore *the anthropological question*."[232]

The conflict between Barth and Brunner intensified during the National Socialist era. In May 1934 Brunner published *Natur und Gnade* ("Nature and Grace"), in which he rejected Barth's critique of his way of natural theology. Barth appeared to him "as a loyal soldier on night duty, who as ordered shoots everyone down who doesn't give the password, and therefore occasionally puts to the sword even a good friend when in his zeal he doesn't hear or correctly understand the password."[233] Barth's reaction, titled *Nein! Antwort an Emil Brunner* ("No! Response to Emil Brunner"), appeared in November 1934. Brunner's son recalls how his father "grew pale" when the mail brought him Barth's pamphlet. Brunner had become accustomed to criticism, but "this Nein!, for the first time so publicly and intensely hurled at him, deeply agitated him, it nagged at him until the end of his life."[234]

Barth began his reply with the ironic introduction:

> I am by nature a gentle creature and utterly averse to all unnecessary conflicts. Whoever—in light of the fact that here he has received a real polemic to read—argues against me that it would be so very much more beautiful if the theologians dwelled together in unity, may be certain of my heartfelt agreement from the onset. And so he may also be explicitly told that in human terms and personally I have absolutely nothing against Emil Brunner, rather very much for him.[235]

Then however Barth explained that he was in no way of the opinion that, as Brunner claimed, "the task of our theological generation is to find our way back to a *correct* natural theology."[236] With that Brunner was expressing the kind of "mediation theology... that has proven itself to be the cause of the current disaster of the Protestant church in Germany."[237] Brunner felt himself completely misunderstood in Barth's text: "The Emil Brunner that you are smearing here *coram publico* (in public)... exists... only in the fantasy of Karl Barth."[238]

Despite this difficult conflict Brunner took a personal interest in Barth's fate during his final months in Germany.[239] They also stayed in casual contact with each other in the years to come and usually addressed one another in letters as "Dear friend." Later they again had words with each other in the context of their work in the Swiss Protestant *Hilfswerk* (Aid Association) for the Confessing Church, because they had different opinions about the significance of the Barmen Declaration of Faith.[240] After the war they fought about the Christian position on Communism.[241]

Barth and Brunner never completely lost sight of each other, whereby this was much truer for Brunner. In 1956, on the occasion of Barth's 70th birthday Brunner wrote him: "Among the thousand voices of grateful and respectful best wishes my own should and would not wish to be absent, coming from a forty-year long 'unhappy love' that despite and in all the battles has proven to be true."[242] Asked in a 1960 interview about the relations between the two, Barth responded with a sad parable:

Can you compare a whale, let's say Moby Dick, with an elephant? Both are God's creatures, but they cannot encounter one another, perhaps from a distance, but it's not a genuine encounter. They cannot speak with one another, they cannot fight one another, they cannot make peace—that is so. My friend Brunner can

10.5. Karl Barth with Emil Brunner, ca. 1935, © Karl Barth-Archive in Basel.

decide whether he prefers to be the whale or the elephant. I hope that the day will come when we see and understand what was planned here—the intention of our good Lord in creating these two, the elephant and the whale.[243]

There had also been tensions between Barth and Rudolf Bultmann since the mid-1920s,[244] which intensified as Bultmann aligned himself more and more with the philosopher Martin Heidegger. Bultmann had become convinced by Heidegger's analysis of the human existence in *Being and Time* (1927): the human being is thrown into existence, is fallen to the "Man," that means onto that which *one* thinks and does, and must be summoned from this inauthentic existence to authentic existence. It was not the new life in Christian faith but the problematic of the inauthentic human existence that Bultmann believed had been appropriately described by Heidegger. He accused Barth of ignoring current philosophy, instead having "naively" adopted "the old ontology of patristic and scholastic dogmatics" in his *Christian Dogmatics in Outline*.[245]

Barth had the impression that in this Bultmann was moving along the same lines as Brunner and Gogarten.

> From my standpoint the concerns of all of you, although differing from mine in different ways, represent a large scale return to the fleshpots of Egypt ... I mean that if I am not deceived, all of you—certainly in a very new way, different from that of the nineteenth century—are trying to understand faith as a human possibility, or, if you will, as grounded in a human possibility, and therefore you are once again surrendering theology to philosophy.

Here they were playing "with the possibility of a natural theology" and were doing "theology in the context of a pre-existing understanding that had not been reached theologically."[246] Through that the shared battle he had once waged together with Bultmann became questionable for Barth: "It might well be that what I understand by the 'Word of God' has never been a concern of yours in this way ... so that our ships were merely ships that passed in the night."[247] Bultmann reacted amicably and invited Barth and Thurneysen to Marburg for a "religious colloquy" with him, Gogarten and Brunner.[248] Because Gogarten then cancelled, the meeting did not take place.[249]

Barth and Bultmann did not write each other at all between October 1931 and July 1933. Bultmann felt fundamentally misunderstood by the accusation that he was advocating a natural theology. After 1933 they met several times to talk, since Bultmann was also active against National Socialism and became a member of the Confessing Church. Barth deceived himself when he thought that Bultmann's theological approach would necessarily lead to support for the "German Christians."[250]

Barth nonetheless was steadfast in his critical position against Bultmann's theological approach. In 1941 Bultmann published his program of a "demythologization of the New Testament": the New Testament contained numerous mythical elements such as images of heaven and hell, angels and demons, or an apocalypse. Bultmann included the divine sonship of Jesus, his death of atonement on the cross, resurrection and ascension, as well as the resurrection of all human beings after death. Because modern people no longer shared this worldview, they could no longer understand the message of the New Testament,[251] although these mythical images expressed a truth about human existence and faith in God that also had a significance in the present. Bultmann attempted to elaborate this significance through an "existential" analysis of the mythically conceptual figures of the New Testament by asking which understanding of existence was being expressed in them.

In 1952 Barth summarized his critique of Bultmann.[252] It was primarily related to the search for an understanding of human existence that was to be articulated in the mythical elements of the New Testament. With that theology again ran "into the dead end of a philosophical anthropology...from which I thought I had summoned it four decades ago."[253]

The course of the conflict between Barth and Friedrich Gogarten ran similarly.[254] Since they had founded the magazine *Zwischen den Zeiten* together in 1922, Barth felt a certain skepticism toward Gogarten's theology.[255] At the time however he still believed that he and Gogarten "were gnawing on the same bone."[256] But with Gogarten's 1929 review of Barth's *Christian Dogmatics in Outline* the substantive differences became apparent. Gogarten felt that Barth was missing a reflection of the essence of history and a thorough anthropology to make it clear who the contemporary human being was who was being addressed by God.[257]

After personal relations between the two became increasingly difficult, the final break came in 1933.[258] That which Barth had incorrectly suspected in Bultmann did in fact occur in Gogarten: following his 1932 *Politische Ethik* in which he had argued for an authoritarian understanding of the state, Gogarten believed that the church too should contribute to the revival of the German people through National Socialism.[259] In August 1933 he joined the "German Christians" for several months,[260] saying that this was "the historical location where it will be decided what our churches have to offer."[261]

The basic *theological* difference between Barth and Gogarten concerned the question of where human beings encounter God's law.[262] Gogarten spoke of the lordship of Jesus Christ meeting people there where they stand under the law of history, to which the law of the nation (*Volk*) especially belongs.[263] Barth saw in this—as he explained in his final contribution to *Zwischen den Zeiten*—an unacceptable proximity to the notion "that God's law for us is identical with the *Nomos* of the German people." Such an identification however was "a betrayal of the Gospel." He and Gogarten were "now divorced people."[264] This was the end of *Zwischen den Zeiten*. Issue 4 in 1933 was the final edition of this publication which had determined the debates for twelve years. Barth, Thurneysen, and Merz each wrote a brief text for this "farewell." Barth was sorry for this break, but attributed it, in an honest self-appraisal, to his own role in it, which "really appears to have its own to some extent explosive or in any case centrifugal effect."[265]

The Barmen Theological Declaration

1934 was the year in which church opposition to National Socialism was most intense. The unacceptable leadership of Reich bishop Ludwig Müller, who had been in office since September 27, 1933, moved the church opposition to consolidate its energies.[266] The most important result of this was the first Confessing synod of the German Protestant Church in Barmen in May 1934, at which the Barmen Theological Declaration, the fundamental document of the Confessing Church, was passed.[267]

On January 23, 1934, the church opposition met in Berlin to consult about what could be undertaken against recent developments. They were united in their rejection of Müller and Jäger and their policies for the Nazification of the church (*Gleichschaltung*), but divided about the relationship to the "German Christians." In a memorandum that was to be presented to Hitler, several wanted to open by thanking God, in the "German Christian" spirit, "for everything that He has done for the German people in 1933 through Adolf Hitler."[268] Barth rejected this: "We have another faith, we have another spirit, we have another God." Over against the "German Christian" positions there could only be "an either/or."[269]

On February 13, 1934, Barth personally wrote another letter to Hitler in which he expressed his regret that Hitler "apparently has never had the opportunity... to take note of an authentic portrayal of what the Protestant church is and should be."[270] He therefore enclosed issues 5 and 7 written by him from the *Theological Existence Today* series.[271]

At the end of March 1934 the bishops of Bavaria and Württemberg, Hans Meiser and Theophil Wurm, decided to bring together the church opposition in an organized way.[272] An important milestone was the "Rally of the Confessing German Protestant Church" in Ulm on April 22, which protested the *Gleichschaltung* policy and announced that the confession of the German Protestant Church was in danger; those gathered were speaking as "the legitimate Protestant Church of Germany."[273] This declaration can be viewed as the birth of the Confessing Church.[274]

To give this new association a more binding organizational form they decided to call a synod, with representatives from all the regional German churches. For the committee that would be preparing a theological declaration, three Lutherans were invited (pastor Hans Asmussen from Altona, High Church councillor Thomas Breit from Munich, and church historian Hermann Sasse from Erlangen), as well as Karl Barth as the Reformed representative.[275] The preparatory committee agreed to meet on May 15–16, 1934, in Frankfurt. It was difficult for Barth to participate in the meeting; he had been interrogated by the Gestapo on April 30, 1934, due to the circular letter from Erica Küppers about statements that Barth had made in October 1933.[276] At the end of the interrogation he was told that "for the foreseeable future he should not take any longer trips, particularly not abroad," but instead should "stay in Bonn and the immediate surrounding area."[277] Barth requested to travel to Frankfurt nonetheless, which was eventually approved.[278] However Sasse was absent due to illness. On the basis of the first morning's consultations Barth wrote during the midday break a first draft of the text in which the basic structure of the subsequently approved Barmen Declaration is evident: the draft includes a preamble that declared why they had decided for a confessional act, and five theses, each of which was constructed in

10.6. At the 1934 Barmen confessional synod: Karl Barth (with pipe) on the left; the two other persons cannot be identified with certainty, © Karl Barth-Archive in Basel.

the form of a biblical citation, a statement of affirmation, and a statement of rejection, with a brief conclusion. At the end of his life Barth commented on this context with a *bon mot*: "The Lutheran church slept and the Reformed church was awake. That was the process of the origin."[279] Afterwards the text underwent an extensive revision by all three present. At the end of the Frankfurt meeting a "Frankfurt *concordia* (agreement)" was on the table, amended by a sixth thesis. According to more recent research this should be viewed as a "text worked out collectively."[280]

When they left Frankfurt, Asmussen, Barth, and Breit assumed that the text would be submitted in this form to the synod. Asmussen was asked to deliver the talk at the synod about this submission.[281] Yet there were objections by Hermann Sasse and his Erlangen colleague Paul Althaus, who accused the text of "syncretism" and of being a union of Lutherans, Reformed, and United[282] reached behind the scenes, leading to a "surrender of Lutheranism to Karl Barth."[283] Althaus wrote Bishop Meiser: "I have discovered that in the entire draft the word 'Volk' does not appear, except in Thesis Six in a different sense. The state is mentioned, but not the people. True Barth!—and Lutherans are going along with it!"[284] With that they had bypassed the fact "that God's claim on us is *also* encountered in the necessities of life of the 'creature' entrusted to us, e.g. our people."[285] Althaus was also displeased with how the state was dealt with: "the concept of state here is that of the liberal constitutional state, as in all of Barth's writings. We Lutherans know that the state is in the service of the life of a *people*."[286]

Meiser finally saw himself compelled to request three further drafts of the text.[287] On May 26 Asmussen traveled to Barth to discuss a revised text that he had worked on together with Sasse. Barth believed that his fear of a "watering down"[288] was confirmed, and convinced Asmussen to adhere more closely to the Frankfurt version. Together they worked on what would be called the "Bonn draft" and agreed that the text as well as Asmussen's presentation would not be submitted for an immediate vote by the synod, but instead as a working text for separate discussion among the different confessional groups during the synod.[289]

On the evening of May 29, 1934, the synod in the Wuppertal district of Barmen opened with a worship service in the church in Barmen-Gemarke. 139 synodal delegates from almost all the regions of Germany were present, with Stephanie von Mackensen from Pomerania as the only woman delegate.[290] Barth had been explicitly forbidden from traveling to the synod. He protested this but sent the letter so late that by the time it arrived he was already consulting with others in Barmen.[291]

After several preliminary discussions the "Bonn draft" was submitted to the synod on May 30. The Lutherans' reservations toward a collective declaration were put aside (except by Sasse) and several suggestions for changes were made.[292] The Lutherans in addition insisted that the declaration for them would not have "the character of a confession in the sense of the Heidelberg catechism and the

Augsburg confession."293 The introductory remarks by Asmussen, in whose sense they wanted to understand the declaration, were essential for Lutheran agreement. The text was revised one more time and in a second reading on May 31 unanimously approved.294

Up until the 1960s Barth presented his own explications of the Barmen Theological Declaration, and the following comments are drawn from those.295 In his view the declaration's decisive advance was that it finally clarified that the protest against the theology of the "German Christians" concerned the heart of Christian faith and therefore had to be unavoidable for every true Christian.296 With the Barmen Declaration's clear affirmations and sharp rejections it rendered impossible what had up to then been the customary response, of "both...and," and gave "the 'free' resistance against the break-in of the German Christians the unambiguous form that until then had been absent."297 Several days after the declaration's ratification Barth during a lecture exclaimed about it with joy: "today the...era of the sleeping church has come to an end!"298

The unity and at the same time the unambiguity of the Barmen Theological Declaration were achieved through different clarifications. At the beginning it invoked the German Protestant Church constitution and with that claimed to be speaking for the rightful German Protestant Church.299 The existing church government had deserted the foundations of its constitution, the "Gospel of Jesus Christ, as it is witnessed to us in the Holy Scripture and has come anew to light in the confessions of the Reformation"300 The confession to Christ, not to political developments, bound the different confessional churches to one federation: "Whatever may divide us, this confession to the *Lord* of the church unites us."301 The "German Christian" ideology that had penetrated the church threatened this confession and this federation, because it introduced *"alien principles"* into the church.302

The first Barmen thesis is the foundation for the Declaration: "Jesus Christ, as he is attested for us in Holy Scripture, is the one Word of God which we have to hear and which we have to trust and obey in life and in death."303 The entire world is indeed in God's hand and God can reveal himself everywhere.304 However: "We do not recognize God in such a way in these figures, events and powers that we could point toward them: Here God is, that this recognition could become a recognition apart from the recognition of God in Jesus Christ."305

In Barth's interpretation of the declaration, this thesis is identical with being oriented toward the first commandment and with the battle against natural theology. Through the statement of rejection in the first thesis—"We reject the false doctrine as though the church could and would have to acknowledge as a source of its proclamation, apart from and besides this one Word of God, still other events and powers, figures and truths, as God's revelation"—the exclusivity of the orientation toward God's revelation in Jesus Christ is sharpened, and it is a warning against "natural theology": "everywhere where one gives natural theology even the little finger" leads "to the denial of God's revelation in Jesus Christ."[306] Following Barth's thinking, he is also saying that it is false to understand certain historical events like the rule of the National Socialists as the revelation of God.

The second Barmen thesis states:

> As Jesus Christ is God's assurance of the forgiveness of all our sins, so in the same way and with the same seriousness is he also God's mighty claim upon our whole life. Through him befalls us a joyful deliverance from the godless fetters of this world for a free, grateful service to his creatures.[307]

It is saying that the life of the Christian cannot be divided in two realms, an internal-spiritual one and an outward-worldly one. With this Christ would cease to be Lord of our entire life.[308] The corresponding rejection reads: "We reject the false doctrine, as though there were areas of our life in which we would not belong to Jesus Christ, but to other lords—areas in which we would not need justification and sanctification through him."[309]

The third thesis distinguishes those who are bound together in the church from any form of blood brotherhood: "The Christian Church is the congregation of the brethren in which Jesus Christ acts presently as the Lord in Word and Sacrament through the Holy Spirit."[310] For this reason the church had to orient itself toward Christ and not—as the rejection explicitly states—around current worldview or political concepts.[311]

The fourth thesis interprets all offices of the church as a special form of that service, which is the task of the entire congregation, and in its statement of rejection turns critically against the Führer principle in the church: "We reject the false doctrine, as though the church, apart from this ministry, could and were permitted to give to itself, or allow to be given to it, special leaders vested with ruling powers."[312] For only Jesus Christ is the "Führer" of the church.[313]

The fifth thesis describes the relationship between church and state. The state is to provide justice and peace, the church is to remind the state of the kingdom of God and make the state aware that it must answer before God's commandment and righteousness.[314] There are two statements of rejection expressed under this thesis: the doctrine of the "totalitarian state" that seeks to dominate all areas of life, including the church, is rejected, as is the teaching that the church should take over the tasks or characteristics of the state. Barth later noted that a strong and vital church would have needed to judge the abuses of the Nazi state even more strongly.[315] Even for these statements however they had to summon all their courage. In light of the ideology of that era the theses were "an immense contradiction."[316]

Finally, in the sixth thesis the task of the church was named and the concept of the people (*Volk*) taken up: "The church's commission, upon which its freedom is founded, consists in delivering the message of the free grace of God to all people in

Christ's stead, and therefore in the ministry of his own Word and work through sermon and sacrament."[317] Swept up into "the steepest ascendance of National Socialist glory," the German people needed this grace of God as well.[318] The church's "popular touch" is due to the proclamation of this grace, not to anything else.[319]

The declaration's conclusion made clear that to reject the declaration would mean a renunciation of Christian faith. At the same time it stressed that while the declaration rejected false teaching, it was not rejecting the human beings who were following these teachings; much more, the declaration invited them to return to the one faith confessed here.[320]

When Barth later looked back at the declaration he was particularly troubled by the "missing seventh thesis" concerning the treatment of the Jews.[321] In a letter to Eberhard Bethge he acknowledged, after reading his Bonhoeffer biography: "I have long since regarded it as guilt on my part that I did not make this [the 'Jewish question'] a decisive issue... at least publicly in the Church Struggle."[322] A statement about it, Barth believed, "would hardly have been acceptable to the mindset of even the 'confessors' of that time.' But this does not excuse the fact that since my interests were elsewhere I did not at least formally put up a fight on the matter."[323]

The Barmen Theological Declaration became the "program"[324] of the Confessing Church. Yet from the onset there was debate about what political consequences it made obligatory for the church. In the subsequent debates about this Dietrich Bonhoeffer, who at the time of the declaration's creation was a pastor of German congregations in London, steadfastly advocated a consistent orientation toward Barmen:

> Either the Barmen Declaration is a true confession to the Lord Jesus effected by the Holy Spirit, in which case its character can be constructive or schismatic for the church; or it is a nonbinding expression of the opinion of several different theologians, and the Confessing Church itself has since then been traveling down a fateful, false path.[325]

Criticism however came from Paul Althaus and the Lutheran church historian and systematic theologian Werner Elert, who together with several other theologians wrote the Ansbach Memorandum on June 11, 1934. There they emphasized against the first Barmen thesis that while the *Gospel* was the message of Jesus Christ, the *law* of God encounters "us in the total reality of our lives, as it has been brought to light through God's revelation. It [the law]... commits us to the natural orders to which we are submitted, such as family, people (*Volk*), race (i.e. to which we are tied by blood)."[326] As late as 1947 Althaus complained in his *Die christliche Wahrheit. Lehrbuch der Dogmatik* (published in English as *Christian Truth: Textbook of Dogmatics*) that the first thesis of the Barmen

Theological Declaration was unbiblical and un-Lutheran, because it had been formed by "Barth's monistic doctrine of revelation."[327]

After the Barmen Synod Barth was under stronger surveillance by the National Socialists. A May/June 1934 report by the Security office of the *Reichsführer SS* stated: "Barth's direction must be characterized as a real danger. In his theology he is creating islands on which people isolate themselves, so as to evade the requirements of the state today for religious reasons."[328] Barth felt the direct effects of a July 9 decree from the Reich Ministry of the Interior, which forbid all public gatherings and publications on the Protestant church battle. All of the existing pamphlets he had written for the *Theological Existence Today* series were confiscated at the end of July at the Chr. Kaiser Publishers offices in Munich.[329] Barth had to send all new texts for the series to the Bavarian Political Police for approval. As he wrote his publisher Lempp, it seemed to him that the prospect of "having to present [his] manuscripts to some uneducated person for review was completely impossible."[330] Could it not be better "now to be demonstratively *silent* than to speak from within some gag order and say whatever such a person is kind enough to consider incontestable"?[331] He even considered stopping the series, to prevent it from becoming a *"harmless publication organ"*: "An armored cruiser cannot be rebuilt into a pleasure yacht."[332] Barth reached an agreement with Lempp to continue the series, but foregoing the prefaces he had written until then about the church situation.[333] In the next issue he explicitly emphasized to his readers that the contemporary aspect of the publication was now to be found "Between the Lines."[334] On October 24, 1934, the order to confiscate Barth's pamphlets was lifted, and after that Barth's prefaces once again appeared.[335]

Barth's son Christoph, at the time sixteen years old, similarly fell into a dangerous situation. In a letter to a friend in England he spoke clearly about the situation in Germany. The letter was read by the censor and Christoph was interrogated for three hours by the police. Because the files were forwarded to the senior prosecutor's office in Leipzig, the family decided it was safer to send him to Switzerland and let him complete his schooling there.[336]

Tensions continued to heighten on the church-political level. Because of their protest actions the bishops of Württemberg and Bavaria, Theophil Wurm and Hans Meiser, were removed from office and placed respectively under house arrest on October 6 and 12, 1934, by August Jäger, who in the meantime had been appointed the "commissar" of the German Protestant Church. Jäger was planning the swearing-in ceremony to Hitler of the Reich bishop and the regional bishops for October 23. The Confessing Church deliberately called the second Confessing synod on October 19–20, 1934, in Berlin-Dahlem, where Martin Niemöller, chair of the Pastors Emergency League, was the pastor. The Dahlem synod drew the practical consequences of the Barmen Declaration, declaring "emergency church law" and strengthening the necessity of having a separate governance system. Along with Charlotte von Kirschbaum Barth participated in the synod.[337]

Similarly to Bonhoeffer and Niemöller, he saw the results of the synod as the necessary continuation of Barmen. The Reformed synodal delegates elected Barth to the two governing bodies of the Confessing Church: the Council of Brethen (*Bruderrat*), which was now expanded from fifteen to twenty-two members, and to the six-member Council of the Confessing Church.[338]

The outcome of Dahlem, as well as the previous resistance against Jäger's *Gleischschaltung* policies and foreign political pressures from the ecumenical world, led Hitler to become personally involved. He put an end to Jäger's undertakings.[339] The swearing-in of the bishops was cancelled, Jäger was forced to resign, and the house arrests of Bishops Wurm and Meiser were lifted.[340] Hitler invited Meiser and Wurm, as well as the Bishop of Hanover, August Marahrens, and Reich Interior Minister Wilhelm Frick to meet with him. At this meeting the bishops presented a paper in which they suggested something other than the new church order that had been decided on in Dahlem: Reich Bishop Ludwig Müller should step down, and an administrator for the Reich Bishop's office as well as a five-member provisional church government should be installed.[341]

At the November 20, 1934, meeting of the Council of Brethren an open fight broke out over this development. Asmussen, Barth, Hermann A. Hesse (moderator of the Reformed Federation), Karl Immer (chair of the Coetus of Reformed Preachers, a forerunner of the Confessing Church), and Niemöller could not agree with the founding of a provisional church government or with naming Marahrens, who up to then had not shown any solidarity with the cause of the Confessing Church, as the administrator for the Reich Bishop's office. They

10.7. Hans Asmussen, Karl Barth, and Heinrich Vogel in Doorn, Netherlands, 1935, © Karl Barth-Archive in Basel.

declared their resignation from the Council of Brethren.[342] Tensions escalated further after Barth was attacked again that night: Wurm's representative Wilhelm Pressel told Barth that he was a great burden for the German Protestant Church, both confessionally and politically.[343] The next day the Reformed group left. The remaining members of the Council of Brethren reached agreement that the line possible with Marahrens was right; one should not ask too much of the state.[344] On November 22 they agreed to the structure suggested by the bishops. With that the decisions of Dahlem were de facto rescinded. Barth believed that in this development

> everything that we have fought for has been called into question. But it is not over, the battle goes on. The ranks will dwindle. The grain will still have to be winnowed. Now is the time to get serious in an entirely new way with the premises with which we went into battle.[345]

Suspension, Ban on Public Speaking, Dismissal

Even before these church political developments, disciplinary proceedings against Barth were being prepared. Emanuel Hirsch played a not minor role in the outcome of this process.[346] He was well informed about the developments by a former student who had become the officer for theological faculties in the Reich Ministry of Culture, and could therefore skillfully maneuver behind the scenes.

The reason for the proceedings was Barth's position on the loyalty oath to Adolf Hitler that was demanded of all civil servants in August 1934. The required wording was: "I swear that I will be loyal and obedient to the leader of the German Reich and people, Adolf Hitler, obey the laws and fulfill my official duties conscientiously, so help me God."[347] Barth did not show up for the first appointment to take the oath. On November 5, 1934, the new rector of the University of Bonn, Hans Naumann, had to report to the Reich Minister for Science, Education, and Public Culture Bernhard Rust that Barth had called on him and declared that "he could only take the oath with an addendum [following the phrase 'loyal and obedient']: 'so far as I can answer for this as a Protestant Christian.'" Naumann added that he

> had the impression that Barth seeks martyrdom and that his dismissal perhaps would be a wished-for signal for a new, major uproar in the Protestant church. This is after all a world-renowned theologian, the head of an enormous following throughout the world... It would be very good if a scandal could be avoided.[348]

After Barth did not appear for a second appointment to take the oath on November 7,[349] he was told by telephone on November 26 that he was immediately suspended from his position as professor of theology at the University of Bonn.[350] Barth's request that he be permitted to personally share this decision with his students the following morning was refused. "Barth ended the telephone call with the comment that he would 'then tomorrow finally [be able to] sleep in.'"[351]

The Reich Ministry press release that was shared widely in the German media stated incorrectly that Barth had refused completely to take the oath, thereby as a civil servant evading every claim of the state. Giving this reason, the Reich leadership of the Nazi Party demanded that the Confessing Church distance itself from Barth.[352]

On November 27, 1934, Barth was questioned for the first time at the Bonn district court.[353] The state prosecutor's office confined itself to his declaration that he desired to take the oath but with the addendum, but reserved possible further charges against him.[354] Barth submitted his protest for the record and gave reasons for his desire for the addendum:

> The taking of an oath is only possible where the content of the commitment stressed in the oath is clear to the one taking it... The previous commitment to the constitution and even the much earlier commitment to the Kaiser and King were clear commitments concerning their content... The commitment to the Führer Adolf Hitler, according to the interpretation of the normative National Socialist way of thinking is an commitment of unending, and therefore unclear content... If the commitment to the Führer Adolf Hitler is to be strengthened by an oath, this can only occur with an addendum that limits its content, i.e., that makes it finite and therefore clear... The reference I make in the addendum suggested by me, to my character as a Protestant Christian, means a reference to the authority by which even the loyalty and obedience to the Führer Adolf Hitler are necessarily limited.[355]

Stated briefly: it was the "totalitarian claim of this one man" against which he believed he had to rebel.[356] With the addendum to the oath and his argumentation Barth sought to uncover this totalitarian claim—thereby revealing that the Hitler state was acting against the first commandment.

Barth's position on the loyalty oath question was very controversial in the Confessing Church. Some had no understanding for it at all. Others, who had already taken the oath without any restrictions, felt discredited by Barth's position. Marburg theology professor Hans von Soden, a member of the Council of Brethren, wrote openly to Barth:

> in what kind of light are you putting the colleagues who stand somehow close to you theologically or personally, such as Bultmann and myself, who have taken the oath with no stipulation, with your demand for a proviso? Are we less

conscientious Christians, who by taking an oath to a person have offhandedly let ourselves dispense with obedience to God?... Or are we those who do not take their oath to the state seriously at all and therefore avoid hedging the careful and conscientious formulation of it? Your demand brings us others unavoidably under suspicion of being insincere toward one side or the other. And consider further: how your behavior burdens our entire community struggling for the Confessing Church!... [by the fact that] a leading theological teacher—at the moment undoubtedly the most respected among all of them—here does not give the state what in my opinion and that of many theologians is the state's [right] and with that unwillingly but unavoidably supports the suspicion that the Confessing front stands in opposition to the legitimate claim of the state...[357]

In his reply to von Soden, Barth emphasized the special nature of the oath to Adolf Hitler:

The sense and intent of National Socialism however is that in Adolf Hitler we have a czar and pope in one person, strictly speaking in theological terms one doubtless would have to say: we are dealing with an incarnate God. In the National Socialist interpretation that is normative here, an oath to Hitler means that the one who takes it devotes himself totally and with body and soul to this one man above whom there is no constitution, no law and order, that I from the outset and unconditionally trust that he knows, desires and will carry out what is best for the whole of Germany and for me under all circumstances, and it would be treason to only assume of him that he could lead me into a conflict in which he was wrong and I was right.[358]

Barth believed it was important to confront the state with a qualification so that it must declare, "consistent with its words and deeds up to now [it] is determined to truly be a 'totalitarian state'... If it [the state] ousts me, then it is documenting... that it indeed *wants* to be understood as anti-Christian."[359]

Following this, state pressure on the Confessing Church continued to build. On December 7, 1934, Reich Interior Minister Wilhelm Frick publicly threatened:

The state is not even considering interfering into church matters. But unfortunately there is well-grounded reason here for determining that all kinds of subversive and treasonous elements are gathering under the cloak of Christian concerns... With respect to this I declare that the Reich government is not willing to watch these goings-on forever, but rather that it is resolute, where political necessity requires it, to crack down against such subversives and traitors... The Reich government in any case has no interest in co-financing churches that should be serving the internal edification of the German people but are only bringing quarrels and fights to the people.[360]

In response Bishop Marahrens wrote to mollify Frick: "The provisional church government of the German Protestant Church is decided to make it unequivocally clear that it will not tolerate any efforts among its members against the National Socialist state."[361] They had "no other wish...than, in obedience under God's word and the task that God has placed upon us in this word, to serve the German people and its Führer and assist in the great work of building it up."[362]

Barth's position was however also supported by many in the Confessing Church who urged that a public declaration be issued about the question of the loyalty oath, acknowledging that Barth was right.[363] From London Dietrich Bonhoeffer intervened with a letter to Westphalian provincial synod president Karl Koch: "If the new church regime cannot find a word...of solidarity...on Barth's behalf, this will seriously threaten the interest in the Confessing Church that has been shown thus far by the ecumenical community."[364] The developments were indeed followed very actively from abroad. There were numerous letters between Alphons Koechlin, president of the Swiss Protestant Church Federation, and the Bishop of Chichester George Bell about the status of the Barth cause.[365]

In the meantime Barth declared to the provisional church government that he was prepared to take the oath without the addendum if the provisional church government passed a declaration making it clear that the totalitarian claim of Adolf Hitler was limited for every Protestant Christian by God's commandment "as it is attested for us in Holy Scripture," and if the state in eloquent silence did not contradict such a declaration, thereby in practical terms recognizing this limitation on its claims.[366]

On December 7, 1934, Barth was officially charged on three points. The first was his demand for an amendment in the oath matter; the second concerned statements in Erica Küppers' circular letter that Barth had reportedly made at the meeting of opposition pastors and to Charles Macfarland on October 30, 1933, "that were likely to damage badly the well-being of the Reich and the reputation of the Reich government"; and the third concerned Barth's refusal to give the Hitler greeting in the context of his lecture classes.[367]

Barth waited in the meantime for an official statement from the Confessing Church. On December 6 the provisional church government took a position on the loyalty oath question only in a non-public letter to a Göttingen student, in which it formulated a limitation on the oath: the oath included "through its reference to God an action that is counter to God's commandment as attested for us in Holy Scripture."[368] The letter was immediately circulated in the Confessing Church, and on December 8 was sent to Reich minister Bernhard Rust by Barth's Bonn colleagues, Friedrich Horst and Hans Emil Weber, with the comment that this was in agreement with Barth's views.[369] On December 12 Marahrens also sent an official letter from the provisional church government to Rust and enclosed the letter of December 6. While Barth's name did not appear,

Marahrens made it clear that this was "*a fundamental statement about the question of the significance of the loyalty oath to the Führer* from the church's standpoint."[370]

On December 14 Rust received another letter, from Reformed theologians Hermann A. Hesse and Karl Immer, stating that the position of the provisional church government was in agreement with Barth's position. At the instigation of Barth's friends, the letter and position statement were published on December 17 on the front page of the *Basler Nachrichten* (one of the main daily newspapers in Basel). In Barth's eyes, this meant that an official church declaration had appeared that limited the scope of the loyalty oath. On December 18 he declared in a letter to the university rector in Bonn, with a copy to Rust and the disciplinary court, that he was now prepared to take the oath without an addendum. The addendum had become superfluous because it had become self-evident through this church declaration.[371]

Nonetheless on December 20, 1934, a disciplinary criminal process against Barth began in the division for criminal matters of the Cologne regional governmental board. The loyalty oath question[372] was at the center of the oral proceedings, although the other charges against Barth, as well as his membership in the SPD, were also touched on. The state attorney Hans Kasper now publicly showed that Barth's assessment of the totalitarian claim had been correct:

> The reference to God in the wording of the oath simply implies: *The person swearing calls on God as witness that in the oath he has promised loyalty and obedience to the Führer*. The decision as to whether what is being demanded of civil servants on the basis of this commitment to be loyal and obedient, is consistent with the commandments of God does not rest with individual civil servants, *but solely and exclusively with the Führer himself,* whom God has placed at his post, and whom for that reason can and must be given *blind trust that because of his special relationship to God he will not demand anything of his subordinates that God forbids*. The very sense of this loyalty oath sworn to the person of the Führer is that the civil servant should have unconditional and unreserved confidence in the Führer and therefore leaves entirely up to him once and for all the decision as to whether there is a contradiction between his commands and orders and the will of God. *Loyalty can always be promised only unconditionally. A loyalty with reservations doesn't exist.*[373]

Barth protested that such an understanding of the state contradicted the first commandment and turned Hitler into a second god. As he reported to Thurneysen, he then took out his edition of Plato and read from Socrates' *Apology*:

> Men of Athens, I honor and love you; but I shall obey God rather than you...
> I believe that to this day no greater good has ever happened in the state than my

service to the God...And now, Athenians, I am not going to argue for my own sake, as you may think, but for yours, that you may not sin against the God, or lightly reject his boon by condemning me."[374]

And so it was true today: "By its recognition of the church, the state affirms for its own sake the limit that is set for the state [by the church], and state professors of theology are the guardians of this limit, put there by the state itself."[375] The court was not impressed by this. At the end of the proceedings Barth was punished by dismissal from service.[376]

On January 3, 1935, the Council of Brethren decided to urge Barth to submit an appeal against this verdict and after studying the reasons for the verdict to negotiate with the state about the loyalty oath.[377] But Barth already had new professional perspectives on the horizon. The University of Basel had promised him an appointment.[378] At the suggestion of the Reformed Federation the theological college at Elberfeld decided to appoint Barth as director should his dismissal not be reversed.[379] In addition, a letter reached Barth from Willem Adolf Visser 't Hooft, the general secretary at the time of the World Student Christian Federation and subsequently the first general secretary of the World Council of Churches, telling Barth of his intent to found an ecumenical seminary in Geneva for which they wanted to win him as teacher.[380]

When on January 12, 1935, the official opinion of the Cologne criminal court appeared in the Cologne newspaper, the *Kölner Zeitung*, Barth's irritation was not inconsiderable. For there it was declared that Barth had *not* been dismissed due to his position on the loyalty oath, and that this had played a very minor role in the proceedings. Barth had been "dismissed due to several politically suspicious statements, due to his refusal to perform the German greeting in university lecture classes and due to his rejection of the new state, which is unacceptable for a German civil servant who educates young people."[381] The written justification for the court's judgement was similarly broad in scope. Barth could not be kept on as someone who educated young people because, as a member of the banned SPD and as a Democrat, the required loyalty was missing.[382] Instead, "the accused has moved gradually toward an ever stronger position of opposition that goes against everything that the state or Reich government does and requires of its civil servants."[383] The question of the oath had been "the least significant" matter in the verdict, since Barth indeed had been prepared to take the oath without an addendum.[384] In reality "in the National Socialist German Reich...in its position that affirms religion and God [there is]...not any possibility of an order by the Führer and Reich Chancellor going against God's commandment, let alone that such a commandment could be expected."[385] Moreover it had been emphasized that Barth had in no way acquired German citizenship when he was appointed professor.[386] His German passport apparently did not count.

Barth's attorney Otto Bleibtreu submitted an appeal against the verdict on January 16, 1935.[387] On February 2 Hitler personally demanded the files on Barth's case from Reich minister Rust.[388] On February 5 Barth expressed his expectation to the provisional church government that the Confessing Church would stand by him and that in his appeal he would be represented by its attorney, Eberhard Fiedler; otherwise he would withdraw his appeal.[389] The provisional church government however initially did not respond, wanting to see whether Barth would pursue the appeal.[390]

In the meantime the possibility that Barth might accept an appointment in Basel was provoking unrest among his Swiss relatives. Rumors about the ménage à trois in Barth's home made the rounds.[391] Theology professors from Bern called on the Barth family because of the "unbearable" situation. This was unpleasant for Barth's siblings and his mother; they had the feeling that they had to suffer for the way he was conducting his life, while he did as he pleased.[392] On February 10, 1935, Barth's mother Anna, Heinrich Barth, and Gertrud and Karl Lindt consulted about whether Karl Barth would be able to continue his previous living arrangement in Switzerland.[393] As the outcome of this family council Gertrud Lindt wrote Charlotte von Kirschbaum on February 11, 1935, that they believed it was more appropriate if she in Basel did not live in the same household as Karl and Nelly or accompany Barth to all his events.[394] She wrote this, she stated, for the sake of the credibility of Barth's theology. "Your life together as three started in Bonn and has become almost self-evident for you."[395] In Basel however the situation was different:

> Karl is returning to his hometown and will have to be much more active as a member of the "city community," to use this pleasant word. It really would not be thinkable for you all to live in Basel the same way you have grown accustomed to in Bonn without opening the door to rumors about you all.[396]

Furthermore Nelly surely could only give genuine consent to this lifestyle

> if you could step back much more and would really just be an "assistant" to Karl, less a friend and life partner, which is what you really are but should not publicly be, out of love for Karl. Karl's marriage to Nelly should after all remain, and I always understood that you wanted to make this easier through your presence.[397]

Heinrich Barth intervened actively as well. He visited Eduard Thurneysen and warned him that as pastor of the Basel Münster congregation he was "co-responsible for the city community, indeed for the entire church, and will have to bear the consequences of the catastrophe that would unfold."[398]

Kirschbaum not only showed Gertrud Lindt's letter to Karl Barth, but to her friends Marguerite and Eduard Thurneysen as well. Marguerite encouraged her to live in Basel as before: "We friends say 'yes' to your path because we see your life together as *guided*, not arbitrarily lived... That makes us believe in the rightness, indeed necessity of your exposed walk along the ridge."[399] Over against that, the rumors that would now arise were secondary. Perhaps at a certain point in time a different way of life would show itself to be more appropriate. "But just to dismantle your unity of life and work out of caution or prudence or even for convention's sake—I do not yet see this command!"[400] The two would have to take Nelly more into consideration than previously. She expected however that Nelly in Basel, with more people around her to whom she could talk, would do somewhat better.[401]

Kirschbaum was more than irritated by Gertrud Lindt's letter, which awakened in her the impression that Gertrud and her husband had no understanding of the situation of the three and had not seen how Barth and she were genuinely trying to follow this path with a sense of responsibility. After Marguerite Thurneysen had given her fresh courage she wrote Lindt that during the years in Bonn numerous people, including students from Switzerland, had seen the situation up close. Conversations to clarify the situation had not been necessary very often, and they had never led to the result that "Karl's teaching became non-credible" for that person.[402]

During this time Barth's situation in Germany continued to worsen. On March 1, 1935, a country-wide ban was ordered on his public speaking that on April 3 was explicitly expanded to include his preaching as well.[403] While the Council of Brethren had asked the provisional church government on February 12, 1935, to "do everything to keep Professor Dr. h.c. Karl Barth in Germany and in the German Protestant Church," it could not resolve itself to comply with Barth's request for legal help from the Confessing Church.[404] Nor did they present a reliable alternative offer to the Bonn professorship.

In addition to this, Bavarian bishop Meiser demanded, as a condition for holding the next Confessing synod of the German Protestant Church in Augsburg at the end of May, that Barth not participate.[405] In January 1935 Barth had been in Basel for a conversation about his possible appointment and was asked about Switzerland's defense of its nation; jokingly Barth replied "he was in favor of a very strong defense on the northern border."[406] On May 10, 1935, Reich Bishop Müller picked up this remark with outrage, since it cast a new light on Barth's refusal to take the oath. Now the accusation of treason against the Fatherland was raised. As a result Karl Immer traveled to Barth on May 18, 1935, and asked him to stay away from the Augsburg synod.[407]

Disappointed, Barth attacked the Confessing Church several days later in a letter:

> That which from the summer of 1933 on I comprehended as the real crisis in the Confessing Church and fought against with all my might: its almost complete

lack of theological principle and its almost never overcome pitiful fearfulness of humans on the political side...has become apparent once more...I am only surprised that you still dare to use this boastful word "front" [Confessional front] to characterize yourselves. And this "front"...now wants to impose the great ban on me? Don't make me laugh. I have only scorn for this.[408]

Initially things on the legal level unfolded differently than expected: on June 14, 1935, the higher administrative court in Berlin dismissed the judgement against Barth due to procedural errors.[409] In light of his refusal to take the oath Barth's salary was reduced by one-fifth for one year; the two other charges were dropped. Barth wrote Ernst Wolf in relief: "There are still judges in Berlin!!" and signed it "Full Professor, Bonn *quasimodogenitus*"[410]—like new born.

To follow up Barth turned to Minister Rust with the question as to whether he still wanted to keep Barth on.[411] Rust replied on June 21, 1935, that Barth was being placed in retirement, based upon paragraph six of the law for the Restoration of the Civil Service.[412] The university was simultaneously informed that payments of Barth's salary were to end after September 1935. On June 22 the press agency of the German Reich issued a commentary about the matter, in which it specifically warned that the totalitarian interpretation of the oath that Barth was fighting against was the only permissible one.[413]

On June 25 the councils of the Confessing synods in Rhineland and Westphalia met to consider the establishment of a "free faculty" to which Barth could be appointed,[414] but in the meantime Barth had informed Basel of the new situation and declared his readiness to accept an appointment. The Basel governmental council decided on June 25 to appoint Barth as professor of systematic theology and homiletics.[415] Despite his doubts about fleeing his responsibility in Germany, but with the feeling that he was forced to this decision by the behavior of the Confessing Church leadership, Barth accepted the appointment.

Numerous members of the Confessing Church publicly thanked Barth for his efforts. The Council of the Protestant Church of the Old Prussian Union declared that Barth "had effectively made the word of God once again the sole guiding principle for church doctrine and law among us"[416] and the Reformed Federation also expressed its gratitude. In contrast August Marahrens, chair of the German Protestant Church's provisional church government, expressed his views clearly in his weekly letter of July 17/18, 1935: primarily in the early 1920s Barth had a stimulating effect on the younger generation and he had taken an early position in the Protestant Church Struggle. But he was of course also Reformed and Swiss, so that "in his thinking about state and authority certain aspects have the upper hand that from the perspective of the Lutheran confession would be impossible." Unable to resist the suggestive question, Marahrens asked: "Is it possible by the way that Karl Barth was not much more strongly influenced by the circumstances and characteristics of his life, rather than fundamentally by the Holy Scripture?"[417]

These events left Barth deeply wounded. Despite the support that he found for his course he had wished for a clearer position from the Confessing Church, which in his opinion had been too hesitant about his trial, in the question of making a public statement and the attempt to find an alternative for him in Germany. He wrote his student Wilhelm Niesel, member of the Council of the Old Prussian Union Church, that he had "finally lost [his] ... confidence in the leadership of the Confessing Church for the future... Everything has its limits, including the possibility of giving oneself into the hands of people whose unreliability one has had to experience again and again."[418] And he summed things up to Hermann A. Hesse: "One [i.e., the Confessing Church] cannot just call a man when he simultaneously is given to understand so often and so clearly that [the church] ... thinks he is dangerous."[419]

Barth sent regular reports to his friend Eduard Thurneysen about the events in the German church and his role in them. In these final weeks Thurneysen had the growing impression, as he wrote Barth, that Barth was like the "lonely bird on the roof," as Barth had described the theologian at the end of his polemic *Theological Existence Today!* Whenever Thurneysen thought of Barth, he always thought of a condor or golden eagle in a cage. Many people were too small for Barth's "beat of his great wings."

> Don't you somehow demand too much of people?... They often don't understand that you are so angry and what they have done and that once again they haven't pleased you... I am naturally convinced that you will not simply be happy in Basel—but rather that even there you will once again be the lonely bird, the bird in the cage which is even narrower than was the case outside.

All the same, wherever he lived, Barth would have to "settle down ... among all the smaller birds."[420]

Barth seems to have been moved by his friend's open letter. He wanted to "take to heart, that for Germans and Swiss I am such a loathsome animal that some secretly like to see leave, the others secretly do not like to see come."[421] He hoped that at his funeral someone would not fail to mention that his way of living had led him to be encircled "more by fear than by love."[422] At the same time Barth could not refrain in his reply to Thurneysen from persisting in the special nature of his own viewpoint: not only was he trapped in a cage, so were the others. His distinction however was that "I know somewhat more about the existence of our shared cage better than those who ... can at least occasionally forget about it."[423]

Notes

1. On Schmidt, cf. Wengst, "Theologie und Politik im Jahr 1933," 37f.
2. Letter of June 5, 1930, to Wilhelm Loew, cited in *Briefwechsel Barth–Thurneysen* III (GA 34), 11, n. 8.

3. Information given the author by Schmidt's grandson, Thomas A. Schmidt.
4. Cf. *Briefwechsel Barth–Thurneysen* III (GA 34), 27, n. 39, and 51, n. 14.
5. Cf. letter of July 28, 1961, to Ernst Wolf, *Briefe 1961–1968* (GA 6), 18.
6. *Schweizerköpfe der Gegenwart*, 119.
7. Cf. the editor's introduction, *Vorträge und kleinere Arbeiten 1930–1933* (GA 49), vii.
8. Letter of July 24, 1931, from Dietrich Bonhoeffer to his Swiss friend Erwin Sutz, in Bonhoeffer, *Ecumenical, Academic, and Pastoral Work: 1931–1932*, 37–38. Translation revised.
9. Letter of January 9, 1931, to Thurneysen, *Briefwechsel Barth–Thurneysen* III (GA 34), 89. Regarding Barth's classes cf. the list of academic courses in the KBA. In the 1933/4 winter semester, 1934 summer semester and 1934/5 winter semester Barth lectured on the second part of the Prolegomena, which then became *Church Dogmatics* I/2. In the 1932/3 winter semester he lectured on the "Pre-history of the newer Protestant theology" and in 1933 summer semester on "The history of Protestant theology since Schleiermacher." Barth also repeated his exegetical lectures: in the 1930 summer semester on the Letter of James, in the summer semester of 1933 on the Gospel of John, in winter semester 1933/4 on the Sermon on the Mount and in 1934/5 winter semester on the Letter to the Colossians. Anselm of Canterbury, Thomas (together with Bonaventura), Luther, Calvin, Ritschl, and Schleiermacher were topics in his seminars and student societies, but also justification and sanctification. In addition there were exercises in preparing sermons as well as a seminar on "The problem of natural theology" (1931/2 winter semester), one on the theology of the Formula of Concord (1934 summer semester), and one on the Lord's Supper (1934/5 winter semester). Barth also continued the tradition in Bonn of holding open evenings, one on the ideologies of the German parties in the 1930/1 winter semester and one on ethics in the 1932/3 winter semester.
10. Gollwitzer, *Skizzen eines Lebens*, 60.
11. Steck also joined the Confessing Church and became a lecturer at its preachers' seminary in Frankfurt a. M. In 1953 he became professor of systematic theology in Frankfurt, moving to Münster in 1963.
12. Gollwitzer, *Skizzen eines Lebens*, 60.
13. Letter of April 2, 1931, to Thurneysen, *Briefwechsel Barth–Thurneysen* III (GA 34), 130.
14. Letter of May 29, 1931, to Thurneysen, *Briefwechsel Barth–Thurneysen* III (GA 34), 142.
15. Letter of November 24, 1931, to Thurneysen, *Briefwechsel Barth–Thurneysen* III (GA 34), 189.
16. Letter of August 21, 1931, from Thurneysen, *Briefwechsel Barth–Thurneysen* III (GA 34), 170f.
17. Gollwitzer, *Skizzen eines Lebens*, 61.
18. Gollwitzer, *Skizzen eines Lebens*, 57f.
19. Gollwitzer, *Skizzen eines Lebens*, 63.
20. Cf. Peterson, "Was ist Theologie?," 132f. Regarding the debate between Peterson and Barth, cf. Jüngel, "Von der Dialektik zur Analogie. Die Schule Kierkegaards und der Einspruch Petersons," in Jüngel, *Barth-Studien*, 127–79, and Beintker, *Die Dialektik*, 132–9.

21. Peterson, "Was ist Theologie?," 134.
22. Peterson, "Was ist Theologie?," 136.
23. Peterson, "Was ist Theologie?," 138.
24. Letter of June 23, 1925, from Erik Peterson, cited in *Vorträge und kleinere Arbeiten 1922-1925* (GA 19), 644.
25. Letter of September 25, 1925, to Bultmann, *Barth-Bultmann Letters* (GA 1), 24.
26. Barth, "Kirche und Theologie," *Vorträge und kleinere Arbeiten 1922-1925* (GA 19), 644-82.
27. Circular letter of October 25, 1925, to his friends, *Briefwechsel Barth-Thurneysen* II (GA 4), 378.
28. Letter of October 11, 1925, from Peterson to Bultmann, cited in *Briefwechsel Barth-Bultmann* (GA 1), 47f., n. 8.
29. Cf. Barbara Nichtweiß, "Lebendige Dialektik. Zur Bedeutung Erik Petersons für die theologische Entwicklung Karl Barths," in Beintker et al., eds., *Karl Barth in Deutschland*, 324.
30. Cf. Jüngel, "Von der Dialektik zur Analogie," in Jüngel, *Barth-Studien*, 144, and Beintker, *Die Dialektik*, 137.
31. Barth, "Kirche und Theologie," *Vorträge und kleinere Arbeiten 1922-1925* (GA 19), 670. See also pp. 128-129 and 134-136.
32. Barth, "Kirche und Theologie," *Vorträge und kleinere Arbeiten 1922-1925* (GA 19), 670.
33. Cf. Beintker, *Die Dialektik*, 138.
34. Barth, "Kirche und Theologie," *Vorträge und kleinere Arbeiten 1922-1925* (GA 19), 655.
35. Barth, "Kirche und Theologie," *Vorträge und kleinere Arbeiten 1922-1925* (GA 19), 657.
36. Cf. Beintker, *Die Dialektik*, 139f.
37. Letter of August 30, 1933, from Peterson to P. Anselm Stolz, cited in Nichtweiß, "Lebendige Dialektik," in Beintker et al., eds., *Karl Barth in Deutschland*, 324.
38. Cf. Barth's preface to the first edition (1931), *Fides quaerens intellectum* (GA 13), 1.
39. Letter of October 19, 1930, to Thurneysen, *Briefwechsel Barth-Thurneysen* III (GA 34), 49f.
40. Beintker, "Fides quaerens intellectum," in Beintker, ed., *Barth Handbuch*, 211.
41. Barth, *Fides quaerens intellectum* (GA 13), 40.
42. Cf. Beintker, *Die Dialektik*, 183.
43. Cf. Beintker, *Die Dialektik*, 282.
44. Cf. Beintker, *Die Dialektik*, 280.
45. Cf. Beintker, *Die Dialektik*, 283. Cf. Barth's definition of the term in *CD* II/1 § 27, 225: "In distinction to both likeness and unlikeness 'analogy' means similarity, i.e., a partial correspondence and agreement (and, therefore, one which limits both parity and disparity) between two or more different entities."
46. Cf. the pointed formulation in *The Humanity of God* (translation of *Die Menschlichkeit Gottes*), 48: "We do not need to engage in a free-ranging investigation to seek out and construct who and what God truly is, and who and what man truly is, but only to read the truth about both where it resides, namely, in the fullness of their togetherness, their covenant which proclaims itself in Jesus Christ."
47. Barth, *How I Changed My Mind*, 43.
48. Barth, *How I Changed My Mind*, 44.

49. Barth, *Die Menschlichkeit Gottes*, 3 and 8.
50. Barth, *Die Menschlichkeit Gottes*, 15.
51. Barth, *Die Menschlichkeit Gottes*, 14. Translation (revised) from *The Humanity of God*, 50.
52. *CD* IV/3 § 69, 119. Translation revised.
53. Barth, *Die Menschlichkeit Gottes*, 16.
54. Barth, *Die Menschlichkeit Gottes*, 17.
55. Barth, *Die Menschlichkeit Gottes*, 18.
56. See pp. 346–347.
57. Barth, "Antwort [auf die Frage: Welches Buch des Jahres halten Sie für wesentlich?]," *Vorträge und kleinere Arbeiten 1934–1935* (GA 52), 624.
58. Barth, *How I Changed My Mind*, 45.
59. Dehn, *Die alte Zeit*, 143.
60. Dehn, *Die alte Zeit*, 221.
61. Cf. editor's introduction to Barth, "An den Rektor der Universität, Prof. Dr. Gustav Aubin, Halle," *Offene Briefe 1909–1935* (GA 35), 160.
62. Cf. Scholder, *Churches and the Third Reich*, vol. 1, 172.
63. Cited in Scholder, *Churches and the Third Reich*, vol. 1, 172.
64. Cf. Scholder, *Churches and the Third Reich*, vol. 1, 172.
65. Cf. Scholder, *Churches and the Third Reich*, vol. 1, 173.
66. Cf. editor's introduction to Barth, "An den Rektor der Universität, Prof. Dr. Gustav Aubin," *Offene Briefe 1909–1935* (GA 35), 160; regarding Gertrud Staewen, see *Barth-Thurneysen Briefwechsel* III (GA 34), 79f., n. 15.
67. Barth, "An den Rektor der Universität, Prof. Dr. Gustav Aubin," *Offene Briefe 1909–1935* (GA 35), 161.
68. Cf. the editorial notations for "An den Rektor der Universität, Prof. Dr. Gustav Aubin," *Offene Briefe 1909–1935* (GA 35), 162.
69. Letter of October 20, 1931, to Dehn, *Offene Briefe 1909–1935* (GA 35), 162f.
70. Cited in Scholder, *Churches and the Third Reich*, vol. 1, 173.
71. Dehn, *Kirche und Völkerversöhnung. Dokumente zum Halleschen Universitätskonflikt*, 89f., cited in Scholder, *Churches and the Third Reich*, vol. 1, 174.
72. Emanuel Hirsch/Hermann Dörries, "Zum halleschen Universitätskonflikt, 31 January 1932," cited in *Offene Briefe 1909–1935* (GA 35), 171.
73. Cf. *Briefwechsel Barth–Thurneysen* III (GA 34), 225, n. 3. On January 4, 1926, Barth received a German passport; for this he did not have to relinquish his Swiss citizenship.
74. Letter of February 9, 1932, to Leopold Cordier, cited in *Offene Briefe 1909–1935* (GA 35), 172.
75. Cf. the editor's introduction to "An die Frankfurter Zeitung," *Offene Briefe 1909–1935* (GA 35), 172.
76. Barth, "Warum führt man den Kampf nicht auf der ganzen Linie? Der Fall Dehn und die 'dialektische' Theologie," *Offene Briefe 1909–1935* (GA 35), 177.
77. Barth, "Warum führt man den Kampf nicht auf der ganzen Linie?," *Offene Briefe 1909–1935* (GA 35), 175.
78. Open Letter of February 27, 1932, from Emanuel Hirsch, *Offene Briefe 1909–1935* (GA 35), 188–95.

79. Open letter of April 17, 1932, to Emanuel Hirsch, *Offene Briefe 1909–1935* (GA 35), 202.
80. Reply of April 21, 1932, to the editor from Emanuel Hirsch, *Offene Briefe 1909–1935* (GA 35), 206.
81. Cf. *Offene Briefe 1909–1935* (GA 35), 203–4, n. 24.
82. "Officials who, according to their previous political activity cannot guarantee that they will act unreservedly at all times on behalf of the national state, can be dismissed from service." (Law for the Restoration of the Civil Service, § 4 [Dismissal for political unreliability], *Reichsgesetzblatt* I (1933), Nr. 34, 175). Cf. the Personalakte der Universität Halle, UAHW, Rep. 11, PA 5296, Günther Dehn.
83. Cf. Wengst, "Theologie und Politik," 38.
84. Cf. the letter of September 24, 1933, from Karl Ludwig Schmidt, KBA 9333.701.
85. Letter of February 9, 1956, to Andreas Schmidt, KBA 9256.43.
86. Letter of January 30(-1), 1933, to Thurneysen, *Briefwechsel Barth–Thurneysen* III (GA 34), 348.
87. Letter of January 30(-1), 1933, to Thurneysen, *Briefwechsel Barth–Thurneysen* III (GA 34), 348.
88. Barth, "Das erste Gebot als theologisches Axiom," *Vorträge und kleinere Arbeiten 1930–1933* (GA 49), 209–41.
89. Barth, "Das erste Gebot," *Vorträge und kleinere Arbeiten 1930–1933* (GA 49), 239.
90. Cf. Busch, *Karl Barth: His Life*, 217.
91. Information about Barth's payment of party dues given the author from Dr. Peter Zocher at the KBA. The official letter that Barth received in August may have been sent to compel civil servants to repudiate the SPD (even though it had already been dissolved) as a way of declaring their loyalty to the state.
92. Cf. Prolingheuer, *Der Fall Karl Barth*, 233.
93. Letter of April 4, 1933, to Reich minister Bernhard Rust, cited in Prolingheuer, *Der Fall Karl Barth*, 233f.
94. Cf. Prolingheuer, *Der Fall Karl Barth*, 2f.
95. "Guidelines of the German Christian Faith Movement," English translation from Mary M. Solberg, *A Church Undone*, 49–50. Translation revised.
96. Cf. "Guidelines of the German Christian Faith Movement," in Solberg, *A Church Undone*, 51.
97. Regarding the following, cf. Strohm, *Die Kirchen im Dritten Reich*, 26–8, and the editor's introduction to "Theologische Existenz heute!," *Vorträge und kleinere Arbeiten 1930–1933* (GA 49), 271f.
98. Cf. editor's introduction to "Theologische Existenz heute!," *Vorträge und kleinere Arbeiten 1930–1933* (GA 49), 275, and the signature below the lecture (363). Regarding the reconstruction of the text's origins, cf. Stoevesandt, "'Von der Kirchenpolitik zur Kirche!'".
99. Cf. editors introduction to "Theologische Existenz heute!," *Vorträge und kleinere Arbeiten 1930–1933* (GA 49), 278. As of the eighth printing this text became the first issue of the new series published by Barth and Thurneysen, *Theologische Existenz heute*.
100. Barth, "Theologische Existenz heute!," *Vorträge und kleinere Arbeiten 1930–1933* (GA 49), 280.
101. Barth, "Theologische Existenz heute!", *Vorträge und kleinere Arbeiten 1930–1933* (GA 49), 280f.

102. Barth, "Theologische Existenz heute!," *Vorträge und kleinere Arbeiten 1930–1933* (GA 49), 282.
103. Barth, "Theologische Existenz heute!," *Vorträge und kleinere Arbeiten 1930–1933* (GA 49), 283.
104. Cf. Romans 8:38. For a clearly political allusion, Barth was using a special Greek version of the text that does not read "angels" (*angeloi*), but "forces" (*exousiai*).
105. Barth, "Theologische Existenz heute!," *Vorträge und kleinere Arbeiten 1930–1933* (GA 49), 285f.
106. Barth, "Theologische Existenz heute!," *Vorträge und kleinere Arbeiten 1930–1933* (GA 49), 290.
107. Barth, "Theologische Existenz heute!," *Vorträge und kleinere Arbeiten 1930–1933* (GA 49), 308.
108. Barth, "Theologische Existenz heute!," *Vorträge und kleinere Arbeiten 1930–1933* (GA 49), 327.
109. Barth, "Theologische Existenz heute!," *Vorträge und kleinere Arbeiten 1930–1933* (GA 49), 327.
110. The so-called "Aryan paragraph" stated: "Civil servants who are not of Aryan descent are to be placed in retirement (§§ 8ff.); insofar as this concerns pro bono civil servants, they are to be dismissed from their office." (Law for the Restoration of the Civil Service, § 3, Par. I [Retirement in cases of non-Ayran descent] *Reichsgesetzblatt* I (1933), Nr. 34, 175). This measure was passed in the Old Prussian Union Church in September 1933, at the so-called "Brown Synod." Cf. Scholder, *Churches and the Third Reich*, vol. 1, 477.
111. Cf. Psalm 102:7.
112. Barth, "Theologische Existenz heute!," *Vorträge und kleinere Arbeiten 1930–1933* (GA 49), 362f.
113. Cf. the editor's introduction to "Theologische Existenz heute!," *Vorträge und kleinere Arbeiten 1930–1933* (GA 49), 278, n. 38.
114. Letter of July 13, 1933, from Heinrich Scholz, cited in *Vorträge und kleinere Arbeiten 1930–1933* (GA 49), 278.
115. Thomas Mann, entry for August 29, 1933, in *Tagebücher 1933–1934*, 163. Cf. also the editor's introduction to "Theologische Existenz heute!," *Vorträge und kleinere Arbeiten 1930–1933* (GA 49), 279.
116. Letter of July 1, 1933, to Adolf Hitler, cited in *Vorträge und kleinere Arbeiten 1930–1933* (GA 49), 277.
117. Cf. Strohm, *Kirchen im Dritten Reich*, 29.
118. Cf. Gollwitzer, *Skizzen eines Lebens*, 66.
119. Cf. Prolingheuer, *Der Fall Karl Barth*, 7.
120. About him cf. *Briefwechsel Barth–Thurneysen* III (GA 34), 797f., n. 11.
121. Cf. letter of March 23, 1933, to Kirschbaum, *Briefwechsel Barth–von Kirschbaum* I (GA 45), 275.
122. Letter of April 10, 1933, from Nelly Barth to Thurneysen, *Briefwechsel Barth–Thurneysen* III (GA 34), 382. Cf. also the letter of March 31, 1933, to Nelly Barth (371).
123. Cf. letter of March 23, 1933, to Kirschbaum, *Briefwechsel Barth–von Kirschbaum* I (GA 45), 275. Thurneysen had already pondered the option of a divorce for Barth in

1932 (cf. letter of April 22, 1932, from Thurneysen, *Briefwechsel Barth–Thurneysen* III (GA 34), 233). And Nelly had already thought about a divorce in 1923, before Kirschbaum had entered their lives (cf. Barth's letter of April 22, 1933, to the Stoevesandts, in Busch et al., eds., *Briefe des Jahres 1933*, 166).

124. Letter of March 24, 1933, from Kirschbaum, *Briefwechsel Barth–von Kirschbaum* I (GA 45), 276.
125. Letter of March 24, 1933, from Kirschbaum, *Briefwechsel Barth–von Kirschbaum* I (GA 45), 277.
126. Letter of March 24, 1933, from Kirschbaum, *Briefwechsel Barth–von Kirschbaum* I (GA 45), 276.
127. Cf. letter of April 15, 1933, from Kirschbaum, *Briefwechsel Barth–von Kirschbaum* I (GA 45), 286.
128. Letter of March 31, 1933, to Nelly Barth, *Briefwechsel Barth–Thurneysen* III (GA 34), 372.
129. Cf. letter of March 31, 1933, to Nelly Barth, *Briefwechsel Barth–Thurneysen* III (GA 34), 373.
130. Cf. letter of March 31, 1933, to Nelly Barth, *Briefwechsel Barth–Thurneysen* III (GA 34), 372.
131. Letter of March 31, 1933, to Nelly Barth, *Briefwechsel Barth–Thurneysen* III (GA 34), 373.
132. Cf. letter of March 31, 1933, to Nelly Barth, *Briefwechsel Barth–Thurneysen* III (GA 34), 373.
133. Letter of March 31, 1933, to Nelly Barth, *Briefwechsel Barth–Thurneysen* III (GA 34), 373.
134. Letter of March 31, 1933, to Nelly Barth, *Briefwechsel Barth–Thurneysen* III (GA 34), 373f.
135. In the letter he mentioned this option in such a way that Nelly would not have the feeling that this idea was coming from her. Cf. Letter of March 31, 1933, to Nelly Barth, *Briefwechsel Barth–Thurneysen* III (GA 34), 372f.
136. Cf. letter of March 31, 1933, to Nelly Barth, *Briefwechsel Barth–Thurneysen* III (GA 34), 374.
137. Cf. letter of March 31, 1933, to Nelly Barth, *Briefwechsel Barth–Thurneysen* III (GA 34), 374.
138. Letter of March 31, 1933, to Nelly Barth, *Briefwechsel Barth–Thurneysen* III (GA 34), 374.
139. This letter has not been preserved, but Nelly Barth's reply can be reconstructed from her husband's reaction; cf. letter of April 5, 1933, to Nelly Barth, *Briefwechsel Barth–Thurneysen* III (GA 34), 376f.
140. Cf. letter of April 5, 1933, to Nelly Barth, *Briefwechsel Barth–Thurneysen* III (GA 34), 376f.
141. Cf. letter of April 5, 1933, to Nelly Barth, *Briefwechsel Barth–Thurneysen* III (GA 34), 377.
142. Letter of April 5, 1933, to Nelly Barth, *Briefwechsel Barth–Thurneysen* III (GA 34), 377.
143. Cf. letter of April 5, 1933, to Nelly Barth, *Briefwechsel Barth–Thurneysen* III (GA 34), 379.

144. Cf. letter of April 5, 1933, to Nelly Barth, *Briefwechsel Barth-Thurneysen* III (GA 34), 380.
145. Letter of April 5, 1933, to Nelly Barth, *Briefwechsel Barth-Thurneysen* III (GA 34), 381.
146. Letter of April 10, 1933, from Nelly Barth to Thurneysen, *Briefwechsel Barth-Thurneysen* III (GA 34), 382.
147. Letter of April 10, 1933, from Nelly Barth to Thurneysen, *Briefwechsel Barth-Thurneysen* III (GA 34), 382.
148. Cf. the editor's introduction to the letter of April 22, 1933, to the Stoevesandts, in Busch et al., eds., *Briefe des Jahres 1933*, 161.
149. Cf. letter of April 12, 1933, from Dorothee Stoevesandt, cited in Busch et al., eds., *Briefe des Jahres 1933*, 162.
150. Cf. letter of April 12, 1933, from Karl Stoevesandt, cited in Busch et al., eds., *Briefe des Jahres 1933*, 162.
151. Letter of April 16, 1933, from Kirschbaum, *Briefwechsel Barth-von Kirschbaum* I (GA 45), 288.
152. Letter of April 22, 1933, to the Stoevesandts, Busch et al., eds., *Briefe des Jahres 1933*, 163.
153. Letter of April 22, 1933, to the Stoevesandts, Busch et al., eds., *Briefe des Jahres 1933*, 163.
154. Cf. letter of April 22, 1933, to the Stoevesandts, Busch et al., eds., *Briefe des Jahres 1933*, 164.
155. Letter of April 22, 1933, to the Stoevesandts, Busch et al., eds., *Briefe des Jahres 1933*, 166.
156. Letter of April 22, 1933, to the Stoevesandts, Busch et al., eds., *Briefe des Jahres 1933*, 166.
157. Cf. letter of April 24, 1933, from Anna Barth, cited in *Briefwechsel Barth-Thurneysen* III (GA 34), 403, n. 7.
158. Letter of May 4, 1933, from Kirschbaum to Anna Barth, Busch et al., eds., *Briefe des Jahres 1933*, 196.
159. Cf. letter of April 19, 1933, to Nelly Barth, Busch et al., eds., *Briefe des Jahres 1933*, 152f.
160. Letter of April 19, 1933, to Nelly Barth, Busch et al., eds., *Briefe des Jahres 1933*, 153.
161. Letter of May 4, 1933, from Kirschbaum to Thurneysen, *Briefwechsel Barth-Thurneysen* III (GA 34), 406f.
162. Cf. letter of June 2, 1933, from Kirschbaum to Thurneysen, *Briefwechsel Barth-Thurneysen* III (GA 34), 418.
163. Cf. letter of June 2, 1933, from Kirschbaum to Thurneysen, *Briefwechsel Barth-Thurneysen* III (GA 34), 418f.
164. Cf. letter of June 2, 1933, from Kirschbaum to Thurneysen, *Briefwechsel Barth-Thurneysen* III (GA 34), 419.
165. Cf. letter of June 9, 1933, from Nelly Barth to Marguerite Thurneysen, *Briefwechsel Barth-Thurneysen* III (GA 34), 425.
166. Letter of June 9, 1933, from Nelly Barth to Marguerite Thurneysen, *Briefwechsel Barth-Thurneysen* III (GA 34), 425.

167. Cf. letter of July 22, 1934, from Kirschbaum to Thurneysen, *Briefwechsel Barth-Thurneysen* III (GA 34), 674.
168. Cf. for example the letter of September 20, 1934, to Kirschbaum, *Briefwechsel Barth-von Kirschbaum* I (GA 45), 363f.
169. In January 1935 Barth wrote tenderly to Kirschbaum from his holidays in the Bernese Highlands: "I know indeed what or who I am missing here. Who here tends to taking care of my vitamins? No one. Who here is organizing my collar and tie? No one. Who here occasionally raves in front of me? No one. Who here now and then smashes precious china to the floor? No one. Who here prevents me from succumbing to the zone of the Swiss bourgeoisie? No one. Who here explains to me how the dear God basically thought in terms of orders etc.? No one. Who here accompanies me lovingly, laughingly, weeping, teaching, protesting...? No one. Who here is my delight, by virtue of her full spiritual-physical being, by virtue of her little voice, by virtue of the contours of her shape and the changing colors of her clothes, by virtue of the 921 possibilities of her face and posture, by virtue of the richness of her heart and intellect, by virtue of the energy of her will and by virtue of the depth of her soul? Who? No one, no one. Indeed, so it is." (Letter of January 17, 1935, to Kirschbaum, *Briefwechsel Barth-von Kirschbaum* I (GA 45), 437. Ellipsis in the original).
170. Letter of September 19, 1933, from Kirschbaum, *Briefwechsel Barth-von Kirschbaum* I (GA 45), 317.
171. Letter of June 23, 1935, to Kirschbaum, *Briefwechsel Barth-von Kirschbaum* I (GA 45), 484.
172. Barth too showed some of his letters to Charlotte to his wife, and the letters of his wife to Charlotte.
173. Cf. for example the letter of September 7, 1930, to Kirschbaum, *Briefwechsel Barth-von Kirschbaum* I (GA 45), 147.
174. Letter of February 27, 1935, from Kirschbaum to Gertrud Lindt, *Briefwechsel Barth-Thurneysen* III (GA 34), 839.
175. Letter of April 23, 1933, to Anna Barth, in Busch et al., eds., *Briefe des Jahres 1933*, 170.
176. Letter of April 24, 1933, from Anna Barth, cited in *Briefwechsel Barth-Thurneysen* III (GA 34), 403, n. 7.
177. Letter of September 20, 1930, to Kirschbaum, *Briefwechsel Barth-von Kirschbaum* I (GA 45), 162. Similarly the letter of February 27, 1935, from Kirschbaum to Gertrud Lindt, *Briefwechsel Barth-Thurneysen* III (GA 34), 838f.
178. Letter of March 18, 1947, to William Lachat, cited in *Briefwechsel Barth-von Kirschbaum* I (GA 45), xxi, n. 2.
179. *CD* III/3 preface, xiii.
180. Cf. Erler, "Biographische Daten zu Charlotte von Kirschbaum von 1899 bis 1935," in *Briefwechsel Barth-von Kirschbaum* I (GA 45), xl.
181. Cf. the letters of January 15 and 16, 1935, from Kirschbaum, *Briefwechsel Barth-von Kirschbaum* I (GA 45), 423–5 and 427–35.
182. Published in Zollikon-Zurich in 1949 (the title means "The Real Woman"; an English translation can be found in Kirschbaum, *The Question of Woman*. The ninety-six-page book distances itself from Gertrud von le Fort's Catholic doctrine of women as well as from Simone de Beauvoir's *The Second Sex* (see the foreword to *Die wirkliche*

Frau, 5). With an explicit reference to *Church Dogmatics* (*CD* III/1 § 41, 176ff.; cf. *Die wirkliche Frau*, 7) Kirschbaum defines the image of God in human beings as the human's way of existing in the relation of man and woman: "This is the basic form in which the human being exists: the unequal duality of the male and the female person" (*Die wirkliche Frau*, 8). Man and woman are "*with one another* that human being... upon whom God's pleasure rests... This is the final and deepest equality of rights, or should we say equality of mercy, of man and woman" (*Die wirkliche Frau*, 10). Karl Barth mentions her book in *CD* III/4 § 54, 172.

183. Cf. Stoevesandt, "Charlotte von Kirschbaum," in Beintker, ed., *Barth Handbuch*, 58.
184. Cf. Bergner, *Um der Sache willen*, 42.
185. Cf. Bergner, *Um der Sache willen*, 42–4.
186. For Barth this included the fact that he had the impression that Kirschbaum had given him her trust because of his books and that Nelly had fallen in love with him because of his faith (cf. letter of February 28, 1926, to Kirschbaum, *Briefwechsel Barth–von Kirschbaum* I (GA 45), 25).
187. Letter of February 28, 1926, to Kirschbaum, *Briefwechsel Barth–von Kirschbaum* I (GA 45), 25.
188. Letter of February 28, 1926, to Kirschbaum, *Briefwechsel Barth–von Kirschbaum* I (GA 45), 26.
189. Cf. letter of April 22, 1933, to the Stoevesandts, in Busch et al., eds., *Briefe des Jahres 1933*, 167f.
190. Letter of February 28, 1926, to Kirschbaum, *Briefwechsel Barth–von Kirschbaum* I (GA 45), 26.
191. Letter of February 28, 1926, to Kirschbaum, *Briefwechsel Barth–von Kirschbaum* I (GA 45), 26.
192. Cf. letter of October 6, 1929, to Kirschbaum, *Briefwechsel Barth–von Kirschbaum* I (GA 45), 117.
193. Letter of June 7, 1926, to Kirschbaum, *Briefwechsel Barth–von Kirschbaum* I (GA 45), 50.
194. Letter of August 8, 1926, to Kirschbaum, *Briefwechsel Barth–von Kirschbaum* I (GA 45), 72f.
195. Letter of August 8, 1926, to Kirschbaum, *Briefwechsel Barth–von Kirschbaum* I (GA 45), 72.
196. Letter of August 8, 1926, to Kirschbaum, *Briefwechsel Barth–von Kirschbaum* I (GA 45), 72.
197. Cf. the letter of October 6, 1929, to Kirschbaum, *Briefwechsel Barth–von Kirschbaum* I (GA 45), 118: "Life is simply too short, that we constantly come back to this, constantly stay hanging in the fact that and why the dear God did not do something very different with us."
198. Cf. letter of May 25, 1926, to Kirschbaum, *Briefwechsel Barth–von Kirschbaum* I (GA 45), 47f.
199. Letter of March 29, 1930, to Kirschbaum, *Briefwechsel Barth–von Kirschbaum* I (GA 45), 127.
200. Letter of March 18, 1947, to William Lachat, cited in *Briefwechsel Barth–von Kirschbaum* I (GA 45), xxiif., n. 3. This understanding of order was central to

Barth. Also in his letter of May 25, 1926, to Kirschbaum (45), he describes holding on to his marriage to Nelly and the simultaneous comradeship with Charlotte under the keyword "orders." The seventh commandment "Thou shalt not commit adultery" was valid, Barth affirms explicitly in his ethics on marriage in *Church Dogmatics*: "But to love... means to *choose*, selecting *this* woman or man and *no* other. The man who thinks it is possible and permissible to love many women simultaneously or alternately has not yet begun to love. He is still in the stage of experiment and if he does not overcome his inconstancy he will always be a bungler in this sphere... If marriage is the proof of love, it is the proof, confirmation and expression of the *choice* made in love. It is life on the basis of this choice. Hence it is *monogamy*" (*CD* III/4 § 54, 195). Divorce was only "ultima ratio, extreme case" (211).

201. Letter of April 22, 1933, to the Stoevesandts, in Busch et al., eds., *Briefe des Jahres 1933*, 166f. with n. 3.
202. Letter of April 22, 1933, to the Stoevesandts, in Busch et al., eds., *Briefe des Jahres 1933*, 167.
203. Letter of April 22, 1933, to the Stoevesandts, in Busch et al., eds., *Briefe des Jahres 1933*, 167.
204. Letter of February 27, 1935, from Kirschbaum to Gertrud Lindt, *Briefwechsel Barth-Thurneysen* III (GA 34), 837.
205. Letter of February 27, 1935, from Kirschbaum to Gertrud Lindt, *Briefwechsel Barth-Thurneysen* III (GA 34), 837.
206. Letter of March 18, 1947, to William Lachat, cited in *Briefwechsel Barth-von Kirschbaum* I, xxf., n. 1.
207. Tügel (the translation of the title of his article is: "Impossible Existence! A statement against Karl Barth"), cited in Prolingheuer, *Der Fall Karl Barth*, 8f.; Michael Hüttenhoff, "Theologische Existenz heute," in Beintker, ed., *Barth Handbuch*, 216.
208. Barth, "Abschied," *Zwischen den Zeiten* 11 (1933), 543.
209. Letter of January 27, 1934, to Karl Garthe, cited in Prolingheuer, *Der Fall Karl Barth*, 14. To Barth's political theology, cf. Timothy Gorringe, "Barth and Politics," in Jones and Nimmo, eds., *Oxford Handbook of Karl Barth*, 178-92.
210. Cf. the circular letter of November 11, 1933, of Erica Küppers to friends, cited in Prolingheuer, *Der Fall Karl Barth*, 236-40; editor's introduction to Barth, "Reformation als Entscheidung," *Vorträge und kleinere Arbeiten 1930-1933* (GA 49), 519 with n. 17.
211. Cf. editor's introduction to Barth, "Reformation als Entscheidung," *Vorträge und kleinere Arbeiten 1930-1933* (GA 49), 520f.
212. Cf. the circular letter of November 11, 1933, of Erica Küppers to friends, cited in Prolingheuer, *Der Fall Karl Barth*, 238.
213. Circular letter of November 11, 1933, of Erica Küppers to friends, cited in Prolingheuer, *Der Fall Karl Barth*, 238. The reference to "Ludwig the Child" relates to King Ludwig III, who at age seven became king, but with a guardian; it is intended to illustrate Ludwig Müller's dependence on Hitler. Cf. Prolingheuer, *Der Fall Karl Barth*, 10, n. 26.
214. Cf. editor's introduction to Barth, "Reformation als Entscheidung," *Vorträge und kleinere Arbeiten 1930-1933* (GA 49), 521f., n. 32.
215. Cf. Prolingheuer, *Der Fall Karl Barth*, 10.

216. Cf. letter of December 16, 1933, to Reich minister Rust, cited in Prolingheuer, *Der Fall Karl Barth*, 240.
217. Cf. letter of December 16, 1933, to Reich minister Rust, cited in Prolingheuer, *Der Fall Karl Barth*, 241.
218. Cf. Goeters, "Karl Barth in Bonn," 146.
219. Cf. letter of December 19, 1933, from Rector Fritz Pietrusky to Reich minister Rust, cited in Prolingheuer, *Der Fall Karl Barth*, 242.
220. Letter of December 16, 1933, to Reich minister Rust, cited in Prolingheuer, *Der Fall Karl Barth*, 240f.
221. Letter of December 19, 1933, from Rector Fritz Pietrusky to Reich minister Rust, cited in Prolingheuer, *Der Fall Karl Barth*, 243.
222. Neuser, *Karl Barth in Münster*, 5.
223. Cf. editor's foreword, *Briefwechsel Barth–Brunner* (GA 33), xvii–xix.
224. Letter of January 30, 1918, from Brunner to Barth and Thurneysen, *Briefwechsel Barth–Brunner* (GA 33), 19.
225. Letter of November 28, 1918, from Brunner, *Briefwechsel Barth–Brunner* (GA 33), 25.
226. Cf. letter of November 28, 1918, from Brunner, *Briefwechsel Barth–Brunner* (GA 33), 26f.
227. Brunner, *Das Gebot und die Ordnungen*, v.
228. Cf. Jehle, *Emil Brunner*, 165f.
229. Letter of February 3, 1930, from Thurneysen, *Briefwechsel Barth–Thurneysen* II (GA 4), 713.
230. Letter of December 13, 1932, from Brunner, *Briefwechsel Barth–Brunner* (GA 33), 211.
231. Brunner, "Die andere Aufgabe der Theologie," 275.
232. Brunner, "Die Frage nach dem 'Anknüpfungspunkt,'" 506.
233. Brunner, *Natur und Gnade*, 5f.
234. Hans Heinrich Brunner, *Mein Vater und sein Ältester*, 89f.
235. Barth, "Nein! Antwort an Emil Brunner," *Vorträge und kleinere Arbeiten 1934–1935* (GA 52), 437.
236. Brunner, *Natur und Gnade*, 44.
237. Barth, "Nein!" *Vorträge und kleinere Arbeiten 1934–1935* (GA 52), 444.
238. Letter of November 12, 1934, from Brunner, *Briefwechsel Barth–Brunner* (GA 33), 268.
239. Cf. letter of December 21, 1934, from Brunner, *Briefwechsel Barth–Brunner* (GA 33), 272–74.
240. Regarding this, see Chapter 11, n. 158.
241. Regarding this, see pp. 325–326.
242. Letter of May 9, 1956, from Brunner, *Briefwechsel Barth–Brunner* (GA 33), 382.
243. Interview von Vernon Sproxton 1960, *Gespräche 1959–1962* (GA 25), 60f.
244. Cf. the letter of February 15, 1925, to his friends, *Briefwechsel Barth–Thurneysen* II (GA 4), 306f.; letter of January 16, 1927, to Thurneysen (454).
245. Letter of June 8, 1928, from Bultmann, *Barth–Bultmann Letters* (GA 1), 38. Translation revised.
246. Letter of February 5, 1930, to Bultmann, *Barth–Bultmann Letters* (GA 1), 49. Translation revised.

247. Letter of February 5, 1930, to Bultmann, *Barth–Bultmann Letters* (GA 1), 50.
248. Cf. letter of February 16, 1930, from Bultmann, *Barth–Bultmann Letters* (GA 1), 51f.
249. Cf. letter of September 30, 1930, to Bultmann and letter of October 2, 1930, from Bultmann, in *Barth–Bultmann Letters* (GA 1), 55 and 56.
250. Cf. Konrad Hammann, "Barth und Bultmann," in Beintker, ed., *Barth Handbuch*, 98.
251. Cf. Bultmann, *Neues Testament und Mythologie*, 12–20.
252. Cf. Barth, *Rudolf Bultmann. Ein Versuch, ihn zu verstehen*.
253. Barth, "Selbstdarstellung," KBA 11294, 3.
254. Cf. Wilhelm Hüffmeier, "Barth und Gogarten," in Beintker, ed., *Barth Handbuch*, 85–90.
255. Cf. the circular letters of February 26, 1922, and December 19, 1922, to his friends, *Briefwechsel Barth–Thurneysen* II (GA 4), 46f. and 125f.
256. Circular letter of December 19, 1922, to his friends, *Briefwechsel Barth–Thurneysen* II (GA 4), 126.
257. Cf. Gogarten, "Karl Barths Dogmatik," in *Gehören und Verantworten*, 19; Hüffmeier, "Barth und Gogarten," in Beintker, ed., *Barth Handbuch*, 87; and Beintker, "Barths Abschied von 'Zwischen den Zeiten,'" 211.
258. Cf. Beintker, "Barths Abschied," 210.
259. Cf. Gogarten, "Predigt über Johannes 15, 26–27," *Zwischen den Zeiten* 11 (1933), 465.
260. Cf. Beintker, "Barths Abschied," 215f.
261. Letter of September 20, 1933, from Gogarten to Georg Merz, cited in Beintker, "Barths Abschied," 216.
262. Cf. Beintker, "Barths Abschied," 217.
263. Cf. Gogarten, "Die Selbständigkeit der Kirche," in *Deutsches Volkstum* 15 (1933), 448, cited in Beintker, "Barths Abschied," 217.
264. Barth, "Abschied," *Zwischen den Zeiten* 11 (1933), 539f.
265. Barth, *How I Changed My Mind*, 41.
266. Cf. Nicolaisen, *Der Weg nach Barmen*, 2.
267. In *Der Weg nach Barmen* Nicolaisen carefully describes the history leading up to the Barmen Declaration and how it took shape; the volume also includes a synopsis of the various drafts of the text. The text of the final declaration is in Heimbucher and Weth, eds., *Die Barmer Theologische Erklärung*, 33–43; a recent English version can be found in Hockenos, *A Church Divided*, 179–80. The Barmen Declaration marked the first time since the confessional divisions after the Reformation that Lutheran, Reformed, and United representatives joined to issue a public statement. It is one of the most significant documents in Protestant Christianity, and is part of numerous constitutions of German regional churches today as well as cited in the constitution of the Protestant Church in Germany (EKD). It is also part of the creed of many non-German churches, e.g. the Presbyterian Church and the United Church of Christ in the United States.
268. Cited in Scholder, *Churches and the Third Reich*, vol. 2, 37.
269. Barth reported this in the preface to *Gottes Wille und unsere Wünsche*, 4.
270. Letter of February 13, 1934, to Chancellor Adolf Hitler, cited in Prolingheuer, *Der Fall Karl Barth*, 16.
271. Issue 7 included Barth's "Erklärung über das rechte Verständnis der reformatorischen Bekenntnisse in der Deutschen Evangelischen Kirche der Gegenwart," which he wrote

for the free synod in Barmen on January 4, 1934; it can be considered an early version of the Barmen Theological Declaration. Cf. editor's introduction to the "Erklärung," *Vorträge und kleinere Arbeiten 1934–1935* (GA 52), 65.
272. Cf. Nicolaisen, *Der Weg nach Barmen*, 14.
273. Cited in Nicolaisen, *Der Weg nach Barmen*, 19.
274. Cf. Schmidt, "Fragen zur Struktur der Bekennenden Kirche," 269.
275. Cf. Nicolaisen, *Der Weg nach Barmen*, 24 and 26.
276. Cf. the letter of May 2, 1934, from Kirschbaum to Thurneysen, *Briefwechsel Barth–Thurneysen* III (GA 34), 626 with n. 3.
277. "Protokoll der Vernehmung durch Ministerialrat Dr. Schnoering vom 30. April 1934," cited in Prolingheuer, *Der Fall Karl Barth*, 18.
278. Cf. Prolingheuer, *Der Fall Karl Barth*, 18f.
279. Barth, "Gespräch mit Tübinger 'Stiftlern'" (March 2, 1964), *Gespräche 1964–1968* (GA 28), 113.
280. Editor's introduction to "Theologische Erklärung zur gegenwärtigen Lage der Deutschen Evangelischen Kirche," *Vorträge und kleinere Arbeiten 1934–1935* (GA 52), 270.
281. Cf. Nicolaisen, *Der Weg nach Barmen*, 35f.
282. Letter of May 21, 1934, from Hermann Sasse to Hans Meiser, cited in Nicolaisen, *Der Weg nach Barmen*, 84f.
283. Letter of May 21, 1934, from Paul Althaus to Hans Meiser, cited in Nicolaisen, *Der Weg nach Barmen*, 88.
284. Letter of May 21, 1934, from Paul Althaus to Hans Meiser, cited in Nicolaisen, *Der Weg nach Barmen*, 87.
285. Letter of May 21, 1934, from Paul Althaus to Hans Meiser, cited in Nicolaisen, *Der Weg nach Barmen*, 87.
286. Letter of May 21, 1934, from Paul Althaus to Hans Meiser, cited in Nicolaisen, *Der Weg nach Barmen*, 88.
287. Cf. Nicolaisen, *Der Weg nach Barmen*, 41.
288. Letter of May 26, 1934, to Hermann A. Hesse, cited in *Vorträge und kleinere Arbeiten 1934–1935* (GA 52), 272, n. 33.
289. Cf. editor's introduction to "Theologische Erklärung," *Vorträge und kleinere Arbeiten 1934–1935* (GA 52), 272.
290. Cf. editor's introduction to "Theologische Erklärung," *Vorträge und kleinere Arbeiten 1934–1935* (GA 52), 273.
291. Cf. Prolingheuer, *Der Fall Karl Barth*, 19f.
292. Cf. Nicolaisen, *Der Weg nach Barmen*, 54–6.
293. Report by Seiz of June 8, 1934, cited in Nicolaisen, *Der Weg nach Barmen*, 56.
294. Cf. Nicolaisen, *Der Weg nach Barmen*, 56–8.
295. These have been compiled in Rohkrämer, ed., *Texte zur Barmer Theologischen Erklärung*.
296. Cf. Barth, "Die theologische Erklärung der Barmer Bekenntnissynode (Fragment von 1934)," *Vorträge und kleinere Arbeiten 1934–1935* (GA 52), 339.
297. Barth, "Die theologische Erklärung," *Vorträge und kleinere Arbeiten 1934–1935* (GA 52), 338 and 340.
298. Barth, "Kurze Erläuterung der Barmer Theologischen Erklärung (June 9, 1934)," *Vorträge und kleinere Arbeiten 1934–1935* (GA 52), 306.

299. Barth, "Kurze Erläuterung," *Vorträge und kleinere Arbeiten 1934–1935* (GA 52), 309; "Die theologische Erklärung" (342).
300. From Hockenos, *A Church Divided*, 179.
301. Barth, "Die theologische Erklärung," *Vorträge und kleinere Arbeiten 1934–1935* (GA 52), 355.
302. From Hockenos, *A Church Divided*, 179.
303. From Hockenos, *A Church Divided*, 179.
304. Cf. Barth, "Kurze Erläuterung," *Vorträge und kleinere Arbeiten 1934–1935* (GA 52), 314.
305. Barth, "Kurze Erläuterung," *Vorträge und kleinere Arbeiten 1934–1935* (GA 52), 314.
306. Barth, "Kurze Kommentierung des ersten Satzes der Theologischen Erklärung der Barmer Synode vom 31. Mai 1934. Vorlesung im Wintersemester 1937/38," in Rohkrämer, ed., *Texte*, 69.
307. Hockenos, *A Church Divided*, 179.
308. Cf. Barth, "Kurze Erläuterung," *Vorträge und kleinere Arbeiten 1934–1935* (GA 52), 314f.
309. Hockenos, *A Church Divided*, 179.
310. Hockenos, *A Church Divided*, 179. Cf. Barth, "Kurze Erläuterung," *Vorträge und kleinere Arbeiten 1934–1935* (GA 52), 315.
311. Cf. Barth, "Kurze Erläuterung," *Vorträge und kleinere Arbeiten 1934–1935* (GA 52), 315f.
312. Hockenos, *A Church Divided*, 180.
313. Cf. Barth, "Kurze Erläuterung," *Vorträge und kleinere Arbeiten 1934–1935* (GA 52), 316.
314. Cf. Barth, "Kurze Erläuterung," *Vorträge und kleinere Arbeiten 1934–1935* (GA 52), 317.
315. Cf. Barth, "Barmen. Martin Niemöller zum 60. Geburtstag am 14. Januar 1952," in Rohkrämer, ed., *Texte*, 169.
316. Cf. Barth, "Barmen. Martin Niemöller zum 60. Geburtstag am 14. Januar 1952," in Rohkrämer, ed., *Texte*, 169.
317. Hockenos, *A Church Divided*, 180.
318. Cf. Barth, "Barmen. Martin Niemöller zum 60. Geburtstag am 14. Januar 1952," in Rohkrämer, ed., *Texte*, 171.
319. Barth, "Kurze Erläuterung," *Vorträge und kleinere Arbeiten 1934–1935* (GA 52), 318.
320. Cf. Barth, "Kurze Erläuterung," *Vorträge und kleinere Arbeiten 1934–1935* (GA 52), 319.
321. Talk of the "missing seventh thesis" goes back to the eight "Theses of Pomeyrol," written in September 1941 in France. The theses used Barmen as a starting point but related the declaration to the French situation. The seventh thesis explicitly took a position on the persecution of the Jews. Cf. Scherffig, "Die fehlende siebte Barmer These," 296–9.
322. Letter of May 22, 1967, to Eberhard Bethge, *Letters 1961–1968* (GA 6), 250. Translation revised. In the literature Barth's omission on this issue has been criticized as a "deliberate result" of his concentration on the "theological existence" of the church (Scholder, *Churches and the Third Reich*, vol. 1, 439). In his study *Unter*

dem Bogen des einen Bundes Eberhard Busch attempted a differentiated approach to this. Barth had already determined self-critically in 1935 that the Confessing Church "had been silent e.g. about the measures against the Jews, the astonishing treatment of political opponents, the suppression of truth in the press of the new Germany and so much else, on which the Old Testament prophets for sure had spoken up... One can and must therefore call its 'confession' a very insufficient one." (Barth, "Bekennende Kirche im nationalsozialistischen Deutschland," *Vorträge und kleinere Arbeiten 1934-1935* (GA 52), 803f.) Regarding Barth's theological attitudes toward Judaism with respect to the Holocaust, see also Mark Lindsay, *Covenanted Solidarity* and *Reading Auschwitz with Barth*. It is also noteworthy that in 1947 Barth was invited to the meeting in Seelisberg, Switzerland, of the International Conference of Christians and Jews (although he declined). "Especially in the Jewish community in Switzerland Barth was well known... for his outspoken calls for the defeat of the Nazi regime" and acknowledged for "his engagement and advocacy for refugees and rescue groups." (Victoria J. Barnett, "Karl Barth and the Early Postwar Interfaith Encounters, 1945-1950," in Hunsinger, ed., *Karl Barth, the Jews, and Judaism*, 108. Barnett however also refers to Barth's 1950 discussion with Emunah, a group of young Swiss Jews who found some of Barth's theological responses quite problematic (111-12).)

323. Letter of May 22, 1967, to Eberhard Bethge, *Letters 1961-1968* (GA 6), 250.
324. Nicolaisen, *Der Weg nach Barmen*, 1.
325. Bonhoeffer's questions were posed in 1936 in "Essay and Discussion on Church Communion," in *Theological Education at Finkenwalde: 1935-1937*, 694.
326. The Ansbach Memorandum, commenting on the Barmen Theological Declaration, cited in Schmidt, ed., *Die Bekenntnisse*, vol. 2, 103.
327. Althaus, *Die christliche Wahrheit*, vol. 1, 71.
328. Cited in Prolingheuer, *Der Fall Karl Barth*, 21.
329. Cf. Barth, foreword to "Der Christ als Zeuge," *Vorträge und kleinere Arbeiten 1934-1935* (GA 52), 426.
330. Letter of July 29, 1934, to his publisher Albert Lempp, cited in *Vorträge und kleinere Arbeiten 1934-1935* (GA 52), 329.
331. Letter of July 29, 1934, to his publisher Albert Lempp, cited in *Vorträge und kleinere Arbeiten 1934-1935* (GA 52), 329.
332. Letter of August 18, 1934, to Albert Lempp, cited in *Vorträge und kleinere Arbeiten 1934-1935* (GA 52), 330.
333. Cf. the editor's introduction to Barth, "Die theologische Erklärung," *Vorträge und kleinere Arbeiten 1934-1935* (GA 52), 330.
334. Cf. Barth, foreword to "Der Christ als Zeuge," *Vorträge und kleinere Arbeiten 1934-1935* (GA 52), 427. This is a play on words: "Between the Lines" (*Zwischen den Zeilen*) picks up on "Between the Times" (*Zwischen den Zeiten*).
335. Cf. *Vorträge und kleinere Arbeiten 1934-1935* (GA 52), 620, n. 7.
336. Cf. the editor's introduction to Barth, "Die theologische Erklärung," *Vorträge und kleinere Arbeiten 1934-1935* (GA 52), 328, n. 5.
337. Cf. letter of October 22, 1934, to Thurneysen, *Briefwechsel Barth-Thurneysen* III (GA 34), 715-18.
338. Cf. Scholder, *Churches and the Third Reich*, vol. 2, 274.

339. Cf. Strohm, *Kirchen im Dritten Reich*, 60.
340. Cf. Scholder, *Churches and the Third Reich*, vol. 2, 260-2.
341. Cf. Besier, *Die Kirchen und das Dritte Reich*, vol. 3, 20.
342. Cf. Besier, *Die Kirchen und das Dritte Reich*, vol. 3, 38. On May 16, 1935, Hermann A. Hesse, Immer, and Niemöller once more became part of the Council of Brethren with Barth's approval (cf. letter of April 27, 1935, to Thurneysen, *Briefwechsel Barth-Thurneysen* III (GA 34), 875 with n. 5).
343. Cf. Prolingheuer, *Der Fall Karl Barth*, 39f.
344. Cf. the minutes of the session in Prolingheuer, *Der Fall Karl Barth*, 40.
345. Barth, "Gedanken über die Lage vom 1. Dezember 1934," *Vorträge und kleinere Arbeiten 1934-1935* (GA 52), 589f. Later too Barth stayed by his judgement that the way in which people had dealt with the Dahlem decisions had been the Confessing Church's decisively "false... setting of the agenda," because people no longer wanted to "stand with" the insights that had been gained there about the "life and... orders of the *body* of Christ in the *battle* situation with which we had at the time been tasked" (Letter of June 29, 1946, to Martin Niemöller, KBA 9246.237).
346. Regarding this cf. Assel, "Barth ist entlassen..."
347. German Civil Service law, § 4, Par. I, in: Reichsgesetzblatt I (1937), Nr. 9, 42.
348. Letter of November 5, 1934, from Rector Hans Naumann to Reich minister Rust, cited in Prolingheuer, *Der Fall Karl Barth*, 26. With this Rector Naumann echoes Rector Pietrusky's fear of Barth becoming a "martyr", see p. 226.
349. Cf. the protocols of the interrogation on December 1, 1934, cited in Prolingheuer, *Der Fall Karl Barth*, 258.
350. Cf. Prolingheuer, *Der Fall Karl Barth*, 47.
351. Prolingheuer, *Der Fall Karl Barth*, 47, with a quote from the December 1934 notes taken by Ernst Wolf.
352. Cf. Prolingheuer, *Der Fall Karl Barth*, 47f. and 52.
353. Cf. Prolingheuer, *Der Fall Karl Barth*, 53.
354. Cf. the ministerial introductory decision of November 26, 1934, cited in Prolingheuer, *Der Fall Karl Barth*, 53.
355. Cited in Prolingheuer, *Der Fall Karl Barth*, 54.
356. Internal position taken by Barth on December 2, 1934, toward the draft by Friedrich Horst for a public declaration by the provisional church government, cited in Prolingheuer, *Der Fall Karl Barth*, 68.
357. Letter of December 2, 1934, from Hans von Soden, cited in *Barth-Bultmann Letters* (GA 1), 135f.
358. Letter of December 5 to Hans von Soden, cited in *Barth-Bultmann Letters* (GA 1), 137. Translation revised.
359. Letter of December 5 to Hans von Soden, *Barth-Bultmann Letters* (GA 1), 137f.
360. *Hannoverscher Kurier* of December 8, 1934, cited in Prolingheuer, *Der Fall Karl Barth*, 79.
361. Letter of December 8, 1934, from August Marahrens to Wilhelm Frick, cited in Prolingheuer, *Der Fall Karl Barth*, 79.
362. Letter of December 8, 1934, from August Marahrens to Wilhelm Frick, cited in Prolingheuer, *Der Fall Karl Barth*, 79f.

363. Cf. the editor's introduction to Barth, "Zur Frage des Hitlereides," *Vorträge und kleinere Arbeiten 1934-1935* (GA 52), 610.
364. Letter of December 1, 1934, from Dietrich Bonhoeffer to Karl Koch. In Bonhoeffer, *London: 1933-1935*, 263. Translation revised.
365. Cf. Prolingheuer, *Der Fall Karl Barth*, 98, 115f., 122, and 186.
366. Cf. Barth, "Zur Frage des Hitlereides," *Vorträge und kleinere Arbeiten 1934-1935* (GA 52), 617.
367. Text of the charges against Barth, cited in Prolingheuer, *Der Fall Karl Barth*, 78.
368. Letter of December 6, 1934, from synod president Karl Koch to Heinrich Harms, cited in Prolingheuer, *Der Fall Karl Barth*, 74.
369. Cf. letter of December 6, 1934, from synod president Karl Koch to Heinrich Harms, cited in Prolingheuer, *Der Fall Karl Barth*, 80f.
370. Letter of December 12, 1934, from Marahrens to Rust, cited in Assel, "Barth ist entlassen...," 467. On December 29 Marahrens distanced himself again in another letter to Rust; cf. Prolingheuer, *Der Fall Karl Barth*, 108.
371. Cf. Prolingheuer, *Der Fall Karl Barth*, 87-91.
372. Cf. Assel, "Barth ist entlassen...," 471.
373. Cited in Prolingheuer, *Der Fall Karl Barth*, 96.
374. Letter of December 24-6, 1934, to Thurneysen, *Briefwechsel Barth-Thurneysen* III (GA 34), 800. The translation from Socrates' *Apology* is from Pelliccia, ed., *Selected Dialogues of Plato*, 301-3.
375. Letter of December 24-6, 1934, to Thurneysen, *Briefwechsel Barth-Thurneysen* III (GA 34), 800.
376. Cf. the verdict, cited in Prolingheuer, *Der Fall Karl Barth*, 97.
377. Cf. the decision, cited in Prolingheuer, *Der Fall Karl Barth*, 114.
378. Cf. the protocol of the Council of Brethren meeting of January 3, 1935, cited in Prolingheuer, *Der Fall Karl Barth*, 114.
379. Cf. Prolingheuer, *Der Fall Karl Barth*, 115.
380. Cf. the letter of December 23, 1934, from Willem Visser 't Hooft, in *Barth-Visser 't Hooft Briefwechsel* (GA 43), 24.
381. Cited in Prolingheuer, *Der Fall Karl Barth*, 120.
382. Cf. the verdict of December 20, 1934, of the Cologne criminal court against Karl Barth, cited in Prolingheuer, *Der Fall Karl Barth*, 291.
383. Cf. the verdict of December 20, 1934, of the Cologne criminal court against Karl Barth, cited in Prolingheuer, *Der Fall Karl Barth*, 292.
384. Cf. the verdict of December 20, 1934, of the Cologne criminal court against Karl Barth, cited in Prolingheuer, *Der Fall Karl Barth*, 295.
385. Verdict of December 20, 1934, of the Cologne criminal court against Karl Barth, cited in Prolingheuer, *Der Fall Karl Barth*, 295.
386. Cf. letter of January 30, 1935, to Maxime de Stoutz, director of the Office for Foreign Affairs in the Political Department in Bern, cited in *Briefwechsel Barth-Thurneysen* III (GA 34), 825, n. 26.
387. Cf. Otto Bleibtreu, *Berufungsbegründung* of March 14, 1935, cited in Prolingheuer, *Der Fall Karl Barth*, 306-26.
388. Cf. Prolingheuer, *Der Fall Karl Barth*, 133.

389. Cf. Prolingheuer, *Der Fall Karl Barth*, 134.
390. Cf. the decision cited in Prolingheuer, *Der Fall Karl Barth*, 144.
391. Cf. letter of January 14, 1935, to Kirschbaum, *Briefwechsel Barth–von Kirschbaum* I (GA 45), 420: "By the way here a little cloud of gossip about 'us' is going around."
392. Cf. letter of February 25, 1935, from Thurneysen, *Briefwechsel Barth–Thurneysen* III (GA 34), 830f.
393. Cf. *Briefwechsel Barth–Thurneysen* III (GA 34), 827, n. 1.
394. Cf. the letter of February 11, 1935, from Gertrud Lindt to Kirschbaum, cited in *Briefwechsel Barth–Thurneysen* III (GA 34), 827, n. 1.
395. Letter of February 11, 1935, from Gertrud Lindt to Kirschbaum, cited in *Briefwechsel Barth–Thurneysen* III (GA 34), 827, n. 1.
396. Letter of February 11, 1935, from Gertrud Lindt to Kirschbaum, cited in *Briefwechsel Barth–Thurneysen* III (GA 34), 838, n. 4.
397. Letter of February 11, 1935, from Gertrud Lindt to Kirschbaum, cited in *Briefwechsel Barth–Thurneysen* III (GA 34), 828, n. 1.
398. Letter of February 25, 1935, from Thurneysen, *Briefwechsel Barth–Thurneysen* III (GA 34), 830.
399. Letter of February 18, 1935, from Marguerite Thurneysen to Kirschbaum, *Briefwechsel Barth–Thurneysen* III (GA 34), 828.
400. Letter of February 18, 1935, from Marguerite Thurneysen to Kirschbaum, *Briefwechsel Barth–Thurneysen* III (GA 34), 829.
401. Cf. letter of February 18, 1935, from Marguerite Thurneysen to Kirschbaum, *Briefwechsel Barth–Thurneysen* III (GA 34), 829.
402. Letter of February 18, 1935, from Marguerite Thurneysen to Kirschbaum, *Briefwechsel Barth–Thurneysen* III (GA 34), 838.
403. Cf. Prolingheuer, *Der Fall Karl Barth*, 157 and 169.
404. Position on the case of Karl Barth, cited in Prolingheuer, *Der Fall Karl Barth*, 144.
405. Cf. Prolingheuer, *Der Fall Karl Barth*, 180.
406. Cited in Boerlin, "Karl Barth als Staatsbürger," 639; cf. *Briefwechsel Barth–von Kirschbaum* I (GA 45), 534, n. 13.
407. Cf. Prolingheuer, *Der Fall Karl Barth*, 178 and 181.
408. Letter of May 22, 1935, to Julius Sammetreuther, cited in Prolingheuer, *Der Fall Karl Barth*, 185.
409. Cf. Prolingheuer, *Der Fall Karl Barth*, 195.
410. Cited in Prolingheuer, *Der Fall Karl Barth*, 195.
411. Cf. Prolingheuer, *Der Fall Karl Barth*, 196.
412. Cf. Prolingheuer, *Der Fall Karl Barth*, 198. "For administrative simplification civil servants can be placed in retirement, even when they are not yet incapable of service" (Law for the Restoration of the Civil Service, § 6 [Placement in retirement], *Reichsgesetzblatt* I (1933), Nr. 34, 176).
413. Cf. Prolingheuer, *Der Fall Karl Barth*, 198f.
414. Cf. Prolingheuer, *Der Fall Karl Barth*, 202.
415. Cf. *Briefwechsel Barth–Thurneysen* III (GA 34), 913, n. 2.
416. "Zum Weggang von Professor D. Karl Barth nach Basel," cited in Prolingheuer, *Der Fall Karl Barth*, 207.

417. August Marahrens, *Wochenbrief* Nr. 4571.II of July 17/18, 1935, cited in Prolingheuer, *Der Fall Karl Barth*, 214f.
418. Letter of June 15, 1935, to Wilhelm Niesel, in Freudenberg, ed., *Karl Barth–Wilhelm Niesel. Briefwechsel 1924–1968*, 183.
419. Letter of June 30, 1935, to Hermann Hesse, cited in Prolingheuer, *Der Fall Karl Barth*, 347.
420. Letter of June 10, 1935, from Thurneysen, *Briefwechsel Barth–Thurneysen* III (GA 34), 897–902.
421. Letter of June 13, 1935, to Thurneysen, *Briefwechsel Barth–Thurneysen* III (GA 34), 903.
422. Letter of June 13, 1935, to Thurneysen, *Briefwechsel Barth–Thurneysen* III (GA 34), 904.
423. Letter of June 13, 1935, to Thurneysen, *Briefwechsel Barth–Thurneysen* III (GA 34), 903.

11

"We Who Can Still Speak"

Basel, 1935–45

At the beginning of July 1935 Karl Barth returned to Basel.[1] The family moved into a corner house at St. Albanring 186 in the Gellert quarter on the left bank of the Rhine—and despite the objections of Swiss relatives, together with Charlotte von Kirschbaum. In July 1941 they moved several houses down to St. Albanring 178. They were next door to Barth's daughter Franziska, who had married businessman and authorized signatory Max Zellweger in 1935 and started her own family with him.[2]

Life Goes On: Professor in Basel

In Basel Barth was initially appointed as an extraordinary professor and then three years later named full professor.[3] Shortly after beginning his work there he preached at the Basel Münster Church before "an audience numbering in the thousands," since many wanted to hear the renowned repatriate.[4]

On the Basel theological faculty Barth was soon working together with two colleagues from Bonn who had already been dismissed in 1933. One was the New Testament scholar Karl Ludwig Schmidt, who after his dismissal initially was active as a pastor in Switzerland, becoming a professor in Basel in 1935.[5] The other was Fritz Lieb, whose research was on the eastern churches and who had initially left Bonn for Paris, where he was in contact with other emigrants such as Walter Benjamin, Heinrich Mann, and Nikolai Berdyaev before his 1937 appointment in Basel as professor for dogmatics and the history of theology, with a focus on the eastern churches.[6] Lieb became an especially important friend to Barth.[7] Another was Wilhelm Vischer, who since 1936 had been private lecturer for Old Testament in Basel as well as pastor at the St. James Church, where Barth was a member.[8] Together with him Barth subsequently became involved in refugee assistance and in this context he played an essential role in Barth's position on the theological significance of Judaism. In addition to his pastorate at the Basel Münster Church, Eduard Thurneysen was private lecturer on the faculty for practical theology.[9] During Barth's time in Germany there had been a very close exchange between the two. Now this relationship began to slacken, among other things because each in the meantime had different areas of work.[10] In the *Festschrift* for Thurneysen's

70th birthday Barth wrote that each of them had had "a special mission." Over the years Thurneysen had become "a little more 'pastoral' and I for my part... a little more 'professorial'" than they had been in earlier years.[11]

In Basel however Barth also encountered previous opponents, particularly Eberhard Vischer, in whose home he had argued in 1920 with Adolf von Harnack about the nature of theology.[12] Vischer nonetheless welcomed Barth in Basel "naturally and chivalrously."[13]

Barth was to teach on the Basel faculty for a good twenty-five years. During that time his relationship with his immediate colleagues remained distant. Several days before his death a younger colleague, the ethicist Hendrik van Oyen, complained that in the many years of working together he "had never really gotten very close" to Barth. Barth replied that

> in all the years with most... of the other faculty members it was only occasionally, if at all, that I cultivated any closer relation... Each of us turned to his own way, partly for practical and technical reasons, and partly for deeper ones. This was far from being an ideal situation.[14]

As with Ernst Staehelin, a church historian who was Barth's colleague until 1961, and Alfred de Quervain, private lecturer in Basel since 1930 and professor for ethics in Bern since 1944, "the cogwheels never noticeably engaged with each other, here and there."[15]

In the lectures that he held after the winter semester of 1935/6, Barth presented successive parts of his manuscripts for the next volumes of *Church Dogmatics*.[16] The second volume in the series I/2 appeared in 1938; the last completed volume IV/3 in 1959.[17] For Barth the work on his dogmatics, amidst all the political and church debates that followed, ultimately took priority. "Where I am not *needed*, there it is also not necessary for me to be too far away from my desk," he explained when he once declined an invitation. He had to "concentrate on the most important things if I am not to be frivolous about the ongoing work on my 'mammoth volumes.'"[18] Barth maintained the conceptual vigor of working on this major project for over a quarter century. During this time the text emerged through its integration in Barth's teaching "year-in, year-out in direct contact with the students."[19]

The additional seminars and societies that Barth held in Basel focused on central dogmatic topics like justification, church, Lord's Supper, or baptism. He partly based his societies on already published volumes of his dogmatics. He regularly handled the major confessions of faith in the Christian tradition.[20] In his seminars shortly before the beginning of the Second World War he addressed the developments in Germany with seminars on natural theology (winter semester 1937/8) and the state as a theological problem, as well as texts of the German Church Struggle (summer semester 1939). But he also turned to Catholic authors and topics again and again.[21] Beginning in 1943 he offered additional colloquiums in French and after 1951 in English as well. In the first semesters he also continued his open evenings.[22]

Several weeks after his start in Basel Barth could report to Elberfeld pastor Hermann Klugkist Hesse that his life there went on, even if "along a somewhat more modest and sedate course than in recent years outside." He was trying to acquaint the Basel students with "church dogmatics" and to get the Swiss church "accustomed very slowly to the idea that there could also be something like confession."[23] In general however Barth was somewhat disappointed that the Basel student body did not have "the zest that had been the case in Göttingen, Münster and Bonn."[24]

In the first semesters there were still German students who came to Basel to study with Barth. Several of his German doctoral students continued their doctoral work under him, including Helmut Gollwitzer, an engaged member of the Confessing Church.[25] But at the beginning of 1937 Reich minister of church affairs Hanns Kerrl issued a decree that semesters abroad at the University of Basel would no longer be counted for German theology students as long as Barth was teaching there.[26] This did not only relate to attending Barth's lectures; because of Barth the entire faculty was placed under this verdict. Gollwitzer was still able to complete his doctorate under Barth and in the summer of 1937 took over the Dahlem pastorate of the arrested Martin Niemöller.

International Honors and Lack of Appreciation

Barth had won much international renown through his involvement in the German Church Struggle. In the summer of 1935 he was invited by the University of Aberdeen to deliver the famous Gifford Lectures.[27] In his final testament Adam Lord Gifford had designated part of his estate to the four Scottish universities of Aberdeen, Edinburgh, Glasgow, and St. Andrews for the establishment of lectures "for 'Promoting, Advancing, Teaching, and Diffusing the study of Natural Theology.'"[28] In this he was especially concerned about laying the foundation of a universal ethic. Invited lecturers were to follow the methods of argumentation used in natural science, not those relying on a revelation. Until that point speakers had included William James ("The Variety of Religious Experience," 1900–2), Henri Bergson ("The Problem of Personality," 1913/14), Alfred North Whitehead ("Process and Reality," 1927/8), Albert Schweitzer ("The Problem of Natural Theology and Natural Ethics," 1934/5), and Werner Jaeger ("The Theology of the Early Greek Philosophers," 1936/7), holding epoch-making lectures.[29]

For his series of lectures in the springs of 1937 and 1938 Barth chose the theme "The Knowledge of God and the Service of God according to the Teaching of the

Reformation," basing it upon the 1560 Scottish confession. In his introductory remarks he addressed the curious circumstance that he—a declared opponent of natural theology—had been invited to give these lectures. He had also explicitly informed the university's senate of this after the invitation, which however did not cause it to withdraw the invitation. Barth continued that the natural theology that Gifford held to be true did indeed exist, but it was thanks to "a radical mistake."[30] He did however wish to follow the concerns of the founder at least indirectly by now giving a hearing for that theology from which natural theology sets itself off: a theology oriented around God's revelation.[31] As a Reformed theologian he could do nothing else. The Reformers had been of the opinion that each human being has a faith in God and an idea of God's commandment. That is, they had acknowledged a certain truth in the natural theology advocated by Gifford. However they had also made clear that they wanted salvation for human beings and the church to be "based *solely* on the word of God, on the *revelation in Jesus Christ* as attested in the Holy Scriptures and on faith in this word of God."[32]

After returning from Aberdeen in March 1937 Barth reported on his trip with some irritation to Ernst Wolf. People in Scotland understood the Church Struggle as a struggle "for the freedom *from* the church"[33] and not as one for the church's survival, were unable to follow his theological points, and continued ingenuously to do natural theology.

In the fall of 1937 Barth traveled once more to Scotland, since the University of St. Andrews bestowed a juristic honorary doctorate on him on September 28.[34] He had already received honorary doctorates from the universities of Glasgow and Utrecht. In 1938 he was honored by Oxford University. In total Barth received this distinction eleven times.

At the ceremony in St. Andrews Professor Donald Macpherson Baillie highlighted the fact that Barth was with certainty the most famous and influential theologian in the world at the time.[35] The "Barthian movement" had been the decisive factor for the radical change in the theological landscape of the past twenty-five years. Barth had succeeded in confronting theology anew with the transcendent word of God. And in light of the religious persecution in continental Europe he had taken up the task of "Mr-Valiant-for-Truth"[36] "and has suffered for it, with Christian courage upon his brow, and even with a twinkle in his eye. Such men we will always delight to honour."[37]

A further credential for Barth's reputation and an important public symbol after his dismissal from Bonn was the fact that already for his 50th birthday on May 10, 1936, a *Festschrift* was dedicated to him, and not first in the context of retirement, as is customary. The volume was to bear the title "The Freedom of Those who are Bound," but the German censor did not permit it, nor did he allow Hans Asmussen's contribution on "Karl Barth and the Confessing Church."[38] Thus the originally planned neutral subtitle "Theological Essays" became the title of the volume.[39] The book, which included German-speaking and international authors, was not intended to be the "expression of esprit de corps...of something like the 'Karl Barth school,'" but the testimony of self-confident pupils who take seriously Barth's warning "Be a man and do *not* follow me!"[40] Despite censorship, publisher Albert Lempp of the Munich Chr. Kaiser Publishers and editor Ernst Wolf did not shy away from saying in the preface that at that time the commandment "Thou shalt not bear false witness against thy neighbor" was frequently disobeyed when it came to Barth. In the church, slandering Barth was regarded "as proof of having a 'German' (he is Swiss!), 'Lutheran' (he is a Calvinist!), or 'Reformed' (he is a unionist!) ethos."[41]

In addition, Hermann Klugkist Hesse,[42] who together with Karl Immer was editor of the Confessing Church-oriented magazine *Unter dem Wort* ("Under the Word"), published in that magazine a personal congratulatory letter for Barth's 50th birthday in which he stressed that Barth was the "teacher of our church... given to us. The borders do not change any of this."[43] Barth replied in the same magazine that the *Festschrift* to which Hesse had contributed as well had shown him "that whatever is yet to come and where and to whom else however I might belong, *in any case I belong to the German protestant church* and to those Christian people who are gathered in it."[44]

Battle for the Confessing Church

Barth retained his ties to the Confessing Church even in Basel. In the fall of 1935 he traveled with Kirschbaum to Barmen-Gemarke to deliver a lecture on October 7 about "Gospel and Law."[45] As Charlotte von Kirschbaum reported, he was not however permitted to give the lecture himself

> but instead he had to let Pastor Immer read it to the overfilled Barmen church in the presence of the Gestapo, who then that same evening, shocked by the crowds pushing forward and the stormy welcome for Karl Barth by his students and followers, found it necessary to accompany us on the night train that brought us back to the border. All this transpired in a humane manner but the fact naturally remains distressing.[46]

In his lecture Barth pursued his thoughts about the first thesis of the Barmen Theological Declaration. "Gospel" and "Law," he noted, are the two ways in which we encounter the *one* word of God. In this, Barth was reacting critically to the widespread interpretation in German Lutheranism of the time that there were *two* words of God, the Gospel and the Law, God's promise and God's claim. The content of the Gospel was the message of Jesus Christ. The content of the law however could also be determined independently of that. From this perspective the content of the divine law could include certain racial rules or ethno-nationalist regulations. In this spirit the sixteenth Lutheran regional synod in Saxony had approved twenty-eight theses on December 10, 1933, in which was stated:

> Because the German national church (*Volkskirche*) regards race as God's creation, it acknowledges as God's commandment the requirement to keep the race pure and healthy... God places people in orders of life which are family, nation (*Volk*), and state. Therefore, in the totalitarian claim of the National Socialist state the national church recognizes God's call to family, nation, and state.[47]

To reinforce the indivisibility of Gospel and Law against this, in 1935 in Barmen Barth formulated what can be seen as the basic principle of his further theological ethic: "Out of what God here [in Jesus Christ] does *for* us, we read what God *wants with* us and *from* us... God's action... is aimed at *our* action, at a conformity of our actions with God's."[48] Whoever does not derive ethics from the Gospel loses himself in his own ethical ideas and attempts to justify himself with the "tatters of the Law."[49] As an example of this Barth mentioned the "*Volksnomoi*," that is, the ethno-nationalist laws. In this separation of Law and Gospel, Jesus Christ and his grace is then merely "the great credit-giver" who is to give our own ethical projects "the necessary cover."[50]

11.1. Karl Barth in 1937, © Karl Barth-Archive in Basel

Following his return from Barmen Barth was very often asked by members of the Confessing Church to give his opinion on the questions that arose. He answered letters, some of them smuggled over the border, and had personal conversations in Basel or at the "Bergli" as well as in the Netherlands.[51] Moreover he commented about the situation in Germany in international publications. In a Swedish newspaper for example he spoke to the question of whether the Confessing Church should cooperate with the state church committees as the German government demanded of it in December 1935.[52] Despite these opportunities to consult Barth suffered under the situation that "in all these things... [I have to] stand so much on the sidelines as is now my destiny!... the joy in not having to see brown uniforms and fear the Gestapo has indeed come at a high cost."[53]

Nor did the National Socialist regime lose sight of the theologian who had gone to Switzerland. It attempted to put pressure on Barth's publishing activities. His books and pamphlets were published as before by the Chr. Kaiser Publishers in Munich; in early 1936 state agencies intervened in the payment of royalties to Barth.[54] In October 1936 publisher Albert Lempp received a letter from the Reich Ministry of Public Enlightenment and Propaganda. It objected that the series *Theologische Existenz heute*, for which Barth continued as a co-editor, was no longer treating "purely church... theological... statements and problems," but that the series, because Barth was writing in it more frequently, "is giving more room for outspoken opponents of the National Socialist state."[55] Barth would no longer be tolerated as an editor and must be induced by the publisher to give up his editorship. In a tone that was simultaneously fuzzy and intimidating, the letter stated: "I see myself compelled to request that you dissolve the connection to Professor Barth and hope that after his withdrawal the series will again as in the beginning contain a purely theological character. Otherwise I would feel obliged to take sharper measures."[56]

Lempp wrote Barth that he assumed Barth would "be able to fulfill this wish in the interest of this series."[57] Nonetheless he planned to write the Reich ministry that the series profile was in no way political, but that since stopping Barth's prefaces its issues "more clearly had only a theological character."[58]

Lempp was torn. Through Walter Gut, professor of dogmatics in Zurich, he sent Barth a message in January 1937:

> For the sake of the German church, which is suffering terribly, he [Lempp] sends the equally heartfelt and urgent request to you not to make statements that could give an anti-church government occasion for further measures. He however added explicitly that he did not want to hamstring your conscience where you feel an inner duty to take a position. Certainly his publishing firm is dependent on you for almost half of its income. Yet that should not be the deciding factor, but your prophetic vocation in contemporary Protestantism in Germany and in

the world. In this regard you should however exercise all caution that the matter really requires.[59]

After another issue from Barth's pen appeared in December 1936, the Reich Ministry of Propaganda explicitly threatened Lempp in February 1937 that it would ban the magazine if Barth continued to be associated with it.[60] In his reply of February 20, 1937, Lempp inquired "whether you wish that in the future nothing at all by Professor Barth appears from my publishing house." Barth was "recognized as one of the most famous theologians in the entire world" and the continuation of his volumes on dogmatics was being planned by the Chr. Kaiser publishers. At the same time Lempp warned in his own way:

The second volume is likely to be ready in the course of this year and through its large sales, primarily overseas, it will also bring us economic benefits including the inflow of foreign currency. If now this volume should not appear, or must be published abroad, these advantages would become their opposite and the change in publishers would possibly make a bad impression.[61]

After this incident Barth expected that the Gestapo would prevent the volume's publication by Chr. Kaiser Publishers.[62] Arthur Frey, director of the Swiss Protestant Press Service, looked around for a Swiss publisher for the publication of Barth's further works and convinced the publishing house Evangelischer Verlag Zollikon, located in Zollikon near Zurich, to take it on. In May 1937 he wrote Barth: "I am simply delighted to see today the possibility that a good Swiss publishing house will publish decisive theological works. It makes it enjoyable once again to live in Switzerland."[63] Frey immediately began concrete negotiations with Lempp and wanted to arrange with him "how many of the books still in stock at Christian Kaiser Publishers should be sent over to Switzerland already today, to avoid their possible confiscation by the state."[64] From that point on Barth's writings appeared at this publishing house.[65]

In February 1938 the question of the oath to Adolf Hitler once more became an urgent issue for the Confessing Church. On the occasion of Hitler's birthday on April 20, 1938, the president of the Old Prussian Union Church's Church Council ordered pastors to take the oath to Adolf Hitler, using the same wording as German civil servants. Refusal would mean mandatory dismissal.[66]

In the Confessing Church there were lengthy discussions about whether this concerned a state requirement, meaning that under the dominant understanding of state authority in the church at that time individuals would have to obey, or whether this was the demand of an illegitimate church leadership that people could resist. They also discussed whether the oath could be toned down with an addendum.[67] In a May 18, 1938, statement that was sent to members of the Confessing Church[68] Barth categorically advised against such an oath, "*with or without an addendum.*"[69] He referred back to his final position in 1935 about the oath. It was not up to the person taking the oath to decide what it meant exactly; that was decided by the person requiring the oath—whether this came from a church or state body. What National Socialism demanded was clear: "the integration of the ministry into the ranks of its, the totalitarian state's, troops" and

> the unconditional external *and internal* recognition *and affirmation* of the present system of government, including its underlying worldview and the ethic necessary for its evolution and preservation, including the entirety of its actual practices as it has carried them out until now and will carry them out for the yet unknown future.[70]

One could not take such an oath without violating the first commandment and serving an alien god. While an addendum was conceivable in principle, in light of the absolute claim it was de facto a different oath. The protesting nature of such a different oath would certainly go unheeded in the present state. In conclusion Barth stressed that he would not judge anyone who behaved differently, since he was no longer exposed to this situation.

Some 60 percent of the pastors in the Old Prussian Union church gave the oath to Hitler on May 31, 1938.[71] The president of the Westphalian synod Karl Koch formulated an explanation for the pastors belonging to the Confessing Church in Westphalia that attempted to limit the oath's absolute claim.[72] After this declaration was accepted by the Old Prussian Church Council the sixth Confessing synod of the Old Prussian Union Church decided at the end of July that its member pastors should take the oath.[73]

At the beginning of August Barth wrote an outraged open letter to the synod[74] in which he accused it of now having abandoned the Barmen confession and fallen into the state's trap. Helmut Gollwitzer countered that with the adoption of the synod's explanation the oath had become "a different one, no longer totalitarian, a Christian oath."[75] "This is no long of any use for the Ministry of Church Affairs' intent to liquidate the Church Struggle through the oath, and all sides recognize this."[76] In Gollwitzer's view Barth was misled.

The battle within the Confessing Church about the oath became the subject of ridicule after a statement by the high-ranking Nazi politician Martin Bormann became known on September 8, 1938. Bormann declared the entire oath question for pastors to be a purely internal church matter.[77] Given this public humiliation Barth exclaimed to his friend Heinrich Vogel, who was also a member of the Confessing Church:

> When oh when, my dearest Heinrich Vogel, will our dear God give you German theologians, in addition to your depth and sagacity that cannot be admired enough, just a little simple political sense so that on such occasions, instead of

poring over the *Augustana*[78] etc., you smell what's cooking!—or at the very least are willing to listen when others tell you that they smell from a distance what's cooking.[79]

Anti-Appeasement: The Call to the Czechs to Resist

Barth was also taking public stands on the foreign political questions of Germany. In the spring of 1938 he grew deeply concerned about Hitler's aggressive policies in the Sudetenland, which were aimed at annexing the Sudeten region that had belonged to Czechoslovakia since 1918/19. As an expression of his support for Czechoslovakia he sent his lecture "Need and Promise in the German Church Struggle"[80] to Josef L. Hromádka, professor for systematic theology at the Hussite theological faculty at the University of Prague.[81] Hromádka thanked Barth on March 21, 1938, for this "sign of friendship" from abroad and reported about the situation in Prague by referring to Barth's wording from *Theologische Existenz heute!*:

> We proceed with our message of Christ *as if nothing had happened*...as citizens of this state however we are prepared to fight with all our might against this ghastly and violent power of blood-mysticism and the newly awakened Germanic lust for dominion. Our situation is not enviable, we do indeed find ourselves as if in a pair of pincers, but the mood in our country is unanimous, from the state president to the simplest market woman there is one single voice: rather death than slavery, rather struggles to annihilation than the loss of freedom, law and self-determination.[82]

In the months that followed Hitler's stance against Czechoslovakia and that of the German media propaganda continued to intensify.[83] Barth observed Hitler's course of action with horror and the appeasement politics of the Western powers skeptically and with great disappointment.[84] He wrote Hromádka at noon on September 19, 1938. That same day, when he learned that the Western powers at a conference in London agreed to cede the Sudetenland to Germany,[85] he added a handwritten comment to the letter: "You can make any use of this letter that you wish. Everyone there may know that there are people in western Europe who think differently from the English and French statesmen!"[86] Hromádka sent Barth's letter to the German-speaking *Prager Presse* (Prague Press), which published excerpts from it on September 25.[87]

Barth expressed himself in the letter pointblank: "Today as far as anyone can judge the freedom of Europe, and perhaps not just of Europe, stands or falls with the freedom of your people."[88] He hoped "that the sons of the old Hussites...will show the Europe that has grown too soft that there are still men today."[89] Further:

11.2. Karl Barth in Moravia, 1935, © Karl Barth-Archive in Basel.

Every Czech soldier who then fights and suffers will be doing this for us as well—and, I say this today without any reservation: he will also be doing it for the church of Jesus Christ, which in the orbit of Hitler and Mussolini can only succumb to ludicrousness or to extinction.[90]

It was "imperative for the sake of the faith ... to put our fear of violence and our love for peace decisively into second place and to put our fear of injustice and our love for freedom just as decisively into first place!"[91] Waging this battle with a clear conscience would depend on

> as many people as possible placing their faith not in people, statesmen, artillery and airplanes but in the living God and father of Jesus Christ ... The German battalions may be stronger but I don't know how and from where they would have this confidence, which ultimately is the only important and lasting one.[92]

Excerpts from Barth's letter appeared in October 1938 in the Netherlands, Switzerland, and, translated back from the Dutch under the title "Karl Barth as Warmonger,"[93] in Germany as well.[94] Shortly after that the German Ministry of Propaganda launched a campaign against Barth, accusing Barth's sympathizers of committing "treason against Christian truth, the Reformation position of faith and the German nation."⁹⁵ Church historian Ernst Barnikol, who taught in Halle, published an article, "Barth as the Anti-German Pope in the Realm of His Church." Barth, he wrote, was now doing exactly that which he had previously criticized in others, mixing politics and religion. "The theological mask of the dialectical politician and tactician" had finally fallen, and Barth "the ruthless theologian of war and anti-German agitator" was now publicly revealed.⁹⁶ A Lutheran pastor in Jena aired his anger in his parish newsletter:

> We German pastors...protest very adamantly against having our theology placed on the same level as that of Herr Barth. Our Christianity and our theology are much too German, much too healthy, much too Christian, for them to be even slightly infected by the Jewish-Marxist-international spirit of Barthian theology. We German Protestant pastors stand body and soul with our *Führer* Adolf Hitler and the Third Reich.⁹⁷

The theological faculty at Giessen drew the conclusion that "all the writings of Karl Barth are to be removed from our seminary library...to preserve the honor of German theology."⁹⁸

The Confessing Church provisional church government requested the letter in its entirety from Barth.⁹⁹ In his cover letter Barth stressed that "despite taking into consideration the strategic situation of the Confessing Church" he still must take the liberty to take a position on his own responsibility for the sake of the Protestant church in other countries and based upon the "overview" possible to him from abroad.¹⁰⁰ The provisional church government however had little understanding for this liberty and distanced itself from Barth's position in a October 28 letter to the all regional church governments and Councils of Brethren, in order to invalidate the SS charge against it of "treason against their country and people."¹⁰¹ Barth's letter to Hromádka, the letter stated, "is deeply painful to us."¹⁰² They did not forget that it had been Barth who had "uncovered and condemned the fanaticism of the 'German Christians' in their amalgamation of Gospel, politics, and worldview."¹⁰³ Barth had worked decisively on the Barmen Theological Declaration, which had stressed that the word and works of Jesus Christ were not to be misused for one's own wishes and purposes. With his letter about the Czechoslovakian situation Barth had "departed from the path that as a teacher of the church he once had pointed to. In his words it is no longer the teacher of theology who speaks, but the politician."¹⁰⁴ The freedom of the church was not dependent on weapons but solely on the will of God. "Therefore it is forbidden to the Christian to call anyone to weapons in order to defend the church of Jesus Christ."¹⁰⁵ The only valid appeal from the church could be one for prayer for peace, law, and justice.

To Hungarian students who had also sent a protest note Barth explained his opinion that "every Czech soldier" was fighting "also for the church of Jesus

Christ." His letter to Hromádka was in no way intended to address the question of territorial boundaries, but rather the danger "of a further incursion on the rest of Europe by German National Socialism."[106] Because in its totalitarian nature National Socialism made the free existence and proclamation of the church impossible, "on the borders of these lands not yet dominated by this system... the church too is being defended indirectly."[107]

Barth's letter had consequences for him in Germany. As of October 1938 his books could no longer be sold.[108] In 1939 the University of Münster withdrew the honorary doctorate it had given him in 1922.[109] A similar petition had already been submitted on October 21, 1936, by the dean of the Protestant theological faculty there, Friedrich Wilhelm Schmidt, because Barth "recently was also *politically* active in Switzerland as an enemy of the Third Reich;"[110] Schmidt however "quietly" withdrew this[111] when word of his intent reached outside circles. Only under the new dean Helmuth Kittel, a National Socialist and "German Christian," did the process once again get under way. In his letter of March 30, 1939, to the rector's office Kittel referred to Barth's position "in the September crisis [i.e., the Sudeten crisis] of the previous year" "against the German nation and its leadership."[112] On May 17, 1939, the university board of the rector and the deans determined unanimously "that Professor Dr. Barth had attempted to inflict serious damage against the German Reich and people and therefore has become unworthy of holding a German academic honor."[113]

After the war the university didn't want to have anything to do with its decision. On January 23, 1946, the dean wrote the rector of the university that the title had been withdrawn "at the initiative of the National Socialist government" and requested that this decision be reversed.[114] Only two weeks later, on February 9, 1946, the request was granted by the responsible university advisory body.[115] The document signed by the rector stated that the withdrawal of the title had been "undertaken by the Nazi regime."[116] It was "a source of satisfaction for the university... that it could be allowed to redress the injustice that occurred against Professor Barth, a leader in the battle against this oppressive regime."[117] In his letter to Barth the rector spoke of the wrong "that the Nazis committed against an extraordinary scholar, honorable character and a courageous fighter."[118] Barth reacted with aplomb, saying that he had "never taken [the decision] seriously and therefore also never ceased... to think [of myself] as a Doctor from Münster." It was "good that the legal position was now formally settled once again."[119]

The Political Responsibility of a Christian

In 1933 Barth had still written in his widely read *Theologische Existenz heute!* that one had to "do theology and only theology... just as before and as if nothing had happened."[120] Why did he now take such a clear political position to Hromádka? Since 1933 the totalitarian claim of the National Socialist state had become clear to Barth. In October 1938 he explained the change to his French friend Pierre Maury,[121] secretary at the time of the World Student Christian Federation:

> I have often enough accused myself that I was silent in Germany between 1921 and 1933 about everything that I saw around me in the political arena, to avoid any confusion between the Kingdom of God and any kind of political ideology. Perhaps this puritanism was necessary or at least excusable at the time. Today that is no longer the case. Today the totalitarian state is not on the scene as an idea, but as an effective power, and I can't understand how one should say anything but No—out loud or quietly—to this thing... But we who *can* still speak, must *do* so, and in particular when I myself have a voice that is widely listened to, then I don't see how I could be silent in a moment whether everything is at stake.[122]

In June 1938 Barth succeeded at an initial conceptual clarification of the relationship between theology and politics, in a lecture on *Rechtfertigung und Recht* (literally: "Justification and Justice," but usually translated as "Church and State").[123] In 1945 he believed that this text made "the theological precondition"[124] of his political engagement since 1938 understandable. In this lecture Barth developed his idea of the kingly lordship (*Königsherrschaft*) of Christ.

The background for Barth's new approach was his observation that it was the Lutheran conception of the church-state relationship, the so-called Two Kingdoms doctrine, which had contributed to the catastrophic implementation of National Socialism in Germany.[125] Barth found the concept of some Lutherans of "Eigengesetzlichkeit" (autonomy) especially dangerous.[126] The Lutheran church historian Hermann Jordan had defined the meaning of this in 1917:

> the significance of Luther's view of the state... rests in the incorporation and general conceptual reification of the idea of the separateness and autonomy of the two realms, the kingdom of God and that of the state... In each, religion and politics [have] to follow their respective laws.[127]

For that reason the church was not in the position to develop criteria for judging the political situation and had to restrain itself completely in political matters.

In *Rechtfertigung und Recht* Barth asks instead:

> Is there a relationship between the reality of the justification of sinners entirely through faith, achieved once and for all time by God in Jesus Christ, and the problem of human justice: an internal, necessary relationship that is such that, through divine justification, human justice also in some sense becomes a subject

of Christian faith and Christian responsibility, and thereby also of Christian confession?[128]

Is there a relationship between God's peace and peace in the world, between the freedom given by God and political freedom?

Barth says yes to these questions, basing worldly justice and the state not in divine law, as in Lutheran thought, but in the divine gospel.[129] For him, the criteria for human justice can be derived from the divine justification of human beings, just as the criteria for earthly peace and earthly freedom can be derived from the peace and freedom given by God. Barth seeks—fully consistent with the first thesis of the Barmen Theological Declaration—a "christological foundation" for political ethics.[130]

In unconventional exegeses of verses from the New Testament Barth then develops the following fundamental ideas: Justice is the duty of the state. There are states that measure up to this. Yet even the "demonic state"[131] that negates this duty is subject to the lordship of Christ. While according to the New Testament the state in the person of Pontius Pilate did indeed unjustly condemn Jesus, at the same time it carried out the will of God—since by this the justification of human beings through Jesus's death was made possible—therefore: "The demonic state in particular may wish evil so as then to be compelled in the utmost way to do good. The state cannot escape its service."[132] Barth derives from this the basic character of the kingly lordship of Christ, which consists in "that the state as such belongs to Jesus Christ originally and ultimately, so that in its relatively independent substance, value, function and purpose it must serve the person and work of Jesus Christ and thereby the justification of sinners that has occurred in him."[133]

This yielded the inherent criteria for the relationship of Christians to the state. The true state (*politeuma*), Jerusalem, the true polis of Christians, is in heaven (cf. Rev. 21). There Christians have their real citizenship. They can recognize only the future, heavenly state as divine. Because in Jesus's death God has established God's justice over sinful humanity, a theological ethic of the political has to be developed out of this justice as realized in Jesus Christ.

Because of this the earthly state must guarantee the church's freedom to preach about justification and divine justice. The state is then a just state when it "not only positively allows but actively gives" the church this freedom of proclamation.[134] If the state suppresses this free preaching, then the church must publicly name this suppression and in that way remind the state of its basic duty. "This will occur not *against* the state but as the church's service *for* the state!"[135] For its part, the church should pray for the earthly state. This prayer illustrates the state's limit: "The state is far away from being able to become an object of devotion, it is much more that the state and its representatives and supporters are in need of being prayed for."[136]

Out of these foundational reflections Barth concludes that Christians fundamentally recognize the state and its laws. However they can only swear an oath required by the state if this is not tied to any totalitarian claim. Because humans are sinners, human law must also be guaranteed by force. Therefore "a fundamentally Christian No" to military service "is impossible because this would have to be a fundamental No to the earthly state as such."[137] Barth emphasized this particularly in connection to the Swiss defensive army, probably also to combat the charge of pacifism that was frequently raised against him. And in light of the often criticized wording in his Tambach lecture,[138] he made it clear that the constitutional Swiss state in no regard stood as "the beast from the bottomless pit"[139] vis-à-vis the church. Because at that time however other states could absolutely be viewed as such, the defense of the Swiss "constitutional order was worth the effort."[140]

Finally, Barth developed the idea that the modern democratic state is the form of state closest to the considerations in the New Testament. Even the Christian prayer for the state is not a servile subordination but an exercise in responsibility. "Over the long term a serious prayer [cannot] remain without the corresponding work" and "one [cannot] ask God for anything that one is not at that moment decided and prepared to bring about within the limits of one's possibilities."[141] Therefore the obligation to pray brings with it the precedence of democracy—therefore over the course of time the democratic form of state had evolved in countries influenced by Christianity. Every Christian is *"answerable* for the character of the state as a *state under the rule of law"*—and for that reason the state can expect special engagement from Christians in particular.[142]

> The saying about the same affinity or non-affinity of all possible forms of state to the Gospel is not only outdated but false. It is true that one can go to hell in a democracy and that one can become saved under a state led by the mob or a dictator. But it is not true that one as a Christian can just as seriously affirm, wish, aim for the mob state or dictatorship as for a democracy.[143]

Church Struggle and Refugee Aid

In the years to come Barth's own political and social engagement would be focused on refugees who were fleeing the National Socialist terror. In the spring of 1937 Zurich Pastor Paul Vogt,[144] who had become the point of contact for refugees coming from Germany, approached Barth for support.[145] Vogt was moved by the "needs of German Confessing pastors and their children" and asked Barth whether these could be helped by finding homes for the children in church institutions or pastors' families in Switzerland.[146] Barth was taken with Vogt's considerations and offered concrete suggestions about how this could be organized and financed.[147] Through Barth's solidarity with the project, which was named *Bekenntnis-Pfarrer-Familien-Hilfe* (Confessing-Pastors'-Family-Aid), Vogt won the confidence of important figures in the Confessing Church such as Niemöller and Gollwitzer.[148] In September 1937 the program had already sponsored holidays for ninety-one children and sixteen adults in Switzerland.[149]

Through his travels in Germany Vogt was directly informed about the increasingly difficult church situation in Germany. In light of this the group decided to send a memorandum, written by Barth, to the Reformed pastors of Switzerland in Advent 1937.[150] The so-called "Church Struggle" had become a "*war of annihilation* against the internal and external existence of the Christian church."[151] "In place of faith in Jesus Christ there is to be self-adoration of the German 'new man,' glorification of German ethnic culture (*Volkstum*) and religious submission *to the German Führer*, and the National Socialist party intends simply to put itself in the place of the church."[152] The church was only being tolerated and would surely soon be persecuted openly, God's word could no longer be preached freely, there was no more freedom of church gatherings and publications.

This development was also a concern for Swiss pastors because "Christian faith...[knows] no national boundaries or declarations of neutrality...Can and may we follow our own concerns and duties, as if nothing had happened, as if our neighbor's house were not going up in flames?"[153] Help could be given through vacation offers for German pastors' families, invitations to theology students, and prayers for the German church, particularly in the Sunday worship service.[154] Soon almost 700 pastors signed on to the declaration.[155]

In early April 1938 the *Bekenntnis-Pfarrer-Familien-Hilfe* was renamed the Swiss Protestant Aid Association for the Confessing Church in Germany (*Schweizerisches Evangelisches Hilfswerk für die Bekennende Kirche in Deutschland*).[156] The work that had been done was now to be expanded: in addition to the welfare committee, in which from that point Charlotte von Kirschbaum also worked, a commission was founded for theological and church matters in which Barth was active as well as a commission for press and public speaking, which included Arthur Frey among others.[157] Soon Eduard Thurneysen and Emil Brunner were involved as well in the Aid Association.[158] During the war it became a prominent Swiss refugee organization, even if its significance was secondary to that of the engagement of the Swiss Jewish community.[159]

After the November 9, 1938 pogroms in the German Reich the Aid Association—as well as church bodies in Bern, Geneva, and Zurich—protested publicly against what had happened[160] and criticized the November 24, 1938, decision by the Swiss government to refuse visas for Jews.[161] Already since March 31, 1933, the regulation in Switzerland was that Jews emigrating from Germany received a temporary stay but no permission to work, which was being justified by a reference to "the situation of the Swiss job market and the already existing foreignization of the country."[162]

From 1938 to 1942 the Aid Association held yearly conferences in Zurich-Wipkingen for clergy and laypeople.[163] At the first conference Barth spoke clearly about the "Jewish question" in his lecture "The Church and the Political Question of Today." He began by describing how after scarcely six years it had become evident that German National Socialism was a "totalitarian...dictatorship...on principle" that put a complete claim on people and destroyed their humanity.[164] National Socialism had also been spreading for some time in Switzerland, namely when people tried to distinguish "between the thing itself and its so-called 'excesses'" and went so far as to display a certain amount of good will toward National Socialism.[165] The "new...Helvetic...nationalism," extolled as defense of the country, and its "indigenous antisemitism" were symptoms of this.[166]

But particularly because of its antisemitism National Socialism was "the fundamental anti-Christian opposing church."[167]

> For what would we be, what are we [Christians] without Israel? Whoever rejects and persecutes the Jews is also rejecting and persecuting the one who died for the sins of the Jews and then and *thereby* also died for our sins. Whoever is on principle an enemy of the Jews reveals himself, even if by the way he would be an angel of light, as a principled enemy of Jesus Christ. Antisemitism is a sin against the Holy Spirit. For antisemitism means the rejection of God's *grace*.[168]

Christian faith and approval of National Socialism were incompatible. The church therefore had to pray for the end of National Socialism.

The impression made by Barth's talk is illustrated by a letter from a pastor of Jewish ancestry who had fled to Switzerland with the help of Charlotte von Kirschbaum and Paul Vogt.[169] He felt "only gratitude" for Barth's clear position because it "comforts those who come from Germany homeless and driven out;" moreover until then hardly anyone had named antisemitism as "a sign for recognizing the anti-Christian nature [of Nazism]."[170] Barth's lecture however met also with sharp criticism. A lead article of March 5, 1939, in the *Neue Zürcher Zeitung* accused him of his political positioning: "The leaders familiar with the harsh reality of life who are filled with deep experience serve the people more than clergy who are politically aligned."[171]

During the war the Aid Association cared for numerous refugees despite constant financial problems. In 1941 it approached the Swiss Protestant Church Federation because of the continuing deportation of the Jews and in 1944 it helped publicize the documentation about the deportation and murder of Hungarian Jews.[172]

Ecumenical Silence at the Onset of the War

Like many other European church figures Barth followed the political developments of March and April 1939 with worry and outrage.[173] On March 15, 1939, the German army marched into the Czechoslovakian territory not yet under occupation. In the so-called Godesberg Declaration[174] the Reich church "German Christians" committed themselves at the end of March 1939 to a nationalistic and antisemitic course. In early April leaders of eleven regional churches adopted four lightly revised articles from the declaration. This revised version stated among other things: "Every transnational or international church body...is the political degeneracy of Christendom. True Christian faith develops fruitfully only within the given orders of creation...Christian faith is the unbridgeable religious opposite of Judaism."[175]

In April Barth suggested two things to Willem Visser 't Hooft, the general secretary of the World Council of Churches in process of formation (the organizational title until its official founding in 1948) since early 1939. First, the Council should publish an ecumenical statement that clearly condemned these principles; secondly, it should issue a statement directed toward the Germans in order to still avoid war or at least to shorten it.[176] Visser 't Hooft was convinced by the first suggestion and Barth composed a draft,[177] which Visser 't Hooft combined with one written by Archbishop of York William Temple. It was officially announced by the provisional committee of the World Council of Churches in early May 1939.[178] In opposition to the Godesberg Declaration, the statement emphasized:

> The structuring of the Christian church by nation is not a necessary element of its life...The acknowledgment of the spiritual unity of all who are in Christ, irrespective of race, nation, and sex (Gal. 3:28; Col. 3:11) is part however of the nature of the church... "Salvation comes from the Jews" (John 4:22).[179]

German foreign bishop Theodor Heckel reacted immediately in a telegram to Geneva in which he refused to tolerate such "unbearable interference in internal German matters" that came from "a false evaluation of the real general church situation in Germany."[180]

According to Barth the statement to Christians in Germany needed to contain two things: first, in case Christians in other nations enter a war against Germany, that this was not directed "against the German people, but rather instead against their usurpers who had become homicidally dangerous"; and secondly, to pose the question of conscience to Christians in Germany about "whether it was not their cause to do everything in their power to prevent this war or a victory of the usurpers."[181] Visser 't Hooft agreed with the first part of the message, but after discussions with Pierre Maury believed that the World Council should not try to influence the conscience of Christian Germans with direct or indirect appeals to them to refuse military service.[182]

Barth disagreed, saying that the first message stopped at giving the military opponents of Germany a "kind of cleansed conscience."[183] It could not be that "the church...—out of the fear that it did not seek 'to dictate conscience'—only reassures the good consciences of Christians outside of Germany—but fails to say the most decisive word to Christians in Germany."[184] The representatives in Geneva however were unable to reach such a resolution. Although some of his friends had similar views Barth stood alone in this demand to the ecumenical movement.[185]

The Second World War began on September 1, 1939. When the war broke out Barth was together with Charlotte von Kirschbaum at a course for German theologians in the Appenzell region in Switzerland. The group immediately began discussions about how the participants should now behave: "Stay on this side of the border? Refuse military service? Shoot into the air?" Barth was relieved "that this time around there is no false peace and that the wartime goal of the western powers is so unambiguous—which will mean not the destruction of Germany, but that of Hitler and his entire system."[186]

One month after the beginning of the war he did not disguise his disappointment from Visser 't Hooft that "on the point where ecumenical Protestantism could have had something like a voice" it had been silent. Those in Geneva justified themselves with the difficulties of structure and legitimation that such a statement would pose. Barth commented cynically that the World Council of Churches in process of formation "would then in the best case" say something "five years after peace is declared (and against the background of the rubble and ruins that would then have emerged)—and even then certainly only something despairingly academic, mediatory and vague."[187] He called upon his friend: "At all costs and for God's sake, away with this respect for the majesty of 'committees' and the prescribed channels—especially...in a moment when the world is in flames."[188] The church in its statements must no longer describe the pros and cons but clearly say Yes or No, for example to the question about whether the church could merely pray for peace or whether it should not much moreso pray "for a *just* peace and therefore consciously and decisively (if it is the will of God, which can make even losing the best thing!) pray for the victory of these and not those weapons." Barth ended his letter by asking Visser 't Hooft that he not request a new draft of a text that would then again be "corrected" by them so that "only half of something emerges." The ecumenical movement now had to give its own independent answer. "Do not seek for yourselves and us all any further delay, but instead—here I must bring the already very worn-out words of Zwingli: 'For God's sake do something courageous!'"[189]

Family Intrigues and Grief

The death of his brother Peter on June 20, 1940, was a crucial event for Barth. Apparently Peter Barth had been very ill for some time so that his death spared him greater suffering.[190] One hour after Barth learned of the death of his brother he wrote an empathetic letter to Peter's life partner Dora Scheuner, thanking her "for all you have been to Peter. It was a great deal and you may and should think back on this in peace." His letter offered insight into the relationship between the brothers:

> He has been my first and for many years also most trusted mate in this earthly life... You will know what it meant that I supposedly or really burdened him like a Napoleon, that he for his part had to emancipate himself from me a little, and what that came to mean once we became men.

This however had never really led to an estrangement between the two. But as he faced the death of his brother Barth asked himself: "whether and how I could have done more and better for him than I did."[191]

Shortly before Peter's death there had been an incident that brought to light the tensions that had long simmered in the family. Increasingly Karl Barth's brother-in-law Karl Lindt, the husband of Barth's sister Gertrud, found the relationship between Dora Scheuner and Peter Barth, who was married to Helene Barth-Rade, unbearable—particularly in light of Peter Barth's office as president of the theological working group in Bern.[192] Lindt was also offended by Karl Barth's relationship to Kirschbaum.[193] Therefore he tried to "mobilize" Albert Schädelin, pastor of the Bern Münster church, as well as Thurneysen, against the two brothers. Lindt's wife and Barth's brother Heinrich also were involved in these plans. One day before Peter Barth's death Gertrud had sent him a letter in the hospital that in Karl Barth's opinion "fortunately" never reached him, in which she blamed him and Karl "more or less for Mama's death."[194]

Barth was deeply disappointed by the behavior of his relatives. He had the impression that they were trying "to utilize Christianity... to 'choke one's fellow servants.'"[195] Barth was especially angered not only that Karl Lindt had not tried to speak to him but had avoided a conversation, instead trying to stir others' opinions against him. "I do not know what to do with this and *whatever* my mistakes may have been and even *if* I were the hound of hell that he has had to endure silently for such a long time... I have neither earned nor invited *this*."[196]

Barth was also distressed that his sister Gertrud and brother Heinrich had "once again united themselves as the family council that functioned so successfully when Mama was alive." They were now behaving as his mother had: "'Loving very, very much'... combined with the constant reproach of the law (the so-called law!) in the form of very expressive head-shaking, at times wordless, at times spoken." He wrote his sister and brother clearly: "I have already unhappily received this deliberate hot and cold bath from Mama, and not without damage to my inner relationship to her. I cannot...take this at all from the two of you." Gertrud would have to choose between the game of "Nice kitty/bad cat!"[197] and "any further closeness between you and me." As long as she stayed by the former he could not trust her and her husband and would not see any obligation "to speak a single word to you both about the question of my marriage."[198] While later they again corresponded amicably with each other, at that time the situation was tense.

The family had to deal with a further tragic event the following year. Barth's son Matthias began to study theology in the spring of 1941, as had his brothers Markus and Christoph previously.[199] Shortly after the beginning of the semester he went climbing with a fellow student on the Fründenhorn mountain in the Bernese Highlands. In the early morning of June 21 they left as a roped party but fell when one "lost hold of the rock."[200] Matthias Barth's companion was only slightly injured but Matthias's skull was fractured. He died at the age of twenty on June 22, 1941, in the hospital in Frutigen.[201] The burial took place on June 25 in Bubendorf in the Basel countryside where his brother Markus had been pastor since 1940. After the burial Karl Barth held a moving sermon that reveals much about how he was dealing personally with the question of why God allows suffering. He did not bypass the shock of this early death but examined what had happened from the perspective of Jesus Christ's overcoming of suffering and death. His sermon reads like a personal spelling out of what he would later assert in Vol. III/3 of *Church Dogmatics,* namely that in Jesus Christ "everything that creation needs and at the heart of creation, man, is already provided."[202] Four days after the burial Barth wrote to his friend Wilhelm Spoendlin that the "so unexpected...passing of our Matthias...has gotten to me more than every previous death...it was a great help to me to give the sermon myself."[203]

Barth chose 1 Corinthians 13:12 as the sermon text: "For now we see in a mirror, dimly, but then we will see face to face"[204]—a verse that had been important to his son even as a child. Barth portrayed to his listeners how Matthias Barth had been a child filled with fantasy and longing who could lose himself in time and space. In light of his son's nature as a "wanderer from afar and into far places" Barth found something merciful in the circumstances of his death: "he was allowed to be and to remain the wanderer that he always was."[205] Jesus's death and resurrection provided the connection between the "now" of death and the "then however" of life with God.[206] Because of that the mourners could

> not only mourn today, despite all our grief. If we ourselves are unable to rejoice, we do hear a very different voice rejoicing even above the evil place on the Fründenhorn where everything happened, even above the grave that we have just left. It speaks of the perfection even of this imperfect [one]...What else can we

11.3. Hiking with his sons Christoph and Markus Barth in the summer of 1941, a month after the death of son Matthias, © Karl Barth-Archive in Basel.

do, when we hear this voice, than be grateful to our God—even in tears—that God has been benevolent and good to our Matthias in his life and in his death?[207]

A Call for Military Resistance, and Swiss Censorship

Barth did not leave Switzerland during the Second World War.[208] In numerous talks he called upon his fellow Swiss to resist, even militarily. In the early months of 1940 he delivered a lecture on several occasions, "Des Christen Wehr und Waffen" ("The Defense and Weapons of a Christian") that created an uproar.[209]

Barth began by laying the theological foundation about God's victory through Jesus Christ over all powers, which was indirectly intended to apply to the power of contemporary evil. He followed by expressing the conviction that in the previous fall "the worse," that is, the war against Hitler, had been a necessary choice "to prevent something far worse."[210] "Peace at any price" was dangerous.[211] Barth asked the radical pacifists who continued to refuse to defend Switzerland militarily: "Can you take responsibility for *not* offering any resistance against the execution of that program?"[212] The old motto of the Benedictine order, "to pray and to work" was the appropriate position today, whereby "in this case 'to work'... unfortunately has to mean: to shoot."[213]

Many of his listeners were irritated that Barth in reference to Adolf Hitler said that Jesus Christ had "also died and risen for him." Hitler and his like, as well as those seduced by him, were like the "poor victims... of a very real but all too human demon." Barth added that it was "perhaps true... that the main figure in this war is very simply a sick man."[214] That sentence in particular was to have consequences.

Before the lecture was printed Hans Herren, director of the publishers of Barth's work in Zollikon, gave a copy of the text to the Swiss Army Office for Press and Radio. This office had been set up to prevent the betrayal of military secrets. In vetting publications it followed a directive of September 8, 1939, that stated in part: "Publication, other forms of dissemination and transmission of reports and statements that influence or damage Switzerland's assertion of independence to the outside world, the preservation of its internal security and maintenance of neutrality, is forbidden."[215]

The copy of Barth's text led to an extensive review process and correspondence, at the end of which it was demanded that the sentence "that the main figure in this war is very simply a sick man" be deleted.[216] The censorship officials had further reservations about the content, but they were unable to arrive at a decision within an acceptable time frame for the publishers, which then printed the text and made the one sentence in question unreadable.[217]

On March 29, 1940, Barth volunteered for military service.[218] In contrast to his recruitment in his youth, this time he was found fit for military duty. Now however they wanted to give him an office job in light of his profession. In response Barth explicitly stated his wish: "to be assigned to the armed auxiliary forces, with an obligation to fight in the event of war."[219] He was assigned to the Guard Company V on the Rhine, in the Jura mountains, and in Brunnen at Lake Lucerne for several weeks in each location, for a total of 104 days.[220] He wrote his uncle Ernst Sartorius about this experience that he especially liked his "comrades from the less distinguished and especially the less pious Basel."[221] He enjoyed looking back at this period after the war, because "it brought me intimately face to face with the common men of my country, with whom I lived day and night."[222]

Switzerland was surrounded by fascist states after the German victory over France in June 1940 and Italy's entry into the war.[223] In response the Swiss federal councilor Marcel Pilet-Golaz, foreign minister and at the time president of the Swiss Confederation, gave a speech that awakened the impression that he was in agreement with German domination of Europe.[224] Five days later Barth spoke up. In a lecture on "Der Dienst der Kirche an der Heimat" (The Service of the Church to Its Homeland), Barth warned: if into Switzerland with its "comforting mountains, valleys and lakes... foreign masters come over us, if a foreign spirit moves into our newspapers and offices and schools, into our constitution and our laws and customs, then it will become very sinister for us in our homeland."[225] Then the Swiss people would forget how to call injustice by its name. Switzerland would

11.4. Karl Barth as a soldier, 1940, © Karl Barth-Archive in Basel.

no longer be a refuge for the persecuted but conformed and *gleichgeschaltet* (Nazified). Switzerland's honor would be over.

Responsibility for the homeland had to look different. It included the military defense of the country because there were "more terrible things...than war."[226] Barth reminded his listeners of the words of the Rütli oath in Schiller's *William Tell*:[227] "'Rather death than to live in slavery!'—if it becomes necessary, will we stand by these words? Will we then rather see piles of ashes where Basel, Zurich and Bern now stand than a foreign flag above their towers?"[228]

In his talk Barth quoted the statement by the general of the Swiss Army Henri Guisan: "Better to die comforted than to live comfortlessly."[229] In light of the threat at the time Guisan decided for a Réduit defense strategy, that is a high concentration of the army's force in the Alps. On July 25, 1940, Guisan explained this strategy in the so-called "Rütli report"[230] to the commandants of the Swiss army and the Swiss people, urging them to absolute, courageous resistance against the Axis powers.

From Barth's viewpoint, what he was suggesting to the Swiss people was entirely in line with Guisan's thinking.[231] Therefore he sent his lecture on July 29, 1940, to the general with the comment: "More than one of your public statements suggests to me that my recently published brochure...might find your sympathy." Barth signed the letter giving his military service rank: "H.D. Soldier, Bew. Komp. 5, B.S."[232]

It was entirely in keeping that Barth was also among the founders of the *Aktion Nationaler Widerstand* (National Resistance Action), a coalition that on September 7, 1940, "was founded [as] a direct riposte against the...acutely threatening *Gleichschaltung*"[233] and secretly sought to work toward the inner forces of resistance of the Swiss in the case of an invasion.[234] Soon they had involved several hundred Swiss men and women who held important social and political positions of influence in this "Aktion."[235] Barth composed for the group an open letter in November 1940 to the board of the Swiss Protestant Church Federation, signed by twenty-eight politicians.[236] He himself did not want to sign it so that his name could not arouse "disputes" between the "Barthians and anti-Barthians" in the clergy.[237]

In November 1940 Barth also held the lecture "Unsere Kirche und die Schweiz in der heutigen Zeit" ("Our Church and Switzerland in the Present Time"), which he delivered on several occasions.[238] Once again he presented the special danger posed by the National Socialist dictatorship. It demanded not only outward obedience "but, by veiling itself in the robes of divinity, goes further to [demand] everything from everyone." Every person who resists was neutralized and everyone who is not useful for the state's purposes was systematically annihilated. Because of this, in no case could one be comforted by "correct relationships of friendship" to Germany; "the great steamroller of the so-called new European order" would at some point reach Switzerland.[239] This could happen through a military invasion but also if Swiss authorities and the people succumbed increasingly to National Socialist propaganda and ideology. Barth turned around the question as to why God had allowed this war. It was not a matter of God's responsibility here, but rather that of humanity. God was waiting "to...eventually encounter a bunch of men and women who are decent enough not to fall for the perfidy, swindles and fraud of this era and who will avoid making any contracts with the devil."[240] Finally he said: "Whether Switzerland still stands in the future will depend on whether we Swiss believe, will believe as Christians."[241] For it was Christian faith that offered the internal strength to resist the seductions of National Socialism or defeatism.

Barth's lecture appeared in February 1941—no longer published in Zollikon but by a small publisher in St. Gallen—and within two months 7,000 copies had been sold. While the Army Office for Press and Radio had refrained from banning the text, the German embassy councilor Baron von Bibra protested against it so that the Swiss state prosecutors' office became involved. Based upon the previous positive decision by the censorship office however the prosecutors' office could not act. The director of the section on book trade in the Office for Press and Radio, Herbert Lang, was then asked to speak to Barth personally.[242]

On May 2, 1941, Lang called on Barth. In his final report about the activity surrounding Barth's lecture on "The Defense and Weapons of a Christian" Lang had already told his supervisor: "We cannot orient our position by the sensitivity of a foreign state, instead we have to act according to our own national Swiss principles."[243] It is not surprising, then, that the conversation proceeded with great agreement. In his official letter of reply on the same day Barth declared his willingness in the future to present before publication all his Swiss books that touched directly on themes of international politics. But he immediately added: "There are other things besides *book* publications, other things besides *printed* and other printed publications besides those in *Switzerland*," that is, he reserved the option for uncensored publications. And he clarified: "By their very nature theological statements in particular always have an indirect relationship to internal and external political decisions."[244]

Barth also declared himself willing to discuss specific wording in the essay for a new edition. But it would be objectively impossible for him to give up as demanded the talk about the National Socialist state power "veiling itself in the robes of divinity." For this content

> in the present situation [has] the character of a Christian statement of faith and confession, to the extent that the faith in the one and only true God...in the present situation cannot be expressed clearly without this characterization of its opposite, which currently threatens. Already in the Church Struggle in Germany (not without my involvement) this sentence was the parting of the ways.[245]

He emphasized at the end of his letter: "Whatever the fate of this lecture is, I will continue to express myself in the sense of this lecture and will be concerned that these statements...reach the people in one way or another."[246]

In his official response to the conversation Barth enclosed a personal note to Lang, expressing his delight in their agreement. He explained to Lang that in the official letter he had also written things for those who might still be able to see the letter. "You will understand correctly, then, if things are stated that do not need to be said to you."[247]

Federal councilor Eduard von Steiger, who as the head of the departments of justice and police also oversaw the Office for Press and Radio, and to whom Barth had turned because of the censorship of "Unsere Kirche und die Schweiz in der heutigen Zeit," wrote Barth a sharp letter in early June 1941. Barth had

> previously fought against militarism and in this connection described the state as the "beast from the bottomless pit"...We don't allow ourselves to intervene in

theological matters, but perhaps we may indeed pose the modest question as to whether *you* are called to champion the duties and necessary actions of the Swiss state through public political lectures and publications, even if "veiled in church robes."[248]

Barth was unshaken by this reprimand and in July 1941, on the occasion of the 650th anniversary of the Swiss Confederation, delivered his lecture "Im Namen Gottes des Allmächtigen! 1291–1941" ("In the Name of God the Almighty! 1291–1941") twice before large audiences.[249] There he explained his idea of the political self-understanding of Switzerland and especially of Swiss neutrality. His title refers to the first words of the preamble of the Swiss constitution. Barth used it as a reminder that the cohesion of Switzerland came about through the oath that constituted the Swiss Confederation, not through linguistic commonalities or ethno-nationalist concepts. The original motivation for coming together had been "the *concept of a community of free peoples consisting of free people bound together by law.*"[250]

It was of vital importance to Switzerland that it be independent and neutral over against every quest for domination by individual European powers. At the same time however it had never been independent of the fates of the West and therefore could not remain neutral to the European duty "to find our path through the chaos that has arisen to a new order." Switzerland was "at once for everyone and against no one" but it had to be against those "who as disturbers of the peace, criminals, revolutionaries and tyrants are for their part against everyone." The political character of Switzerland is "comparable to the Alpenglow, a *reflection*" of the Gospel of Jesus Christ, "a confirmation of his resurrection."[251] If however National Socialism were to triumph in Switzerland as well, no more light would shine from it. It would have lost its right to exist.

In conclusion Barth addressed several concrete abuses in Switzerland, including censorship: "Not everyone knows this but it is so: today in Switzerland we have censorship."[252] It issued warnings and reprimands, banned newspapers as well as books and prevented lectures and public gatherings. "Even this lecture [might] not be secure from its grasp."[253] This censorship suppressed the kinds of reports and opinions that could be uncomfortable for the Axis powers and did not tolerate public mention or criticism of their activities. "Thanks to this censorship we learn only a part of the truth from the public word about European matters and especially only part of what there would be to say with good reason and necessity from the Swiss side."[254] Just as clearly, Barth broached the issue of the economic relationships between Switzerland and Germany. Through arms exports and trade relationship, which made Switzerland "indirectly, yes, but really to the *financier* of the Axis might" it "had become its *helper in war.*"[255]

The text was printed quickly and Barth sent it to General Guisan as well as the president of the Swiss Confederation Ernst Wetter before it was banned by the censor on July 29, 1941.[256] The reason given by the censor was that Barth had used "the theological framework, through the mirror that he held up to his fellow citizens, to take a position against a foreign state in such a way that is likely to disturb the correct relationships between Switzerland and this state and endanger Switzerland's neutral position."[257]

On August 10, 1941, Barth submitted an appeal against this ban and stressed that the charge of a theological "framework" was an insult, because it made "my theological as well as my political position appear to be an insincere camouflage," whereas precisely based upon his Reformed theology he held "a certain view of the Swiss state as necessary."[258] Sternly he continued: "The moment has yet to arrive where Bern will be happy that it can point out to England and America that during these years there were also Swiss like me on the scene, who spoke and acted, and that it was allowed to them in particular for the sake of the 'neutral position' of Switzerland."[259]

Barth's appeal was rejected on October 25, 1941. The statement of rejection indeed agreed with his claim that he had not used theology as a framework.[260] But it repeated that his "extremely hostile...position against the current German state" was "likely to disturb our peaceful relations with a neighboring land and thereby endanger the claim of our independence and neutrality."[261]

In the meantime another lecture by Barth in September 1941 in Muristalden, Bern Canton, had been forbidden.[262] Barth was informed by Colonel Ernst Adolf Bäschlin about the reasons for the police treatment of the matter: they wanted to avoid that Barth, as someone who had no political responsibilities, attacked the federal council in these tense times. The colonel assured him that the cantonal councilor of the Bern Canton, Hugo Dürrenmatt, read Barth's theological writings with genuine enthusiasm but that he viewed Barth's political activities as going too far.[263] Barth replied combatively to the colonel:

> By what right...do they dare to draw this line? Are they clear that this is an attack on the Reformed confession, when it is demanded of a theologian that while he may speak theologically he is by no means allowed to speak politically? Was not this separation of territories, this "doctrine of two drawers," the fatal mistake of German Lutheranism, which not incidentally may bear the guilt that in Germany today things are as they are?[264]

Barth was familiar with how things stood in Germany primarily through Dietrich Bonhoeffer. Through his brother-in-law Hans von Dohnanyi Bonhoeffer had become involved in the coup plan against Hitler that was being put together in the Foreign Military Intelligence Office, the German military counterintelligence. Bonhoeffer was assigned to the Foreign Military Intelligence Office and so was able to travel outside Germany during the war—officially with the assignment to gather information about foreign countries. In fact however he informed theologians and church figures whom he trusted about the conspiracy plans. In this context Bonhoeffer traveled three times to Switzerland in 1941 and 1942, where he met together with Visser 't Hooft and Barth.[265] He informed Barth about the generals' plans to remove Hitler and their hope that after the overthrow of Hitler they could negotiate with the Allies about an independent rebuilding of Germany. Both also discussed whether it would be better to have a conservative-authoritarian form of government (as was Bonhoeffer's view) or a Democratic form in postwar Germany.[266]

In December 1941 Barth allowed a "Christmas Message to Christians in Germany" to be read on the BBC, which Bishop of Chichester George Bell had invited him to do, via the British embassy in Switzerland.[267] Although and especially because in the past year things had "fallen silent" between the German church and other churches, Barth sent Christians in Germany "greetings from the entire holy and universal church," thereby emphasizing Christian unity beyond nationalities.[268] He mentioned the price currently being paid in Germany "for the confession of the Gospel" and explicitly "the horrors that your and our brothers and sisters of Israel [have to] endure in Germany."[269] Against the National Socialist masters and their military victories he then hinted "that the eternal God...became and is our brother with the aim...of being as our savior the true Lord and victor over all kingdoms, powers, and authorities of this dark earth;" there was "no human lie, arrogance and disorder...that does not have its boundary in His truth, in His justice and in His peace."[270] At the same time he warned Christians in Germany that Christian responsibility could not be limited to the private sphere of individuals or to church life.

Barth's message was printed on December 31, 1941, by the Swiss Protestant Press Service, but several days later it was forbidden by the Swiss censors.[271] Federal councilor von Steiger shortly afterward ordered the surveillance of Barth's telephone, which was in place from February 5, 1942, until spring 1943 with the goal—as one surveillance report records—"of determining whether Barth maintains direct or indirect relations with official or semi-official persons of foreign states."[272] When Barth learned of the surveillance on October 26, 1942[273] he was deeply offended because this treated him exactly like the National Socialists living in Switzerland and because this process reminded him all too well of his treatment by the German Gestapo.[274]

In April 1942 a new message from Barth was read on the BBC. Again requested by Bell, this time it was aimed at Christians in Norway. At the beginning of 1942 the Norwegian Church Struggle had intensified against the German occupation and Norwegian National Socialists. On Easter Sunday countless pastors resigned their offices in protest against the policies on religion and the church.[275] Barth's message openly showed how appropriate he found this action of the Norwegian pastors and how much he viewed the suffering being demanded of them as an expression of a "special calling" in which their faith should prove to be worthwhile and emerge strengthened. With this they were performing "the greatest and decisive service to the restoration of freedom and justice in your fatherland"[276] and were an example for Christians of all nations.

Following this, Swiss censorship officials intensified their efforts to find out "in what way the incomprehensible behavior of Professor Barth can be brought to an end."[277] The German legation wrote the Swiss government and criticized the fact that although they had raised the issue numerous times, "Professor Karl Barth, well-known for his anti-German position... today is still able to instigate against the Reich." They found it especially questionable that "here is a case of active support for enemy propaganda by a Swiss citizen who apparently is in [a position of] public service in a canton."[278] In reaction, Federal councilor von Steiger turned to the state prosecutor who concluded that "there is not a punishable infringement of neutrality here"; nonetheless Barth's outspokenness could pose damage to the policy of neutrality.[279] Following this von Steiger and Pilet-Golaz agreed on June 24, 1942, to undertake no further measures for the time being but to continue to observe Barth's behavior.[280]

A few days before, on June 12, 1942, the Basel Stadt Canton department that oversaw university education requested that Barth take a position on the facts of the case.[281] Barth replied three days later, now completely tactically, that in responding to an inquiry from Bishop Bell he had wanted to support Bell in his activities to strengthen ties between partner churches that had been divided by the war. Despite the unavoidably "political aspect" there could be no doubt about the "*church* nature... of the entire affair," and for that reason he "can and could" not find it right to withhold a positive answer to such an inquiry.[282]

On August 18, 1942, the University of Basel curatorium responded. With his BBC contributions Barth had given "assistance *for English propaganda*" and had slipped "into the service of the war efforts of a foreign power."[283] This however had been forbidden by a 1939 decree about political activity by university personnel. Barth had to follow this in the future, otherwise they would be forced to take further measures.

Barth's conflict with the Swiss government and censors was based on a different understanding of Swiss neutrality. Barth was reacting against a line of thinking like that expressed in a speech by president of the Swiss Confederation Wetter on November 21, 1941: "We have always held the standpoint that the battle of opposing systems in other countries has *nothing to do* with our state, since from our viewpoint every national people is free to create its own establishment of its choice."[284] Barth saw in this a reinterpretation of the military neutrality that had been established since the nineteenth century. After the war Barth summarized that the government had wanted to prescribe to the Swiss people

> whereas the others were fighting and bleeding for the "light of freedom"[285]... to make a stupid face toward the outside and act as though whether... Hitler or

Churchill, it was all the same... we should act as if with every conceivable war outcome we would equally ring our bells and return to planting our cabbages.

In 1945 Barth declared: "The speeches that I and others were forbidden to give were not a danger to our country; the danger to our country was the silence that they wanted to command of us."[286]

A Friend of the Germans, Nonetheless

In the final months of the war Barth came into contact with the National Committee for Free Germany (NKFD), which had been founded by German prisoners of war in July 1943, following the battles of Stalingrad and at the instigation of the Soviet government.[287] Officers, soldiers, and members of other professions united here to send a message to the German people: "Put an end to Hitler! Rescue what can still be saved! Make peace, fight for a free, independent and democratic Germany!"[288] Soon a movement aligned with this cause, "Free Germany," arose in Switzerland, as it did in other European countries.[289] Barth became acquainted with it at the beginning of 1945, when one of its leading figures approached him with "the request to introduce him and some of his friends to representatives of the Protestant emigration [German Protestant refugees who had fled Nazism]."[290] There was a meeting of the two sides in Barth's home. Barth gained an "excellent" impression "of the humane character, particularly of the Communists who attended" and therefore—"naturally as a Swiss citizen without playing any direct role"—let many of the Germans in his acquaintance know about the movement.[291] Since this movement until then had been influenced primarily by Communists, a Protestant member was needed to give the movement credibility. For that reason Charlotte von Kirschbaum joined the movement at the end of March 1945 out of "personal... responsibility and decision."[292] After the war ended she was elected to the three-person board.[293]

As the end of the war and the defeat of Germany became foreseeable, Barth became loudly and distinctly engaged that the Swiss should take a position of "friendship *despite*"[294] everything that had happened. In early 1945 he frequently delivered his lecture in Switzerland on "Die Deutschen und wir" (published in English as "The Germans and Ourselves").

In his lecture Barth noted that among all Swiss people there was now a "thorough distrust against the Germans as such, a deep alienation against our neighbors." Because however the Swiss had not been directly affected by the German actions and therefore "have no one and nothing to avenge against the Germans" it now befitted them well "to be among the first" who could now pursue a "*new* statement" toward the Germans.[295]

One knew very little of the "German people," of their involvement and responsibility for the National Socialist system or of their resistance against it. When the "iron curtain" of the lack of available information fell, the Swiss would have to be prepared to see the Germans as they had really been in recent years.[296] For "there are not just optimistic illusions but pessimistic ones."[297]

The Germans now faced the recognition "of having done, endured and sacrificed so much for a corrupt and futile undertaking, for the sake of pure stupidity and evil and with a purely negative result."[298] This time it would be impossible for them to glorify this war:

> This time...there will be no romantically-driven youth marching through the German lands with guitars and songs as if nothing had happened, in order to turn right back into a murderously dangerous mob of warriors...This time too much has been...shattered, made superfluous, problematic, impossible... However things may develop, the new Germany will be a country full of grief... There can be nothing else but for its role for a long time to come to be a very humble, very miserable one.[299]

In the face of the impending defeat of Germany the Swiss should feel neither triumph nor satisfaction nor pity. Much more they should be "*genuine* witnesses of this *genuine* tragedy...in *horror*, in *sympathy*, in *humility*."[300] The Swiss owed the Germans, who now had only enemies, primarily one thing today: to be their friends, for the Germans lacked "a concrete experience of what forgiveness is: that human beings nonetheless can be for one another—despite when they have much against each other, despite what they cannot overlook and forget." Forgiveness was "the deepest wisdom of a strong politics."[301]

In his argumentation for friendship the explosive power of Barth's theology becomes clear: the Swiss people understood Christianity namely as "first the Gospel and only then the Law."[302] The Gospel meant that Jesus Christ was also *for* the Germans—and indeed *unconditionally*. Barth made Jesus's call "Come unto me all who are heavily laden!" (Matt. 11:28) radically concrete. With that he made irritatingly visible the unconditional nature of the Christian message of God's care for all people, and the justification of sinners "regardless of the quality of the object":[303]

> How, when suddenly it would be: "Come to me, you unpleasant ones, you evil Hitler young men and women, you brutal SS soldiers, you bad Gestapo scoundrels, you sad compromisers and collaborators, you herd of people who all ran after your so-called *Führer* for so long, patient and stupid! Come to me, you who are guilty and co-responsible, to whom now befalls and must befall what your deeds have earned! Come to me, I know you well, I ask however not who you are and what you have done, I see only that you are at your end, and whether you like

it or not must start from the beginning, I will refresh you, precisely with you I will now begin anew from point zero!"[304]

The reactions to this talk in Germany were varied. Kurt Müller, pastor of the Protestant-Reformed parish in Stuttgart, publicized the lecture in September 1945 in Germany because behind Barth's clear "No" to National Socialism he noted the "greater... 'Yes' to responsibility and to the bond with us," a bond for which precisely in this time in Germany one had to be grateful.[305]

Ernst Friedlaender, born in Wiesbaden and with one Jewish parent, who in the meantime lived in Liechtenstein and in 1946 became associate head editor of the newly founded newspaper *ZEIT*, criticized Barth in a letter of March 8, 1945, accusing him of supporting the thesis of a German "collective guilt."[306] Friedlaender rejected this perspective. Every people consisted of genuine criminals, potential criminals (who in a constitutional state would not commit crimes), and an "enormous majority of 'orderly citizens.'" Among the latter there was "only a tiny minority of true heroes" who resisted.[307] According to Friedlaender, 99 percent of the Germans had neither participated in crimes nor been heroes, and they had not known of the crimes; the same was true of most National Socialist civil servants.

Barth countered by arguing that such a view would lead the Germans to continue mostly looking on or collaborating, rather than actively taking their future in hand. The concept of guilt was not what mattered to him but rather that the Germans take responsibility for the *path* that all the Germans had followed to these crimes, even when they themselves had not committed them. Heroes had not been necessary back then, rather only "politically rationally thinking... and decisively acting... citizens of the state" who would have resisted in "civil health" and "maturity."[308] There was by all means a middle ground between heroes and "wimps."[309]

Notes

1. While during Barth's time in Germany his intensive correspondence with Thurneysen documented many events as a diary would, this source ended after 1935 once both were living again in the same place. Beginning in 1935 Barth's pocket calendars with entries for his appointments have been preserved, but they are unable to replace the detailed reports to Thurneysen. For the chronology of events after 1935, cf. Busch, *Karl Barth: His Life*, 263ff.
2. Cf. letter of October 5, 1934, to Thurneysen, *Briefwechsel Barth–Thurneysen* III (GA 34), 708, n. 3; and Busch, *Karl Barth: His Life*, 311 (as well as 260).
3. Cf. Busch, *Karl Barth: His Life*, 268.
4. Letter of September 29, 1935, to Hellmut Traub, KBA 9235.280.
5. Cf. Wengst, "Theologie und Politik," 38.

6. Regarding his history after 1933, cf. Rohkrämer, "Fritz Lieb 1933–1939."
7. Regarding this, cf. Barth's tribute to Professor Fritz Lieb in the *Basler Nachrichten*, Nr. 447, October 22, 1958, and Barth, "Offener Brief an Fritz Lieb 1962," *Offene Briefe 1945–1968* (GA 15), 501–6.
8. Regarding him, cf. *Briefwechsel Barth–von Kirschbaum* I (GA 45), 166, n. 6.
9. He was named extraordinary professor in 1941.
10. Cf. Stoevesandt, "Eduard Thurneysen," in Beintker, ed., *Barth Handbuch*, 52.
11. Barth, "Lebendige Vergangenheit," 14.
12. See p. 123.
13. Barth, "Zum Andenken an Eberhard Vischer," 55.
14. Letter of December 4, 1968, to Prof. Hendrik van Oyen, *Letters 1961–1968* (GA 6), 337. Translation revised.
15. Letter of December 4, 1968, to Prof. Hendrik van Oyen, *Letters 1961–1968* (GA 6), 337.
16. Occasionally he also lectured on exegetical themes, as for example in the 1937/8 winter semester on the Letter to the Colossians and in the 1938 summer semester on the 1 Letter of Peter. Cf. the list of academic courses in the KBA.
17. *Church Dogmatics* IV/4 was published in fragmentary form in 1967. Regarding the content of *Church Dogmatics*, see Chapter 13.
18. Letter of June 28, 1944, to Alphons Koechlin, KBA 9244.97.
19. *CD* IV/4 (Fragment), Preface, p. vii. Translation revised.
20. Many of his courses were dedicated to individual authors: Anselm of Canterbury, Luther, Zwingli, Melanchthon, Calvin, Immanuel Kant, Johann Caspar Lavater, repeatedly Schleiermacher, and over several semesters the newly reissued (1935) textbook on Reformed theology, *Christianae theologiae compendium* by Johannes Wolleb. They also discussed Alois Emanuel Biedermann's Reformed *Christliche Dogmatik* (1869), Albrecht Ritschl, Wilhelm Herrmann, Paul Tillich, and the debate about Bultmann's demythologization program.
21. In his courses Barth dealt with the spiritual exercises of Ignatius of Loyola, the doctrine of justification from the Council of Trent, post-Tridentine texts on Mariology, Matthias Joseph Scheeben's *Mysterien des Christentums*, the *Missale Romanum* (the liturgical book for the Roman Catholic mass) as well as the 1943 papal encyclical *Mystici Corporis*.
22. Cf. the list of academic courses in the KBA.
23. Letter of November 16, 1935, to Hermann Klugkist Hesse, KBA 9235.348. In the Reformed church in German-speaking Switzerland there has been no obligatory confession since the middle of the nineteenth century. The so-called *Apostolikumsstreit* about the use particularly of the Apostles' Creed in worship ended with the decision to make the confession optional. Cf. Rudolf Gebhard, *Umstrittene Bekenntnisfreiheit*, 455.
24. Letter of August 21, 1936, to Wilhelm Niesel, in Freudenberg, ed., *Barth–Niesel Briefwechsel*, 195.
25. Cf. Gollwitzer, *Skizzen eines Lebens*, 67. Gollwitzer wrote his doctoral dissertation in 1937 under Barth on the Lord's Supper.
26. Cf. "Der Reichs-Boykott gegen Prof. Barth," in *Sonntagsblatt Staats-Zeitung und Herold*, report of February 18, 1937, KBA 3986.
27. Cf. Barth, *Gotteserkenntnis und Gottesdienst nach reformatorischer Lehre*, 44.

28. Lord Adam Gifford's Will, https://giffordlectures.org/lord-gifford/will (accessed April 30, 2020).
29. Regarding the Giffords Lectures cf. https://giffordlectures.org/lectures (accessed April 30, 2020).
30. Barth, *Gotteserkenntnis und Gottesdienst*, 43.
31. Cf. Barth, *Gotteserkenntnis und Gottesdienst*, 44f.
32. Barth, *Gotteserkenntnis und Gottesdienst*, 46.
33. Letter of March 30, 1937, to Ernst Wolf, KBA 9237.49; author's italics.
34. Cf. letter of April 30, 1937, from Andrew Bennett, Secretary of the University of St. Andrews, KBA 9337.233.
35. Rev. Professor D. John Baillie, "Presentation of Graduands, Doctor of Laws" on Karl Barth, in *The Scotsman*, September 29, 1937, KBA 3692: "It may safely be said that there is in the whole world today no more celebrated theologian than Professor Barth, and his influence is as wide as his reputation."
36. The name refers to a figure from John Bunyan's allegory *The Pilgrim's Progress*.
37. Rev. Professor D. John Baillie, "Presentation of Graduands, Doctor of Laws," on Karl Barth, in *The Scotsman*, September 29, 1937, KBA 3692.
38. Cf. the open letter to Hermann Klugkist Hesse, *Offene Briefe 1935–1942* (GA 36), 22 with n. 19. Asmussen's contribution is listed in the volume's table of contents but on p. iv it is noted that it "had to be omitted."
39. Cf. letter of August 21, 1936, to Niesel, Freudenberg, ed., *Barth–Niesel Briefwechsel*, 196.
40. Albert Lempp and Ernst Wolf, foreword, in *Theologische Aufsätze. Karl Barth zum 50. Geburtstag*, v f., referring to the motto of Goethe's second German edition (1775) of *The Sorrows of Young Werther*.
41. Albert Lempp and Ernst Wolf, foreword, in *Theologische Aufsätze. Karl Barth zum 50. Geburtstag*, vi.
42. Regarding him, cf. *Briefwechsel Barth–von Kirschbaum* I (GA 45), 534, n. 14.
43. Open letter of May 16, 1936, from Hermann Klugkist Hesse, *Offene Briefe 1935–1942* (GA 36), 20.
44. Open letter of May 16, 1936, from Hermann Klugkist Hesse, *Offene Briefe 1935–1942* (GA 36), 22.
45. Barth, "Evangelium und Gesetz," in *Rechtfertigung und Recht*, 81–109. The occasion was a theological week organized by the Council of Brethren of the Old Prussian Union Church.
46. Letter of October 10, 1935, from Kirschbaum to Albert Lempp, KBA 9235.288.
47. "Die 28 Thesen der sächsischen Volkskirche zum inneren Aufbau der Deutschen Evangelischen Kirche," in Schmidt, ed., *Bekenntnisse* (1933), 99f.
48. Barth, "Evangelium und Gesetz," in *Rechtfertigung und Recht*, 87f.
49. Barth, "Evangelium und Gesetz," in *Rechtfertigung und Recht*, 97.
50. Barth, "Evangelium und Gesetz," in *Rechtfertigung und Recht*, 99f.
51. Cf. Busch, *Karl Barth: His Life*, 272, 287, 294.
52. Cf. open letter of 1935 to the *Svenska Morgonbladet*, *Offene Briefe 1935–1942* (GA 36), 8–12.
53. Letter of August 21, 1936, to Niesel, in Freudenberg, ed., *Barth–Niesel Briefwechsel*, 194f.

54. Cf. letter of August 21, 1936, to Niesel, in Freudenberg, ed., *Barth–Niesel Briefwechsel*, 195, where Barth reported that he had not been paid royalties since January.
55. Letter of October 10, 1936, from Stephan to Lempp, cited in letter of October 16, 1936, from Lempp, KBA 9936.815.
56. Letter of October 10, 1936, from Stephan to Lempp, cited in letter of October 16, 1936, from Lempp, KBA 9936.815.
57. Letter of October 16, 1936, from Lempp, KBA 9936.815.
58. Letter of October 16, 1936, from Lempp, KBA 9936.815.
59. Letter of January 7, 1937, from Walter Gut, KBA 9337.8.
60. Letter of February 11, 1937, from Berndt from the Reich Ministry for Public Enlightenment and Propaganda, KBA 17304.
61. Letter of February 20, 1937, from Lempp to the Reich minister for Public Enlightenment and Propaganda, KBA 17304.
62. Cf. the letter of March 29, 1937, to Hermann Albert Hesse, which was smuggled over the border, KBA 9237.47.
63. Letter of May 22, 1937, from Arthur Frey, KBA 9337.312.
64. Letter of May 22, 1937, from Arthur Frey, KBA 9337.312.
65. After 1970 the publisher was named Theologischer Verlag Zürich. To replace the *Theologische Existenz heute* series, where he could no longer publish, Barth founded the series *Theologische Studien* in Zollikon. His lecture on "Rechtfertigung und Recht" opened the series.
66. Cf. the editor's introduction to the 1938 open letter to the Confessing Church in Germany, *Offene Briefe 1935–1942* (GA 36), 84.
67. Regarding this, cf. Tietz, *Theologian of Resistance*, 73–4.
68. Cf. the editor's introduction to the "Consilium zur Frage des 'Treueides' der 'Geistlichen'" in 1938, *Offene Briefe 1935–1942* (GA 36), 86.
69. "Consilium zur Frage des 'Treueides,'" *Offene Briefe 1935–1942* (GA 36), 87.
70. "Consilium zur Frage des 'Treueides,'" *Offene Briefe 1935–1942* (GA 36), 88.
71. Cf. the editor's introduction to the "Consilium zur Frage des 'Treueides,'" *Offene Briefe 1935–1942* (GA 36), 86. See also the discussion of the loyalty oath controversy in Barnett, *For the Soul of the People*, 156–8.
72. Cf. the text of this declaration on the loyalty oath, formulated by synod president Koch, in Gerlach-Praetorius, *Die Kirche vor der Eidesfrage*, 132. This states that through the reference to God the oath ruled out "an act that goes against God's command as witnessed in the Holy Scripture." By virtue of the ordination vows, for the pastor there was only one Lord, Jesus Christ; with this "the official duties assumed in the ordination vows were neither expanded nor restricted through the oath taken to [state] authority" (132).
73. Cf. the editor's introduction to the open letter to the sixth Confessing synod of the Evangelical Church of the Old Prussian Union, *Offene Briefe 1935–1942* (GA 36), 94.
74. Cf. the open letter to the sixth Confessing synod of the Evangelical Church of the Old Prussian Union, *Offene Briefe 1935–1942* (GA 36), 96–103.
75. Letter of August 20, 1938, from Gollwitzer, KBA 9338.614.
76. Letter of August 20, 1938, from Gollwitzer, KBA 9338.614.
77. Cf. the editor's introduction to the open letter to the sixth Confessing synod of the Evangelical Church of the Old Prussian Union, *Offene Briefe 1935–1942* (GA 36), 95.

78. The Augsburg Confession of 1530, the central confession of the imperial estates that were in agreement with Luther's Reformation.
79. Letter of September 19, 1938, to Heinrich Vogel, cited in *Offene Briefe 1935–1942* (GA 36), 96, n. 12.
80. Barth, "Not und Verheißung im deutschen Kirchenkampf."
81. Cf. the editor's introduction to the open letter of September 19, 1938, to Prof. Dr. Josef L. Hromádka in Prague, *Offene Briefe 1935–1942* (GA 36), 107. Hromádka had visited Barth while he was still in Bonn and invited him to give a lecture at a pastors' conference in the fall of 1935 in Myslibořice in Moravia; the two had been in contact since then. Regarding the background cf. Rohkrämer, "Karl Barth in der Herbstkrise 1938."
82. Letter of March 21, 1938, from Hromádka, cited in *Offene Briefe 1935–1942* (GA 36), 107.
83. Cf. the editor's introduction to the open letter to Hromádka, *Offene Briefe 1935–1942* (GA 36), 110.
84. Cf. open letter to Hromádka, *Offene Briefe 1935–1942* (GA 36), 114, and the letter of September 28, 1938, to D. Buxton (123, n. 68).
85. Cf. the editor's introduction to the open letter to Hromádka, *Offene Briefe 1935–1942* (GA 36), 111 with n. 22.
86. Postscript to letter to Hromádka, *Offene Briefe 1935–1942* (GA 36), 115.
87. Cf. the editor's introduction to the open letter to Hromádka, *Offene Briefe 1935–1942* (GA 36), 111. Later, after the end of the Second World War, the letter became important again during the 1950 debate about the rearmament of the German Federal Republic and in the discussion about upgrading atomic weapons in 1983. See p. 330.
88. Open letter to Hromádka, *Offene Briefe 1935–1942* (GA 36), 113.
89. Open letter to Hromádka, *Offene Briefe 1935–1942* (GA 36), 114.
90. Open letter to Hromádka, *Offene Briefe 1935–1942* (GA 36), 114.
91. Open letter to Hromádka, *Offene Briefe 1935–1942* (GA 36), 114f.
92. Open letter to Hromádka, *Offene Briefe 1935–1942* (GA 36), 115.
93. Rohkrämer, "Karl Barth in der Herbstkrise 1938," 526.
94. Cf. the editor's comments about the open letter to Hromádka, *Offene Briefe 1935–1942* (GA 36), 118 and 126.
95. Rohkrämer, "Karl Barth in der Herbstkrise 1938," 527.
96. Barnikol, "Barth als antideutscher Papst," 27.
97. Oberpfarrer H. Leidenfrost, "Ein Wort zur Aufklärung," *Blatt der Kirchengemeinde Jena*, December 1938, cited in *Offene Briefe 1935–1942* (GA 36), 121, n. 59.
98. "Erklärung des Dekans der Gießener Fakultät Vogelsang," October 25, 1938, cited in *Offene Briefe 1935–1942* (GA 36), 119, n. 48.
99. Cf. the editor's comments on the open letter to Hromádka, *Offene Briefe 1935–1942* (GA 36), 119.
100. Cf. the letter of October 15, 1938, to the provisional church government of the Confessing Church, *Offene Briefe 1935–1942* (GA 36), 120.
101. In the SS-journal *Das Schwarze Korps* the provisional church government was accused on October 27 of "treason and betraying the German people" after it called for a

prayer service. Cf. the letter of October 28, 1938, from the Confessing Church provisional church government to the regional church governments and councils of brethren in *Kirchliches Jahrbuch für die Evangelische Kirche in Deutschland 1933–1944*, 266.

102. Letter of October 28, 1938, from the Confessing Church provisional church government in *Kirchliches Jahrbuch 1933–1944*, 265.
103. Letter of October 28, 1938, from the Confessing Church provisional church government in *Kirchliches Jahrbuch 1933–1944*, 265.
104. Letter of October 28, 1938, from the Confessing Church provisional church government in *Kirchliches Jahrbuch 1933–1944*, 265.
105. Letter of October 28, 1938, from the Confessing Church provisional church government in *Kirchliches Jahrbuch 1933–1944*, 265.
106. Open letter to the students of reformed theology in Budapest 1938, *Offene Briefe 1935–1942* (GA 36), 154.
107. Open letter to the students of reformed theology in Budapest 1938, *Offene Briefe 1935–1942* (GA 36), 154.
108. Cf. the announcements in the *Zofinger Tagblatt* of October 19, 1938, and the *St. Galler Tagblatt* of October 20, 1938, cited in the editor's comments on the open letter to Hromádka, *Offene Briefe 1935–1942* (GA 36), 126, n. 74.
109. Regarding this, see Happ, "Streng vertraulich," and Hammerschmidt, "Zum Gedenken an Karl Barth, 7–9.
110. "Antrag des Dekans der Evangelisch-Theologischen Fakultät, Friedrich Wilhelm Schmidt, auf Einleitung des Verfahrens zur Aberkennung des Ehrendoktortitels von Karl Barth vom 21. Oktober 1936," Universitätsarchiv Münster, Bestand 5, Nr. 8.
111. Cf. the archival note of February 25, 1937, from Rector Karl Hugelmann, cited in Happ, "Streng vertraulich," 360.
112. "Antrag des Dekans der Evangelisch-Theologischen Fakultät, Helmuth Kittel, auf Entziehung des Ehrendoktortitels von Karl Barth vom 30. März 1939," Universitätsarchiv Münster, Bestand 4, Nr. 1092.
113. "Mitteilung Rektor Mevius' an den Reichsminister vom 5. Juni 1939," cited in Hammerschmidt, "Zum Gedenken," 9.
114. "Brief von Dekan Herrmann an Rektor Schreiber vom 23. Januar 1946," Universitätsarchiv Münster, Bestand 18, Nr. 12.
115. Hammerschmidt, "Zum Gedenken," 10.
116. "Schreiben von Rektor Schreiber an Dekan Herrmann vom 11. Februar 1946," Universitätsarchiv Münster, Bestand 18, Nr. 12.
117. "Schreiben von Rektor Schreiber an Dekan Herrmann vom 11. Februar 1946," Universitätsarchiv Münster, Bestand 18, Nr. 12.
118. "Schreiben von Rektor Schreiber an Karl Barth vom 11. Februar 1946," Universitätsarchiv Münster, Bestand 18, Nr. 12.
119. "Schreiben an Rektor Schreiber 1946," Universitätsarchiv Münster, Bestand 9, Nr. 1375.
120. Barth, "Theologische Existenz heute!," *Vorträge und kleinere Arbeiten 1930–1933* (GA 49), 280.
121. On him, cf. *Briefwechsel Barth–Thurneysen* III (GA 34), 214, n. 10.

122. Letter of October 12, 1938, to Pierre Maury, cited in *Offene Briefe 1935–1942* (GA 36), 124–6.
123. Barth, "Rechtfertigung und Recht," in *Rechtfertigung und Recht*, 5–45.
124. Barth, foreword, "Ein Schweizer Stimme," 11.
125. Cf. the open letter of December 1939 to France, *Offene Briefe 1935–1942* (GA 36), 220. Barth did not stand alone in his understanding of Lutheran political theology. In 1912 for example Ernst Troeltsch had critically noted: "Lutheranism [has] suffered under the influence of dominating powers everywhere. The weakness of its completely internal spirituality huddled together with the respective dominant powers" (Troeltsch, *Die Soziallehren*, 602).
126. Barth, *How I Changed My Mind*, 48. The English edition of these essays translated *Eigengesetzlichkeit* as "self-determination." Cf. also "Rechtfertigung und Recht," in *Rechtfertigung und Recht*, 8, where Barth speaks of the "unfruitful and dangerous divisions."
127. Jordan, *Luthers Staatsauffassung*, 191f. Author's italics.
128. Barth, "Rechtfertigung und Recht," in *Rechtfertigung und Recht*, 5.
129. In Lutheran thought, law and the state have their respective duties within the context of the so-called "political use" of divine law.
130. Barth, "Rechtfertigung und Recht," in *Rechtfertigung und Recht*, 7.
131. Barth, "Rechtfertigung und Recht," in *Rechtfertigung und Recht*, 13.
132. Barth, "Rechtfertigung und Recht," in *Rechtfertigung und Recht*, 13.
133. Barth, "Rechtfertigung und Recht," in *Rechtfertigung und Recht*, 18f.
134. Barth, "Rechtfertigung und Recht," in *Rechtfertigung und Recht*, 43.
135. Barth, "Rechtfertigung und Recht," in *Rechtfertigung und Recht*, 37.
136. Barth, "Rechtfertigung und Recht," in *Rechtfertigung und Recht*, 34.
137. Barth, "Rechtfertigung und Recht," in *Rechtfertigung und Recht*, 40.
138. See Chapter 8, n. 109.
139. Barth, "Rechtfertigung und Recht," in *Rechtfertigung und Recht*, 40.
140. Barth, "Rechtfertigung und Recht," in *Rechtfertigung und Recht*, 40.
141. Barth, "Rechtfertigung und Recht," in *Rechtfertigung und Recht*, 41f.
142. Barth, "Rechtfertigung und Recht," in *Rechtfertigung und Recht*, 42.
143. Barth, "Rechtfertigung und Recht," in *Rechtfertigung und Recht*, 41f., n. 30b.
144. Cf. the short biography of Vogt in Rusterholz, *Nachbars Haus*, 32.
145. Cf. Rusterholz, *Nachbars Haus*, 64f.
146. Letter of May 1, 1937, from Vogt, cited in Rusterholz, *Nachbars Haus*, 64.
147. Cf. letter of May 4, 1937, to Vogt, cited in Rusterholz, *Nachbars Haus*, 65f.
148. Cf. Rusterholz, *Nachbars Haus*, 69 and 72.
149. Cf. Rusterholz, *Nachbars Haus*, 69f.
150. Cf. editor's introduction to the "Memorandum an die Pfarrer der reformierten Kirchen der Schweiz 1937," *Offene Briefe 1935–1942* (GA 36), 53f., as well as the text, 57–64.
151. Barth, "Memorandum an die Pfarrer," *Offene Briefe 1935–1942* (GA 36), 57.
152. Barth, "Memorandum an die Pfarrer," *Offene Briefe 1935–1942* (GA 36), 57f.
153. Barth, "Memorandum an die Pfarrer," *Offene Briefe 1935–1942* (GA 36), 61f.
154. Cf. Barth, "Memorandum an die Pfarrer," *Offene Briefe 1935–1942* (GA 36), 62f.

155. Cf. "An die kantonalen Kirchenräte und die Kirchenpflegen und Kirchgemeinden der reformierten Kirchen in der Schweiz 1938," *Offene Briefe 1935-1942* (GA 36), 67. For an overview of the responses, see Rusterholz, *Nachbars Haus*, 86-8.
156. Editor's introduction to the open letter "An die kantonalen Kirchenräte," *Offene Briefe 1935-1942* (GA 36), 66.
157. Cf. Rusterholz, *Nachbars Haus*, 122.
158. In 1940 there was a new conflict between Brunner and Barth because Brunner had criticized that the first thesis of the Barmen Declaration was also the basis for the Aid Association and with that "the order of creation [remained] unconsidered." Cf. Rusterholz, *Nachbars Haus*, 193.
159. Cf. Rusterholz, *Nachbars Haus*, 24.
160. Cf. Evangelischer Presse Dienst 49/5 December 1938, p. 3, cited in Rusterholz, *Nachbars Haus*, 139. Regarding the other organizations see Rusterholz, 139f.
161. Cf. Rusterholz, *Nachbars Haus*, 159.
162. Quotation from the protocol of the Swiss Federation Council of March 31, 1933, in "Diplomatische Dokumente der Schweiz online": http://dodis.ch/45798 (accessed April 30, 2020).
163. Cf. Rusterholz, *Nachbars Haus*, 243-88.
164. Cf. Barth, "Die Kirche und die politische Frage von heute," in *Eine Schweizer Stimme*, 84.
165. Barth, "Die Kirche und die politische Frage," in *Eine Schweizer Stimme*, 78.
166. Barth, "Die Kirche und die politische Frage," in *Eine Schweizer Stimme*, 78.
167. Barth, "Die Kirche und die politische Frage," in *Eine Schweizer Stimme*, 89f.
168. Barth, "Die Kirche und die politische Frage," in *Eine Schweizer Stimme*, 90. This quotation illustrates both the complexities and problems of Barth's thought on this. On Barth's theological attitudes toward Judaism, see ch. 10, note 322.
169. Cf. the letter of October 26, 1937, from Kirschbaum to Vogt, cited in Rusterholz, *Nachbars Haus*, 227f.
170. Letter of December 8, 1938, from Heinz Gordon, KBA 9338.944, cited in Rusterholz, *Nachbars Haus*, 248.
171. J. B. T., "Kirche und Politik," *Neue Zürcher Zeitung*, Jg. 160, Nr. 401, March 5, 1939, in *Offene Briefe 1935-1942* (GA 36), 176.
172. Cf. Rusterholz, *Nachbars Haus*, 209-21, 266-75, 417-58.
173. Cf. letter of April 13, 1939, to Visser 't Hooft, *Barth-Visser 't Hooft Briefwechsel* (GA 43), 91. An especially prominent figure was Archbishop of Canterbury Cosmo Gordon Lang, who appealed to the British House of Lords on March 29 to decisively resist Hitler's aggressive conduct, an appeal that unleashed a vehement reaction in Germany (cf. Herwig, *Barth und die Ökumenische Bewegung*, 60f.).
174. Cf. "Die Godesberger Erklärung," in *Kirchliches Jahrbuch 1933-1944*, 293-4.
175. "Bekanntmachung," in *Kirchliches Jahrbuch 1933-1944*, 294.
176. Cf. the letters of April 13 and 22, 1939, to Visser 't Hooft, *Barth-Visser 't Hooft Briefwechsel* (GA 43), 89-92 and 95.
177. Cf. letter of April 15, 1939, from Visser 't Hooft, *Barth-Visser 't Hooft Briefwechsel* (GA 43), 92.
178. Cf. the editor's introduction to "An die deutschchristlichen und nationalkirchlichen Landeskirchenführer in Deutschland 1939," *Offene Briefe 1935-1942* (GA 36), 164.

179. "Eine Kundgebung an die christlichen Kirchen," in *Kirchliches Jahrbuch 1933–1944*, 330–1.
180. Telegram of May 6, 1939, from Bishop Theodor Heckel, in *Kirchliches Jahrbuch 1933–1944*, 331.
181. Letter of April 13, 1939, to Visser 't Hooft, *Barth–Visser 't Hooft Briefwechsel* (GA 43), 91f.
182. Cf. Letter of April 15, 1939, from Visser 't Hooft, *Barth–Visser 't Hooft Briefwechsel* (GA 43), 93.
183. Letter of April 22, 1939, to Visser 't Hooft, *Barth–Visser 't Hooft Briefwechsel* (GA 43), 95.
184. Letter of April 22, 1939, to Visser 't Hooft, *Barth–Visser 't Hooft Briefwechsel* (GA 43), 95.
185. Cf. Gollwitzer, *Skizzen eines Lebens*, 166.
186. Letter of September 7, 1939, to Franziska Zellweger, KBA 9239.149.
187. Letter of October 7, 1939, to Visser 't Hooft, *Barth-Visser 't Hooft Briefwechsel* (GA 43), 101f.
188. Letter of October 7, 1939, to Visser 't Hooft, *Barth-Visser 't Hooft Briefwechsel* (GA 43), 104.
189. Letter of October 7, 1939, to Visser 't Hooft, *Barth-Visser 't Hooft Briefwechsel* (GA 43), 109f.
190. Cf. the letter of September 10, 1940, to Ernst Sartorius, KBA 9240.156.
191. Letter of June 20, 1940, to Dora Scheuner, KBA 9240.116.
192. Email of January 20, 2018, from Dr. Hans-Anton Drewes to the author.
193. Cf. the letter of July 17, 1940, to Gertrud Lindt, KBA 9240.127.
194. Letter of July 17, 1940, to Gertrud Lindt, KBA 9240.127.
195. Letter of July 17, 1940, to Gertrud Lindt, with a reference to Matt. 18:21, KBA 9240.127.
196. Letter of July 17, 1940, to Gertrud Lindt, KBA 9240.127.
197. Barth had used "Büseli" for "kitty," which is the Swiss term of affection for a cat.
198. Letter of July 17, 1940, to Gertrud Lindt, KBA 9240.127.
199. Christoph Barth completed his doctorate in Old Testament, *Die Errettung vom Tode in den individuellen Klage- und Dankliedern des Alten Testaments*, under Walter Baumgartner in 1947 in Basel, and then went to Indonesia as a theological teacher. From 1967–79 he was professor of Old Testament in Mainz. During his time in Indonesia Karl Barth frequently wrote him long letters in which he reported on the events in his life. After 1940 Markus Barth was a pastor in Bubendorf. He had submitted his dissertation on *Der Augenzeuge. Eine Untersuchung über die Wahrnehmung des Menschensohnes durch die Apostel* in Basel but withdrew it after he read the evaluation by Karl Ludwig Schmidt, which in his eyes demanded "such a methodical and material reworking...which would completely alter...the essence and purpose of the work." (Letter of June 29, 1945, from Markus Barth to Schmidt, KBA 9345.461). Markus Barth then published the work in 1946 with the Evangelische Verlag Zurich, and with it attained his doctorate retroactively in 1947 under Ernst Wolf in Göttingen (cf. the letter of May 7, 1947, from Wolf, KBA 9347.519). Markus Barth became professor of New Testament in 1953 at Presbyterian Theological

Seminary in Dubuque (Iowa), in 1956 at the University of Chicago, in 1963 at Pittsburgh Theological Seminary, and finally from 1973 until his retirement in 1985 at the University of Basel. Of Karl Barth's sons only the youngest, Hans Jakob, followed a different path, becoming a gardener and artist (painter). Cf. Busch, *Karl Barth: His Life*, 312ff.

200. "Zwei Basler Studenten am Fründenhorn abgestürzt," in *Nationalzeitung*, Nr. 284, June 24, 1941, 5.
201. Cf. "Zwei Basler Studenten," in *Nationalzeitung*, Nr. 284, June 24, 1941, 5.
202. *CD* III/3, § 49, p. 271.
203. Letter of June 29, 1941, to Wilhelm Spoendlin, KBA 9241.127.
204. Barth, Sermon of June 25, 1941, on 1 Corinthians 13:12 (NRSV translation in the text), *Predigten 1935-1952* (GA 26), 224. See also Christiane Tietz, "Standing on the Boundary, where Now and Yet Then Touch Each Other: Barth on Theodicy and Eschatology," in Dugan and Ziegler, eds., *The Finality of the Gospel*.
205. Barth, Sermon of June 25, 1941, on 1 Corinthians 13:12, *Predigten 1935-1952* (GA 26), 238.
206. Barth, Sermon of June 25, 1941, on 1 Corinthians 13:12, *Predigten 1935-1952* (GA 26), 225.
207. Barth, Sermon of June 25, 1941, on 1 Corinthians 13:12, *Predigten 1935-1952* (GA 26), 230f.
208. Cf. Barth, *How I Changed My Mind*, 52.
209. Barth, "Des Christen Wehr und Waffen," in *Eine Schweizer Stimme*, 123-46. The title draws from Martin Luther's hymn "A Mighty Fortress is Our God" (the second line of the German text would be translated literally as "the Christian's bulwark and weapon").
210. Barth, "Des Christen Wehr und Waffen," in *Eine Schweizer Stimme*, 142.
211. Cf. Barth, "Des Christen Wehr und Waffen," in *Eine Schweizer Stimme*, 134.
212. Barth, "Des Christen Wehr und Waffen," in *Eine Schweizer Stimme*, 134f.
213. Barth, "Des Christen Wehr und Waffen," in *Eine Schweizer Stimme*, 141.
214. Barth, "Des Christen Wehr und Waffen," in *Eine Schweizer Stimme*, 141-3.
215. "Grunderlass der Abteilung Presse und Funkspruch vom 8. September 1939," cited in Busch, ed., *Die Akte Karl Barth*, 699.
216. Cf. letter of April 27, 1940, to Alexander J. Bronkhorst, KBA 9240.81.
217. Regarding this event cf. Busch, ed., *Die Akte Karl Barth*, 18-57.
218. Cf. letter of March 29, 1940, to the district commandant in Basel, Major R. Saladin, cited in *Offene Briefe 1935-1942* (GA 36), 259.
219. Letter of March 29, 1940, to Major R. Saladin, cited in *Offene Briefe 1935-1942* (GA 36), 259.
220. Cf. Barth, *How I Changed My Mind*, 53. Cf. Busch, *Karl Barth: His Life*, 315. The information about the dates is in pp. 308-15. At the end of 1946 Barth was discharged from the army at his own request (cf. editor's introduction to the open letter to Swiss soldiers 1940, *Offene Briefe 1935-1942* (GA 36), 260, n. 1).
221. Letter of September 10, 1940, to Ernst Sartorius, KBA 9240.156.
222. Barth, *How I Changed My Mind*, 53.
223. Cf. Reinhardt, *Geschichte der Schweiz*, 110.

224. Cf. Reinhardt, *Geschichte der Schweiz*, 111.
225. Barth, *Der Dienst der Kirche an der Heimat*, 6.
226. Barth, *Der Dienst der Kirche an der Heimat*, 11.
227. Schiller, *Wilhelm Tell*, 62 (end of the second act).
228. Barth, *Der Dienst der Kirche an der Heimat*, 12.
229. Barth, *Der Dienst der Kirche an der Heimat*, 20.
230. Cf. Reinhardt, *Die Geschichte der Schweiz*, 438f.
231. Regarding this cf. Barth's letter of May 3, 1946, to the Office for Press and Radio in the Army Staff, KBA 9241.94.
232. Letter of July 29, 1940, to General Guisan, KBA 9240.145. The abbreviation stands for Auxiliary Soldier, Observation Company 5, City of Basel.
233. Letter of January 31, 1942, to Fritz Frei, cited in *Offene Briefe 1935-1942* (GA 36), 255, n. 13.
234. Cf. Barth, *How I Changed My Mind*, 53; editor's introduction to "An den Vorstand des Schweizerischen Evangelischen Kirchenbundes," *Offene Briefe 1935-1942* (GA 36), 252f.
235. Cf. Alice Meyer, *Anpassung oder Widerstand*, 192. Whoever signed the following declaration belonged to the "*Aktion*": "I am decided and prepared and I swear to fight by every means: for freedom, honor and the independence of the Swiss Confederation, based upon a Christian foundation; for the freedom of the person and conscience; for freedom of the community on a federalist foundation; for the government of the people on the foundation of personal responsibility; for the securing of work and bread for every citizen; against every defeatist wherever he may stand."
236. Cf. the editor's introduction to "An den Vorstand des Schweizerischen Evangelischen Kirchenbundes," *Offene Briefe 1935-1942* (GA 36), 254, and the letter itself, 255-58.
237. Cf. Lindt, *Die Schweiz das Stachelschwein*, 63, cited in *Offene Briefe 1935-1942* (GA 36), 254, n. 8.
238. Cf. Busch, ed., *Die Akte Karl Barth*, 83f.
239. Barth, "Unsere Kirche und die Schweiz in der heutigen Zeit," in *Eine Schweizer Stimme*, 160-2.
240. Barth, "Unsere Kirche und die Schweiz," in *Eine Schweizer Stimme*, 170.
241. Barth, "Unsere Kirche und die Schweiz," in *Eine Schweizer Stimme*, 178.
242. Cf. Busch, ed., *Die Akte Karl Barth*, 84.
243. Herbert Lang, "Zusammenfassender Bericht über die Angelegenheit der Schrift Karl Barth: 'Des Christen Wehr und Waffen' vom 21. September 1940," in Busch, ed., *Die Akte Karl Barth*, 82.
244. Letter of May 3, 1941, to the Army Office for Press and Radio, in Busch, ed., *Die Akte Karl Barth*, 163.
245. Letter of May 3, 1941, in Busch, ed., *Die Akte Karl Barth*, 163f.
246. Letter of May 3, 1941, in Busch, ed., *Die Akte Karl Barth*, 165.
247. Letter of May 3, 1941, in Busch, ed., *Die Akte Karl Barth*, 162.
248. Letter of June 3/9, 1941, from federal councilor Eduard von Steiger, in Busch, ed., *Die Akte Karl Barth*, 203f.
249. Barth, "Im Namen Gottes des Allmächtigen! 1291-1941," in *Eine Schweizer Stimme*, 201-32; cf. Busch, ed., *Die Akte Karl Barth*, 219.

250. Barth, "Im Namen Gottes," in *Eine Schweizer Stimme*, 209.
251. Barth, "Im Namen Gottes," in *Eine Schweizer Stimme*, 209–11.
252. Barth, "Im Namen Gottes," in *Eine Schweizer Stimme*, 221.
253. Barth, "Im Namen Gottes," in *Eine Schweizer Stimme*, 222.
254. Barth, "Im Namen Gottes," in *Eine Schweizer Stimme*, 222.
255. Barth, "Im Namen Gottes," in *Eine Schweizer Stimme*, 226.
256. Cf. Busch, *Unter dem Bogen*, 340.
257. "Schreiben der Abteilung für Presse und Funkspruch an die Buchhandlung der Evangelischen Gesellschaft St. Gallen vom 29. Juli 1941," in Busch, ed., *Die Akte Karl Barth*, 254.
258. Letter of August 10, 1941, to Lieutenant Plancherel from the Office for Press and Radio to the attention of the Confederation Commission on Appeals, in Busch, ed., *Die Akte Karl Barth*, 311f.
259. Letter of August 10, 1941, to Lieutenant Plancherel, in Busch, ed., *Die Akte Karl Barth*, 315. Barth emphasized his original text with a vertical marginal line.
260. Cf. the decision of October 25, 1941, by the Confederation Commission on Appeals, in Busch, ed., *Die Akte Karl Barth*, 372.
261. Decision of October 25, 1941, in Busch, ed., *Die Akte Karl Barth*, 373.
262. Cf. Busch, ed., *Die Akte Karl Barth*, 352f.
263. Cf. letter of September 18, 1941, from Lieutenant Ernst Adolf Bäschlin, in Busch, ed., *Die Akte Karl Barth*, 362.
264. Letter of September 22, 1941, to Lieutenant Bäschlin, in Busch, ed., *Die Akte Karl Barth*, 364.
265. Cf. Tietz, *Theologian of Resistance*, 82.
266. Cf. letter of September 7, 1956, to Jørgen Glenthøj, KBA 9256.267.
267. Regarding the occasion and publication history cf. the editor's introduction to "An die Christen in Deutschland Weihnachten 1941," *Offene Briefe 1935–1942* (GA 36), 321f.
268. Barth, "Weihnachtsbotschaft an die Christen in Deutschland," *Offene Briefe 1935–1942* (GA 36), 324.
269. Barth, "Weihnachtsbotschaft," *Offene Briefe 1935–1942* (GA 36), 325.
270. Barth, "Weihnachtsbotschaft," *Offene Briefe 1935–1942* (GA 36), 325.
271. Cf. Busch, ed., *Die Akte Karl Barth*, 408.
272. "Überwachungsbericht vom März 1942," in Busch, ed., *Die Akte Karl Barth*, 473.
273. Cf. Busch, ed., *Die Akte Karl Barth*, 473.
274. Cf. letter of October 27, 1942, to Arthur Frey, in Busch, ed., *Die Akte Karl Barth*, 572.
275. Cf. editor's introduction to "An die Christen in Norwegen 1942," *Offene Briefe 1935–1942* (GA 36), 327–9.
276. Barth, "An die Christen in Norwegen," *Offene Briefe 1935–1942* (GA 36), 330.
277. Letter of June 2, 1942, from federal councilor Eduard von Steiger to federal councilor Marcel Pilet-Golaz, in Busch, ed., *Die Akte Karl Barth*, 526.
278. Note of June 2, 1941, from the German legation to the Swiss government, cited in *Offene Briefe 1935–1942* (GA 36), 333f.
279. Editor's comments on Barth, "An die Christen in Norwegen," *Offene Briefe 1935–1942* (GA 36), 334, with quote from the "Expertise der Schweizerischen Staatsanwaltschaft an den Vorsteher des Justiz- und Polizeidepartements vom 18. Juni 1942."

280. Cf. editor's comments on Barth, "An die Christen in Norwegen," *Offene Briefe 1935–1942* (GA 36), 335.
281. Cf. editor's comments on Barth, "An die Christen in Norwegen," *Offene Briefe 1935–1942* (GA 36), 335.
282. Letter of June 15, 1942, to cantonal councilor Carl Miville, cited in the editor's comments on Barth, "An die Christen in Norwegen," *Offene Briefe 1935–1942* (GA 36), 336.
283. Letter of August 18, 1942, from the curatorium, in Busch, ed., *Die Akte Karl Barth*, 557.
284. Cited in Barth, foreword, *Eine Schweizer Stimme*, 9.
285. Cited from the address delivered by federal president Eduard von Steiger on the evening of May 8, 1945, Diplomatische Dokumente der Schweiz online: https://dodis.ch/30882 (accessed April 30, 2020).
286. Barth, preface, *Eine Schweizer Stimme*, 9f.
287. Cf. Bungert, *Das Nationalkomitee und der Westen*, 22.
288. "Call to Action," cited in Langhoff, *Die Bewegung Freies Deutschland*, 15.
289. Cf. Bungert, *Das Nationalkomitee und der Westen*, 88f.
290. Letter of May 11, 1945, to Friedrich Siegmund-Schultze, KBA 9245.88.
291. Letter of May 11, 1945, to Friedrich Siegmund-Schultze, KBA 9245.88.
292. Letter of May 11, 1945, to Friedrich Siegmund-Schultze, KBA 9245.88. Cf. Bergmann, *Die Bewegung "Freies Deutschland,"* 62.
293. Cf. Bergmann, *Die Bewegung "Freies Deutschland,"* 156.
294. Cf. letter of March 12, 1945, to Ernst Friedlaender, *Offene Briefe 1945–1968* (GA 15), 23.
295. Barth, "Die Deutschen und wir," in *Eine Schweizer Stimme*, 335–7.
296. Cf. Barth, "Die Deutschen und wir," in *Eine Schweizer Stimme*, 338 and 343.
297. Barth, "Die Deutschen und wir," in *Eine Schweizer Stimme*, 344.
298. Barth, "Die Deutschen und wir," in *Eine Schweizer Stimme*, 346.
299. Barth, "Die Deutschen und wir," in *Eine Schweizer Stimme*, 347.
300. Barth, "Die Deutschen und wir," in *Eine Schweizer Stimme*, 348.
301. Barth, "Die Deutschen und wir," in *Eine Schweizer Stimme*, 352.
302. Barth, "Die Deutschen und wir," in *Eine Schweizer Stimme*, 354.
303. Letter of March 12, 1945, to Ernst Friedlaender, *Offene Briefe 1945–1968* (GA 15), 24.
304. Barth, "Die Deutschen und wir," in *Eine Schweizer Stimme*, 354f.
305. Kurt Müller, foreword to Barth, *Zur Genesung des deutschen Wesens*, 7.
306. Letter of March 8, 1945, from Ernst Friedlaender, cited in *Offene Briefe 1945–1968* (GA 15), 5.
307. Letter of March 8, 1945, from Ernst Friedlaender, cited in *Offene Briefe 1945–1968* (GA 15), 6.
308. Letter of March 12, 1945, to Ernst Friedlaender, *Offene Briefe 1945–1968* (GA 15), 22.
309. Cf. letter of March 12, 1945, to Ernst Friedlaender, *Offene Briefe 1945–1968* (GA 15), 23.

12

"In Political Respects a Dubious Will-o'-the-Wisp"

Basel, 1945–62

War's End and the Declaration of Guilt

On May 8, 1945, the Second World War ended with the unconditional surrender of the German military. Karl Barth watched the events of the final weeks of the war "partly joyful, partly concerned and in any case thoughtful"[1] and like most people at the time, with uncertainty about what would now happen. "Whether the history of the world has raved enough so that it will now take a rest so that the times return like those of my youth—1890–1910, it is like a fairy tale when one thinks of it—or whether now everything will become even wilder?"[2] He was deeply moved when on May 16, 1945, he could "for the first time in so many years again put a German address on a letter."[3]

The day the war ended Barth was delivering a lecture in Spiez at Lake Thun on "The Spiritual Preconditions for Reconstruction in the Postwar Era." He hoped there would now be "attempts to live along somewhat *different* lines."[4] It would be a matter of showing that people in these horrible years had learned something. One however could not be too innocent in this hope. For there was no longer any need for more proof: "The human being is not good."[5]

That's why the time had come "to become clear about that which is hidden and dominant in human beings and therefore in ourselves, and to tame that with the necessary discipline, without which it apparently can become monstrous." Barth was referring to the human spirit, or more concretely: the "spirit of our weekday lives" as realized in politics and economy, in the life of society and in technology. For if the human spirit was not controlled in everyday life "then it goes to the devil despite and amidst all the work of culture, then the Schiller and Goethe homes with all their solemn memories cannot prevent the possibility and reality of a Buchenwald [concentration camp] in their immediate vicinity."[6]

Barth didn't think much of making only the political leadership responsible for the years that had just ended. Every single individual had failed to live up to his responsibility:[7]

People can flee into the herd in very noble ways, they can also do so with Christian arguments, but whoever does this should not be surprised when one day the butcher arrives for him as well. Who is to blame for Hitler and Mussolini? It is the countless people who were not involved, those back then who were waiting it out and looking on... It is all of us, we who did not think of seeing to justice ourselves by mobilizing all our powers under all circumstances... rather than letting ourselves be driven by the current of history.[8]

A genuine restoration would only be possible if there were "now... more men and women... who do not let their liability for that which takes place in public life be taken away."[9] Pragmatic and skeptical of ideology, Barth concluded with the warning that, in light of the concrete tasks of helping and rebuilding that were now urgent, one needed to be willing "to live and if it must be to die for genuine life," not just for ideas. And so: "Our baggage of *principles* has to be very light if it is not to hinder us in this task."[10]

In the late summer of 1945 Barth took his first journey in the Germany of the immediate postwar period. This was made possible for him by the American military,[11] which hoped to get insights from his trip about the ideological incrimination of the Protestant churches and their representatives as well as German views of the American occupation.[12] In Frankfurt/Main Barth participated in the reconstitution of the Confessing Church Council of Brethren, in which he was momentarily accepted again.[13] There he sat for a long time with his friend Martin Niemöller, whom the U.S. Army had liberated from Nazi captivity a few days before the war's end in South Tirol.[14] After that Barth traveled to Treysa in northern Hesse to attend the church conference for the founding of the Evangelical (Protestant) Church in Germany (EKD).[15] He visited the universities in Freiburg, Marburg, and Bonn, meeting there with colleagues who in his impression "under the external cover of *Gleichschaltung* had held high the spirit of humanity and also conveyed that to their students."[16]

Afterwards Barth reported to the American occupation forces of certain "elements who were hindering, indeed were reactionary" that he had noticed in the Protestant church, but asked the Americans at the same time "to meet the Protestant Church in Germany and particularly its provisional government that was appointed in Treysa—provisionally!—with trust and grant it the necessary easements for its important functions."[17]

What Barth afterward conveyed about his impressions of the trip for a Swiss weekly newspaper is surprising because it seems like a relativization of his criticisms of the Germans' behavior. It can be understood as an attempt to bring a differentiated view of the German people to the Swiss public in the sense of Barth's goal of "friendship, despite." Barth related how during the trip

12.1. Karl Barth with Pierre Maury, 1945, © Karl Barth-Archive in Basel.

in an extremely evocative manner my always cherished conviction became firm that the German people was never the unified block behind Hitler that Goebbels' propaganda and the apparent hushing of all contradiction made it seem. There were extensive circles that throughout the entire time said a clear "No," and if they did not move on to deeds, they nonetheless never tried to make their position a secret, despite the unimaginable terror that threatened them daily, and they never capitulated.

He therefore warned Swiss readers that they should "in light of these opposition groups stop thinking of seeing the Germans simply as *one* great band of Nazis. Swiss people could not at all conceive of what terror on such a large scale is capable of." The people whom he met indicated to him that the majority of Germans were "in fact not in favor of National Socialism," "rather in a certain sense this came over them like a dreadful catastrophe and their only guilt consists of their passivity—of not having been heroes."[18]

Barth did however critically mention the tendency of some Germans to evade responsibility through religious ideas. He had heard statements like "We looked Satan in the eye."[19] Instead, the Germans should say soberly: "We have been political fools."[20]

In the months that followed Barth hoped that the Germans and particularly the church in Germany would find their way to a clear statement about their failures in the previous years, since only an honest dealing with guilt can make forgiveness and a genuine new beginning possible.[21] He was hoping for a short declaration of the church in which it would pronounce "pointblank and without addition and qualification" that "we Germans lost our way, hence the chaos today, and we Christians in Germany were Germans as well!"[22]

On October 19, 1945, the Council of the Protestant Church approved the Stuttgart Declaration of Guilt. A delegation from the World Council of Churches with Willem A. Visser 't Hooft, Alphons Koechlin, and George Bell hoped that such a declaration would make trust among the churches possible once more.[23] In the declaration the German church stated:

> We... know ourselves to be not only in a community of suffering, but also in a solidarity of guilt. With great anguish we state: Through us, inestimable suffering was inflicted on many peoples and lands... Indeed we have fought for long years in the name of Jesus Christ against the spirit that found horrible expression in the violent National Socialist regime, but we charge ourselves for not having confessed more courageously, prayed more conscientiously, believed more joyously, and loved more ardently.[24]

Barth articulated his own view of how to deal with German guilt when on November 2, 1945, at the invitation of the Württemberg interior ministry in Stuttgart, he directed "A Word to the Germans" before an audience of 1,500. Shortly afterward he gave the talk again at the University of Tübingen.[25] Barth began by recalling that the Swiss peoples' defensiveness against Germany in the past twelve years had been due to the fear of the expansion of the Third Reich, and that the Swiss however had always attempted to distinguish "between the swastika and the German people, and among the German people between the Nazis and the others."[26] Many Swiss now would like to be friends with the Germans. Barth then emphasized the special task of the church "to let the old be in the past, to begin a new part of the path," since it lived from the Gospel that "absolves and liberates."[27] The Germans should take this Yes of God and of the church to heart and "not let themselves fall;" and they should not ever stop thinking and wanting independently, nor surrender themselves to such an alien force as they had to Adolf Hitler.[28]

The systematic theologian Helmut Thielicke, who had also belonged to the Confessing Church and had lost his professorship in 1939 for political reasons, reacted publicly to Barth's lecture. First he praised Barth as an "honest... friend of our people,"[29] who "had come as one of the very first among the leading personalities from abroad" and had been ready "to hold a speech unpopular in many respects... among men, eye to eye."[30] Then however, like so many other Germans after the war, he rejected the claim that there was guilt for which they needed forgiveness. Guilt was always two-way. The 1919 "Versailles dictate" had "at the very least created the prerequisites" for German guilt. After 1933 it was also the foreign countries that had not unambiguously distanced themselves from Hitler, although such a distancing would have been much easier from abroad than it was "in the pincers of a system of extortion."[31]

At the same time, Thielicke was critical that Barth was expressing himself about the German situation at all, although Barth—Thielicke apparently overlooked Barth's years in Germany—had not lived through the economic and social crises that "Versailles" had meant for Germany. "There are simply some things in life that a person can only hear from someone else if he too has bled and been wounded"—not by someone who like Barth only speaks "at occasional visits to the trenches in the front."[32] One-sided public confessions of guilt led all too easily to one-sided plans for revenge. Thielicke therefore stated polemically:

> It does not suffice for a well-meaning teacher to dare to cross our borders from abroad like Noah's peace dove... in order to give his beloved but wayward pupils a word of direction and encouragement. Instead, we await a dove that would have a little letter with one line in its beak: that the *others* also begin beating *their* breasts.[33]

Only such a person could expect "that we speak with him about our guilt, who instead of being a hypocrite includes himself in the general solidarity of those in need of forgiveness."[34] One should not speak publicly about true guilt. It was better to speak only among themselves about the colliding obligations that had confronted the officers or about the internal conflicts in the hearts of dead soldiers.[35] Finally, "all of us (French, Americans, British, Germans, Japanese—and Jews) have need of forgiveness seventy times seven."[36] In Germany Thielicke's position—in contrast to that of Barth—met with widespread positive approval.[37]

Only a few months after the Stuttgart Declaration of Guilt Barth himself was sobered by the "still shocking unwillingness to repent... in so many places."[38] Although he himself publicly acknowledged the Declaration so as not to undo its positive effects on the ecumenical world,[39] he could not see the comprehensive conversion for which he had hoped. Instead of dealing with their own guilt Germans were "basically much more concerned about what they had against the others."[40] In February 1946 Barth wrote a pastor whom he considered to be from the "'other' Germany" that understood its guilt: "How mistaken one would have been when one thought that such a catastrophe must and somehow would automatically lead them to new attitudes, spiritual and intellectual reversals!"[41] In June 1946 Barth complained to Martin Niemöller, who saw the guilt question similarly and was even booed for his talks about German guilt,[42] that some church representatives in their subsequent statements were giving the Stuttgart Declaration the "fatal taste of being a throwaway and passing" document.

> What should we now do, dear Martin?... Perhaps the main thing is not to let ourselves grow tired, to say our little sentence today after the Great Flood, as we

also said before the Great Flood, as we also said in November 1934 [after the decisions of the Dahlem synod were not followed]...You especially...should not let yourself be put off, and continue to be the energetically biting louse in the thick, all too thick coat of this animal.[43]

To combat the powers of restoration in the EKD that became evident at the beginning of the Cold War, the Council of Brethren of the EKD issued the Darmstadt Statement on August 8, 1947. Barth, Hans-Joachim Iwand, and Martin Niemöller worked on the drafts. Regarding the Third Reich the text acknowledged German guilt by repeating the statement "We went astray" and bemoaning the "formation of political, social, and philosophical fronts" that overlooked "that the economic materialism of Marxist teachings ought to have reminded the Church of its task and its promise for the life and fellowship of human beings in this world."[44] For many in the EKD this went politically too far. Both the Stuttgart Declaration and the Darmstadt Statement remained controversial statements in the postwar Protestant Church of Germany.

Privately, Barth in April 1946 was about to move again. Together with his family and Charlotte von Kirschbaum he moved to Pilgerstrasse 25, a lovely one-family house close to the university. In September 1955, six and a half years before his retirement, came the final move with his wife and Charlotte, to Bruderholzallee

12.2. Barth's final home on Bruderholzallee. Photo: Christiane Tietz.

26, on a hill on the outskirts of Basel. Barth bought half of a modest duplex that had a small garden.[45] His office was in the first story, directly adjoining Kirschbaum's office.[46]

In the postwar years Barth now and then spent vacation weeks at the "Bergli" but it no longer felt so much like home for him after a certain distance developed between its owner Rudi Pestalozzi and Barth.[47] Instead he traveled frequently to Saint-Luc in the canton of Wallis or, when he was in need of resting more than hiking in the mountains, he went to Gyrenbad, a hotel well-known for its spa treatments, above the Töss valley near Winterthur.[48]

Back to Bonn and, Once Again, State and Church Issues

Together with Charlotte von Kirschbaum Barth spent the summer semester of 1946 and 1947 as a visiting professor at his old university in Bonn. Of those who had been forced to leave the university under National Socialism he was the first to return to his old place of work.[49] He described his impressions to the family: "the...great poverty and scarcity, tensions and technical complexity in which people here live is the strongest external impression with which one has to deal."[50] He was struck by the "many peaked, pale, worn out faces" and shocked by the "horizon of ruins."[51] Barth felt that the situation in which the world found itself was again "a time 'between the times.'"[52]

In Bonn Barth met old friends like Günther Dehn or his former defense attorney Otto Bleibtreu, celebrating his 60th birthday with them. The social circumstances were even part of this day: for the occasion Dehn gave Barth potatoes, Bleibtreu potatoes, lettuce, and parsley.[53]

During the semester Barth held his lecture on "Dogmatics in Outline" ("Dogmatik im Grundriss") mornings at 7 a.m. "in the half-ruins of the once so grand Kurfürsten Castle" where the Rhinish Friedrich-Wilhelms University had been since 1818.[54] They convened this early because as of 8 a.m. there were machines taking away the rubble.[55] Barely half of the attendees were theologians; most were students from other disciplines. The men attending had only just returned from the war and captivity as prisoners of war. Barth noted that his listeners, given all that they had "lived and gone through...had to learn once more how to smile."[56]

In the lecture Barth again gave an exegesis of the apostolic creed. Differently from his usual practice, he did not read from a prepared manuscript but spoke freely about the previously formulated thesis statements of the individual parts of the creed. In light of the situation he had the impression that he could not simply "read" but had to "speak."[57]

Barth felt that the summer in Bonn—his fiftieth semester as a university teacher—was "the finest up to now."[58] He mourned at the end of the semester that he "could not create a double of myself and be allowed to contribute my part to rebuilding the church and state here."[59] He wrote a farewell to his students in the university newspaper. On the trip there on one of the Rhine tugboats he had asked himself whether after his numerous criticisms of Germany during the war he would not in Bonn "run into...a wall of reserve and distrust," and whether after the years in the Hitler Youth, on the front, under bomb attacks, and in prison of war camps his listeners would not be so changed that he and his students would be unable to understand each other.[60] But he then "found everything so much easier, simpler and nicer...than I could ever have dreamed."[61] Knowledge, education, and linguistic ability had indeed declined, sometimes he still encountered a propagandistic tone, and the daily worries could not be overlooked. But the students were open and interested in theology. Here Barth was an early witness to the boom in theology and the church in the postwar decades that would lead during the 1950s and 1960s to a high point in church membership. Barth never asked his students whether they were still "Nazis" or in the meantime had become good democrats. "This will all work itself out," he believed, when German students are "once again addressed on a very objective foundation without prejudice, taken seriously and at the same time should find themselves a little cheered up."[62] In Barth's view the semester in general went as well as it did because he was teaching dogmatics, for there they encountered "words that remain steadfast even in the midst of ruins and of which one cannot grow weary, even in such a time in which all words have been exhausted."[63]

During his period at the Bonn university Barth delivered a lecture, *Christengemeinde und Bürgergemeinde* ("The Christian Community and the Civil Community") in different German cities.[64] It is his most important text on the relationship between church and state, which here he gave sharper contours than in his 1938 *Rechtfertigung und Recht*. He now also more strongly emphasized the significance of democracy.

Barth chose *Christengemeinde und Bürgergemeinde* as his title in order to point to a similarity of church and state from the onset: both are not primarily institutions but consist of people who form a community because of shared tasks. Both rely on a spatial reality in a way that can be local, regional, or national.

Barth used the Greek word for church, *ecclesia*, as the basis for his description of the Christian community: its members were *those* people from an area who were *called out* and *brought together* through the word of God. Internally the members of the Christian community were borne through faith, love, and hope; externally they were visible through their creed, proclamation, and prayer. The task of the Christian community was: "It proclaims the lordship of Jesus Christ and the hope in the coming kingdom of God."[65]

All people in a geographical area belong to the civil community since they stand under a legal order that holds for all and for each individual. The purpose of this community is freedom, peace, and humanity, ensured through the legislative, executive, and judicial branches.

In contrast to the civil community, the Christian community *knows more*, inasmuch as its insight into "arrogance" and the sinfulness of human beings leads to knowledge about the *necessity* of an established legal order. The Christian community knows "how dangerous human beings are and how endangered they are through themselves."[66] It therefore affirms the civil community as the "endeavour...that occurs in the state's being for the sake of an external, relative, provisional humanization of human existence to prevent the worst. This [humanization] is guaranteed through a political order that is for everyone (for non-Christians and Christians: both have need of this)."[67]

In the eyes of the church the state is something divinely endowed, a divine "*order.*" This does not mean that any kind of political system has the character of revelation. It means that the establishment of the state can be understood as a "means of divine grace"[68] because it works against human sin and indeed does so irrespective of whether those who carry out political office are Christians or not.

Since the state suppresses evil and prevents chaos the civil community serves from the Christian perspective to give people "time: time to proclaim the gospel, time for repentance, time for faith." For that reason the church can be "in no way indifferent, in no way neutral to an order that has such a clear connection with its own task."[69]

Barth developed a model of politics with two concentric circles—the civil community as the larger, the Christian community as the smaller—with the gospel of Jesus Christ as the shared center. The Christian community is above all responsible for the proclamation of the gospel of Jesus Christ. This however in no way signifies that the Christian community is indifferent toward the question of political formation. It is more the case that the Christian community, by recalling the fifth thesis of the Barmen Theological Declaration "calls to mind the Kingdom of God, God's commandment and righteousness, and thereby the responsibility both of rulers and ruled," criteria that are given to distinguish "between the just and unjust state, i.e., between the respective political form and reality as better or worse."[70]

That which should apply in the state can and must be analogous to that which applies in the kingdom of God. If the state exists as "*parable...corresponding... analogue* to the kingdom of God that is believed and proclaimed by the church" then it is a just state.[71] Concretely this means, for example: Since God became human in Jesus Christ, from the Christian perspective politics must above all concern human beings: "After God became human, the human became the measure of all things."[72]

The power of the state must allow itself to be measured to this analogy. The power of the police and courts to carry out order must be accepted, but when a government no longer lives up to its task, violent resistance is legitimate. This as well as state violence, including that of war, may however always only be the *ultima ratio*.

The analogies between the Christian community and the civil community do not have to be realized only in a democracy, and there they do not do so inevitably. But it was Barth's conviction that there is indeed "an *affinity* between the Christian community and the civil community of *free* peoples!"[73]

Barth thought that a Christian political party was inappropriate, because this relinquished the claim of an analogy of the *entire* civil community to the kingdom of God, and distinguished between those Christians who became involved in such a party and other Christians. Because of the pluralism of worldviews in the civil community, the decisions of the Christian community could not be defended by Christian arguments, but rather "solely because they are politically better, factually are more healing for the preservation and construction of the commonwealth, [and] ... are made ... plausible [as being so]."[74]

Because of the analogous structures of the Christian and political community Barth thought that the Gospel was "originally political."[75] The lifestyle of the church must be "*exemplary*" with respect to politics so that what it means to exist in this world based upon the gospel becomes visible. Barth called out critically to the German church:

> What rubbish, when e.g. in a country and people who today must relearn the elements of justice, freedom, responsibility, equality etc., the elements of democracy from the ground up, that it is precisely the church that finds it necessary to be increasingly hierarchical, increasingly more bureaucratic, becoming a refuge for nationalism precisely where it should portray itself as the holy, universal church, thereby helping lead German politics out of an old bottleneck![76]

In February 1946 Barth wrote a letter along the same lines as his lecture to Gustav Heinemann, who after 1945 was among the founders of the Christian Democratic Union and whom Barth had known since the Barmen synod.[77] In his letter he viewed the founding of a Christian party critically. Barth feared that the term "Christian" could be misused and that without a solid foundation that which was "democratic" would be ridiculed. Instead of a Christian party Barth advocated a "program" that would place Christians in the situation where they first had to learn democracy from the roots up, in the Christian community. That is how it would come to a "construction [of democracy] from below." Thus equipped, Christians should work in one of the already existent parties or found "a new party that better corresponds to their political views" "but without the title or claim to be Christian!"[78]

Barth also taught in Bonn the following summer of 1947. He lectured on "Christian doctrine according to the Heidelberg Catechism" and "The Christian understanding of Revelation."[79] Once again he and Charlotte von Kirschbaum arrived with a ship via the Rhine. As he reported back home, among the ruins along the Rhine they now already saw "unmistakable signs of all kinds of attempts to bring the order of creation and culture that was so torn apart back into equilibrium as far as they could. Roofs are half or completely covered, bridges passably rebuilt, the iron debris at least organized in large piles."[80]

Barth again traveled throughout Germany to lecture and have conversations.[81] In light of these many demands he longed for a quieter life: "now I'm thinking, we're thinking... of a certain Alp with grazing cows that do not demand to know my views about God, the world, and human beings either in lectures or private interviews, rather simply want to graze and then also let me, us, graze a little."[82]

Barth believed his possibilities to have direct influence in Germany were limited after the church reconstituted itself differently than he had hoped.[83] Public appearances, he thought, would only "be the hoarse screeching of an old crow, injustice against well-behaving people, incitement of fruitless confusion etc."[84] He therefore turned down a request from Wilhelm Niesel, moderator of the Reformed Federation and a member of the EKD council, to make a contribution about the question of the Lord's Supper in the Council. He had gotten intensively involved in the German church between 1933 and 1935, back then "as the Greek ships were burning."[85] In the "Lord's supper question that is on the agenda for today's EKD, its councils and other bodies I don't see any burning ship in sight."[86]

Back in Basel Barth reduced his lecture travels. Increasingly he turned down invitations with the reason that he wanted to concentrate on the ongoing work on *Church Dogmatics*.[87] He continued to participate by taking stands in public debates. To his own surprise he observed that he had become

> more peaceable and readier to see that, after all, one is in the same boat with one's opponents; readier also now and then to suffer unjustified attacks without stepping forward to defend myself, and so less zealous to attack others... Signs of weakness? Perhaps. But... I am still able to put up a good fight when that is absolutely called for.[88]

"God's Beloved Eastern Zone": Against Anti-Communism

At the end of March 1948 Barth traveled to Hungary at the invitation of the Reformed church there. He met with leading representatives of that church, with church members, and with the Hungarian state president Zoltán Tildy, who at the time was for the most part powerless, shortly thereafter would lose his office and be placed under house arrest by the Communist party.[89]

The church conversations particularly concerned what position should be taken toward the destruction of the political party system by the Communists and the growth of their power.[90] Barth gave talks in six cities in which he asked how "the Christian community" should behave "when the state forms of government were changing."[91] Once again he began with the reality of God, with the "great change ... in earthly and heavenly history" that had already occurred in Jesus Christ's death and resurrection and toward whose revelation, when he returns, human history is moving.[92] By beginning Christian reflection with attention to this, one gained distance to contemporary political developments and could "see them more calmly, clearly and better."[93]

Barth initially suggested calm in light of the political changes, since those happened under the lordship of Christ. Therefore the Christian community should neither identify with a political system nor reject one out of principle. And the church was not permitted to let any political system divert it from its duty to proclaim the word of God. The church's accompaniment of the state consisted of praying for the state and in what Barth with the Reformed tradition called the church's "prophetic office of watchman."[94] The church had to say Yes to certain political developments and No to others. In the current Hungarian situation Barth had the impression there was no need to say an immediate No, instead "to wait a little and observe the matter in detail."[95]

In his report about the Hungarian trip Barth described the situation of Hungarian Christians as a walk along a ridge. "From the perspective of social concerns" they were "too open to be able to completely reject Communism. They also knew the weaknesses of the West well enough that they did not now see themselves as obligated by the election of the second possibility [sc. fundamental political resistance against Communism] to become party followers [of the West.]"[96] He was impressed that he had not encountered in Hungary the nervousness against Communism that he had so frequently noted in the West. Instead of being preoccupied primarily with the East-West problematic or the "Russian atrocities" or "the question about the justice or injustice of their current government," the Hungarians were reflecting again on "the new proclamation of the old word of God."[97]

Barth's previous dialectical companion Emil Brunner reacted to Barth's travel report on June 10, 1948, with an open letter: "How should one understand this?" Brunner himself could "see no difference between Communist and any other kind of *totalitarianism*, e.g. the National Socialist one." Even if social concerns had been the origin of Communism it was simply a form of totalitarianism and as such necessarily atheist. Brunner asked rhetorically: Did not the church therefore also have to "say an unconditional, unmistakable and passionate No" to Communistic totalitarianism?[98] Barth was masking the problem of Communism's oppression of entire people when he spoke only of the "East-West problem." Brunner attacked Barth directly:

> I ... cannot get it into my head that you of all people, you who so severely judged even the appearance of *church* collaboration under Hitler, now make yourself the spokesmen of those who not only judge the external but even the inner resistance and mock it as "nervousness," which is simply nothing other than *turning one's back in horror* to a truly devilish system of injustice and inhumanity.

Brunner had the impression that Barth in his delight that the Hungarian Reformed church was only dealing with the question of proclamation had returned again to his "position of a passive lack of concern" that he had already advocated in 1933 in *Theologische Existenz heute!*, when he thought that one had to do theology as if nothing had happened.[99]

Barth responded to Brunner with the open letter "Theological Existence 'Today'" ("Theologische Existenz 'heute'").[100] In his report, he stated, he had wanted primarily to reject a *principled* anti-Communism. The church "does not deal timelessly with these or those -isms and systems, but always with the historical reality in the light of the word of God and faith...It thinks, speaks, and acts for that reason never 'on principle'...[but rather] from case to case."[101]

During the period of National Socialism the "seduction" that this posed had summoned him to battle. National Socialism was like "a magic spell...that showed notoriously that it had the power to take over our souls and win us over to believe its lies and to participate in its injustice." Today however in the West there is unanimity that the Soviet form of state was "not a form of life that we can call acceptable or good...because it is not corresponding to any of our well-grounded concepts of justice and freedom." For that reason it would never come to a *seductive* power of Communism. "I cannot...admit that it would be a Christian or church task to say again on theological grounds what every citizen anyway, head nodding in agreement, reads daily in the newspaper." No final words, no confession directed to fight against the current was needed here. The church should "wait calmly...whether and in what way the situation may become serious again and merit comment."[102]

The publication of Barth's Hungarian texts and his correspondence with Brunner[103] led to strong reactions in the Swiss press. The Social Democrat paper *Volksstimme* mocked the subtitle of Barth's publication "Documents from a 1948 Trip to Hungary": "Barth sees in *everything* that he has to offer 'documents'—and these *are* of that nature, namely, documents of the stupidity of this era." Barth over the years had "remained the same—the same ambiguous, short-sighted and very self-assured 'interpreter' of Christendom that he has always been."[104] After Barth returned to Switzerland in September 1948 from the World Council of Churches conference in Amsterdam and realized the uproar in the press, he wrote soberly to his friend Alphons Koechlin: "Ten days in Engadin—and an unusually lively rain of rotten eggs and dead cats bestowed upon me again by the Swiss press—have helped to find my way back to normal again in my fatherland."[105]

In 1949 Barth again summarized his position on Communism: "I am...of the opinion that communism can be warded off only by a 'better justice' on the part of the Western world, not by the all too cheap denials in which the fear of the West is not expressing itself."[106] He condemned a sweeping anti-Communism that did not even consider the social questions raised by Communism as valid.[107] Barth refused to simply fly the flag of the "Christian West." For he could not declare his "allegiance to this 'Christian West'; rather I think that the locus of Christianity is to be sought above today's conflict between East and West."[108]

In the years that followed Barth saw many occasions on which he was engaged on behalf of Protestants in the German Democratic Republic (GDR). In 1953 he was asked to intervene against the growing state pressure on the Protestant church and the arrests of pastors. In March 1953 Barth wrote Wilhelm Zaisser, the first minister of state security in the GDR, about this. While the letter was not intended to be made public, three weeks later it reached the Western press and it was disseminated throughout the GDR in late April.[109] In his letter Barth commended himself to Zaisser as someone who "since 1945 has consistently advocated a position of understanding toward the East" and therefore had even been "strongly attacked as a purported secret Communist."[110] When now however pastors were being arrested, the criticism of socialism's opponents would be substantiated that in the GDR only "a church conformed to the regime, that is, an unfree, necessarily un-Christian church [could] have a legitimate place," whereas "a church that wanted to keep itself as a Christian church [would have to] withdraw into the 'catacombs.'"[111] Barth received no reply to his letter. After a meeting of church representatives with the GDR government on June 10, 1953, the church's relationship to the regime became somewhat better.[112] One of the pastors arrested in early 1953 later believed that Barth's letter had contributed to "the announcement that all the measures taken [against them] would be re-examined."[113]

From the mid-1950s the relationship between the GDR regime and the Protestant church again grew worse. One young pastor, Friedemann Goßlau, who knew Barth from his student years in Basel in 1951/2,[114] urged Barth in the summer of 1958 to say something about the current situation.[115] Goßlau was angry that the West German church circles that had been close to the tradition of the Confessing Church lacked the courage "to state with bitter level-headedness that the socialism being steered from Moscow constantly defaults to the temptation to muzzle the Christian communities, on principle and rigorously."[116] He reported about the government's growing animosity toward the church, structural hindrance of the *Christenlehre* (church-sponsored classes on religion), and the ridicule directed toward children who attend these classes. "In one [public school] class of beginning students, the teacher had all the children stand up who still attended *Christenlehre*, and all the other children taunted these children by yelling 'Ba, ba.'"[117] Similarly the confirmation classes were hindered since the only children permitted to move on to the secondary high school were almost exclusively those who had participated in the *Jugendweihe* [the secular coming-of-age ceremony in East Germany that substituted for the church confirmation]. In the GDR Christians were being "subjected to an unashamedly atheist state power."[118]

Barth's lengthy reply of August 1958 was not allowed to appear in the GDR.[119] Quite a few of the copies that nonetheless made it into the country were confiscated by the censor, because they contained "incitement against the GDR."[120] In fact however Barth was somewhat reserved in his evaluation of the situation in the GDR and emphasized that one should not as a Christian engage in wholesale resistance against Communism. But when Communism "takes the form and power of a seducer, who prompts and misleads people...to active godlessness" then resistance was necessary.[121] Barth added that of course there were also attempts in the West to take away what was essential for the Christian community. If in the East it was the "omnipotent...party, propaganda, and police" that worked against the church's preaching, in the West it was the "just as omnipotent...press, private sector, pretentiousness, and public opinion."[122] Even the socialism framed by Russia had—here Barth harked back to his reflections in *Rechtfertigung und Recht*—a "function" in God's plan. Therefore one could hope "for a better development of this socialism"[123] and he saw no difficulties in the declaration of loyalty that the GDR leadership wanted. Later Barth acknowledged that here he had "failed to think everything through and missed the goal."[124]

Finally Barth asked, in light of the loss of the church's previous social position and its freedom to operate under the Communist systems, "whether Christianity [can] fulfil its task really only...in light of that public support, recognition or even toleration." Barth's clear No to this question was followed by his challenging questions to Goßlau and his colleagues about whether it might not be "that your particular call could be to live as an example of a Christian community which seeks out and perhaps already walks on a new path for the church *for* the people (instead *of* the people) as 'God's (quite seriously especially) beloved eastern zone.'"[125]

In his letter Barth wanted to make the East German pastors accept their task where they were, and to take that seriously. This is evident in an anecdote that the theologian Eberhard Jüngel liked to tell. He had started his theology studies in the GDR, but in 1957 was commuting between Gerhard Ebeling in Zurich, Martin Heidegger in Freiburg, and Barth in Basel. After an evening of intense discussion Barth had given him all the volumes of *Church Dogmatics* that had been published so far with the inscription "To Eberhard Jüngel on the way to God's beloved eastern zone."[126]

Barth's August 1958 letter provoked critical reactions. One GDR pastor attested that he showed little knowledge about the situation in the East, which made them "sometimes *grow weary*."[127] Barth's reflections on loyal opposition overlooked that it was almost impossible to assert the reservations expressed by such opposition over against the state offices. The liberal newspaper *Neue Zürcher Zeitung* criticized him, arguing that the question of political and civil freedom was "not an important question for Barth," who was interested only in the freedom of God's grace. If Barth would not continually express himself about current political questions one could characterize his position as "consistent a-politicism." Finally, Barth's "somehow more benevolent...attitude toward Marxism" was evident here. "Here we must protest that the theologian whose authority throughout the entire theological world is like no other, now emerges as a Socialist and makes theological propaganda for his subjective leaning."[128] The *Basler Nachrichten* diagnosed in Barth's "pamphlet" "an almost manic-like...testimony...to the resentment against everything that the so-called West means." Barth even offered directions for how one could "collaborate" with the Communist state.[129]

In 1959 Barth regarded this lack of understanding with disappointment:

> I have been accused of disdainful ingratitude against the privileges and benefits of the "free world." My statements and especially my non-statements [Barth was silent about the 1956 Hungarian uprising] have been pilloried as documents of dangerously weakening bones and confusion (explicable only due to my advanced age!). In the leading political and church circles of West Germany I have become even more unpopular than I already was even in the best of times—though I should also note that several Soviet-German official places have attested to my representing views of an explicitly "antidemocratic," indeed "antihumanistic" character. It has been especially difficult for me in my native Switzerland where, remarkably enough, there are numerous little McCarthys... Oh, I already anticipate reading the necrology in which they will sum everything up about me to say that while I have made certain contributions to the renewal of theology and performed certain services during the German Church Struggle, in political respects I was a dubious will o' the wisp![130]

In no way did Barth overlook how greatly people in Communist countries were oppressed. He often spoke of the injustice of the Soviet system, which had treated the social question "with very dirty and bloody hands in a manner that rightly outrages us." What was encountered there in "despotism, trickiness and ruthlessness" aroused "great revulsion and horror."[131] As already mentioned, socialism was also for him "not a form of life that we can call acceptable or good...because it does not correspond to any of our well-grounded concepts of justice and freedom."[132] Nonetheless Barth was convinced that a radical enmity against this system would not help the people there and overshadowed the problems in the West.

Wolf Krötke has documented Barth's actual significance for the real life of Christians in the GDR. Krötke was imprisoned from 1958 to 1959 for political reasons and at the time of the peaceful revolution in 1989 was a lecturer at the *Sprachenkonvikt*, the church college in East Berlin in which students could study theology free of state oversight. He decisively rejects the claim that Barth had stood "in the service of the GDR communists."[133] The church college was much more able to practice "freedom over against socialist ideology and in solidarity with the people" in the GDR because it had been influenced by Barth's theology.[134] In his battle against blind anti-Communism Barth also wanted to prevent a nuclear war between East and West.[135] On this point, he believed, the churches should not take a one-sided position. Barth's "third way" posed a much greater danger for socialism than the usual other blanket condemnations. At the same time Barth

> from Switzerland [could] only have an approximate idea of what it meant to live in the GDR... For us in any case it was a gain for freedom that precisely this Swiss who was more experienced in this struggle against bondage accompanied and advised us on along the way.[136]

A Pacifist after All? Protest against Rearmament and Nuclear Weapons

Since the beginning of the Korean War in June 1950 the establishment of a European army including West German soldiers was discussed in Western Europe.[137] Because Federal Chancellor Konrad Adenauer conducted secret negotiations about this on his own authority and without consulting his cabinet, the federal interior minister Gustav Heinemann, at the time also president of the EKD synod and by virtue of this office also a member of the EKD council, submitted his resignation on August 31, 1950. In a declaration on September 11 about his resignation Heinemann took a clear position against German rearmament. Martin Niemöller, the deputy chair of the EKD council, joined in this opinion, accusing Adenauer in an open letter of October 4 of falsifying the true reasons for rearmament before the German people. The "remilitarization of West Germany," which was already underway for some time, in truth served to raise fears of another war and make the people "more willing to throw themselves into a new armament adventure." Emphatically Niemöller declared: "The Protestant Church in Germany has left no doubt that it cannot speak for remilitarization—neither in the East nor the West."[138]

In the debate that followed, which almost led to a split among Protestant Christians in Germany,[139] rearmament advocates seized upon Barth's letter to Hromádka during the 1938 Sudeten crisis. The situation in West Germany was similar, they claimed, to the situation back then in Czechoslovakia.[140] In October 1950 the Bonhoeffer student Wolf-Dieter Zimmermann turned to Barth for clarification: was his letter being cited with justification or unjustly?[141] Barth's opinion on the political situation was exactly the same as that of Heinemann and Niemöller. In his reply, which was then circulated as a pamphlet in Germany on November 1,[142] he made it clear however that in his view European freedom had been at stake in 1938. "To my knowledge such a turning point, decision and catastrophe as back then, in which everything was at stake with the Yes or No, has not arisen since." While today's Russia was in Barth's eyes hardly a "peaceful power," war was "only unavoidable...when it is there." In 1938 the war, differently from today, had already been there. The churches had to combat the fear and hatred of Russia so that the "already rising natural lust for war, eagerness for war" was not realized in a new war.[143]

Barth brought a list of reasons against the rearmament of Germany: The German people could not be expected to accept that their youth would die for a third time in war or that Germans would fight against Germans. After the attempt of the past five years to drive out any positive connection the Germans had to the military, one could not now get them to "seek their salvation in the preparation of a further war." Moreover the armament of West Germany could pose a provocation for the Soviet Union. Only as a final reason, and "somewhat hesitantly" Barth mentioned his fear that the German soldier could quickly again become the "total soldier."[144]

The debate continued in 1954 when Barth was invited by the Social Democrat-led Hessian regional government for a state ceremony in Wiesbaden on the German National Day of Mourning. In his speech he made it clear that the rearmament of Germany would lead directly to a third world war, because the East would necessarily feel itself "offensively threatened." It was an "illusion that Communism, under whose dominion none of us want to enter, will be attacked or even only repelled, let alone conquered, by panzer divisions and atomic weapons rather than with social renewal and reform!" Barth went even further: he saw a "parallel to National Socialism" not in the threat of Communism but in West German rearmament, a "re-establishment of a German authoritarian state" and a division of Germany and Europe into two blocs, because here the same "panic and mass suggestion" was the basis.[145]

Once more there were fierce attacks in the press. Barth had called for "decisive rejection of the German federal government's foreign and domestic politics." To Barth's disappointment the Hessian government did not defend him as he thought they should, but distanced itself from his statements.[146]

Four years later Barth's uncompromising position against German rearmament led to another scandal. In 1958 when the philosopher Karl Jaspers, who taught in Basel, received the Peace Prize of the German Book Trade for his book *The Atom Bomb and the Future of Man*, the rumor began that they had originally considered giving the prize to Barth, but that the German Federal President Theodor Heuss had declared that he would not participate in the award ceremony for Barth. The Social Democrat magazine *Politische Verantwortung. Evangelische Stimmen* ("Political Responsibility: Protestant Voices") picked up the matter. In a letter to the editor Heuss made it clear that he had told a publisher: "I myself will then not be able to come." As a "private person" he would probably have been interested in what Barth "with his art of paradoxical formulations would have said, as a piece of individual and intellectual history." But in the parliamentary council, in regard to the question of German rearmament, he had "tried to portray" general military

12.3. Karl Barth in Italy, 1954, © Karl Barth-Archive in Basel.

conscription "as a function of democracy" and believed that in this he had even represented Barth's view of the Swiss national defense. He was unable to comprehend Barth's position on the rearmament issue and he had the impression that Barth was judging Switzerland and Germany by different measures: "I cannot get it into my head, and not theologically either, that what is considered virtue south of Riehen, Basel's border village to the Markgräflerland, should be vice and hubris north of it [in Germany]."[147]

As early as 1957 the debate about the military equipping of Germany had intensified. Two years after the establishment of the German army the question was raised about whether it should be armed with tactical nuclear weapons. Chancellor Konrad Adenauer advocated this on April 5, 1957, saying that these were "almost normal weapons" and one needed "to go along with the newest development."[148] In opposition to this assessment leading atomic scientists, including Werner Heisenberg, Otto Hahn, and Carl Friedrich von Weizsäcker, published the Göttingen Manifesto on April 12, 1957. In it they avowed to secure Western freedom against socialism, but emphasized strongly the contaminating and "life-exterminating...effect" of atomic and hydrogen bombs.[149] As a small country Germany should explicitly renounce the possession of atomic weapons.

After the dropping of the atomic bombs in 1945 on Japan Karl Barth had already stated that the question of war would now be fundamentally different.[150] Further use of an atomic weapon would presumably "be the end of most, perhaps all things."[151] After this the question that confronted him was "the avoidance of any possible war and therefore the question about a solid and definitive peace."[152] After the publication of the Göttingen Manifesto Barth was immediately asked by the West Berlin weekly paper *SOS* what he thought of it. Barth's reply on April 19, 1957, was published under the title: "It's a matter of life."[153] Similarly to Albert Schweitzer[154] at the time, Barth appealed to the citizens:

> You must let your government and your press understand with all means that you neither want to annihilate nor be annihilated: not even for the defense of the "free world," nor even for the defense of socialism! You should shout Stop! to those in responsibility in West and in East so that their ears ring: Put an end to the preparation of a war with weapons that make it senseless from the very onset for all those involved! Put an end to the mutual threat of the use of such weapons!...It's not a matter of principles, ideologies and systems. It's not a matter of questions of power. It's a matter of life. It's a matter of human beings. Before it's too late, they should support the rightness of this issue of the most basic, simple reason.[155]

In a further declaration requested of Barth by Radio Warsaw in May 1957, he sent a statement via telegraph supporting a one-sided renunciation of nuclear tests: "A sincere and credible will to peace will be from that world power that first declares that it will commit itself to renouncing all further nuclear experimentation, without consideration for the behavior of the opposing side."[156]

Barth was in solidarity during this period with the church brotherhoods (these were Protestant communities that arose during the 1950s in the theological tradition of the Confessing Church) that were intensely fighting against nuclear armament. In January 1958 he formulated ten theses for them.[157] In the tenth thesis he insisted: "A converse standpoint or neutrality toward this question is not defensible for a Christian."[158] Barth again requested that his name not be mentioned so that the contents of the theses would not be rejected from the onset.[159] However they pulled Barth "yet again into the German melee" out of which he had "proposed to withdraw after the experience in 1954 (Wiesbaden!)."[160] His theses were inserted in a question from the church brotherhoods to the synod of the Protestant Church in Germany.[161] Gustav Heinemann also referred back to

Barth's theses during the German parliamentary debate on nuclear weapons on March 25, 1958.[162] Heinemann unmistakably formulated his position: "I call nuclear weapons a method for eradicating vermin, in which this time the human being is to be the vermin."[163]

In 1957/8 there was also a Swiss discussion about possible nuclear armament. The theological commission of the Swiss Protestant Church Federation, to which Barth had belonged since 1950, was asked to compose a position statement.[164] Barth presented a statement for the meeting of June 14, 1958, according to which the churches should canvass among the Swiss people for a renunciation of nuclear weapons.[165] In 1951 in *Church Dogmatics* Barth had written that a country could arrive at a "wholly abnormal situation of emergency" in which its existence and sovereignty is threatened; only the self-defense against this situation could be a "legitimate reason for war."[166] Now he explained: a nuclear war because of its power to annihilate could in no respect be understood as self-defense.[167] The majority of the commission members could not adopt his position as their own, but his statement went into the minority report that was published along with the statement of the majority in 1958 by the Church Federation.[168]

The question of nuclear weapons was so important to Barth that he became involved in the board of an initiative that wanted to lay down a ban on nuclear weapons in Switzerland in the constitution.[169] He acknowledged to his children: "I would be prepared in this matter if necessary to enter an alliance with the devil's grandmother!"[170] On April 1, 1962, the bill came up for a popular vote. In the battle for the vote Barth worked politically with the novelist Friedrich Dürrenmatt and the Nobel Prize winning chemist Leopold Ružička.[171] Barth claimed in a contribution to the discussion that the "political existence of Switzerland" deserved to be secured militarily, but also needed biological and economic foundations as well as a legal system that respected the dignity of human beings. The political existence of Switzerland included especially the "continuation and revival of its mission as an independent and therefore mediating and reconciling element and factor in the life of the nations, over against the conflicts of interests and ideologies of its surroundings." All this would be endangered by stationing nuclear weapons in Switzerland. "The Switzerland defended with their help would no longer be Switzerland and would also be lost over against the threat of world Communism."[172]

In 1959 the European Congress against Nuclear Armament took place in London, to which the Munich writer Hans Werner Richter and the English philosopher Bertrand Russell along with Barth and others had extended invitations.[173] Barth was asked to give a talk because people were convinced that "particularly your participation and your voice could offer new courage to many people who are in despair due to the general paralysis that has set in."[174] Barth was unable to participate but via his friend Fritz Lieb sent a greeting to the gathering that was aimed at overcoming the ideological contradictions of the Cold War.[175]

"IN POLITICAL RESPECTS A DUBIOUS WILL-O'-THE-WISP" 335

12.4. *Der Spiegel* cover of December 23, 1959, © DER SPIEGEL 52/1959.

For the cover story of its 1959 Christmas issue the German magazine *Der Spiegel* offered a balance of Karl Barth's involvement in the political debates of these years. In the past years Barth had "a reputation in the western world as a disturber of the peace of western self-satisfaction... Where and whenever the West erected golden or paper calves to itself, Karl Barth was prepared to attack them with wrathful and scornful words, clenching the banner of non-conformism."[176]

Yes to Ecumenism, but without the Catholics

In addition to his multifaceted political engagement Barth became involved in ecumenism in the postwar years. Already in 1935 he had defined the main features of his ecumenical approach in a Geneva lecture on "The Church and the Churches."[177] The unity of the church was dependent on Jesus Christ being the "head and Lord...of the Church."[178] For Barth however the diversity of confessions was not an expression of richness and diversity, as many in the ecumenical movement claimed at the time, but rather of sin and guilt. The point of departure for a new life together among the confessions had to be the unity that was already given in Christ. Therefore the unification of confessions cannot be made by human beings, "but can only be *found* and *acknowledged* in obedience to the unity of the church that is already fulfilled in Jesus Christ."[179]

From August 22 to September 4, 1948, the constitutive full assembly of the World Council of Churches took place in Amsterdam.[180] Now, finally, 147 churches of different confessions participated to consolidate institutionally the ecumenical work that had grown in the previous decades but had become problematic because of wartime enmities. Barth participated in the preparatory meetings and on August 23 held the opening talk on the conference theme "The Disorder of the World and God's Plan of Salvation." The theme had been chosen because "the devastation of the Second World War and the worries about a new 'cold' war stood clearly before everyone."[181]

In his speech Barth invited the delegates to read the theme in reverse: only from the perspective of God's plan for salvation can one think at all about the disorder of the world. He was missing this perspective in the prepared material for the meeting, which began with analyses of the problems and worries of the world. From these however one could not infer God's plan for salvation.[182] He advised emphatically that for the discussion of social and international questions, they should not follow their own ideas and criteria, "laws," for the "office of political watchmen...and social Samaritan service," but rather the Gospel. Only from the Gospel could "our Yes and our No to the acting of society and the states" be won.[183] Barth welcomed the non-participation in Amsterdam of the Roman Catholic Church and Moscow Patriarchate, because this meant that perhaps conversation partners had stayed away who "do not want to implement the movement away from a focus on an institutional church culture and toward Jesus Christ."[184]

In a further address during the meeting of the Reformed delegates in Amsterdam Barth formulated it more sharply:

> We should...not lose any sentimental tears about it, that the Roman Catholic Church is not here among us...you truly didn't belong here, not to us. There where one no longer believes in Jesus *alone*, but rather in Jesus *and* Maria, there where one sets up an infallible authority on earth and wants to indicate itself as such, for our part we can only say equally decisively No to this, our ecumenical task is solely to have the form of mission and evangelization.[185]

Understandably there were protests after the conference against this perspective. The Jesuit Jean Daniélou, professor of practical theology at the Paris Catholic Institute, reacted on October 16, 1948, with an open letter. The Roman Catholics had not been able to be in Amsterdam because of "their loyalty to the good entrusted to them that they must adamantly protect." He had followed the Amsterdam conference attentively and in prayer and enjoyed reading many of its texts. Barth's words before the Reformed group however had deeply wounded him. These were words "that were not Christian"; in them one heard a nasty laugh "that is closer to Nietzsche than to Jesus." As much as Catholics had loved Barth and had much to thank him for, today they had to say No to him. "We cannot approve of the blithe fashion with which he accepts the separation [of the churches.]"[186]

Barth responded immediately. The separation between the Roman Catholic Church and the other Christian churches was "a sad, embarrassing, galling matter for all of us, not any less for me than for you." But he would not back down from his position. For when Daniélou admitted that they were unable to participate because of the good that had to be adamantly protected, he was simply repeating what the Pope had also stated: the Roman Catholic Church could "not sit at the same table with other 'churches' to consult with them about the question of unity in Jesus Christ with the same standing, same humility and openness."[187] Instead it demanded that other churches refrain from their errors and return to the Roman church.[188] None of the churches present in Amsterdam had appeared with the claim "to be the only church of salvation and infallability, i.e. by its very existence to have already answered the question that was moving us together."[189]

Barth's harsh statements may seem surprising from today's perspective, after many decades of the fruitful Protestant-Catholic dialogue that followed the Second Vatican Council in 1962–5. One must be aware however that the Roman Catholic Church only changed its own stance toward ecumenism through that Council.

In contrast it is difficult to find sympathy for Barth's statements on the commission on "Life and Work of Women in the Church" even in the context of the times. Presumably his participation can be traced to the intercession of Henriette Visser 't Hooft, the wife of his friend, who had frequent conversations with Barth about a Christian concept of the relationship of man and woman.[190] Very few men besides Barth worked on this commission; they included the

American theologian Reinhold Niebuhr and Martin Niemöller. The women on the commission advocated the general admission of women to the pastorate and other leadership offices.[191] In their arguments Barth saw a tendency that he had criticized in his keynote speech: these were not arguments based on biblical texts but on humanistic ideas. As he declared at the Reformed meeting, he had "genuine...sympathy" for the women's issue. But the biblical texts spoke of a "subordination of the woman to the man that Paul parallels to the subordination of the congregation under Christ."[192] Not only do we find the sentence "in Christ there is neither male nor female" (Gal. 3:27) in Paul that was cited by the women on the commission, but other texts as well that simply spoke of this established order. Barth strongly polemicized the argument that Paul's words reflected his own times and one had to understand the text "in the spirit of Jesus": "Whoever refers genuinely and justifiably to the spirit of Jesus cannot allow themselves a balloon trip in the heavens of humanistic theology. The genuine spirit of Jesus cannot be separated from the words of the apostles and prophets."[193] It must be asked critically whether Barth himself does not succumb here to the idea of the Bible's word for word authority that his scriptural hermeneutics help us avoid.[194]

Barth's difficulty in empathizing with the women's concerns is evident in a letter of August 31, 1948, to Charlotte von Kirschbaum about his participation in this commission:

> I talked until I was blue in the face to make Gen. 1–2, 1 Cor. 11, Eph. 5[195] etc. clear and acceptable to them... But the *women* always fall back with bared teeth on their *equality*, want to be "ordained" to all and everything, preach from the pulpit of the Münster churches [i.e., the important pulpits of Switzerland] and everything else.[196]

Henriette Visser 't Hooft wrote Barth afterward of how angry she was that Barth in this section of the conference had "such an unconstructive, indeed almost destructive" effect.[197] She reminded Barth of a conversation they had had: "Do you recall, Herr Professor, your spontaneous and assertive 'No!' when I asked you: 'Should the church too be a patriarchy?'"[198]

After his return from Amsterdam Barth's relationship at least to Catholicism began to change. Partly responsible for this was the Catholic theologian Hans Urs von Balthasar who had come to Basel in 1940 as a student chaplain. In the winter of 1948/9 he spoke in a lecture series about "Karl Barth and Catholicism."[199] Von Balthasar came from a patrician family in Lucerne and had become a Jesuit in 1929 after his studies and his doctorate in Germanistics; Erich Przywara and Henri de Lubac had been influential in his subsequent theological studies. The theological work of von Balthasar is considered some of the most original Catholic work of the twentieth century. In a 1951 book Balthasar compiled his lectures on Barth, where his intent was not "to theologize with a hammer," but help bridge the gap between the confessions, with "doubled caution, a quiet...nature and much patience."[200] Barth attended several of von Balthasar's lectures and discussed them with him afterward in a Basel wine cellar. Subsequently he reported to his son Christoph: "the speaker [is trying] to do nothing less than square the circle...to approve of all the main positions in my dogmatics and nonetheless remain and speak as a Catholic. The stake at which I was supposedly to be burned again and again will not catch fire." Barth had the impression that von Balthasar was working—almost fifteen years before the reforms of the Second Vatican Council—toward "a kind of Reformation of the Catholic church and theology from within, toward its implementation...I am now being pulled in as a new Trojan horse."[201]

For the preparations of the second world assembly of the World Council of Churches, with the theme "Christ: the Hope of the World," "twenty-five of the most outstanding and influential Christian thinkers now living" were invited to undertake preliminary work during the period between 1951 and 1953, among them Karl Barth.[202] He participated with his own theses and wrote the final section of the commission report.[203] Barth was asked as an official "advisor" to the world assembly itself, which met in Evanston, Illinois, in 1954.[204] He now planned to travel to the United States for the first time, but then cancelled the trip because among other things he "could not abandon work on the Dogmatics for so long" and because he had noticed in the meantime how much energy such occasions cost him. Barth asked Visser 't Hooft to understand his decision, which he also regretted "because I must now come to terms that by human measures I will only get to see America from that corner in one of the lower sections of heaven which I will be granted."[205]

In 1957 a Catholic dissertation about Barth, the work of Swiss Hans Küng about justification, found an ecumenical echo. Küng inquired about whether the central Protestant insights about the doctrine of justification as Barth represented them were not also represented by Catholic theologians.[206] Küng did not want to be satisfied with what a professor at the Pontifical Gregorian University in Rome had once told him: "If you don't find any Catholic witnesses for certain Barthian teachings, that is a clear sign that Karl Barth is on the wrong track."[207] In his doctoral work Küng arrived at the conclusion "that in the doctrine of justification, seen as a whole, there is fundamental agreement between Barth's teaching and that of the Catholic Church."[208] This thesis was ecumenically explosive because the differences in the doctrine of justification had been considered as the central reason for the split between the Roman Catholic and the Protestant church in the sixteenth century. Küng's work on Barth was an important step in the ecumenical process that led to the 1999 Joint Declaration on the Doctrine of Justification by the Lutheran World Alliance and the Catholic Church, which represented "a consensus about the basic truths in the doctrine of justification" and illustrated

12.5. Karl Barth with Willem A. Visser 't Hooft at a 1960 conference of the World Student Christian Federation in Strasbourg, © Karl Barth-Archive in Basel.

"that the continuing different interpretations are no longer occasion for condemnations."[209]

Barth was delighted by Küng's work. He viewed it as a sign that the old confessional battles were gradually passing and that new provisions for the relationship were being attempted. Recording his ecumenical basic concepts he wrote in a foreword to Küng's work: "divided *in faith*, namely within the *same* faith, because and as we here and over there can believe *in the same Lord*." While both confessions believed "'differently' they do not believe in a different One."[210] Barth therefore concluded for himself toward Küng:

> *If* that which you take from the Holy Scripture, the old and new Roman Catholic theology and then also the "Denzinger"[211] as well as the texts of the Council of Trent[212] *is* truly the teaching of your church and can be confirmed as such... *then* I will indeed hasten to the church of San Maria Maggiore of Trent, having been there twice, for a third time: this time for a confession with a contrite *patres peccavi* [Fathers, I have sinned]![213]

The Master with the Crumpled Tie

After his two guest semesters in Bonn in 1946 and 1947 Barth only taught in Basel until his retirement in 1962. The philosopher Karl Jaspers had been his colleague there since 1948. Jaspers heard Barth for the first time in September 1949 at the Rencontres Internationales de Genève, an annual interdisciplinary meeting in Geneva on current global problems. Moved, Jaspers wrote Barth afterward "how happy I am to have seen and heard you. It made an unforgettable impression on me. Perhaps I will understand you better in the future."[214] Although Jaspers continued to criticize Barth as a "believer in revelation,"[215] on Barth's 70th birthday in May 1956 Jaspers sent a letter in which he expressed his admiration for this so very different thinker:

> In the eight years I have spent in your sphere your immediate effect on students has been perceptible and it has been a joy to observe it. Even though I know that philosophy cannot be taken seriously by you, the presence of a different kind of seriousness from which you teach is for your philosophical colleague a constant encouragement: namely that this seriousness is there at all.[216]

The impression made by Barth is evident in Jaspers' confession that in Basel he had "for the first time personally experienced the power of theology, of which I only knew theoretically."[217] In Heidelberg where he had been previously he had learned much from the New Testament scholar Martin Dibelius, but "[t]heologically I never asked him: His faith, at least as I encountered it, was not very different from philosophy and that was all right with me and allowed some friendly conversations. But through your charisma I have seen something of the great opponent that I otherwise only knew historically."[218]

For his part Barth wrote Jaspers on his 70th birthday in February 1953 in respectful acknowledgment of his philosophical life achievements, that they were both

> agreed in our effort to recognize the mystery that limits and determines the micro- and macro-cosmos. It shows itself to you and to me from an entirely different point of view, and so your teaching and mine from the very first word cannot be the same. But we are also agreed that this mystery itself is one and the same—and agreed as well that it is worthwhile to devote oneself with utter seriousness to its testimony.[219]

For several generations of Swiss and German theology students it became automatic to spend at least one semester in Basel with the "master," as some put it. Internationally the prospect of hearing Barth drew many from the United States, the Netherlands, and Asia to the ancient university town.

Barth supervised over thirty dissertations in all.[220] Several of his doctoral students later themselves became influential in their discipline, such as Hans Ruh, professor of social ethics at the University of Zurich until 1998, or Walter Kreck, professor in Bonn until 1973, or the already mentioned Helmut Gollwitzer. Among those who became important for American theological discussions during the second half of the twentieth century were Paul van Buren and John D. Godsey.

The impression that Barth's appearance left among his students is described by Rudolf Smend, who studied in Basel from 1954 to 1955 and later became professor of Old Testament in Göttingen:

> He did not particularly attend to his appearance, his hair drifted whichever way it wanted, his tie was often 'crumpled' and never tied a la Windsor... When you encountered him, he greeted you with a friendly smile and put his hand on his Basque beret, which next to his pipe was one of his attributes. Another attribute, the heavy horn-rimmed glasses, covered only a little of the proportions of his highly expressive and by the way very photogenic face... One didn't immediately notice that behind those glasses and the bushy eyebrows were his eyes, but they were there, observed sharply and could twinkle. The thing least worth seeing, if you allow me, were his teeth, which certainly had to do with the pipe-smoking.[221]

In his lectures Barth continued to read from the most recently worked-on manuscript pages of the next section of *Church Dogmatics*. He often finished his preparations as shortly before the beginning of the class session as he had done when he first started to teach, which probably also was connected to his diminishing energy for work. Already in 1949 he told his son Christoph

> that the class lectures demand much, much more of me than before (perhaps due to increasing age) so that I regularly devote not just the entire mornings, but also the evenings before and the free Wednesdays and Saturdays, primarily to this central duty, tightening and correcting the text almost until the last quarter-hour before the lecture.[222]

Barth began his lecture class unpretentiously, with a short summary of the previous hour, and then he started off anew by looking at his text and a "Here we will continue today." He ended the classes by saying "Here we will continue next time" and marking the place in his manuscript.[223] Rudolf Smend, who first experienced Barth's lecture style at a large 1953 conference of the *Gesellschaft für Evangelische Theologie* (Society for Protestant Theology), reported that Barth read from the complete formulated text. This reading however was not in a monotone, but "was in truth a proclamation, in a loud voice, emphatically and dramatically and such that the speaker was devoting his entire strength and completely overextending himself. There could be no doubt that he stood behind every half sentence, every word."[224] Barth set up his points by slowing the tempo and through a "wily smile."[225]

The Swiss poet and pastor Kurt Marti, who could write phrases like "The Holy Spirit is no African linden,"[226] also studied under Barth and recalled that Barth's lengthy, difficult to read sentences revealed "in the oral presentation all the more their musicality and so to speak Baroque sensuousness." "The fact that his light blue eyes often looked up from the typewritten page and briefly established eye contact with his listeners from above the slipped down glasses additionally showed how dialogical his magisterial discourse was in nature."[227]

In his seminars Barth was open to the contributions of the students and moderated the discussion discreetly.[228] Barth's motto for his seminars was "learn to read!"[229] Eberhard Jüngel observed that Barth was not lacking in self-irony in his classes. He replied to students who wanted "to flatter him, and there were not a few such 'Barthians' among the students... with an irony that sent them all packing."[230]

12.6. Karl Barth in Bossey, 1958, © Karl Barth-Archive in Basel.

As Smend confirms, in the required examinations Barth was genuinely concerned with what he described in one publication:

> An examination is, correctly understood by both sides, an amicable conversation of several older and several younger theology students about certain themes of mutual interest—a conversation whose sense is to give the younger participants the opportunity to show that and how they have worked on the topic and the extent to which they hope to promise to do so in the future.[231]

Barth succeeded in performing academic theology in a way that would be usable later in the ministry. He reported happily "that the *Church Dogmatics* is to be found in not a few pastors' homes, is read, studied (if sometimes only as a reference work!), and profitably used in sermon, instruction, and counseling, and thus indirectly comes even into congregations that are far away."[232]

Barth enjoyed working with the students. "I can truly say that this is a pleasure for me, to talk with them, listen to their questions and interjections and to reply, directing them along the path that I hold to be the right one."[233] At the same time he ensured repeatedly that he did not want to found a Barthian school of thought. "If there are 'Barthians,' I am not among them. We are there to learn from each other... and then—not in a theological 'school' but in the church and therefore independently—to go our way."[234]

The Discovery of Optimism in Prison

In 1954 Martin Schwarz, the pastor at the Basel prison, asked if Barth could not come and preach to the prisoners sometime.[235] Barth had not preached in Basel since 1947 and only three times elsewhere,[236] but after participating in a prison worship service he agreed. From this time on he asked regularly whether he could preach again there.[237] Even on the morning of his 70th birthday it was important for him to begin the day by celebrating worship with the prisoners.[238] Afterward he sent his birthday sermon to Karl Jaspers in the hope that it would make clear to him "that I am in my element, firstly and finally, in such speaking *to* the people, in such an attempt to *pray* with them."[239]

Until 1964, when he stopped for health reasons, Barth held twenty-eight worship services at the Basel prison.[240] Referring to this he commented that he hardly ever preached elsewhere: "There are but few theology professors whose sermons one can only listen to after having committed a serious violation of the civil order."[241]

In addition to his sermons Barth participated in the community evenings at the prison where he replied to questions from the prisoners. And from time to time he visited individual prisoners in their cells.[242] Barth found the prisoners in very different moods. From the letters in which he reported of these visits it is evident how deeply he was moved by these impressions: "A sad case however is that of … a real victim of his background, and in addition rather helpless intellectually: are you in contact with his wife? But everything here seems so complex that one really feels powerless."[243] With others he was happy to see that they "apparently know how to deal meaningfully with their punishment."[244] Not infrequently he gave prisoners a cigar at the end of a conversation. The prisoners were evidently happy about his visits not only because of that and talked willingly about much in their lives. Barth saw his task here primarily as listening and asking about things.[245]

Barth's prison sermons are not dogmatic or moralistic. He addressed his listeners directly and always included himself. The accent was on God's grace and closeness, which applied very especially to the prisoners, who were "not just criminals but human beings."[246] Barth's sermon on his 70th birthday, Ascension Day of 1956, shows vividly how he wanted to change the situation of the prisoners through the message of God's grace. Barth preached on Psalm 34:5: "Look to him, and be radiant; so your faces shall never be ashamed."[247]

A simple "keep your head up," as some kind of "looking up," was not what was here intended. It could be that one would look up to a heaven "that was a hard reflection of our entire human misery."[248] It was far more a matter of looking up to Jesus Christ, who has taken the guilt and needs of human beings on himself and overcome them. In light of the fear that they might have completely forfeited and ruined their lives—in God's eyes as well—Barth promises the prisoners that this is not the case, because God's care specifically applies to them.

In a 1960 conversation that Barth had with prison chaplains he rebelled against a sharp boundary between the imprisoned and people outside. Even if it might eventually be the case—as someone asked him—that there was such a thing as an "ineradicable disposition" of prisoners, all human beings had such an "ineradicable disposition: ineradicable egotism, spiritual laziness, know-all attitude, ambition, histrionics, etc." It was very certain that such dispositions however should not be mistaken for some kind of divine predestination. There was only *one* divine predestination, that of divine election of grace: "In Jesus Christ every human being is called to God."[249] Against the possible charge that such a message for prisoners was reckless, even dangerous, Barth responded: "Should it really be dangerous to see the residents of a penitentiary—prisoners and personnel—unconditionally as the community of Christ? Is then the community of Jesus Christ something other than such a community in a penitentiary, 'lost, damned, but rescued and redeemed through Jesus Christ'?"[250]

Barth observed in himself that he "could not simply leave any of these men shaking my head and worried, but it was much more the case that I saw in each of them something that was encouraging and gladdening for me."[251] In light of that Barth asked himself ironically: "Might it be the case that I have become after all something like an optimist or even a wandering illustration of the heresy of *apokatastasis panton* [the restoration of all[252]]?...Do I listen to too much Mozart?"[253]

Courage, Tempo, Purity, Peace: Confession to Mozart

During 1956, the 200th anniversary of Mozart's birth, Barth expressed his lifelong love for the composer on numerous occasions. Barth could not imagine his daily routine without Mozart, for he had "for years and years begun each day with listening to Mozart" and only then turned to dogmatics.[254] Because of this for some time "the gramophone... [had been] really a central piece of furniture" in his home.[255] In his study "the pictures of Calvin and Mozart are to be seen hanging next to each other and at the same height."[256] Barth often acknowledged "that if I should ever come to heaven I would first of all ask after Mozart and only then after Augustine and Thomas, Luther, Calvin and Schleiermacher."[257]

In a fictional almost tender letter to Mozart, which Barth wrote in 1955 at the invitation of a Swiss newspaper, he expressed his deep gratitude to the composer: Barth pertly apologized that he did not play an instrument, nor was he a scholar of music, which is why he could not say with certainty "in which of the thirty-four periods into which Wyzema and St. Foix have divided your life you appeal to me the most." But he comforted himself that he had read about Mozart "that you sometimes played hours on end for very simple people, merely because you sensed that they enjoyed listening to you. This is the way I have always heard you playing and still do, with a constantly renewed enjoyment of ear and heart."[258]

Barth was fascinated that Mozart could play, which was not so easy. "Beautiful playing presupposes a childlike awareness of the center—as also the beginning and the end—of all things."[259] Barth had the sense that with Mozart's music he could *live*.

> What I thank you for is simply this: Whenever I listen to you, I am transported to the threshold of a world which in sunlight and storm, by day and by night, is a good and ordered world. Then, as a human being of the twentieth century, I always find myself blessed with courage (not arrogance), with tempo (not an exaggerated tempo), with purity (not a wearisome purity), with peace (not a slothful peace).[260]

In Mozart he discovered a "dialectic" with which "one can be young and become old, can work and rest, be cheerful and sad."[261] Mozart had been neither an optimist nor pessimist. "What he translated into music was real life, in all its discord. But in defiance of that, and on the sure foundation of God's good creation..."[262]

In Mozart's music Barth found what he himself attempted to express theologically: that all tension and difficulty in life can always be viewed already from the vantage point of having overcome it. For Barth this lay in God's already granted turn toward the world in Jesus Christ. To him Mozart's music was a parable for this.[263]

In contrast Barth had by his own account "simply no instinct" for contemporary music, nor for the painting and literature of his era. "I do not have a negative judgement of it, to my knowledge I have never said a bad word about it. It is simply a sad fact that I have no understanding, no eyes, no ears for it... Perhaps I was born too deeply in the nineteenth century?"[264] To the question about whether he had never had the wish for any other music besides that of Mozart, he once replied to his son-in-law Max Zellweger: "it was just this way with him: during the playing of musical pieces by other composers he had to constantly think about how lovely it would be, if he could spend this time listening to Mozart's music, then the time would not be wasted!"[265] That's why Barth once brought his admiration for Mozart to the point: "it may be that when the angels go about their task of praising God, they play only Bach" but he was "sure, however, that when they are together *en famille* they play Mozart and that then too our dear Lord listens with great pleasure."[266]

During the 1956 Mozart Jubilee year Barth celebrated his 70th birthday. Three *Festschriften* were given to him at the birthday celebrations at the university on May 11.[267] On this occasion Barth's friend Benedikt Vischer presented the university with a portrait of Barth that had been painted by his cousin, the painter Paul Basilius Barth,[268] who had died shortly before.[269] In 1949 a proposal for such a portrait had been rejected by the Basel Art Credit Commission. Barth wrote his son Christoph at the time about the reason: "whoever flirts like that with Communism will *not* be painted at the state's cost!" His cousin Paul Barth was furious and ironically commented that after Barth's death they would "erect a memorial in bronze on the Münster square." Barth himself took the rejection with humor: "the thought that on the wall of the *Regenzzimmer* [a conference room at the university] I would then have had to attend all the meetings of this council over the centuries (which I now almost always skip) would have been dreadful indeed."[270]

Children, Grandchildren, and the Rejection of His Desired Successor

To the outside world Barth during the 1950s said that he did not want to "think of becoming old—except when it is unavoidable as a practical matter" and wanted to "go calmly on, simply being a man."[271] He had two things to thank that he continued to do so well:

> first the *Church Dogmatics*, which calls for completion and does not allow me to hang my head or rest my hands—and then the invitation of the cantonal council

12.7. Karl Barth and the painter Paul Basilius Barth in 1954, © Karl Barth-Archive in Basel.

of Basel Stadt to continue teaching at the university beyond the customary age limit, so that I can continue to let myself be disturbed and refreshed by the demands of the studying youth.[272]

The theological faculty in 1955 had applied for an extension of Barth's professional activity beyond the 70th year because "it cannot be expected of any serious candidate to come on as Barth's successor as long as he is in the condition to continue teaching."[273] The department for education of the canton of Basel Stadt wrote in support to the cantonal council:

> Even those who do not agree with everything that Barth teaches and writes recognize the unique, almost epoch-making significance Barth has in Protestant theology. His influence on theological thought in Europe as in America is—in any case for our century—unique. Barth enjoys worldwide prestige as a teacher as well.[274]

Barth admitted to his children however how tired and exhausted he felt in the meantime with his massive *Dogmatics* project:

> what an undertaking! And what travail from week to week. Lollo says that she has never known me any differently than in this gasping way of moving forward...

but subjectively I do feel that the burden is getting heavier. Now and then Lollo orders me to cancel a class so that I can catch my breath.[275]

On the whole however he continued to enjoy fairly good health, despite the frequent pipe-smoking.[276]

Since the 1950s Barth had become more interested than before in the lives of his children and grandchildren. A moving 1952 letter to his friend Lukas Christ shows how Barth saw his relationship to his sons:

> I raised them on a very long leash—or rather I hardly raised them, but instead (because I myself was always busy up to my neck) let them be and do. They then became—each of them on his own—theologians, have always shown great confidence in me and understood me, just as I in their particular paths also understood them as they grew older and, as well as I could, accompanied them. There were never tensions or scenes between us, but many exchanges that were comfortable and for me too always instructive. Meanwhile each in his own way is his own person. And when criticism on my part was necessary I certainly never suppressed it. But everything has increasingly been on the basis of a free, masculine friendship.

He felt clearly how difficult they had it "always in the shadow of the 'famous' father. Always to be compared with him!...For many people to be the welcome target for saying things that they were afraid to say to me!" Barth was at the same time grateful that he had "such a warm...relationship" to his children and their spouses. He was aware that this was "astonishing enough...because it has turned out this way over the years and decades despite the great turbulence [of Barth's difficult marriage situation]. This is a great gift for me: undeserved."[277]

Barth was a loving grandfather to his grandchildren. When they visited him at the home on Bruderholzallee, not seldom for lunch, he wanted to know exactly what was happening in their lives. Barth's grandson Dieter Zellweger (born in 1947) reported in 2017 how sensitively Barth had noticed his needs:

> I grew up in a bourgeois milieu in which much value was put on correct manners. My grandfather soon sensed that this pressure didn't suit me, and so he smilingly made an agreement with me that when we said farewell we no longer politely shook hands, but instead looked each other sharply in the eyes and then with a brusque hand movement made it clear to the other: "You may leave!"[278]

As Barth began to feel more clearly that his ability to work was diminishing he asked to retire after the 1961 summer semester at age seventy-five. At the end of the semester he addressed his students:

12.8. Karl Barth with grandson Dieter Zellweger in 1955, © Karl Barth-Archive in Basel.

I must truly... thank you. I live just as much from the students as the students live at least in part from *me*: I have always needed a certain encouragement from young academics, and over the last almost forty years during which I have been a professor this has basically never been lacking, so that these forty years... cannot seriously be called a wandering in the wilderness. In any case I have never lacked entirely for manna and quail and water from the rock, and when I... certainly often enough disgraced myself, I nonetheless now have the promised land in very clear view, although admittedly I need to realize that there will be Pheresites and Jebusites and Canaanites and certainly Philistines who will continue to make my life even in the promised land of retirement... a little sour...[279]

Barth hoped that his former doctoral student Helmut Gollwitzer, who in the meantime was professor at the Free University in Berlin, could be his successor in Basel.[280] The faculty voted almost unanimously for him and the leadership of the university also agreed.[281] Through his political activities however Gollwitzer had incurred the charge of being "pro-Communist."[282] In June 1961 this led to a media uproar in the Swiss press: "Communist-friendly education for Reformed Theologians. Professor Karl Barth's chair in Basel is to be occupied by a Berlin friend of the Communists."[283] Barth's own political engagement came once more in focus.[284] There were also intense fights in the Swiss church about the planned appointment.[285] The media controversies dragged out for weeks. Finally there was even an intelligence report about Gollwitzer compiled in Switzerland.[286] In the end, the cantonal council decided for Barth's previous doctoral student, the Swiss Heinrich Ott.[287] Barth was deeply hurt by the entire process. He wrote Gollwitzer on July 31, 1962: "The University of Basel is now for me deeply ruined. I will continue to hold a few colloquia strictly privately in an inn close by, but in the catalogue of lectures I'll let a bleak 'will not lecture' appear."[288]

Barth had still stepped in for himself in the 1961/2 winter semester. He dedicated his final lecture before a large audience to *Evangelical Theology: An Introduction*. There he described once more what in his eyes was the special nature of the scholarship that had preoccupied him now for forty years:

> whoever wants to do this will never come with their options settled by already resolved questions, already worked-through results, already secured outcomes, will in no way be able to build today on the foundations that he has already laid yesterday, or live from the interest of the accumulated capital of yesterday, but instead must rely on having to begin anew each day, indeed each hour, at the beginning.[289]

Notes

1. Letter of May 13, 1945, to Hans Jakob Barth, KBA 9245.89.
2. Letter of May 13, 1945, to Hans Jakob Barth, KBA 9245.89.
3. Letter of May 16, 1945, to Gotthilf Weber, KBA 9245.97.
4. Barth, "Die geistigen Voraussetzungen für den Neuaufbau in der Nachkriegszeit," in *Eine Schweizer Stimme*, 415.
5. Barth, "Die geistigen Voraussetzungen," in *Eine Schweizer Stimme*, 415 and 431.
6. Barth, "Die geistigen Voraussetzungen," in *Eine Schweizer Stimme*, 418.
7. With regard to the German developments, in his 1945 text "An die deutschen Theologen in der Kriegsgefangenschaft" Barth acknowledged his own guilt as well, that he had "neglected to warn against the tendencies that since I stepped on German soil in 1921 were visible to me and sinister enough in the church and world that surrounded me: not only implicitly but explicitly, not only privately but also publicly to warn!...back then I did not speak out as loudly and clearly as would have had to be spoken at that time." *Offene Briefe 1945–1968* (GA 15), 50.
8. Barth, "Die geistigen Voraussetzungen," in *Eine Schweizer Stimme*, 421.
9. Barth, "Die geistigen Voraussetzungen," in *Eine Schweizer Stimme*, 421.
10. Barth, "Die geistigen Voraussetzungen," in *Eine Schweizer Stimme*, 430. Author's italics.
11. Cf. Peter Zocher, "Karl Barth und Emil Brunner nach 1945," in Beintker et al., eds., *Karl Barth im europäischen Zeitgeschehen*, 292.

12. Cf. Barth's report about his trip to Germany from August 19–September 4, 1945, given to the Organization I of the U. S. Army in Germany: "Bericht über eine Deutschlandreise," in Vollnhals, ed., *Die evangelische Kirche nach dem Zusammenbruch*, 117.
13. Cf. Barth's report on his trip in "Und vergib uns unsere Schuld," 7; regarding his temporary acceptance cf. his letter of June 29, 1946, to Martin Niemöller, KBA 9246.237, in which Barth reported that he had been "again stricken on the quiet" from the list of the Council of Brethren.
14. Cf. Barth, "Und vergib uns unsere Schuld," 7. On Niemöller cf. Ziemann, *Martin Niemöller. Ein Leben in Opposition*, 355.
15. Cf. Barth, *How I Changed My Mind*, 55.
16. Cf. Barth, "Und vergib uns unsere Schuld," 7.
17. Cf. Barth, "Bericht über eine Deutschlandreise," in Vollnhals, ed., *Die evangelische Kirche*, 117.
18. Barth, "Und vergib uns unsere Schuld," 7.
19. Barth, "Und vergib uns unsere Schuld," 12. This is how Helmut Thielicke formulated it in "Die Kirche inmitten des deutschen Zusammenbruchs, ihre Beurteilung der Lage und ihre Ziele," in Besier et al., ed., *Kirche nach der Kapitulation*, 205: "We Christians in Germany looked from afar at the 'beast from the bottomless pit'; we lived very close to the demons."
20. Barth, "Und vergib uns unsere Schuld," 12.
21. Cf. Beintker, "Karl Barth und die Frage nach der Schuld der Deutschen," in Beintker et al., eds., *Karl Barth im europäischen Zeitgeschehen*, 229–42.
22. Letter of September 28, 1945, to Martin Niemöller, in Greschat, ed., *Die Schuld der Kirche*, 86–7.
23. Cf. Greschat, ed., *Die Schuld der Kirche*, 91.
24. English translation from Barnett, *For the Soul of the People*, 209.
25. Cf. letter of January 18, 1946, to Mary Hottinger, KBA 9246.27.
26. Barth, "Ein Wort an die Deutschen," in *"Der Götze wackelt,"* 88.
27. Barth, "Ein Wort an die Deutschen," in *"Der Götze wackelt,"* 89.
28. Barth, "Ein Wort an die Deutschen," in *"Der Götze wackelt,"* 90.
29. Thielicke, "Exkurs über Karl Barths Vortrag in Tübingen," 371.
30. Thielicke, "Exkurs über Karl Barths Vortrag," 371.
31. Thielicke, "Exkurs über Karl Barths Vortrag," 373.
32. Thielicke, "Exkurs über Karl Barths Vortrag," 376.
33. Thielicke, "Exkurs über Karl Barths Vortrag," 377.
34. Thielicke, "Exkurs über Karl Barths Vortrag," 377.
35. Cf. Thielicke, "Exkurs über Karl Barths Vortrag," 382.
36. Thielicke, "Exkurs über Karl Barths Vortrag," 382.
37. Cf. Lepp, *Tabu der Einheit?*, 52. Regarding Thielicke's lecture, cf. also Greschat, ed., *Die Schuld der Kirche*, 156f.
38. Barth, "Unser Malaise muss fruchtbar werden," 7.
39. Cf. letter of June 8, 1946, to Hans Asmussen, KBA 9246.204. Cf. the tribute in Barth, "Ein Wort an die Deutschen," in *"Der Götze wackelt,"* 94.
40. Letter of June 8, 1946, to Hans Asmussen, KBA 9246.204.

41. Letter of February 12, 1946, to Heinrich Graffmann, KBA 9385.65.
42. Cf. letter of June 29, 1946, to Martin Niemöller, KBA 9246.237; letter of February 12, 1946, to Heinrich Graffmann, KBA 9385.65.
43. Letter of June 29, 1946, to Martin Niemöller, KBA 9246.237.
44. English translation of the Darmstadt Statement from Hockenos, *A Church Divided*, Appendix 6, 193. Translation revised.
45. Cf. letter of November 18, 1955, to Paul van Buren, KBA 9255.189.
46. Today the house is the site of the Karl Barth-Archive. The two offices with a large section of Barth's library and some of the original furniture can still be seen.
47. Cf. letter of January 13, 1948, to Rudi Pestalozzi, KBA 9248.13; letter of January 21, 1948, from Pestalozzi, KBA 9348.90.
48. Cf. Busch, *Karl Barth: His Life*, 370, 469.
49. Cf. Christian George, *Studieren in Ruinen*, 256.
50. Letter of May 17, 1946, to the family, KBA 9246.174.
51. Letter of May 17, 1946, to the family, KBA 9246.174.
52. Barth, *Dogmatik im Grundriß*, 6.
53. Letter of May 17, 1946, to the family, KBA 9246.174.
54. Barth, *Dogmatik im Grundriß*, 5.
55. Cf. Barth, *Dogmatik im Grundriß*, 5.
56. Barth, *Dogmatik im Grundriß*, 5.
57. Barth, *Dogmatik im Grundriß*, 6.
58. Barth, *Dogmatik im Grundriß*, 5.
59. Cf. "Autobiographical Sketches II. Bonn, B. 1946," in *Barth–Bultmann Letters* (GA 1), 158.
60. "Prof. Karl Barth's Gruß an die Studenten," in *Bonner Universitäts-Zeitung*, Nr. 7, October 18, 1946, 1.
61. "Prof. Karl Barth's Gruß," in *Bonner Universitäts-Zeitung*, Nr. 7, October 18, 1946, 1.
62. "Prof. Karl Barth's Gruß," in *Bonner Universitäts-Zeitung*, Nr. 7, October 18, 1946, 1.
63. "Prof. Karl Barth's Gruß," in *Bonner Universitäts-Zeitung*, Nr. 7, October 18, 1946, 2.
64. Barth, "Christengemeinde und Bürgergemeinde," in *Rechtfertigung und Recht*, 47–80.
65. Barth, "Christengemeinde und Bürgergemeinde," in *Rechtfertigung und Recht*, 54.
66. Barth, "Christengemeinde und Bürgergemeinde," in *Rechtfertigung und Recht*, 51.
67. Barth, "Christengemeinde und Bürgergemeinde," in *Rechtfertigung und Recht*, 52.
68. Barth, "Christengemeinde und Bürgergemeinde," in *Rechtfertigung und Recht*, 52.
69. Barth, "Christengemeinde und Bürgergemeinde," in *Rechtfertigung und Recht*, 52f.
70. Barth, "Christengemeinde und Bürgergemeinde," in *Rechtfertigung und Recht*, 57f. Cf. the Barmen Declaration, Hockenos, *A Church Divided*, 180.
71. Barth, "Christengemeinde und Bürgergemeinde," in *Rechtfertigung und Recht*, 63.
72. Barth, "Christengemeinde und Bürgergemeinde," in *Rechtfertigung und Recht*, 66.
73. Barth, "Christengemeinde und Bürgergemeinde," in *Rechtfertigung und Recht*, 74.
74. Barth, "Christengemeinde und Bürgergemeinde," in *Rechtfertigung und Recht*, 75.
75. Barth, "Christengemeinde und Bürgergemeinde," in *Rechtfertigung und Recht*, 76.
76. Barth, "Christengemeinde und Bürgergemeinde," in *Rechtfertigung und Recht*, 78.
77. Cf. editor's introduction to the open letter to attorney Dr. Gustav W. Heinemann, Essen, *Offene Briefe 1945–1968* (GA 15), 58.

78. Open letter of February 16, 1946, to Gustav Heinemann, *Offene Briefe 1945-1968* (GA 15), 62f.
79. Cf. the lists of academic courses in the Karl Barth-Archive.
80. Letter of May 9, 1947, to the family, KBA 9247.135.
81. Cf. letter of August 1, 1947, to the family, KBA 9247.258.
82. Letter of August 13, 1947, to the family, KBA 9247.295.
83. Cf. letter of August 8, 1950, to Niesel, in Freudenberg, ed., *Barth-Niesel Briefwechsel*, 236.
84. Letter of August 20, 1949, to Wolfgang Scherffig, KBA 9249.177.
85. Letter of August 8, 1950, to Niesel, in Freudenberg, ed., *Barth-Niesel Briefwechsel*, 236. The reference to the burning of the Greek ships is from Friedrich Schiller's "Das Siegesfest," in *Werke und Briefe*, vol. 1, Frankfurt a.M.: Deutscher Klassikerverlag, 1992, 346:89.
86. Letter of August 8, 1950, to Niesel, in Freudenberg, ed., *Barth-Niesel Briefwechsel*, 236.
87. Cf. for example letter of August 8, 1950, to Niesel, in Freudenberg, ed., *Barth-Niesel Briefwechsel*, 236.
88. Barth, *How I Changed My Mind*, 51. Translation revised.
89. Cf. Barth's report on his journey, "Reformierte Kirche hinter dem 'eisernen Vorhang,'" in *Christliche Gemeinde im Wechsel der Staatsordnungen: Dokumente einer Ungarnreise 1948*, 55-8.
90. Cf. Barth, *How I Changed My Mind*, 56.
91. Barth, "Die christliche Gemeinde," in *Christliche Gemeinde im Wechsel*, 30-46.
92. Barth, "Die christliche Gemeinde," in *Christliche Gemeinde im Wechsel*, 30.
93. Barth, "Die christliche Gemeinde," in *Christliche Gemeinde im Wechsel*, 31.
94. Barth, "Die christliche Gemeinde," in *Christliche Gemeinde im Wechsel*, 43.
95. Barth, "Aus der Diskussion in Budapest am Vormittag des 1. April 1948," in *Christliche Gemeinde im Wechsel*, 51.
96. Barth, "Reformierte Kirche hinter dem 'eisernen Vorhang,'" in *Christliche Gemeinde im Wechsel*, 57.
97. Barth, "Reformierte Kirche hinter dem 'eisernen Vorhang,'" in *Christliche Gemeinde im Wechsel*, 58.
98. Emil Brunner, "Wie soll man das verstehen? Offener Brief an Karl Barth," cited in *Offene Briefe 1945-1968* (GA 15), 150f.
99. Brunner, "Wie soll man das verstehen?," cited in *Offene Briefe 1945-1968* (GA 15), 158.
100. Barth, "Theologische Existenz 'heute.' Antwort an Emil Brunner," *Offene Briefe 1945-1968* (GA 15), 159-66.
101. Barth, "Theologische Existenz 'heute,'" *Offene Briefe 1945-1968* (GA 15), 159.
102. Barth, "Theologische Existenz 'heute,'" *Offene Briefe 1945-1968* (GA 15), 162-5.
103. All texts can be found in Barth, *Christliche Gemeinde im Wechsel der Staatsordnungen*.
104. *Volksstimme St. Gallen*, August 13, 1948.
105. Letter of September 20, 1948, to Alphons Koechlin, cited in *Offene Briefe 1945-1968* (GA 15), 149, n. 7.
106. Barth, *How I Changed My Mind*, 57.
107. Cf. Zocher, "Karl Barth und Emil Brunner nach 1945," in Beintker et al., eds., *Karl Barth im europäischen Zeitgeschehen*, 294.
108. Barth, *How I Changed My Mind*, 57.

109. Cf. editor's introduction to the letter to Minister Wilhelm Zaisser, East Berlin 1953, *Offene Briefe 1945–1968* (GA 15), 332f.
110. Letter of March 2, 1953, to Wilhelm Zaisser, *Offene Briefe 1945–1968* (GA 15), 334.
111. Letter of March 2, 1953, to Wilhelm Zaisser, *Offene Briefe 1945–1968* (GA 15), 336.
112. Cf. editor's introduction to Barth's open letter to a pastor in the GDR 1958, *Offene Briefe 1945–1968* (GA 15), 401. This introduces a series of letter exchanges between Barth and several pastors in the GDR; cf. notes 113, 116–18, 121–3, 125, and 127 below.
113. Letter of February 25, 1977, of a pastor imprisoned in 1953 in the GDR to Diether Koch, cited in *Offene Briefe 1945–1968* (GA 15), 334, n. 10.
114. Cf. Rinse Reeling Brouwer, "Karl Barth und die Suche nach einem Weg zwischen den Fronten des Kalten Krieges," in Beintker et al., eds., *Karl Barth als Lehrer der Versöhnung*, 183.
115. Cf. editor's introduction to Barth's open letter to a pastor in the GDR 1958, *Offene Briefe 1945–1968* (GA 15), 401.
116. Letter of a young pastor from 1958, cited in *Offene Briefe 1945–1968* (GA 15), 403.
117. Letter of a young pastor from 1958, cited in *Offene Briefe 1945–1968* (GA 15), 407.
118. Letter of a young pastor from 1958, cited in *Offene Briefe 1945–1968* (GA 15), 410.
119. Cf. Wolf Krötke, "Die Religion wollte partout nicht sterben," in Krötke, *Karl Barth und der "Kommunismus,"* 15.
120. This is the formulation in the protocol of March 5, 1959, about the confiscation, cited in *Offene Briefe 1945–1968* (GA 15), 439, n. 90.
121. Barth, "Brief an einen Pfarrer in der Deutschen Demokratischen Republik," *Offene Briefe 1945–1968* (GA 15), 415.
122. Barth, "Brief an einen Pfarrer in der Deutschen Demokratischen Republik," *Offene Briefe 1945–1968* (GA 15), 417.
123. Barth, "Brief an einen Pfarrer in der Deutschen Demokratischen Republik," *Offene Briefe 1945–1968* (GA 15), 419.
124. Cf. "Gottes fröhlicher Partisan. Dialektischer Theologe Karl Barth. Kunde vom unbekannten Gott," in *Der Spiegel*, Nr. 52/1959, December 23, 1959, 77.
125. Barth, "Brief an einen Pfarrer in der Deutschen Demokratischen Republik," *Offene Briefe 1945–1968* (GA 15), 426f.
126. Eberhard Jüngel, in *Systematische Theologie der Gegenwart in Selbstdarstellungen*, 191.
127. "Von einem Pfarrer in der DDR, Offener Brief," in *Deutsches Pfarrerblatt* 59 (1959), Nr. 7, April 1, 1959, 146. The pastor's bishop had read him excerpts from the letter and the pastor then ordered the text from Barth's publisher in Switzerland.
128. Max Schoch, "Karl Barth und der Kommunismus," in *Neue Zürcher Zeitung*, December 15, 1958, KBA 6930.
129. Peter Dürrenmatt, "Karl Barth desavouiert Karl Barth," in *Basler Nachrichten*, December 19, 1958, KBA 6826.
130. Barth, *How I Changed My Mind*, 65f. Translation revised.
131. Cf. Barth, "Die Kirche zwischen Ost und West," in *"Der Götze wackelt,"* 136f. In this article Barth penned the sentence that was so often criticized later: "Now it truly flies in the face of all logic,... when one wishes to name a man of the quality of Joseph Stalin even for only one moment in the same breath as charlatans such as Hitler,

Göring, Heß, Goebbels, Himmler, Ribbentrop, Rosenberg, Streicher etc." (137). According to Barth the distinction lay in the fact that in the Soviet Union it concerned at least a "constructive idea," namely the "solution... of the *social* question." In no respect had the West offered a better answer to this question; as an example Barth named the "'freedom' here to throw grain in the sea while people there went hungry" (137). Barth's text played a central role in the 1949-51 church controversy in Bern; cf. Ficker Stähelin, *Karl Barth und Markus Feldmann im Berner Kirchenstreit 1949-1951.*

132. Barth, "Theologische Existenz 'heute'. Antwort an Emil Brunner," *Offene Briefe 1945-1968* (GA 15), 163.
133. This was how Erwin Bischof characterized Barth in *Honeckers Handschlag, Beziehungen Schweiz-DDR 1960-1990*, 136.
134. Krötke, "Die Religion," in *Karl Barth und der "Kommunismus,"* 9.
135. Cf. Krötke, "Die Religion," in *Karl Barth und der "Kommunismus,"* 10.
136. Krötke, "Die Religion," in *Karl Barth und der "Kommunismus,"* 16. This should be distinguished from the so-called "leftist Barthianism," for example of Friedrich-Wilhelm Marquardt, who found in Barth a "conceptual form" of "dialectical materialism." Cf. p. 18.
137. Cf. Kielmansegg, *Das geteilte Land*, 141-4, and the editor's introduction to Barth's open letter to Wolf-Dieter Zimmermann, *Offene Briefe 1945-1968* (GA 15), 202.
138. Martin Niemöller, "Offener Brief an Bundeskanzler Dr. Adenauer vom 4. Oktober 1950," in *Kirchliches Jahrbuch für die Evangelische Kirche in Deutschland 1950*, 174f.
139. Cf. Lepp, *Tabu der Einheit?*, 115.
140. Regarding this cf. the report in the letter of October 13, 1950, from Wolf-Dieter Zimmermann, cited in *Offene Briefe 1945-1968* (GA 15), 203.
141. Cf. letter of October 13, 1950, from Wolf-Dieter Zimmermann, cited in *Offene Briefe 1945-1968* (GA 15), 203.
142. Cf. Lepp, *Tabu der Einheit?*, 115.
143. Letter of October 17, 1950, to Wolf-Dieter Zimmermann, cited in *Offene Briefe 1945-1968* (GA 15), 207-9.
144. Letter of October 17, 1950, to Wolf-Dieter Zimmermann, cited in *Offene Briefe 1945-1968* (GA 15), 212f.
145. "Volkstrauertag 1954," in Barth, *"Der Götze wackelt,"* 173f.
146. Cf. state secretary Walter Strauß (Christian Democrat Union), "Ein Mißklang beim Volkstrauertag," in *Union in Deutschland. Informations-Dienst der Christlich-Demokratischen und Christlich-Sozialen Union Deutschlands*, November 20, 1954, 2. Cf. the letter of November 18, 1954, from Gustav Heinemann and Barth's reply to Heinemann of November 19, 1954, KBA 9125.291 and 9254.233.
147. Letter to editor Johannes Rau of December 17, 1958, from Theodor Heuss, in *Politische Verantwortung* 3 (1959), Nr. 1.
148. Adenauer's press release of April 5, 1957, in *Dokumente zur Deutschlandpolitik*, Reihe III, vol. 3. January 1-December 31, 1957.
149. "Göttinger Manifest der Göttinger 18," in Lorenz, *Protest der Physiker*, 31-2.
150. Regarding this generally, cf. Klappert, *Der Aufstand gegen das Nichtige.*
151. "Rückblick auf das Jahr 1945," in *Schweizer Radio Zeitung* Nr. 2, 1946, 2.
152. Cf. "Rückblick auf das Jahr 1945," in *Schweizer Radio Zeitung* Nr. 2, 1946, 2.

153. Cf. editor's introduction to Barth, "An die Öffentlichkeit," *Offene Briefe 1945–1968* (GA 15), 390.
154. Cf. Albert Schweitzer, "Appell an die Menschheit," in Heipp, ed., *Es geht ums Leben!*, 49–56; the editor's introduction to Barth, "An die Öffentlichkeit," *Offene Briefe 1945–1968* (GA 15), 390.
155. Barth, "An die Öffentlichkeit," *Offene Briefe 1945–1968* (GA 15), 391f.
156. Barth, "An Radio Warschau," *Offene Briefe 1945–1968* (GA 15), 393.
157. Cf. Martin Greschat, "Barth und die Politik," in Beintker, ed., *Barth Handbuch*, 157.
158. Cf. "10 Thesen," in Möller, *Im Prozeß des Bekennens*, 393.
159. Cf. Greschat, "Barth und die Politik," in Beintker, ed., *Barth Handbuch*, 157.
160. Letter of July 28, 1958, to Christoph and Markus Barth and their wives, KBA 9258.146.
161. Cf. the texts in Möller, *Im Prozeß des Bekennens*, 393–7.
162. Cf. Klappert, *Der Aufstand gegen das Nichtige*, 376f.
163. Gustav Heinemann, "Wider die atomare Bewaffnung der Bundeswehr. Rede im Deutschen Bundestag, März 1958," in Heinemann, *Es gibt schwierige Vaterländer*, 304.
164. Cf. Barth, *Gespräche 1963* (GA 41), 70, n. 53. Letter of June 14, 1950, from the Swiss Protestant Church Federation with the announcement of Barth's election to the commission, KBA 9350.361.
165. Cf. the typescript of Barth's vote in the theological commission of the Swiss Church Federation, June 14, 1958, KBA 11266.
166. Cf. *CD* III/4, § 55, 461. Translation revised.
167. Cf. the typescript of Barth's vote in the theological commission of the Swiss Church Federation, June 14, 1958, KBA 11266: a nuclear war "cannot be conceived—not even if necessary such as the war to date!—as a measure of maintaining justice, peace, order (and thus in relation to God's love for humanity as revealed in J.C.)."
168. Cf. Barth, *Gespräche 1963* (GA 41), 70f., n. 53.
169. Cf. the editor's introduction to Barth, "An den Ausschuss gegen Schweizer Atombewaffnung/Heinrich Buchbinder, Zürich 1958," *Offene Briefe 1945–1968* (GA 15), 398. On April 1, 1962, the Confederation Peoples' Initiative "Verbot der Atomwaffen" was rejected.
170. Letter of October 12, 1958, to Christoph and Markus Barth and their wives, KBA 9258.196.
171. Cf. the 1962 flyer on banning nuclear weapons, KBA 6909.
172. "Atomwaffenverbot in die Verfassung? Ein Diskussionsbeitrag zur Volksabstimmung vom 1. April," *Zürcher Woche*, March 23, 1962, 3, KBA 860.
173. Cf. editor's introduction to Barth, "Offener Brief an den Europäischen Kongress gegen Atomrüstung, London 1959," *Offene Briefe 1945–1968* (GA 15), 456.
174. Letter of November 14, 1958, from Hajo Schedlich, cited in *Offene Briefe 1945–1968* (GA 15), 456.
175. Cf. Barth, "Offener Brief an den Europäischen Kongress gegen Atomrüstung, London 1959," *Offene Briefe 1945–1968* (GA 15), 458.
176. "Gottes fröhlicher Partisan," in *Der Spiegel*, Nr. 52/1959, 69.
177. Cf. Thomas Herwig, "Barth und die Ökumene," in Beintker, ed., *Barth Handbuch*, 144f.

178. Barth, "Die Kirche und die Kirchen," in *Theologische Fragen und Antworten, Gesammelte Vorträge*, vol. 3, 217.
179. Barth, "Die Kirche und die Kirchen," in *Theologische Fragen und Antworten*, 225.
180. Regarding Barth's role in the Amsterdam conference, cf. Herwig, *Karl Barth und die Ökumenische Bewegung*, 128–94.
181. Raiser, *Ernstfall des Glaubens*, 67.
182. Cf. Barth, "Die Unordnung der Welt und Gottes Heilsplan," 183.
183. Barth, "Die Unordnung der Welt und Gottes Heilsplan," 187.
184. Cf. Barth, "Die Unordnung der Welt und Gottes Heilsplan," 185.
185. "Unsere reformierten Kirchen und der Weltrat der Kirchen," in Barth et al., *Amsterdamer Fragen und Antworten*, 15.
186. Jean Daniélou, S. J., "Frage an Karl Barth," *Offene Briefe 1945–1968* (GA 15), 169f.
187. Letter of October 23, 1948, to Jean Daniélou, *Offene Briefe 1945–1968* (GA 15), 171f.
188. In his letter Barth cites a lecture given in Amsterdam by the Jesuit Charles Boyer who is said to have expressed himself in this manner; cf. *Offene Briefe 1945–1968* (GA 15), note on p. 175.
189. Letter of October 23, 1948, to Jean Daniélou, *Offene Briefe 1945–1968* (GA 15), 174.
190. Cf. Herwig, *Karl Barth und die Ökumenische Bewegung*, 168–71.
191. Cf. Herwig, *Karl Barth und die Ökumenische Bewegung*, 171.
192. "Unsere reformierten Kirchen," in Barth et al., *Amsterdamer Fragen und Antworten*, 14.
193. "Unsere reformierten Kirchen," in Barth et al., *Amsterdamer Fragen und Antworten*, 14.
194. On this, see pp. 364–365.
195. Biblical passages that Barth viewed as legitimizing the submission of women.
196. Letter of August 31, 1948, to Kirschbaum, cited in Herwig, *Karl Barth und die Ökumenische Bewegung*, 172, n. 188. Cf. Barth's exegesis of the different New Testament passages in *CD* III/2, 309–16, which focusses on super- and subordination In a 1932 exchange of letters about a woman taking a pastorate in Graubünden, however, Barth had taken a different viewpoint (cf. open letters to pastor D. Wilhelm Kolfhaus, *Offene Briefe 1909–1935* (GA 35), 235–53.
197. Letter assumed to be October 6, 1948, from Henriette Visser 't Hooft, in *Barth–Visser 't Hooft Briefwechsel* (GA 43), 374.
198. Letter assumed to be October 6, 1948, from Henriette Visser 't Hooft, in *Barth–Visser 't Hooft Briefwechsel* (GA 43), 379.
199. Cf. Busch, *Karl Barth: His Life*, 362.
200. Balthasar, *Karl Barth. Darstellung und Deutung*, 11.
201. Letter of December 30, 1948, to Christoph Barth, KBA 9248.345.
202. Cf. letter of November 13, 1950, from George Chichester, Henry P. Van Dusen and Willem Visser 't Hooft, *Barth–Visser 't Hooft Briefwechsel* (GA 43), 235.
203. Cf. Herwig, "Barth und die Ökumene," in Beintker, ed., *Barth Handbuch*, 146f.
204. Cf. letter of August 28, 1953, from Willem Visser 't Hooft, *Barth–Visser 't Hooft Briefwechsel 1930–1968* (GA 43), 275–6.
205. Letter of October 18, 1953, to Willem Visser 't Hooft, *Barth–Visser 't Hooft Briefwechsel 1930–1968* (GA 43), 278.
206. Cf. Küng, *Erkämpfte Freiheit*, 169.
207. Küng, *Erkämpfte Freiheit*, 170.

208. Küng, *Rechtfertigung*, 274.
209. "Joint Declaration on the Doctrine of Justification by the Lutheran World Federation and the Catholic Church": http://www. vatican.va/roman_curia/pontifical_councils/chrstuni/documents/rc_pc_chrstuni_doc_31101999_cath-luth-joint-declaration_en.html (accessed January 15, 2020).
210. Barth, "Ein Brief an den Verfasser," in Küng, *Rechtfertigung*, 13f.
211. The "Denzinger" is a collection of all the official doctrinal decisions of the Roman Catholic church (the ecclesiastical ministerium) from the third century AD until the twentieth century, edited by Heinrich Denzinger.
212. The post-Reformation council of Trent, 1545–63.
213. Barth, "Ein Brief an den Verfasser," in Küng, *Rechtfertigung*, 12.
214. Letter of September 15, 1949, from Karl Jaspers, in Jaspers, *Korrespondenzen*, 60.
215. Cf. Jaspers, *Der philosophische Glaube*, 174–9 and 485–8.
216. Letter of May 8, 1956, September from Karl Jaspers, in Jaspers, *Korrespondenzen*, 75.
217. Letter of May 8, 1956, September from Karl Jaspers, in Jaspers, *Korrespondenzen*, 75.
218. Letter of May 8, 1956, September from Karl Jaspers, in Jaspers, *Korrespondenzen*, 75.
219. Letter of February 21, 1953, to Karl Jaspers, KBA 9253.27.
220. Cf. letter of December 20, 1963, to Christoph and Marie Claire Barth, KBA 9263.236.
221. Smend, "Studium bei Karl Barth," in *Zwischen Mose und Karl Barth*, 312f.
222. Letter of June 25, 1949, to Christoph Barth, KBA 9249.138.
223. Smend, "Studium bei Karl Barth," in *Zwischen Mose und Karl Barth*, 318f.
224. Smend, "Studium bei Karl Barth," in *Zwischen Mose und Karl Barth*, 316.
225. Smend, "Studium bei Karl Barth," in *Zwischen Mose und Karl Barth*, 319.
226. Cf. Kurt Marti, *Der Heilige Geist ist keine Zimmerlinde*.
227. Marti, *Ein Topf voll Zeit*, 183.
228. Cf. Smend, "Studium bei Karl Barth," in *Zwischen Mose und Karl Barth*, 322f.
229. Smend, "Studium bei Karl Barth," in *Zwischen Mose und Karl Barth*, 330.
230. Jüngel, *Die Leidenschaft, Gott zu denken*, 23.
231. Barth, *Einführung in die evangelische Theologie*, 188, confirmed in Smend, *Studium bei Karl Barth*, 331.
232. Barth, *How I Changed My Mind*, 68.
233. Barth, *How I Changed My Mind*, 70.
234. Preface to the first edition, in Weber, *Karl Barths Kirchliche Dogmatik*, 5.
235. Cf. Martin Schwarz, "Bericht des evangelischen Strafanstaltspfarrers 1968," in *Karl Barth in der Strafanstalt*, private publication (1969), KBA R3T6B184, 5.
236. Cf. editor's foreword, Barth, *Predigten 1954–1967* (GA 12), viii.
237. Cf. Schwarz, "Bericht des evangelischen Strafanstaltspfarrers" (KBA R3T6B184), 5.
238. Barth, "Blicket auf zu ihm! Psalm 34,6," May 10, 1956 (Ascension), Strafanstalt Basel, *Predigten 1954–1967* (GA 12), 39–47.
239. Letter of May 18, 1956, to Karl Jaspers, in Jaspers, *Korrespondenzen*, 76.
240. Cf. editor's foreword, Barth, *Predigten 1954–1967* (GA 12), ix.
241. Barth, *How I Changed My Mind*, 68.
242. Cf. Schwarz, "Bericht des evangelischen Strafanstaltspfarrers" (KBA R3T6B184), 7.
243. Letter of July 19, 1957, to Martin Schwarz, KBA 9257.124.
244. Letter of July 19, 1957, to Martin Schwarz, KBA 9257.124.

245. Cf. Letter of July 19, 1957, to Martin Schwarz, KBA 9257.124.
246. Barth, "Grundsatzfragen der Gefangenenseelsorge," in *Karl Barth in der Strafanstalt* (KBA R3T6B184), 17.
247. Barth, "Blicket auf zu ihm!," *Predigten 1954–1967* (GA 12), 39–47.
248. Barth, "Blicket auf zu ihm!," *Predigten 1954–1967* (GA 12), 41.
249. Barth, "Grundsatzfragen der Gefangenenseelsorge," in *Karl Barth in der Strafanstalt* (KBA R3T6B184), 11f.
250. Barth, "Grundsatzfragen der Gefangenenseelsorge," in *Karl Barth in der Strafanstalt* (KBA R3T6B184), 16.
251. Letter of August 1, 1955, to Martin Schwarz, KBA 9255.139.
252. The belief that at the end all human beings will be with God and that no one will be separated from God for eternity, i.e., literally end up in hell. On this Barth had his own opinion. See p. 371.
253. Letter of August 1, 1955, to Martin Schwarz, KBA 9255.139.
254. Barth, "A Testimonial to Mozart," in *Wolfgang Amadeus Mozart*, 16.
255. Letter of June 25, 1949, to Christoph Barth, KBA 9249.138.
256. Barth, *How I Changed My Mind*, 72.
257. Barth, "A Testimonial to Mozart," in *Mozart*, 16.
258. Barth, "A Letter of Thanks to Mozart," in *Mozart*, 21.
259. Barth, "A Testimonial to Mozart," in *Mozart*, 16. Translation revised.
260. Barth, "A Letter of Thanks to Mozart," in *Mozart*, 22.
261. Barth, "A Letter of Thanks to Mozart," in *Mozart*, 22. Translation revised.
262. Barth, "Wolfgang Amadeus Mozart," in *Mozart*, 33.
263. Cf. Barth, "Mozart's Freedom," in *Mozart*, 55. (Originally a speech given on January 29, 1956, at a commemoration at the Musiksaal in Basel.) See also Barth, *How I Changed My Mind*, 71–72.
264. Letter of June 22, 1963, to Kurt Lüthi, *Briefe 1961–1968* (GA 6), 145.
265. Max Zellweger-Barth, "Erinnnerungen in Splitterform," in *Mein Schwiegervater*, 46.
266. Barth, "A Letter of Thanks to Mozart," in *Mozart*, 23.
267. Cf. the invitation of May 11, 1956, by the theological faculty to this ceremony, KBA 9356.811.
268. On him, cf. Irene Rehmann, Barth, Paul Basilius, in *Lexikon zur Kunst in der Schweiz*: http://www.sikart.ch/KuenstlerInnen.aspx?id=4000021 (accessed May 1, 2020).
269. Cf. Busch, *Karl Barth: His Life*, 416.
270. Letter of June 25, 1949, to Christoph Barth, KBA 9249.138.
271. Barth, *How I Changed My Mind*, 61. Translation revised.
272. Barth, *How I Changed My Mind*, 61–2.
273. "Protocol of the faculty meeting of 9 September 1955," cited in Kuhn, "McCarthy-Schwierigkeiten," 56.
274. Communication of the department for education to the cantonal council, March 26, 1956, cited in Kuhn, "McCarthy-Schwierigkeiten," 57.
275. Letter of July 28, 1958, to Markus and Christoph Barth and their wives, KBA 9258.146.
276. Cf. Barth, *How I Changed My Mind*, 61.
277. Letter of May 18, 1952, to Lukas Christ, KBA 9552.84. With respect to the marital side of his "family life" Barth still felt in 1952 like a "so-called badly war-wounded soldier."

278. Dieter Zellweger, "Ermutigung und Infragestellung. Berufs- und Lebenserfahrungen als Enkel Karl Barths. Festvortrag an der Diplomfeier der Theologischen Fakultät Basel," October 26, 2017, 1. Copy in the author's possession.
279. "Mitschrift von Barths quasi-Abschiedsrede am 4. Juli 1961," KBA 11288.
280. Cf. Kuhn, "McCarthy-Schwierigkeiten," 58.
281. Cf. Kuhn, "McCarthy-Schwierigkeiten," 62 and 67.
282. Cf. Kuhn, "McCarthy-Schwierigkeiten," 61.
283. *Badener Tagblatt* of June 7, 1961, cited in Kuhn, "McCarthy-Schwierigkeiten," 69, and other newspaper reports on pp. 69ff.
284. Cf. Kuhn, "McCarthy-Schwierigkeiten," 72 and 80.
285. Cf. Kuhn, "McCarthy-Schwierigkeiten," 76f.
286. Cf. Kuhn, "McCarthy-Schwierigkeiten," 84–8.
287. Cf. Kuhn, "McCarthy-Schwierigkeiten," 96.
288. Letter of July 31, 1962, to Gollwitzer, cited in Kuhn, "McCarthy-Schwierigkeiten," 99. The *Laudatio* given by the university vice president Edgar Salin at Barth's farewell at his final lecture on March 1, 1962, was considered for some time to be a "scandalous speech" that defamed Barth's political position; in the meantime however it has been described as a brilliant non-theological attempt to honor Barth. Cf. Edgar Salin, "Laudatio von Karl Barth," ed. by Niklaus Peter, in *Zeitschrift für Neuere Theologiegeschichte* 1 (1994), 305–12.
289. Barth, *Einführung in die evangelische Theologie*, 182.

13

"The White Whale"

Church Dogmatics

"A Conceptual Helix": Barth's Monumental Work

Karl Barth's *Church Dogmatics* (*CD*) is the most extensive theological work of the twentieth century. In twelve volumes and over 9,000 narrowly typeset pages Barth completely reconceptualized theology from its very foundations. The first volume (*CD* I/1) appeared in 1932 during his Bonn years, the final volume (*CD* IV/4) appeared in 1967 as a fragment. Barth once explained why he had to write so much: "I could not 'simply go along' with an accepted church doctrine and theological tradition; I had to think through and develop everything anew, from a center which I considered the right one—namely, the Old and New Testament witness to the person and work of Jesus Christ."[1] Barth saw his task as a theologian in the carrying out of this Christ-centered approach. When visitors to his study noticed the reproduction of the crucifixion scene from the Isenheim Altar above his desk, he enjoyed explaining to them that, just as in this scene John the Baptist pointed with his long index finger toward Jesus Christ as the center of Christian faith, this too is what the theologian should do.[2] At the end of his life Barth considered whether he could have rooted his *Dogmatics* even more strongly in a theology of the Holy Spirit.[3]

The enormous scope and the individual volumes bound in white canvas linen soon earned *Church Dogmatics* the nicknames "White Whale" and "Moby Dick." When Barth expressed amazement to Martin Niemöller that "despite the *small amount* of systematic theology that you have done you almost always get it right!" Niemöller responded: "Karl, I am amazed that despite the *copious amount* of systematic theology that you have done you almost always get it right!"[4]

Church Dogmatics is not an easy read. Paraphrasing a popular saying by Mark Twain, an American theologian once commented that a sentence from Barth was "like a dog that jumps into the Atlantic Ocean, swims all the way across to the other side, and climbs out at the end with a verb in its mouth!"[5] The initial impression is usually that Barth constantly repeats himself and in a wearisome manner always comes back to what he has already stated. A more correct description is that this is "a conceptual helix,"[6] for when Barth returns to a previous statement it is always to reach a further conceptual advance.

13.1. Karl Barth's study at the Bruderholzallee home in Basel, doorway to Charlotte von Kirschbaum's office in the background. Photo: Christiane Tietz.

Barth organized this work with thesis statements, as he did in his other dogmatic drafts *Unterricht in der christlichen Religion* and *Die christliche Dogmatik im Entwurf*. Following each thesis statement he explained his own considerations, alternating with extended passages in small print in which he dealt with the biblical texts and theological tradition. Because of this structure Barth was repeatedly accused of using the biblical texts solely to serve as the confirmation of his own position. There are many places however for which it can be shown that only through his exegesis of the biblical text did he arrive at a dogmatic position.[7]

Barth's *Church Dogmatics* was a new start after his 1927 *Die christliche Dogmatik im Entwurf*. In the foreword to the first volume he explained:

> My experience of twelve years ago in re-editing the *Epistle to the Romans* was repeated. I could still say what I had said. I wished to do so. But I could not do it in the same way. What option did I have but to begin again at the beginning, saying the same thing, but in a very different way?[8]

Barth already indicates a fundamental change in the title, for "Christian" dogmatics now became "Church" dogmatics.

In substituting the word Church for Christian in the title, I have tried to set a good example of restraint in using "Christian," since I have protested the light-hearted use of the great word. But materially I have also tried to show that from the very outset dogmatics is not a "free" science. It is bound to the sphere of the Church, where alone it is possible and meaningful as a science.[9]

This was precisely what Barth had explained in his 1931 book on Anselm of Canterbury, *Fides quaerens intellectum*: theology begins with the faith of the church.[10]

Therefore Barth emphatically stressed in 1932 that he had written this book "in and for the ... [community of] the Church."[11] At that time however there was within the church "a heretical non-theology which is to be resolutely denied"[12]—a reference to the theology of the "German Christians." He wanted to show in opposition to this how Protestant theology must be shaped methodically and conceptually; above all it had to start with Jesus Christ.

Barth planned his work in five major parts. Part I, "The Doctrine of the Word of God," contains the prolegomena in which he accounts for his theological methods and sources. Part II discusses "The Doctrine of God," Part III "The Doctrine of Creation," and Part IV "The Doctrine of Reconciliation." The final volume on the doctrine of reconciliation, *CD* IV/4, remained uncompleted.[13] A fifth part, "The Doctrine of Redemption," was intended in which the "last things" such as life after death and the Last Judgement were to be addressed, but Barth did not begin work on it.

The Threefold Form of the Word of God

In his famous 1922 text "The Word of God as the Task of Theology" Barth made it clear that ultimately only God could speak properly of God.[14] Barth adheres to this basic realization throughout *Church Dogmatics* and therefore begins the prolegomena by considering the nature of the *Word of God*. Here he distinguishes three "forms": the preached Word of God proclaimed in the sermon, the written Word of God in the Bible, and the revealed Word of God, that is, Jesus Christ.

The third, but actually fundamental form of the Word of God is Jesus Christ, as "the revealed Word of God." Jesus Christ is "directly ... God's own Word spoken by God Himself."[15] Through him God speaks to human beings. In his words and deeds, in his becoming human, the cross and resurrection, Jesus Christ shows that "[t]his 'God with us [Immanuel]' has happened. It has happened in human history and as a part of human history."[16]

Jesus Christ as the revealed Word of God is the foundation of all church speaking about God. But the church has no direct access to him, only through the biblical texts, "the written Word of God." The biblical texts bear *witness* to Jesus Christ; they give an account of him as the one in whom God's revelation has taken place.[17] "Holy Scripture is the word of men who yearned, waited and hoped for this Immanuel and who finally saw, heard and handled it in Jesus Christ."[18] The Old Testament for Barth expresses the expectation of this "Immanuel," that is, the expectation that God will completely be with human beings. The New Testament expresses the recollection of this "Immanuel," that is, the recollection that in Jesus Christ God was completely with human beings.[19]

Speaking of the *Scripture as the Word of God*[20] can lead to the problematic understanding that every single word of the biblical text was spoken directly by God and therefore is binding in a verbatim sense. In the history of theology there have been repeated attempts, for example to prove the infallibility of the biblical texts, in order to prove their divinity. Over against this Barth first warns that the Bible is a *human word* about the revelation of God in Jesus Christ: "The Bible is a witness of revelation which is really given and really applies and is really received by us just because it is a written word, and in fact a word written by men like ourselves, which we can read and hear and understand as such."[21] With this he clearly distances himself from a biblicistically verbatim reading of the Bible: "It *witnesses* to God's revelation, but that does not mean that God's revelation is now before us in any kind of divine revealedness. The Bible is not a book of oracles; it is not an instrument of direct impartation. It is genuine *witness*."[22]

That the Bible is nonetheless the *Word of God* is due to the particular thing to which it witnesses: the revelation of God. Because these texts, in expectation and recollection, ultimately are directed toward Jesus Christ, they are absolutely essential for the church.[23] Therefore: "We believe in and with the Church that Holy Scripture *has* this priority over all other writings and authorities, even those of the Church. We believe in and with the Church that Holy Scripture as the original and legitimate witness of divine revelation *is* itself the Word of God."[24]

Barth has a very particular understanding of this "has" and "is." It could be said that he constructs it elliptically. The priority of the Bible cannot be established generally. And it cannot be proven through textual analysis that this is the Word of God. It is much more the case that "the 'has' and 'is' speak about a divine disposing, action and decision, to which when we make these statements we have on the one hand to *look back* at something which has already taken place, and on the other to *look forward* at something which is to come."[25] Again and again, the church has had the experience that God made these texts to the Word of God, in that through them human beings began to believe. And the church lives from the hope that God will do this again. The "has" and "is" are therefore a "had" and "will have," and a "was" and "will be." The fact that the Bible *is* the Word of God and *has* primacy over all other human texts is only given in the respective situation through God's acting. With this, Barth makes it clear that the indicative statement "the Bible is the Word of God" can never be understood as if God had "said" certain verses exactly so. The "has" and the "is" are the "*divine* present."[26]

For the church, the Bible has a fundamentally orienting function, in that the church's proclamation takes place as *interpretation* of the biblical text. In its proclamation the church is not sharing its opinion about certain facts, but rather its task is the proclamation of the Word of God which the church is faced with in Jesus Christ and the Bible that witnesses to him.[27] Analogous to his argument about the Bible as Word of God, Barth contends that the proclamation can also become the Word of God. This however does not rest in the power of the preacher, but is equally God's doing: It is "God's own act, when human talk about God is for us *not just* that, *but also and primarily and decisively* God's own speech."[28] Then in the sermon we truly hear God speaking to us. According to Barth, that which holds true for the structure of expectation and recollection in the biblical texts applies to the church as well: It can venture its proclamation "in recollection of past revelation and in expectation of coming revelation."[29] Through God's free decision, the Bible and the proclamation, both human words, can "again and again" become God's Word.[30] Only Jesus Christ is always the Word of God.

God's Three Modes of Being

For Barth's understanding of God it is of vital importance that the Christian God is a Trinitarian God, that is, that the one God exists in three persons or, as Barth preferred to say, in three "modes of being" (*Seinsweisen*).[31] In his view this conception was not esoteric speculation, but the expression of God's self-revelation in Jesus Christ, with which Christian theology starts. The doctrine of the Trinity is nothing other than "a *necessary* and *relevant* analysis of revelation."[32]

Therefore Barth places his thinking about the divine Trinity already in the first part of *Church Dogmatics*, in his reflections about the nature of God's self-revelation. In this order he deviates notably from other positionings of the doctrine of the Trinity. Often one begins with a general doctrine of God, that is, describing that there is *one* God and how God is precisely to be conceived, and only in a second step explains that the Christian God exists in three persons.[33] Barth does not make such a division into two parts, because he wants to derive everything that he states about God exclusively from God's self-revelation.

According to Barth the doctrine of the Trinity discusses three questions: (1) Who is acting in revelation, that is, who is its subject? (2) Through what does revelation happen, that is, what does its subject do? And finally: (3) How does the effect of revelation work and how does it affect the one to whom it befalls?

Barth's answer states: (1) *God* is the subject, the cause of revelation; God is the "Revealer."[34] This is expressed in that Christians believe in God the Father. (2) *God* is also the one in whom this revelation takes place. God does not reveal himself in a stone or in some historical event, but in Jesus Christ, in whom God is present. This is expressed in that Christians believe in "God the Son," who is the "revelation."[35] And (3) *God* brings it about, that the human being recognizes the revelation and answers it with faith and obedience. This is expressed in that Christians believe in God the Holy Spirit who is working within the human heart when we encounter the revelation; the Holy Spirit is "being revealed."[36] In sum in Barth's eyes the doctrine of the Trinity, by speaking of God as Father, Son, and Holy Spirit, is the conceptual expression of the self-revelation of God.

Barth counters the charge that Christian theology thereby advocates a doctrine of three gods by specifically warning: there is not a different God in each of these three modes of being, but rather the same God, each time differently: as Father God reveals Himself as creator; as Son God reveals Himself as reconciler; as Holy Spirit God reveals Himself as redeemer. In each case however God is totally Himself.[37]

This conviction is fundamental for Barth's further theological reflection, because it means that in God's revelation to human beings God reveals Himself as the God he really is. Whereas in the theological tradition there had been a separation made between a "God as such" and a "God for us," the assumption being that God does not reveal all of God, so that besides the revealed God there was also a "hidden God," for Barth God's revelation was "the repetition of God" and God was "His own doppelgänger in His revelation."[38]

God's turn to the world in creation, reconciliation, and redemption is therefore "something *new* in God"[39] but not anything strange to God, since God in Himself exists in relationships: in the loving relationships between Father, Son, and Holy Spirit. God can

13.2. Karl Barth with Charlotte von Kirschbaum at his desk in 1955, © Karl Barth-Archive in Basel.

be *our* God, He can meet us and unite Himself to us, because creation, reconciliation and redemption, the whole being, speech and action in which He wills to be our God, have their basis and prototype in His own essence, in His own being as God. As Father, Son and Spirit God is, so to speak, ours in advance [i.e., before revelation].[40]

"God Is" Means "God Loves"

For Barth his doctrine of the Trinity yielded a central conceptual description for God: God is the one who loves in freedom. God is free because God has no need of anything else besides God, and as Trinitarian God, God is essentially determined through love internally. As the free one God is already a "relationally rich" being.[41] Therefore God does not need human beings to be able to exist in fellowship.

But God wants fellowship with human beings, God wants to be together with human beings. God *determines Himself* to love an other.[42] God is the one "who, without having to do so, seeks and creates *fellowship* between Himself and us. He does not have to do it, because in Himself without us, and therefore without this, He has that which He seeks and creates between Himself and us."[43] In that God turns toward human beings God goes beyond God, but in a way that corresponds to God's most intimate essence.

Through this Barth makes a fundamental concept of Reformed theology fruitful: the concept of a covenant between God and humanity, which God has created and to which the human beings should agree: God

> wills *to be ours*, and He wills *that we should be His*. He wills to belong to us and He wills that we should belong to Him. He does not will to be without us, and He does not will that we should be without Him . . . He does not will to be *Himself* in any other way than He is in this *relationship*.[44]

God's relationship to humanity also includes God's wrath, judgement, and punishment. These however are integrated in the one will of God toward fellowship with human beings.[45] Precisely this is expressed in the concept of *love*: "That He is God—the Godhead of God—consists in the fact that He loves, and it is the expression of His loving that He seeks and creates fellowship with us."[46]

The special nature of this love God has for human beings is first, that God is not using human beings for another purpose; God wants fellowship with human beings "*for their own sake.*"[47] Secondly, God's love is unconditional; human beings do not have to bring anything to be worthy of this love:

> God's loving is concerned with a seeking and creation of fellowship *without any reference* to an existing *aptitude* or *worthiness* on the part of the loved. God's love

is not merely not conditioned by any reciprocity of love. It is also not conditioned by any worthiness to be loved on the part of the loved ... The love of God always throws a bridge over an abyss.[48]

Briefly stated, God's love is grace.

This love is God's nature. "'God is' means 'God loves.'"[49] From this standpoint Barth completely transforms a central teaching of Reformed theology, the doctrine of so-called double predestination.

Whom God Elects

Since the early church father Augustine, the reverse of a strong doctrine of grace was always a strong doctrine of predestination. A strong doctrine of grace means that the relationship between God and humanity, the salvation of humankind, depends solely on God's graceful turning to humankind and *not* on what human beings bring themselves. Augustine and in turn the Reformers deduced from this that even human will cannot contribute anything to human salvation. They concluded that whether a person can believe in God was not a question of human will. On the question of why a person believes, the advocates of a strong doctrine of grace responded: because God has predestined some people. Those who were predestined would enter heaven, the others would enter hell. God's election depends solely on God's free will which needs no reason. The concern of this doctrine was originally liberating: since human beings cannot do anything for their election, they do not need to ask themselves anxiously what they could do for this, or whether they have done enough.

Martin Luther developed this doctrine by using a so-called simple predestination. As sinners, all human beings basically deserve to go to hell, but God chooses some to be able to believe in the gospel of Jesus Christ. The rest are left to the fate they have earned.

The Reformed tradition intensified this doctrine. John Calvin in his late writings assumed that God has determined salvation for the one person and damnation for the other. From this perspective one speaks of a "double predestination." It is "God's eternal decree."[50] Human beings cannot know why God has determined damnation for some and salvation for others. According to Calvin the "sweet fruit" of this doctrine is certainty (everything rests on God's will, not on my desire or achievement), humility, and gratitude.[51] For Calvin Christ is above all the one who realizes this eternal twofold decision of God, for Christ causes that those whom God has elected are in reality granted salvation.[52]

As a Reformed theologian Karl Barth assumes double predestination, but he completely reconceptualizes it. He does not want to subordinate the role of Jesus Christ to election and damnation, but rather the reverse, conceptualizing predestination directly *from Christ*. The doctrine of predestination does not hold for Barth, as for Calvin, a twofold will of God.[53] Its goal is not, as tradition states, the division of human beings into two groups.[54] The doctrine of predestination is much more the "sum of the Gospel."[55]

From this standpoint Barth prefers to speak of God's "election of grace" rather than of predestination. This initially and primarily consists in "the fact that God elects in His grace, that He moves towards man, in his dealings within this covenant with the one man Jesus, and the people represented by Him."[56] It therefore means that God in Jesus Christ "elects to be man and to have dealings with man and to join Himself to man."[57]

In other words: *Before* the creation of the world and of human beings God has already elected that "in His Son He would be gracious towards man, uniting Himself with him."[58] "Election" does not mean "arbitrariness," but is a description of the free willing of God. It is grace that God so wishes. God did not have to do this, but wished to do so.[59] Election is grace precisely because of this, not because there are people who have not been elected.[60]

The special Christological conception that Barth now expounds on is that Jesus Christ is the electing God and the elected human being. The first part of that statement is saying that it is not an unknown, incomprehensible God who elects, but rather God as revealed in Jesus Christ. As God, Jesus Christ elects to become human, to give himself for humanity.[61] With this election, which God makes for the benefit of humanity, God does not remain distant and untouched by the world, but instead puts God's honor at stake, surrendering "God's own impassibility from...the world of evil."[62] In Jesus Christ God becomes *completely* involved in this world. The second part of the statement is saying that as a human being, Jesus Christ is elected to live with God in covenant.[63] This election of God is therefore carried out on this concrete human being, in his life and death.

For Barth too God's election in Jesus Christ is a *double* one—there is election and rejection—but very differently than in the Reformed tradition. In Jesus Christ God elects namely *for himself* rejection. This takes place in Jesus's betrayal through Judas, in the judgement of Pilate, in Jesus's cross and death. God elects for himself the rejection that humanity would have earned because it wished to live without God. And because God elects rejection for himself, all other human beings are freed from rejection.[64] Jesus Christ is thereby the *only one rejected*. Simultaneously he is the *first elected* to fellowship with God. The human being Jesus is elected so that in him the covenant of God with humanity can be fulfilled. And in his election all human beings are included.[65]

Jesus's task as this elected human being was now from his part to elect God.[66] Jesus did this in his life by living it in faith and obedience. In him God's covenant with humanity is joined not only from God's side, but also from the human side. "God elects man [that is Jesus Christ]. On man's side this election becomes actual in *man's own electing of God*..."[67]

Barth's doctrine of election is deliberately constructed asymmetrically: Jesus Christ is the only rejected one, no one besides him is rejected. Jesus Christ is the first elected one, and in him all are elected. No human being can escape this election of grace: the human being

> cannot reverse or change the eternal decision of God...He can certainly hate God and be hateful to God (he does and is so); but he cannot change into its opposite the eternal love of God which triumphs even in his hate...He may let go of God, but God does not let go of him.[68]

Barth was repeatedly asked whether with this he was not teaching a universal reconciliation, that is, that he was claiming that ultimately all human beings are saved. Such teaching had been frequently condemned as heresy in the church, because it would not correspond to the statements in the New Testament and because of the fear this could undermine the efforts of human beings for their salvation and for living a good, responsible life before God. Barth reacted by generally dismissing abstract statements about the circle of those who will be saved. One could not claim "if we are to respect the *freedom* of divine grace" that truly all people at the end of time would say yes to God, but "in grateful recognition of the *grace* of the divine freedom" one also could not say "that there cannot and will not be this final opening up and enlargement of the circle of election and calling." Both statements were "formal conclusions without any actual substance."[69] Therefore Barth argued that we could not be certain that no one would be lost, but only hope for this.[70] "God does not owe eternal patience and therefore deliverance...In this matter there is nothing, nothing at all to postulate even by appealing to the cross and resurrection of Jesus Christ!" At the same time there was also "no good reason why we should not be open to this possibility..."[71] Barth once pointedly answered the question as to whether he taught universal reconciliation: "I do not teach it, but I also do not not teach it."[72]

What God Commands

Since the end of the eighteenth century there has been a distinction in Protestant theology between a "doctrine of faith" and "moral doctrine," that is, between what Christians must believe and what they must do. Since the nineteenth century this has been expressed by the distinction between "dogmatics" and "ethics."[73] Barth rejected such a separation. In his ethical thought he starts from the basic perspective that he had already described in his lecture "Evangelium und Gesetz" ("Gospel and Law") that "out of what God...does *for* us" we must read "what God *wants* with us and *from* us."[74] God's actions as creator, reconciler, and redeemer have immediate consequences for the actions of human beings, for the aim of God's grace "is that our being and action should be conformed to His."[75]

From this, Barth sees in Jesus's behavior the criteria for how every human being should act. In Jesus's election of God he has behaved toward God's election according to God's will. God's command is already fulfilled in him. The duty of all human beings is now to shape their own lives accordingly. God's command demands of human beings "that they *live* according to their having *been* elected."[76]

Because God's election includes all human beings, Barth's approach to Christian ethics is addressed to all people, not only Christians. For Barth there is no "human action which is free, i.e., exempted from decision in relation to God's command, or neutral in regard to it."[77] This is why ethics for Barth is part of dogmatics. Parts II, III, and IV of *Church Dogmatics* end with extensive chapters on ethics in which Barth explores God's commandment in general, the commandment of the creator and that of the reconciler.

Why God Wants the Creation

In wrestling with the theology of his era Barth consistently and sharply rejected all forms of "natural theology." By this term he meant every theological approach (including that of the pro-Nazi "German Christians") that attempted to make statements about God by starting with the world, that is, by contemplating the creation or by using human reason. Barth saw this as a contradiction to a theology grounded in God's revelation in Jesus Christ—a judgement that does not meet the self-understanding of many representatives of natural theology. Barth himself sought a strict orientation toward Jesus Christ.

Therefore Barth did not begin in his doctrine of creation by deriving from the existence and qualities of the world that God is its creator and the world is God's creation. Even the doctrine of creation must consistently be conceived from the standpoint of God's self-revelation in Jesus Christ.[78] The Father of Jesus Christ is the creator of this world.[79] This means in particular that God's intention for the world can only be discerned through how we understand God in Jesus Christ. Only through Christ are we able to recognize that God created the world out of free love.[80]

In his doctrine of creation Barth was not seeking a debate with modern natural science, nor was he attempting, as is today often done in the arguments for intelligent design, to work God into the causal chain that led to the genesis of the world, irrespective of all the knowledge of natural science. According to Barth the perspective of natural science and that of theology were dealing with two different issues.[81] It was not the natural scientific causal chain that was of theological interest, but rather God's intention in the creation of the world.

Why however does God *want* the creation? God

wills and posits the creature neither out of caprice nor necessity, but because He has loved it from eternity, because He wills to demonstrate His love for it, and because He wills, not to limit His glory by its existence and being, but to reveal and manifest it in His own co-existence with it.

Creation, more specifically, is "the presupposition for the realisation of the divine purpose of love in relation to the creature."[82] Barth holds the action and fulfillment of this love of God under the concept of "covenant." The idea is very simple: For a covenant between God and creature to be possible, creature must exist.

The creation for Barth is the "*external basis* of this covenant":[83] "It can be said that it makes it technically possible; that it prepares and establishes the sphere in which the institution and history of the covenant take place; that it makes possible the subject which is to be God's partner in this history."[84] God's covenant with humanity was therefore not established only after the creation or even after the fall, but rather God's will for a covenant is the beginning of everything. The purpose and reason for creation are recognized not in and of creation, but only from God's covenant with humanity. The covenant therefore is "the *inner basis* of creation."[85] This also means that creature was already created under the perspective of God's covenant with humanity: "There is no existence of the creature in which it can originally belong elsewhere than to this compact."[86]

As God's covenant partner, the human being according to Barth is a relational creature. Just as God internally exists in relations, and then relates in loving freedom to humanity, human beings too exist in relationships: "The relationship between the summoning I in God's being and the summoned divine Thou is reflected both in the relationship of God to the man whom He has created, and also in the relationship between the I and the Thou...in human existence itself." For Barth this relationality is realized especially in the correlation of man and woman.[87]

God says "Yes" to creation as the reality that God has willed as different from God. With that God at the same time says "No" to everything "which...by His own nature God cannot will and create, and cannot even tolerate as a reality distinct from Himself."[88] Barth calls this "nothingness."

Nothingness and the Shadow Sides of Creation

"Nothingness" is Barth's response to the question of evil in the world that has preoccupied theology as well as philosophy since their beginnings.[89] In the theological tradition, the discussion usually addresses how it can be that evil exists in God's good creation. Where does it come from, and what is God's relationship to it? Is God responsible for the evil, particularly the suffering, in the world? Martin Luther believed that God works "all in all" and is therefore also at work in evil.[90] This was illustrated especially by the fact that *not* all human beings are elected by God.[91]

Here too Barth follows his own path. Evil in his view is that which stands in "opposition and resistance against God's world-dominion"[92] and therefore can be traced only very indirectly back to God's work. It cannot be traced back to God's willing but to God's non-willing. Because God has disclosed himself *entirely* in Jesus Christ, there are things in this world that cannot in any way be traced back to God's working, since they are indeed in contradiction to God's self-revelation. They exist only because God says No to them.[93] For because God is holy, God separates himself in God's doing and being from those things that stand in opposition to God's nature, that is, from the nothingness as that which God does not will.[94]

This is what gives nothingness its particular mode of being: nothingness "exists, because and as and as long as God is *against* it. It is only because of God's opposition to it...only in the boundary that has been set with that." Nothingness is

> the world which He did not choose or will, which He could not and did not create, but which, as He created the actual world, He passed over and set aside, marking and excluding it as the eternal past, the eternal yesterday. And this is *evil* in the Christian sense, namely, what is alien and adverse to grace, and therefore without it.[95]

Barth distinguishes between this nothingness and the "shadow sides" of creation such as failure, grief, loss, age, and death, all of which belong to the good, finite creation of God, as difficult as they may be to bear. Creation simply includes "the limitations and boundaries of life, not only growth but decline, not only wealth but poverty, not only sweetness but murkiness." These shadow sides are in "certain ways *close*" to nothingness, but in contrast to nothingness Barth believes that we can also praise God in the face of these shadow sides. There is "also a praise of God from the abyss, the night."[96] Barth sees the reason for this again in Jesus Christ. For if God has comprehended the shadow side as part of "creation in its totality and made it His own in His Son, it is for us to acquiesce without thinking that we know better, without complaints, reproach or dismay."[97] It would however be dangerous to see nothingness only as a shadow side. This could lead for example to seeing sin, which for Barth was a form of nothingness, only as something harmless, something that was simply part of the world.[98]

For Barth, Jesus Christ is the evidence that this nothingness, which God does not wish at all, truly exists in the world. Nothingness is that which in Jesus Christ "challenged *Him* and provoked His wrath...what made *Him* yield to nothingness in order to overcome it."[99] God has not only negated nothingness as that which God does not want, but has exposed himself to it in Jesus Christ, in order to destroy it.[100]

He did it by *suffering* death, *this* death, the death of condemnation... He did so in order to take away the power of death, real death, death as the condemnation and destruction of the creature, death as the offender against God and the last enemy. In His resurrection from the dead God reveals that He has done this. His resurrection sums up the whole process of revelation.[101]

Barth concludes from this that the "*controversy* with nothingness, its conquest, removal and abolition, are primarily and properly *God's own* affair."[102] For God nothingness has already been overcome because God negated it for all time when creating the world, but for creation this does not hold true. This is why God in Jesus Christ entered the "confrontation with nothingness," the "threat of temptation,"[103] "the...deepest condescension."[104] God must not do so, God could simply have let the creation run its course. But God wanted to care for God's creature, thereby descending into these depths.[105] Barth develops this further in his doctrine of reconciliation.

The Threefold Office of Christ and the Three Forms of Sin

In the exposition of his Christology in *Church Dogmatics* Barth orients himself to Calvin's doctrine of the threefold office of Christ, in which Calvin explains in connection to conceptions in the Old and New Testaments that Jesus Christ is priest, king, and prophet.[106] Barth constructs a twofold movement of Jesus Christ, the first more emphasizing his divinity and "divine Sonship," the second his humanity and "human sonship." The path of the son of God leads from above to below "into the far country," and the path of the son of man from below to above, as "homecoming" to God.

From this Christological concept Barth derives his understanding about what human sin concretely consists in.[107] Whereas traditionally most have first described human sin in order to introduce Jesus Christ as the one who overcomes sin, for Barth Jesus Christ is the basis for understanding the essence of sin. Behind this is Barth's conviction that human beings *cannot* know about their sinfulness and malice from within themselves.[108] "Access to the knowledge that he is a sinner is lacking to man *because* he is a sinner."[109] Human beings can be aware of the problematic of their existence or some tensions and imperfections of their lives. But these are not sins.[110] Our human measures for good and evil are not those of God.[111] Humans recognize sin only at the point where it has been condemned and overcome: in the death and resurrection of Jesus Christ.[112]

The path of God's son "into the far country" is his obedience; it consists of God's becoming human and in this that Jesus Christ surrendered himself to nothingness. "Without ceasing to be true God,...God *went into the far country* by becoming man in His second person or mode of being as the Son—the far country not only of human creatureliness but also of human corruption and perdition."[113] This path culminated in the cross, where God took upon himself the judgement that we would have earned. Jesus Christ is "the judge judged in our place."[114] The *priestly office* of Christ is in this humiliation of his divinity.

The sin, which contradicts this act of God and is uncovered by it, is the human pride by which human beings seek to be their own lord, judge, and helper.[115] This sin is overcome by the justification of human beings without our own acting and through our faith as the recognition of God's acting.[116]

The counter-movement to this path into the far country is the human being's homecoming to God. This consists in the exaltation of the son of man and is the *kingly office* of Jesus Christ. Jesus of Nazareth is the "royal human," the prototype of how we human beings should and could live: "Jesus Christ... is the new and true and royal man who participates in the being and life and lordship and act of God and honours and attests Him."[117] This exaltation takes place in the incarnation, which as Barth conceives of it is that here the human being of Jesus is taken up in the divine being.[118] It is apparent in Jesus's resurrection and ascension:[119] "this one Son of Man—*returned home* to where He belonged, to His place as true man, to fellowship with God, to relationship with His fellows, to the ordering of His inward and outward existence, to the fullness of His time for which He was made, to the presence and enjoyment of the salvation for which He was destined."[120] Every human being is included in this exaltation.

But human beings contradict this movement through the sin of sloth. As the "counter-movement to the elevation" this sin is that "of evil inaction... of the tardiness and failure."[121] This sin is overcome through the sanctification by which God renews the human and makes the human God's covenantal partner.[122] Reconciliation in Jesus Christ then means generally: "It was God who went into the far country, and it is man who returns home."[123]

The reality of reconciliation in Jesus Christ is ultimately recognized in Jesus Christ himself. Therefore the third office of Christ is his *prophetic office*, for the prophet speaks the truth of God. Christ carries out this office at the right hand of God in that he is the light of the world, that is, he allows humankind to recognize this truth. Jesus Christ is "his own witness."[124]

But human beings contradict this through the sin of lying by which human beings evade this witness.[125] This sin is overcome by the call to human beings to become Christians and on their part witness to Jesus Christ.[126] Barth's famous and surprising doctrine of lights belongs in the context of this third office of Christ.

The Light Shines Where It Wishes

In the penultimate volume (IV/3) of *Church Dogmatics* Barth argues that the light of Christ, the expression of his prophetic office, can also be encountered *outside* the church. Already in the first volume of his work Barth considered the possibility—despite all the focus on Jesus Christ, the Bible, and church proclamation—that God can also speak differently to human beings: "God may speak to us through Russian Communism, a flute concerto, a blossoming shrub, or a dead dog."[127] But he insisted that these other ways through which God speaks cannot become the basis for Christian proclamation.[128] This remains the case for Barth at the end of *Church Dogmatics*, but he now clarifies how we should think of God's way of speaking outside the church and how theology and church can learn from this.

For Barth, Jesus Christ is "the *one* and *only* light of life... there is no other light of life outside or alongside His, outside or alongside the light which He is."[129] As "the one Word of God" he is witnessed to directly in the words of the prophets and the apostles. But this does not mean "that in the Bible, the Church and the world there are not *other* words which are quite notable in their way, other lights which are quite clear and other revelations which are quite real."[130] While it is always Jesus Christ whose light shines through them, "why should not the world have its varied prophets and apostles in different degrees?"[131] Not all revelations outside the Bible and church must a priori be considered false, and outside of what is Christian there are—as Barth now acknowledges—words of the highest wisdom. Christ's lordship encompasses more than the realm of the church. "De iure *all* men and *all* creation derive from His cross, from the reconciliation accomplished in Him."[132] This is why "parables of the kingdom" can also be found elsewhere.[133] But such words encountered outside of the church are only true when they do not stand in competition with the Christian message, that is, when they do not say something other than Jesus Christ. They are only lights, then, when they "do not destroy it [the *one* light] with lies."[134]

The Baptism of Water and of the Spirit

In *Church Dogmatics* IV/4, which Barth published only as a fragment, he concludes with reflections on baptism as "the foundation of the Christian life."[135] They were "a confirmation and strengthening of my opposition to the custom, or abuse, of infant baptism"[136] and therefore a critique of the practice of most Christian churches. Already in 1943 Barth in *Die kirchliche Lehre von der Taufe* ("The Teaching of the Church Regarding Baptism") had spoken out against infant baptism, since the passivity of the infant contradicted the fact that the one to be baptized should be a free partner of Jesus Christ.[137] At that time however baptism for Barth was a sacrament in the Reformed sense, as a symbolic function that portrayed God's act of salvation.[138]

Now, Barth located baptism entirely on the side of human beings. Unlike Calvin, who stressed the work of the divine spirit in the baptism, Barth now joined Zwingli in seeing baptism as the work only of the human person. Therefore Barth like Zwingli drew a strict distinction between the baptism by water and that by the spirit. The baptism of spirit was a divine act that took place when human beings, by the action of the Holy Spirit, recognize that God's acting in Jesus Christ also applies to us, and that we were already included into this event.[139] In contrast, the church ritual of baptism by water is a human act and for that reason belongs to ethics. It is the free act of a human obedient response to the divine act of baptism through the spirit. Baptism of water is "the work and word of men who have become obedient to Jesus Christ and who have put their hope in Him."[140] It marks the beginning of a life that lets itself be determined by God's reconciling act in Jesus Christ.

In baptism it is not the parents of the person to be baptized who are the actors, rather, the one to be baptized is acting. If baptism is truly to be a person's own action, that person must herself be ready and willing. She must herself say Yes to what has become clear to her through the baptism of spirit.[141] When a person allows himself to be baptized, this is "the first step of this life of faithfulness to God, the Christian life" and "the binding confession of his obedience, conversion and hope, made in prayer for God's grace."[142] An infant cannot make such a decision. Children cannot yet independently believe and be obedient to God's will.[143] Therefore they also cannot let themselves be baptized as the expression of their belief and obedience.

Zwingli too viewed the concept of sacrament critically, but held to it. Barth now recognized only one single sacrament: Jesus Christ. Only Christ is "the instrument of grace."[144]

Notes

1. Barth, *How I Changed My Mind*, 59–60. Translation revised.
2. Cf. Küng's memoir, *Erkämpfte Freiheit*, 179.
3. Cf. the reference to this in Barth, "Concluding Unscientific Postscript," *Theology of Schleiermacher*, 278f.
4. Reported by Barth in "Barmen. Martin Niemöller zum 60. Geburtstag am 14. Januar 1952," in Rohkrämer, ed., *Texte zur Barmer Theologischen Erklärung*, 159.
5. From Hunsinger, *How to Read Karl Barth*, 27.
6. Smend, "Studium bei Karl Barth," 317.
7. Regarding this cf. Bergner, *Um der Sache willen*.
8. CD I/1, Preface, xi. Translation revised.
9. CD I/1, Preface, xii–xiii. Translation revised.
10. See p. 204.
11. CD I/1, Preface, xv.
12. CD I/1, Preface, xv.
13. Regarding the end of the project, see p. 399.

14. See p. 134.
15. *CD* I/1, §4, 113.
16. *CD* I/1, §4, 116.
17. Cf. *CD* I/1, §4, 111.
18. *CD* I/1, §4, 108.
19. Cf. *CD* I/1, §4, 116.
20. Regarding this, cf. Tietz, "Das Ringen um das Schriftprinzip."
21. *CD* I/2, §19, 463–4.
22. *CD* I/2, §19, 507. Italics for "witnesses" by the author.
23. Because the biblical texts are oriented in expectation and recollection of Jesus Christ, for the Church the Bible is the "canon," that means literally: the plumb line. "... the Bible constitutes itself the Canon. It is the Canon because it imposed itself upon the Church as such, and continually does so... If we thought we could say why this is so, we should again be acting as if we had in our hands a measure by which we could measure the Bible and on this basis assign it its distinctive position." *CD* I/1, §4, 107.
24. *CD* I/2, §19, 502.
25. *CD* I/2, §19, 502. Author's italics.
26. *CD* I/2, §19, 503.
27. Cf. *CD* I/1, §4, 89ff.
28. *CD* I/1, §4, 93.
29. *CD* I/1, §4, 99.
30. *CD* I/1, §4, 117.
31. Cf. Tietz, "Systematisch-theologische Perspektiven zur Trinitätslehre," 168ff.
32. *CD* I/1, §8, 310.
33. The classical approach is Thomas Aquinas's conception, beginning first with "De Deo uno" ("Treatise on the One God," *Summa Theologica*, first part, questions 2–26) and only afterward the Trinity "De Deo trino" ("Treatise on the Most Holy Trinity," first part, questions 27–43).
34. *CD* I/1, §8, 299.
35. *CD* I/1, §8, 299.
36. Cf. *CD* I/1, §8, 299 and 361. Barth distinguishes *Offenbartheit* (literally "revealedness") and *Offenbarsein* (literally "being revealed"; *CD* translates "revealedness" in 299, but "being revealed" in 361). While *Offenbartheit* would refer to something which "is there" like a thing and thus available for humans (something which Barth of course rejects), *Offenbarsein* emphasizes that God's revelation in Jesus Christ needs an individual event of clarification for each human through the Holy Spirit.
37. Cf. *CD* I/1, §9, 559f.
38. *CD* I/1, §8, 299 and 316 (translation revised). On the idea of the hidden God, cf. ch. 4, note 92.
39. *CD* I/1, §9, 316. Author's italics.
40. *CD* I/1, §9, 383.
41. Regarding this cf. Jüngel, *Gottes Sein ist im Werden*.
42. *CD* II/1, §28, 279f.
43. *CD* II/1, §28, 273.
44. *CD* II/1, §28, 274.

45. Cf. *CD* II/1, §28, 274f.
46. *CD* II/1, §28, 275.
47. *CD* II/1, §28, 276.
48. *CD* II/1, §28, 278.
49. *CD* II/1, §28, 283.
50. Calvin, *Unterricht in der christlichen Religion*, III, 21, 5, 513.
51. Cf. Calvin, *Unterricht in der christlichen Religion*, III, 21, 1, 510.
52. Cf. Calvin, *Unterricht in der christlichen Religion*, III, 21, 7, 515. Cf. also II, 12, 1f., 246f., and III, 24, 5, 538f.
53. Cf. *CD* II/2, §33, 161f. and 171f.
54. Cf. *CD* II/2, §32, 41.
55. *CD* II/2, §32, 3.
56. *CD* II/2, §32, 14.
57. *CD* II/2, §33, 94f.
58. *CD* II/2, §33, 101.
59. Cf. *CD* II/2, §32, 22f.
60. Cf. *CD* II/2, §33, 102.
61. Cf. *CD* II/2, §33, 105f.
62. *CD* II/2, §33, 163.
63. Cf. *CD* II/2, §33, 103f.
64. Cf. *CD* II/2, §33, 164–8.
65. Cf. *CD* II/2, §33, 115f. and §35, 353.
66. Cf. *CD* II/2, §33, 179f.
67. *CD* II/2, §33, 180.
68. *CD* II/2, §35, 317.
69. *CD* II/2, §35, 417f.
70. Cf. *CD* IV/3, §70, 478.
71. *CD* IV/3, §70, 477f.
72. Cited in Jüngel, *Barth–Studien*, 51 (Barth never wrote this down).
73. Regarding this, cf. Martin Honecker, *Einführung in die Theologische Ethik*, 25.
74. Barth, "Evangelium und Gesetz," in *Rechtfertigung und Recht*, 87.
75. *CD* II/2, §36, 512.
76. Jüngel, "Evangelium und Gesetz," in Jüngel, *Barth–Studien*, 202.
77. *CD* II/2, §36, 535.
78. Cf. *CD* III/1, §40, 3f.
79. Cf. *CD* III/1, §40, 11.
80. Cf. *CD* III/1, §40, 28.
81. Cf. *CD* III/1, Preface, x.
82. *CD* III/1, §41, 95f.
83. *CD* III/1, §41, 96. Author's italics.
84. *CD* III/1, §41, 97.
85. *CD* III/1, §41, 97. Author's italics.
86. *CD* III/1, §41, 96.
87. *CD* III/1, §41, 196.
88. *CD* III/1, §42, 330f.

89. Regarding this, cf. Wüthrich, *Gott und das Nichtige*.
90. Cf. Luther, *De servo arbitrio/The Bondage of the Will* (1525), in Luther's Works 33:3–295, 87.
91. Cf. Tietz, "The Crucial Question of Theodicy."
92. *CD* III/3, §50, 289.
93. Cf. *CD* III/3, §50, 352.
94. Cf. *CD* III/3, §5, 350.
95. *CD* III/3, §50, 353.
96. *CD* III/3, §50, 296f. Translation revised.
97. *CD* III/3, §50, 297.
98. Cf. *CD* III/3, §50, 300f.
99. *CD* III/3, §50, 304.
100. Cf. *CD* III/3, §50, 311.
101. *CD* III/3, §50, 312.
102. *CD* III/3, §50, 354.
103. *CD* III/3, §50, 357. Translation revised.
104. *CD* III/3, §50, 358.
105. Cf. *CD* III/3, §50, 357.
106. Cf. Calvin, *Unterricht in der christlichen Religion*, II, 15, 1–6, 263–8.
107. Regarding this, cf. Wolf Krötke, "Sünde und Nichtiges," in Beintker, ed., *Barth Handbuch*, 345f.
108. Cf. *CD* IV/1, §60, 359.
109. *CD* IV/1, §60, 360f.
110. Cf. *CD* IV/1, §60, 360.
111. Cf. *CD* IV/1, §60, 365f.
112. Cf. *CD* IV/1, §60, 390f.
113. *CD* IV/2, §64, 20.
114. *CD* IV/1, §59,2, 211.
115. Cf. *CD* IV/1, §60, 358.
116. Cf. *CD* IV/1, §61, 514.
117. *CD* IV/2, §64, 3.
118. Cf. *CD* IV/2, §64, 41f.
119. Cf. *CD* IV/2, §64, 118.
120. *CD* IV/2, §64, 20f.
121. *CD* IV/2, §65, 403.
122. Cf. *CD* IV/2, §66, 499.
123. *CD* IV/2, §64, 21. Translation revised.
124. Weber, *Karl Barths Kirchliche Dogmatik*, 285.
125. Cf. *CD* IV/3, §70, 434f.
126. Cf. *CD* IV/3, §71, 520f. and 575.
127. *CD* I/1, §3, 55.
128. Cf. *CD* I/1, §3, 55f.
129. *CD* IV/3, §69, 86.
130. *CD* IV/3, §69, 97.
131. *CD* IV/3, §69, 97.

132. *CD* IV/3, §69, 116f.
133. *CD* IV/3, §69, 114.
134. *CD* IV/3, §69, 100. Translation revised. These lights, which are beyond the light of Jesus Christ, are "irruptions...of the one light and expressions...of the one truth" (152).
135. *CD* IV/4, 2.
136. CD IV/4, Preface, x. Cf. Tietz, "Sakramente."
137. Cf. Barth, *Die kirchliche Lehre von der Taufe*, 40.
138. Cf. Jüngel, "Karl Barths Lehre von der Taufe," in *Barth–Studien*, 249.
139. Cf. *CD* IV/4, 27f.
140. *CD* IV/4, 102.
141. Cf. *CD* IV/4, 42.
142. *CD* IV/4, 2.
143. Cf. *CD* IV/4, 187.
144. *CD* IV/4, 102.

14

"All Things Considered, a Little Tired"

The Final Years, Basel, 1962–8

"Fantastic": A Calvinist in the United States

After the unpleasant events at the University of Basel surrounding the rejection of Helmut Gollwitzer as Barth's desired successor, Karl Barth was "very happy to be able to leave Switzerland behind me for a few weeks."[1] From April 7 to May 26, 1962, around six months before the Cuban missile crisis, Barth traveled to the U.S. with his son Christoph and Charlotte von Kirschbaum.[2] In the U.S., they were accompanied by his son Markus, who held a professorship in Chicago and whom Barth had asked in advance to stay with him if possible for the entire time—also to prevent him from speaking too unguardedly to American journalists.[3] A delicate situation might otherwise arise, since through his critical statements about the West in his battle against anti-Communism Barth had acquired "a reputation for anti-Americanism."[4]

American public interest in the Swiss theologian was enormous. On April 23 *Newsweek* magazine reported about Barth's first visit to the United States: "He never visited this country... Last week, after years of staying put while Americans came to the mountain, the mountain at last paid a visit to America."[5]

On April 20, 1962, Barth appeared on the cover of *Time Magazine*; inside there was a multi-page report about him. Barth's portrayal on the title page was admittedly somewhat curious. There is an open tomb, the stone door of the tomb is rolled aside, and a crown of thorns lies on the ground. Barth stands before the grave looking sternly at the reader. Barth himself appears to have been uneasy about this portrait. In a letter to his son-in-law Max Zellweger he tried to mollify it with an explanation that Kirschbaum thought up: The empty grave "could even in a pinch portray the entrance to a wine cellar."[6] This corresponded to a photo in the article itself that shows Barth laughing heartedly over a beer in a Chicago nightclub; beneath the photo is the comment: "A Calvinist—but not a gloomy one."[7]

For the first three weeks Barth visited Chicago and his son Markus's family. He had numerous conversations and gave a press conference in which he was immediately asked about his view of East-West relations. Barth was clear: "In no way have I more sympathy for the East... I think the best use we can make of

14.1. *Time Magazine* cover of April 20, 1962, https://time.com/

the freedom, or liberty, which we have in the West is to see our own faults."[8] These included the plight of African-Americans in the slums of Chicago.[9]

At the University of Chicago Divinity School Barth held lectures from his *Evangelical Theology: An Introduction* and accepted another honorary doctorate. On two evenings there were ecumenical panel discussions, each attended by over 2,000 listeners.[10] The *New York Times* commented on the huge resonance he found: "To hear him and to see him in the flesh...is to ecclesiastics what a personal appearance of Sir Winston Churchill would be in the House of Representatives."[11] The church historian Jaroslav Pelikan, who moderated the discussion, welcomed Barth with the words: "We are what we are, theologically, because of him."[12] Barth's discussants on the panel were six younger theologians of different confessions and faiths, including Rabbi Jakob Josef Petuchowski, the Baptist Hans W. Frei, who had done a dissertation on Barth under H. Richard Niebuhr at Yale, and Schubert M. Ogden, who taught at Southern Methodist University. Barth's concluding remarks in Chicago invited those attending to a "theology of freedom," which if he were an American theologian he would attempt to draw up, with a "freedom from...any inferiority complex over against good old Europe," as well as "freedom from a superiority complex...over against Asia and Africa." American freedom needed to be a "freedom...for humanity." Barth added:

> Being an American theologian, I would then look at the Statue of Liberty in the New York Harbor...That lady needs a little or perhaps a good bit of demythologization. Nevertheless, maybe she may also be seen and interpreted and understood as a symbol of a true theology, not of liberty, but of freedom.[13]

In Chicago Barth also met the famous evangelical preacher Billy Graham,[14] whom he had already gotten to know in Switzerland in August 1960 and had found sympathetic until he experienced Graham at one of his evangelizations.[15] Barth was outraged by Graham's preaching style:

> That was not the Good News, that was pistol-shooting. An urgent appeal was made to the people: You must, you should!...It was a proclamation of the Law...He wanted to scare people. To threaten always makes an impression. People would always much rather be frightened than be made joyful.[16]

Asked again about Graham at a press conference in the U.S., Barth expressed himself similarly: "Christian faith begins with joy and not with fear. Mr. Graham begins by making people afraid."[17]

Barth and his companions journeyed from Chicago to Princeton, where as part of the 150th anniversary of the Reformed seminary he delivered another lecture on *Evangelical Theology: An Introduction*. Here too there was a podium discussion.[18] Barth was amused when he was given a baseball jersey and made an honorary member of the seminary baseball team.[19] He also had a brief meeting with Martin Luther King Jr., whom he heard preach.[20] But the meeting came to nothing more than a photo of the two together in front of the University Church.[21]

In Washington Barth had a conversation with members of President John F. Kennedy's inner circle.[22] After a short trip to Richmond, Virginia, he traveled on to San Francisco, where Barth lectured again. Finally he visited Union Theological Seminary in New York City, walked through East Harlem and spoke with members of the Black civil rights movement. In New York Barth also met with prison officials and was impressed by their desire to reform prison conditions.[23] He expressed his displeasure about prison conditions in another press conference: the narrow "cages" that each prisoner had to share with another were the "sight of Dante's Inferno on Earth."[24] Barth calculated that a flight to the moon and back, with one week's stay, would cost as much as a prison that could imprison twice the entire American population: "Why not spend a fraction of the moonshot's cost on humane prisons?" Barth viewed the living conditions of the prisoners as a "contradiction to the wonderful message on your Statue of Liberty."[25]

During his trip Barth met with many significant U.S. theologians who had been inspired by him, but famous American minds also viewed Barth critically. Reinhold Niebuhr is said to have stated that Barth's theology was "designed for the church of the catacombs" and "irrelevant...to America."[26] Paul Tillich, who had emigrated from Germany to the United States in 1933, praised Barth's greatness to "correct...himself again and again in the light of the 'situation' and that he strenuously tries not to become his own follower." He appreciated Barth's approach from the concept of revelation, but insisted that theology also had to come from the questions of contemporary people and offer them an answer. Barth's approach, which decidedly rejected this, was ultimately "neo-orthodox." In Barth's thought "the message must be thrown at those in the situation—thrown like a stone."[27]

In addition to the many church and academic appointments Barth found time for his personal historical interests. The group visited Gettysburg and other significant battle sites from the Civil War. Barth was excited that he could finally view these sites since he had "long before experienced these events and figures... from afar, through literature."[28] *Der Spiegel* reported:

> Karl Barth, 76, Protestant pope from Basel...grabbed a hundred-year old musket during his tour of a Civil War battlefield near Richmond (Virginia), loaded the gun on his own with the help of a ramrod, and fired at a white handkerchief that his companion had attached to a post thirty meters away. The theology professor was delighted that he had hit the mark: "Like William Tell!"[29]

In general Barth thoroughly enjoyed the trip. He could summarize his impressions

> essentially only with the word "fantastic"...yes, "fantastic": the small endlessness of the winding rivers, plateaus, hills and mountains between the two oceans, which we criss-crossed hurriedly by plane or car—the deserts of Arizona, the Grand Canyon, which for good reason I decided not to descend, the San

14.2. Karl Barth at the Gettysburg battlefield, 1962, © Karl Barth-Archive in Basel.

Francisco Bay and the Golden Gate Bridge—Chicago and New York with their skyscrapers, with their constant glittering movement of countless cars filling the incoming and outgoing streets, with their hubbub of people from all lands, races, occupations and goals... the thorough organization and standardization of all life (including church life, including theological scholarship!) which to some extent competes with divine providence, the American reporter's pertinent and sometimes a little impertinent desire to know and the way they portray things...! "Fantastic" too were the thousands who came together in Chicago and Princeton for my lectures and public discussions and the amount of "publicity"... with which I suddenly saw myself surrounded and was unaccustomed to.[30]

He liked the Americans personally, telling his son-in-law Max Zellweger, "the people... all have something free, open, lively, and so I'm happy to overlook or allow for the occasional kitsch."[31]

"Rules for Older People in Relation to Younger"

Only after his return from the United States did Barth begin to adjust to his life as a retired person, which was not easy for him. Barth had gone to the university almost daily, and he now missed the daily contact with students. He decided to continue to offer a German-speaking society for advanced students as well as colloquia in English and French. A large number of students gratefully accepted the offer. He also met with a smaller circle of doctoral students.[32]

Barth held his final colloquium in the summer semester of 1968. It was dedicated once more to Friedrich Schleiermacher. "I have fought my whole life long against his Romantic theology," he wrote a friend, "and at the end want to try to bring it to light for the young people of today."[33] Barth remained connected to Schleiermacher "with the old love/hate and the even older hate/love," and up to his life's end was "not finished with him."[34]

Generally in the early years after his retirement the number of talks and interviews increased. Right into his final weeks, Barth continued to follow political events with lively interest.[35]

He also attentively followed the paths taken by his children, grandchildren, and great-grandchildren; in 1962 his first great-grandchild had been born.[36] He was delighted when he received detailed letters about how they were doing from the U.S. and Indonesia, where Christoph Barth lived with his family. He encouraged his son Markus that he would certainly soon receive an appointment from the east coast in the U.S. If Markus continued to write his books, "eventually the 'son of the world famous...,' which is surely unbearable for you, will finally disappear."[37]

Barth pondered for himself the correct way to behave toward the younger generation. In 1964 he wrote himself[38] seven "Rules for Older People in Relation to Younger," in which he intended to step back and be grateful for everything coming from younger people:

1) You should make it clear to yourself, that the younger, whether relatives or close in other ways... have a right to go their own ways according to their own (and not your) principles, ideas, and desires, to gain their own experiences, and to find happiness in their own (and not your) fashion. 2) Do not force upon them, then, your own example or wisdom or inclinations or favors... 4) Do not be surprised or annoyed or upset if you necessarily find that they have no time, or little time, for you, that no matter how well-intentioned you may be toward them, or sure of your cause, you sometimes inconvenience and bore them, and they casually ignore you and your counsel.... 7) Never in any circumstances give them up, but even as you let them go their own way, go with them in a relaxed and cheerful manner, while trusting in God and being confident of the best in them, and always loving and praying for them.[39]

After his retirement Barth also attentively kept up with new theological publications, but he viewed very few of the newer developments positively, regarding them primarily as continuations of Tillich, Bultmann, and Bonhoeffer's prison letters.[40] Frequently he commented cantankerously in his letters about many of the new theologians.⁴¹ After the 1965 death of Paul Tillich, who had been four months older than Barth, Barth described himself and Bultmann as "the last somewhat decayed pillars of an older generational era."⁴² Theologically he felt lonely. "At one time I started my new journey by sailing against the wind, and this is just how I also want to continue and to end it, resolutely, but in gratitude and thereby peacefully."⁴³

There were also moments when he held milder views of the contemporary theological situation and acknowledged a few young colleagues. In a 1964 Advent letter he wrote: "I now constantly seek the child of peace and promise, who may improve theology more than I was permitted to. Hopefully I will be alert and humble enough, when he appears in my range of vision, to recognize him as such."⁴⁴

Even outside the theological guild Barth himself achieved wide recognition, for his way of doing theology as "speaking about God," as is illustrated by the major awards he received after his retirement. In April 1963 in Copenhagen he received the Danish Sonning Prize, which was given for significant contributions to "the spread of European culture"; previous recipients had included Winston Churchill and Albert Schweitzer.⁴⁵ In his acceptance speech Barth noted with pleasure that bestowing the prize on a theologian expressed "that a proper European culture not only included proper natural science, art, and politics, but also a proper theology: and perhaps not as the least of these." In his speech Barth also recalled the most famous city son, the philosopher and theologian Søren Kierkegaard, who had been an incorruptible critic of church and society of his time. If Kierkegaard now met him, he would presumably say:

> So, my dear, this is how far you've come at the end of your theological and ordinary existence—this is how far you, the fearless witness to truth, have gotten after your stormy debut in "Epistle to the Romans"...—so far that you've been... given an impressive prize. Didn't I always think: as a small genius perhaps you will be famous, although by my standards there would still be some things to comment on. But an apostle? To my knowledge the real apostles were not given any prize, but rather... well, you know what I mean!⁴⁶

On November 7, 1963, Barth was the first Protestant theologian to receive an honorary doctorate from the Sorbonne in Paris, nominated by the Faculty of Humanities. The *Laudatio* for Barth stated:

> The philosophers recommend a theologian although he does not wish to be a philosopher. In previous centuries the Sorbonne outlawed Reformed theologians. When today it gives one of them a distinction, it is because of the high qualities that this theologian possesses as a thinker and creator of a comprehensive scholarly work.⁴⁷

Finally, at the beginning of 1968 Barth was bestowed the accolade of being elected as one of fifty members of the French Academy of Moral and Political

Sciences that had been founded in 1795 in the spirit of Montesquieu.[48] A few months later he received a letter from the German Academy for Language and Literature that he was the recipient of the Sigmund-Freud Prize, established in 1964, for his "contribution to scholarly prose." Hannah Arendt had received it the previous year.[49] Barth reacted to the general secretary, Ernst Johann, with some amusement:

> Have I really made a "contribution to scholarly prose"? It is from your academy that I have first heard this stated so solemnly, which is an honor for me. So far, when the public has paid attention to me, it has as a rule spoken more about what I said than the way I said it. If my prose is really meritorious and even worthy of a prize according to the judgement of your academy, then in all the decades of my writing there must have been resolutely at work (apart from my conscious concern to write respectably) what Sigmund Freud would have called my unconscious or subconscious.[50]

Secretly however he was very pleased that he, who had thought so little about the *language* of theology, and "not Ebeling, not Fuchs,"[51] in general not any hermeneutics scholar or cybernetics scholar with their talk of "the language event" had been honored with this prize.[52]

"As If Deeply Veiled": Charlotte von Kirschbaum Must Move Out

Already in June 1963 Barth was feeling "all things considered, a little tired and short of breath."[53] In light of the high honors he had received that year, he feared that "my renown in this aeon will grow proportional to the diminishing of my able-bodiedness or my need to sleep and sleep again."[54] In February 1964 he thought "in light of the length and depth of my daily sleeping I could be counted among the Olympic champions for this kind of sport."[55]

He did not intend to take on any more major essays. The things that he still wrote tended to be shorter occasional papers. He described to his son Christoph in June 1963: "Now and then I write something short... With regard to the larger works e.g. [CD] IV/4 and the Eschatology [CD V] I will no longer get to them *rebus sic stantibus* [as things stand] without a special *afflatus Spiritus* [breath of the spirit]." He complained, "People have not yet read the entirety of the volumes already written. Why then are they calling for the next installments?"[56]

At the end of November 1963 Barth wrote his son Markus, who had repeatedly asked him to continue his work on *Church Dogmatics*, and told him what he also told others:

> a) that the fulfillment of your request would demand a physical/psychological/pneumatic dynamism that I no longer possess; b) that the *Summae*[57] and

cathedrals of the medieval age also remained unfinished; c) that I have already written and published more than any other living theologian, and have they already read and worked through what is there? d) that the moment may have arrived in which the younger generation... should first and foremost step up.[58]

Barth experienced his diminishing ability to work along with the smaller physical afflictions as "rather embarrassing. On the other hand this is how it must be, and I try as best I can to refrain from complaining and grumbling."[59] Even now Charlotte von Kirschbaum found the right words: she "reminds me time after time that I am really not a contemptible little wallflower and therefore have no cause for that. I'm sure that she is right."[60] For a while he exhorted himself daily with a verse by Paul Gerhardt: "God has often given me delight in good days—should I now not also endure something?"[61]

Barth had enjoyed good health his entire life but starting in 1964 experienced a steady decline. "Brother body" now gave him more trouble.[62] In the final four years of his life he had to spend a total of nine and a half months in the hospital.[63] Shortly before Christmas in 1964 (after having had prostate problems in August 1964) he suffered a minor stroke that caused him to lose his ability to speak for several hours.[64] For some time after that Barth could not regain his strength. In March 1965 he wrote wearily to his friend Helmut Gollwitzer that he was sitting

> passably cheerful—grateful for all the decades when I was doing better and could do things—but still dejected and horrified by the ocean of paper that breaks in here daily, well aware that there is much that is important among it, still requested and spurred on by naïve people for some kind of great or small mighty deed, [which I] can unfortunately only still do to the smallest extent, and instead much prefer talking by the window with the crows, blackbirds and sparrows, to whom God in the middle of the snow—partly with my assistance—gives food in due season.[65]

In 1965 Barth spent four months in the hospital because of prostate problems; afterward he permanently had to wear a catheter, requiring ambulant care by medical personnel.[66]

An even heavier burden on Barth's daily life however was that since the early 1960s Charlotte von Kirschbaum had begun to show signs of dementia.[67] At the beginning this was most noticeable through "small signs of forgetfulness."[68] In the fall of 1965 a good solution for dealing with the daily post and other duties emerged when Eberhard Busch became Barth's personal assistant and remained so until his death.[69] In early 1966 Kirschbaum had to move into the Sonnenhalde psychiatric clinic in Riehen near Basel.[70] Until his death Barth visited her every Sunday.[71] Almost half a year after her move Barth reported calmly and comforted to his son Markus, that "dear Lollo... [is] subjectively perhaps satisfied at her

14.3. Karl Barth and Charlotte von Kirschbaum, 1967, © Karl Barth-Archive in Basel.

place...[is] happy to hear this and that...and talks [about things] herself, in a somewhat puzzling way." "With a gentle hand" she had "wiped away...[her] memories of the decades-long discord with Mama...Thus some things with time do indeed sort themselves out..."[72] Finally in 1968 Charlotte seemed to him to be "as if deeply veiled."[73] During one visit she said to him: "'Everything is so hard and so beautiful and so much more interesting!' And when she said goodbye: 'We are well off, are we not?!'"[74] Charlotte von Kirschbaum died on July 24, 1975, almost seven years after Karl Barth, and was buried in the Barth family gravesite at the Hörnli cemetery in Basel.[75]

Kirschbaum's move out of the home eased the relationship between Karl and Nelly Barth, who in the meantime was already seventy-two years old. Nelly was interested in Karl's classes, attending for example his colloquium on the Second Vatican Council.[76] Some people have reported that with advancing age the three had already come more to terms with their difficult interrelationship than previously, and that a certain peace had arrived.[77] Other visitors to the home on Bruderholzallee reported that the mood in the household remained as tense as before, as long as Charlotte von Kirschbaum was still living there. Up until she moved out, Barth's letters to third persons usually mentioned only *her* name, and seldom that of Nelly. Barth himself reported in December 1964 to his son Christoph "that in our little home it is now substantially more peaceful than before; the different weaknesses of age and character are borne more patiently."[78] Barth dedicated the final volume of *Church Dogmatics*, Volume IV/4, to "My wife Nelly Barth in deep gratitude," and in his final birthday circular letter he wrote happily that with her, "like a perfect example of Philemon and Baucis, I now celebrate a most harmonious evening of life."[79]

14.4. Karl Barth with Nelly Barth, 1966, © Karl Barth-Archive in Basel.

On May 10, 1966, Karl Barth turned eighty. He received around 1,000 letters and 150 telegrams from friends and acquaintances from throughout the world.[80] At a celebratory event on May 9, 1966, he was given a large Festschrift[81] and the University of Bonn made him an honorary senator.[82] In his thank-you speech Barth protested against being called the "greatest theologian" of the twentieth century. It might well be the case that "perhaps there is a little man or woman who has been holding Bible studies somewhere very quietly... who has been in reality the greatest theologian of this century."[83] At the end he pulled out his personal copy of the second edition of the *Epistle to the Romans* and showed those who were present the dedication with which he had given himself the book back then: "Karl Barth, to his dear Karl Barth, 1922." To keep himself from vanity and arrogance he had added a quote from Luther, written in:

> If you however feel and let yourself think that you... with your own little books, teachings, or writings... have done so exquisitely and preached splendidly... and if you also very much like it when someone praises you to another, and want to be praised... then grab yourself by the ears, and if you are grabbing correctly you will find a lovely pair of big, long, rough donkey ears... adorn them then with golden bells so that wherever you go, people can hear you and point toward you and say: Look, look, there goes that fine animal that can write such exquisite books and... preach splendidly.[84]

Barth then concluded his birthday speech with gratitude that "it [appears] to have pleased God that in our time he used me for his purposes, just as I was, and despite all the fatal things that can and will be said about me."[85]

"Separated Brothers": In Conversation with Rome

From the beginning of the 1960s Barth attentively followed the changes that were taking place in the Roman Catholic Church. He was impressed by Pope John XXIII, who invited the world church in 1962 to Rome for a great council on reform, the Second Vatican Council. After the Pope's death in 1963 Barth wrote his son Christoph that John XXIII had "indeed given the papacy de facto an abundance... in light of which, whatever can be said against this institution, it can no longer simply be said as unbowed as before. He was a good man."[86]

In 1963 Barth was invited by Augustin Cardinal Bea, the chair of the Secretariat for Promoting Christian Unity that had been newly established in 1960 by John XXIII, to attend the second session of the Council from September 29 to December 4, 1963, as an observer.[87] When Hans Küng conveyed the invitation to him by telephone on September 19, 1963, Barth felt honored, for this showed him "that in Bea's secretariat the fear of me as a wild man seems to have been

14.5. Karl Barth with Hans Küng, 1966, © Karl Barth-Archive in Basel.

overcome."[88] But he had to cancel, partly because of concerns about overextending himself physically and partly because the preparatory time was too short in light of his other commitments. His calendar for that period was already filled.[89] From Basel however Barth took careful note of the Council texts and was pleased about the developments there.[90] Barth was well informed about the course of the Second Vatican Council, which lasted until 1965, through Hans Küng, who attended as an advisor, and his Basel colleague, the New Testament scholar Oscar Cullmann, who attended as a Protestant observer.[91]

A half year after the conclusion of the Council Barth felt well enough to inquire of Cardinal Bea whether he could not "at least come post festum to Rome after all," in order to "learn what are the thoughts of the Vatican and its immediate environs, the central precincts of the Roman Catholic church and its theology, as it looks *back* on the finished Council and looks *ahead* from it." He would not be coming in any official church or academic capacity, but on his own responsibility, as a person concerned about the unity of faith and the church that was sought and already existing. Barth wanted to come to Rome "not to speak...but as much as possible to listen, to receive, to understand, to *learn*."[92] Cardinal Bea responded to Barth's inquiry with pleasure and arranged various meetings for Barth's trip.[93] Barth prepared by drawing up a catalog of substantive and critical questions about various Council texts, which he considered bringing up while in Rome.[94]

From September 22 to 29, 1966, Barth traveled with his wife and his family doctor to Rome.[95] He was familiar with Rome from earlier trips and enjoyed the contact that was now possible with the Curia.[96] He met with Jesuits and Dominicans, and had conversations with Cardinal Bea and the Waldensians.[97] By his own account he remained very circumspect with critical questions; he had "really not come there for arguments."[98] In addition he briefly visited the International Congress of Theology, where he was honored with applause and an address, and even—although at a distance—placed on the same level as the cardinals who were present.[99] In conclusion he met with Karl Rahner, S.J., and Joseph Ratzinger.[100]

The successor to John XXIII, Pope Paul VI, who had continued the Council, received Barth and his companions for an hour-long private audience. After Barth had walked through the long rows of rooms, the Pope received him before his study "literally in the doorway, with open arms."[101] They discussed among other things how the formulation *"fratres sejuncti,"* "separated brothers," had been intended in the Council texts to be applied to churches that were not in unity with the Catholic Church. In addition Barth broached the position of Maria, the mother of Jesus, in the church. He was impressed by the Pope's personality and his humility, which was also evident in that in Council texts he did not name himself "Pontifex maximus" or "representative of Christ," but simply "Bishop, servant of the servants of God."[102] Barth particularly commended the fact that Paul VI had been so clearly engaged for peace during the Vietnam War.[103]

At the end the Pope gave Barth the Council medal and a facsimile of the Vatican Codex, one of the most important Greek manuscripts of the Bible. Barth gave the Pope four of his books.[104] In the dedication he boldly wrote in Latin: "In shared service to the one Lord this book is dedicated to Bishop Paul VI, the most humble servant of God, by the separated brother Karl Barth."[105]

Afterward Barth, a Protestant Christian, summarized his Rome journey:

> I have gotten to know a church and theology up close that has entered into a movement whose effects are unforeseeable, a movement that is slow but certainly genuine and no longer reversible, in light of this one could only wish that on our side there would be something similar.

In Rome he had "encountered so many Christian people with whom I could speak in genuine seriousness but could also heartily laugh, that I cannot think of certain garden dwarfs in our preserve without some wistfulness." Barth did not allow himself a naïve hope in ecumenism but thought it appropriate to have a "quietly brotherly hope, connected to the willingness to sweep thoroughly in large and small matters before our own doors." In contrast to Luther's harsh judgement Barth established: "The Pope is not the Antichrist!"[106]

One year later Barth sent warm congratulations to Paul VI on his 70th birthday and expressed concern about his health.[107] The Pope thanked him with a personally signed letter and assured him of how he enjoyed thinking back to Barth's visit: "In you we encountered a scholar who courageously seeks the truth and for whom the concept of brotherly fellowship in Christ signifies a genuine concern."[108]

Several months before his death Barth reacted with a personal letter to the Pope after the appearance of the 1968 papal encyclical *Humanae vitae* about marriage, sexuality, and contraception. Here Paul VI stipulated that all sexual intercourse in marriage "must remain open to the transmission of life" and therefore that all artificial forms of regulating birth as well as abortion were forbidden for Catholic Christians.[109] Barth did not address questions of content, but expressed his criticism that the Pope had based the church's position by appealing to natural law, which Barth could not reconcile with the Constitution on Divine Revelation of the Second Vatican Council.[110]

A Late Friendship with Carl Zuckmayer

During the year before his death Barth sought out a correspondence with the Catholic writer Carl Zuckmayer. "Someone has given me a copy of your book *Als wär's ein Stück von mir* ('A Part of Myself, Portrait of an Epoch')," Barth wrote, "and I read it at one sitting." Barth thanked Zuckmayer for the humanity that he had encountered in this account of Zuckmayer's life. Assuming that Zuckmayer had "perhaps just...heard my name occasionally and then forgotten it," Barth briefly presented his own life's journey and continued that he had written

> many stout and slim volumes of practical, historical, and above all—do not be alarmed!—dogmatic theology. I now live in quiet but busy retirement. I value the presence of loving women, good wine, and a constantly burning pipe...I say all this so as to tell you something about who is writing and who it is that takes such pleasure in thinking about you.[111]

This letter almost got lost in the piles of post that Zuckmayer had received after his autobiography appeared, since it had been sorted by an assistant in the stack of "other letters from unknown people to be answered in a circular letter."[112] But then Zuckmayer, who had lived since 1957 in Saas-Fee, sent a friendly reply:

> It would be a scandal for a writer like myself not to know and respect you. For a long time your work and activity and position have been of particular significance to me...I am one of those for whom God is *not* dead and Christianity, when properly experienced and lived, is still the message of salvation. And you are one of those, of the few, who in our day will not allow Christians to pension

themselves off and live on the legacy of those who have gone before... For my generation, which has had to experience the way in which both confessions gave their blessing to weapons on both sides in two world wars, it was by no means easy to maintain faith. You have been a help to both of us, to both Roman Catholics and Evangelicals.[113]

Therefore he wished Barth: "May your glowing pipe not go out for a long time!"[114]

In the months that followed the two carried on an intensive correspondence and sent each other their publications. During his final vacation in Valais in July 1967 Barth visited Zuckmayer and his wife for one day in Saas-Fee,[115] writing him afterward: "Rarely have I found a personal meeting so delightful as the unexpected one that I had with you."[116] Afterward Barth wrote down what so impressed him in Zuckmayer's writings; it was something that was important to him in his own theology: "the never-failing compassion with which it is constantly given you to view human darkness, corruption, and misery. Mephistopheles is absent."[117] Zuckmayer was convinced that the evil in the world could only be overcome through goodness and empathy: "I believe that the expression of goodness is a stronger weapon in the fight against evil than its depiction, which is not only not totally renounced but is even undertaken with a certain pleasure, and indeed a self-indulgence, by many authors."[118]

Both also shared a similar sense of humor. Barth delighted Zuckmayer with an anecdote about the cellist Pablo Casals, of whom it was said that even at the age of ninety he still practiced four to five hours a day. Asked why he was doing this, Casals supposedly replied: "Because I have the impression that I am making progress."[119] In May 1968 Zuckmayer traveled to Basel for the premiere of his play *The Devil's General* only "because you (and the Zoo) are to be found in Basel."[120] After Barth's death Zuckmayer said that the best thing about the many discussions between them had been "that notwithstanding a deep, basic agreement, there were always things about which we differed."[121] But even more, he was moved by Barth's nature: "Never has any person in our day, with the possible exception of Albert Einstein, so convinced me by his mere existence that faith in God is rational."[122]

In his final years Barth reconciled with his Zurich colleague Emil Brunner, against whom he had thrown his unflinching *Nein!* in 1934. After Pastor Peter Vogelsanger informed Barth on April 2, 1966, about the precarious state of Brunner's health,[123] Barth responded right away and asked Vogelsanger—if it were still possible—to let Brunner know: "the time when I thought I should say No to him is long since past, and we all live only by the fact that a great and merciful God speaks his gracious Yes to all of us."[124] Vogelsanger immediately went to see Brunner and read Barth's letter to him. He remembered: "A fine, infinitely lovely and reconciled smile passed over his face, and he quietly pressed my hand."[125]

Shortly afterward Brunner lost consciousness, and on the following day, April 6, 1966, he died.[126]

Even in his eighties Barth enjoyed visits, but preferred those by individuals who came regularly over the constantly new groups.[127] On his eighty-second birthday, his final one, he was delighted by the numerous letters, presents, and then—as he wrote in his circular thank-you letter—"that so many both near and far should think of me with such love and acceptance and constantly let me know this with such generosity." He immediately added modestly: "I only know myself up close, and truly don't consider myself someone who has deserved such things."[128]

The Uncompleted Mammoth Work

Barth had wanted to continue working on his *Church Dogmatics* in retirement. In May 1961 he had still written the well-wishers for his seventy-fifth birthday: "*C.D.* IV, 4 is being prepared but is far from complete." But even then he faced his plan to write a fifth part on eschatology with the proper respect: "Eschatology? Friends, do not ask or complain or plague me too much about this. Could it not be written by someone else?"[129] Two months later he joked to his friend Ernst Wolf: "In the spring [1962] I shall then retire definitely. In view of my natural indolence and release from daily pressure the problem of how to continue *C.D.* still awaits solution. Lollo will undoubtedly have to keep me afloat with drops and shots to the brain and encouraging words."[130] But basically he already sensed that he lacked the zest and vitality to continue. This was apparently related to a certain resignation in light of the contemporary theological situation. He felt "gripped by a lassitude bordering on acedia...Does it make much sense to write a thirteenth and fourteenth volume if I could not stop this deluge with my previous twelve volumes? Are not other and new voices...needed to check it?"[131] Barth acknowledged to Gollwitzer that he feared that if he were to continue writing *Church Dogmatics*, "I will go back to the provocative style of the second Romans, in which case all the fine books written about me would have to be rewritten or be given a greatly disconcerting concluding chapter."[132]

In the spring of 1967 Barth put an end to the pressure and waiting for a conclusion of his mammoth work by publishing the fragments of what until then he had been working on, for the fourth volume, dealing with ethics, of part IV of *Church Dogmatics*.[133] Barth had published the first volume at the age of forty-five. Since then he had continued working on it year by year, but now "I have to give up the race."[134] As he explained in his preface there were various reasons. The important stimulus of presenting what he had worked on in lectures to his students had ended with his retirement.[135] In addition there were the illnesses, other interests like his autobiography and the developments in Rome, which kept him away from his work on it. The final factor was that Charlotte von Kirschbaum could no longer help him because of her illness. "For the 'late Barth' that I am now," he summed up, "it is in reality too late to still do this in a worthy fashion: he begs understanding and pardon."[136] In terms of the content Barth was aware that with his reflections on baptism, which he had formulated for this final, fragmentary volume—not with his fundamental thinking but with the consequence of rejecting infant baptism—he would be left "in the theological and ecclesiastical isolation which has been my lot for almost fifty years. I am thus about to make a poor exit with it. So be it!"[137]

At the End of His Life Journey

Starting in the summer of 1967 Barth's health worsened. In August he had to be brought urgently in the night to the hospital in Basel from Valais because of an acute prostate infection.[138] In December 1967 Nelly Barth suffered a heart attack and had to spend two months in the hospital.[139] During that time Barth moved in with his daughter Franziska,[140] but at the beginning of 1968 he developed bad pneumonia and had to return to the clinic.[141] His spiritual vitality was diminishing as well. Since the beginning of his retirement Barth suffered repeatedly under depressive moods,[142] from a sadness that was "completely inexplicable" to himself, "in which all the successes that my life has brought me *don't help at all*."[143] The depression became stronger in his final months. His assistant Eberhard Busch reported of "days and nights filled with serious depression and temptations... in which he would whisper: he used to know how to teach 'Before you [God] no one can endure', but only now was he was learning what that meant."[144] In August 1968 Barth suffered a life-threatening twisting of the intestine and had emergency surgery and had to be fed artificially. For a brief time his situation was worsened by pneumonia.[145]

In September and October of 1968 Barth gave interviews on Swiss radio. In a program titled "Music for a Guest," for which he had—naturally—wished only Mozart, he summarized what had been the essential focus of his theological work:

> ultimately I am neither at home in theology nor in the political world nor even in the church... now I come to that where I am basically at home—or I would like to say now: to the *one*, by whom I am basically at home... the last word that I... have to say, is not a concept like "grace" but it's a *name*: Jesus Christ. *He* is grace... We cannot encapsulate him but we have to deal with him. And that over which I have endeavored in my long life was to a growing extent this: to raise up this name and to say: *there!*[146]

In the evenings of the final weeks of his life Barth enjoyed hearing his sermons from his earlier period in Safenwil read to him, listening to Mozart, and smoking his pipe with a glass of good wine. At the end they sang Advent chorales together, or Barth would sing alone the old Basel children's songs by Abel Burckhardt, which had shaped him as a child and in which he had found the events of Jesus's life sung as if they were just happening in his Basel neighborhood.[147]

The Sunday before his death, December 8, Barth visited Charlotte von Kirschbaum as he did every Sunday.[148] That Monday he worked on an ecumenical lecture on the theme "Starting Out—Turning Round—Confessing!"[149] His last telephone call was on December 9, a call from Eduard Thurneysen, with whom he again had close contact.[150] Thurneysen later reported that they talked about the current state of the world, which they both found depressing. Barth ended the call with the words:

Yes, the world is dark. But just don't be downhearted! Never! Because the world is being governed, not only in Moscow or in Washington or in Peking but from above, from heaven. God is sitting in the government. That's why I am not afraid. Let us stay confident, even in the darkest moments! Let's not let our hope sink, hope for all human beings, for the entire world of nations! God will not let us fall, not a single one of us and not us all together! The world is being governed![151]

Karl Barth died in the following night, on December 10, 1968, in his sleep.[152] His burial, attended by family and close friends, took place on December 13 at the Hörnli cemetery in Basel.[153] Eberhard Busch and Barth's parish pastor Hans-Peter Zürcher spoke at the private service.[154]

Nelly Barth outlived her husband by eight years. Shortly after his death she moved into a senior residential home in Basel. She was still living when Eberhard Busch's major biography, *Karl Barth: His Life from Letters and Autobiographical Texts*, appeared in 1975. On October 23, 1976, she died in Basel after an illness of several months.[155]

On December 14, 1968, an overfilled Basel Münster Church hosted Barth's memorial service, which was broadcast live on the radio.[156] The speakers were Max Geiger, dean of the theological faculty; Lukas Burckhardt, the president of the cantonal council of Basel Stadt; Helmut Gollwitzer on behalf of the German churches and universities; Josef Hromádka for the eastern European churches; Hans Küng, representing the Catholics; Eberhard Jüngel, who was only 34 years old and represented the younger theological generation; and Willem A. Visser 't Hooft representing the ecumenical movement.[157]

Max Geiger emphasized Barth's distinctiveness:

Barth dared to do that which before him in Basel Overbeck and since then many others have described as no longer possible: after two thousand years of Christian history, after Kant and Hegel, Feuerbach, Marx and Nietzsche, after the French revolution, after Auschwitz and Hiroshima, to live in an immediate sense from the reality of the Gospel.[158]

Jüngel stated more precisely: "Karl Barth attacked the world with the Gospel." But this attack was not brutal or unmerciful, on the contrary: "His thought and his life was the collective attempt to show that 'God' is a joyful word."[159]

Küng told about a conversation he had with Barth many years ago, in which Barth spoke of what he hoped for after death:

> When the day arrives on which I must appear before my Lord, then I will not come with my works, with my *Dogmatics* volumes on my back in the "pannier." All the angels would laugh at that. Then I will also not say: I always meant well, I had the right belief. No, then I will only say one thing: Lord, receive me, a poor sinner, with mercy![160]

Notes

1. Barth, "Uns fehlt das Bewußtsein der eigenen Relativität," 16.
2. Regarding this, cf. Tietz, "On Reading Karl Barth in the USA," in *Theology Today* 69 (2012), 133–40. Cf. the itinerary in *Letters 1961–1968* (GA 6), 32, n. 1.
3. Cf. letter of February 11, 1962, to Markus Barth, KBA 9262.39.
4. Interview of April 23, 1962, with Mr. Lemon from *Newsweek*, *Gespräche 1959–1962* (GA 25), 445.
5. Interview of April 23, 1962, with Mr. Lemon from *Newsweek*, *Gespräche 1959–1962* (GA 25), 445.
6. Kirschbaum's comment mentioned in a letter of April 18, 1962, to Max Zellweger, *Letters 1961–1968* (GA 6), 43. Translation revised.
7. "Witness to an Ancient Truth," in *Time Magazine*, April 20, 1962, 60.
8. Press conference of April 19, 1962, in Chicago, *Gespräche 1959–1962* (GA 25), 448.
9. Cf. interview of April 23, 1962, with Mr. Lemon from *Newsweek*, *Gespräche 1959–1962* (GA 25), 445.
10. Editor's introduction to the podium discussions of April 25 and 26, 1962, in Chicago, *Gespräche 1959–1962* (GA 25), 231.
11. Cited in editor's introduction to the podium discussions of April 25 and 26, 1962, in Chicago, *Gespräche 1959–1962* (GA 25), 231.
12. Podium discussions of April 25 and 26, 1962, in Chicago, *Gespräche 1959–1962* (GA 25), 457.
13. Podium discussions of April 25 and 26, 1962, in Chicago, *Gespräche 1959–1962* (GA 25), 489.
14. Cf. Letter of April 18, 1962, to Max Zellweger, *Letters 1961–1968* (GA 6), Nr. 34, 43f.
15. Cf. *Gespräche 1959–1962* (GA 25), 180, n. 23.
16. Conversation with Methodist pastors, *Gespräche 1959–1962* (GA 25), 180f.
17. Press conference in San Francisco of May 15, 1962, *Gespräche 1959–1962* (GA 25), 525.
18. Cf. the conversation in Princeton II of May 4, 1962, *Gespräche 1959–1962* (GA 25), 509–521. ("II" refers to a second program Barth participated in.)

19. Cf. letter of June 11, 1962, to Dr. James I. McCord, *Letters 1961–1968* (GA 6), 51.
20. Cf. Busch, *Karl Barth: His Life*, 459.
21. Cf. Barth's draft for a preface to the American edition of *Evangelical Theology: An Introduction*, KBA 10390.
22. Cf. Barth, "Uns fehlt das Bewußtsein," 17.
23. Cf. Barth's draft for a preface to the American edition of *Evangelical Theology: An Introduction*, KBA 10390.
24. Press conference of May 1, 1962, in New York, *Gespräche 1959–1962* (GA 25), 494.
25. Press conference of May 1, 1962, in New York, *Gespräche 1959–1962* (GA 25), 494.
26. Cf. "Witness to an Ancient Truth," *Time Magazine*, April 20, 1962, 65 and 59.
27. Tillich, *Systematic Theology*, vol. 1, 5 and 7.
28. Barth's draft for a preface to the American edition of *Evangelical Theology: An Introduction*, KBA 10390.
29. *Der Spiegel* 21/1962, May 23, 1962, 80.
30. Barth's draft for a preface to the American edition of *Evangelical Theology: An Introduction*, KBA 10390.
31. Letter of April 18, 1962, to Max Zellweger, *Letters 1961–1968* (GA 6), 44. Translation revised.
32. Cf. letter of December 20, 1963, to Christoph and Marie-Claire Barth, KBA 9263.236.
33. Letter of March 16, 1968, to Zuckmayer, *A Late Friendship*, 27.
34. Letter of May 7, 1968, to Zuckmayer, *A Late Friendship*, 43, and Barth, "Concluding Unscientific Postscript," *Theology of Schleiermacher*, 274.
35. Cf. for example the list in his letter of September 26, 1968, to Zuckmayer, *A Late Friendship*, 58.
36. Cf. letter of July 31, 1962, to Gollwitzer, *Letters 1961–1968* (GA 6), 61.
37. Letter of February 26, 1963, to Markus Barth, KBA 9263.35.
38. Cf. letter of May 7, 1968, to Zuckmayer, *A Late Friendship*, 42.
39. Zuckmayer, *A Late Friendship*, 45. Translation revised.
40. Cf. letter of March 1–2, 1965, to Gollwitzer, *Letters 1961–1968* (GA 6), 186. (The date is incorrectly given as March 12 in the English translation.) Cf. also letter of June 18, 1963, to Christoph Barth, KBA 9263.107, and letter of May 7, 1968, to Zuckmayer, *A Late Friendship*, 42.
41. Letter of June 18, 1963, to Christoph Barth, KBA 9263.107.
42. Letter of November 3, 1965, to Jüngel, *Letters 1961–1968* (GA 6), 192.
43. Barth, "Selbstdarstellung," KBA 11294, 4.
44. Letter of December 5, 1964, to Christoph and Marie-Claire Barth, KBA 9264.142.
45. Letter of February 27, 1963, to Christoph Barth and family, KBA 9263.38.
46. Barth, "Dank und Reverenz," 337f.
47. Cited from "Zum ersten Mal ein protestantischer Theologe Ehrendoktor der Sorbonne," *National-Zeitung* of November 15, 1963, 3.
48. Cf. letter of March 16, 1968, to Zuckmayer, *A Late Friendship*, 26.
49. Letter of May 27, 1968, from general secretary Ernst Johann, KBA 9368.273.
50. Letter of June 1, 1968, to Ernst Johann, *Letters 1961–1968* (GA 6), 299.
51. The reference is to Gerhard Ebeling and Ernst Fuchs, two younger systematic theologians whose work Barth viewed critically.

52. Cf. letter of October 30, 1968, to Pastor Richard Karwehl, *Letters 1961–1968* (GA 6), 322. Barth was no longer able to travel to the celebration itself on October 26 in Darmstadt and let his son Christoph, who in the meantime was professor in Mainz, represent him. Cf. letter of June 1, 1968, to general secretary Ernst Johann, *Letters 1961–1968* (GA 6), 299, n. 1.
53. Letter of June 18, 1963, to Christoph Barth, KBA 9263.107.
54. Letter of December 20, 1963, to Christoph and Marie-Claire Barth, KBA 9263.236.
55. Letter of February 11, 1964, to Markus Barth, KBA 9264.29.
56. Letter of June 18, 1963, to Christoph Barth, KBA 9263.107.
57. The great theological texts such as the *Summa Theologica* of Thomas Aquinas.
58. Letter of November 27–29, 1963, to Markus Barth, KBA 9263.224.
59. Letter of December 20, 1963, to Christoph and Marie-Claire Barth, KBA 9263.236.
60. Letter of December 20, 1963, to Christoph and Marie-Claire Barth, KBA 9263.236.
61. Letter of June 6, 1964, to Markus Barth, KBA 9264.91.
62. Cf. for example letter of May 12, 1968, from Zuckmayer, *A Late Friendship*, 46.
63. Cf. editor's introduction, *Gespräche 1964–1968*, xii.
64. Cf. letter of November 8, 1964, to Richard Karwehl (p. 174) and the letter of January 29, 1965, to Emil Brunner (p. 179), *Letters 1961–1968* (GA 6).
65. Letter of March 1–2, 1965, to Gollwitzer, *Letters 1961–1968* (GA 6), 186f. (The date is incorrectly given as March 12 in the English translation.)
66. Cf. Busch, *Karl Barth: His Life*, 472.
67. Cf. Selinger, *Charlotte von Kirschbaum und Karl Barth*, 14.
68. Letter of December 5, 1964, to Christoph and Marie-Claire Barth, KBA 9264.142.
69. Regarding this, cf. Busch, *Meine Zeit mit Karl Barth*.
70. Cf. "Charlotte von Kirschbaum. Einige Angaben aus ihrem Leben," in *Briefwechsel Barth–von Kirschbaum* I (GA 45), xxxiii f. Barth mentioned this in a letter of January 15, 1966, to Lieutenant Commander Alfred Ernst, *Letters 1961–1968* (GA 6), 197f.
71. Cf. the circular letter to those sending congratulations to Barth's 82nd birthday at the end of May 1968, *Letters 1961–1968* (GA 6), 296f.
72. Letter of November 21, 1966, to Markus Barth, KBA 9266.111.
73. Circular letter to those sending congratulations to Barth's 82nd birthday at the end of May 1968, *Letters 1961–1968* (GA 6), 297.
74. Circular letter to those sending congratulations to Barth's 82nd birthday at the end of May 1968, *Letters 1961–1968* (GA 6), 297.
75. Cf. "Charlotte von Kirschbaum. Einige Angaben aus ihrem Leben," in *Briefwechsel Barth–von Kirschbaum* I (GA 45), xxxiv.
76. Cf. letter of November 21, 1966, to Markus Barth, KBA 9266.111.
77. As, for example, Hans Küng, who had lunch in 1955 in the Barth home. Cf. Küng, *Erkämpfte Freiheit*, 181.
78. Letter of December 5, 1964, to Christoph and Marie-Claire Barth, KBA 9264.142.
79. Circular letter to those sending congratulations to Barth's 82nd birthday at the end of May 1968, *Letters 1961–1968* (GA 6), 295.
80. Cf. Circular letter to those sending congratulations to Barth's 80th birthday, *Letters 1961–1968* (GA 6), 212.
81. Cf. Busch et al., eds., *Parrhesia. Karl Barth zum 80. Geburtstag am 10. Mai 1966.*

82. Cf. Barth, "Dankesworte anläßlich der Feier zu seinem 80. Geburtstag am 9. Mai 1966," 618.
83. Barth, "Dankesworte anläßlich der Feier zu seinem 80. Geburtstag am 9. Mai 1966," 616.
84. From Barth, "Dankesworte anläßlich der Feier zu seinem 80. Geburtstag am 9. Mai 1966," 616f.
85. Barth, "Dankesworte anläßlich der Feier zu seinem 80. Geburtstag am 9. Mai 1966," 619.
86. Letter of June 18, 1963, to Christoph Barth, KBA 9263.107.
87. Cf. letter of September 19, 1963, to Hans Küng, *Letters 1961-1968* (GA 6), 126f. with notes 1-3.
88. Letter of September 19, 1963, to Hans Küng, *Letters 1961-1968* (GA 6), 127. In Küng's judgement Barth became "through his influence even in the Catholic church—very indirect and yet very effective, so that it would not be an exaggeration to say this—*one of the spiritual fathers of Catholic renewal* in connection to the Second Vatican Council." (Küng, "Ansprache zum Tode Karl Barths," in *Karl Barth 1886-1968. Gedenkfeier*, 44).
89. Cf. letter of September 19, 1963, to Hans Küng, *Letters 1961-1968* (GA 6), 127.
90. Cf. Barth, "Historischer Bericht," *Ad Limina Apostolorum*, 9f.
91. Cf. letter of February 26, 1963, to Markus Barth, KBA 9263.35 and letter of February 27, 1963, to Christoph Barth and family, KBA 9263.38.
92. Letter of June 2, 1966, to Augustin Cardinal Bea, *Letters 1961-1968* (GA 6), 208.
93. Cf. letter of June 15, 1966, from Augustin Cardinal Bea, KBA 9366.1188.
94. Cf. Barth, "Historischer Bericht," *Ad Limina Apostolorum*, 10f.
95. Cf. Barth, "Historischer Bericht," *Ad Limina Apostolorum*, 11.
96. Cf. Barth, "Historischer Bericht," *Ad Limina Apostolorum*, 11f.
97. Cf. letter of October 3, 1966, to Ernst Wolf, *Briefe 1961-1968* (GA 6), 357; Barth, "Historischer Bericht," *Ad Limina Apostolorum*, 13f.
98. Barth, "Historischer Bericht," *Ad Limina Apostolorum*, 12.
99. Cf. Barth, "Historischer Bericht," *Ad Limina Apostolorum*, 14.
100. Cf. Barth, "Historischer Bericht," *Ad Limina Apostolorum*, 15.
101. Barth, "Historischer Bericht," *Ad Limina Apostolorum*, 15.
102. Cf. Barth, "Historischer Bericht," *Ad Limina Apostolorum*, 16.
103. Cf. Barth, "Historischer Bericht," *Ad Limina Apostolorum*, 17.
104. Cf. Barth, "Historischer Bericht," *Ad Limina Apostolorum*, 16.
105. According to Busch, *Karl Barth: His Life*, 484.
106. Barth, "Historischer Bericht," *Ad Limina Apostolorum*, 17f. In the aftermath of his journey Barth held a weekly colloquium in both the 1966/7 and 1967/8 winter semesters on two central texts of the Second Vatican Council. Cf. letter of November 21, 1966, to Markus Barth, KBA 9266.111; and the letter of November 1, 1967, to Zuckmayer, *A Late Friendship*, 20.
107. Cf. letter of October 3, 1967, to Pope Paul VI, *Letters 1961-1968* (GA 6), 268f.; letter of November 1, 1967, to Zuckmayer, *A Late Friendship*, 21.
108. Letter of November 14, 1967, from Pope Paul VI, *Letters 1961-1968* (GA 6), appendix 16, 356.

109. The text of the encyclical *Humanae Vitae* of July 25, 1968, can be found here: https://www.papalencyclicals.net/paul06/p6humana.htm (accessed May 5, 2020).
110. Cf. letter of September 28, 1968, to Pope Paul VI, *Letters 1961–1968* (GA 6), 501. The reply of November 11, 1968, from Cardinal Cicognani (appendix 17, 357f.).
111. Letter of May 16, 1967, to Zuckmayer, *A Late Friendship*, 3–4. Translation revised.
112. Zuckmayer, "Story of a Late Friendship: In Memory of Karl Barth," *A Late Friendship*, 65. Translation revised.
113. Letter of July 10, 1967, from Zuckmayer, *A Late Friendship*, 5.
114. Letter of July 10, 1967, from Zuckmayer, *A Late Friendship*, 6.
115. Cf. letter of August 15, 1967, to Zuckmayer, *A Late Friendship*, 8.
116. Letter of August 15, 1967, to Zuckmayer, *A Late Friendship*, 8.
117. Letter of August 15, 1967, to Zuckmayer, *A Late Friendship*, 8.
118. Letter of August 20, 1967, from Zuckmayer, *A Late Friendship*, 11.
119. Letter of November 1, 1967, to Zuckmayer, *A Late Friendship*, 21. Translation revised.
120. Letter of April 10, 1968, from Zuckmayer, *A Late Friendship*, 29.
121. Zuckmayer, "Story of a Late Friendship," *A Late Friendship*, 66.
122. Zuckmayer, "Story of a Late Friendship," *A Late Friendship*, 71.
123. Cf. *Letters 1961–1968* (GA 6), 202, n. 1.
124. Letter of April 4, 1966, to Pastor Peter Vogelsanger, *Letters 1961–1968* (GA 6), 202. Barth had already written to Brunner's wife Margrit along the same lines on March 7, 1966; cf. *Letters 1961–1968*, 200.
125. Information from Peter Vogelsanger, *Letters 1961–1968* (GA 6), 202, n. 3.
126. Cf. information from Peter Vogelsanger, *Letters 1961–1968* (GA 6), 202, n. 3.
127. Cf. Busch, *Karl Barth: His Life*, 490.
128. Circular letter to those who sent congratulations to Barth's 82nd birthday at the end of May 1968, *Letters 1961–1968* (GA 6), 295.
129. Circular letter to those who sent congratulations to Barth's 75th birthday in May 1961, *Letters 1961–1968* (GA 6), 3.
130. Letter of July 28, 1961, to Ernst Wolf, *Letters 1961–1968* (GA 6), 16.
131. Letter of July 31, 1962, to Gollwitzer, *Letters 1961–1968* (GA 6), 61.
132. Letter of July 31, 1962, to Gollwitzer, *Letters 1961–1968* (GA 6), 62.
133. See p. 377–8.
134. *CD* IV/4 (Fragment), Preface, vii.
135. Cf. *CD* IV/4 (Fragment), Preface, viif.
136. *CD* IV/4 (Fragment), Preface, viii. Translation revised.
137. *CD* IV/4 (Fragment), Preface, xii.
138. Cf. Letters of August 15 and November 1, 1967, to Zuckmayer, *A Late Friendship*, 9 and 20f.
139. Cf. letter of February 19, 1968, from Zuckmayer (23) and letter of March 16, 1968, to Zuckmayer (25), *A Late Friendship*.
140. Cf. Busch, *Karl Barth: His Life*, 493.
141. Cf. letter of February 19, 1968, from Zuckmayer, *A Late Friendship*, 23.
142. Cf. letter of February 26, 1963, to Markus Barth, KBA 9263.35.
143. Letter of March 7, 1966, to Margrit Brunner, *Letters 1961–1968*, 200. Translation revised.

144. Busch, "Ansprache bei der Trauerfeier am 13. Dezember 1968," in *Karl Barth 1886–1968. Gedenkfeier*, 17.
145. Cf. letter of September 26, 1968, to Zuckmayer, *A Late Friendship*, 56; and letter of October 30, 1968, to Richard Karwehl, *Letters 1961–1968* (GA 6), 322.
146. Interview with Roswitha Schmalenbach (conducted around September 17 and broadcast on November 17, 1968), *Gespräche 1964–1968*, 541f.
147. Cf. Busch, *Karl Barth: His Life*, 497. See p. 15.
148. Cf. Busch, *Karl Barth: His Life*, 497.
149. Cf. Busch, "Ansprache bei der Trauerfeier am 13. Dezember 1968," in *Karl Barth 1886–1968. Gedenkfeier*, 15.
150. Cf. letter of October 30, 1968, to Richard Karwehl, *Letters 1961–1968* (GA 6), 322.
151. "Gespräch mit Eduard Thurneysen am 9. Dezember 1968," *Gespräche 1964–1968*, 562.
152. Cf. "Gespräch mit Eduard Thurneysen am 9. Dezember 1968," *Gespräche 1964–1968*, 562.
153. Cf. Busch, *Karl Barth: His Life*, 499.
154. *Karl Barth 1886–1968. Gedenkfeier*, 11.
155. Cf. Zellweger-Barth, "Lebenslauf," in *Nelly Barth-Hoffmann*, 9.
156. Cf. Busch, *Karl Barth: His Life*, 499.
157. Cf. *Karl Barth 1886–1968. Gedenkfeier*, 27.
158. "Ansprache von Max Geiger," in *Karl Barth 1886–1968. Gedenkfeier*, 30.
159. "Ansprache von Eberhard Jüngel Karl Barth zu Ehren," in *Karl Barth 1886–1968. Gedenkfeier*, 50.
160. Recounted by Hans Küng, "Ansprache zum Tode Karl Barths," in *Karl Barth 1886–1968. Gedenkfeier*, 46.

Epilogue

Over the generations Karl Barth has dominated the theological landscape of the twentieth century like no other. Even his first theological opinions already show his self-confidence. In many controversies he operated almost daredevil-like. When he found it necessary—and this was often the case—he engaged fearlessly with the political and church powers. Soon he himself became an authority. The accusation that as a theologian he was either too political or not political enough was a consistent theme throughout this life.

If one looks behind the facade of his public statements, one discovers someone who particularly at the beginning of his academic career suffered under massive self-doubts and later was troubled by his "centrifugal effect." As decisively as Barth took substantive positions against others, he was deeply wounded when others did so against him in the same manner. Despite his worldwide fame he remained modest to a certain degree and grateful that he was able to work so fruitfully in his life.

Personally Barth never found a resolution for the burden of his "three-way relationship." He was well-aware of his own guilt and did not sugarcoat the situation nor did he attempt to justify it theologically. It is conspicuous that in this matter Barth did not use any Christological concepts of argumentation to lead to clarification. He who otherwise dismissed "experience" as a theological category remained here under the spell of his own experience.

More than fifty years have passed since Barth's death in 1968. In the early decades after his death his theology dominated the German- and English-speaking world, particularly in the United States. Many theologians in the church and the academy had studied under him and followed his approach that centered on God's self-revelation in Jesus Christ. Several of them brought him into conversation with the concepts of others like Bonhoeffer, Bultmann, or Schleiermacher.

Others remained consistently critical, primarily because they had the impression that Barth's understanding of revelation was hermetical, making it impossible to portray Christian faith plausibly as a meaningful option for other people. Many people shared Paul Tillich's critique that Barth had thrown revelation at humanity like a stone. Dietrich Bonhoeffer's enigmatic charge that Barth represented a "positivism of revelation"[1] became a slogan for Barth's opponents.

---

[1] Bonhoeffer, *Letters and Papers from Prison* (*Dietrich Bonhoeffer Works*, vol. 8), 364.

And today? Throughout the world, especially in the United States, Great Britain, and Asia, Karl Barth remains one of the most frequently read theologians. In contrast, in recent years in the German-speaking world there has been an extensive turning away from Barth's theology. It continues to have validity as a plausible attempt in light of the historical challenges faced by Barth and that can be located and contextualized in the history of ideas. But in today's era there is a call for a post-Barthianism that once again picks up on the liberal theological projects of the nineteenth century, implying that Barth's theology would offer too few linkages to culture and scholarship. A prominent voice is that of the systematic theologian Jörg Lauster, who diagnoses:

> In the mid-twentieth century the Word of God theology was for one generation the normative way of thinking in the German-speaking Protestant theological world. This rests admittedly not only on the convincing nature of the theological argument. One must also consider the cultural context, which shows that it satisfies a religious, not just theological, longing for a return to the pre-modern era, i.e., a return to a situation in which the signs of disintegration and the loss of relevance for the Christian religion could be reversed.[2]

The success of Barth's theology was due to the "climate of a hunger for authority" of that era.[3] Lauster critically sums up that

> [t]he Word of God theology has damaged the theological landscape... This intentionally cultivated renunciation of linkages to other academic disciplines promotes a preference for immanent language games and forms of argumentation that cannot be followed outside of these circles. The revival of mystical concepts of God, the tenacious insistence that God speaks, constitutes a tangibly violent infantilization of the concept of God, which to many has a deterrent and excluding effect, because it does not contain any points of connection at all to modern critical thought.[4]

This judgement does not take into account that through his strict distinction between God and the world, Barth was in the position to regard the "world" (particularly of politics and society) critically—more critically than those advocates of liberal theology and cultural Protestantism who were all too ready during the First World War, Weimar republic, Third Reich, and partly even in the early postwar Cold War period to see something divine, albeit distorted, in social and political ideals and myths, and to conceptualize engagement for this as a religious

---

[2] Lauster, *Zwischen Entzauberung und Remythisierung*, 18f.
[3] Lauster, *Zwischen Entzauberung und Remythisierung*, 20.
[4] Lauster, *Zwischen Entzauberung und Remythisierung*, 22.

duty. In particular the critical potential of Barth's theology is as necessary today as it was in Barth's times and could make Barth's thinking relevant far beyond the theological realm once more today.

This was true in his own time, as can be seen by the various non-theological honorary doctorates and scholarly prizes that he received. Barth won interdisciplinary recognition, particularly as a thinker who differed from them in that he spoke of God.

And in theology? According to systematic theologian and philosopher Martin Laube the blanket criticisms like that of Lauster "rashly obscure the question as to whether and how the dialectical critique of religion...formulates justified complaints that could not find consideration in the smoke of post-dialectical polemics of dissociation."[5] Despite the majority's return to liberal theology, a range of German-speaking theologians continue to find Karl Barth's theological approach seminal.[6] The author of this biography is one of them. They remain firmly convinced that theology is not primarily concerned with the human cultural performance of religion, but with God. God for them is not the concept for a certain human reference to transcendence, but rather God and humankind are fundamentally distinct, and only God can bridge the distance to humanity. They therefore believe that theological thinking must begin with God's self-revelation in Jesus Christ, in which the Christian church believes, and orient itself toward that. Such theological talk of God does not simply expound how human beings always understand themselves in their own world. Expressing God as wholly Other is the critical corrective for human self-understanding and human understanding of this world. Ultimately Barth's theology is a continuation of the Reformers' insight that human beings do not get beyond themselves by themselves. Human beings live from God as the One who faces them, the great You who unconditionally affirms the human being. Held by this You, the human being is free.

---

[5] Laube, "Die Unterscheidung von Theologie und Religion," 453.
[6] The events in 2019, which commemorated both the fiftieth anniversary of his death and the centenary of the publication of *The Epistle to the Romans*, showed that there are more such scholars than assumed.

Chronology

1886	May 10. Karl Barth is born in Basel, the eldest son of Fritz and Anna Barth
1889	The Barth family moves to Bern
1904–8	Theology studies in Bern, Berlin, Tübingen, and Marburg
1908–9	Barth joins the editorial team of *Die Christliche Welt*, the journal published by Martin Rade in Marburg
1909–11	Barth serves as a vicar in the German-speaking Reformed congregation in Geneva
1911	Engagement to Nelly Hoffmann
1911–21	Pastor in the working-class and farming congregation in Safenwil
1913	Marriage to Nelly Hoffmann. The couple has five children: Franziska in 1914; Markus in 1915; Christoph in 1917; Matthias in 1921; and Hans Jakob in 1925
1915	Barth joins the Swiss Social Democrat Party
1919	Publication of the first version of *Der Römerbrief*
1921–5	Honorary professor for Reformed Theology in Göttingen
1922	Publication of the second, completely reworked version of *Der Römerbrief* February: Barth receives honorary doctorate from the University of Münster, the first of eleven honorary doctorates August: The journal *Zwischen den Zeiten* is founded, together with Friedrich Gogarten, Georg Merz, and Eduard Thurneysen at the "Bergli" in Oberrieden
1923	Controversy with Adolf von Harnack about the academic nature of theology
1925–30	Professor for Dogmatics and New Testament Exegesis in Münster
1925	August: First encounter with Charlotte von Kirschbaum at the "Bergli"
1926	February: Charlotte von Kirschbaum visits Barth in Münster; beginning of their relationship
1927	Beginning of the working relationship with Charlotte von Kirschbaum Publication of *Die christliche Dogmatik im Entwurf*. vol. I: *Die Lehre vom Worte Gottes. Prolegomena*
1929	October. Charlotte von Kirschbaum moves in with the Barth family
1930–5	Professor for Systematic Theology at the University of Bonn
1931	Publication of *Fides quaerens intellectum. Anselms Beweis der Existenz Gottes im Zusammenhang seines theologischen Programms* Barth joins the German Social Democrat Party

1931/2	Involvement in the controversy about Günther Dehn's appointment to Heidelberg and Halle an der Saale, combative exchange especially with Emanuel Hirsch
1932	Publication of *Die Kirchliche Dogmatik*, vol. I/1: *Die Lehre vom Wort Gottes. Prolegomena*
1933	July. Publication of *Theologische Existenz heute!* (Starting with the 8th edition, it becomes the first issue of the new series *Theologische Existenz heute*) October. Barth refuses to give the Hitler greeting in his lectures The journal *Zwischen den Zeiten* ceases publication
1934	April. Ban on travel issued against Barth May. Barmen Theological Declaration, to which Barth contributed decisively, approved by the first national Confessing synod of the Confessing Church Barth's issues from the *Theologische Existenz heute* series are confiscated for several months October. Barth participates in the second national Confessing synod in Berlin-Dahlem and is elected to the Confessing Church Council and Council of Brethren November. Barth resigns from both offices because of the establishment of a provisional church government, which counteracted the decisions of the Dahlem synod; suspension of the professorship because of his refusal to swear the oath to Adolf Hitler without an addendum limiting its content; publication of *Nein! Antwort an Emil Brunner* December. Opening of disciplinary criminal process against Barth in the Cologne criminal court, among other things because of his position on the oath question, leading to his dismissal
1935	March. Ban on public speaking issued against Barth April. Ban on preaching issued against Barth June 14. Judgement against Barth lifted by the higher administrative court in Berlin June 21. Barth is placed in retirement by Reich minister Bernhard Rust June 25. Basel governmental council decides to appoint Barth
1935–61	Professor for Systematic Theology and Homiletics at the University of Basel
1937	Beginning of Barth's involvement in the Swiss Refugee Aid Association led by Paul Vogt
1937/8	Barth delivers the Gifford Lectures in Aberdeen
1938	September. Letter to Josef L. Hromádka appealing to the Czechs to militarily resist Hitler October. Ban on the sale of Barth's writings in Germany
1939	Withdrawal of Barth's honorary doctorate from Münster During the Second World War Barth urges an appropriate interpretation of Swiss neutrality

1940	Swiss censorship of Barth's lectures and writings begins Barth joins the Swiss Army armed auxiliary
1941	Death of Barth's son Matthias after a mountain climbing accident
1942/3	Surveillance of Barth's telephone by Swiss censorship officials
1945	Contacts with the "Free Germany" movement August/September. First postwar trip to Germany
1946/7	Guest professorship for both summer semesters at the University of Bonn, and active period of giving lectures in Germany
1947	August. Barth is one of the authors of the Darmstadt Statement on the guilt of the Protestant church in Germany; the statement also speaks out against anti-Communism
1948	March/April. Trip to Hungary with lectures about the church's situation under Communism; in the following period Barth becomes a frequent critique of anti-Communism August. Barth delivers the opening address to the first meeting of the World Council of Churches in Amsterdam
As of 1950	Barth becomes involved in opposition to German rearmament
1954–64	Preacher at the Basel prison
As of 1957	Opposition to arming the German and Swiss armies with atomic weapons
1958	August. Letter to a pastor in the German Democratic Republic
1961	Barth becomes emeritus after the summer semester
1961/2	Final lecture at the University of Basel on *Einführung in die evangelische Theologie*. Barth continues to offer colloquia and societies for a smaller number of students
1962	April/May. Lecture tour in the United States
1963	April. Barth receives the Danish Sonning Prize September. Barth is invited to attend the second session of the Second Vatican Council as an observer. Cancels for health reasons among other things
As of 1964	Barth's health declines
1966	January. Charlotte von Kirschbaum moves into a nursing home due to dementia September. Barth travels to Rome, where he meets with the Curia and has an audience with Pope Paul VI
1967	*Die Kirchliche Dogmatik* IV/4 (fragment) appears as the twelfth and final volume
1968	Barth is elected a member of the French Academy of Moral and Political Science and receives the Sigmund-Freud Prize from the German Academy for Language and Literature December 10. Barth dies at his home on Bruderholzallee in Basel

Bibliography

Karl Barth's literary estate is in the Karl Barth-Archive (KBA), located in his final home on Bruderholzallee 26 in Basel. Since 1971 the Theologischer Verlag Zürich has published the Karl Barth-Gesamtausgabe (GA), the critical edition of Barth's collected works, on behalf of the Karl Barth-Stiftung and under the leadership of Hinrich Stoevesandt (until 1998), Hans-Anton Drewes (1998–2012), and Peter Zocher (since 2013). The critical edition of Barth's collected works has six sections: I. Sermons; II. Academic Works; III. Lectures and Minor Works; IV. Conversations; V. Letters; VI. From Karl Barth's Life. In working on this biography the author consulted the editors' introductions as well as the informative annotations in the respective volumes. Titles from the critical edition that were consulted for this biography are listed in the second section of this bibliography.

This bibliography is organized in three sections: writings of Karl Barth (including the *Church Dogmatics* (*CD*), early collections of his writings, journal articles, newspaper articles, and interviews), the GA volumes that were consulted, and secondary literature.

Writings of Karl Barth

"Abschied," *Zwischen den Zeiten* 11 (1933): 536–44.
Ad Limina Apostolorum. Zurich: EVZ Verlag, 1967. Translated as *Ad Limina Apostolorum: An Appraisal of Vatican II* by Keith R. Crim. Eugene, Oregon: Wipf & Stock, 2016.
Amsterdamer Fragen und Antworten. Co-authored with Jean Daniélou and Reinhold Niebuhr. Nr. 15 of *Theologische Existenz heute. Neue Folge*. Munich: Chr. Kaiser Verlag, 1949.
Briefe des Jahres 1933. Ed. Busch, Eberhard, Bartolt Haase, and Barbara Schenck. Zurich: Theologischer Verlag, 2004.
Christliche Gemeinde im Wechsel der Staatsordnungen. Dokumente einer Ungarnreise 1948. Zollikon-Zurich: Evangelischer Verlag, 1948.
"Concluding Unscientific Postscript on Schleiermacher," in *The Theology of Schleiermacher*, 261-79. Ed. Dietrich Ritschl. Translated by Geoffrey W. Bromiley. Grand Rapids, Michigan: Wm. B. Eerdmans, 1982. German: "Nachwort," in *Schleiermacher-Auswahl*, 290–312. Ed. Heinz Bolli. 2nd ed. Gütersloh: Gütersloher Verlagshaus G. Mohn, 1980.
"Dank und Reverenz," *Evangelische Theologie* 23 (1963): 337–42.
"Dankesworte anläßlich der Feier zu seinem 80. Geburtstag am 9. Mai 1966," *Evangelische Theologie* 26 (1966): 615–20.
Der Dienst der Kirche an der Heimat. Zollikon-Zurich: Evangelischer Verlag, 1940.
Dogmatik im Grundriß. 9th ed. Zurich: TVZ Verlag, 2006. Original 1949 ed. translated as *Dogmatics in Outline* by G. T. Thomson. London: SCM Press, 1949.
Einführung in die evangelische Theologie. Zurich: Theologischer Verlag, 1962. Translated as *Evangelical Theology: An Introduction* by Grover Foley. London: T & T Clark, 1979.
Evangelische Theologie im 19. Jahrhundert. Zollikon-Zurich: Evangelischer Verlag, 1957.

Final Testimonies. Ed. Eberhard Busch. Translation by Geoffrey W. Bromiley. Grand Rapids, Michigan: Wm. B. Eerdmans 1977. German: *Letzte Zeugnisse.* Zurich: EVZ-Verlag, 1969.
Gesammelte Vorträge. Vol. 3: *Theologische Fragen und Antworten.* Zollikon-Zurich: Evangelischer Verlag, 1957.
Gottes Wille und unsere Wünsche. Munich: Chr. Kaiser Verlag, 1934.
Gotteserkenntnis und Gottesdienst nach reformatorischer Lehre. 20 Vorlesungen (Gifford-Lectures) über das Schottische Bekenntnis von 1560 gehalten an der Universität Aberdeen im Frühjahr 1937 und 1938. Zollikon: Evangelische Buchhandlung, 1938. Translated as *The Knowledge of God and the Service of God According to the Teaching of the Reformation Recalling the Scottish Confession of 1560: The Gifford Lectures Delivered in the University of Aberdeen in 1937 and 1938* by J. L. M. Haire and Ian Henderson. London: Hodder and Stoughton, 1949.
"Der Götze wackelt." *Zeitkritische Aufsätze, Reden und Briefe von 1930 bis 1960.* Ed. Karl Kupisch. Berlin: K. Vogt, 1961.
How I Changed My Mind. Introduction and epilogue by John D. Godsey. Richmond, Viginia: John Knox Press, 1966.
Die Kirchliche Dogmatik. 4 Vols. Munich: Chr. Kaiser; Zurich: Evangelischer Verlag, 1932–67. Translated as *Church Dogmatics* by G. T. Thomson. Ed. G. W. Bromiley and T. F. Torrance, 4 Vols. Edinburgh: T & T Clark, 1956–77.
Die kirchliche Lehre von der Taufe. Zurich: Evangelischer Verlag, 1943.
"Lebendige Vergangenheit. Briefwechsel zwischen Eduard Thurneysen und Karl Barth aus den Jahren 1921–1925. Vorrede," in *Gottesdienst–Menschendienst. Eduard Thurneysen zum 70. Geburtstag am 19. Juli 1958,* 7–14. Zollikon: Evangelischer Verlag, 1958.
Die Menschlichkeit Gottes. Zollikon-Zurich: Theologischer Verlag, 1956. Translated as *The Humanity of God* by John N. Thomas. Philadelphia: Westminster John Knox Press, 1996. Reprint.
"Möglichkeiten liberaler Theologie heute," *Schweizerische theologische Umschau* 30 (1960): 95–101.
Not und Verheißung im deutschen Kirchenkampf. Vortrag, gehalten am 23. Januar 1938 in der Heiliggeistkirche in Bern. Bern: BEG Verlag, 1938.
"Prof. Karl Barth's Gruß an die Studenten," *Bonner Universitäts-Zeitung* 7 (October 18, 1946): 1–2.
Rechtfertigung und Recht. Christengemeinde und Bürgergemeinde. Evangelium und Gesetz. Zurich: Theologischer Verlag, 1998. Translated as *Community, State, and Church. Three Essays* by A.M. Hall. New York: Doubleday, 1960.
Rudolf Bultmann. Ein Versuch, ihn zu verstehen. Zurich: Evangelischer Verlag, 1952.
"Rückblick," in *Festschrift für D. Albert Schädelin. Das Wort sie sollen lassen stahn,* 1–8. Ed. Hans Dürr. Bern: Herbert Lang, 1950.
"Rückblick auf das Jahr 1945," *Schweizer Radio Zeitung* 2 (1946): 2–3.
Eine Schweizer Stimme 1938–1945. Zollikon-Zurich: Evangelischer Verlag, 1945.
Suchet Gott, so werdet ihr leben! Written with Eduard Thurneysen. Bern: Bäschin, 1917.
"Systematische Theologie," in *Lehre und Forschung an der Universität Basel zur Zeit der Feier ihres fünfhundertjährigen Bestehens, dargestellt von Dozenten der Universität Basel,* 35–8. Basel: Birkhäuser, 1960.
Texte zur Barmer Theologischen Erklärung. Ed. Martin Rohkrämer and with an introduction by Eberhard Jüngel. 2nd ed. Zurich: Theologischer Verlag, 2004.
"Die Unordnung der Welt und Gottes Heilsplan," *Evangelische Theologie* 8 (1948/9): 181–8.
"Uns fehlt das Bewußtsein der eigenen Relativität," *Die Woche* January 23, 1963: 16–17.
"'Unser Malaise muss fruchtbar werden.' Interview mit Prof. Karl Barth," *Die Weltwoche* December 21, 1945: 1–2, 7.

"Und vergib uns unsere Schuld. Ein Interview über das deutsche Problem mit Prof. Karl Barth," *Die Weltwoche* September 14, 1945: 7, 12.
Wolfgang Amadeus Mozart 1756/1956. Zurich: Theologischer Verlag, 1956. Translated as *Wolfgang Amadeus Mozart* by Clarence K. Pott. Eugene, Oregon: Wipf & Stock, 2003.
The Word of God and Theology. Translated by Amy Marga. London and New York: T & T Clark International, 2011. Translation of *Das Wort Gottes und die Theologie*. Gesammelte Vorträge, Munich: Kaiser, 1924.
"Zum Andenken an Eberhard Vischer," *Kirchenblatt für die reformierte Schweiz* 102(4) (February 21, 1946): 54–6.
"Zum Geleit," in *Die Dogmatik der evangelisch-reformierten Kirche, dargestellt und aus den Quellen belegt von Heinrich Heppe*, vii–x. Ed. Ernst Bizer. Neukirchen: Erziehungsverein, 1935.
Zur Genesung des deutschen Wesens. Ein Freundeswort von draußen. Stuttgart: Mittelbau Verlag, 1945.
"Zwischenzeit," *Magnum. Die Zeitschrift für das moderne Leben* (Köln) 35 (April 1961): 38.

Works cited from the Karl Barth Gesamtausgabe (GA). Vols. 1–53. Zurich: Theologischer Verlag Zürich, 1971–2018. (NB: Some of the English translations of these works rely on earlier non-critical editions.)

Briefe 1961–68. GA 6: 1975. Ed. Jürgen Fangmeier and Hinrich Stoevesandt. 2nd expanded ed. of 1979 translated as *Letters 1961–1968* by Geoffrey W. Bromiley. Grand Rapids, Michigan: Wm. B. Eerdmans Publishing, 1981.
Die christliche Dogmatik im Entwurf. Vol. 1: *Die Lehre vom Worte Gottes. Prolegomena zur christlichen Dogmatik 1927*. GA 14: 1982. Ed. Gerhard Sauter.
Erklärungen des Epheser- und des Jakobusbriefes 1919–1929. GA 46: 2009. Ed. Jörg-Michael Bohnet.
Ethik I. Vorlesung Münster Sommersemester 1928, wiederholt in Bonn, Sommersemester 1930. GA 2: 1973. Ed. Dietrich Braun. Translated by Geoffrey W. Bromiley as *Ethics*. Edinburgh: T & T Clark, 1981.
Fides quaerens intellectum. Anselms Beweis der Existenz Gottes im Zusammenhang seines theologischen Programms 1931. GA 13: 1986. 2nd ed. Ed. Eberhard Jüngel and Ingolf U. Dalferth. Translated as *Anselm: Fides Quaerens Intellectum. Anselm's Proof of the Existence of God in the Context of His Theological Scheme* by Ian W. Robertson. Philadelphia: Westminster John Knox, 1960.
Gespräche 1959–1962. GA 25: 1995. Ed. Eberhard Busch.
Gespräche 1963. GA 41: 2005. Ed. Eberhard Busch.
Gespräche 1964–1968. GA 28: 1971. Ed. Eberhard Busch. All three volumes of the *Gespräche* have been translated as *Barth in Conversation* by a team and edited by Eberhard Busch, Karlfried Froehlich, and Darrell Guder, and David Chao. 3 Vols. Princeton: Princeton University Press, 2017–19.
Karl Barth–Emil Brunner Briefwechsel 1916–1966. GA 33: 2000. Ed. by the Karl Barth-Forschungsstelle an der Universität Göttingen under the direction of Eberhard Busch.
Karl Barth–Rudolf Bultmann Briefwechsel 1922–1966. GA 1: 1971. Ed. Bernd Jaspert. Translated as *Karl Barth–Rudolf Bultmann: Letters 1922–1966* by Geoffrey W. Bromiley. Grand Rapids, Michigan: Wm. B. Eerdmans Publishing Company, 1981.
Karl Barth–Charlotte von Kirschbaum Briefwechsel. Vol. 1: *1925–1935*. GA 45: 2008. Ed. Rolf-Joachim Erler.
Karl Barth–Eduard Thurneysen Briefwechsel. Vol. I: *1913–1921*. GA 3: 1973. Ed. Eduard Thurneysen. Sections translated by James D. Smart as *Revolutionary Theology in the Making: Barth–Thurneysen Correspondence 1914–1925*. Richmond: John Knox Press, 1964.

Karl Barth–Eduard Thurneysen Briefwechsel. Vol. II: *1921–1930.* GA 4: 1974. Ed. Eduard Thurneysen. Sections translated by James D. Smart as *Revolutionary Theology in the Making: Barth–Thurneysen Correspondence 1914–1925.* Richmond: John Knox Press, 1964.
Karl Barth–Eduard Thurneysen Briefwechsel. Vol. III: *1930–1935.* GA 34: 2000. Ed. Caren Algner.
Karl Barth–Willem Visser 't Hooft Briefwechsel 1930–1968. GA 43: 2006. Ed. Thomas Herwig.
Konfirmandenunterricht 1909–1921. GA 18: 1987. Ed. Jürgen Fangmeier.
Offene Briefe 1909–1935. GA 35: 2001. Ed. Diether Koch.
Offene Briefe 1935–1942. GA 36: 2001. Ed. Diether Koch.
Offene Briefe 1945–1968. GA 15: 1984. Ed. Diether Koch.
Predigten 1911. GA 51: 2015. Ed. Eberhard Busch and Beate Busch-Blum.
Predigten 1914. GA 5: 1974. Ed. Ursula and Jochen Fähler.
Predigten 1916. GA 29: 1998. Ed. Hermann Schmidt.
Predigten 1935–1952. GA 26: 1996. Ed. Hartmut Spieker and Hinrich Stoevesandt.
Predigten 1954–1967. GA 12: 1979. Ed. Hinrich Stoevesandt.
Der Römerbrief (first version/1919). GA 16: 1985. Ed. Hermann Schmidt.
Der Römerbrief (second version/1922). GA 47: 2010. Ed. Cornelis van der Kooi and Katja Tolstaja. Translated from the 6th ed., including the introduction to the first version, as *The Epistle to the Romans* by Edwin C. Hoskyns. New York: Oxford University Press, 1968.
Die Theologie Calvins. Vorlesung Göttingen Sommersemester 1922. GA 23: 1993. Ed. Hans Scholl. Translated by Geoffrey W. Bromiley as *The Theology of John Calvin.* Grand Rapids, Michigan: Wm. B. Eerdmans Publishing Company, 1995.
"Unterricht in der christlichen Religion." Vol. 1: *Prolegomena 1924.* GA 17: 1985. Ed. Hannelotte Reiffen. Translated by Geoffrey W. Bromiley as *The Göttingen Dogmatics.* Vol. 1. Grand Rapids, Michigan: Wm. B. Eerdmans Publishing Company, 1991.
"Unterricht in der christlichen Religion." Vol. 3: *Die Lehre von der Versöhnung/Die Lehre von der Erlösung 1925/1926.* GA 38: 2003. Ed. Hinrich Stoevesandt.
Vorträge und kleinere Arbeiten 1905–1909. GA 21: 1992. Ed. Hans-Anton Drewes and Hinrich Stoevesandt.
Vorträge und kleinere Arbeiten 1909–1914. GA 22: 1993. Ed. Herbert Helms, Friedrich W. Marquardt, et al.
Vorträge und kleinere Arbeiten 1914–1921. GA 48: 2012. Ed. Hans-Anton Drewes.
Vorträge und kleinere Arbeiten 1922–1925. GA 19: 1990. Ed. Holger Finze.
Vorträge und kleinere Arbeiten 1925–1930. GA 24: 1994. Ed. Hermann Schmidt.
Vorträge und kleinere Arbeiten 1930–1933. GA 49: 2013. Ed. Michael Beintker, Michael Hüttenhoff, et al.
Vorträge und kleinere Arbeiten 1934–1935. GA 52: 2017. Ed. Michael Beintker, Michael Hüttenhoff, et al.

Secondary Literature

Adam, Karl. "Die Theologie des Krisis (1925/26)," in *Gesammelte Aufsätze zur Dogmengeschichte und Theologie der Gegenwart,* 319–37. Ed. Fritz Hofmann. Augsburg: P. Haas & Cie, 1936.
Althaus, Paul. "Theologie und Geschichte. Zur Auseinandersetzung mit der dialektischen Theologie," *Zeitschrift für Systematische Theologie* 1 (1923): 741–86.
Althaus, Paul. *Die christliche Wahrheit. Lehrbuch der Dogmatik.* Vol. 1. Gütersloh: C. Bertelsmann, 1947.

Anzinger, Herbert. *Glaube und kommunikative Praxis. Eine Studie zur "vordialektischen" Theologie Karl Barths.* Munich: Chr. Kaiser Verlag, 1991.
Assel, Heinrich. "'Barth ist entlassen...'. Emanuel Hirschs Rolle im Fall Barth und seine Briefe an Wilhelm Stapel," *Zeitschrift für Theologie und Kirche* 91 (1994): 445–75.
Balthasar, Hans Urs von. *Karl Barth. Darstellung und Deutung seiner Theologie.* 4th ed. Einsiedeln: Johannes Verlag, 1976.
Barnett, Victoria. *For the Soul of the People: Protestant Protest against Hitler.* New York: Oxford University Press, 1992.
Barnikol, Ernst. "Barth als antideutscher Papst im Raum seiner Kirche. Eine kirchengeschichtliche Feststellung der Säkularisierung der konsequenten dialektischen Theologie," in *Dialektische Exegese!*, 24–31. Halle: Akademischer Verlag, 1938.
Barrett, Lee C. "Karl Barth: The Dialectic of Attraction and Repulsion," in *Kierkegaard's Influence on Theology.* Vol. 1: *German Protestant Theology*, 1–41. Ed. Jon Stewart. Farnham: Ashgate, 2012.
Barth, Fritz. "Tertullians Auffassung des Apostels Paulus und seines Verhältnisses zu den Uraposteln," *Jahrbuch für Protestantische Theologie* 8 (1882): 706–56.
Professor D. Fritz Barth 1856–1912. Bern, 1912.
Barth, Fritz. *Christus unsere Hoffnung. Sammlung von religiösen Reden und Vorträgen.* Bern: A. Francke, 1913.
Barth, Fritz. *Die Hauptprobleme des Lebens Jesu. Eine geschichtliche Untersuchung.* 5th ed. Gütersloh: Bertelsmann, 1918.
Beauvoir, Simone de. *The Second Sex.* Translation of *Le Deuxième Sexe* by Constance Borde and Sheila Malovany-Chevalier. London: Jonathan Cape, 2009.
Beintker, Michael. *Die Dialektik in der "dialektischen Theologie" Karl Barths. Studien zur Entwicklung der Barthschen Theologie und zur Vorgeschichte der "Kirchlichen Dogmatik."* Munich: Chr. Kaiser, 1987.
Beintker, Michael. "Barths Abschied von 'Zwischen den Zeiten.' Recherchen und Beobachtungen zum Ende einer Zeitschrift," *Zeitschrift für Theologie und Kirche* 106 (2009): 201–22.
Beintker, Michael, ed. *Barth Handbuch.* Tübingen: Mohr Siebeck Verlag, 2016.
Beintker, Michael, Christian Link, and Michael Trowitzsch, eds. *Karl Barth in Deutschland (1921–1935). Aufbruch—Klärung—Widerstand. Beiträge zum Internationalen Symposion vom 1. bis 4. Mai 2003 in der Johannes a Lasco Bibliothek Emden.* Zurich: Theologischer Verlag, 2005.
Beintker, Michael, Christian Link, and Michael Trowitzsch, eds. *Karl Barth im europäischen Zeitgeschehen (1935–1950). Widerstand—Bewährung—Orientierung. Beiträge zum Internationalen Symposion vom 1. bis 4. Mai 2008 in der Johannes a Lasco Bibliothek Emden.* Zurich: Theologischer Verlag, 2010.
Beintker, Michael, Georg Plasger, and Michael Trowitzsch, eds. *Karl Barth als Lehrer der Versöhnung (1950–1968). Vertiefung—Öffnung—Hoffnung.* Zurich: Theologischer Verlag, 2016.
Bergmann, Karl Hans. *Die Bewegung "Freies Deutschland" in der Schweiz 1943–1945.* Munich: Hanser, 1974.
Bergner, Gerhard. *Um der Sache willen. Karl Barths Schriftauslegung in der Kirchlichen Dogmatik.* Göttingen: Vandenhoeck & Ruprecht, 2015.
Besier, Gerhard. *Die Kirchen und das Dritte Reich.* Vol. 3: *Spaltungen und Abwehrkämpfe 1934–1937.* Berlin/München: Propyläen, 2001.
Besier, Gerhard, Jörg Thierfelder, and Ralf Tyra, eds. *Kirche nach der Kapitulation*, Vol. 1: *Die Allianz zwischen Genf, Stuttgart und Bethel.* Stuttgart: Kohlhammer Verlag, 1989.

Bietenhard, Benedikt. "Freies Gymnasium Bern 1859–2009, 150 Jahre Schulgeschichte," in *Das Jubiläumsbuch. 150 Jahre Freies Gymnasium Bern*, 2009, 13–82. http://www.fgb.ch/fileadmin/user_upload/_temp_/fgb._Geshichte_1859-2009.pdf (accessed May 2, 2018).

Bischof, Erwin. *Honeckers Handschlag, Beziehungen Schweiz–DDR 1960–1990. Demokratie oder Diktatur*. Bern: Interforum, 2010.

Blaser, Klauspeter, Article on Barth, in *Historisches Lexikon der Schweiz*. http://www.hls-dhs-dss.ch/textes/d/D10516.php (accessed February 3, 2020).

Blumhardt, Christoph. *Haus-Andachten nach Losungen und Lehrtexten der Brüdergemeine*. Stuttgart/Basel: Liesching, 1916.

Boerlin, Gerhard. "Karl Barth als Staatsbürger," *Schweizer Monatshefte für Politik und Kultur* 14(12) (1934–5): 639.

Bonhoeffer, Dietrich. *Act and Being: Transcendental Philosophy and Ontology in Systematic Theology*. Translation by Martin Rumscheidt of *Akt und Sein. Transzendentalphilosophie und Ontologie in der systematischen Theologie*. Gütersloh: Chr.Kaiser/Gütersloher Verlagshaus, 1988. Ed. Wayne Whitson Floyd Jr., *Dietrich Bonhoeffer Works*, Vol. 2. Minneapolis: Fortress Press, 1996.

Bonhoeffer, Dietrich. *Ecumenical, Academic, and Pastoral Work: 1931–1932*. Translation by Nicolaus Humphreys, Marion Pauck, Anne Schmidt-Lange, and Douglas W. Stott of *Ökumene, Universität, Pfarramt 1931–1932*. Gütersloh: Chr.Kaiser/Gütersloher Verlagshaus, 1994. Ed. Victoria Barnett, Mark Brocker, and Michael Lukens, *Dietrich Bonhoeffer Works*, Vol. 11. Minneapolis: Fortress Press, 2012.

Bonhoeffer, Dietrich. *London: 1933–1935*. Translation by Isabel Best and Douglas W. Stott of *London: 1933–1935*. Gütersloh: Chr. Kaiser/Gütersloher Verlagshaus, 1994. Ed. Keith Clements, *Dietrich Bonhoeffer Works*, Vol. 13. Minneapolis: Fortress Press, 2007.

Bonhoeffer, Dietrich. *Theological Education at Finkenwalde: 1935–1937*. Translation by Douglas W. Stott of *Illegale Theologenausbildung, Finkenwalde 1935–1937*. Gütersloh: Chr. Kaiser/Gütersloher Verlagshaus, 1996. Ed. H. Gaylon Barker and Mark S. Brocker, *Dietrich Bonhoeffer Works*, Vol. 14. Minneapolis: Fortress Press, 2013.

Bonhoeffer, Dietrich. *Letters and Papers from Prison*. Translation by Isabel Best, Lisa E. Dahill, Reinhard Krauss, Nancy Lukens, and Douglas W. Stott of *Widerstand und Ergebung*. Gütersloh: Chr. Kaiser/Gütersloher Verlagshaus, 1998. Ed. John W. de Gruchy, *Dietrich Bonhoeffer Works*, Vol. 8. Minneapolis: Fortress Press, 2010.

Brazier, Paul. "Barth and Expressionism—Some Further Considerations," *Zeitschrift für dialektische Theologie* 2(1) (2005): 34–52.

Brunner, Emil. "Die andere Aufgabe der Theologie," *Zwischen den Zeiten* 7 (1929): 255–76.

Brunner, Emil. "Die Frage nach dem 'Anknüpfungspunkt' als Problem der Theologie," *Zwischen den Zeiten* 10 (1932): 505–32.

Brunner, Emil. *Natur und Gnade. Zum Gespräch mit Karl Barth*. Tübingen: J. C. B. Mohr (Siebeck), 1934. Translated as *Natural Theology: Comprising "Nature and Grace" by Emil Brunner and the Reply "No!" by Karl Barth*, by Peter Fraenkel. London: G. Bles, 1946.

Brunner, Emil. *Das Gebot und die Ordnungen. Entwurf einer protestantisch-theologischen Ethik*. 3rd ed. Zurich: Theologischer Verlag, 1939.

Brunner, Hans Heinrich. *Mein Vater und sein Ältester. Emil Brunner in seiner und meiner Zeit*. Zurich: Theologischer Verlag, 1986.

Buess, Eduard and Markus Mattmüller. *Prophetischer Sozialismus. Blumhardt—Ragaz—Barth*. Freiburg: Edition Exodus, 1986.

Buff, Walter. "Karl Barth und Emanuel Hirsch. Anmerkungen zu einem Briefwechsel," in *Christliche Wahrheit und neuzeitliches Denken. Zu Emanuel Hirschs Leben und Werk*, 15–36. Ed. Hans Martin Müller. Tübingen/Goslar: Katzmann Verlag, 1984.

Bultmann, Rudolf. "Ethische und mystische Religion im Urchristentum," *Die Christliche Welt* 34 (1920): 725–31, 738–43.
Bultmann, Rudolf. *Glauben und Verstehen*. Vol. 1. Tübingen: Mohr, 1933.
Bultmann, Rudolf. *Neues Testament und Mythologie. Das Problem der Entmythologisierung der neutestamentlichen Verkündigung*. Ed. Eberhard Jüngel. Reprint, 3rd ed. Munich: Chr. Kaiser, 1988.
Bungert, Heike. *Das Nationalkomitee und der Westen. Die Reaktion der Westalliierten auf das NKFD und die Freien Deutschen Bewegungen 1943–1948*. Stuttgart: F. Steiner, 1997.
Burckhardt, Abel. *Kinder-Lieder von Abel Burckhardt. Eine Weihnachtsgabe für die Kinder und Mütter der Heimath*. Basel: F. Schneider, [1845].
Busch, Eberhard. *Karl Barth: His Life from Letters and Autobiographical Texts*. Translation of *Karl Barths Lebenslauf. Nach seinen Briefen und autobiographischen Texten*. 2nd ed. Munich: Chr. Kaiser, 1976 by John Bowden. Eugene, Oregon: Wipf & Stock Publishers, 1975.
Busch, Eberhard. *Unter dem Bogen des einen Bundes. Karl Barth und die Juden 1933–1945*. Neukirchen-Vluyn: Neukirchener Verlag, 1996.
Busch, Eberhard, ed. *Die Akte Karl Barth. Zensur und Überwachung im Namen der Schweizer Neutralität 1938–1945*. Zurich: Theologischer Verlag, 2008.
Busch, Eberhard. *Meine Zeit mit Karl Barth. Tagebuch 1965–1968*. Göttingen: Vandenhoeck & Ruprecht, 2011.
Busch, Eberhard, Jürgen Fangmeier, and Max Geiger. *Parrhesia. Karl Barth zum 80. Geburtstag am 10. Mai 1966*. Zurich: EVZ-Verlag, 1966.
Calvin, Johannes. *Unterricht in der christlichen Religion. Institutio Christianae Religionis*. Revised and edited by Otto Weber, revised and newly edited by Matthias Freudenberg. 2nd ed. Neukirchen-Vluyn: Neukirchener Verlag, 2009.
Chalamet, Christophe. *Dialectical Theologians: Wilhelm Herrmann, Karl Barth and Rudolf Bultmann*. Zurich: Theologischer Verlag, 2005.
Cohen, Hermann. *Logik der reinen Erkenntnis*. Introduced by Helmut Holzhey. Hermann Cohen Werke, Vol. 6/1. 4th ed. Hildesheim: Olms, 1977.
Dehn, Günther. *Kirche und Völkerversöhnung. Dokumente zum Halleschen Universitätskonflikt*. Berlin: Furche Verlag, 1931.
Dehn, Günther. *Die alte Zeit, die vorigen Jahre. Lebenserinnerungen*. Munich: Kaiser Verlag, 1962.
Denzinger, Heinrich. *Kompendium der Glaubensbekenntnisse und kirchlichen Lehrentscheidungen*. Ed. Peter Hünermann. 45th ed. Freiburg: Herder Verlag, 2017.
Drewes, Hans-Anton. *Das Unmittelbare bei Hermann Kutter. Eine Untersuchung im Hinblick auf die Theologie des jungen Karl Barth*. Dissertation, Tübingen University, 1979.
Dugan, Kaitlyn, and Philip Ziegler, eds. *The Finality of the Gospel: Karl Barth and the Tasks of Eschatology*. Leiden: Brill, 2021.
Ficker Stähelin, Daniel. *Karl Barth und Markus Feldmann im Berner Kirchenstreit 1949–1951*. Zurich: TVZ, 2006.
Foerster, Erich. "Marcionitisches Christentum. Der Glaube an den Schöpfergott und der Glaube an den Erlösergott. Vortrag auf der Eisenacher Tagung des Bundes für Gegenwartschristentum am 3. Oktober 1921," *Die Christliche Welt* 35 (1921): 809–27.
Freudenberg, Matthias. "Die Errichtung der Professur für Reformierte Theologie an der Georg-August-Universität Göttingen," *Jahrbuch der Gesellschaft für niedersächsische Kirchengeschichte* 94 (1996): 237–57.
Freudenberg, Matthias. *Karl Barth und die reformierte Theologie. Die Auseinandersetzung mit Calvin, Zwingli und den reformierten Bekenntnisschriften während seiner Göttinger Lehrtätigkeit*. Neukirchen-Vluyn: Neukirchener Verlag, 1997.

Freudenberg, Matthias and Hans-Georg Ulrichs, eds., *Karl Barth–Wilhelm Niesel. Briefwechsel 1924–1968*. Göttingen: Vandenhoeck & Ruprecht, 2015.
Gadamer, Hans-Georg. *Wahrheit und Methode. Grundzüge einer philosophischen Hermeneutik*. 3rd expanded ed. Tübingen: Mohr Verlag, 1972.
Gebhard, Rudolf. *Umstrittene Bekenntnisfreiheit. Der Apostolikumsstreit in der Reformierten Kirche der Deutschschweiz im 19. Jahrhundert*. Zurich: Evangelischer Verlag, 2003.
George, Christian. *Studieren in Ruinen. Die Studenten der Universität Bonn in der Nachkriegszeit 1945–1955*. Bonn: Bonn University Press, 2010.
Gerlach-Praetorius, Angelika. *Die Kirche vor der Eidesfrage. Die Diskussion um den Pfarreid im "Dritten Reich."* Göttingen: Vandenhoeck & Ruprecht, 1967.
Gilliard, Charles. "Zofingia," *Historisch-Biographisches Lexikon der Schweiz*. Vol. VII: 673–4. Neuenburg: Administration des Historisch-Biographischen Lexikons der Schweiz, 1934.
Göckeritz, Hermann Götz, ed. *Friedrich Gogartens Briefwechsel mit Karl Barth, Eduard Thurneysen und Emil Brunner*. Tübingen: Mohr Siebeck, 2009.
Goeters, J. F. Gerhard. "Karl Barth in Bonn 1930–1935," *Evangelische Theologie* 47 (1987): 137–50.
Goethe, Johann Wolfgang von. *Aus meinem Leben. Dichtung und Wahrheit*. Book 1, Hamburger Ausgabe. Ed. Erich Trunz. Vol. 9. 12th ed. Munich: C. H. Beck, 1994.
Gogarten, Friedrich. "Karl Barths Dogmatik (1929)," in *Gehören und Verantworten. Ausgewählte Aufsätze*, 14–30. Ed. Hermann Götz Göckeritz together with Marianne Bultmann. Tübingen: J. C. B. Mohr, 1988.
Gogarten, Friedrich. "Predigt über Joh. 15, 26-27," *Zwischen den Zeiten* 11 (1933): 465–72.
Gollwitzer, Helmut. *Skizzen eines Lebens. Aus verstreuten Selbstzeugnissen gefunden und verbunden von Friedrich-Wilhelm Marquardt, Wolfgang Brinkel und Manfred Weber*. Gütersloh: Chr. Kaiser, 1998.
"Gottes fröhlicher Partisan. Dialektischer Theologe Karl Barth. Kunde vom unbekannten Gott," *Der Spiegel* 52 (December 23, 1959): 69–72, 74–81.
Graf, Rüdiger. "Either-Or: The Narrative of 'Crisis' in Weimar Germany and in Historiography," *Central European History* 43 (2010): 592–615.
Greschat, Martin, ed. *Die Schuld der Kirche. Dokumente und Reflexionen zur Stuttgarter Schulderklärung vom 18/19. Oktober 1945*. Munich: Kaiser Verlag, 1982.
Gruner, Paul. *Menschenwege und Gotteswege im Studentenleben. Persönliche Erinnerungen aus der christlichen Studentenbewegung*. Bern: BEG Verlag, 1942.
Hägglund, Bengt. *Geschichte der Theologie. Ein Abriß*, 2nd ed. Munich: Kaiser, 1990.
Haitjema, Theodorus L. *Karl Barths "kritische" Theologie*. Leipzig: Wageningen, 1926.
Hake, Claudia. *Die Bedeutung der Theologie Johann Tobias Becks für die Entwicklung der Theologie Karl Barths*. Frankfurt am Main: Lang, 1999.
Hammerschmidt, Bernd. "Zum Gedenken an Karl Barth," 7–9. http://www.flurgespraeche.de/wp-content/uploads/2016/12/Gedenkblatt_Barth-Karl.pdf (accessed April 22, 2018).
Happ, Sabine. "'Streng vertraulich.' Das Verfahren zur Aberkennung des Ehrendoktors von Karl Barth an der Universität Münster (1936–1939)," *Westfälische Forschungen* 61 (2011): 345–63.
Härle, Wilfried. "Der Aufruf der 93 Intellektuellen und Karl Barths Bruch mit der liberalen Theologie," *Zeitschrift für Theologie und Kirche* 72 (1975): 207–24.
Harnack, Adolf von. *What is Christianity? Lectures delivered in the University of Berlin during the Winter Term 1899–1900*. Translation by Thomas Bailey Saunders of *Das Wesen des Christentums. Sechzehn Vorlesungen vor Studierenden aller Fakultäten im*

Wintersemester 1899/1900 an der Universität Berlin gehalten von Adolf v. Harnack. 2nd revised ed. New York: G. P. Putnam's Sons, 1908.

Harnack, Adolf von. *Marcion. Das Evangelium vom fremden Gott.* Leipzig: J.C. Hinrichs, 1921.

Heimbucher, Martin and Rudolf Weth, eds. *Die Barmer Theologische Erklärung. Einführung und Dokumentation.* Mit einem Geleitwort von Wolfgang Huber. 7th revised and expanded ed. Neukirchen-Vluyn: Neukirchener Verlag, 2009.

Heinemann, Gustav. *Es gibt schwierige Vaterländer... Reden und Schriften.* Vol. 3: *Reden und Aufsätze 1919–1969.* Ed. Helmut Lindemann. Frankfurt a. M.: Suhrkamp, 1977.

Heipp, Günther, ed. *Es geht ums Leben! Der Kampf gegen die Bombe 1945–1965. Eine Dokumentation.* Hamburg: Hamburg Reich, 1965.

Herrmann, Wilhelm. *Ethik.* 3rd ed. Tübingen: J. C. B. Mohr, 1904.

Herrmann, Wilhelm. *Der Verkehr des Christen mit Gott. Im Anschluß an Luther dargestellt,* 7th ed. Tübingen: J. C. B. Mohr, 1921.

Herwig, Thomas. *Karl Barth und die Ökumenische Bewegung. Das Gespräch zwischen Karl Barth und Willem Adolf Visser 't Hooft auf der Grundlage ihres Briefwechsels 1930–1968.* Neukirchen-Vluyn: Neukirchener Verlag, 1998.

Hirsch, Emanuel. *Die Reich-Gottes-Begriffe des neueren europäischen Denkens. Ein Versuch zur Geschichte der Staats- und Gesellschaftsphilosophie.* Göttingen: Vandenhoeck & Ruprecht, 1921.

Historisches Wörterbuch der Philosophie. Ed. Joachim Ritter, Karlfried Gründer and Gottfried Gabriel. Vols. 1–12. Darmstadt: Wissenschaftliche Buchgesellschaft, 1971–2004.

Hockenos, Matthew. *A Church Divided: German Protestants Confront the Nazi Past.* Bloomington: Indiana University Press, 2004.

Honecker, Martin. *Einführung in die Theologische Ethik. Grundlagen und Grundbegriffe.* Berlin: De Gruyter, 1990.

Hong, Liang. *Leben vor den letzten Dingen. Die Dostojewski-Rezeption im frühen Werk von Karl Barth und Eduard Thurneysen (1915–1923).* Neukirchen-Vluyn: Neukirchener Theologie, 2016.

Horne, John and Alan Kramer. *German Atrocities 1914: A History of Denial.* New Haven: Yale University Press, 2002. Translated as *Deutsche Kriegsgreuel 1914. Die umstrittene Wahrheit* by Udo Rennert. Hamburg: Hamburger Edition, 2004.

Hunsinger, George. *How to Read Karl Barth: The Shape of His Theology.* New York: Oxford University Press, 1991. Translated as *Karl Barth lesen. Eine Einführung in sein theologisches Denken* by Marianne Mühlenberg. Neukirchen-Vluyn: Neukirchener Verlag, 2009.

Hunsinger, George, ed. *Karl Barth, the Jews, and Judaism.* Grand Rapids: Wm. B. Eerdmans, 2018.

Jaspers, Karl. *Der philosophische Glaube angesichts der Offenbarung.* Munich: Piper Verlag, 1962.

Jaspers, Karl. *Korrespondenzen: Philosophie.* Ed. Dominic Kaegi and Reiner Wiehl. Göttingen: Wallstein Verlag, 2016.

Jehle, Frank. *Emil Brunner. Theologe im 20. Jahrhundert.* Zurich: Theologischer Verlag, 2006.

Jones, Paul Dafydd and Paul T. Nimmo, eds. *The Oxford Handbook of Karl Barth.* Oxford: Oxford University Press, 2019.

Jordan, Hermann. *Luthers Staatsauffassung. Ein Beitrag zu der Frage des Verhältnisses von Religion und Politik.* Munich: Mueller and Froehlich, 1917.

Jüngel, Eberhard. *Gottes Sein ist im Werden. Verantwortliche Rede vom Sein Gottes bei Karl Barth. Eine Paraphrase*. Tübingen: Mohr Siebeck, 1965.

Jüngel, Eberhard. *Barth-Studien*. Zurich-Köln/Einsiedeln: Benzinger et al., 1982.

Jüngel, Eberhard. *Die Leidenschaft, Gott zu denken. Ein Gespräch über Denk- und Lebenserfahrungen*. Ed. Fulvio Ferrario. Zurich: Theologischer Verlag, 2009.

"Eberhard Jüngel," in *Systematische Theologie der Gegenwart in Selbstdarstellungen*, 189–210. Ed. Christian Henning and Karsten Lehmkühler. Tübingen: Mohr Siebeck, 1998.

Kaftan, Julius. *Dogmatik*. Freiburg i.Br./Leipzig/Tübingen: J. C. B. Mohr, 1897.

Kaftan, Julius. *Kant, der Philosoph des Protestantismus. Rede gehalten bei der vom Berliner Zweigverein des evangelischen Bundes veranstalteten Gedächtnisfeier am 12. Februar 1904*. Berlin: Reuther & Reichardt, 1904.

Karl Barth 1886–1968. Gedenkfeier im Basler Münster. Zurich: EVZ Verlag, 1969.

Kielmansegg, Peter Graf. *Das geteilte Land. Deutschland 1945–1990*. Siedler Deutsche Geschichte, Vol. 4. Munich: Siedler Verlag, 2000.

Kierkegaard, Søren. *Einübung im Christentum. Von Anti Climacus*. Translated by Emanuel Hirsch. Part 26 of *Gesammelte Werke*. Düsseldorf: Diederichs, 1962.

Kirchliches Jahrbuch für die Evangelische Kirche in Deutschland 1933–1944. Evangelische Kirche im Dritten Reich. Ed. Joachim Beckmann. Gütersloh: C. Bertelsmann, 1948.

Kirchliches Jahrbuch für die Evangelische Kirche in Deutschland 1950. Ed. Joachim Beckmann. Gütersloh: C. Bertelsmann, 1951.

Kirschbaum, Charlotte von. *The Question of Woman: The Collected Writings of Charlotte von Kirschbaum*. Ed. Eleanore Jackson. Grand Rapids/Cambridge: Eerdmans, 1996.

Klappert, Bertold. "Der Aufstand gegen das Nichtige. K. Barths Stellungnahme zu den Massenvernichtungsmitteln," in *"Wenn nicht jetzt, wann dann?" Aufsätze für Hans-Joachim Kraus zum 65. Geburtstag*, 365–82. Ed. Hans-Georg Geyer, Johann Michael Schmidt et al. Neukirchen-Vluyn: Neukirchener Verlag, 1983.

Köbler, Renate. *Schattenarbeit. Charlotte von Kirschbaum–Die Theologin an der Seite Karl Barths*. Cologne: Pahl-Rugenstein, 1987. Translated as *In the Shadow of Karl Barth: Charlotte von Kirschbaum* by Keith Crim. Louisville, Kentucky: Westminster John Knox Press, 1989.

Kooi, Cornelis van der. *Anfängliche Theologie. Der Denkweg des jungen Karl Barth (1909–1927)*. Munich: Kaiser Verlag, 1987.

Korsch, Dietrich. *Dialektische Theologie nach Karl Barth*. Tübingen: Mohr, 1996.

Krötke, Wolf. *Karl Barth und der "Kommunismus." Erfahrungen mit einer Theologie der Freiheit in der DDR*. Zurich: TVZ, 2013.

Krumwiede, Hans-Walter, Martin Greschat, Manfred Jacobs, and Andreas Lindt, eds. *Kirchen- und Theologiegeschichte in Quellen*. Vol. IV/2. Neukirchen-Vluyn: Neukirchener Verlag, 1980.

Kuhn, Thomas K. "'McCarthy-Schwierigkeiten.' Der Streit um Helmut Gollwitzer als Nachfolger Barths 1961/62," *Basler Zeitschrift für Geschichte und Altertumskunde* 109 (2009): 53–102.

Küng, Hans. *Rechtfertigung. Die Lehre Karl Barths und eine katholische Besinnung. Mit einem Geleitbrief von Karl Barth*. Einsiedeln: Johannes Verlag, 1957. Translated as *Justification: The Doctrine of Karl Barth and a Catholic Reflection* by Thomas Collins. London: Thomas Nelson, 1964.

Küng, Hans. *Erkämpfte Freiheit. Erinnerungen*. Munich: Piper, 2002.

Kutter, Hermann. *Sie müssen! Ein offenes Wort an die christliche Gesellschaft*. Zurich, 1904.

Langhoff, Wolfgang. *Die Bewegung Freies Deutschland und ihre Ziele*. Zurich and New York: Europa Verlag, 1945.

Laube, Martin. "Die Unterscheidung von Theologie und Religion. Überlegungen zu einer umstrittenen Grundfigur in der protestantischen Theologie des 20. Jahrhunderts," *Zeitschrift für Theologie und Kirche* 112 (2015): 449–67.
Lauster, Jörg. *Zwischen Entzauberung und Remythisierung. Zum Verhältnis von Bibel und Dogma.* Leipzig: Evangelische Verlagsanstalt, 2008.
Leiner, Martin and Michael Trowitzsch, eds. *Karl Barths Theologie als europäisches Ereignis.* Göttingen: Vandenhoeck & Ruprecht, 2008.
Lepp, Claudia. *Tabu der Einheit? Die Ost-West-Gemeinschaft der evangelischen Christen und die deutsche Teilung 1945–1969.* Göttingen: Vandenhoeck & Ruprecht, 2005.
Lexikon für Theologie und Kirche. 11 Vols. 3rd completely new revised ed. Ed. Walter Kasper. Freiburg/Basel/Wien: Herder, 1993–2001.
Lienert, Meinrad. *Schweizer Sagen und Heldengeschichten.* Aarau: Sauerländer, 1974.
Lindsay, Mark. *Covenanted Solidarity: The Theological Basis of Karl Barth's Opposition to Nazi Antisemitism and the Holocaust.* New York et al.: Peter Lang, 2001.
Lindsay, Mark. *Reading Auschwitz with Barth: The Holocaust as Problem and Promise for Barthian Theology.* Eugene, Oregon: Pickwick Publication, 2014.
Lindt, August R. *Die Schweiz das Stachelschwein. Erinnerungen.* Bern/Gümlingen and Bonn: Zytglogge, 1992.
Loewenich, Walther von. *Erlebte Theologie. Begegnungen—Erfahrungen—Erwägungen.* Munich: Claudius Verlag, 1979.
Lohmann, Johann Friedrich. *Karl Barth und der Neukantianismus. Die Rezeption des Neukantianismus im 'Römerbrief' und ihre Bedeutung für die weitere Ausarbeitung der Theologie Karl Barths.* Berlin and Boston: De Gruyter, 1995.
Lorenz, Robert. *Protest der Physiker. Die "Göttinger Erklärung" von 1957.* Studien des Göttinger Instituts für Demokratieforschung zur Geschichte politischer und gesellschaftlicher Kontroversen, Vol. 3. Bielefeld: transcript Verlag, 2011.
Luther, Martin. *Werke. Kritische Gesamtausgabe.* Weimar: H. Böhlau, 1883–. Translated as *Luther's Works*, 55 Vols., Vols. 1–30 edited by Jaroslav Pelikan, Vols. 31–55 edited by Helmut Lehmann. Philadelphia and Minneapolis: Fortress Press, 1972—.
Mann, Thomas. *Tagebücher 1933–1934.* Ed. Peter de Mendelssohn. Frankfurt a. M.: S. Fischer, 1977.
Marquardt, Friedrich-Wilhelm. *Theologie und Sozialismus. Das Beispiel Karl Barths.* Munich: Kaiser Verlag, 1972.
Marti, Kurt. *Der Heilige Geist ist keine Zimmerlinde. Achtzig ausgewählte Texte.* Stuttgart: Radius Verlag, 2000.
Marti, Kurt. *Ein Topf voll Zeit 1928–1948.* Zurich: Nagel & Kimche, 2008.
McCormack, Bruce L. *Karl Barth's Critically Realistic Dialectical Theology: Its Genesis and Development, 1909–1936.* Clarendon: Oxford University Press, 1995. Translated as *Theologische Dialektik und kritischer Realismus. Entstehung und Entwicklung von Karl Barths Theologie 1909–1936* by Matthias Gockel. Zurich: TVZ, 2006.
Merz, Georg. "Die Begegnung Karl Barths mit der deutschen Theologie," *Kerygma und Dogma* 2 (1956), 157–75.
Merz, Georg. *Wege und Wandlungen. Erinnerungen aus der Zeit von 1892–1922.* Ed. posthumously by Johannes Merz. Munich: Chr. Kaiser, 1961.
Meyer, Alice. *Anpassung oder Widerstand. Die Schweiz zur Zeit des deutschen Nationalsozialismus.* Frauenfeld: Huber, 1965.
Möller, Ulrich. *Im Prozeß des Bekennens. Brennpunkte der kirchlichen Atomwaffendiskussion im deutschen Protestantismus 1957–1962.* Neukirchen-Vluyn: Neukirchener Verlag, 1999.

Moltmann, Jürgen, ed. *Anfänge der dialektischen Theologie.* 2 Vols. Munich: Kaiser, 1962/63.
Müller, Ernst Friedrich Karl. Karl Barth's Römerbrief, *Reformierte Kirchenzeitung* 71 (1921): 103-5.
Natorp, Paul. *Die logischen Grundlagen der exakten Wissenschaften.* Leipzig/Berlin: Teubner, 1910.
Nelly Barth-Hoffmann 26. August 1893-23. Oktober 1976, without place and year.
Neuser, Wilhelm H. *Karl Barth in Münster 1925-1930.* Zurich: Theologischer Verlag, 1985.
Nicolaisen, Carsten. *Der Weg nach Barmen. Die Entstehungsgeschichte der Theologischen Erklärung von 1934.* Neukirchen-Vluyn: Neukirchener Verlag, 1985.
Niemeyer, Christian. *Heldenbuch. Ein Denkmal der Grossthaten in den Befreiungskriegen von 1808-1815.* 3rd ed. Leipzig: Baumgärtner, 1818.
Otto, Rudolf. *Das Heilige. Über das Irrationale in der Idee des Göttlichen und sein Verhältnis zum Rationalen.* Munich: Beck, 2014. Translated as *The Idea of the Holy: An Inquiry into the Non-Rational Factor in the Idea of the Divine and Its Relation to the Rational* by John W. Harvey. 2nd ed. New York: Oxford University Press, 1958.
Overbeck, Franz. *Christentum und Kultur.* Werke und Nachlass. Vol. 6/1. Stuttgart: Metzler, 1996.
Pelliccia, Hayden, ed. *Selected Dialogues of Plato: The Benjamin Jowett Translation.* Revised and with an introduction by Hayden Pelliccia. New York: Modern Library Classics, 2000.
Peterson, Erik. "Was ist Theologie?," in *Theologie als Wissenschaft. Aufsätze und Thesen,* 132-51. Ed. Gerhard Sauter. Munich: Chr. Kaiser, 1971.
Peterson, Erik. *Theologie und Theologen,* Ausgewählte Schriften. Vol. 9/2. Ed. Barbara Nichtweiß. Würzburg: Echter, 2009.
Pfister, Rudolf. *Kirchengeschichte der Schweiz.* Vol. 3: 1720-1950. Zurich: Theologischer Verlag, 1984.
Prolingheuer, Hans. *Der Fall Karl Barth. 1934-1935. Chronographie einer Vertreibung.* 2nd ed. Neukirchen-Vluyn: Neukirchener Verlag, 1984.
Przywara, Erich. *Religionsphilosophie katholischer Theologie.* Munich/Berlin: Oldenbourg, 1926.
Przywara, Erich. *Ringen der Gegenwart. Gesammelte Aufsätze 1922-1927.* Vols. 1 and 2. Augsburg: Filser, 1929.
Ragaz, Leonhard. *Das Evangelium und der soziale Kampf der Gegenwart.* 2nd ed. Basel: C. F. Lendorff, 1907.
Ragaz, Leonhard. "Antwort an Herrn Pfarrer Gottfried Traub, Dr. der Theologie, in Dortmund," *Neue Wege* 8 (1914): 438-48.
Ragaz, Leonhard. *Religiöser Sozialist, Pazifist, Theologe und Pädagoge.* Published by Leonhard-Ragaz-Institut. Darmstadt: Lingbach Verlag, 1988.
Ragaz, Leonhard and Emil Brunner. "Von Gottesreich und Weltreich. Ein Gedankenaustausch," *Neue Wege* 9 (1915): 262-82.
Raiser, Konrad. *Ernstfall des Glaubens. Kirche sein im 21. Jahrhundert.* Göttingen: Vandenhoeck & Ruprecht, 1999.
Ramstein, Christoph. *Die Evangelische Predigerschule in Basel. Die treibenden Kräfte und die Entwicklung der Schule.* Bern: Lang, 2001.
Reichel, Hanna. *Theologie als Bekenntnis. Karl Barths kontextuelle Lektüre des Heidelberger Katechismus.* Göttingen: Vandenhoeck & Ruprecht, 2015.
Reinhardt, Volker. *Die Geschichte der Schweiz.* 2nd ed. Munich: C. H. Beck, 2013.
Reinhardt, Volker. *Geschichte der Schweiz.* 5th ed. Munich: C. H. Beck, 2014.

Religion in Geschichte und Gegenwart. Handwörterbuch für Theologie und Religionswissenschaft. Vols. 1–8. Ed. Hans Dieter Betz, Don S. Browning, Bernd Janowski and Eberhard Jüngel. 4th completely revised ed. Tübingen: J. C. B. Mohr, 1998–2005.

Rohkrämer, Martin. "Karl Barth in der Herbstkrise 1938," *Evangelische Theologie* 49 (1988): 521–45.

Rohkrämer, Martin. "Fritz Lieb 1933–1939. Entlassung–Emigration–Kirchenkampf–Antifaschismus," in *Theologische Fakultäten im Nationalsozialismus,* 181–97. Ed. Leonore Siegele-Wenschkewitz and Carsten Nicolaisen. Göttingen: Vandenhoeck & Ruprecht, 1993.

Rohls, Jan. *Philosophie und Theologie in Geschichte und Gegenwart.* Tübingen: Mohr Siebeck, 2002.

Rusterholz, Heinrich. "*...als ob unseres Nachbars Haus nicht in Flammen stünde.*" *Paul Vogt, Karl Barth und das Schweizerische Evangelische Hilfswerk für die Bekennende Kirche in Deutschland 1937–1947.* Zurich: TVZ, 2015.

Salin, Edgar. "Laudatio von Karl Barth." Ed. Niklaus Peter, *Zeitschrift für Neuere Theologiegeschichte* 1 (1994): 305–12.

Scherffig, Wolfgang. "Die fehlende siebte Barmer These. Französische Christen sprechen 1941 zur Judenverfolgung," *Evangelische Theologie* 55 (1995): 296–9.

Schiller, Friedrich. *Wilhelm Tell. Schauspiel, mit einem Kommentar von Wilhelm Große.* Frankfurt a. M.: Suhrkamp, 2002.

Schmidt, Kurt Dietrich, ed. *Die Bekenntnisse und grundsätzlichen Äußerungen zur Kirchenfrage des Jahres 1933.* Göttingen: Vandenhoeck & Ruprecht, 1934.

Schmidt, Kurt Dietrich, ed. *Die Bekenntnisse und grundsätzlichen Äußerungen zur Kirchenfrage.* Vol. 2: *Das Jahr 1934.* Göttingen: Vandenhoeck & Ruprecht, 1935.

Schmidt, Kurt Dietrich. "Fragen zur Struktur der Bekennenden Kirche (1962)," in *Gesammelte Aufsätze,* 267–93. Ed. Manfred Jacobs. Göttingen: Vandenhoeck & Ruprecht, 1967.

Schneider, Jörg. "Oswald Spenglers 'Der Untergang des Abendlandes' als Katalysator theologischer Kriseninterpretation zum Verhältnis von Christentum und Kultur," *Journal for the History of Modern Theology* 10 (2003): 196–223.

Scholder, Klaus. *Die Kirchen und das Dritte Reich.* Vol. 1: *Vorgeschichte und Zeit der Illusionen 1918–1934.* Berlin/Vienna: Ullstein, 1977. Translated as *The Churches and the Third Reich: Preliminary History and the Time of Illusions 1918–1934* by John Bowden. Philadelphia: Fortress Press, 1988. Vol. 2: *Das Jahr der Ernüchterung 1934 Barmen und Rom.* Berlin: Propylaen, 1985. Translated as *The Churches and the Third Reich: The Year of Disillusionment, 1934 Barmen and Rome* by John Bowden. Eugene, Oregon: Wipf & Stock, 2018.

Schweitzer, Albert. *Geschichte der Leben-Jesu-Forschung.* 9th ed. Tübingen: Mohr, 1984. Translated by John Bowden as *The Quest of the Historical Jesus.* Minneapolis: Fortress Press, 2001.

Schweizerköpfe der Gegenwart. Vol. 1, 117–21. Zurich: Verlag Schweizerköpfe der Gegenwart 1945.

Schwöbel, Christoph ed., *Karl Barth–Martin Rade. Ein Briefwechsel.* Gütersloh: Mohn, 1981.

Selinger, Suzanne. *Charlotte von Kirschbaum and Karl Barth: A Study in Biography and the History of Theology,* University Park, PA: Pennsylvania State University Press, 1998. Translated as *Charlotte von Kirschbaum und Karl Barth. Eine biografisch-theologiegeschichtliche Studie.* Zurich: Theologischer Verlag, 2004.

Smend, Rudolf. "Studium bei Karl Barth," in *Zwischen Mose und Karl Barth. Akademische Vorträge*, 311–40. Tübingen: Mohr Siebeck, 2009.
Solberg, Mary M. *A Church Undone: Documents from the German Christian Faith Movement 1932-1940*. Minneapolis: Fortress Press, 2015.
Stählin, Wilhelm. *Via Vitae. Lebenserinnerungen*. Kassel: Stauda, 1968.
Stoevesandt, Hinrich. "'Von der Kirchenpolitik zur Kirche!' Zur Entstehungsgeschichte von Karl Barths Schrift 'Theologische Existenz heute!' im Juni 1933," *Zeitschrift für Theologie und Kirche* 76 (1979): 118–38.
Strohm, Christoph. *Die Kirchen im Dritten Reich*. Munich: C. H. Beck, 2011.
Theologische Aufsätze. Karl Barth zum 50. Geburtstag. Munich: Kaiser, 1936.
Theologische Realenzyklopädie. Ed. Gerhard Krause and Gerhard Müller. Vols. 1–36, Berlin/New York: De Gruyter, 1977–2004.
Thielicke, Helmut. "Exkurs über Karl Barths Vortrag in Tübingen, gehalten am 8. November 1945 im Festsaal der Neuen Universität in Tübingen innerhalb der Vorlesungsreihe 'Die geistige und religiöse Krise des Abendlandes,'" in *Rudolf Bultmann—Briefwechsel mit Götz Harbsmeier und Ernst Wolf 1933-1976*, 370–83. Ed. Werner Zager. Tübingen: Mohr Siebeck, 2017.
Tietz, Christiane. "Systematisch-theologische Perspektiven zur Trinitätslehre," in *Trinität*, 163–94. Ed. Volker Henning Drecoll. Tübingen: Mohr Siebeck, 2011.
Tietz, Christiane. "On Reading Karl Barth in the USA," *Theology Today* 69 (2012): 133–140.
Tietz, Christiane. *Theologian of Resistance: The Life and Thought of Dietrich Bonhoeffer*. Minneapolis: Fortress Press, 2016. Translation by Victoria J. Barnett of *Dietrich Bonhoeffer: Theologe im Widerstand*. Munich: C. H. Beck, 2013.
Tietz, Christiane. "Karl Barth and Charlotte von Kirschbaum," *Theology Today* 74:2 (2017): 86–111.
Tietz, Christiane. "The Crucial Question of Theodicy: Predestination in Martin Luther's Theology," in *Game Over? Reconsidering Eschatology*, 293–311. Ed. Christophe Chalamet, Andreas Dettwiler, Mariel Mazzocco, und Ghislain Waterlot. Berlin: De Gruyter, 2017.
Tietz, Christiane. "Sakramente," in *Gottesdienst in der reformierten Kirche. Einführung und Perspektiven*, 162–75. Ed. David Plüss, Katrin Kusmierz, Matthias Zeindler, and Ralph Kunz. Zurich: Theologischer Verlag, 2017.
Tietz, Christiane. "Das Ringen um das Schriftprinzip in der modernen evangelischen Theologie," *Jahrbuch für Biblische Theologie*. Vol. 31: *Der Streit um die Schrift*, 283–302. Neukirchen/Vluyn: Neukirchener Verlag, 2018.
Tietz, Christiane. "Standing on the Boundary, where Now and Yet Then Touch Each Other. Barth on Theodicy and Eschatology." in *The Finality of the Gospel: Karl Barth and the Task of Eschatology*. Ed. Kaitlyn Dugan and Philip Ziegler, Leiden: Brill, 2021.
Tillich, Paul. *Ein Lebensbild in Dokumenten. Briefe, Tagebuch-Auszüge, Berichte*. Ed. Renate Albrecht and Margot Hahl. Stuttgart: Evangelisches Verlagswerk, 1980.
Tolstaja, Katja, ed. *"Das Römerbriefmanuskript habe ich gelesen." Eduard Thurneysens gesammelte Briefe und Kommentare aus der Entstehungszeit von Karl Barths Römerbrief II (1920-1921)*. Zurich: TVZ, 2015.
Trillhaas, Wolfgang. "Emanuel Hirsch in Göttingen," *Zeitschrift für Theologie und Kirche* 81 (1984): 220–40.
Troeltsch, Ernst. *Die Soziallehren der christlichen Kirchen und Gruppen*. Reprint of 1912 ed. Tübingen: Mohr, 1994.
"Um die Wahl eines Professors für die systematische Theologie," *Der Bund* 407 (September 22, 1927).

Vischer, Eberhard. "Overbeck und die Theologen," *Kirchenblatt für die reformierte Schweiz* 35 (1920): 122–4, 125–7.
Vollnhals, Clemens. *Die evangelische Kirche nach dem Zusammenbruch. Berichte ausländischer Beobachter aus dem Jahre 1945*. Göttingen: Vandenhoeck & Ruprecht, 1988.
Walser, Martin. *Über Rechtfertigung. Eine Versuchung*. Hamburg: Rowohlt, 2012.
Weber, Otto. *Karl Barths Kirchliche Dogmatik. Ein einführender Bericht zu den Bänden I, 1 bis IV, 3, 2*. 5th ed. Neukirchen-Vluyn: Neukirchener Verlag, 1963.
Wengst, Klaus. "Theologie und Politik im Jahr 1933—Karl Barth (1886-1968) und Karl Ludwig Schmidt (1891–1956)," in *Gesichter der Demokratie. Porträts zur deutschen Zeitgeschichte. Festschrift für Udo Wengst*, 37–51. Ed. Bastian Hein, Manfred Kittel, and Horst Müller. Munich: Oldenbourg, 2012.
"Witness to an Ancient Truth," *Time Magazine* April 20, 1962: 59–62, 65.
Wittekind, Folkart. *Geschichtliche Offenbarung und die Wahrheit des Glaubens. Der Zusammenhang von Offenbarungstheologie, Geschichtsphilosophie und Ethik bei Albrecht Ritschl, Julius Kaftan und Karl Barth (1909–1916)*. Tübingen: Mohr Siebeck, 2000.
Wüthrich, Matthias D. *Gott und das Nichtige. Zur Rede vom Nichtigen ausgehend von Karl Barths KD § 50*. Zurich: Theologischer Verlag, 2006.
Zellweger, Max. *Mein Schwiegervater. Erinnerungen an Karl Barth*. Zurich: Theologischer Verlag, 1981.
Ziemann, Benjamin. *Martin Niemöller. Ein Leben in Opposition*. Munich: Deutsche Verlagsanstalt, 2019.
Zuckmayer, Carl. *A Late Friendship: The Letters of Karl Barth and Carl Zuckmayer*. Grand Rapids, Michigan: Wm. B. Eerdmans Publishing, 1983. Translation of *Späte Freundschaft. Carl Zuckmayer—Karl Barth in Briefen* by Geoffrey Bromiley. Ed. Hinrich Stoevesandt. 2nd ed. Zurich: TVZ, 1978.
Zur Erinnerung an Frau Professor Anna Barth-Sartorius (15 April 1863–5. September 1938). Privately printed, undated.

Index

Not indexed: Basel; Karl Barth (with the exception of a very specific list of references). Barth family members are indexed under their individual names.

For the benefit of digital users, indexed terms that span two pages (e.g., 52–53) may, on occasion, appear on only one of those pages.

Aarau student Christian conferences 68, 122, 125–6
Academic Protestant Theological Association (Bern) 26
Achelis, Ernst Christian, critique of Barth 40
Acts of the Apostles, Barth's work in Harnack seminar 29–30
Adam, Karl, reaction to *Epistle to the Romans* (first version) 90
Adenauer, Konrad 330, 332–3
Aeschbacher, Robert 23
Alpine imagery, in Barth's theology 11, 15, 35, 134–5, 160–1, 295, 325
Althaus, Paul
  criticism of *Epistle to the Romans* (second version) 130–1
  critique of Barmen Declaration 233, 236–7. *See also* Lutherans; nationalism
Analogia entis (analogy in being) 166
Ansbach memorandum 236–7. *See also* Lutherans; nationalism
Anselm of Canterbury 163, 202, 364
  Barth's study of 203–4
Anti-Communism
  Barth's engagement against 324–30
  controversies about Barth in U.S. 383
  Swiss controversy about 326, 350–1. *See also* Communism
Antisemitism
  and Christianity 285
  as sin 285
  in Reich Church 286. *See also* Aryan paragraph; German Christians; Jews; National Socialism
Arendt, Hannah 389–90
Aryan paragraph 213. *See also* antisemitism; Church Struggle; Civil Service laws; "German Christians"
Asmussen, Hans 231–4, 238–9, 271–2. *See also* Barmen Synod; Lutherans
Atheism, and belief in Jesus 63
Augsburg Synod (1935), Barth asked not to attend 246

Augustine of Hippo 53, 166, 186, 346, 369
Auschwitz 401
Autonomy (*Eigengesetzlichkeit*) 90, 281
Awakening movement (*Erweckungsbewegung*) 157

Bad Oeynhausen conference (1935) 220. *See also* Barmen Synod; Confessing Church; Dahlem Synod
Baillie, Donald M. 271
Balthasar, Hans Urs von 338–9
Baptism
  Basel seminar on 269–70
  in *Church Dogmatics* 377–8
  church racial laws 213
  infant baptism 377–8
Barmen Declaration 210, 231–9, 260n.267, 272–3, 279
  first thesis 234–5
  second thesis 235
  third thesis 235
  fourth thesis 235
  fifth thesis 235
  sixth thesis 235–6
  approval of final version 233–4
  Barth's postwar evaluation of 234, 236
  Barth's work on 231–3
  and Dahlem 237–8
  debates over the text 233–4
  failure to address persecution of Jews 236 and 263n.322
  and political ethics 282
Barmen Synod 231–9. *See also* Barmen Declaration; Confessing Church
Barmen-Gemarke, Barth's 1935 lecture 272
Barnikol, Ernst 278–9
Barth, Anna neé Sartorius (Barth's mother; 1863-1938) 5–6, 9, 11–12, 14, 288–9
  and Barth's marital tensions 12, 189, 217, 219–20, 245
  death of 12

Barth, Christoph (son; 1917–86) 74, 338–9, 347, 388, 390, 392–3
  interrogated by Gestapo 237
  theological studies 309n.199
  1962 visit to U.S. 383
Barth, Franz Albert 2–3
Barth, Franziska (daughter; 1914–94) 74, 177, 268, 400
Barth, Gertrud. *See* Lindt, Gertrud
Barth, Hans Jakob (ancestor) 2
Barth, Hans Jakob (son; 1925–84) 103
Barth, Heinrich (brother; 1890–1965) 13
  and Barth's marital tensions 245
  theological influences on Barth 14, 95n.9, 125–6
Barth, Johann Friedrich (Fritz/Barth's father; 1856–1912) 8–11, 23, 26, 33
  academic career 10–11 and 20n.60
  death of 11
  marriage to Anna Sartorius 12
  theological influences on Barth 8–11, 24, 28–9, 40–1, 96n.20
Barth, Karl
  autobiography 1, 3, 15
  childhood and family influences 5–8, 12–18
    schooling 16–18
    theological influences on his later theology 5–6, 11–12, 15–16, 18, 37, 39–40
  early theological influences 23
    decision to study theology 23
    earliest theological writings 24–6
  personality 2–3, 156, 163, 167–8, 201–2, 248, 324, 397
  relationship to his children 167, 349, 388
  theological legacy 411
Barth, Katharina (sister; 1893–99) 13
Barth, Markus (son; 1915–94) 74, 177, 309n.199, 383, 388, 390
Barth, Matthias (son; 1921–41) 74,
  death of 289–90
  Barth's funeral sermon 289–90
Barth, Nelly neé Hoffmann (wife; 1893–1976) 154–7, 196n.100, 319–20, 392–3
  and Barth's relationship to Kirschbaum 183–9, 245–6
  and Barth's theological work 221
  death of 401
  discussions about divorce 214–18
  education and early years 55–6
  engagement and marriage to Barth 55–6, 73–6
  heart attack 400
Barth, Paul Basilius 347
Barth, Peter (brother; 1888–1940) 13–14, 70, 124
  death of 288
Barth, Samuel 2
Barth, Sara neé Lotz 3, 13
Barthians
  Barth's attitude toward 167–8, 293, 343–4
  theological influence of 271
Barth-Rade, Helene 288
Bäschlin, Ernst Adolf 296
Basel Mission Society 7, 24–5
Baur, Ferdinand Christian 24
BBC, Barth's wartime broadcasts 297–8
Bea, Augustin Cardinal 394–6
Beck, Johann Tobias 8–9
  influence on *Epistle to the Romans* (first version) 95n.8
Beckmann, Max 87
Beethoven, Ludwig van 80n.72
Bell, George 242, 297–8, 317
Bengel, Johann, influence on *Epistle to the Romans* (first version) 95n.8
Benjamin, Walter 268–9
Benn, Gottfried 87
Berdyaev, Nikolai 268–9
Bergson, Henri 270–1
Berlin theological faculty, Barth's studies in 28–31
Bern Canton Theological Working Group 14
Berneuchen Circle 156
Bertholet, Alfred 111
Bethge, Eberhard 236
Bethmann-Hollweg, Theobald 69
Beza, Theodore 48
Bible 96n.24, 122, 126–7, 132, 143
  historical study of 24, 127
  as witness of revelation 365, 379n.23. *See also* exegesis; historical-critical method; scripture; Word of God
Bismarck, Otto von 2
Bleibtreu, Otto 214, 245, 320
Bloch, Ernst 125, 205–6
Blue Cross 66
Blumhardt, Christoph 33, 72–3, 85, 101–2
Blumhardt, Johann Christoph 72–3, 85
Bodelschwingh, Friedrich von 211–12
Bonhoeffer, Dietrich 199–200, 242, 296–7, 388–9
  and Barmen Declaration 236–8
  on Barth's theology 132, 409
  and Jewish question 236
Bormann, Martin 276
Bousset, Wilhelm 39
Brand, Gertrud 6
Breit, Thomas 231–3
Brunner, Emil 137–8, 284
  criticism during Cold War 325–6
  disagreements about Barmen 308n.158

early friendship with Barth 137–9, 158, 228–9
ethics and natural theology 226–7
ethics of dialectical theology 226–7
and *Epistle to the Romans* (first version) 90
late reconciliation with Barth 398–9
Brunner, Hans Heinrich 223
Buber, Martin 166
Buchenwald concentration camp 314
Bullinger, Heinrich 7
Bultmann, Rudolf 37, 158, 202, 388–9, 409
differences about natural theology 229–30
friendship with Barth 137, 139
and loyalty oath 240–1
responses to *Epistle to the Romans* (second vision) 131–2, 139. *See also* Confessing Church; demythologization
Burckhardt, Abel 15, 401
Burckhardt, Christoph 6
Burckhardt, Jacob 7–11
Burckhardt, Johanna 5–8
Burckhardt, Johannes Rudolf 6–7
Burckhardt, Lukas 401
Burckhardt-Burckhardt, Hans 13
Buren, Paul van 342, 391–2, 401
Busch, Eberhard
Barth biography viii, 401
on Kirschbaum relationship 177–8

Calvin, John 14, 48, 62, 107, 126–7, 163, 346, 369
Barth's lectures on theology of 105–7
influence on Barth's thought 53–4
influence on *Epistle to the Romans* (first version) 95n.8. *See also* predestination
Capitalism 63, 68. *See also* Communism; socialism
Casals, Pablo 398
Catholic Church. *See* Roman Catholic Church
Catholic theology
Barth's first encounter with 165–6, 269–70
understanding of justification 339–40. *See* Küng, Hans; Roman Catholic Church; Second Vatican Council; University of Münster
Censorship of Barth
in Nazi Germany 271–2, 274, 280
in wartime Switzerland 291, 293–9. *See also* Gestapo; Lempp, Albert; loyalty oath; Nazi Germany
Christ. *See* Jesus Christ; Christology
Christendom
conformation to the world and Barth's critique 121
Christengemeinde und Bürgergemeinde (1946) 321–3

Christian community
as analogy to civil community 323
as Ecclesia 321–2
role toward state power 293, 322–3
task of 321. *See also* Christian political parties; church; church/state issues
Christian political parties, Barth's critique of 323. *See also* church/state issues; nationalism; Christian community; church
Christian Student Movement 26
Christliche Dogmatik im Entwurf/Christian Dogmatics in Outline (1927) 160–2, 168, 186, 200, 203, 363
influence on Brunner 227
Bultmann's critique of 229
Gogarten's review of 227
reworking of 200–2
Christliche Welt 35–6, 133–4, 142
Barth's work for 37–9
and First World War 69–70
Christology 36, 370, 375
Barth's developing 204–5
in *Church Dogmatics* 375–6
and political ethics 282
prophetic office of Christ 376. *See also* Historical Jesus; Jesus Christ; Herrmann, Wilhelm
Church
Basel seminar on 269–70
as boundary of the state 213
centrality of Holy Scripture 365–6
central task of 235–6
duty to address social issues 63
freedom of proclamation of 282
not defined by ethnic/racial/ideological categories 235–6
as "religious" 130
as understood in Catholicism 166. *See also* church/state issues; proclamation
Church Dogmatics 16, 29, 162, 324, 334
Barth's hopes for completion 347–9
in Barth's teaching and lectures 269, 342
as Christ-centered 362, 364
as conceptual helix 362
early work on 195n.82
end of work on 390–1, 399–400
Kirschbaum's contribution to 220–1, 399–400
organization of 363–4
title change from "Christian," 363–4
Church of the Holy Ghost (Bern) 14
Church Struggle (*Kirchenkampf*) 167, 212–14, 231, 276, 294
Barth's role 269–70, 284

Church Struggle (*Kirchenkampf*) (*cont.*)
  international impressions of 271
  and Jewish question 236. *See also* Barmen Declaration; church/state issues; Confessing Church; "German Christians"; nationalism; Nazi Germany
Church/state issues 240–1, 281–3, 296, 321
  as addressed in Barmen 235
  under Communism 324–5
  in German Democratic Republic 327–8. *See also* Barmen Synod; *Christengemeinde und Bürgergemeinde*; loyalty oath; *Rechtfertigung und Recht*
Churchill, Winston 389
Civil Service laws (1933) 209 and 252n.82
Civil War (U.S.) 386
Cohen, Hermann 36–7
Cold War 324–30, 410
  Barth's statements in U.S. 383–4
  Christianity as above the conflict 326–7
  and German rearmament 330–6. *See also* Communism; controversies; nuclear weapons; pacifism; rearmament
Collective guilt, Barth perspective on 301. *See also* Germany
Cologne criminal court, and Barth's case 244
Colossians, Barth's lectures on 162
Communism 228, 299, 326–7
  Barth's criticisms of 327–30
  Christianity under 327–8
  controversies about Barth 331, 355n.131
Confessing Church 167, 228, 241, 272, 274, 315
  Barmen 236
  and Barth 240, 242–3
  and Barth's 1935 refusal to take loyalty oath 240–8, 279
  Barth's disappointment 247–8, 264n.345
  Barth's dismissal from Bonn 245
  beginning of 167, 231
  and Bultmann 229
  Dahlem synod 237–9
  1938 loyalty oath debate 275–7 and 302n.27
  and Barth's objections 276
  Kirschbaum participation in 220
  pastors who fled Nazi Germany 283–4. *See also* Barmen Declaration; Church Struggle; "German Christians"; German Evangelical Church; nationalism
Confessions, Basel seminar on 269–70
Confirmation instruction 50–2, 55
Council of Brethren 238–7
  Barth elected to 237–8
  relation to Barth's dismissal due to loyal oath 244, 246. *See also* Confessing Church

Council of Trent 340
Covenant
  between God and humanity 204, 368, 370
  creation and 373
Creation 367–8, 372–5
Cremer, Hermann 85
Cullmann, Oscar 394–5
Cultural Protestantism 121, 140, 410
Czechoslovakia 277–80
  Barth solidarity with 277–8, 280
  German invasion of 286

Dahlem church 270
Dahlem Synod (1934) 237–8, 318–19
  aftermath of 238–9
  Barth's judgment about 264n.345
Daniélou, Jean 337
Darmstadt Statement of Guilt (1947) 319
Darwinism 63
Dehn, Günther
  Barth's solidarity with Dehn 207–8
  "Dehn affair," 206–9
  dismissed April 1933 209
  friendship with Barth 206, 320
Democracy 321, 323
  relationship to Gospel 283. *See also* church/state issues
Demythologization 230
Der Spiegel, 1959 cover story on Barth's politics 335–6
Dialectical theology 15, 94, 111–12, 133–6, 158–9
  beginnings of 93
  and Bultmann 139–40
  Catholic perspective on 165
  debates about 142–4, 202–3, 226–31
  and Dehn affair 207–8
  in the *Epistle to the Romans* 205
Dibelius, Martin 341
Dibelius, Otto 159–60
Dilthey, Wilhelm 71
Divorce
  discussions about 214 and 253n.123
  Barth's theological understanding of 222–3. *See also* Barth, Nelly; Kirschbaum, Charlotte von; marital tensions
Dix, Otto 87
Dogma, importance of 203
Dogmatics
  early approach toward 29, 109
  first publication of 160–2
  Göttingen lectures on 108–9
  Münster lectures on 160–2

postwar course in Bonn 320–1
understanding of 34, 36, 162, 371–2. *See* Church Dogmatics; Prolegomena
Dogmatism, Barth's rejection of 134–5
Dohnanyi, Hans von 296–7
Dorries, Hermann, and Dehn affair 207
Dostoevsky, Fyodor 85, 94, 125
Drews, Paul 40
Duns Scotus 166
Dürrenmatt, Friedrich 334
Dürrenmatt, Hugo 296

Ebeling, Gerhard 328, 390
Economic depression (interwar), in Germany 113–14
Ecumenical movement
 Barth's post-1945 involvement 336–40
 question of German guilt 317
 Second World War 286–7. *See also* Visser 't Hooft, Willem; World Council of Churches
Eichendorff, Joseph von 31
Einstein, Albert 398
Elert, Werner 236–7. *See also* Lutheran theologians
Ephesians, Barth's Göttingen lectures on 103
Epistle of James, Barth's lectures on 117n.40, 162, 249n.9
Epistle to the Romans (first version)
 Brunner's reaction to 138 and 150n.208, 226
 Bultmann's reaction to 139
 as foundation for his Tambach lecture 92, 94
 and professorship in Göttingen 100
 publication and early reception 87, 90–1, 94
 writing of 85–7. *See also* Lempp, Albert; Tambach lecture; Thurneysen, Eduard
Epistle to the Romans (second version)
 Barth's decision to revise 121–2, 124, 126–7, 363
 Barth's 1922 inscription to himself 394
 Bultmann's reaction to 139
 continuing impact of 132
 criticisms of 130–2
 dialectics of 136
 four central factors influencing the second version 125
 Harnack's critique of 142
 overview of 125–30
Epistle to the Romans 36–7, 53, 223–4
 and Barth's understanding of Luther 107
 and Christian dogmatics 161–2
Eschatology 129
 Barth's only lectures on 160
 section planned for *Church Dogmatics* 399

Ethics 31, 129–30, 205, 371–2
 lectures on 162, 200
 place of in theology 107
European Congress against Nuclear Armament 334
Evangelical Church of Germany (after 1945) 315, 319, 324
 guilt question 317
 postwar debates about rearmament 330–1, 333–4
Evangelicalism (in U.S.), Barth's statements about 385
Evil, and nothingness 373–4
Exegesis 85, 162
 and Barth's dogmatics 363. *See also* preaching; scripture; sermons
Existentialism 16
Experience (*Erlebnis*) as theological motive of war theology 71
 Barth's rejection of 97n.43, *See also* Dilthey, Wilhelm; Herrmann, Wilhelm

Faith 16, 51, 53, 90, 93, 129–30, 204, 229, 385
 and dialectical formula 136
 distinction from history 54–5
 knows no boundaries 284
Family tensions, over Barth's marital issues 245–6, 288–9
Feuerbach, Ludwig 401
Fichte, Johann Gottlieb 69, 140
Fides quaerens intellectum (1931) 204, 364
Fiedler, Eberhard 245
First Commandment 209–10
First World War 95n.4, 410
 Barth's critique of German theological support for 69–71
 Barth's opposition to 69, 71–2
 German militarism 27 and 80n.72
 German theological responses to 137, 140, 206, 223–4
 influence on Barth's thought 68–73, 82n.115, 89–90
 postwar crisis 125
 propaganda 70. *See also* Schweitzer, Albert; Spengler, Oswald
Fleiner, Fritz 33
Foerster, Erich 135–6
 critique of Barth's comments on culture 149n.165
Forgiveness 5, 122
 of Germans 300
Formula of Concord, Barth's 1934 seminar on 249n.9
Fourth Lateran Council (1215) 166

France, honors received 389–90
Francis of Assisi 25–6
Franco-Prussian War 2
Free Germany movement (National Committee for Free Germany) 299
Freedom
 of church 282
 of God and world 282
 of God 205, 368
 of human action 372
 in U.S. 384–6
Frei, Hans 384–5
French Revolution 401
Frey, Arthur 275, 284
Frick, Wilhelm 238, 241
Friedlaender, Ernst 301
Fuchs, Ernst 390
Führer principle 212, 244, 284
 rejected in Barmen Declaration 235
Die Furche 157

Gadamer, Hans-Georg 90–1
Geiger, Max 401
Geneva, Barth's ministry in 48–58
Gender equality in the church, Barth's statements on 337–8
Gerhardt, Paul 1
"German Christian" movement 211–12, 214, 230–1, 234, 286
 Barth's opposition to 212–13, 223–5, 279
 reference to in Church Dogmatics 364
 and natural theology 372. See also Barmen Declaration; Church Struggle; National Socialism; Reich Church
German Christian Student Association 157
German Democratic Republic 327–30
 Barth's protests against state pressures on churches 327–8
German Evangelical Church (pre-1945) 211–14
 and Barmen 234
 Barth's solidarity with 272
 Barth's warnings 213
 official position on loyalty oath 242. See also Church Struggle; Confessing Church
German Federal Republic, controversies about Barth 331–2. See also Adenauer, Konrad; Evangelical Church of Germany; nuclear weapons; pacifism; rearmament
"German greeting," Barth's opposition to 225–6. See also Führer principle; University of Bonn
German militarization, Barth's postwar fears of 331

German nationalism
 among theologians 208–9
 Barth's opposition to 113, 163, 224
 interwar 206–9
German people
 Barth's postwar friendship with 299–301, 315
 postwar attitudes toward guilt 318–19
German Propaganda Ministry, attacks on Barth 278–9
German Protestant Church Federation 211
German Reformed church, Geneva 48
German Religious Social Association 91–2
German theologians
 attacks on Barth's theology 223–6
 Barth's criticism of 112, 131
 beginning of Second World War 287
 and First World War 69–71
 nationalism of 159–60
 support for Barth in 1933 213. See also Church Struggle; Manifesto; nationalism
Germany 18
 attacks on Barth 271–2
 Barth's attitudes toward 91–2, 101, 113–14, 153, 163–4, 206, 269–70, 314
 Barth's wartime perspective on 299–301
 Barth's post-1945 perspectives 315, 317, 320–1, 323–4
 and Germans' reactions 301
 military counterintelligence resistance circles 296–7
 popular interest in Barth 113
 post-1945 rearmament debates 330–4 and 305n.87, See also Church Struggle; Nazi Germany
Gestapo, and Barth 225, 231–3, 237, 272, 275. See also censorship; loyalty oath
Gettysburg, 1962 visit to 386
University of Giessen, theological faculty protest vs. Barth 279
Gifford, Adam 270
Gifford lectures 270–1
Gilliard, Charles 26–7
Gleichschaltung (nazification) 211, 231, 238, 293, 315
God 36, 71–2, 122–3, 134, 136, 138–9, 162, 202–4, 272–3, 376–7, 401
 and the Bible 122
 became human in Christ 202–6, 375–6
 as bridge to humanity 122, 126, 136, 203, 227, 365–6, 368–9, 371–2, 411
 and creation 372–3
 and human history 128, 138
 judgement 128–9, 136, 368
 knowledge of 127, 270–1

in Luther's thought 70–1, also 81n.92, 166
nature of God's love 368–9
and "nothingness," 374–5
and redemption 88, 93
self-revelation in Christ 372, 411
self-revelation in trinity 366–8
"sole significance of," 90–2
as "wholly other," 92, 121–2, 125–7, 130, 143, 162, 205
wrath of 368. *See also* Christology; covenant; Epistle to the Romans; kingdom of God; revelation; trinity; Word of God
Godesberg Declaration (1939) 286
Godet, Frédéric, influence on *Epistle to the Romans* (first version) 95n.8
Godsey, John 342
Goethe, Johann Wolfgang von 1, 34, 80n.72
Gogarten, Friedrich 104, 124, 140–1, 158, 166, 229
Barth's theological differences with 230–1
early friendship with Barth 137, 140–1
and *Zwischen den Zeiten* 141–2
Gollwitzer, Helmut 200–1, 270, 283–4, 342, 391, 399, 401
as Barth's possible successor in Basel 350–1, 383
and 1938 loyalty oath 276
Göring, Hermann, 1929 encounter with 169
Gospel and Law, Barth's 1935 lecture on 272–3
Gospel 5–6, 10, 24, 30, 54, 58, 65, 133, 143, 168–9
in Barmen Declaration 234
in Barth's refutation of Christian nationalism 209, 212–13
"German Christian" interpretations of 236–7
and God's word 272–3
political implications of 68, 70, 207–8, 272–3, 279, 282–3, 323. *See also* preaching
Goßlau, Friedemann 327–8
Göttingen, Barth family move to 101–3. *See also* University of Göttingen
Göttingen Manifesto (antinuclear statement) 332–3
Barth's support for 333
Grace 88, 90, 129, 132, 136, 188–9, 235–6, 345
and doctrine of election 369–71
and God's love 123, 368–9
Graham, Billy 385
Grisebach, Eberhard 166
Großmünster Church (Zurich) 7
Grünewald, Matthias 123
Guilt
Barth's acknowledgment of his own personal 181, 184–5, 215, 222
Barth's acknowledgement of his own political 351n.7

collective 301
German, after First World War 70–1
German, after Second World War 296, 300–1, 317–19
means to reconciliation and forgiveness 316–17
theological 5, 336, 345
toward Jews 236
Guisan, Henri 292, 295–6
Gunkel, Hermann 29, 39
Gut, Walter 274

Habsburg monarchy 1
Hahn, Otto 332–3
Haitjema, Theodorus 168
Haller, Max 101
Hamlet 25
Harnack, Adolf von 8–9, 12, 26, 69, 101–2, 140, 151n.249, 269,
critique of Barth's understanding of God 123–4
and Barth's response 123
critique of dialectical theology 142–4
and Barth's response 143–4
final meeting with Barth 152n.252
influence on Barth 29–31, 201
What is Christianity 25
Heckel, Theodor 286
Hegel, Georg Wilhelm Friedrich 8–9, 69, 93, 136, 401
Heidegger, Martin vii, 166, 229, 328
Heidelberg Catechism, Barth's opinion of 103–4
Heilmann, Johann 100
Heinemann, Gustav, stance against rearmament 323, 330–1, 333–4
Heisenberg, Werner 332–3
Heitmüller, Wilhelm 37
Hermeneutics, significance of *Epistle to the Romans* 90–1
Herpel, Otto 94
Herren, Hans 291
Herrmann, Wilhelm 39, 51–4, 68–9, 71
Barth's study under 31, 35–6
Hesse, Hermann (novelist) 205–6
Hesse, Hermann (Reformed theologian) 238–9, 248
and Barth loyalty oath case 243
Hesse, Hermann Klugkist 270, 272
Heuss, Theodor 331–2
Heym, Georg 87
Hiroshima 401
Hirsch, Emanuel 110–12
clashes with Barth 208–9
and Dehn affair 207
role in Barth's suspension from Bonn 239

Historical Jesus 10–11, 16, 52
    and faith 54–5
    and social issues 63
Historical relativism 39–40
Historical-critical approach to the Bible 10, 84, 143
    and Barth 26, 87–8, 126, 143–4
    and Lord's Prayer 26
    and miracle accounts 25
History 93, 111, 122
    God's action in 130–1
    and lordship of Christ 230–1
Hitler, Adolf 212, 238, 296–7, 315
    Barth's 1933 letter to 213–14
    Barth's 1934 letter to 231
    Barth's critique of 241, 243, 291
    involvement in case vs. Barth 245
    loyalty oath to 239, 275. *See also* Barmen Declaration; Confessing Church; "German Christians"; National Socialism; nationalism
Hofacker, Ludwig 7
Hoffmann, Adolph 55
Hoffmann, Anna neé Hugentobler 55
Hoffmann, Joseph Marzell 55
Hoffmann, Robert 55
Holl, Karl 29, 165
Hölscher, Gustav 214
Holy Scripture. *See* scripture
Holy Spirit 11, 128, 162, 213, 235–6, 285, 362, 367, 377–8
    as revealed 366–7 and 379n.36. *See also* trinity
Honorary doctorates 271, 389
Honors received 389–90
    on his 80th birthday 394
Horst, Friedrich 242–3
Hromádka, Josef L. (1889–1969) 280–1, 401
    Barth's 1938 letter to 277–80, 330–1
    meeting with in Bonn 305n.80, 277
Huber, Achilles 4
Huber, Sophie 4–5
Human being 136, 314–15
    in relation to God 139–40, 206, 227, 373. *See also* God
Humanae vitae (1968 encyclical) 397
Humanistic education 16–17
"Humanity of God," 1956 lecture 205
Hungarian Reformed church, Barth's postwar visit 324–6
Hungarians, protests to Barth during Sudeten crisis 279–80. *See also* Hromádka, Josef L.; Sudeten crisis

Husserl, Edmund 166
Hüssy, Gustav 64–5
Hüssy, Walter 63–4

Immer, Karl 238–9, 243, 246, 272
India, caste system 24–5
Injustice, not God's will 62
Inner life of faith 56–8, 61–3
Inner Mission (Netherlands) 168
Institutes of the Christian Religion (Calvin) 48, 62, 108, 369
Isenheim Altar 123, 362
Iwand, Hans 319

Jacobi, Gerhard 224–5
Jäger, August 211–12, 231, 237–8
Jaeger, Werner 270–1
James, William 270–1
Jaspers, Karl, friendship with Barth 331–2, 341, 344
Jesus Christ 33–4, 90, 202, 235, 281–2, 366–7, 376–8
    Barmen Declaration 210
    death and resurrection 289
    and doctrine of predestination 369–70
    as "ethical personality" 35–6
    as grace 400
    as humankind's bridge to God 127–8
    Jewishness of 17
    and nothingness 374–5
    as revealed word of God 143, 204–5, 209–10, 364–6
    Tambach lecture 92
    as the "unconditionally New," 92–3
    unity of the church in 336. *See also* Barmen Declaration; Christology; resurrection, revelation; trinity; Word of God
Jewish community, in Switzerland 284
Jews
    Barth's response to persecution of 285
    not mentioned in Barmen Declaration 236, and 263n.322
    persecution in Germany 297
    status of converts to Christianity under Nazi law 213. *See also* Judaism; "Kristallnacht" pogroms; refugees; Swiss Aid Association
Johann, Ernst 389–90
John the Baptist 123, 362
Jordan, Hermann 281
Judaism, Barth's theological understanding of 263n.322, 285. *See also* Jews
Judas, betrayal of Jesus 370
Jugendbewegung 156

Jülicher, Adolf 37, 101–2
  critique of *Epistle to the Romans* (first version) 91
Jüngel, Eberhard 328, 343, 401
  eulogy for Barth 402
Jünger, Ernst 71
Justice 129, 281–3
Justification
  1927 lecture on 157
  1999 Joint Lutheran-Catholic Declaration on 339–40
  Basel seminar on 269–70
  different understandings of 132
  by grace 88
  Küng's work on 339–40
  relation to justice 281–2
  of sinners 300

Kaftan, Julius 8–9, 29–31
Kaiser Wilhelm II 69
Kant, Emanuel 24, 29, 31, 35, 80n.72, 125, 401
  Critique of Pure Reason 24
  influence on *Epistle to the Romans* (first version) 85
Kasper, Hans 243
Kautzsch, Emil 8
Keller, Adolf 48, 56, 74
Keller, Gottfried 224
Kennedy, John F. 385–6
Kennicott, M. B. 205–6
Kerrl, Hanns 270
Kierkegaard, Søren 16, 123, 125–6, 128, 389
  influence on Barth's theology 85, 127
King, Martin Luther Jr., Barth meets 385
Kingdom of God 33, 39, 129
  distinction from human and political agendas 89–90, 92, 122
  on earth 63, 137–8
  and First World War 72
  social dimension of 61–2, 72–3
  as synthesis 93–4. *See also* God; religious socialism
Kirschbaum, Charlotte von 33, 154–5, 157–8, 168, 178–9, 218, 224–5, 287, 319–20, 324, 383
  and Church Struggle 214, 237–8, 272
  discussions of marriage 214–16
  early correspondence with Barth 179–83
  education and career training 179
  and feminism 257n.182, 338
  final years 391
    health decline 391–3
    final visit to 401
  friendship with the Thurneysens 246
  interest in theology 179, 220
  moves in with the Barth family 170, 188–91
  and Nelly Barth 185, 188–90
  support for Barth's theological work 185–6, 220–1, 399–400
  and Swiss Aid Association 284–5, 299
  tensions with Barth 188 and 197nn.104,114, 198n.133
  tensions with Barth family and friends 177–8, 216, 245–6
  theological significance of relationship with Barth 220–3
Kirschbaum, Henriette von 178
Kirschbaum, Maximilian von 178
Kittel, Helmuth 280
Köberle, Adolf 158
Koch, Karl 242, 276
Koechlin, Alphons 242, 317, 326
Kohlbrügge, Hermann 159–60
Körner, Theodor 17
Kreck, Walter 342
"Kristallnacht" pogroms (1938) 284–5
Krötke, Wolf 329–30
Küng, Hans 394–5, 401
  dissertation on Barth's understanding of justification 339–40
  eulogy for Barth 402
Küppers, Erica 224–5, 231–3, 242
Kutter, Hermann 68, 85, 137
  influence on *Epistle to the Romans* (first version) 85 and 95n.8, 101–2, 125, 138
  religious socialism of 72–3
  support for First World War 72

Lang, Cosmo Gordon Archbishop of Canterbury 308n.173
Lang, Herbert 293–4
Laube, Martin 411
Lauster, Jörg 409–10
Lauterburg, Otto 30–1, 37–8
Lempp, Albert 94, 121, 212, 218, 237, 271–2, 274–5
Lerber, Theodor von 16–17
Lessing, Gotthold Ephraim 16
Liberal theology 35, 139–40, 410
  Barth family attitudes toward 3, 5–6
  Barth's early interest in 23, 37
  Epistle to the Romans (first version) as critique of 91
Liberalism 16
Lieb, Fritz 199, 268–9, 334
Lietzmann, Hans 95n.8, 112
Lindt, Gertrud neé Barth (sister; 1896–1979) 13–14, 219, 288–9
  and Barth's marital tensions 245–6

Lindt, Karl (married to Gertrud Barth) 14, 288–9
  and Barth's marital tensions 245
Literature, Barth's preferences 205–6
Loew, Wilhelm 53, 156
Loewenich, Walther von 108, 110
Lord's Prayer 26, 51
Lord's Supper
  Basel seminar on 269–70
  1934/35 seminar on in Bonn 249n.9
Lotz, Burkhard 2
Lotz, Peter Friedrich (great-grandfather) 2–3
Loyalty oath to Hitler for civil servants (1935) 210, 239
  Barth's position on 239–42
  and Christian freedom 282–3
  state interpretation of 243, 247
Loyalty oath to Hitler, 1938 controversy 275–7
Lubac, Henri 338–9
Lüdemann, Hermann 24, 34, 163
Lukacs, Georg 125
Luther, Martin 53, 106, 157, 163, 165, 211, 346, 373–4
  concept of state 281
  ethical questions 107
  and predestination 369
  understanding of God 81n.92, 166
Luther Renaissance 29, 165
Lutheran World Alliance 339–40
Lutherans
  and Barmen Synod 233
  and German nationalism 272–3. See also Asmussen, Hans; Church Struggle; German Evangelical Church; Marahrens, August; Meiser, Hans; Wurm, Theophil

Macfarland, Charles 225, 242
Mackensen, Stephanie von 233
Manifesto (1914) of German intellectuals supporting First World War 69
  history of 80n.72 and 80n.78
Mann, Heinrich 268–9
Mann, Thomas 205–6
  on Barth's critique of National Socialism 213
Mannheim, Karl 205–6
Marahrens, August 238–9
  and Barth loyalty oath controversy 242–3
  critique of Barth 247
Marburg, Barth's 1908–1909 studies in 35–41
  theological faculty 28–9, 140
Marcion 143 and 151n.249
Marital tensions 360n.277
  crisis of 1933 214–16
  friends and family react to 184, 216–17, 219–20, 245–6

and his theological work 220–3 and 258n.200, 409. See also Barth, Nelly; Kirschbaum, Charlotte von; Thurneysen, Eduard
Marti, Karl 24
Marti, Kurt 343
Marx, Karl 401
Marxism, postwar German church perspectives on 319
Maury, Pierre 280–1, 286–7
Mayer, Marguerite 67
Meiringen 32
Meiser, Hans 231, 233
  church-state tensions 237–8
  pressures on Barth 246
Merian, Christoph 5
Merian, Peter 3–4
Merz, Georg 94, 160–1, 179
  and Kirschbaum 184, 220
  and Zwischen den Zeiten 141–2, 230–1
Military service 17
  Barth's 291
  for Christians 282–3, 286–7
Ministry of Church Affairs 270, 276
Miracle accounts in scripture 25
Möhler, Johann Adam 165
Molina, Luis de (1535–1600) 166
Morgarten, battle of 1
Mozart 345–6, 400–1
  as analogy for God's relation toward the world 205
  Barth's lifelong love for 346–7
Müller, Alfred Dedo 91
Müller, Ernst Friedrich Karl 100
Müller, Kurt 301
Müller, Ludwig 211–12, 225, 231, 238, 246
Münch, Alexander 94
Münger, Rosy, Barth's relationship to 32–3
Münster Church (Basel) 68
  Barth baptized in 13
  Barth preaches in 268
  Barth's funeral 401
  elects Thurneysen 168–9
Münster Church (Bern) 163
Music, family interest in 17–18, 113, 157–8, 167
  and Barth 347. See also Mozart
Mussolini, Benito 315
Mysticism 16, 138

Napoleon I Bonaparte 2
Napoleon III 17
National Committee for Free Germany. See Free Germany movement

National Socialism 206, 285
  Barth's first encounter with 169
  demands on church 275-7
  during interwar period 207
  early postwar legacy of in Germany 299-300, 315-17, 326
  as false religion 209-10, 272-3, 284, 294. See also Church Struggle; Hitler; loyalty oath; nationalism
Nationalism, and German churches 272-3, 278-9, 323
  among German theologians 110-11, 230-1, 286
  Barth's early opposition to 169. See also First World War; German theologians; Hirsch, Emanuel; nationalism
Natorp, Paul 36-7
Natural law, Barth's opposition to 397
Natural theology, Barth's opposition to 119n.107, 209-10, 226-7, 229-30, 234-5, 270-1, 372
Naumann, Hans 239
Nazi Germany
  actions against Barth 242-6
  Barth's critique from Switzerland 286-7
  Barth's opposition to 226
  controversies about Barth 223-6
  early period 209-14
  pressure on Confessing Church in Barth case 240
  pressures on Barth in Switzerland 274, 298
  refugees from 283-4
  totalitarian claim on church 241-4. See also Barmen Declaration; Church Struggle; Gestapo; loyalty oath; National Socialism; totalitarianism; University of Bonn
Neo-Kantianism 14, 36-7
Netherlands, Barth's 1926/1927 lectures 168
Neuchâtel, Barth lecture in 54
Neumünster Church (Zurich) 68
  Barth called to (1925) 153
New Testament 103, 121, 127. See also exegesis; preaching; scripture
Niebuhr, H. Richard 384-5
Niebuhr, Reinhold 337-8, 386
Niemeyer, Christian 17
Niemöller, Martin 14, 237-9, 270, 337-8, 362
  postwar debate about German guilt 315, 318-19
  and rearmament 330-1
  and Swiss aid to Confessing pastors' families 283-4
Niesel, Wilhelm 248, 324
Nietzsche, Friedrich 8-9, 121, 401

Norway, and Barth's support for church resistance there 297-8
Nothingness 373-5
  God's negation of 374-5
Novalis (Georg Philipp Friedrich von Hardenburg) 31
Nuclear weapons
  Barth's statements on 333-4
  Barth's Ten Theses against 333-4
  debates about 332-4. See also Cold War; Göttingen manifesto; rearmament
Nydegg Church (Bern) 74

Ogden, Schubert 384-5
Old Prussian Union Church 247, 275. See also Confessing Church
Old Testament 24, 364-5
Orders of creation 162
Origen 53
Ott, Heinrich 350-1
Otto, Rudolf 122, 131
Overbeck, Franz 8-9, 125
  influence on Barth's *Epistle to the Romans* 85, 121-2 and 144n.10
Oxford, honorary doctorate 271
Oyen, Hendrik van 269

Pacifism 71-2
  Barth's critique of during Second World War 290-2
  post-1945 330-6
  war as *ultima ratio* 322
Parish ministry 84, 100. See also preaching; Safenwil; sermons
Pastors Emergency League 14, 237-8
Paul (apostle) 9, 24, 30, 85, 125, 138
  Barth's exegetical approach to 87-8. See also *Epistle to the Romans*
Pelikan, Jaroslav 384-5
Pestalozzi, Gertrud 67, 184, 219
Pestalozzi, Rudolf 67, 85
  and Kirschbaum relationship 184, 320
Peterson, Erik 111-12
  argument with Barth about dialectical theology 202-3
Petuchowski, Jakob 384-5
Peyer, Amalie 7
Philippians, Barth's lectures on 162
Pietism
  Barth's estrangement from 167-8
  in family history 7-8
Pilet-Golaz, Marcel 291-2, 298
Piper, Otto 158

Plato 53, 125
  influence on Barth's *Epistle to the Romans* (first version) 85
Political responsibility
  Barth's developing thought in response to Nazism 280-3
  Barth's theological view 89, 212, 323
Politics, Barth's model of 322. *See also* church/state issues
Pontius Pilate 282, 370
Pope John XXIII 394
Pope Paul VI, Barth's audience with 396-7
Positive theology, Barth's opposition to 28-9, 35, 131
Prayers, for state 283
Preaching 109
  Barth's attitude toward 73, 105
  as theological question 109, 133-4, 143. *See also* proclamation; sermons
Predestination
  Barth's transformation of this doctrine 369-71
  Calvin 369
  and Christology 369. *See also* election
Pressel, Wilhelm 238-9
Princeton, Barth's 1962 visit to 385
Prison ministry, Barth's 344-6
Prisons, Barth calls for reform in U.S. 385-6
Proclamation, as interpretation of biblical text 365-6, 376-7. *See also* preaching; sermons
Prolegomena to Dogmatics 108, 160-1, 168, 200 and 249n.9, 364-8. *See also* *Christliche Dogmatik im Entwurf*
Protestant Church Welfare Society of Bern 10, 12
Protestant Preachers Seminary (Basel) 10
Protestant theology
  Barth's lectures on history of 160
Provisional church government 238-9, 242-3, 245-7. *See also* Confessing Church; Council of Brethren; Dahlem Synod; Marahrens, August
Prussian ministry of culture 225. *See also* Rust, Bernhard
Przywara, Erich 165-6, 338-9
  praise for dialectical theology 165

Quervain, Alfred de 269

Racism, in U.S. 383-6
Rade, Helene 14

Rade, Martin 14, 37, 39, 41, 133-4, 142
  Barth's appreciation for 41
  support for First World War 69-71
Ragaz, Leonhard 68, 87, 163-4
  farewell in *Epistle to the Romans* to (second version) 125
  First World War 72
  religious socialism of 72-3
Rahlfs, Alfred 108
Rahner, Karl 396
Rathje, Johannes 41
Rationalism 16
Ratzinger, Joseph 396
Rearmament. *See* Germany, rearmament of
Rechtfertigung und Recht (1938) 281-3, 321. *See also* church/state issues; political responsibility
Reconciliation
  Barth's doctrine of 371, 375
  in Christ 376-7
  and God 367-8
Reformation Confessions
  as foundation of church 234
Reformation 107, 270-1
Reformed Confessions
  Barth's lectures on 105
Reformed Federation 110, 244, 247
Reformed theology, Barth's courses on in Göttingen 101, 103, 105
Refugee work, in Switzerland 268-9, 283-5, 299
Reich bishop 211-12, 237-8. *See also* Müller, Ludwig; Ministry of Church Affairs
Reich church, early calls for 211-12. *See also* "German Christians"
Reich Ministry of Culture
  Bonn case vs. Barth 240
  oversight of universities 239
Reich Ministry of Interior, and churches 237
Reich Ministry of Propaganda, pressures on *Theological Existence Today* 275
Reichstag fire 224
Religion
  understanding of 29, 89, 92, 122, 129-30
  and cultural crisis of the early twentieth century 140-1
Religious experience 51, 92
Religious socialism 89, 91-2
  in Switzerland 68
Rembrandt van Rijn 168
Resurrection of the dead 375-6
  Barth's lecture on 154
  and knowledge of God 92-3, 122, 128

Retirement
  Barth's activities in 387–90
  health issues 390–1, 400
Revelation 51, 130, 270–1, 409
  and dialectical theology 203
  and doctrine of election 370
  of God in Christ 11, 143–4, 162, 202, 365, 372, 379n.36
  historicity of 130
  and natural theology 372
  and trinity 366–7. *See also* God; Jesus Christ; Word of God
Richter, Hans Werner 334
Rickenbach, Margaretha 5
Rieger, Carl, influence on *Epistle to the Romans* (first version) 95n.8
Ritschl, Albrecht 8–9, 37, 40, 163
Roman Catholic Church
  Barth's changing relationship to 338–9, 394
  and Protestant ecumenical movement 337
  reception of Barth 337, 397–8
Rome, Barth's 1966 visit 395–6. *See also* Küng, Hans; Przywara, Erich; Second Vatican Council; University of Münster
Romanticism, Barth's early appreciation for 31
Roth, Karl Ludwig 4
Ruh, Hans 342
Ruhr occupation (1923) 111
Russell, Bertrand 157–8, 334
Rust, Bernhard 210–12, 225, 239, 242–3, 245, 247
Ružička, Leopold 334

Safenwil
  Barth's recollections of 73, 104, 153
  Barth's theological development in 84
  controversies about Barth's political views 63–5
  economic demographics of 62–3, 65–6
  end of Barth's ministry there 95
  Thurneysen's summary of Barth's time there 101–2. *See also* Ragaz, Leonhard; sermons; Social Democrats
Salvation
  human longing for 134
  and predestination 369
  and social questions 336
  Word of God and revelation 136, 270–1
San Francisco, 1962 visit to 385–6
Sartorius, Ernst (uncle) 291
Sartorius, Karl (for whom Barth was named) 5, 12–13
Sartorius, Karl Achilles (grandfather) 5–6
  theological profile of 5–8

Sartorius, Karl Friedrich (great-grandfather) 3–5
Sasse, Hermann 231–4
Schädelin, Albert 163, 288
Scheeben, Matthias Joseph 165
Schelling, Friedrich Wilhelm Joseph 5
Scheuner, Dora 14, 288
Schiller, Friedrich 17, 291–2
Schlatter, Adolf 10, 12, 69
  Barth's study under 33
  criticism of *Epistle to the Romans* (second version) 131
  influence on *Epistle to the Romans* (first version) 95n.8
Schleiermacher, Friedrich 24, 69, 124, 131, 163, 346, 409
  Barth's reading of 31, 48, 134
  Barth's lectures and courses on 105, 201, 388
  Barth's perspective about 53–4, 388
  Brunner's critique and Barth's response 138–9
  Christliche Sitte 5
  early influence on Barth 5–6, 35, 37, 101–2
Schmidt, Friedrich Wilhelm 280
Schmidt, Karl Ludwig 207, 210
  friendship with 199, 268–9
  leaves Nazi Germany 209
Schmitz, Otto 157, 167
Scholastic theology 53
Scholz, Heinrich 43n.56, 203, 213
  friendship with 157–8
Schürch, Ernst 164
Schwarz, Martin 344
Schweitzer, Albert 89–90, 270–1, 389
  anti-nuclear stance 333
  influence on *Epistle to the Romans* (first version) 95n.8
Scottish confession (1560) 270–1
Scripture 162
  Barth's understanding of scripture and revelation 364–5
  as bearing witness to Christ 364–5
  doctrine of verbal inspiration 23
  problems with literal interpretation of 365. *See also* exegesis; preaching; sermons
Second Vatican Council 337–9
  Barth's influence on 405n.88
  Barth's interest in 395
  colloquium on 405n.106
  invitation to Barth 394–5. *See also* Roman Catholic Church; Rome
Second World War
  beginning of 287
  Barth's BBC talks 297

Second World War (*cont.*)
  early ecumenical reactions to 286–7
  end of 314
  defends military service 290–1
  postwar destruction in Bonn 320
  Swiss surveillance of Barth's activities 297–8
  volunteers for military service 291
  wartime publications and lectures 291–6.
    See also censorship; Switzerland
Seeberg, Reinhold 29
Sempach, battle of 1
Sermons 133
  Barth's preaching style 48–50, 100–1
  during First World War 73
  prison ministry 344–5
  as proclamation of God's word 162, 227
  in Safenwil 137
  Seek God and You Shall Live! (book of sermons co-authored with Thurneysen) 137–8
  task of 143. *See also* parish ministry; preaching; proclamation
Sermon on the Mount 117n.40, 249n.9
Sigmund-Freud Prize 389–90
Sin
  and Christology 375–6
  human 163
  reality of 143
Smend, Rudolf 342–3
Social analysis, Barth's early thinking 27–8
Social democracy, early praise for 63. *See also* socialism
Social Democrat Party
  Barth's membership in 72, 210–11, 243–4
  in Germany 209–11
  in Switzerland 27
  tensions with church 68
Social justice, Christian 68
Socialism 92
  Barth's 61–5, 72, 78n.43, 124
  failure during First World War 71–2. *See also* Kingdom of God; Social Democrats
Socrates 53, 243–4
Soden, Hans von 240–1
Sonning Prize 389
Spengler, Oswald 89–90, 113, 140–1
Spitteler, Carl 85
Spoendlin, Willy 33–4
St. Elisabeth Church (Basel) 5
St. James Church (Basel) 7, 268–9
St. Peter's Church (Basel) 6–7
St. Peter's Church (Geneva) 48
Staehelin, Ernst 101, 269
Staewen, Gertrud 207
Stählin, Wilhelm 156–7

Stalingrad 299
Stange, Carl 108, 111
State
  Barth's critical attitude toward 164
  Christian understanding of 89, 283
  nature of 322
  as theological problem 269–70. *See also* church/state issues; loyalty oath; totalitarianism
Steck, Karl 201
Steck, Rudolf 24, 30–1, 164
Steiger, Eduard von 294–5, 297–8
Stigmata, Barth's writing on 25–6
Stoevesandt, Dorothee 216–17
Stoevesandt, Karl 216
Students
  Barth's relationship to 159–60, 199, 201, 270, 349–50
  in retirement 387–8
Stuttgart Declaration of Guilt (1945) 317
  German reactions to 318–19
Sudeten crisis 1938
  Barth's responses 277–81, 330–1
  Nazi state pressure on Confessing Church 305n.101
Sutz, Erwin 199
Swiss Army Office for Press and Radio, censors Barth's lecture 291
Swiss Confederation, 650th anniversary of 295
Swiss Protestant Aid Association 284
  and Hungarian Jews 285
Swiss Protestant Church Federation
  position on nuclear weapons 334
  wartime position 293
Switzerland, and Nazi propaganda 293, 295
Switzerland 26–7, 163–4
  anti-German popular sentiment 299, 316–17
  Barth's critical positions 295–6, 298–9
  church solidarity with Confessing Church 283–4
  church responses to Jewish refugees 284–5
  nationalism in 285
  in Second World War 291–3, 295
Synoptic question 24

Tambach lecture (1919) 91–5, 174n.109, 206
  and *Epistle to the Romans* 121
  remarks about the state 282–3
Teaching
  Barth's attitudes toward 101, 104–5, 109, 158–60
  Barth's style 342–4
  relationship with his students 109–10.
    See also students

Tell, William 17, 292, 386
Temple de l'Auditoire, Geneva 48
Temple, William 286
Tertullian 9
Theological Existence Today! 212–13, 231, 277, 280–1
  attacks on 224
  Barth sends to Hitler 213–14
  Nazi state pressures on 237, 274–5
  praise for 213
Theological vocation 133–4
Theology 134, 400
  foundation of 84, 202, 204
  and politics, Barth's comment in 1933 224
Thielicke, Helmut 317–18
Thiess, Frank 205–6
Third Reich 131, 212–13, 280, 319
  religious attitudes about 410. *See also* National Socialism; Nazi Germany
Thomas Aquinas 23, 163, 166, 346
Thurneysen, Eduard 8, 101, 103–4, 109–10, 123, 141, 153–4, 163–6, 168–9, 201, 209, 219, 268–9, 284, 288
  and Barth's marital situation 214, 216–17, 246, 248
  and Charlotte von Kirschbaum 177, 185, 188, 190–1, 197n.112
  early friendship 66–8, 72, 75–6, 101–2
  and Emil Brunner 137–9, 226–7
  and *Epistle to the Romans* 84–6, 124–5
  final phone call 401
  and *Zwischen den Zeiten* 141–2, 230–1
Thurneysen, Eduard senior 8
Thurneysen, Marguerite 75–6, 190, 217–18, 246
Tildy, Zoltan 324
Tillich, Paul 125, 386, 388–9, 409
Time Magazine, cover of Barth 383
Titius, Arthur 102–3
Totalitarianism
  Barth's critique of 243
  claims of state 225–6
  comparison of Third Reich and Soviet Union 325
  and theological response 213, 235, 281. *See also* Barmen Declaration; church/state issues; Cold War; Communism; Hitler; loyalty oath; Nazi Germany
Trent, council of 166
Treysa conference (1945) 315
Trinity
  Barth's understanding in *Church Dogmatics* 366–8
Troeltsch, Ernst 39, 68, 140, 307n.125
  Barth's conversation with 54

Tügel, Franz 223–4
Two Kingdoms doctrine 281, 296

Ulm 1934 rally 231
Union Theological Seminary (NY), 1962 visit to 385–6
United States, Barth's 1962 visit
  general impressions from 1962 visit 386–7
  work with military occupation in postwar Germany 315
University of Aberdeen 270. *See also* Gifford Lectures
University of Basel 168–9, 244, 350–1, 383
  Barth accepts professorial appointment 247
  colleagues 269
  courses offered 269–70 and 302nn.16, 20, 21
  final lecture 351
  final years of teaching 341–4
  relationship to students 270, 341–2
  wartime pressures 298
University of Bern
  Barth's 1904/5 studies 24–6
  Barth's 1907 studies 32–3
  potential appointment and controversy (1927) 163–4
  theological faculty of 10, 24
University of Bonn
  appointment to 158, 160, 169–70
  Barth's dismissal 244, 247–8
  Barth's suspension 239–48
  controversies over Barth's politics 225–6
  list of classes taught 249n.9
  postwar honors 394
  postwar lectures 320, 324
  students 270
University of Chicago, Barth's visit 384–5
University of Glasgow, honorary doctorate 271
University of Göttingen
  beginning of his teaching there 100–1
  courses taught 103–8
  first semester 103–4
  students 270
  tensions with the faculty 108, 110, 112, 156
University of Greifswald, theological faculty 28–9
University of Halle 28–9, 39
  and Dehn affair 207
University of Heidelberg, and Dehn affair 207
University of Münster
  Barth called as professor 153–4
  becomes dean 158
  controversy over honorary doctorate 154, 280
  courses taught 160–3

University of Münster (*cont.*)
   first encounter with Catholicism 165–6
   relationship with faculty 156
   students 156, 270
University of St. Andrews, honorary doctorate 271
University of Tübingen
   Barth's 1907 studies 33–4
   postwar speech 317–18
University of Utrecht, honorary doctorate 271

Versailles Treaty 317–18
Vietnam War 396
Vischer, Benedikt 347
Vischer, Eberhard 123, 144n.10, 269
Vischer, Wilhelm 268–9
Visser 't Hooft, Henriette 337–8
Visser 't Hooft, Willem 244, 317, 339, 401
   and German resistance 296–7
   and Second World War 286–7. *See also* ecumenical movement; World Council of Churches
Vogel, Heinrich 276
Vogelsanger, Peter 398–9
Vogt, Paul 283–5

Wackernagel, Jakob 100
Wackernagel, Wilhelm 5
Walser, Martin 132
War. *See* First World War; military service; pacifism; Second World War
Weber, Hans Emil 214, 242–3
Weimar Republic 410
Weiß, Johannes 68
Weizsäcker, Carl Friedrich von 332–3
Werner, Martin 164
Wernle, Paul 65
Westphalian regional church 276
Wetter, Ernst 295–6, 298
Whitehead, Alfred North 157–8, 270–1
Wobbermin, Georg 108
Wolf, Ernst 199, 214, 247, 270–2
Women's movement, Fritz Barth support for 10
Word of God 134
   and ethics 162
   preaching 133

theology of 410
"three forms of," 162, 364–6. *See also* God; preaching; proclamation; scripture
"Word of God as the Task of Theology" (1922 lecture) 57–8, 139, 364
Working class 68, 92
   in Safenwil 62–6
World Council of Churches 244
   condemns Godesberg Declaration 286
   1948 Amsterdam meeting 326, 336
      Barth's talk 336–7
      Barth's address to Reformed delegates 337
   1954 Evanston assembly 339. *See also* ecumenical movement; Visser 't Hooft, Willem
Wurm, Theophil 231, 237–9
Württemberg revivalist movement 7

Young Men's Christian Association 67
Young Reformation Movement 211–12, 214
Youth, Barth's perspective on younger generation 388

Zahn, Theodor, influence on *Epistle to the Romans* (first version) 95n.8
Zahn-Harnack, Agnes von 30–1
Zaisser, Wilhelm 327
Zeitschrift für Theologie und Kirche 39, 41
Zellweger, Dieter (grandson; 1947–) 349
Zellweger, Max (son-in-law; 1903–2003) 268, 347, 383, 387
Zeltner, Hermann 108
Zimmermann, Wolf-Dieter 330–1
Zofingia 26–8, 32–3, 206
   Barth's leadership in 28
Zollikon publishers 275, 291
Zuckmayer, Carl, friendship with 397–8
Zündel, Friedrich, influence on *Epistle to the Romans* (first version) 95n.8
Zürcher, Hans-Peter 401
Zurich, Barth called to 153
Zwingli, Huldrych 7, 53, 106–7, 287, 378
Zwischen den Zeiten 140–2, 157, 168, 230
   end of 230–1. *See also* dialectical theology; Gogarten, Friedrich; Merz, Georg; Thurneysen, Eduard